THE STAMP ACT CRISIS

The Institute of Early American History and Culture is
sponsored jointly by the College of William and Mary
and Colonial Williamsburg, Incorporated

THE STAMP ACT CRISIS

Prologue to Revolution

By EDMUND S. MORGAN
and HELEN M. MORGAN

PUBLISHED FOR

*The Institute of
Early American History and Culture
at Williamsburg, Virginia*

BY

THE UNIVERSITY OF NORTH CAROLINA PRESS

Chapel Hill

For
E. M. M.

PREFACE

THE book before you is an attempt to recreate two years of American history. If the attempt is successful, it will be apparent that these years were decisive ones in the several colonies that later became the United States. In a book dealing with so brief a span of time it might have been possible to furnish the reader with a comprehensive account of what happened in each of these colonies. To have done so, however, would have meant repeating a dozen times a train of events in which the variations had only local significance. Such tedious reproduction of a pattern would have robbed the story of its movement and given it the deceptively static quality of a wall-paper print. On the other hand to have described the pattern in purely general terms would have been to lose contact with actual persons and places.

Our solution has been to see general issues so far as possible through the eyes of particular men. The large attention given these men is not meant to magnify their individual importance. To be sure, they did play important roles in the crisis, but they have been singled out because their experiences exhibit most strikingly the impact of the crisis on human beings.

A word about our collaboration—the original conception of the book and the actual writing of it have been carried out by Edmund S. Morgan, but both the structure of the thought and the final expression have been the product of so close a cooperation that it would be misleading to assign the book to a single author. We have considered and reconsidered every word so often that the book has become ours far more completely than if each of us had written separate parts of it.

We wish to express our gratitude to the other people who have helped us: to Professor Donald Fleming of the History Department at Brown University who read the manuscript and offered many valuable suggestions, and to the librarians at the John Hay Library, the John Carter Brown Library, the William L. Clements Library, the Henry E. Huntington Library, the Harvard College Library, the Yale University Library, the Boston Public Library, the New York Public Library, the Free Library Company of Philadelphia, the Library of Congress, the New Hampshire Historical Society, the Massachusetts Historical Society, the Massachusetts Archives, the American Antiquarian Society, the Rhode Island Historical Society, the Newport Historical Society, the Connecticut Historical Society, the New York Historical Society, the Historical Society of Pennsylvania, the American Philosophical Society, the Maryland Historical Society, the Virginia Historical Society, and the South Carolina Historical Society. The last two of these societies we did not visit, but their librarians furnished us with copies of documents.

Finally we owe a debt of gratitude to Brown University, where a genuine respect for scholarship, on the part of faculty, students, and administration, has been a constant encouragement and inspiration.

E. S. M.
H.M.M.

CONTENTS

PART III

Patterns of Loyalty

PART IV

Revolution Delayed

PART I

Absolute Authority and Inalienable Right

ONE

PROLOGUE

THE place was something out of a fairy tale, a ghost town in the wilderness, empty houses lining the street on one side, savage plants creeping toward them to recover their domain, and on the other side—an enchanted castle, where a gentleman lived with his wife and her young sister. They might have been king, queen, and princess, and the two tame deer which wandered about the house were doubtless a lord and lady transformed by some magic into their present shape. There was a rich meadow, surrounded on three sides by a winding river, and shady lanes which led past a marble fountain, and a covered bower where the princess sat and bewailed the suitor who did not come.

This was Germanna, on the Rapidan River in Spotsylvania; the king was Colonel Alexander Spotswood, former Governor of Virginia, and the queen was the wife whom he had brought from London to live in this improbable paradise. The empty houses had once been the homes of the German settlers whom Spotswood had planted there but who had since deserted him. In September, 1732, the place was visited by a traveller who, like the Spotswoods, would have looked more at home on Regent Street than on the frontier of Virginia. William Byrd had come to consult with the Colonel about iron-mining, but he had a gift for recording scenes and conversations, and in his journal he snatched the whole episode out of time and left it to us, complete with Spotswood's oracular pronouncements not only on iron-mining, but also on tar-burning, hemp, the Spaniards, the post-office, and British politics.[1] In this fantastic setting, so far from the

1. J. S. Bassett, ed., *The Writings of "Colonel William Byrd of Westover in Virginia"* (New York, 1901), 356-470.

civilized world, far it might seem from the world at all, Spotswood spoke of events in London or Boston as though he could abolish at will the desert of woods and water that separated him from them. He told Byrd how the British government had demanded that the people of Massachusetts settle a standing salary upon the governor whom the King appointed for them. The New Englanders had refused, and now, said Spotswood, the Ministry were receding from their demand. "He said further," Byrd recorded, "that if the Assembly in New England would stand Bluff, he did not see how they cou'd be forct to raise Money against their Will, for if they shou'd direct it to be done by Act of Parliament, which they have threaten'd to do, (though it be against the Right of Englishmen to be taxt, but by their Representatives,) yet they wou'd find it no easy matter to put such an Act in Execution." [2]

It was a prophecy delivered in the wilderness, and those magic words "the Right of Englishmen," which more than once had measured the tread of marching feet, would continue to lay their spell long after Spotswood was in his grave and his castle in ruins. But this book is concerned with history, and though history may sometimes take on the guise of a fairy story, as it did on the banks of the Rapidan in 1732, it must shortly come back to earth. In sober fact, Spotswood's prophecy need not be ascribed to second sight, for he had been Governor of Virginia, and he knew from bitter experience how jealously a colonial assembly guarded its right to levy taxes. In 1715 the House of Burgesses had refused to grant the supplies necessary for defense against the Indians, because they thought that he had called some of their prerogatives in question. He had denounced them and finally dissolved them, but he had not beaten them.[3] And he knew that any attempt by Parliament to beat them would have met with doubled resistance.

In 1732 the Assembly of Massachusetts "stood Bluff," as the Virginia Assembly stood in 1715, and the Ministry did recede from their demand. For a generation thereafter, as for three generations before, New Englanders and other Americans went about their business unhampered by Parliamentary taxes. Yet the assemblies did not relax their vigilance, and wise governors avoided so far as possible any conflicts which might prompt a discussion of rights. They knew, as Ed-

2. *Ibid.*, 365-366. The episode is treated in L. W. Labaree, *Royal Government in America* (New Haven, 1930), 359-366.
    3. H. R. McIlwaine, ed., *Journals of the House of Burgesses of Virginia, 1712-1714, 1715-1718 1720-1722, 1725-1726* (Richmond, 1912), 121-170.

mund Burke was to say, that when people begin to define their rights, it is "a sure symptom of an ill-conducted state."

During the first six decades of the eighteenth century Britain allowed her children to grow in their own way: though the internal quarrels of the colonies were constant, there were only occasional points of friction with the mother country, such as the episode which Spotswood discussed with Byrd; and before the colonists had time to formulate a definition of their rights, the British receded—without any disclaimer of their own right—and the colonists went about their business of catching fish or growing tobacco without further philosophizing. The happy result of this policy was that by 1760 the British Empire was the strongest and most prosperous power and British subjects the freest inhabitants in the western world. A less propitious result was that the rights of the colonists in relation to the mother country had never come up for close examination, and hence no one knew exactly what they were.

The colonies had been founded under the authority of the King but had taken advantage of three thousand miles of ocean to achieve a considerable independence of him and of the royal governors he sent to rule them. From a comfortable distance they watched Parliament assume the same powers in Great Britain that their assemblies were assuming in America. The growing impotence of the King was the symbol of their freedom, for it separated them effectively from the real power of the British government. As long as Parliament continued to deal with them through the King, as long as its power reached them in the diluted form of royal instructions, they need fear no interference. To be sure Parliament did direct the operation of their commerce in the Acts of Trade and Navigation, but except in this area it acted through the King and even set up a Board of Trade to assist him and his Privy Council in formulating colonial policy. The colonies in turn devised an informal method of keeping England informed of their views: they hired agents to represent their interests in London, and these agents, though without official standing or power, could go to the Privy Council or the Board of Trade and offer petitions or explain the effects which might be expected from any measure affecting the welfare of their clients.

To persons with tidy minds an empire which required such unofficial handymen to keep it running might seem in need of overhauling. But the British Empire had the great advantage of success. The structure might not appeal to an architect, but it seemed adequate to most of the people who lived in it. So long as they did not have to decide who had what rights and what authority, they could get along well together. Early in 1764 it became apparent that they would have to decide. Governor Spotswood had not predicted what would happen if a dispute should arise in which both Parliament and the colonies "stood Bluff." The ensuing pages try to tell what did happen.

TWO

FRANCIS BERNARD
Royal Governor

WHEN Englishmen and Americans finally found themselves quarreling about the rights of Englishmen, anyone could look back and see that the trouble had been brewing ever since Colonel Washington surrendered his force of Virginians to the French at Fort Necessity in the summer of 1754. For five years after that skirmish, through disaster and defeat, Englishmen and Americans fought the French in North America. After the enemy crumbled on the Plains of Abraham in 1759, England joined America in rejoicing, but at the same time Englishmen looked at their possessions across the ocean with new eyes. When they counted the cost in blood and money of the victory at Quebec, they could not fail to see that most of the blood and most of the money had come from England, and they naturally asked what they would gain from the sacrifice. The colonies had benefited enormously by their attachment to England. What could England expect in return?

Once the question was put, the answer was bound to follow, that the colonies ought to contribute more to imperial support than could be found in the records of the Treasury. Quebec had scarcely fallen before short-sighted ministers began to talk of a colonial tax. At Whitehall and Westminster there was little comprehension of the effect such an innovation could have in America, and the ignorance was even greater in Parliament and among the people at large. But here and there a clear-headed individual who had had experience with bumptious Americans anticipated their antagonism if Parliament should try to tax them before settling its right to do so. Instead of forcing such a premature measure it would be wiser to proceed at once to reorganize the colonies. Most of them had been founded before the vindication of Parliamentary supremacy in England, and a careful reconstruction to make this new authority as clear in the forests of America as in the streets of London must be accomplished before any foolhardy attempt at taxation should crystallize colonial sentiment against it. Unfortunately the Ministry was so occupied with winding up the war and playing politics inside Parliament that it had little time to examine its authority in territories three thousand miles away. Consequently, while statesmen and politicians pulled and hauled to hold their parties together, the problem of taking up the slack in the British Empire was ignored except by a few zealous men, mostly on the outer fringes of government, who cried out in vain for reform.

Best known, perhaps, was Thomas Pownall, the former Governor of Massachusetts. His plans for reorganization were published in a book called *The Administration of the Colonies*. Through six editions, each larger than its predecessor, he urged his schemes and died without finding a receptive audience.[1] Less conspicuous than Pownall was his successor in Massachusetts, who also perceived from the vantage point of New England that the empire needed remodeling. Francis Bernard's plans were clearer, simpler, and more concise than Pownall's, and though he too failed to make himself heard in Whitehall, his efforts to do so and the forces which frustrated him are a part of the story this book attempts to tell.

Bernard was an altogether improbable man to become the architect of a new British Empire, and it seems likely that the defects of his character and birth led his superiors to underestimate the merit of his proposals. The son of a country rector, he had gone through Oxford, the Middle Temple, and twenty years as a barrister in Lincolnshire by the time Washington surrendered at Fort Necessity.[2] His only qualification for a place in the colonial service was the fact that he had managed to marry a cousin of Lord Barrington, one of the most remarkable politicians of the age. From 1755 until 1778, while other cabinet officers came and went, Lord Barrington stayed in office, mostly as Secretary at War. There were those who inferred that he was able to hold his post because he was not troubled by principles, but the fact that he held it was indisputable.

From the day of his marriage in 1741 Bernard cultivated a close acquaintance with his wife's cousin. During seventeen years, while Mrs. Bernard bore him a succession of children, he went about his

1. London, 1764, 1765, 1766, 1768, 1774, 1777.
2. On Bernard's early life see the *Dictionary of National Biography* and E. A. Jones, *American Members of the Inns of Court* (London, 1924), 17-18.

legal business, contenting himself with the small honors of serving as local steward or receiver or recorder. By 1758, when he was forty-six years old, his family had grown to eight children, and the cost of bringing them up in the manner to which he had become accustomed was beginning to exceed his income. For assistance he turned to his influential relative. In eighteenth-century England gentlemen of power frequently showed their affection for needy friends and relations by finding them comfortable positions in the pay of the government. The position which Barrington found for Bernard was no sinecure. In 1759 when General Wolfe was taking Quebec, Bernard had been royal Governor of New Jersey for a little more than a year.

It must have been a considerable wrench for a small city lawyer with a large family to pull up stakes and head for America. The salary which rewarded this move was £800 a year, an attractive sum, but Bernard had to pay £400 in fees for his commission, and it cost him £1200 to bring his family and furnishings across the ocean.[3] After a year's service he could count a net loss of £800. Money meant a lot to him, and he worried about it as he tried his hand at governing an American colony. He worried, in fact, about a great many things. Essentially a parvenu, he always had to wonder whether people were treating him with the proper respect. He never knew when to leave a matter alone but must constantly take up his pen to complain about some injury, real or imaginary. He did not know, in fact, how to deal with people, and the mantle of authority only magnified his difficulty. In view of these handicaps his success as Governor of New Jersey was remarkable. Shrewdly perceiving that the Quakers held the balance of power in the colony, and that they had been badly treated by the former governor, he courted their support and was rewarded by an unprecedented harmony in his dealings with the Assembly.[4] So well did he show up in this situation that after two years Lord Barrington was able to get him transferred to the stormy, intractable, and important colony of Massachusetts Bay.

Bernard was happy with the promotion, for his new salary would be £300 a year larger. He was still badly in debt and anxious to increase his income by every possible means, so much so that he made a fool of himself trying too hard to sell his house and various knickknacks to his successor in New Jersey.[5] The move to Massachusetts temporarily embarrassed his finances still further: besides the cost of

3. Bernard to John Pownall, January 13, 1761, to Barrington, January 17, 1761, Bernard Papers, I, 289-295, Harvard College Library.

4. Bernard to Bishop of Bristol, January 7, 1760, to John Taylor, October 12, 1759, to Halifax, July 18, 1760, Bernard Papers, I, 190-192, 212, 266-271.

5. Bernard to Boone, June 3, 10, 1760, Bernard Papers, I, 252-259, 261.

moving there was again the £400 in fees on his new commission. On top of this came the death of King George II, a real disaster, for it meant that he must renew the commission, at the cost of still another £400.[6]

But the government of Massachusetts would bring other than monetary rewards, and Bernard, though no longer a young man, was ambitious and fired by the possibilities he saw before him. He had been as impressed as his superiors by what he took to be his political abilities in governing New Jersey; and in Massachusetts he would have more room to exercise them. In Massachusetts he might also expand his perspective to view the colonies as a whole; eventually, who could tell, he might rise from a provincial governor to an imperial statesman. As he entered the colony and received the plaudits of the citizens, he already took a larger view of things than he had at Perth Amboy or in Lincolnshire. In New Jersey he had rested his policy on an alliance with the Quakers. Here he would rise above the sordid bickerings of provincial politics and found his administration "on the broad bottom of the people in general." [7]

Such a course might have been possible for a man with the Olympian character to carry it out. Bernard had already persuaded himself that he had such a character and continued to believe during the next few years that he was displaying it. But the fundamental insecurity of his temperament betrayed him. Even before he left New Jersey his trivial troubles preceded him to Massachusetts. A servant girl who was preparing his Boston residence ran off with a man who had already seduced two of his maids at Perth Amboy, and Bernard could not forbear writing tedious letters to people in Boston complaining of the rascal.[8]

From first to last there was always someone abusing him. After a gratifying welcome by the people of Massachusetts he was disappointed to find the merchants combining against him. He consoled himself that this was the consequence of his dutiful attention to the Laws of Trade. He was sure too that the merchants were encouraged by a few designing politicians, particularly James Otis, Jr., who bore him an undeserved grudge for not appointing the elder Otis to the bench of the Superior Court.[9] There were also some unscrupulous customs officers siding with the merchants, and the plot reached serious proportions late in 1761 when John Temple, the new Surveyor

6. See note 3.
7. Bernard to John Pownall, May 12, 1761, Bernard Papers, I, 317.
8. Bernard to Andrew Oliver, June 15, 1760, Bernard Papers, I, 262-263.
9. Bernard to John Pownall, January 19, February 21, July 6, 1761, to Thomas Pownall, August 28, 1761, Bernard Papers, I, 296-298, 322-323; II, 9.

General of the Customs, not only upheld this insubordination but himself failed to accord the proper respect to His Majesty's Governor. This was insufferable, and Bernard wrote petulantly to England of all the insults he had borne. "There never," he cried, "was a governor so ill treated by a subject of the government, since the Colonies were first planted." [10] Even the British Navy joined the conspiracy when Admiral Colville claimed Bernard's share of vessels condemned in Massachusetts for violating the Laws of Trade.[11] On every hand heartless men were scheming to deprive him of the dignity and profit that were rightly his.

To all of these trials Bernard responded by dashing off letters to England, complaining of his persecutors and protesting that the mass of the people loved him. Perhaps because of the bad judgment he too evidently displayed, the Board of Trade and the Privy Council paid little attention to the other letters he was writing. Though he deluded himself about the popularity of his administration, Bernard did have the vision and the perspective and the insight to see that the American governments must be reformed in order to secure colonial submission to Parliament's unlimited authority. In New Jersey he had become acquainted with the deficiencies of imperial control in the middle colonies. At Boston he discovered that Massachusetts was constitutionally incapable of functioning effectively as part of the empire, and that nearby Connecticut and Rhode Island were no better than independent republics. A reform of colonial administration was glaringly needed, and by December of 1761 he knew who ought to direct that reform. On the fifteenth of the month he wrote to Lord Barrington that "when a Revisal and settlement of the political state of North America should have a place in the British Councils, I might possibly be of some service." [12] During the next two years he sent over a barrage of letters informing everyone who might be interested that he was ready at a moment's notice to take sail for England and advise the Ministry on the proper procedure for reorganizing the colonies.[13]

After the peace treaty with France had been signed in February,

10. To John Pownall, May 6, 1765, Bernard Papers, III, 288. The first three volumes of the Bernard Papers are full of letters dealing with Bernard's troubles with the merchants and customs officers. See especially I, 315-320; II, 24-26, 30.

11. Bernard to Colville, April 25, 1764, to Halifax, February 18, 1764, Bernard Papers, III, 39, 141-144.

12. Bernard Papers, II, 21-23; Edward Channing and Archibald Cary Coolidge, eds., *The Barrington-Bernard Correspondence* (Cambridge, 1912), 42-45.

13. See letters to Charles Townshend, May 18, 1763; to Richard Jackson, May 21, 1763, and August 3, 1763; to Lord Shelburne, July 25, 1763; Bernard Papers, II, 60-62, 65-68, 92-94, and 84-85 respectively.

1763, Bernard's eagerness quickened. His friend Richard Jackson, agent of the colony of Connecticut, Member of Parliament, and intimate of George Grenville, wrote that the Crown was considering a union of Rhode Island, Connecticut, and Massachusetts in one government. Though Jackson indicated his own coolness to the suggestion, Bernard jumped at it. The government of Connecticut was a "monster in politicks," he said, and both Rhode Island and Connecticut must be made more dependent upon the mother country. He continued with a measure of political philosophy: "I consider Government not to be a Right but a trust, and that the Royal Grants of Jurisdiction in America either to private persons or Corporations are no more than temporary provisions untill the Parliament that is the whole Legislature, shall settle the Government, . . ." This was strong medicine. According to Bernard, the charters of Connecticut and Rhode Island, dating from 1662 and 1663 respectively, and that of Massachusetts, dating from 1691, were temporary trusts and could be revoked by Parliament at will. Perhaps he realized that these ideas would go down in New England like chopped hay, even though they should come from so popular a man as he considered Francis Bernard to be. He encouraged himself by adding, "Surely this is law now, whatever it was before the Revolution," which might be translated as "I think this is law now, even though many will deny it." [14]

In spite of his easy dismissal of colonial charters Bernard did not intend to oppress the Americans. He had no grudge against the people he governed. What he had was an orderly mind that foresaw trouble in the imperfect subordination of the colonies to Parliament. His diagnosis of the difficulty was doubtless assisted by the fact that Parliament's position in the colonies closely resembled his own position in the world. Both were insecure and untried. The insults he received or fancied were a token of the larger ones Parliament received daily in colonial violations of the Laws of Trade. Through the office he held Bernard saw his personal sufferings transfigured: an insult to Francis Bernard, Governor of Massachusetts, became an insult to Parliament; and his personal anxiety and ambition were exalted to anxiety and ambition for the empire. What he wanted for himself was wealth, distinction, and perhaps power; what he wanted for Parliament was a benevolent despotism over the colonies. The two aims were fused in his vision of a new colonial empire of which he should be the guiding genius, or in which at least his own dignity would be firmly established under the aegis of a supreme Parliament.

In the spring of 1764, while events of the greatest importance for

14. Bernard to Jackson, August 2, 1763, Bernard Papers, III, 89-92.

him and for the colonies were preparing in England, Bernard was in Concord, Massachusetts, where he had convened the Assembly in order to avoid the small-pox at Boston. Here in the country air that later generations would also find congenial to health and to writing, he began to put his ideas on paper. With characteristic tidiness he reduced them to a set of propositions numbered consecutively from one to ninety-seven, beginning with principles he considered self-evident and proceeding relentlessly until the necessary steps for reorganization were plainly marked out.[15]

Bernard began by defining the sovereignty of Great Britain, which he placed in the King, acting with the advice and consent of Parliament. This was the axiom which all British subjects took for granted. It was not necessary to point out that Parliament was the final authority in any conceivable contest with the King. The propositions went on to distinguish the areas under the control of the sovereign power into Great Britain herself and the external dominions which, together with Great Britain, made up the empire. The American colonies were, of course, a part of these external dominions. As such they were subject to the King in Parliament just as much as Great Britain was herself. And Bernard went on with the ideas he had already expressed to Jackson, that the colonial governments with their representative assemblies were simply convenient temporary arrangements which Parliament could alter at will. He did not shrink from the conclusion that this line of reasoning led to: "The rule that a *British* subject shall not be bound by laws, or liable to taxes, but what he has consented to by his representatives, must be confined to the inhabitants of *Great Britain* only; and is not strictly true even there." [16] Parliament, in other words, had every right to tax and legislate for the colonies, although they were unrepresented in it. And yet why should they not be represented? Bernard thought they should: though it was impracticable for all parts of the empire to send members to Parliament, it was not, in his opinion, impracticable for the Americans. He could foresee no detrimental consequences for the mother country, and though the Americans could not properly claim representation as a right, to make them a gift of it would effectively quiet their protests when Parliament began to exercise its authority more broadly over them.

Coming to the colonial governments themselves, Bernard insisted

15. The propositions were not printed until 1774 in *Select Letters on the Trade and Government of America, and the Principles of Law and Polity, Applied to the American Colonies* (London, 1774).

16. *Ibid.*, 75.

on uniformity. Their constitutions varied as widely as the different times and conditions of their founding. But now that they had reached maturity, it was improper for the people of one colony to have fewer rights and privileges than those of another, since all were subject to one King and one law and all equally fit for one form of government. It was unfair, for example, for the people of Rhode Island and Connecticut to elect their own governors, who permitted them to ignore the Acts of Trade, while the faithful royal governor of Massachusetts kept his people within the law.[17] All colonies should have royal governors. And all should retain their assemblies, which were still convenient arrangements for conducting local affairs; but the assemblies must be altered to provide for an independent upper house, to be neither the tool of the lower house nor yet an executive council of the governor. In Parliament the independence of the upper house rested on the hereditary succession of the Lords. Bernard thought the new colonial governments should resemble England's as closely as possible, and though he believed that America was not yet ready for the establishment of a hereditary nobility, still "A *Nobility* appointed by the *King* for life, and made independent, would probably give strength and stability to the *American* governments, as effectually as an hereditary *Nobility* does to that of *Great Britain*." [18]

With a royal governor and an influential house of nobles in every colony, both ready to support the power that created them, Parliament would be in a better position to exercise its authority over the Americans. But though Bernard granted Parliament's unlimited authority, he recommended that in the matter of colonial taxation it confine itself to duties on trade. Taxes, he felt, should be levied on those who benefited most from them. Since the protection of trade was the most expensive part of imperial defense, Parliament, as the imperial legislature, might appropriately tax trade to pay for it. The expenses of local government, on the other hand, should be met by internal taxes, and these could best be left for the local representative assemblies to levy. Parliament might establish a "civil list," naming the offices of government and the salaries required for each, but it need not step in unless the colonists failed to raise the requisite amount. In this way royal officials would be freed from servile dependence on the assemblies, but at the same time a colony's internal

17. This point was made by Bernard in letters to William Pitt, October 3, 1761, to Lord Egremont, October 25, 1763, to John Pownall, February 10, 1764, and to Lord Halifax, December 14, 1764, Bernard Papers, II, 14-16; III, 99-100, 130, 200.

18. *Select Letters*, 83.

economy would not be disrupted through unwise taxes levied by a Parliament unacquainted with local conditions.

Bernard wrote as an Englishman brought up on the doctrine of Parliamentary supremacy; but he knew, as few Englishmen did, the pitfalls waiting in America for the minister who should attempt to wield Parliamentary authority there in the existing political chaos. His plan aimed at complete recognition of Parliament's authority. To secure this without unduly antagonizing the Americans he was willing to continue their privilege of raising their own internal taxes and in addition to allow them representation in Parliament.

It is remarkable how closely Bernard's ideas conformed to those of the men who were to become his bitter enemies. While he was writing his *Principles of Law and Polity, Applied to the Government of the British Colonies in America* (the title he gave to his ninety-seven propositions), James Otis, who also attended the meeting of the Assembly at Concord, was writing *The Rights of the British Colonies Asserted and Proved.*[19] Otis's pamphlet was a passionate denial of Parliament's right to tax the colonies, either internally or by duties on trade, but though he differed from Bernard on the question of right, he agreed, in part at least, that the remedy was to grant the colonies representation in Parliament. Unfortunately Parliament offered the two men no opportunity to work together for this reform, but forced them to take their respective stands on the question of right.

As Bernard and Otis were agreed on the desirability of colonial representation in Parliament, Bernard and John Adams were agreed on the necessity of an independent, aristocratic upper house in a properly constituted legislature. The principle of "balanced" government—and Bernard used the word "balanced" to describe it—was John Adams's great contribution to the governments of the independent United States. In 1764, before Adams began to stress the idea, Bernard fully understood it and wished to see it established throughout America. If his recommendations had been accepted in London, it is not impossible that Adams and Otis might have been found by his side in supporting the reformation of colonial government.

Even as it was, Bernard felt that he could count on the backing of many influential colonists. In Massachusetts he was sure that the most prudent men were behind him, in spite of the grumbling at his strict attention to the Laws of Trade. In at least three other colonies he knew there were strong elements in favor of reform. The situation in

19. Boston, 1764.

Pennsylvania was familiar to him from his service in nearby New Jersey. During his years there he had written to Lord Barrington that the government of Pennsylvania must be taken over by the Crown and the governor made independent of the people. "Till these things are done," he had said, "there will be no restoring peace to that distracted province." [20] Now, he heard, the most enlightened Pennsylvanians were taking the matter into their own hands: a petition had been circulated asking the King to revoke the governmental powers of the Penn family and make Pennsylvania a royal colony. The Assembly approved it and sent it to Bernard's friend Richard Jackson for presentation. Bernard, following the whole affair in the newspapers, admired the masterly manner in which it had been brought to a crisis and recognized the hand of his friend Benjamin Franklin behind it.[21] In November, 1764, Franklin himself left for London to further it.[22]

Similarly from Rhode Island came news that the sensible people were sick and tired of the corruption and quarrelling in the popular government there. The *Boston News Letter* for May 3, 1764, reported from Newport that "Many of the Inhabitants seem desirous of an alteration of their present Form of Government, and are willing to be on the Footing which the Inhabitants of Pennsylvania have requested, viz. to be a Royal Government." The Rhode Islanders did in fact take their cue from Pennsylvania: by October a petition was on its way to the King, asking for a revocation of the charter, and influential Rhode Islanders were writing to Franklin, asking him to support their petition along with his own.[23]

In Connecticut too signs of readiness appeared. The quarrel there between the "Old Light" and the "New Light" factions of the Congregational Church had sent moderately disposed members in disgust to the Anglican Church. And the feeling of the Anglican ministers about the Connecticut charter was no secret. They had been pushed around for years by a government which supported only the established Congregational Church. In letters to their headquarters in London they had more than once suggested that the only salvation for the colony would be a royal governor and an Anglican bishop, and when Samuel Johnson, a leader of the Church in Connecticut, heard that Franklin was off for London to apply for royal government,

20. Bernard to Barrington, May 23, 1759, *Barrington-Bernard Correspondence*, 4-6.
21. Bernard to [Richard Jackson] April 7, 1764, Bernard Papers, III, 229-230.
22. On the Pennsylvania petition see below, ch. 14.
23. Martin Howard to Benjamin Franklin, November 16, 1764, and May 14, 1765; Thomas Moffat to Benjamin Franklin, May 12, 1764. Franklin Papers, I, 108; II, 127; I, 88, American Philosophical Society.

he wrote to him, "Would to God you were charged with pleading the same cause in behalf of all the governments that they might all alike be taken into the Kings immediate protection. It would certainly be best for us all to be under one form of Government, and I beg that your best influence may be so directed that the Government at home, when they take yours in hand may make one work of it." [24]

The men backing these pleas for reorganization were undeniably some of the most substantial citizens of the new world—men of property, influence and judgment. There was one point in Bernard's program which would probably attract them as much as it attracted him: the American nobility. Resounding titles appeal to men in any age, and this was an age when aristocracy had not yet had to do battle with the philosophy of social equality. Even in America, ten years before the Declaration of Independence, scarcely anyone doubted the rightness and desirability of social distinctions. Though Boston was soon to see mobs roaming the streets, they would not be seeking to haul down the banners of aristocracy. In fact one of the mortifying scenes about to be enacted before Governor Bernard was that in which gentlemen, who should have known better, disguised themselves in working-men's clothes and led the mob in attacking officers of the King's government.

An American nobility was by no means a fanciful idea in 1764, and might have served to forestall some of the troubles which were close at hand. Bernard would not have found it difficult to name suitable candidates in the colonies of his acquaintance. In every nothern colony there were the merchants, those of large fortune, that is, and with wide investments, who could be expected to weather the storms of depression and shipwreck which made colonial commerce a matter of large risks and large returns. Besides the merchants in the north and the correspondingly wealthy planters in the south, there were professional men, lawyers and doctors, and the more important officials in the customs service or government. In Massachusetts the Lieutenant-Governor, Thomas Hutchinson, was an obvious candidate: dignified, conservative, and prudent; so were Andrew Oliver, Secretary of the province, and Colonel Israel Williams of Hatfield

24. Bancroft Transcripts, undated, New York Public Library. The letter was undoubtedly written late in 1764 or early in 1765. See also letters by Samuel Johnson, April 14, 1751, and July 13, 1760, in Francis L. Hawks and William S. Perry eds., *Documentary History of the Protestant Episcopal Church ... containing Numerous Hitherto Unpublished Documents concerning the Church in Connecticut* (New York, 1863), I, 278, 312, and a letter signed "Ecclesanglicus," dated New London, August 10, 1764, which says, "Great God incline his Majesty and Privy Council to send us a Bishop for his church, and a Governor for the Colony." Chalmers Papers, Harvard College Library.

and the other so-called "River Gods," who dominated the western part of the colony. Then of course there was Francis Bernard.

In Connecticut, despite its present "republican" form of government, there were some properly qualified men, like Jared Ingersoll, the New Haven attorney, and Joseph Harrison, the Customs Collector there, who was on intimate terms with the Marquis of Rockingham, and Thomas Fitch, who did as good a job as could be expected of an elected governor. Even in Rhode Island, the most disgracefully radical and lawless colony, there were gentlemen on whom a title would sit becomingly, those for example who were petitioning for a royal government. Martin Howard, Jr., an attorney, was a man of proper sentiments, and so was Doctor Thomas Moffat, a Scotch physician who had come to Newport in the wake of Bishop Berkeley and who maintained a distinguished library and collection of paintings. John Robinson, the recently arrived Collector of the port, was a likely person also, though Bernard was soon to find him too much under the influence of the Surveyor General of the Customs, John Temple. Temple was one of those pushing people who might well be left out of any colonial aristocracy.

If proper candidates for an aristocracy could be found in Rhode Island and Connecticut, they could surely be found in every colony. The fact that Benjamin Franklin was taking the lead for royal government in Pennsylvania was a good omen, for Franklin had already demonstrated his influence by getting his son William appointed Governor of New Jersey. It was possible that Franklin himself would be the first royal governor of Pennsylvania,[25] and he would doubtless be glad to have his government supported by a local peerage, made up of his abler and more well-to-do friends, like John Hughes and Joseph Galloway.

All in all, the prospect seemed favorable for realizing Bernard's scheme. Not only were there influential colonists who might support it strongly in hopes of gaining a seat in the new aristocracy, but people in general appeared reconciled to some kind of reorganization. Although alarmed by new restrictions on their trade and impending Parliamentary taxation, they showed no particular concern about reports that the structure of the colonial governments would be altered. The newspapers printed rumors from London of boundary readjustments for the northern colonies: "It is said there will be but four, viz. Nova Scotia, Province of Main, New Hampshire and New York—the Massachusetts Rhode Island and Connecticut are to be divided

25. See William Allen to Thomas Penn, March 11, 1765, Penn Correspondence 1765-1771, Historical Society of Pennsylvania.

between New York and New Hampshire." [26] The likelihood of a colonial representation in Parliament was also suggested and even the establishment of an American nobility.[27] The Boston newspapers which expressed themselves with greatest vehemence on the taxation of the colonies printed these items without comment.

The succession of rumors must have been provocative to a man of Bernard's ambition. He knew that his analysis of the situation was a penetrating one and that the ministry in England would profit by studying it. He saw the mood for reorganization ripe in both England and America, and he felt strongly that it was now or never. The concluding paragraphs of his ninety-seven propositions were prophetic:

96. The people of *North America,* at this time, expect a revisal and reformation of the *American* Governments, and are better disposed to submit to it than ever they were, or perhaps ever will be again.
97. This is therefore the proper and critical time to reform the *American* governments upon a general, constitutional, firm, and durable plan; and if it is not done now, it will probably every day grow more difficult, till at last it becomes impracticable.[28]

Filled with the urgency of the situation Bernard sent a copy of his plan to Lord Barrington as soon as it was finished and asked him to show it to Lord Halifax and Lord Hillsborough, each of whom might be expected to have a hand in the coming reorganization.[29] Three weeks later he sent copies to Richard Jackson. Jackson could show it to other persons of influence in the administration and if they approved its sentiments might have it printed.[30]

Jackson apparently did not find it advisable to publish the piece, but Bernard continued to press advice on him.[31] On November 9, 1764, he finally abandoned the indirect approach and wrote to Lord Halifax himself, now Secretary of State for the Southern Department and charged with control of the colonies.[32] Barrington had told him that Halifax praised the ninety-seven propositions as "the best thing of the kind by much that he ever read." [33] Taking this as a license to open correspondence on the subject, Bernard plunged in with a ten-page letter amplifying some details of his scheme. In the ninety-seven

26. *Boston Gazette,* April 22, 1765.
27. *Boston Post-Boy and Advertiser,* February 25, 1765; *Boston Gazette,* supplement, May 27, 1765.
28. *Select Letters,* 84-85.
29. June 23, 1764, *Barrington-Bernard Correspondence,* 75-77.
30. July 9, 1764, Bernard Papers, III, 237-238.
31. October 22, 1764, Bernard Papers, X, 230-236.
32. Bernard Papers, X, 238-247.
33. Barrington to Bernard, October 3, 1764, *Barrington-Bernard Correspondence,* 81.

propositions he had recommended that colonial boundaries be re-
drawn to conform better to physiography. What he proposed now
was a union of Massachusetts, Rhode Island, and eastern Connecticut,
with western Connecticut attached to New York. In this enlarged
government of Massachusetts a governor's council and a separate
upper house of the legislature should both be appointed by the King,
the former for life, the latter during his pleasure. The reform should
be brought about by act of Parliament. This was not the complete
colonial reorganization he envisaged, but it was at least a beginning.[34]

Bernard never had the opportunity of observing the reaction of
New England to such an act or to any other act for reorganizing the
colonies. Lord Halifax may have been sympathetic with his schemes,
for he himself had long felt the need of reform in colonial administration, but no one in England sensed the urgency of the situation as
Bernard did. The members of the Privy Council had not experienced
the insults of uncouth Americans and might have dismissed them
with the assurance of birth and breeding if they had. Yet they would
have been wise to listen to Bernard, for however secure they might
be in rank and fortune, they were conducting a government whose
position in the colonies was no more secure than Francis Bernard's.
When their government finally felt the sting of colonial insubordination, it would respond with the same petulance that Bernard had
shown to the insults of James Otis and John Temple, but it would be
unable to translate its sense of injury into a larger scheme of colonial
reform. Now, however, instead of heeding Bernard's advice, they sent
him two revenue acts to enforce. These were the premature measures
he had feared, acts which he had expressly urged the Ministry not to
pass. In the repercussions that followed, his wishful identification
with Parliament became a reality, for the colonists struck at royal
officers with a violence that Parliament could not fail to resent. But
the fulfillment, coming as it did, reduced the would-be imperial
statesman to a provincial pariah and reorganization of the colonies
to a hopeless dream.

34. November 9, 1764, Bernard Papers, X, 238-247.

⋙ THREE ⋘

THE SUGAR ACT

THE ministers at Whitehall who neglected the advice of the royal governor of Massachusetts-Bay were not as reckless as they seemed from across the water. Although the acquisition of Canada sharpened the imperial vision of men like Bernard, it also presented the British government with problems that could not wait for an answer. It was all very well to draw up schemes for reorganizing the colonies—Bernard was not the only one doing that—but to get a plan accepted by Parliament and into operation might be a long and ticklish business. In the meantime the empire must be administered and protected. The problem was not new, but to the men responsible for balancing the British budget, it looked a great deal more difficult than it had before the war.

In the black years when Englishmen fought with their backs to the wall, they gave freely of blood and money, and succeeded in winning the war. They did not succeed in paying for it. The arrival of peace found the national debt rising at a perilous rate; it had grown from £72,289,673 in 1755 to £122,603,336 in 1763 and to £129,586,789 in 1764.[1] Merely to pay the interest would require a heavier burden of taxation than had been known before, but besides increasing the debt, the war had fastened a great new peace-time expense on the budget. Though Canada and the Mississippi Valley were doubtless a glorious addition to the empire, in terms of pounds and shillings they were a long-term investment. They might pay off heavily in the dis-

---

1. *Journals of the House of Commons,* XXVII, 167; XXIX, 432, 760. Grenville told Parliament that the debt had risen from £67,000,000 to £140,000,000 (Jasper Mauduit to the Speaker of the Massachusetts House of Representatives, April 7, 1764, Massachusetts Archives, XXII, 361-363, and Israel Mauduit, *Mr. Grenville's Offer to the Colony Assemblies to raise the Supply Themselves,* n.p., n.d.), but this was apparently an exaggeration.

21

tant future when filled by the prolific, burgeoning people of the American colonies, who doubled their numbers every twenty-five years. For the present they were a liability: until the Englishmen outnumbered the hostile French and Indian population, there would be constant danger of repossession by France in a future war. It was essential therefore that the British maintain a standing army in America. What greater folly than to expend blood and money in the conquest of Canada only to give it up because of the high cost of defense? No one was surprised when the government decided to maintain 10,000 regular troops in America,[2] and its wisdom was demonstrated when an Indian uprising under Pontiac in 1763 threatened to drive the British back to the coast. Troops there must be in America whatever the cost.

The cost was not small. The annual expense of 10,000 troops was estimated at more than £220,000.[3] Other peacetime expenses, quite apart from interest on the national debt, had also increased,[4] so that the problem of making ends meet was desperate. Obviously new sources of revenue must be found, and obviously the new world was the place to look for them. In all fairness the Americans should help support the army protecting them. Though an American tax would be a novelty, few members of Parliament would doubt their authority to levy it, nor, considering the circumstances, its equity. It might be more judicious to proceed by the old method of sending requisitions to the colonial governors, requests for a contribution, but that method had proved unreliable even in wartime. The Treasury needed money at once, and if requisitions were sent, there would be delay after delay in getting a response and perhaps nothing to show for it in the end. Likewise if taxation were postponed until a colonial reorganization smoothed the way, years might pass before anything was accomplished. Reorganization, like the settlement of Canada, was a gradual and long-range matter. The gaping hole in the British Treasury demanded immediate action.

The man who undertook to balance Britain's budget was George Grenville, brother-in-law of the great William Pitt, but a man with a mind and will of his own. George Grenville was nobody's fool. Al-

2. *Journals of the House of Commons,* XXIX, 506, 530 (March 7, 1763). See Clarence W. Alvord, *The Mississippi Valley in British Politics* (Cleveland, 1917), ch. 4.

3. *Journals of the House of Commons,* XXIX, 681. Grenville said that American expenses had risen to £350,000 (see references cited in note 1), but this figure included other expenses than the military. Actual disbursements for the military were only a little over £200,000. Treasury Papers, class I, bundle 433, f. 404, Public Record Office, Library of Congress transcripts.

4. See the figures in *The Annual Register . . . for the Year 1764,* 155-163.

though he thought Americans grossly undertaxed by comparison with Englishmen, he had no intention of saddling them with any part of the interest charges on the British national debt.[5] He did not even intend to assign them the whole expense of the new standing army,[6] for their protection was an imperial concern as well as a local American one. Yet something they must pay.

On taking office in the summer of 1763, Grenville found laws already on the books which offered the possibility of some income from the Americans. Some of the Acts of Trade made use of customs duties to regulate the flow of colonial commerce for the advantage of the mother country. The returns from these duties demonstrated equally the success of the American smugglers and the failure of the royal customs collectors. Surely the latter ought to be collecting more than the ridiculous sum of £1800 a year.[7] Too many of them sat placidly in England enjoying their large salaries, while their ill-paid and irresponsible deputies collected bribes instead of customs in America. Grenville promptly ordered the office-holders to perform their duties in person or forfeit their jobs; and in order to check on them and facilitate their work he instructed colonial governors to report regularly on contraband trade, and the Navy to patrol American ports and inlets for smugglers.[8] Now perhaps the customs returns would begin to look respectable. But Grenville did not wait to see, for even if strictly enforced, the existing laws were inadequate. The customs duties had been designed to regulate the flow of trade rather than fill the Treasury. To obtain a satisfactory revenue from them, he would have to get Parliament to revise them with this purpose in view. While customs officers hurried to their posts and naval officers took up stations along the Atlantic coast, he was already preparing recommendations and by March 9, 1764, had them ready. On that day and the days following, his suggestions were presented to an

5. "Mr. Grenville, after the kindest expressions of regard to the Colonies, assured my brother, that whatever were the distresses bro't upon the revenue by the extravagant Expences of the War, they did not mean to draw anything from America for the relief of them." Jasper Mauduit to the Speaker of the Massachusetts House of Representatives, February 11, 1764, Massachusetts Historical Society, Collections, 74 (1918), 146n.

6. Thomas Whately, The Regulations Lately Made concerning the Colonies and the Taxes Imposed upon Them, Considered (London, 1765), 101-103. This pamphlet, though written by Whately, was widely attributed to Grenville and doubtless represented his views, for Whately was one of his secretaries in the Treasury Department. The third edition of the pamphlet bore Grenville's name on the title page. See Massachusetts Historical Society, Collections, 6th ser., 9 (1897), 77.

7. W. L. Grant and James Munro, eds., Acts of the Privy Council of England, Colonial Series (London, 1908—), IV, 569; Whately, Regulations Lately Made, 57.

8. Treasury Papers, Class I, Bundle 430, ff. 332-334; Acts of the Privy Council, Colonial, IV, 570-572.

attentive House of Commons in a series of resolutions. He himself introduced the first proposals, covering a new schedule of duties.[9]

The proposals would affect many branches of colonial commerce. Madeira, the staple of trade with the Wine Islands, was for the first time to bear a duty, £7 a ton. Drawbacks (customs duties refunded on re-exportation) on European and Asian textiles exported from Great Britain to the colonies were to be discontinued, and new duties placed on coffee, pimiento, foreign indigo, and foreign sugar. Lumber and iron bound for Europe must be shipped first to England. Foreign rum was to be prohibited. Most important of all, the duty on foreign molasses was to be reduced from 6d. to 3d. a gallon.

Two days after proposing these alterations in duties the Ministry called for an amendment in the means of collecting and enforcing them.[10] Violators were to be detected through an elaborate system of bonds and cockets which would reveal exactly what a vessel was carrying and where she had previously called. More important, once a violation had been detected it should be prosecuted in the admiralty courts. These courts had been deciding maritime cases in the colonies since 1696, but were highly unpopular because they operated without juries. The common-law courts, seizing upon an ambiguity in the statute of 1697, denied them jurisdiction over the Acts of Trade. As a result smugglers were regularly tried—and acquitted—by sympathetic juries of their peers. The Ministry now proposed at long last to put an end to this practice by giving the existing admiralty courts clear jurisdiction over the Acts of Trade. As further insurance against local meddling, a new admiralty court would exercise original jurisdiction over any case which the collectors chose to take before it. Lord Colville, the Admiral in charge of American waters, had warned the Ministry that the admiralty judges in New York and New England were hand in glove with the merchants, or else afraid of the mobs which the merchants seemed to have at their disposal. Colville suggested that the remedy was to have cases tried at Halifax, where his flagship was stationed.[11] Grenville approved, and while Parliament was extending admiralty jurisdiction, he arranged for an order in Council to establish the new court.[12] He wanted to free the cus-

9. *Journals of the House of Commons*, XXIX, 934-935. Accounts of Grenville's speech may be found in a letter of Edward Montague April 11, 1764, quoted in *Virginia Gazette* (Purdie & Dixon), October 3, 1766; and in a letter of Israel Mauduit, March 10, 1764, Massachusetts Archives, XXII, 357.

10. *Journals of the House of Commons*, XXIX, 940.

11. Colville to Philip Stephens, October 25, 1763, Admiralty Secretary In Letters 482, Public Record Office, Library of Congress transcripts.

12. *Acts of the Privy Council, Colonial*, IV, 663-664.

toms officers still further from local pressures by giving them immunity from retaliatory damage suits by merchants. If a collector seized a ship but failed to prove his case against her, he should not be liable for his error, provided the judge was satisfied there had been a probability of guilt.[13]

If Parliament was at all interested in reforming the administration of the colonies, here was a profitable place to begin.[14] If not, the Ministry could defend its recommendations on more familiar ground: though designed to raise money, the new duties, like the old, would regulate colonial trade for the welfare of the mother country. They would, in fact, bring new benefits to British merchants and manufacturers. The heavy duty on Madeira was designed to break the monopoly which that Portuguese product had acquired over the colonial wine market. American ships carried pipe staves and provisions to the Azores and had hitherto returned with pipes of Madeira in the hold duty free. As a result Madeira was plentiful in America, and the colonists had grown fond of it. Though they would still be able to buy it—at a price—they were expected to shift to cheaper wine, obtainable from English merchants. The abolition of the drawback on foreign textiles would increase the revenue, because the goods included in this group were a luxury on which the rich could well afford to pay a higher tax. The rest of the colonists could get along very well on British textiles. British linens might not be as good as French, but they were adequate and would improve with the encouragement thus given them. To be sure, the high prices might lead the Americans to set up linen manufactures themselves, but the possibility seemed remote, since labor was so dear in the colonies. If the Americans for any reason should attempt to embark on such a manufacture, the drawback could be restored.

The reduction of the molasses duty was also designed to benefit both trade and Treasury. Molasses duties, whether large or small, were an advantage to the British sugar planters. But in order to benefit the Treasury, the duties must be set at a figure which, though high enough to yield a good income, would not be so high as to stop the flourishing trade and hence the revenue. Grenville had received a good deal of advice, asked and unasked, on this question, and had

---

13. These measures will be found in the Act as passed, 4 George III, c. 15, Danby Pickering, ed., *The Statutes at Large* . . . (Cambridge, 1762-1807), XXVI, 40-52. They were apparently not embodied in specific resolutions beforehand.

14. The official ministerial defense was offered by Thomas Whately in *The Regulations Lately Made*, which seems to have followed the lines laid down by Grenville in his speech of March 9. The ensuing two paragraphs are based largely on *The Regulations Lately Made*, 58-87.

finally concluded upon 3d. a gallon as the figure likely to bring in
the largest revenue. Governor Bernard and Jasper Mauduit, the agent
of Massachusetts, had both warned that 3d. was too much,[15] but he
did not agree with their reasoning. It was well known that the cost of
smuggling molasses was about 1½d. a gallon, the price for which collectors generally agreed to look the other way. The trade, having
grown to its present strength with this sum as one of the fixed costs,
could surely bear a little more now. The collection of a 3d. tax would
in reality add only 1½d. to the amount already paid in smuggling.
From these considerations Grenville and his advisers calculated that
a 3d. duty would not reduce the trade by more than 2/9. If they levied
only 1d., as Jasper Mauduit had urged, trade might continue un-
abated, but the total revenue would be less.[16] Grenville therefore
stuck to his figure, and Parliament accepted it without a murmur.

The only resolution that did not call for immediate action by
Parliament was the fifteenth, which provided that "towards further
defraying the said Expences, it may be proper to charge certain
Stamp Duties in the said Colonies and Plantations." [17] Grenville evidently doubted that the revenue from the new duties would be as
much as he wanted from the colonies. By the fifteenth resolution he
simply announced his intention of levying a stamp duty—that is, an
excise tax on various documents and articles made of paper—sometime in the future. With the exception of this resolution, which called
for no action, and with minor revisions, his proposals were drawn
into a bill, and enacted into law—the Sugar Act of 1764, it was usually
called, because the part of it which drew most attention was the
three-penny tax on molasses.

Although the new law was formally a revision in the regulations of
trade, there was no attempt to conceal its main purpose: it was offered
as a revenue act, and the preamble affirmed that it was "just and necessary, that a revenue be raised, in your Majesty's said dominions in
America." [18] The colonists were at last to be taxed.

15. Bernard to Jackson, August 3, 1763, Bernard Papers, Harvard College Library,
III, 93-94; Jasper Mauduit to the Lords of the Treasury, read February 27, 1764, Treasury Papers, Class I, Bundle 430, ff. 204-205.

16. Treasury Papers, Class I, Bundle 434, f. 52. These calculations were, of course, not
borne out by events. Grenville's measures did put the customs service on a paying basis,
so that a net total of about £20,000 was extracted from the North American colonies
between September 29, 1764, and October 10, 1765 (Treasury Papers, Class I, Bundle
430, f. 228), but of this amount the duty on molasses probably accounted for less than
£5000 (ibid., Bundle 434, f. 53). Later, when the duty was reduced to 1d. a gallon, it
netted a much larger amount (ibid., Bundle 434, f. 70). See also O. M. Dickerson, Letter
to the Editor, William and Mary Quarterly, 3d ser., 6 (1949), 353.

17. Journals of the House of Commons, XXIX, 935.

18. Statutes at Large, XXVI, 33.

From the very beginning the colonies greeted the attentions of George Grenville with consternation. Of his first effort to enforce existing customs regulations Governor Bernard reported that "the publication of orders for the strict execution of the Molasses Act has caused a greater alarm in this country than the taking of *Fort William Henry* did in 1757 ... the Merchants say, There is an end of the trade in this Province. ..." [19] The Act had been due to expire in a few months, but now the colonists correctly surmised the intention of the Ministry to continue it.[20] If they could no longer evade the duty on molasses, the future of some colonies would be dismal indeed. Probably none of the Acts of Trade had been universally complied with, but in the case of the Molasses Act violation had been wholesale, for by their own admission New England merchants could not have obeyed it and stayed in business.

The Americans blamed both the establishment and the enforcement of the sugar duties on the influence of the British West Indian sugar planters. These nabobs, who drew huge incomes from the labor of their slaves, were able to spend their lives in England, where a judicious use of their wealth secured legislation favoring their interests above those of the mainland colonies, in fact above those of England herself.[21] To defeat this sinister power, the colonists relied on the good sense of the mother country. They could not believe that, if awakened to the facts, she would allow her trade with a whole continent to be sacrificed to these grasping plutocrats.

The Assembly of Rhode Island, that colony which sometimes seemed to regard itself as the ally, rather than the subject of Great Britain, put the case in a remonstrance to the Board of Trade.[22] Rhode Island, they pointed out, consumed £120,000 sterling of British manufactures every year and herself produced little more than £5000 worth of exports. Only the profits from the molasses trade enabled the colony to pay for her consumption of British goods. As the British sugar islands could supply less than a fifth of the molasses that poured into Rhode Island's thirty distilleries, the other four-fifths

---

19. *Select Letters on the Trade and Government of America* (London, 1774), 9.

20. The House of Commons, in March of 1763, had actually voted a bill to extend it, but the final reading had been postponed and never resumed. *Journals of the House of Commons*, XXIX, 623. When the Sugar Act was passed, it contained a provision extending the old duties until the end of September, 1764, when the new ones were to take effect.

21. Bernard, *Select Letters*, 9. The North Americans seem to have credited the West Indians with greater influence in England than they actually possessed. See L. B. Namier, *England in the Age of the American Revolution* (London, 1930), 271-279.

22. John R. Bartlett, ed., *Records of the Colony of Rhode Island and Providence Plantations* (Providence, 1861), VI, 378-383.

must be French and subject to duty, the collection of which would entail a prohibitive increase in price and put an end not only to the molasses trade but to the distilling industry, the African trade in rum, and the sale of fish and produce in the West Indies, and consequently to the profits which British manufacturers were drawing from Rhode Island. A memorial to Parliament from New York rehearsed these same arguments but with more impressive figures: the preponderance of New York's imports over her exports amounted to nearly £470,000 sterling, all of which was made up through the trade deriving from French molasses.[23] The New York memorial was not approved by the House of Representatives until April 20, 1764, when the Sugar Act—though news had not yet reached America—had already passed both houses of Parliament; nor unfortunately had the Rhode Island remonstrance and one from the Massachusetts Assembly[24] reached England by March 9, when Grenville introduced his resolutions for revision and continuation of the molasses duty.

Even though the colonies had surmised the Ministry's intention to continue some duty,[25] when news arrived early in May, 1764, that Grenville had called for 3d. per gallon, they were taken by surprise. Rumor had led them to suppose that the figure would be 1d. or 2d. a gallon.[26] It was conceivable that the trade might have borne a 2d. duty, though even this would have caused hardship. A 3d. duty would be as prohibitive as a 6d. one, and would entail all the disastrous consequences described in the protests that had gone to England.

Although the duty on molasses was the most distressing provision of the Sugar Act, it was by no means the only one to cause alarm in the colonies. The new restrictions on the export of lumber threatened to ruin a branch of business almost as vital as that based on molasses. America's forests were one of her greatest economic assets, and colonial merchants had built up a substantial lumber trade at several European ports. Now all shipments must go to England.

23. *Journal of the Votes and Proceedings of the General Assembly of the Colony of New York* (New York, 1766), II, 740-744.

24. On the Massachusetts protest, see *Journal of the Honorable House of Representatives* . . . (Boston, 1763), 132; Connecticut Historical Society, *Collections*, 18 (1920), 261-273. Jasper Mauduit, the agent, failing to receive the protest in time, drew up a petition to the Lords of the Treasury himself (Treasury Papers, Class I, Bundle 430, ff. 204-205; see also Massachusetts Historical Society, *Collections*, 74 (1918), 144 n., 146 n.), but it evidently had no effect. No petition against the bill reached Parliament.

25. A committee of the Massachusetts General Court appointed to consider the question, conjectured that the policy of enforcing the 6d. duty had been adopted in order to secure acquiescence in the renewal at a lower figure. Thomas Cushing to Jasper Mauduit, January, 1764, Massachusetts Historical Society, *Collections*, 74 (1918), 145.

26. *Massachusetts Gazette and Boston News-Letter*, May 26, 1763, March 29, April 5, 1764.

Though from there they could be reshipped, the increased costs might well destroy the trade. The new wine duties, while drying up the consumption of Madeira as intended, would also shrink the profitable island market for American provisions. The abolition of drawbacks on foreign textiles would curb another branch of commerce. Thus all the minor avenues of trade, through which the colonists might have recovered from the ruin of their molasses business, were also blocked. Furthermore the old solution of smuggling was no longer practical, for the risk of seizure was so great that the added cost of smuggling would have the same effect as the payment of duties.

The terms of the Sugar Act undoubtedly caused genuine distress to colonial merchants, but this was heightened by a number of circumstances not directly connected with the Act itself. Most annoying, perhaps, was the literal-mindedness of naval officers. The Navy lives in a world of its own, and when the commanders of ships in American waters received instructions to assist in collecting the customs, they went about the business with no regard whatever for the facts of economic life. It is not likely that Parliament intended the new restrictions to apply to every dory that crossed an American river, but the Navy thought it necessary to exact the full measure of obedience from everything that floated, especially since the officers claimed a share of the prize money on every seizure they made.[27] By November of 1764 William Allen, the Chief Justice of Pennsylvania, was complaining to a business correspondent in London, that "even the Intercourse between here and New Jersey is, in a great Measure interrupted, which was carried on in Flats and small Boats, and the produce of the Western part of that Colony shipped off from this City, but now, one of those poor fellows cannot take in a few Staves, or Pig Iron, or Bar Iron, or Tar &c. but they must go thirty or forty Miles, or more to give Bond, the Charge of which and his travelling, make the Burthen intollerable. It never was the intention of the Legislature at home to destroy this little River-Trade, which is carried on in a kind of Market Boats, but their Regulations were only for Sea Vessels. This is a general Complaint all over the Continent."[28] Allen

27. This was a matter of dispute between the Navy and the colonial governors, the latter maintaining that the share claimed by the Navy should go to the governor of the colony where the ship was seized. See letters of Lord Colville to Philip Stephens, November 24, 1763, September 22, 1764, Admiralty Secretary In Letters 482, Public Record Office, Library of Congress transcripts; Francis Bernard to Lord Colville April 25, 1764, to J. Pownall, December 29, 1763, and to Lord Halifax, February 18, 1764, Bernard Papers, III, 39, 119, and 141-144 respectively.

28. William Allen to D. Barclay & Sons, November 20, 1764, Lewis B. Walker, ed., The Burd Papers: Extracts from Chief Justice William Allen's Letter Book (n.p., 1897), 65.

was right. Not merely in Philadelphia, but in Boston, Newport, Charleston, and the other centers of shipping, merchants found that the men-of-war were so completely unbending that, as one Boston merchant said, "no vessel hardly comes in or goes out, but they find some pretence to seize and detain her." [29]

To be sure the merchants fought back. They boycotted pilots who brought naval vessels into port,[30] offered mates and midshipmen higher wages than the Navy was allowed to pay,[31] and raised howling mobs when the Navy consequently had to impress seamen to fill out its crews.[32] In Boston, where people had already had a good deal of practice in minding their neighbors' business, they even wrote anonymous letters to the authorities in England complaining of the "immodest women" that the naval officers brought with them.[33] But these tactics probably served to make the Navy more determined in carrying out what it took to be its duties.

Another circumstance adding to colonial irritation was that Parliament followed the Sugar Act almost immediately by an act prohibiting paper money.[34] Such a prohibition had already been applied to New England in 1751; now it was extended to all the American colonies. Although the use of paper money had sometimes resulted in inflation, with hardship for creditors, the lack of it would be a hardship to almost everyone. The balance of trade with England prevented the colonies from acquiring a supply of hard money there, and the new restrictions on trade would prevent them from acquiring it elsewhere, so that without paper money they would be without any medium of exchange with which to carry on business. Economic life would be reduced to bartering. As one Philadelphia merchant expressed it, "the Inhabitants will be reduced to the necessity of primitive Times in this Place, of going to Market for the Provisions of their Families with Rum Sugar Melasses Ozenbrigs &c &c instead of Money. . . ." [35] The effect on commerce, in combination with the

29. *Massachusetts Gazette*, May 17, 1764. See also *Newport Mercury*, June 10, 1765. Governor Bull of South Carolina wrote to Charles Garth, the colony's agent, complaining of the Navy's treatment of "Decked Pettiaugers and Schooners in their Necessary Coasting Voyages." Charles Garth to Committee of Correspondence of the South Carolina Assembly, December 23, 1765, South Carolina Historical Society.

30. Lord Colville to Philip Stephens, November 9, 1764, Admiralty Secretary In Letters 482.

31. Lord Colville to Philip Stephens, November 9, 1764, and August 8, 1765, *ibid.*

32. For an example see ch. 4.

33. Lord Colville to Philip Stephens, August 8, 1765, Admiralty Secretary In Letters 482.

34. 4 George III, c. 34, *Statutes at Large*, XXVI, 103-105.

35. November 9, 1765, Daniel Roberdeau to Meyler & Hall, Roberdeau Letter Book, Historical Society of Pennsylvania.

Sugar Act, was obvious. Samuel Rhoads, Jr., another Philadelphian, wrote to his business correspondents in England: "If you will deprive us of all Medium of Trade among ourselves, we shall not be able to export Provisions &c. in the same Degree as formerly, and if we are not on any Terms allow'd a Trade to get Money from abroad, we shall have none to pay you for Goods, and then unless you will send them Gratis our Dealings must end." [36]

The final and most serious circumstance aggravating the burden of the Sugar Act, was a post-war depression. The initial depression probably had no connection with the Sugar Act. Colonial credit had expanded during the war, and the post-war contraction brought a number of large-scale bankruptcies. From Philadelphia Chief Justice Allen wrote in May, 1765, "I think we have a gloomy Prospect before us, as there are of late some Persons failed, who were no way Suspected, and a probability of some others, as the whisper goes, . . ." [37] In Boston there was the most alarming failure in the history of the town, when Nathaniel Wheelwright stopped payment on January 16, 1765. According to James Otis, this event gave as great a shock to credit in Massachusetts as the collapse of the South Sea Bubble did in England. Wheelwright had been heavily engaged in war contracts for the government in England, and had consequently acquired "such an undue Credit that he became next to the Treasurer, Banker General for the province and almost for the Continent." His failure carried a wave of lesser failures in its wake, and "such was the Consternation for some little time that people appeared with pale Horror and Dread, and when a little recovered run about the City. Widows and Orphans that are ruined can only bewail their fate, the more resolute have been pulling and hauling, attaching and summoning to secure themselves, but it was too late to shut the Stable door, . . ." [38] Wheelwright's failure could not be attributed directly to the Sugar Act, but the accompanying depression could be and was. When merchants found themselves in a tight spot and prevented from extricating themselves because of the Sugar Act, it was natural to blame the Act for everything.

The colonists were unwilling to die an economic death without a struggle and threw themselves into a fight for repeal. Their most effective weapon was the fact that such a large part of English in-

36. June 22, 1764, Pennsylvania Magazine of History and Biography, 14 (1890), 423.
37. William Allen to D. Barclay & Sons, May 19, 1765, Burd Papers, 67.
38. James Otis to George Johnstone et al., June 27, 1765, Massachusetts Historical Society, Proceedings, 43 (1909), 204-207. Governor Bernard told the Board of Trade that Wheelwright's failure "was like an Earthquake . . . and a general Bankruptcy was apprehended for a time." April 8, 1765, Bernard Papers, III, 203-204.

dustry and commerce was supported by the American market. An impoverished America would be unable to buy English manufactures. The assemblies of New York, Rhode Island, and Massachusetts had pointed this out to Parliament; the colonial merchants now impressed it on their British business correspondents. Upon learning of Grenville's resolutions, Samuel Rhoads, Jr., wrote, "I need not say much of future Dealings, because I fear that all our Trade with you must come to an End, for nothing can be more certain than its Intirely ceasing if your Legislature will carry into Execution those Resolves. . . ." [39] William Allen likewise warned that the Sugar Act must put an end to all remittances from America to England, a fact which would "soon be perceived by the London Merchants, and by all the Manufacturers in England." [40]

Time alone would have proved the truth of these warnings, and probably soon with the assistance of the post-war depression, which was also being felt in England; but the colonists knew that a determined boycott of English goods would further hasten the day. They urged one another to replace British manufactures with American.[41] Widows and widowers should stop wearing the costly mourning clothes fashionable at the time and stop handing out fancy gloves and scarves to other mourners at funerals.[42] Such luxuries must be foregone until American manufacturers could supply them. American thirst should be quenched with American brew,[43] and American ladies should set aside "gaudy, butterfly, vain, fantastick, and expensive Dresses brought from Europe" and appear in "decent plain Dresses made in their own Country." [44] In New York a society for the promotion of colonial manufactures was established which offered bounties for the production of articles generally imported from England.[45] In Philadelphia the several volunteer fire companies pledged themselves to eat no more lamb and to drink no imported beer, in order to encourage the local brewing industry and the raising of wool.[46]

39. *Pa. Mag. of Hist.*, 14 (1890), 423.

40. *Burd Papers*, 65-66.

41. *Massachusetts Gazette and Boston News-Letter*, July 5, 1764; *Boston Post-Boy and Advertiser*, October 1, 1764. See A. M. Schlesinger, *The Colonial Merchants and the American Revolution*, 1763-1776 (New York, 1918), ch. 2.

42. *Boston Post-Boy and Advertiser*, October 1, 8, 29, 1764; *Newport Mercury*, August 20, 1764.

43. *Pennsylvania Journal*, August 23, 1764; *Massachusetts Gazette and Boston News-Letter*, September 6, 13, 1764.

44. *Pennsylvania Journal*, August 23, 1764.

45. *London Chronicle*, January 26-29, 1765; *Pennsylvania Journal*, December 27, 1764; Schlesinger, *Colonial Merchants*, 64.

46. *Pennsylvania Gazette*, February 28, March 7, 1765.

This was language which merchants and manufacturers could understand, a sure means to enlist their support in the fight for repeal. And Parliament would have to listen when they spoke up. If exports to the colonies fell off sharply, the cries of rage and distress throughout the kingdom would drown out the voice of the West Indies planters and be heard inside the House of Commons.

Undoubtedly the drastic economic effects the colonists anticipated from the Sugar Act prompted the alarm they felt, but it was natural for them to inquire into the right of the matter. The whole structure of constitutional government has grown out of resistance to the unwise or irresponsible use of authority, and the colonists were following the example of their English ancestors when they asked whether a measure which threatened such disastrous consequences could be enacted of right. They found the answer too in the constitutional principles which Englishmen had fought for on a hundred battlefields. Examining the Sugar Act, they saw that it curtailed the right of trial by jury, and they saw that the British Parliament was assuming the authority to tax them. Here was the ground upon which they could challenge the body that threatened them, the very ground on which that body had fought and gained its own supremacy over the King.

They had heard rumors of a colonial tax for some time, a tax to support a standing army in America. Ever since Wolfe captured Quebec this had been in the air,[47] and when in 1763 an army of 10,000 was definitely decided on, the rumors of taxation multiplied. Joseph Sherwood, the Rhode Island agent, wrote on August 4 that the colonies would be expected to bear the whole expense of the troops, and this was also reported in the newspapers.[48] There were assorted theories of how the money would be raised: by a poll tax,[49]

47. See Cecilius Calvert to Horatio Sharpe, January 19, 1760, *Archives of Maryland,* XXXI, 527.

48. "Official Letters of Rhode Island Agents in London 1746-1769," transcripts, John Carter Brown Library. Thomas Hutchinson wrote to Israel Williams, November 17, 1763, that "A revenue from the Colonies will certainly be attempted the next Parliament sufficient at least to support the troops to be kept up here." Bancroft Transcripts, New York Public Library. *The London Chronicle* reported in the issue of March 5-8, 1763, just after Parliament had voted to establish the troops (*Journals of the House of Commons,* XXIX, 506, 530, March 7, 1763), that they were "to be paid the first year by Great Britain, but afterwards by the colonies." This item was copied in colonial newspapers, e.g. *Pennsylvania Journal,* May 12, 1763. See also *Annual Register . . . for the Year 1763,* 21.

49. Cecilius Calvert to Governor Sharpe, March 1, 1763. Sparks Mss. 9, f. 46a, Harvard College Library; *Archives of Maryland,* XIV (1895), 92.

by a stamp tax,[50] by a tax on imports.[51] These advance rumors elicited no extensive reaction, perhaps because they were too uncertain to form the basis of a protest; but there was no uncertainty left after the resolutions for the Sugar Act appeared. England intended to raise a revenue by taxes on trade and probably by a stamp tax. The passage of the Sugar Act, if we may believe James Otis, "set people a thinking, in six months, more than they had done in their whole lives before." [52] And what they thought about was the rights of Englishmen. The incantation of those potent words was heard from Portsmouth to Savannah.

In Massachusetts, the town of Boston, exhibiting what was to become a characteristic colonial attitude, detected the entering wedge of a movement to deprive the colonists of all their rights. The instructions prepared on May 24, 1764, for Boston's representatives in the General Assembly declared:

But what still hightens our Apprehensions is that those unexpected proceedings may be preparatory to new Taxations upon us: For if our Trade may be taxed why not our Lands? Why not the produce of our Lands and every Thing we possess or make use of? This we apprehend annihilates our Charter Right to Govern and Tax ourselves.—It strikes at our British Privileges which as we have never forfeited them we hold in common with our Fellow Subjects who are Natives of Britain: If Taxes are laid upon us in any shape without ever having a Legal Representation where they are laid, are we not reduced from the Character of Free Subjects to the miserable state of Tributary Slaves? [53]

It was also about this time that James Otis, one of the assemblymen from Boston, wrote his *Rights of the Colonies Asserted and Proved*.[54] Otis insisted that a Parliament without American representatives, though supreme in authority, could have no more right to tax Americans than to make two plus two equal five. He explicitly rejected a distinction which Bernard was simultaneously setting down in his ninety-seven propositions, that external taxes on trade be levied by Parliament and internal taxes by the colonial assemblies. Otis affirmed flatly (had he and Bernard perhaps argued this together at Concord?) that "there is no foundation for the distinction

50. *Newport Mercury*, May 30, 1763.
51. Governor Sharpe to Cecilius Calvert, June 4, 1763, Sparks Mss. 9, f. 52; *Boston Post-Boy and Advertiser*, May 14, 1764.
52. *The Rights of the British Colonies Asserted and Proved* (Boston, 1764), 54.
53. *A Report of the Record Commissioners of the City of Boston, Containing the Boston Town Records, 1758 to 1769* (Boston, 1886), 121-122.
54. Boston, 1764.

some make in England between an internal and an external tax on the colonies." [55] Parliament had no right to levy either.

The Massachusetts House of Representatives listened while Otis's lengthy pamphlet was read and read again. Then they voted their approval and sent it to their agent in London with a letter further developing their views along the same lines.[56] By October they had drawn up and approved a petition to the King, informing him too that "we look *upon those Duties as a tax* [i.e. the duties imposed by the Sugar Act], and which we humbly apprehend ought not to be laid without the Representatives of the People affected by them." [57] The petition drafted by the House of Representatives so firmly denied Parliamentary authority that the Council feared it would give offense in England and do more harm than good. Under the leadership of Lieutenant-Governor Hutchinson they met in conference with a committee of the Representatives and pleaded so successfully that the House withdrew their strong words in favor of tamer ones submitted by the Lieutenant-Governor.[58] The new document was directed not simply to the King but to the House of Commons, a significant recognition of that group's authority. Omitting entirely the question of rights, even the word, it asked instead for continuation of the "privilege" which the colonies had hitherto enjoyed of levying their own internal taxes. This argument was aimed at the proposed stamp tax. The Sugar Act itself was condemned on the familiar economic grounds. The address was such a model of restraint and loyalty that Governor Bernard himself endorsed it.[59] The members of the House of Representatives, though they accepted it, were not so enthusiastic. Their Speaker advised the agent that they

were clearly for making an ample and full declaration of the exclusive Right of the People of the Colonies to tax themselves and that they ought not to be deprived of a right they had so long enjoyed and which they held by Birth and by Charter; but they coud not prevail with the Councill, tho they made several Tryalls, to be more explicit than they have been in the Petition sent you . . . You will

55. *Ibid.*, 42.

56. *Journal of the Honourable House of Representatives* . . . (Boston, 1764), 53, 66, 72-77.

57. Oxenbridge Thacher Papers, Massachusetts Historical Society, and Massachusetts Archives, XXII, 414.

58. Alden Bradford, ed., *Speeches of the Governors of Massachusetts from 1765 to 1775* . . . (Boston, 1818), 21-24. On Hutchinson's role, see Governor Bernard's letters to Lord Halifax, John Pownall, and Richard Jackson, November 17, 18, 1764; Bernard Papers, III, 181-187, 189, 260-264.

59. Bernard Papers, III, 181-187; *Select Letters*, 13-22.

therefore collect the sentiments of the Representative Body of People rather from what they have heretofore sent you than from the present Address.[60]

In Rhode Island where the whole government was popularly elected, no conservative politicians hampered the preparation of a spirited protest. Governor Stephen Hopkins himself stated the colony's objections to Parliamentary taxation in a pamphlet entitled *The Rights of Colonies Examined.*[61] Though Hopkins rehearsed all the woeful effects on trade to be expected from the Sugar Act, his principal concern, as the title indicated, was rights, and he reserved his specific arguments on this head for the proposed stamp tax. This, he said, would be "a manifest violation of their [the colonists'] just and long enjoyed rights. For it must be confessed by all men, that they who are taxed at pleasure by others, cannot possibly have any property, can have nothing to be called their own; they who have no property, can have no freedom, but are indeed reduced to the most abject slavery." [62] The Assembly approved the Governor's pamphlet and sent it to the agent along with a petition to the King, which they had drawn themselves. This concluded with the request "that our trade may be restored to its former condition, and no further limited, restrained and burdened, than becomes necessary for the general good of all Your Majesty's subjects; that the courts of vice admiralty may not be vested with more extensive powers in the colonies than are given them by law in Great Britain; that the colonists may not be taxed but by the consent of their own representatives, as Your Majesty's other free subjects are." [63]

Both Rhode Island and Massachusetts, in demonstrating the unconstitutionality of Parliamentary taxation, concentrated their constitutional objections on the proposed stamp tax. In spite of the preamble which clearly announced the Sugar Act as a revenue measure, they skirted the question of right and protested it only as a crippling regulation of trade—unwise but within the authority of Parliament. It remained for the Assembly of New York, the colony which later became the stronghold of loyalism, to tell Parliament flatly that the Sugar Act violated colonial rights. On October 18, 1764, in petitions to the King, the House of Lords, and the House of Commons, the New Yorkers claimed an absolute exemption from

60. Massachusetts Historical Society, *Collections,* 74 (1918), 170-171.
61. Providence, 1764, reprinted in John R. Bartlett, ed., *Records of the Colony of Rhode Island and Providence Plantations* (Providence, 1861), VI, 416-427.
62. *Ibid.,* 423.
63. *Ibid.,* 414-416.

taxes not granted by their own representatives.[64] The people of New York, they said, "nobly disdain the thought of claiming that Exemption as *a Privilege.*—They found it on a Basis more honourable, solid and stable; they challenge it, and glory in it as their Right." [65] New York, like other colonies, had no quarrel with Parliament's power to regulate their trade. They would not, for example, ask for liberty to import woolens from France. But they demanded that regulations of trade be regulations of trade. Parliament could "model the Trade of the whole Empire, so as to subserve the Interest of her own, . . . But a Freedom to drive all Kinds of Traffic in a Subordination to, and not inconsistent with, the *British* Trade; and an Exemption from all Duties in such a Course of Commerce, is humbly claimed by the Colonies as the most essential of all the Rights to which they are intitled, . . ." The exemption from duties in all commerce not detrimental to the mother country was essential, in the opinion of the Assembly, to a proper enjoyment of the right of self-taxation. Any distinction between different kinds of taxes was futile, for,

since all Impositions, whether they be internal Taxes, or Duties paid, for what we consume, equally diminish the Estates upon which they are charged; what avails it to any People, by which of them they are impoverished? Every Thing will be given up to preserve Life; and though there is a Diversity in the Means, yet, the whole Wealth of a Country may be as effectually drawn off, by the Exaction of Duties, as by any other Tax upon their Estates.

And therefore, the General Assembly of *New-York,* in Fidelity to their Constituents, cannot but express the most earnest Supplication, that the Parliament will charge our Commerce with no other Duties, than a necessary Regard to the particular Trade of *Great-Britain,* evidently demands; but leave it to the legislative Power of the Colony, to impose all other Burthens upon it's own People, which the publick Exigences may require.

Latterly, the Laws of Trade seem to have been framed without an Attention to this fundamental Claim.[66]

The Sugar Act by this reasoning infringed colonial rights not only by extending the jurisdiction of admiralty courts but by imposing duties on branches of colonial commerce which did not conflict with British interests. The molasses duty might be beneficial to

64. *Journals of the Votes and Proceedings of the General Assembly of the Colony of New York . . .* (New York, 1766), II, 769-779.
65. *Ibid.,* II, 777.
66. *Ibid.,* II, 778.

the West Indies planters but certainly not to the commerce or manufactures of the mother country. It was therefore an abuse of the Parliamentary power to regulate trade.

North Carolina was the only other colony which took the Sugar Act squarely for what it was, a revenue act. The North Carolina Assembly, in a message to Governor Dobbs, on October 31, 1764, objected to the "new Taxes and Impositions laid on us without our Privity and Consent, and against what we esteem our Inherent right, and Exclusive privilege of Imposing our own Taxes." [67] The rest of the colonies, depending to some extent on how it would affect them, either ignored the Act or, like Massachusetts and Rhode Island, argued against it on economic grounds. But the colonies were not therefore ignoring Grenville's challenge to their rights. Several of those that failed to take issue with him over the Sugar Act, raised their voices against his resolution for a stamp tax: Connecticut, Pennsylvania, Virginia, and South Carolina sent their protests and denials that Parliament had the right to enact it into law. [68]

The remarkable thing about these various remonstrances both against the Sugar Act and the proposed stamp tax is that their denial of Parliament's right to tax the colonies was wholesale and unqualified. Hopkins in Rhode Island did not specify that one kind of tax would be more acceptable than another. Governor Thomas Fitch, writing for Connecticut, focused his strictures on internal taxes, but did not acknowledge that external taxes would be acceptable. Otis's pamphlet specifically rejected any distinction between taxes on trade and internal taxes. New York, of course, rejected "all Taxes not granted by themselves." [69] Pennsylvania instructed her agent to prevent the stamp tax "or any other Impositions or Taxes on the Colonists from being laid by the Parliament, inasmuch as they neither are or can be represented, under their present Circumstances, in that Legislature," and because such taxes would "have a Tendency to deprive the good People of this Province of their most essential Rights as British Subjects." [70] Virginia, in three petitions to King, Lords, and Commons, declared it a funda-

67. William L. Saunders, ed., *The Colonial Records of North Carolina*, (Raleigh, 1886-1890), VI, 1261.

68. J. H. Trumbull and C. J. Hoadly, eds., *Public Records of the Colony of Connecticut* (Hartford, 1850-1890), XII, 651-671; *Pennsylvania Archives*, 8th ser., VII (1935), 5643-5645, 5678-5682; J. P. Kennedy, ed., *Journals of the House of Burgesses of Virginia, 1761-1765* (Richmond, 1907), liv-lviii, 302-304; R. W. Gibbes, *Documentary History of the American Revolution* (New York, 1855), I, 1-6.

69. *Journal of the Votes and Proceedings*, II, 776.

70. *Pennsylvania Archives*, 8th ser., VII (1935), 5643-5645.

mental principle of the British constitution "that the People are not subject to any Taxes but such as are laid on them by their own Consent, or by those who are legally appointed to represent them." [71] North Carolina claimed the "Exclusive privilege of Imposing our own Taxes," [72] and South Carolina the "inherent right of every British subject, not to be taxed but by his own consent, or that of his representative." [73]

With such a universal denial of Parliament's right to tax, it is surprising that the protests against the Sugar Act did not emphasize the question of right more than they did. Most colonies chose to regard it as a regulation of trade, which it was, rather than a revenue measure, which it also was. Because of its dual purpose they hesitated to question Parliament's authority to pass it, for it could always be defended as a mere regulation of trade. Only North Carolina, New York, and Massachusetts dared raise the question, and even they might have been content to overlook it had the duty been set at 1d. a gallon instead of 3d. In any event George Grenville did set the duty at 3d., and he did announce his intention of levying a stamp tax. This would be a naked and indisputable act of taxation. By these two steps he plunged the empire into the discussion of colonial rights which earlier ministers had been able to avoid, and which later ministers were unable to halt.

71. *Journals of the House of Burgesses, 1761-1765,* lv, 302.
72. *Colonial Records of North Carolina,* VI, 1261.
73. Gibbes, *Documentary History,* I, 2.

≫ FOUR ≪

JOHN ROBINSON
Collector of Customs

THE old road from Dighton, on Narragansett Bay, to the town of Taunton, Massachusetts, was eight miles, not too long for an afternoon's walk if you liked walking, and not unpleasant to travel as it wound past farms and fields, a trifle too muddy perhaps in April, and as full of holes and stumps as other American roads, yet not unpleasant. It was not the road that bothered the tight-lipped man stumbling along it on Friday afternoon, the twelfth of April, in the year 1765. It was not the road or the weather or the countryside, but the people. Who would enjoy walking eight miles, led by a jeering mob and an impudent sheriff, with Taunton jail at the end of the road? The procession that afternoon would have been fitting for some monstrous enemy of society, a murderer perhaps. But John Robinson was no murderer. John Robinson was the man George Grenville had sent to collect His Majesty's customs in Narragansett Bay, and his only crime was enforcing the Laws of Trade.

Robinson had left England a little more than a year before, with only a hazy idea of what to expect from his new post. He knew of Rhode Island's bad reputation, for the other colonies hopefully propagated the idea that all smuggling was carried on from there. He knew that Newport, a town of eight or nine thousand inhabitants, was an appropriate place for the custom-house he was to occupy, for it was strategically located on an island commanding the entrance to Narragansett Bay. Beyond this he was innocent. His predecessor could not have told him much, because that happy individual had never seen the shores of Narragansett. Thomas Clift had acted by deputy, and when Grenville ordered all customs officers to their posts, he was one of those who thought the comforts of home in

England more valuable than the profits of office in America.[1] His loss was John Robinson's gain, if anything could be called a gain that led a man along the road to Taunton with the sheriff by his side. As he tramped along, grimly ignoring the insults hurled at him, proudly ignoring the sword which that young devil Smith brandished over him, Robinson had to admit that his present predicament was not surprising after his experiences of the past year.

His education in the tribulations of American customs officers must have begun before he reached his post, for he had come by way of Boston [2] and undoubtedly learned from John Temple, the Surveyor General of Customs for the Northern District (Connecticut northward) what had occurred only a few months before, when a new Comptroller of Customs was installed in Rhode Island. The Governor of the colony, by instruction from the Assembly, had refused to administer the oaths of office, and Temple himself had been obliged to go to Providence for the ceremony. There, under his very nose, a vessel had landed a cargo from Surinam, without so much as a look in the direction of the customs officers. He had immediately ordered her seized, but that night a crowd of people with blackened faces boarded her, loaded an export cargo, and put her to sea before morning. Temple was pained, but not surprised, to discover that the ship belonged to a judge of the Rhode Island Superior Court.[3]

Thus forewarned and filled with misgivings about the people he was to live among, Robinson could hardly have been prepared for the civilized, almost sophisticated community that he found in Newport. People still talked of Bishop Berkeley, who had once lived there, and the Redwood Library furnished a meeting place for the gentlemen who continued to inhabit the intellectual world which he represented. The town was filled with fine houses, only a few of brick or stone, but many showing a taste that would not be complained of in London. Some were surrounded by the elaborate landscaping that was now regarded by Englishmen as one of the fine arts, and the farms that covered the rolling countryside were laid out in neat and prosperous fields, divided by beautiful stone walls that even England could not have matched. In May, when

1. Samuel G. Arnold, *History of the State of Rhode Island and Providence Plantations* (3d edn., New York, 1878), II, 246.

2. Ezra Stiles, *Extracts from the Itineraries and other Miscellanies of Ezra Stiles*, Franklin B. Dexter, ed. (New Haven, 1916), 204; *Providence Gazette*, May 26, 1764.

3. Francis Bernard to John Pownall, February 10, 1764, Bernard Papers, III, 130, Harvard College Library; Ezra Stiles to John Hubbard, January 30, 1764, Stiles Papers, Yale University Library.

Robinson arrived, the whole island was a thing of beauty, rippling meadows, gardens ablaze with tulips, white sails and blue water glittering in the harbor. Any man would have been impressed, for Newport was truly one of the most delightful spots in eighteenth-century America.

After finding quarters with a British Army officer who had retired to this haven, Robinson settled down to business and found at once that the white sails were doing dirty work. The Newport merchants, whose houses looked so dignified and respectable, had fingers sticky with French molasses upon which they had paid no duties. With the zeal of a good housewife, he set about to scrub things clean. The merchants, he found, would be glad to make a bargain with him as they had with former customs officers, seventy thousand pounds per annum colonial currency, in return for freedom to take their ships in and out as they pleased.[4] But John Robinson preferred the hard way: backed by the new Sugar Act, he was confident he could collect duties as the law demanded. With the assistance of the royal Navy and of his subordinate customs officers he quickly began to catch Rhode Island ships in the act of smuggling molasses. It was not until he brought his prizes to the Admiralty Court for legal condemnation that he discovered what he was up against: the Rhode Island merchants knew more than one way to skin a customs officer. Both the Judge and the Advocate (prosecuting attorney) of Rhode Island's Admiralty Court were natives of the place and sympathetic, to say the least, with the merchants. The Judge called trials on short notice in Providence at times when he knew that the Collector was occupied by his duties at Newport, and the Advocate frequently failed to appear at all, so that merchants and ship captains who had been caught red-handed were dismissed on the pretext of a lack of evidence. If ever a smuggler had to be convicted and his ship consequently forfeited, the Court assumed the right of selling the vessel in the name of the King and generally did so at a trifle of her real value, perhaps to the culprit himself. Thus in one way or another the Sugar Act was evaded in the Admiralty Court as easily as the old Molasses Act had been in the common-law courts. To be sure, Robinson could take his cases to the Court at Halifax if he wished, but Halifax was several hundred miles away. If all his cases were to be tried there, he would never have time for his official duties in Rhode Island.[5]

4. Ezra Stiles, *Extracts from the Itineraries*, 204.

5. John Robinson and John Nicoll to Governor Ward, February 22, 1766, in Gertrude S. Kimball, ed., *The Correspondence of the Colonial Governors of Rhode Island, 1723-1775* (Boston, 1903), II, 376-381; *Records of the Colony of Rhode Island*, VI, 457-459.

The only real assistance that Robinson obtained was from the Navy. Two or three naval vessels were generally to be found in Newport Harbor, and under the new regulations some of their officers were commissioned as deputies to assist in the collection of customs duties. This did not make it any easier to win a case in Rhode Island's Admiralty Court, but it did make the initial seizure of smugglers possible. Unfortunately the assistance given him by the Navy added to the unpopularity he was winning only too rapidly by himself, for the British Navy was not welcome in American ports. The press gangs which came ashore from British warships to recruit sailors for the service had always aroused bitter resentment. In 1747, the people of Boston had greeted a press gang with a riot lasting three days.[6] But even if there was no attempt to impress American seamen or to enforce the Acts of Trade, there was apt to be friction whenever the Navy met up with civilians. A typical example was reported in the *Newport Mercury* on December 10, 1764. The officers of the *Cygnet* and the *Jamaica*, both men-of-war, had boarded a passenger ship running from Newfoundland to Boston and engaged in an altercation with the passengers. The incident concluded with a lieutenant running his sword through the belly of one of the passengers. When the *Cygnet* arrived in Newport Harbor a week after the news of this episode, she could scarcely have had a friendly reception. The newspapers failed to report, and probably few people ever learned, the part of the story which Robinson doubtless heard from Captain Leslie: the lieutenant's sword had come into play only after he was attacked with a broad axe and after several of his party had been thrown overboard by the passengers, who were suspected of being deserters from British warships.[7]

Such conflicts were by no means unusual. During Robinson's first year of residence the Rhode Islanders fought more than once with the men of the Navy. In fact he had been in Newport less than two months when he witnessed a most shocking incident. The naval schooner *St. John* had been impressing men in and around Narragansett Bay and had also seized a brig loaded with molasses. These actions, though legal, were cause enough for indignation in Rhode Island. The inhabitants of Newport found an opportunity to make their indignation righteous when three men from the schooner came ashore and stole some pigs and chickens. The indignation and its righteousness grew as the Sheriff, rowing out to arrest the offenders,

6. Thomas Hutchinson, *History of the Colony and Province of Massachusetts Bay*, L. S. Mayo, ed. (Cambridge, 1936), II, 330-333.

7. Lord Colville to Philip Stephens, February 16, 1765, Admiralty Secretary In Letters 482, Public Record Office, Library of Congress transcripts.

was prevented from boarding the ship. Then, on the same day, one of the impressed seamen, having escaped, showed himself on shore in plain view of the *St. John*. Her commander lowered a boat with a contingent of armed men to capture him, for he was now regarded as a deserter. On shore a mob was assembling. As the boat touched land they seized the officer in charge and rained a shower of brickbats on his men, who quickly pushed off again without him. Meanwhile the Sheriff had reported to the civil authorities that he had not been allowed to serve his warrant. Two of the Governor's Council therefore gave orders to the gunners at Fort George in Newport Harbor that the *St. John* should not leave the harbor. When she got under sail late in the afternoon, the fort hailed her, and upon her refusal to answer, opened fire. About eight or ten shots were sent, none of which took effect, and the *St. John* came to safely under the stern of the *Squirrel* man-of-war, which was anchored outside the harbor. In the next few days the thieves were delivered to the authorities, but the incident had resulted in colonial guns' firing upon a ship of His Majesty's Navy.[8]

People who dared fire on a ship of the royal Navy would dare— who could say what they would dare do to a mere customs collector? As John Robinson made his forced march to Taunton he must have realized that he could expect even worse treatment than he was now getting. The episode that landed him in Taunton jail began as a routine check on a suspicious cargo. The sloop *Polly* had sailed into Newport on April 2, 1765, after a voyage to Surinam. Her home port was Taunton, Massachusetts, which because of its location off Narragansett Bay was included in the jurisdiction of the custom-house at Newport. The captain reported a cargo of sixty-three casks of molasses, and Job Smith of Taunton, the owner, came to Newport and paid the 3d. a gallon tax required by the Sugar Act. The vessel then proceeded down the bay.[9]

Two days later John Robinson, looking over the record, decided that sixty-three casks of molasses was a surprisingly small cargo for a sloop the size of the *Polly* to be carrying. He communicated his suspicions to Captain Antrobus of the *Maidstone* man-of-war, and the two men, accompanied by Robinson's servant, Daniel Guthridge, and by Nicholas Lechmere, a minor customs officer, set off in a boat

8. *Records of the Colony of Rhode Island*, VI, 428-430; *Newport Mercury*, July 16, 1764; *Acts of the Privy Council, Colonial*, VI, 374-376, 384-387.

9. The account which follows, except as otherwise noted, is based on the documents in Treasury Papers, Class I, Bundle 442, Library of Congress transcripts. Some of these are listed in *Acts of the Privy Council, Colonial*, VI, 382-383.

to have another look. They overtook the *Polly* at Dighton on April 6, and upon boarding her found double the reported quantity of molasses. In the name of the King they seized the vessel, together with the undeclared part of her cargo.

The next step was to have their prize brought to Newport for safekeeping until she could be properly condemned in court, but no one in Dighton would serve the King on such a voyage. Leaving the vessel in charge of Guthridge and Lechmere, Robinson and Antrobus returned to Newport in search of a crew and sent them off on the morning of April 8. By this time Guthridge and Lechmere were on their way back with a sad story.

On Sunday afternoon, April 7, after Robinson and Antrobus had left, the two custodians grew thirsty and rowed to an enticing tavern which stood on the shore less than a hundred yards away. While they refreshed themselves, their boat was carried away, and darkness falling they saw some forty men in old clothes and blackened faces hurrying to the waterside. In boats and scows the mob swarmed aboard the *Polly,* and quickly carried away her whole cargo and everything else they could pry loose. Guthridge and Lechmere were given to understand that it would not be healthy to interfere. The next morning when they applied for aid to Colonel Richmond, a local justice of the peace, he told them darkly that earlier the same morning a party of men with guns, cutlasses, and blackened faces had come by looking for customs officers, and had dispersed only when he convinced them that Antrobus and Robinson were not at hand. There was no telling when they might assemble again. Lechmere and Guthridge decided that prudence lay in the direction of Newport and departed.

When they heard this story, Robinson and Antrobus set off at once for Dighton with a party of thirty marines and forty armed sailors. They soon met the crew they had despatched, returning without the *Polly* after a warm send-off by about a hundred people. And on reaching Swansea they were approached by Colonel Richmond, who did his best to discourage them from going farther, because "the handfull of men they had with them would be nothing against a whole Country." They replied by asking him and another justice of the peace for writs of assistance—warrants empowering them to search any building for suspected goods—but the justices held that only the Superior Court could grant such writs, and so the royal officers pressed on toward Dighton, giving no attention to the silent hostility of the farmhouses they passed. At Dighton they found that the mob had done its job well. The *Polly* had been run aground at a spring tide, her sails, rigging, cables, anchors, and entire cargo carried away and her bottom bored full of holes. Robinson again took possession of his devalued prize in the name of the King and went ashore to see what could be done about recovering the stolen goods. He had no doubt that they would be found somewhere in the possession of Job Smith.

No sooner had he landed than a sheriff appeared with a warrant for his arrest in an action brought by Job Smith: Smith wanted £3000 damages for seizure of the *Polly* and her cargo. Though Robinson could surmise that Smith had recovered everything but the hull already, he was obliged to submit; and so he found himself slogging through the mud, listening to the curses of the country people who now lined the road to watch him pass. He might well have been suffering more than verbal insults, had not Captain Antrobus sent along some of his men to accompany the procession, for a number of the "incensed Rabble" were armed, among them the son of Job Smith. Antrobus himself remained in Dighton to guard the *Polly*.

Upon arrival in Taunton, Robinson immediately sent messages to John Temple, the Surveyor General, but since he had no friends in the town to stand bail for him, he had to spend the night in custody. But John Robinson was not the man to be intimidated by a lawsuit, or by sore feet, or even by a mob. The letter he wrote to Temple showed that he had no intention of giving up. "My Antagonist," he said, "by his Friends has made several Overtures for an Accomodation but as it is no more my Inclination than it is in my Power, to favour a Wretch deserving of the severest Treatment that the Law can inflict, I continue Inflexable, and ready to suffer anything that their malice and Wickedness can suggest, tho' happy in the Consolation that the whole is the Effect of my doing my Duty," —brave words, written no doubt for transmittal to appreciative eyes in Whitehall, but the words of a man who was not afraid to do things the hard way. This was Friday, April 12; it was not until Sunday evening that a messenger arrived from the Surveyor General to bail him out. During the interval Job Smith and his friends had plenty of time to hide their molasses. The local justices of the peace had shown no disposition to help in recovering it. Rather, it seemed to Robinson, they offered every possible obstacle. And Samuel White, a local attorney and former Speaker of the Massachusetts Assembly, refused to give him any legal advice, on the ground that he had already been retained on the other side of the case. By the time Robinson was able to search buildings for the lost molasses, he could discover only eight hogsheads. These he sent to Newport, and Captain Antrobus after much difficulty floated the *Polly* and brought her back too. The prize had been plucked bare, but Robinson had at least maintained his dignity and in some measure the authority of the British government. He went at once to Boston to confer with the Surveyor General and to protest against the failure of the justices of the peace to assist him. On Temple's advice he decided to have the case of the *Polly* tried by the new Admiralty Court at Halifax.[10] The move would further aggravate the local feeling against him, but what of that? Popularity was not among the rewards which a customs officer could hope for.

The whole experience had been a trying one, and even though it had occurred in Massachusetts it must have made Robinson sympathize strongly with the aims of a group in Newport with whom he was becoming friendly. This was a small club of men, probably not more than fifteen or twenty, who had become thoroughly disgusted with the licentiousness of Rhode Island politics and wished to see a royal government established there.[11] It is not possible to identify all the members, but probably one was Benjamin Wickham, the officer who shared bachelor's quarters with Robinson and who may have introduced him to the other members. The winter of 1764-1765 in Newport was unusually severe,[12] with the harbor frequently clogged by ice, so that Robinson had plenty of time to sit by the fire and enjoy the company of his new friends. There was George Rome, an agent sent by the English firm of Champion and Hayley to collect debts owed them in Rhode Island. Rome had come to Newport only in 1761, but other members of the group were residents of long standing: Peter Harrison, the amateur architect who had designed the Redwood Library, Dr. Thomas Moffat, who had come in the 1730's to enjoy the company of Bishop Berkeley, Martin Howard, Jr., the son of a respected citizen of the town, and perhaps Augustus Johnston, another native, who was Attorney General of the colony. These men were of conservative temper and united in their distaste for the popular form of government which prevailed under Rhode Island's charter of 1663. Since the election of 1757 the annual contest for the governor's chair had degenerated into a personal feud between Samuel Ward of Newport and Kingstown and Stephen Hop-

10. Francis Bernard to Lord Halifax, May 11, 1765, Bernard Papers, III, 211-215.
11. The membership of this group can be inferred from the events discussed below. In particular, however, consult *Providence Gazette*, September 15, 1764, February 23, 1765; James Otis, *Brief Remarks on the Defence of the Halifax Libel* (Boston, 1765); and Carl Bridenbaugh's discussion in his *Peter Harrison, First American Architect* (Chapel Hill, 1949), 124-126.
12. *Newport Mercury*, January 7, 28, February 4, 1765.

kins of Providence. Each side battled for votes with all the tricks
known to politics, with polemic, bribery, flattery, slander, and even
the devastating truth. The results were discouraging to those who
thought that stability and decorum were essential attributes of good
government. To the members of the Newport club the disorderly
character of these elections was one more indication that the Rhode
Islanders had more freedom than they knew how to use.

The cause and the cure for this unhappy situation they agreed
on: "the colonies have originally been wrong founded.—They ought
all to have been regal governments, and every executive officer
appointed by the King. Until that is effected, and they are properly
regulated, they will never be beneficial to themselves nor good subjects to Great-Britain." [13] So wrote George Rome to Doctor Moffat in
1767, after the group had been scattered far and wide by the events
which were approaching when John Robinson returned from Taunton. But Rome's views in 1767 could not have come as a surprise
to his correspondent, for the club had been doing their best to make
them a reality ever since 1764. Doctor Moffat and Martin Howard, Jr.,
had taken the lead in the attempt to have the charter of Rhode
Island revoked and the government of the colony placed in the
hands of the Crown. The campaign began on April 23, 1764, with
a letter signed Z.Y., printed on the front page of the *Newport Mercury*. The writer (probably Moffat or Howard) lamented the evils
of party contention in Rhode Island and urged as a solution an act
of Parliament revoking the colony's charter and establishing royal
government. The letter was too straightforward. Had the conservatives been more experienced in the political maneuvering they
despised so much, they would not have tipped their hands so early
in the game. Perhaps they were overconfident, because they believed
that the change they were suggesting was in the cards. Like Bernard
they had noticed the reports that Parliament was going to overhaul
the colonial governments, and surely their own would be one of the
first to require attention. The letter of Z.Y. showed what the conservatives were expecting when it concluded, "Upon the whole, I hope
every honest man in the colony will seriously think of these things,
and join to facilitate and hasten that general reformation of the
colonies, which, we have reason to think, is now under the consideration of our rulers at home." The letter gladdened the heart and
quickened the pulse of Francis Bernard in Boston, but to most Rhode
Islanders the proposal to revoke their charter must have come as

13. *The Representations of Governor Hutchinson and Others, Contained in Certain
Letters Transmitted to England . . .* (Boston, 1773), 53.

a shock. And the next move in the conservative campaign was no more subtle. On June 11 the *Mercury* carried, by request of "some of our Customers," a copy of the commission which Charles I had issued to Archbishop Laud and others in 1634, with power to revoke all colonial charters. This was presumably intended to suggest that a similar move by George III would not be a novel one; but in a country which had not been sorry to see Charles I lose his head and perhaps had harbored the regicides, the suggestion was ill designed to win sympathy. Not until August 20 did the conservatives begin to clothe their sentiments in more appealing colors. On that date the *Mercury* began the first of a series of letters signed "O.Z. &c. &c." They were published over the next seven months and aimed principally at encouraging local industry, particularly the growth and manufacture of flax, hemp, and wool. Home industries were already popular with the most ardent local patriots as a possible means to turn British public opinion against the Sugar Act and the proposed Stamp Act, but the conservatives had no such end in view. They were not interested in bringing pressure to bear on Parliament but rather in diverting their countrymen's energies away from disloyal protests against its enactments. O.Z. and his colleagues discovered new reason for satisfaction with the policies of the mother country. "We cannot repress our filial Gratitude," they said, "when we consider that at the same Time Molasses is reduced to Three Pence per Gallon Duty, a Bounty of £8 Sterling per Ton is granted for Hemp raised in the Colonies. The Benefits the Colonies receive, we think, overbalance the Impositions supposed to be laid upon them." [14] There followed much good advice about the methods of growing hemp.

Mingled, however, with the sober information about husbandry were occasional sarcastic jabs at the truculent pamphlets against the Sugar Act printed at Boston and the insubordinate petitions sent home by New York. There were also persistent hints that Rhode Island would be better off under a royal government. In commending a humble attention to home industry the writers would be led to attack the pride of their countrymen and from there to a suggestion that neither the people nor the government of Rhode Island were so nearly perfect as to be incapable of improvement. "If we are so vain as to think either ourselves or our government too perfect to need an ammendment, it is a sure mark that we are in a reprobate state." [15] (No pious New Englander could ignore that warning!)

14. *Newport Mercury*, September 17, 1764.
15. *Ibid.*, November 19, 1764.

The legislature of Pennsylvania was commended for seeking to have that colony's charter revoked, and Benjamin Franklin was hailed as "the friend of liberty and of mankind," for going to England with their petition.[16] Though the Rhode Island charter was corporate, and not proprietary like that of Pennsylvania, nevertheless "undue power and influence, in whatever mode it appears, should be opposed, when it breaks the harmony or destroys the equilibrium of government." Obviously in Rhode Island the undue power and influence were in the hands of the people.

In singing the praises of Franklin and the Pennsylvanians the Newport group were slyly complimenting themselves. Though they could not hope that the Rhode Island Assembly would imitate Pennsylvania's, they had already prepared a private petition of their own, asking for royal government. Joseph Harrison (formerly a member of the group but now Collector of Customs at New Haven) obliged his friends by taking the petition with him on a trip to London in October, 1764, and Martin Howard, Jr., wrote to Franklin urging him to forward the good cause for Rhode Island as well as Pennsylvania.[17] Franklin was no stranger to the Newport group, for both Howard and Moffat had corresponded with him before, and evidently found reason to believe that he would be sympathetic with their aims. Only the preceding May, Moffat had informed him that Rhode Island was agitated with rumors about the abolition of charter governments and that "The (few) Friends to regular and good Government are wishing for a deprivation [of the charter] while the Herd deplore it as a Calamity." [18] So confident were the Newport royalists of Franklin's support that Howard wrote him of Rhode Island, "it is now nothing but a Burlesque upon Order and Government, and will never get right without the Constitution is altered, I have not time to enlarge and indeed your thorough knowledge of the subject would anticipate all and more than I could say." [19]

Whether Benjamin Franklin actually did sympathize with the aims of Moffat and Howard and their friends is a question to which that shrewd philosopher left no answer, but there was no doubt about the attitude of the "herd," and of a good many people who could not be included in that category, in Rhode Island. They had not been taken in by the O.Z. letters in spite of the current popularity of home industries, and the revelation that the authors were also

16. *Ibid.*
17. Martin Howard, Jr., to Benjamin Franklin, November 16, 1764, Franklin Papers, I, 108, American Philosophical Society.
18. *Ibid.*, I, 88.
19. November 16, 1764, *ibid.*, I, 108.

behind a petition for royal government was enough to damn them completely. On September 15 a correspondent of the *Providence Gazette* who signed himself "I ***" had attacked the motives of O.Z. and charged "that some, if not all, of the Members of this wonderful club are at this Time actually conspiring against the Liberties of the Colony, and that they have, with other Enemies of the Colony, formed a Petition, and sent it to the King, praying that our most valuable Charter Privileges may be taken away, notwithstanding their specious Pretences in the News-Papers of promoting the Welfare of the Government." Governor Hopkins confirmed the charge in a message to the Assembly on November 4, 1764,[20] and shortly thereafter published his *Rights of Colonies Examined*,[21] which included a diatribe against those who were ready to surrender colonial liberties.

Hopkins' pamphlet was no mean performance, and Martin Howard, Jr., felt obliged to answer it with a new appeal for submission to the authority of Parliament. In February, 1765, he published anonymously *A Letter from a Gentleman at Halifax to his Friend in Rhode Island,* [22] a point-by-point reply to Hopkins, written in a haughty, condescending tone. The title deceived no one. Everybody knew that the gentleman at Halifax was Martin Howard, Jr., just as everybody knew, beyond much doubt, that Martin Howard, Jr., and Dr. Moffat were the authors of the O.Z. letters and the leaders in the anti-charter petition.

Governor Hopkins answered Howard's Halifax Letter in the *Providence Gazette*,[23] but James Otis, the Boston patriot, gave a more stinging rebuttal in a pamphlet entitled *A Vindication of the British Colonies against the Aspersions of the Halifax Gentleman in his Letter to a Rhode Island Friend.* [24] And when Howard came back with *A Defense of the Letter from a Gentleman at Halifax,* [25] Otis replied again with *Brief Remarks on the Defense of the Halifax Libel.* [26] This last pamphlet lowered the controversy to a level that had hitherto been approached but never quite reached. The other pamphlets had confined themselves mainly to a discussion of principles; Otis struck at persons. Though he lived in Boston, he had relatives in Newport and was well acquainted with the situation

20. *Records of the Colony of Rhode Island*, VI, 414.
21. Providence, 1764, reprinted in *Records of the Colony of Rhode Island*, VI, 416-427.
22. Newport, 1765.
23. *Providence Gazette,* February 23, March 2, 9, 1765, and *Providence Gazette,* postscript, April 8, 1765.
24. Boston, 1765.   25. Newport, 1765.   26. Boston, 1765.

there.[27] He branded the Newport conservatives in words that had just enough truth in them to lend plausibility to his most extravagant charges. He accused them of drinking toasts to the pretender and concluded: "Such is the little, dirty, drinking, drabbing, contaminated knot of thieves, beggars and transports, or the worthy descendents of such, collected from the four winds of the earth, and made up of Turks, Jews and other Infidels, with a few renegado Christians and Catholics, and altogether formed into a club of scarce a dozen at N—p—t. From hence proceed Halifax-letters, petitions to alter the colony forms of government, libels upon all good colonists and subjects, and every evil work that can enter into the heart of man." [28] Scurrilous as these remarks were, they expressed a growing bitterness that was shared by many Newporters against the band of royalists in their midst.

Besides his damnation of the club as a whole, Otis had some special epithets for the two men who were recognized as its leaders. Howard he called Martinus Scriblerus, and Moffat was variously Dr. Smallbrain, Dr. Murphy, or "that mawgazeen of knowledge Dr. Mumchance." Referring to the O.Z. letters, Otis advised Howard to find better ways of spending his time, "instead of teaching people to spin and manufacture wool before they know where to get it, as he and the Dr. have been employed for these 12 months, with regard to the good people of R——— Island." [29] Otis had nothing to say about John Robinson, but Robinson's association with the club, his vigorous collection of duties, and his employment of the Navy to assist him rendered him one of the most hated men in Rhode Island. With the approach of November, when the Stamp Act was to go into effect, an explosive situation was developing in Newport; and though Robinson would have no immediate part in enforcing the Act, he was as obvious a target for popular wrath as the other members of the group when the pent-up hatred finally broke loose. Four years later, when the smoke had cleared a little, he would have occasion to remember, and to avenge, the contribution which James Otis had made to the terror which struck at him and his friends only a few months after his return from Taunton.

27. Major Jonathan Otis of Newport, one of the Sons of Liberty there, was a relative of Otis's. Ezra Stiles, Stamp Act Notebook, Stiles Papers, Yale University Library.
28. *Brief Remarks,* 5.
29. *Ibid.,* 28.

⇒ FIVE ⇐

THE STAMP ACT[1]

WHEN George Grenville tightened up the administration of the colonial customs service and revised the rates to make them produce a revenue, he knew that he was only beginning, that the colonies could and should contribute more to the cost of their defence. During the summer of 1763 he had already begun to consider the possibility of a stamp tax, and had assigned two different individuals to prepare drafts of an American Stamp Act. When these were presented to him on September 30, 1763, and October 10, 1763, respectively, he found neither satisfactory. The men who drew them up simply did not know the details of American judicial procedures well enough to name and describe the documents upon which a tax should be collected. In fact it is unlikely that anyone in the offices at Whitehall knew enough. Consequently, although Grenville was anxious to increase the revenue as rapidly as possible, a stamp tax would have to wait until the necessary information could be gathered.[2]

Since he could not present Parliament with an American Stamp Act in the spring of 1764, why did Grenville offer his resolution that one might be proper in the future? Why not wait until he had it ready, before introducing the subject? Unfortunately he left no answer to this question, and we can only infer his motives from things he did and said. From these one fact emerges: Grenville was

1. I have treated parts of this subject in greater detail in an article entitled "The Postponement of the Stamp Act," *William & Mary Quarterly*, 3d ser., 7 (1950), 353-392.
2. Additional Mss., 35910, ff. 136-159; 35911, ff. 17-37; 36226, f. 353, British Museum, Library of Congress transcripts. Cf. George Bancroft, *History of the United States* (Boston, 1834-1874), V, 151.

worried, though probably not greatly, about the reaction to a stamp tax both in Parliament and in the colonies. When introducing the resolution, he affirmed, a little too confidently, that he "hoped that the power and sovereignty of Parliament, over every part of the British dominions, for the purpose of raising or collecting any tax, would never be disputed. That if there was a single man doubted it, he would take the sense of the House, having heard without doors hints of this nature dropped." [3] No one in Parliament rose to this challenge, and it is doubtful that a majority ever would have dis-avowed the authority to tax the colonies. Legislative bodies are not fond of setting limits on their own competence, and Parliament had long since accustomed itself to the idea of its own omnipotence. Yet Grenville had heard hints dropped outside Parliament. Perhaps he knew that his great brother-in-law did not share the general view, and a view which William Pitt did not share was possibly not so general after all. One way to establish its acceptance, however, was by a Parliamentary resolution. Once Parliament agreed that it had the right to levy stamp duties in the colonies, it was not likely to reverse its opinion when asked to exercise the right. An assertion of the right, in such a resolution, would be more acceptable if un-encumbered with the details of any immediate application; and the application, in the bill he was preparing, would be more acceptable if the question of right had already been settled.[4]

There was also the question of how a stamp act would be received in the colonies. Grenville saw a way to take care of this problem too with his advance resolution: when introducing it to Parliament he managed to maneuver the colonists into a position where a stamp act would appear to be the result of their own failure to come to the assistance of the mother country in an hour of need. Although he had almost certainly made up his mind to have the tax enacted at the next session of Parliament, he gave the impression that the colonies might avert it if they took proper action during the inter-vening year. There is no official record of what he said in Parliament

3. Edward Montague, letter of April 11, 1764, quoted in *Virginia Gazette* (Purdie & Dixon), October 3, 1766. Cf. Eliphalet Dyer to Jared Ingersoll, April 14, 1764, New Haven Colony Historical Society, *Papers*, 9 (1918), 291, "Mr. Grenville strongly urg'd not only the power but the right of Parliament to tax the colonys, and hop'd in Gods Name as his Expression was that none would dare dispute their Sovereignty."

4. It was implied in one newspaper report (see *Pennsylvania Gazette*, May 10, 1764) that Parliament had previously debated the constitutionality of taxing the colonies and had determined the question in the affirmative. This does not seem to be supported by the records, though it is clear that a stamp tax had been suggested many times during the eighteenth century and as recently as the previous year. See *Newport Mercury*, May 30, 1763; cf. Bancroft, *History of the United States*, V, 88 n.

on March 9, 1764, and in the several accounts by private hands most
of the space is devoted to his remarks on the deplorable condition
of English finances and his explanation of the resolutions which
were to form the basis of the Sugar Act.[5] With regard to the fifteenth
resolution (which affirmed that a stamp tax might be necessary), the
accounts are meager, but a few facts stand out: Grenville announced
that he wished no action on this subject until the next session, that
his reason for delay was a desire to consult the ease, the interest
(or the quiet), and the good will of the colonies, and that the colonies
might take advantage of the delay to offer any objections they might
have to the tax, or to suggest some more satisfactory tax, or—and
here was the most misleading suggestion—to raise the money themselves in any way they saw fit. Two accounts of the speech clearly
affirm that Grenville offered the colonies this alternative of raising
the money themselves. Jasper Mauduit, the agent of Massachusetts,
was not present when the speech was delivered, but his brother Israel
was, and on the basis of Israel's report, Jasper transmitted to the
Massachusetts Assembly on March 13 copies of the resolutions which
had been passed, with comments upon them. Of the fifteenth resolution he wrote, "The Stamp duty you will see, is deferr'd till next
Year. I mean the actual laying it: Mr. Grenville being willing to give
to the Provinces their option to raise that or some equivalent tax,
Desirous as he express'd himself to consult the Ease, the Quiet, and
the Goodwill of the Colonies." [6] Here Mauduit speaks in the first two
sentences as though the tax was certain to be passed the next session,
but then he adds that the colonies have an "option" to raise some
other tax, presumably through their own assemblies.

The report by Edward Montague, the agent of Virginia, stated
even more explicitly that Grenville had given the colonies this alternative: "Mr. G—— then suggested that this [his?] great object,
being the relief of this kingdom from the burthen which in justice
America should bear, it would be as satisfactory to him if the several
provinces would among themselves, and in modes best suited to their
circumstances, raise a sum adequate to the expense of their defence." [7]

According to these two accounts Grenville definitely proposed in
his speech of March 9, that the colonies might avert the stamp tax. If
they would prefer to tax themselves rather than be taxed by Parlia-

5. Besides the accounts cited in note 3, see *Archives of Maryland*, XIV (1895), 144;
Connecticut Courant, September 16, 1765; New Haven Colony Historical Society, *Papers*,
9 (1918), 294; Massachusetts Historical Society, *Collections*, 6th series, 9 (1897), 20;
Massachusetts Archives, XXII, 359.
6. Massachusetts Archives, XXII, 359.
7. *Virginia Gazette* (Purdie & Dixon), October 3, 1766.

ment they had a year in which to take action. Having made this magnanimous gesture, Grenville put in motion the machinery for drawing up a stamp bill to present to the next session of Parliament. For reasons that will become apparent Grenville was probably certain that the colonies would do nothing, and he wanted to have his bill ready by 1765. He gave to Thomas Whately in the treasury office the task of preparing it,[8] and Whately wrote to persons he knew in America to get the necessary information. He wrote to Jared Ingersoll of Connecticut, asking, "Would it yield a considerable Revenue if the Duty were low upon mercantile Instruments, high upon gratuitous Grants of lands and moderate upon Law Proceedings? Would the Execution of such a Law be attended with great Inconveniencies, or open to frequent Evasions which could not be guarded against?"[9] He asked more detailed questions of John Temple at Boston:

I know there has been a stamp act in your Colony [referring to a Massachusetts stamp act of 1755]. I should be glad to know what was its product and on what articles it chiefly produced. What difficulties have occurr'd in executing it? What objections may be made to it, and what additional provisions must be made to those in force here? The greatest difficulty will be to ascertain the law proceedings that ought to be stampt. I should be much obliged to you if you could procure me the names of your several courts and of the respective instruments and proceedings used therein, which any lawyer of your acquaintance can readily furnish you with. Have you any fines and recoveries? Have you any inferior Courts that hold plea to a certain sum only? What appeals have you from one Court to another? And are your writs the same as are mentioned in our stamp acts? It will be a principal object of attention here to make this tax as little burthensome as possible, but for this purpose it will be necessary to know whether the same duties as are imposed in England on obligations, instruments of conveyance, and indentures of apprenticeship would be too heavy on the Colonies. Which of the English duties will be burthensome? which should be omitted? and which lighten'd and why? I should also be glad to be inform'd whether you use stampt cards and dice, how many newspapers are circulated in the Province, and what may reasonably be expected to be the produce of a stamp act, should the duty be laid at an average in any given proportion to that imposed in England.[10]

8. This is clearly established in Additional Mss., 35911, ff. 17-37 British Museum. See also Additional Mss., 35910, ff. 311-323. The two previous drafts of a Stamp Act had been drawn by Henry McCulloh and by a Mr. Cruwy. See note 2.

9. New Haven Colony Historical Society, *Papers*, 9 (1918), 294.

10. Massachusetts Historical Society, *Collections*, 6th series, 9 (1897), 22-23.

Whately did not have to rely wholly on information obtained informally from his friends. On August 11, 1764, the Earl of Halifax, Secretary of State for the Southern Department, sent a circular letter to the colonial governors announcing the resolution for a future stamp tax and asking for "a list of all instruments made use of in public transactions, law proceedings, grants, conveyances, securities of land or money within your government, with proper and sufficient descriptions of the same, in order, that if Parliament should think proper to pursue the intention of the aforesaid resolution, they may thereby be enabled to carry it into execution, in the most effectual and least burdensome manner." [11] On the basis of the various reports he received Whately drew up a tentative schedule of duties, and most of his recommendations were accepted in the bill that was eventually laid before Parliament. In general the American rates were lower than the corresponding English ones. They could be raised after the colonists were used to the tax. In a few cases, however, the American charges were higher at the outset. If any incipient American democrats had seen Whately's report, there would surely have been howls of rage when they read that "the Duties upon Admissions to any of the professions or to the University degrees should certainly be as high as they are in England; it would indeed be better if they were raised both here and there considerably in order to keep mean persons out of those situations in life which they disgrace." [12] Accordingly the colonial tax was set at £2 for matriculation and the same amount for a degree, though in England it was two shillings for one and two shillings, sixpence for the other; admission to the bar in America was £10, in England £6; and taxes on admission to minor public offices were also slightly higher in America.[13]

While Thomas Whately was busy preparing the Stamp Act, the colonial agents, to say nothing of the colonists, were puzzling over the meaning of the alternative proposal that Grenville had made in his speech of March 9. For a reason which is obvious enough if we assume that Grenville had already made up his mind to have a stamp tax, he had not communicated the proposal to the colonial assemblies through the channel normally used. Had he really intended to allow the colonies a chance to raise the money themselves, he would have made his offer in the regular manner by having the Secretary of State for the Southern Department write to the governors of the

11. *Records of the Colony of Rhode Island*, VI, 404.

12. Additional Mss., 35910, ff. 317-318, British Museum.

13. *Ibid.*, ff. 167-203, lists conveniently the English duties at the time, which may be compared with those of Grenville's Stamp Act in *Statutes at Large*, XXVI, 179-204 (5 George III, c. 12).

colonies. He had had Halifax write for the information about colonial judicial transactions needed in draughting the Stamp Act, but
he made no communication on the subject of letting the colonial
assemblies tax themselves. There was a good deal of justice in a complaint published later in the *Boston Gazette,* after the Stamp Act had
become a law:

It has been said the Stamp Act was put off a year, that the colonies
might have notice to object and give their reasons against it. What
notice the other colonies had, I know not. The Massachusetts never
had a line about it from one of the public offices. Mr. Jasper M-ud-t
indeed told them, that his brother Israel told him, that Mr. Gr-v-ll
haughtily told him, to tell his brother to tell his constituents, that if
they would not stamp themselves, he would have them stamped, or
very nearly to that effect.[14]

Yet in spite of the fact that Grenville did not make the offer in
proper form, he did make it, and the agents did report it to their
constituents—Israel did tell Jasper, and Jasper did tell the Massachusetts Assembly. It was only a short time after the speech, however,
before the agents realized that the terms of the proposal they had
communicated to the colonies were not entirely clear. Grenville had
said that if the colonies would raise among themselves an adequate
sum or sum equivalent to that expected from the stamp tax, he would
accept it in lieu of a stamp tax. But how much was an "adequate" or
"equivalent" sum? If the colonies were to lay an equivalent tax
themselves, they would have to know either how much was needed in
all, or else what were the intended taxable items and rates. Without
this information it would be impossible for them to act upon Grenville's proposal. The agents, before they could have had time to
hear from their constituents about it, decided to have a talk with the
Minister. He met them on May 17, 1764, in a conference which was
afterwards described in some detail by three of the participants.[15]

Grenville opened by stating that he had not changed his mind, but
he then proceeded to propose something he had not so much as mentioned in his speech.[16] The agents were trying to find out "the sort of

14. *Boston Gazette,* January 20, 1766.
15. By Jasper Mauduit, whose brother Israel attended the conference for him, in a
letter to the Speaker of the Massachusetts House of Representatives, May 26, 1764,
Massachusetts Archives, XXII, 375; by Charles Garth in a letter to the Committee of
Correspondence of South Carolina, June 5, 1764, *English Historical Review,* 54 (1939),
646-648; and by William Knox, in *The Claim of the Colonies to an Exemption from
Internal Taxes (London,* 1765), 31-33.
16. But Grenville may have discussed it with some of the agents or other friends of
the colonies, for Thomas Penn, one of the Proprietors of Pennsylvania, wrote from

proposition, which would probably be accepted from them to Parliament," [17] in other words how much he wanted the colonies to raise. But Grenville, rather than stating the sum he wanted from them, now proposed that they assent in advance to the Parliamentary tax and thereby set a precedent for being consulted about any future taxes! He also spoke strongly of the difficulties which "would have" [18] attended any scheme of letting them tax themselves, as though that issue were closed. But he did not expressly repudiate his offer; and the agents, although they could not help seeing that he was discouraging action by the colonies, apparently did not recognize that he was precluding it. They did not, however, press for a statement of the exact sum with which the colonies might satisfy him. Grenville had steered the conference beyond that subject, and they probably feared to upset his evident good humor by insisting on a matter so obviously distasteful. They must prolong the conference and find out, if possible, the terms of the act he expected to bring in if the colonies did not raise the money themselves. They must know the terms, one of the agents explained, "in order that our respective constituents might have the whole, both substance and form under their deliberation, when they would be far better able to determine whether or how far, to approve or disapprove." [19] But the details of the act were, of course, unknown to Grenville himself, for it had not yet been drawn up. Israel Mauduit pointed out that to ask the colonies to assent in advance to a bill without giving the provisions of it was asking them "to assent to they did not know what." [20] To this Grenville answered simply that it was not necessary to bother with details, "That everyone knew the stamp laws here; and that this Bill is intended to be formd upon the same plan." [21] He did agree to consult with the agents on this matter just before the meeting of Parliament, provided that in the meantime the colonial assemblies should signify their assent to the general idea of a stamp tax. He warned that any protests based on the financial inability of the colonies to pay would carry little weight in Parliament. In his speech of March 9 he had already made it plain that he would listen to nothing which called in

London on March 9, 1764, that a stamp tax had been proposed, but "we have endeavoured to get this last postponed, as it is an internal Tax, and wait til some sort of consent to it shall be given by the several Assemblys, to prevent a Tax of that nature from being laid without the consent of the Colonys, ..." Penn Correspondence, VIII (1763-1766), 33, Historical Society of Pennsylvania.

17. *Claim of the Colonies*, 31-32.
18. *English Historical Review*, 54 (1939), 647.
19. *Ibid.*, 646-647.
20. Massachusetts Archives, XXII, 375.
21. *Ibid.*

question the right of Parliament to levy the tax, so that he left the colonies very little room either for criticism or for constructive action.

It is evident from this conference that Grenville was determined upon a stamp tax. Though he was willing to make magnanimous gestures, he had no intention of allowing the colonies to prevent passage of his measure either by objections to it or by raising an "equivalent" sum. They would not thwart him by levying a substitute tax themselves: by witholding the necessary information he made sure of that. Nor would he be troubled by their objections: thanks to his foresighted resolution he could safely predict Parliament's unsympathetic reaction here. Grenville must have felt comfortably satisfied with all his maneuvers. He had made it useless for the colonies to attempt any action to avert the tax, and yet he had carried out his interview so smoothly, and expressed his affection for the colonies so convincingly, that the agents did not perceive, nor inform their clients, of the hopelessness of their efforts.

It was only when a colony set about to tax itself that the hollowness of Grenville's offer became apparent. Massachusetts made the attempt. Though Governor Bernard was convinced that the Ministry really intended to let the colonies raise all internal taxes themselves, yet when several members of the Assembly approached him in the summer of 1764, asking for a special session in order that the colony might tax itself to avoid being taxed by Parliament, Bernard refused, because he saw that nothing could be done without more information from Grenville. He related the entire incident to his friend Richard Jackson, in a letter dated at Boston, August 18, 1764:

Dear Sir

Yesterday the members for Boston came to me to signify that it was the desire of many Members of the House that the Assembly might meet as soon as possible, that proper measures might be taken to prevent an inland parliamentary Taxation. That their Agent had wrote word that Mr. Grenville had told him that such a taxation might be prevented, if they would tax themselves to the same purposes as were intended by the former. That they were desirous of immediately setting about such taxation themselves or at least of doing something to prevent a parliamentary tax.

I told them that in the present state of things I did not see that they could do anything more than they might have done last session: that is to signify their desire that they might be allowed to tax themselves and not be taxed by the parliament. That it was impossible at present to proceed to an actual taxation, untill the demands of the ministry should be further explained. That If every province was to be left to raise the Money in what manner they pleased, the particular sum expected from each province as their proportion must be first ascertained. That if a stamp Duty was to be imposed by provincial Acts as forming of itself a proportion of charge, the Duties themselves must be first settled, as they ought to be the same in every province; otherwise they will not be a proportional charge. That neither of these things can be done by the provinces themselves, they must be settled by some authority that can mediate between the Provinces and moderate their partialities for themselves. That in regard to the Provinces preferring to tax themselves rather than to be taxed by Parliament, there can be no doubt of that being the desire of the Ministry. The Friends of the Provinces had been long aware of that preference; you had particularly urged it: and I had wrote upon the same subject. In short it could never be doubted but that if the parliament should require certain sums of the provinces, It is of no little Consequence to them that such sums should be raised by provincial Acts. For thereby the forms of their priviledges (which are no little part of them) are kept up, tho' the Substance is impeached, as it frequently must be in Subordinate Governments, whose relation to the Sovereign power has never been formally settled nor is generally understood.

But I promised them that I would Call the Assembly together about the middle of october, when there would be time enough to send instructions to the agent before this business could be brought on in parliament. However, if the Ministry should be settling their plan before hand, I wish you would interpose on the behalf of the province that they may at least have the liberty of enacting internal taxations themselves: which I have no doubt, but that they will readily do, when it shall be positively required of them. I am Sir

your most faithfull and obedient servant.[22]

This letter shows plainly enough why the colonies did not take advantage of Grenville's offer to let them tax themselves. Not only was the offer never made them in a regular manner by letters from the Secretary of State, but it was never couched in terms that were definite enough to permit of action. Several colonies signified their willingness to contribute if requested in a regular manner for a specific sum,[23] but such a request was never made.

What the colonies did do was to take up the challenge which Grenville had thrown to Parliament and which Parliament had endorsed

22. Bernard Papers, III, 248-249, Harvard College Library.

23. Pennsylvania included such a statement in instructions to her agent, *Pennsylvania Archives*, 8th ser., VII (1935), 5678-5682, and so evidently did other colonies, for according to Charles Garth the agents decided later to acquaint Grenville with the fact that "most of the Colonies had signify'd their inclinations to assist their Mother Country upon proper requisitions from hence." *English Historical Review*, 54 (1939), 649.

and passed on to them. The Americans read the fifteenth resolution correctly, as a declaration of Parliament's right to tax them.[24] And since the challenge was no more than a declaration, albeit by a body which regarded its own declarations as final, they replied in the mode, infuriating to omnipotence, of talking back. In the petitions to Parliament and letters to their agents that we have already examined, they denied that Parliament had any right to tax them. This denial was by no means limited to the dusky halls of legislative assemblies. The people at large were as much concerned over the measure as their representatives. Jared Ingersoll, in answer to Thomas Whately's inquiries, warned the man who was drafting the Stamp Act, that the minds of the people "are filled with the most dreadfull apprehensions from such a Step's taking place, from whence I leave you to guess how Easily a tax of that kind would be Collected; tis difficult to say how many ways could be invented to avoid the payment of a tax laid upon a Country without the Consent of the Legislature of that Country and in the opinion of most of the people Contrary to the foundation principles of their natural and Constitutional rights and Liberties. Dont think me impertinent, Since you desire Information, when I tell you that I have heard Gentlemen of the greatest property in Neighbouring Governments say, Seemingly very Cooly, that should such a Step take place they would immediately remove themselves with their families and fortunes into some foreign Kingdom." [25] Ingersoll also told Whately, much as Bernard had told Jackson, that "If the King should fix the proportion of our Duty, we all say we will do our parts in the Common Cause, but if the Parliament once interpose and Lay a tax, tho' it may be a very moderate one . . . what Consequences may, or rather may not, follow?" [26]

With his two secretaries, Jackson and Whately, receiving communications of this kind, and with other colonial agents spreading petitions and pamphlets to the same effect around London, Grenville could see for himself that the champions of colonial reorganization were right in crying that the authority of Parliament in America needed bolstering, but he did not therefore agree that reorganization would provide the best reinforcement. The way to get authority recognized was to exercise it, and Grenville was prepared to do just that with his stamp tax. Twenty-three years before, in 1742, Sir William

24. In referring to the fifteenth resolution Americans frequently spoke of it as an assertion of Parliament's right to tax the colonies, e.g. *Records of the Colony of Rhode Island,* VI, 422.

25. Ingersoll to Whately, July 6, 1764, New Haven Colony Historical Society, *Papers,* 9 (1918), 299–300.

26. *Ibid.,* 299.

Keith had proposed such a tax precisely because he thought it would establish among the Americans "a more just and favourable opinion of their dependency on a British Parliament, than what they generally have at present." [27] And doubtless Thomas Whately voiced Grenville's own view when he called the Stamp Act "the great measure of the Sessions . . . on account of the important point it establishes, the Right of Parliament to lay an internal Tax upon the Colonies." [28]

If Parliament was not as aware as Grenville that its authority in America needed support, the colonists themselves completed the awakening. As the protests from across the ocean poured into England, Parliamentary hackles rose, and the Minister could rejoice, for, as he had calculated, the members reacted to the denial of their authority with the wrath of injured dignity. The unfortunate colonial agents, fighting frantically to stave off the coming blow, saw that because of their clients' declarations the battle was being transformed into a test of Parliament's authority. The main issue was no longer raising a revenue, but putting the Americans in their place. The agents knew that Parliament would refuse to hear any arguments calling its authority into question, and yet they had specific instructions, or else petitions to present, which required them to contest the bill on the question of right. A few of them, led by William Knox of Georgia, thought that all the agents should unite in a petition of their own, leaving out offensive expressions against Parliamentary authority. It would at least get a hearing and thereby establish a precedent in Parliament for receiving petitions from the colonies before taxing them, whatever that might be worth. The petition was drawn up, but most of the agents did not feel free to sign it, and the project was dropped.[29]

Some of the agents tried to enlist the aid of the merchants. The colonial non-importation movement, combined with the depression, was making itself felt in England, but though they were generally opposed to the stamp tax, the merchants had not yet become sufficiently alarmed to mobilize and concert their opposition. As Jasper Mauduit put it in a letter to the Massachusetts Assembly on January 16, 1765, "The Merchants talk much, but cannot bring them to Act." [30]

By this time the situation was becoming desperate. Parliament was due to open, and though a good deal of propaganda had been pub-

27. Additional Mss., 33028, British Museum.
28. Thomas Whately to John Temple, February 9, 1765, Temple-Whately Letter Book, Stowe Collection, Huntington Library.
29. Knox, *Claim of the Colonies*, 35.
30. Massachusetts Archives, XXII, 426.

lished, most of it probably at the instigation of the agents, there was
no organized opposition in the House of Commons to contest the bill
when Grenville should bring it in.[31] The agents decided to make one
last attempt to stop the tax at its source and deputed four of their
number to call on the Minister again and point out to him that most
of the colonies had expressed their willingness to contribute to the
British Treasury if called upon to do so in a regular, constitutional
manner. The agents who met with Grenville on February 2, 1765,
were Charles Garth, agent of South Carolina and Member of Parliament for a borough in Wiltshire, Richard Jackson, agent of Connecticut and now also of Pennsylvania and Massachusetts, also Member of
Parliament for Weymouth and secretary to Grenville, Benjamin
Franklin, who had recently come over to urge a royal government for
Pennsylvania, and Jared Ingersoll, who had also just arrived, on private business. Ingersoll left the most complete account of the conference in a letter to Governor Fitch, dated February 11, 1765. He
wrote:

The Agents of the Colonies have had several Meetings, at one of
which they were pleased to desire Mr. Franklin and myself as having
lately Come from America and knowing more Intimately the Sentiments of the people, to wait on Mr. Grenville, together with Mr.
Jackson and Mr. Garth who being Agents are also Members of Parliament, to remonstrate against the Stamp Bill, and to propose in Case
any Tax must be laid upon America, that the several Colonies might
be permitted to lay the Tax themselves. This we did Saturday before
last. Mr. Grenville gave us a full hearing—told us he took no pleasure
in giving the Americans so much uneasiness as he found he did—that
it was the Duty of his Office to manage the revenue—that he really
was made to believe that considering the whole of the Circumstances
of the Mother Country and the Colonies, the later could and ought to
pay something, and that he knew of no better way than that now pursuing to lay such Tax, but that if we could tell of a better he would
adopt it. We then urged the Method first mentioned as being a
Method the people had been used to—that it would at least seem to
be their own Act and prevent that uneasiness and Jealousy which
otherwise we found would take place—that they could raise the
Money best by their own Officers &c &c

Mr Jackson told him plainly that he foresaw [by] the Measure now
pursuing, by enabling the Crown to keep up an armed Force of its
own in America and to pay the Governours in the Kings Governments and all with the Americans own Money, the Assemblies *in* the

31. See Fred J. Ericson, "The Contemporary British Opposition to the Stamp Act,"
Michigan Academy of Science, Arts, and Letters, *Papers*, 29 (1943), 489-505.

Colonys would be subverted—that the Governors would have no Occasion, as for any Ends of their own or of the Crown, to call 'Em and that they never would be called together in the Kings Goverments. Mr. Grenville warmly rejected the thought, said no such thing was intended nor would he beleived take place.[32]

One may doubt whether Grenville's judgment on this last point was as acute as Jackson's. Though Grenville himself may have had no intention of subverting the colonial assemblies, the colonial governors would have been glad to free themselves from the control of those bodies, and if Parliament were to collect taxes in the colonies, the assemblies might very well lose the power of the purse entirely.

The conference up to this point was no more than what could have been expected: the agents had urged that the colonies be allowed to tax themselves, and the Minister had urged that a stamp tax levied by Parliament was preferable. But now the meeting took a new turn. In answer to the request that he let the colonies raise the money in their own assemblies, Grenville asked the agents if they "could agree upon the several proportions Each Colony should raise." [33] A more fatuous question can scarcely be imagined, and if the agents had not been so soothed by the Minister's personal charm, they would probably have shown some indignation at his asking it. Grenville himself, in his speech of March 9, had been the first to propose that the colonies raise the money themselves but had failed to provide them with the details of how much was wanted from each or from all. When the agents had sought these details in the conference of May 17, he had refused them and had made a different proposal, that the colonial assemblies assent in advance to a tax by Parliament, but even in this connection he had not offered the details of the bill he wanted them to assent to. The colonial assemblies had ignored this second proposal, which would have meant resigning the very function for which they existed; yet they had stated their willingness to comply with any requisition made in the normal, constitutional manner. Now the agents were asking once more that the colonies be allowed to do so. Grenville's answer was to ask the agents if they were empowered to do what he himself should have done in the first place, namely to set the proportion of a total sum which each colony should bear. "We told him no," says Ingersoll, "He said he did not think anybody here was furnished with Materials for that purpose. . . ." [34]

32. Connecticut Historical Society, *Collections*, 18 (1920), 324-325.
33. *Ibid.*
34. *Ibid.*

If Grenville did not think that anyone in England was furnished with information to set the proportion for each colony, who did he think was furnished with it? It was his business, or the business of his Secretary of State, to have this information, and the Board of Trade existed to provide him with it. The colonies had no connection with one another except through the British government. They could not have settled the proper proportions except by an inter-colonial congress, but such a congress could not properly have been called without authorization from Great Britain, and could not have acted anyhow without knowing the total sum expected from the colonies.[35] When members of the Massachusetts Assembly wished to take up Grenville's offer by taxing themselves, Governor Bernard had rightly told them that they could do nothing until the Minister gave them more information. The Minister now wanted to know whether the colonial agents could provide the information which *he* should have given *them*.

When the conference of February 2 was over the agents must have realized at last that Grenville's offer had never been made in good faith, that a year ago, even while making the offer, he had already made up his mind to levy a stamp tax. The willingness he had then expressed to let the colonies tax themselves or offer objections was nothing more than a rhetorical gesture, designed to demonstrate his own benevolence. In the conference of February 2, 1765, he even told the agents that "he had pledged his Word for Offering the Stamp Bill to the house." [36] What he had given the colonies was not an opportunity to tax themselves but an opportunity to refuse to tax themselves.

In the time that was left the agents continued their preparation for the ensuing battle in Parliament, but the impudence of the Americans had so irritated the law-makers, that the issue was a foregone conclusion. One member wrote to a friend that the insubordinate declarations against Parliamentary right were going to be examined, "but first it is thought proper to establish that Right by a new execu-

35. Benjamin Franklin discussed the possibility of such a congress with Richard Jackson (Carl Van Doren, ed., *Letters and Papers of Benjamin Franklin and Richard Jackson, 1753-1785*, Philadelphia, 1947, p. 175), but there is no indication that Grenville ever suggested calling one. When the Stamp Act Congress was held, after passage of the Stamp Act, Parliament refused to receive its communications, because, among other reasons, the Congress "partook too much of a federal Union assembled without any Requisition on the Part of the Supreme Power." Charles Garth to Ringgold, Murdoch, and Tilghman, February 26, 1766, *Maryland Historical Magazine*, VI, 282-287. This indicates how Parliament might have treated the proceedings of a congress assembled without authorization from England.

36. Connecticut Historical Society, *Collections*, 18 (1920), 325.

tion of it, and in the strongest instance, an internal Tax, that of the Stamp duty." [37] On February 6, when Grenville reminded the House of their resolution of the preceding year, there followed a lively debate, but though a great deal was said in demonstration of Parliament's right to levy the tax, no one argued the other side of the question. Even the most eloquent opponents of the tax spoke in terms of equity and expediency and did not venture to deny the absolute authority of Parliament.

The staunchest supporter of the colonies in this first debate was Colonel Isaac Barré, a veteran of the French and Indian War. According to one observer, "He most strongly recommended that if there must be a tax laid, tho' he could wish there was to be none, that the Provinces might be indulged with the liberty as heretofore of furnishing their quotas of any sums required and colecting it in their own modes." [38] Barré, in other words, advocated the proposal that Grenville himself had first made but failed to carry through. Charles Townshend, author-to-be of the Townshend Duties, spoke with some warmth in the debate, asking on one occasion: "And now will these Americans, Children planted by our Care, nourished up by our Indulgence untill they are grown to a Degree of Strength and Opulence, and protected by our Arms, will they grudge to contribute their mite to relieve us from the heavy weight of that burden which we lie under?" To this Barré answered with words that would soon make him famous throughout the American Colonies:

They planted by your Care? No! your Oppressions planted em in America. They fled from your Tyranny to a then uncultivated and unhospitable Country—where they exposed themselves to almost all the hardships to which human Nature is liable, and among others to the Cruelties of a Savage foe, the most subtle and I take upon me to say the most formidable of any People upon the face of Gods Earth. And yet, actuated by Principles of true english Lyberty, they met all these hardships with pleasure, compared with those they suffered in their own Country, from the hands of those who should have been their Friends.

They nourished by *your* indulgence? they grew by your neglect of Em: as soon as you began to care about Em, that Care was Exercised in sending persons to rule over Em, in one Department and another, who were perhaps the Deputies of Deputies to some Member of this house—sent to Spy out their Lyberty, to misrepresent their Actions

37. Edward Sedgwick to Edward Weston, February 14, 1765, Charles Fleetwood Weston Underwood Mss., Historical Manuscripts Commission, *Tenth Report*, [pt. 1] (1885), 382.

38. John Nelson to John Temple, n.d., Massachusetts Historical Society, *Collections*, 6th ser., 9 (1897), 46.

and to prey upon Em; men whose behaviour on many Occasions has caused the Blood of those Sons of Liberty to recoil within them; men promoted to the highest Seats of Justice, some, who to my knowledge were glad by going to a foreign Country to Escape being brought to the Bar of a Court of Justice in their own.

They protected by *your* Arms? they have nobly taken up Arms in your defence, have Exerted a Valour amidst their constant and Laborious industry for the defence of a Country, whose frontier, while drench'd in blood, its interior Parts have yielded all its little Savings to your Emolument. And beleive me, remember I this Day told you so, that same Spirit of freedom which actuated that people at first, will accompany them still.—But prudence forbids me to explain myself further. God knows I do not at this Time speak from motives of party Heat, what I deliver are the genuine Sentiments of my heart.[39]

Even Barré's eloquence, which did not, after all, deny the authority of Parliament, could not alter the determination of the members to prove their unlimited authority by taxing the colonies. With regard to the ability of the colonies to pay, Grenville had figures ready at hand to show that their total public debts amounted to only about £900,000, all of which was scheduled to be paid off before the year 1769.[40] The per capita indebtedness of the colonists was thus only a fraction of that in England. The sentiment in favor of the tax was so strong that the opposition, instead of bringing the matter to a vote on the immediate question, tried to get through a vote to adjourn. Mr. Beckford, a former West Indian, made the motion, and Colonel Barré seconded it, remarking that he "should with greater pleasure second a motion that it might never be bro't on the carpet again." [41] The motion was lost by a vote of 245 to 49, taken at about midnight, and on the following day the House of Commons passed, without a division, the fifty-five resolutions which formed the basis of the Stamp Act.[42]

Grenville, having thus secured the approval of Parliament, brought in the bill itself on February 13. It received its first reading then and its second on February 15.[43] This was the crucial reading, and the opposition prepared to present petitions against it. After the debate of February 6, Charles Garth, agent for South Carolina, had written to his clients that "the power of Parliament was asserted and so uni-

39. Connecticut Historical Society, *Collections*, 18 (1920), 322-323.
40. Treasury Papers, Class I, Bundle 433, f. 402; Charles Garth to Committee of Correspondence of South Carolina, February 8, 1765, *English Historical Review*, 54 (1939), 649-650.
41. Massachusetts Historical Society, *Collections*, 6th ser., 9 (1897), 46.
42. *Journal of the House of Commons*, XXX, 97-101.
43. *Ibid.*, 131, 148.

versally agreed to, that no petition disputing it will be received." [44]
Accordingly he had drawn up a petition in which he tried to avoid
the question of Parliamentary authority. Since he was a Member of
Parliament, he could not sign it himself, but he secured the signatures of a few South Carolinians who happened to be in London. It
was to no avail, because Parliament refused to hear any petitions
against the bill. When Sir William Meredith, a London merchant,
presented the petition from Virginia, two reasons were given for refusing to consider it: first, that it was contrary to the custom of the
House of Commons to hear petitions against money bills, second and
more important, that it cast doubt on the authority of Parliament.
According to Garth, "The House declared they would not suffer a
petition that should hint at questioning the supremacy and authority
of Parliament to impose taxes in every part of the British Dominions." [45] In spite of his efforts to avoid the contentious subject Garth's
own carefully contrived petition on behalf of South Carolina met
the same fate. He was called upon to state its contents, "Which done,
the House were of opinion it tended to question the right of Parliament to exercise this power of taxation, and being likewise against a
Money Bill, was also refus'd." [46] Richard Jackson had no better success with the petitions from Connecticut and Massachusetts, which
were likewise denied a hearing.[47] The one from New York was
couched in such strong terms that no Member of Parliament could be
persuaded to present it.[48]

The refusal of Parliament to hear these petitions did not pass without debate. General Conway, another veteran of the late war though
not of the American branch of it, was the principal defender of the
colonies at this juncture. He made a telling point when he reminded
the members that they had postponed the Stamp Act the preceding
year in order to give the colonies time to send messages representing
their objections to it. "This time has been given," said Conway. "The
Representations are come from the Colonies; and shall we shut our
Ears against that Information, which, with an Affectation of Candour,
we allotted sufficient Time to reach us? . . . from whom, unless from
themselves, are we to learn the Circumstances of the Colonies, and
the fatal Consequences that may attend the imposing of this Tax?" [49]

44. *English Historical Review*, 54 (1939), 650.
45. *Ibid.*
46. *Ibid.*, 651.
47. *Ibid.*, and Connecticut Historical Society, *Collections*, 18 (1920), 341. It is possible
that the petition from Massachusetts was never formally presented. See Jared Ingersoll's
account, *ibid.*, 334-335.
48. *Ibid.*, 335.
49. *Maryland Gazette*, June 13, 1765.

Conway's plea on February 15 was no more effective than Barré's had been on February 6. The bill survived the second reading without even a division. The third reading was a mere formality, and by March 22 the Stamp Act was a statute of the realm.[50] It remained to be seen whether it would establish, or destroy, the authority of Parliament in America.

50. *The Parliamentary History of England* . . . (London, 1806-1820), XVI, 40.

SIX

DANIEL DULANY
Pamphleteer

WHEN news reached America that the Stamp Act had passed, anger erupted first in a torrent of words. Of these millions of words which the Act provoked and which found their way into print, probably none were more widely read or more universally approved than those of a Maryland lawyer, Daniel Dulany, in a pamphlet called *Considerations on the Propriety of imposing Taxes in the British Colonies, for the Purpose of raising a Revenue, by Act of Parliament.*[1]

When his pamphlet appeared, Dulany was already an outstanding provincial lawyer and politician. He was one of those able sons of an able father, who by starting life with the accumulated advantages of their parents' brains and industry, are able to use their own brains and their own industry to maintain and increase the family fortunes and prestige. Dulany's father had come to Maryland a penniless immigrant.[2] By hard work and shrewd investments he had built himself a fortune and won a place in the confidence of Lord Baltimore, the Proprietor of the colony. When his son Daniel was ready for serious schooling, he was able to send him to England to study successively at Eton, Cambridge, and finally the Middle Temple. The father, who had himself earned a place on the Maryland bar and had even returned to England to study at Gray's Inn, decided early that his son too should be a lawyer, and Daniel acquiesced readily.[3] At Eton and

1. First edition, North America [Annapolis], 1765; second edition, Annapolis, 1765. I have used the second edition.

2. On the elder Dulany, see the article by Newton D. Mereness in *Dictionary of Amer. Biog.*, and Aubrey C. Land, "Genesis of a Colonial Fortune," *William and Mary Quarterly*, 3rd ser., 7 (1950), 255-269.

3. Daniel Dulany, Sr., to Peter Goddard, 1741, Dulany Papers, Maryland Historical Society.

Cambridge he lived frugally [4] and studied the "law of Nature and Nations," a step which his father endorsed as good preparation for his future calling.[5] At the Middle Temple in London he went through the regular training of a lawyer,[6] so that when he returned to Maryland in 1746 to take up the career which his father had laid out for him, he was as well equipped to practise as any English barrister and far better equipped than most Americans.

Daniel Dulany was admitted to the bar in Maryland in 1747 and quickly made a name for himself, not only in the law but in politics as well. By 1751 he had been elected to the Assembly and was earning a reputation similar to his father's as a defender of the Proprietor.[7] At this time, as always in Maryland's colonial history, the Assembly was divided between the friends of the Proprietor and those who wanted to curb his lordship's political power and to reduce the quitrents which he collected on the lands in the province. Daniel Dulany became so closely associated with the proprietary party that in 1754 Lord Baltimore apologized for not appointing him to the Governor's Council (a more distinguished position than that of an elected member of the Assembly), on the grounds that he was needed in the Assembly to protect the proprietary interests there.[8]

But Dulany was no mere tool of Lord Baltimore. Though he recognized the Proprietor's legal rights and was ready to defend them, he was not afraid to defend the rights of the people as well, whenever the occasion should arise. After he was finally appointed to the Governor's Council in 1757, the Governor found him somewhat too independent, and wrote to the Proprietor's secretary that "he is fond of being thought a Patriot Councillor and rather inclined to serve the People than the Proprietary." [9] Though Dulany, as it turned out later, was no demagogue, and finally lost his popularity in Maryland by supporting the interests of the Proprietor, in this early period at least, before 1765, he kept a sharp eye on contests in which popular rights seemed to be at stake. Through books and newspapers he maintained an interest in political events in England as well as America, and in May, 1764, he read in the *Maryland Gazette* that the House of

4. Daniel Dulany, Sr., to Mr. Hyde, June 7, 1747, says that his son's expenses at Eton "did not Exceed £50 a year and seldom reached it." *Ibid.*

5. Daniel Dulany, Sr., to Peter Goddard, 1741, *ibid.*

6. Jones, *American Members of the Inns of Court*, 68.

7. Daniel Dulany, Sr., to Cecilius Calvert, December 26, 1752, Dulany Papers.

8. Cecilius Calvert to Daniel Dulany, April 17, 1754, *ibid.*

9. Governor Sharpe to Cecilius Calvert, May 8, 1764, *Archives of Maryland*, XIV, (1895), 160.

Commons in England had debated the question of its right to tax the colonies and had decided in favor of such a right.[10]

As far as Dulany was concerned the Parliamentary resolution did not settle the question. He had been thinking about the matter himself for some ten years, and he had come to the conclusion that there were colonial rights involved which could not be overthrown simply by the fiat of Parliament. When he had first considered the idea of a Parliamentary tax, it had not seemed entirely unreasonable to him. In 1755, at the beginning of the French and Indian War, the rumor had gone around that Parliament might tax the colonies. At that time Dulany had written a friend that it was reasonable for the mother country to expect a contribution from the colonies toward the expense of the war and that a Parliamentary tax appeared to be necessary, but even this early he went on to say that "so many things are to be considered in making a regulation of this sort just and effectual, that I dread the consequence of the Parliament's undertaking it." [11] By summer of 1764 the consequences had come to appear even more dreadful, and Dulany must have given the problem increasing attention as he read in the newspapers not only that Parliament would lay a tax of some sort but that there would be a general reorganization of the colonial governments, that boundaries would be adjusted, and that proprietary titles would be returned to the Crown. He did not know of the sweeping changes which Governor Bernard was advocating in private letters, but he did receive from his bookseller in London a number of pamphlets and books which advocated a thorough overhaul of colonial affairs and which denied, almost in advance of colonial protests, that the colonists were exempt from Parliamentary taxation.

One of the most substantial of these, Thomas Pownall's *Administration of the Colonies*,[12] struck Dulany as a pompous piece of work. Pownall apparently thought himself the only person in the world with sufficient experience of colonial affairs to direct the management of them. Dulany thought otherwise. He could remember that Pownall had come to the colonies only a dozen years ago, as a mere secretary to the new governor of New York, Sir Danvers Osborne. After Osborne hanged himself in a fit of despondency, Pownall by a series

10. *Maryland Gazette,* May 17, 1764; *Considerations,* 33. The debate referred to in the *Maryland Gazette* may have been simply the debate over the fifteenth resolution of March 10, which was evidently regarded as an assertion of Parliamentary right. See ch. 5, n. 4.

11. *Pa. Mag. of Hist.,* 3 (1879), 148.

12. The first edition was published in March, 1764, the second edition in March, 1765.

of intrigues raised himself from one post to another and now paraded on the title page of his book as "Late Governor and Commander in Chief of his Majesty's Provinces, Massachusetts-Bay and South-Carolina, and Lieutenant-Governor of New-Jersey." Dulany could think of another title given him in a satirical piece published in Boston four or five years before, called *Proposals for Printing by Subscription the History of the publick life and distinguished actions of vice-admiral Sir Thomas Brazen.*[13] Dulany had read this piece of invective and thought that the label "Brazen" suited admirably the character of the man who had written *The Administration of the Colonies.* Dulany's views were perhaps prejudiced, but he may have been particularly irked by the fact that Pownall suggested, with no apparent concern for the violation of colonial rights, that a stamp tax was a suitable mode of raising money in America.[14]

In the spring of 1765, probably along with news of the passage of the Stamp Act, Dulany received three anonymous pamphlets which disposed of colonial rights even more cavalierly than Pownall had done. *The Objections to the Taxation of our American Colonies by the Legislature of Great Britain briefly Considered* [15] Dulany recognized, by what means is hard to say, as the work of one of the Lords of Trade.[16] The author was Soame Jenyns, a man who fancied himself a wit and who affirmed the absolute authority of Parliament without any salvos whatever to the rights of Englishmen or Americans. Jenyns denied unequivocally the principle that an Englishman cannot be taxed without the consent of his representatives and disposed of all objections with such flourishes as this: "The Liberty of an *Englishman* is a Phrase of so various a Signification, having within these few years been used as a synonymous Term for Blasphemy, Bawdy, Treason, Libels, Strong Beer, and Cyder, that I shall not here presume to define its meaning; but I shall venture to assert what it cannot mean; that is, an Exemption from Taxes imposed by the Authority of the Parliament of *Great Britain;* . . ." [17] Dulany was nettled but thought that such fuming scarcely deserved an answer.[18]

Another piece which affirmed the Parliamentary right to tax was *The Claim of the Colonies to an Exemption from Internal Taxes im-*

13. Boston, 1760; see *Considerations,* 13. Dulany may have been in Boston or nearby when this pamphlet, attributed to Samuel Waterhouse, was published. One of his few surviving letters indicates that he was in Rhode Island September 21, 1760. Dulany Papers.

14. First edition, pp. 66-67; second edition, pp. 90-92.

15. London, 1765.

16. *Considerations,* 35.

17. *Objections to Taxation,* 9.

18. *Considerations,* 35.

posed by Authority of Parliament, Examined.[19] The author, as one might learn from the context, was one of the colonial agents in London (William Knox of Georgia), and it was clear that this agent had sold out the interests of his clients. He had nothing but praise for the fair-mindedness of the Minister who had inaugurated the Stamp Act and even implied that he had given the colonists an opportunity to avert it. Dulany knew well enough what kind of opportunity the colonists had actually had; he knew that no requisition had been sent in the regular form, no request made of the colonial assemblies before this naked act of power.

These pamphlets were irritating, because the authors all seemed unworthy of the great question they had undertaken to discuss. But there was a fourth publication, which could not be dismissed so lightly—the pamphlet entitled *The Regulations Lately Made concerning the Colonies and the Taxes Imposed upon Them, considered.*[20] This was evidently written by someone close to the Ministry. Dulany, like other Americans, attributed it to Grenville himself. Though the author was actually Thomas Whately, one of Grenville's secretaries, there can be little doubt that it was written under Grenville's direction and represented his views.[21] Because of the source from which it came and the seriousness of its approach this was a much more important piece of work than the others which Dulany had seen, but it was full of pious self-congratulation on the wisdom of the present Ministry. Dulany could not help reflecting that the members of the present Ministry had formerly shown little enthusiasm for the great additions made to the empire in the last war by William Pitt but that now they seemed to regard themselves as the only ministers who had ever given attention to the empire.[22]

The Regulations Lately Made devoted most of its space to demonstrating the wisdom of the Sugar Act of 1764 as a means of directing the trade of the American colonies into proper channels; but in its last pages the author took up the question of Parliament's authority to tax the colonies and supported it with a plausible line of reasoning, all the more irritating because of the assurance with which it was delivered. After reading this and the other pamphlets and the

19. London, 1765.

20. London, 1765.

21. See ch. 3, n. 8. For evidence that other Americans as well as Dulany, attributed the pamphlet to Grenville, see James C. Ballagh, ed., *The Letters of Richard Henry Lee* (New York, 1911), I, 7-10; article signed "Freeman," reprinted from *New York Gazette* in *Maryland Gazette*, August 1, 1765: and article signed "Colonus" in *Providence Gazette Extraordinary*, August 24, 1765.

22. *Considerations*, 18-19. The quotation on these pages is compounded from pp. 5-15 of *The Regulations Lately Made.*

accounts in the newspapers of the small opposition which the Stamp
Act had met in Parliament, Dulany's indignation rose in the same
way that the indignation of other Americans was rising all over the
continent. Finally he set pen to paper and, with just enough anger to
make his words bite, undertook to answer some of the specious con-
tentions of the British pamphleteers and to prove to the satisfaction
of both Englishmen and Americans that Parliament had no right to
tax the colonies.

In the various apologies for Parliamentary taxation that had come
into his hands during the preceding six months Dulany had been
particularly struck by the absurdity of the argument for "virtual"
representation. He could read in the *Pennsylvania Gazette* (May 16)
in an extract of a letter from London that the Ministry had argued
for the Stamp Act in Parliament on the ground "that the colonies
were all virtually represented in Parliament, in the same manner as
those of the subjects in Great Britain, who did not vote for representatives." [23] That the Ministry were founding their right to tax the
colonies on this ground was evident also from the last pages of *The
Regulations Lately Made*.

In reading this pamphlet Dulany could not have failed to perceive
that Grenville had admitted that no British subject could be taxed
without the consent of his representatives. Grenville had argued that
Parliament had authority to tax the colonies only because they were
represented in Parliament, not represented to be sure by delegates
whom they themselves had chosen, but virtually represented by the
delegates chosen in England. Grenville (speaking through Whately)
had said:

... they [the colonies] claim it is true the Privilege, which is common
to all *British* Subjects, of being taxed only with their own Consent,
given by their Representatives; and may they ever enjoy the Privilege
in all its Extent. May this sacred Pledge of Liberty be preserved in-
violate, to the utmost Verge of our Dominions, and to the latest Page
of our History! but let us not limit the legislative Rights of the
British People to Subjects of Taxation only: No new Law whatever
can bind us that is made without the Concurrence of our Representatives. . . . For the Fact is, that the Inhabitants of the Colonies are
represented in Parliament: they do not indeed chuse the Members
of that Assembly; neither are Nine Tenths of the People of *Britain*
Electors; . . . The Colonies are in exactly the same Situation: All

23. The letter was designated as coming from a gentleman in London to his friend
in Charleston, South Carolina. Actually it was written by Charles Garth, the London
agent of South Carolina, to the Assembly's Committee of Correspondence and is quoted
in full in *English Historical Review*, 54 (1939), 649-650.

British Subjects are really in the same: none are actually, all are virtually represented in Parliament; for every Member of Parliament sits in the House not as Representative of his own Constituents, but as one of that august Assembly by which all the Commons of *Great Britain* are represented. Their Rights and their Interests, however his own Borough may be affected by general Dispositions, ought to be the great Objects of his Attention, and the only Rules for his Conduct.[24]

Grenville went on to argue that not only the majority of the people of Great Britain but most of the land itself was represented in Parliament only by virtual representation; for there were many large towns, like Birmingham and Leeds, which elected no members. Later Grenville and his followers would drop this admission that the right to tax rested on the representative character of Parliament and rest the right simply on the all-powerful sovereignty of Parliament.[25] But in this pamphlet and in their arguments for passage of the Stamp Act, they upheld the principle for which the colonists would be contending during the next ten years, that a legislative body can tax only those persons who are represented in it. Dulany must have discerned that Grenville's whole position could be destroyed by showing that the colonies were not represented, either virtually or actually, in the British Parliament. If he did not perceive this obvious fact, a newspaper article, appearing first in the *New York Gazette,* and reprinted both in the *Pennsylvania Journal* (June 13, 20, 27) and in the *Maryland Gazette* (August 1) pointed it out to him. The author of this article, signing himself "Freeman," observed:

that it was admitted in Parliament, even by the greatest Enemies to the Colonies, that they had in the fullest Sense, a Right to be Taxed only by their own Consent, given by their Representatives, but it was said by these Gentlemen, that the Colonies were *virtually* represented in the *English* Parliament—Here let the Reader note well, That the Minister grounds his Pretence of the Parliament's Right to Tax the Colonies, entirely upon this, *that they are* virtually *represented in Parliament:* If therefore he fails in the Proof of their being

24. *Regulations Lately Made,* 104-109.
25. Dulany called attention to the shift when it took place. In a letter to General Conway, c. 1766, he wrote, "this idea of the Right to tax the Colonies by Statute, tho' they are not represented in Parliament, in any manner, has, it should seem, occurred since the Stamp Act, for if the right to tax and the right to regulate had been imagined by Mr. Grenville to be inseparable why did he task his ingenuity to find out a virtual Representation. Why did not some able friend intimate to him his Hazard on the Slippery ground, he chose, when the all powerful Sovereignty of Parliament might have afforded so safe a footing?" Sparks Mss., 44, Harvard College Library. Cf. the similar views expressed in a letter to Walter Dulany, c. 1766, in *Maryland Historical Magazine,* 14 (1919), 381.

so Represented, he must, by his own Argument, give up the Point, and allow that the Parliament has no Manner of Right to tax the Colonies.

Dulany knew that it would be easy to convince his fellow-Americans that they were not virtually represented in Parliament. Not only was the idea repugnant to their interests, but it was repugnant to their whole conception of representative government. Within a week after he had written and published his pamphlet, and probably before they had read it, the people in Anne Arundel County declared in instructions to their members in the Maryland Assembly that "The MINISTER'S *virtual Representation* adduced argumentatively, in Support of the TAX on us is fantastical and frivolous." [26] In this declaration the people of Anne Arundel denied the idea of virtual representation not only by the substance of their statement but by their very manner of making it, in an instruction to their assemblymen, for the idea of virtual representation assumed that a legislator was not bound to his particular constituents or subject to their directions after his election, but that he represented the whole nation. Actually it had not been common for the electors in the southern colonies to direct their representatives because of the inconvenience of gathering the people of a whole county in order to draw up instructions. In the northern colonies, where representation in the assemblies was by town, the town meeting frequently instructed its delegate, not only on local matters but on general questions as well. The representative, in other words, was regarded as the agent of his constituents, and this conception prevailed in the southern colonies as well as the northern, even though the southerners could not readily act upon it. Consequently the idea of a virtual representation, in which the legislator acted for nobody in particular but everybody in general, was indeed "fantastical and frivolous" to the colonists. [27]

Dulany knew, however, that the idea had vogue in England. The great Algernon Sidney himself, in his *Discourses Concerning Government,* had affirmed that the members chosen for the various counties and boroughs were representatives of the whole nation, "and tho it be fit for them as Friends and Neighbors (so far as may be) to harken to the Opinions of the Electors for the Information of their Judgments, and to the end that what they shall say may be of more weight, when every one is known not to speak his own thoughts only,

26. October 24 supplement to *Maryland Gazette,* October 10, 1765.

27. See Kenneth Colegrove, "New England Town Mandates," Colonial Society of Massachusetts, *Publications,* 21 (1911), 411-449. Cf. *Colonial Records of North Carolina,* VII, 249-252.

but those of a great number of men; yet they are not strictly and properly oblig'd to give account of their Actions to any, unless the whole Body of the Nation for which they serve, and who are equally concern'd in their Resolutions, could be assembled." [28] Perhaps Dulany remembered a debate that took place in Parliament in 1745 while he was a student at the Middle Temple. Thomas Carew had argued for annual elections to the House of Commons in order that members might be kept in closer contact with their constituents, but Sir Thomas Yonge had ridden the bill down with a speech in which he pointed out that a member of Parliament after his election is "the attorney of the people of England, and as such is at full freedom to act as he thinks best for the people of England in general. He may receive, he may ask, he may even follow the advice of his particular constituents; but he is not obliged, nor ought he to follow their advice, if he thinks it inconsistent with the general interest of his country." [29]

This was the general belief in England by 1765. Within a few months William Blackstone reaffirmed it in his famous *Commentaries*,[30] and nine years later Edmund Burke gave it classic expression in his *Address to the Electors of Bristol*.[31] Thomas Whately and George Grenville in 1765 were simply extending the idea to cover the whole empire. Probably most Americans thought it had been stretched beyond the elastic limit in reaching Leeds and Birmingham. Dulany, however, was willing to concede all of Great Britain to the Ministry; he drew the line at the Atlantic Ocean, and he believed that he could demonstrate in terms irresistible to Englishmen as well as Americans, that the colonists were not represented in Parliament in the way that Englishmen were.

In a preface to his pamphlet Dulany acknowledged that "It would, now, be an unfashionable Doctrine, whatever the ancient Opinion might be, to affirm that the Constituent can bind his Representative by Instructions." The reason why instructions were not generally considered binding in England was that, as Grenville said, each member was considered the representative of those who did not participate in choosing him as well as of those who did. But this idea, despite its currency, had never been defined or carefully scrutinized. Dulany, accepting it as far as England was concerned, attempted to determine the meaning, and the only way in which he could make sense of it

28. *Discourses Concerning Government*, sec. 44.
29. *Parliamentary History*, XII, 1078.
30. Bk. I, ch. 2, sec. 2.
31. *Works* (4th edn., Boston, 1871), II, 94-98.

was to assume that a dual representation was involved, whereby those who could participate in elections represented those who could not. In this way the members of Parliament actually represented the voters and virtually represented the non-voters. When this supposition was applied merely to England, it could be defended with some pretence of reason: it could be argued, for example, that voteless Leeds and Birmingham were adequately represented in a Parliament containing members from other industrial boroughs with similar interests. To extend the concept to the whole empire, however, was to reduce it to absurdity; to say that the voters of England had similar interests to the colonists' was so far from true that in the matter of taxation the very reverse was true. The author of *The Claim of the Colonies* admitted that it would be advantageous to both the Parliament and the people of Great Britain to load America with taxes, for every shilling that came to the Treasury from the colonies meant one shilling less to be collected at home.[32] A tax raised in England would affect the legislators who voted for it and the electors who chose them as well as the non-voting population, but a tax raised by Parliament in America would affect the people who levied it only by reducing their total tax bill. In this situation to say that the Americans were virtually represented in Parliament was ridiculous.

It was not true, moreover, that there was a great deal of English land not represented in Parliament. Grenville, in maintaining this proposition, had been thinking only of the borough representation. It was well known that this was based on a distribution of population which had long since changed, leaving empty shells of towns with representatives while newly risen industrial centers had none. But in addition to borough representatives Parliament contained two members from each county, so that every square foot of English land was represented, if not by a special borough member, then at least by the two county members. No English property-holder, therefore, was in the same situation as an American, who could not participate in the election of any member. Not one acre of American ground was represented in Parliament; not one acre of English ground was unrepresented.

Dulany pursued these arguments to show that Americans were not represented in Parliament even by the standards of virtual representation, but he did not leave the matter there. He knew, whatever might be said about the representative's independence of his constituents, that in practice many members did follow instructions. Twenty-two years before, in 1743, just after he had taken his cham-

32. *Claim of the Colonies*, 28-30; cited in *Considerations*, 11.

bers at the Middle Temple, there had been a remarkable series of instructions sent by various boroughs to their members. In fact there was still among the family papers a letter he had written to his good father at the time, remarking that "The People are very bold in their instructions to their representatives, and insist very much upon having their Grievances redressed, before they grant any Supplies." [33] Dulany could agree with Sidney and with Sir Thomas Yonge, that the representatives were not bound by these instructions, but what representative, facing reelection, would be apt to ignore them? Even the most ardent advocates of virtual representation, as the conception had been defended before Grenville's time, had admitted the propriety of a member's hearing and possibly heeding the advice of his constituents and the right of his constituents to replace him at the next election if he did not. But to what member of Parliament could the Americans give advice? What member could they replace at the next election for violating their wishes? Instead of giving instructions they must appear as petitioners, humbly begging for favors. How could it be said, then, that Americans were represented in Parliament in anything like the way that Englishmen were?

Having demonstrated that virtual representation, as applied to America, was a fantasy, Dulany might have rested his case. He had shown that Grenville's policy of taxation was unwarranted by Grenville's own principles. But he had more to say. Like other Americans he was full of indignation at the easy gestures with which English writers dismissed colonial rights. Something must be said on that score. Moreover, he did not want to leave the statement of the colonial position with a mere refutation of the idea of virtual representation. In a sense, if one accepted Grenville's avowed position, that no laws whatever could be made for Englishmen (including Americans) without the consent of their representatives, then a mere proof that Americans were not represented in Parliament would prove too much, for it would leave Parliament with no authority whatever in America, and such a result did not accord with Dulany's own views. What he wanted to do was to ascertain the limits of Parliament's authority, not to dissolve it utterly.

Dulany was careful to point out near the beginning of his essay that he was concerned with propriety and not with power.[34] Like other Englishmen and Americans he acknowledged that the power of Parliament was supreme: there was no institution or authority superior to Parliament which could legally call it to account. And

33. January 22, 1743, Dulany Papers.
34. *Considerations,* 7.

yet there were admittedly things that it could not with propriety do. That excellent newspaper article by "Freeman" had pointed out: "No Parliament can alter the Nature of Things, or make that good which is really evil. If they could do this, then they might alter the whole Frame of the Constitution where they are chosen— They might make themselves independent on their Constituents, and be perpetual Dictators—or they might do any Thing— But this cannot be: There is certainly some Bounds to their Power, and 'tis Pity they were not more certainly known." [35] Englishmen were constantly sounding out the limits of Parliament's power in England, but in America, where that power had been so seldom exercised, the limits had not been ascertained. Dulany must have read "Freeman's" article, and he agreed that bounds should be prescribed beyond which Parliament could not with propriety wield its power over Americans. This was necessary not only to arouse the colonists against Parliament's transgressions but also, he felt, to prevent the development of extravagant colonial claims of the type that were already beginning to appear, to the effect that Parliament had no power at all in America.

On May 30, for example, the *Maryland Gazette* had reprinted a piece from one of the northern newspapers in which the author maintained that the only relation between the people of England and those of the colonies was "that we are all the common subjects of the same King; and by any Thing that hath been said in the present controversy, I cannot find that the Inhabitants of the Colonies are *dependent* on the *People* of *Britain,* or the *People* of *Britain* on them, any more than *Kent* is on *Sussex,* or *Sussex* on *Kent.*" Before the controversy was over the newspapers would be filled with shrill assertions that Parliament had "no more Legislative Authority over us than those that lived before the Flood." [36] On this basis even the Acts of Trade and Navigation would be unconstitutional, and indeed one writer in New York affirmed that the colonists had submitted to them only because of their expediency and not because of their legality. [37] This kind of talk, in Dulany's opinion at least, went a good deal too far. He was ready to acknowledge a dependence on

35. *Maryland Gazette,* August 1; *Pennsylvania Journal,* June 13, 20, 27.

36. *Pennsylvania Journal,* February 6, 1766; *Maryland Gazette,* February 20, 1766; *Boston Gazette,* February 24, 1766.

37. *Considerations upon the Rights of the Colonists to the Privileges of British Subjects* (New York, 1766), 11. For other statements of the view that Parliament had no authority in the colonies and that the only connection between England and the colonies was a common King, see *Providence Gazette,* August 18, 1764; *Boston Gazette,* March 17, 1766.

Parliament; the question was how much, for it seemed to him perfectly reasonable that the colonists should be dependent without being reduced to the status of slaves. To be sure one English pamphleteer had maintained that any line between absolute dependency and independence was "a whimsical Imagination, a chimerical Speculation against Fact and Experience." This assertion, said Dulany, contained "more Confidence than Solidity," and he determined to disprove it.[38]

Dulany was a lawyer, and he set about establishing the bounds of Parliament's authority with a lawyer-like regard for tradition and precedent. Other spokesmen for the colonial cause had already begun to argue in terms of the natural rights of man,[39] but Dulany knew that however such arguments might appeal to Americans, they would carry small weight in the British Parliament. The question, as he saw it, did not hinge so much on natural rights as it did on constitutional rights. As long as the colonists had the constitution on their side—and he was sure that they had—it would be best for them to ground their arguments upon it.

On the other hand Dulany did not make the mistake of supposing that the British constitution was so exact a body of principles that its interpretation could be left to the determination of legal experts. He could remember several opinions of legal experts employed by ministries in the past, opinions on American affairs, and they all declared that to be legal which the Minister for the time being deemed to be expedient. Dulany knew that the law was a fallible instrument, and when it came to deciding what was constitutional and what was not, the opinion of a lawyer was to be trusted only in so far as his arguments were convincing. In determining the bounds of Parliament's authority in the colonies, therefore, Dulany made no pretence of relying upon bare legal precedents but sought to rest his case upon what he took to be acknowledged principles

38. *Considerations,* 14. I have not been able to identify the quotation which Dulany refers to. In citing his opponents' arguments Dulany generally stated what he took to be their position, sometimes quoting word for word, more often summarizing or paraphrasing, but always including the whole in quotation marks as though it were an exact transcription. Most of his quotations can be traced to one of the pamphlets discussed above, but this one has eluded me.

39. For the statements of natural rights during the Stamp Act period, see James Otis, *The Rights of the Colonies Asserted and Proved,* 34; the New York Assembly's Petition to the House of Commons of October 18, 1764, *Journal of the Votes and Proceedings . . .* (New York, 1766), II, 776-779; Pennsylvania Resolves and Massachusetts Resolves of 1765, cited in Chapter 7; articles in *Boston Gazette,* November 18, 1765, December 2, 1765; *Boston Post-Boy and Advertiser,* December 30, 1765; and resolves by Sons of Liberty in various towns, cited in Chapter 11.

of the constitution and upon the manner in which those principles had hitherto been applied in English and American history.

The fundamental principle of the British constitution, as Dulany understood it, prescribed a mixed government, compounded of monarchy, aristocracy, and democracy, represented respectively by the King, the House of Lords, and the House of Commons. This was not a peculiar belief of Dulany's but rather a commonplace of political theory at the time. In the threefold division, Dulany observed, the levying of taxes was generally considered "the Province of the House of Commons as the Representative of the People." [40] Taxation was regarded, in other words, not as an act of sovereign power by the whole legislature, but as a free gift of the people by their representatives. In support of this statement he had only to point out that the House of Commons alone could originate a bill of taxation and the other branches of the government were allowed merely to assent to it without modification. This procedure embodied the principle which Grenville had acknowledged, that no British subject could be taxed except by the consent of his representatives. Though the American colonists were British subjects, they were not represented in Parliament but only in their colonial assemblies. Therefore the colonial assemblies could tax them, but Parliament could not. Parliament had authority to tax only those persons who were represented in the House of Commons, namely the people of England, Scotland, and Wales.

Dulany, though insistent that Parliament's right to tax was limited, upheld its right to legislate for all British subjects, including the Irish and the Americans, who were not represented in it. He saw no inconsistency here, because for him taxation and legislation were two separate functions, the former associated with the representative character of the House of Commons, the latter with the supreme authority of Parliament. Parliament was entitled to legislate for both mother country and colonies, because its legislative power derived not from its representative character (as Grenville apparently believed) but from its sovereignty over the whole empire.

Since Dulany was concerned about the issue of Parliamentary taxation rather than Parliamentary legislation, he did not define the latter except on points where confusion between the two might arise. For instance, while admitting that the colonies by their very nature were dependencies of their mother country and that "the supreme authority vested in the King, Lords, and Commons may justly be exercised to secure, or preserve their Dependance whenever

40. *Considerations*, 5.

necessary for that Purpose," [41] he hastened to deny that this implied a right to tax. As Dulany put it, "tho' the Right of the Superior to use the proper Means for preserving the Subordination of his Inferior is admitted, yet, it does not necessarily follow, that he has a Right to seize the Property of his Inferior when he pleases." [42] And again, "The Right of Exemption from all Taxes *without their Consent,* the Colonies claim as *British* Subjects. . . . On the other Hand, they acknowledge themselves to be subordinate to the Mother-Country and that the Authority vested in the supreme Council of the Nation, may be justly exercised to support and preserve that Subordination." [43]

What Dulany meant by supporting and preserving the subordination of the colonies he made clear in several places: he meant that Parliament might regulate the trade of the empire, as it had done in the Acts of Trade and Navigation, in order to insure that the colonies subserve the economic interests of the mother country. He even admitted that regulations of trade might take the form of import or export duties levied in the colonies and that such duties might produce an "incidental Revenue," but he put those words in italics and followed them by a demonstration that regulations of trade in the past could not be regarded as taxes, for they had clearly not been made with an intention of producing revenue. [44] This he could prove readily by evidence which Grenville himself had provided. In *The Regulations Lately Made* Grenville had supplied figures on customs duties in America which indicated that the average annual remittance from such duties during the past thirty years had been less than £2000, while the cost of collecting them had been £7600. Duties which cost four times as much to collect as they produced might well be justified as regulations of trade, but they could scarcely be regarded as taxes levied for the purpose of revenue. [45]

The gist of Dulany's whole argument was that taxation formed no part of the authority which Parliament enjoyed as the supreme power in the empire. Taxation was the function of representative bodies, and the only representative bodies in America were the colonial assemblies, so that an American could "give his Consent in no other Manner than in Assembly." [46] In maintaining this position Dulany was unable to refrain from lashing out in digression after digression against various absurdities he had found in the British

41. *Ibid.,* 15. 42. *Ibid.,* 15. 43. *Ibid.,* 28. 44. *Ibid.,* 34-35.
45. *Regulations Lately Made,* 57; *Considerations,* 35.
46. *Considerations,* 29.

pamphleteers. He was too angry to keep his remarks entirely on the high level of constitutional theory; and he found occasion to make effective use of a number of ideas and episodes that had been rankling in his mind. Remembering, for example, that the stamp tax had been levied ostensibly to help defray the expense of the troops stationed in America, he made sarcastic reference to an episode he had read of in the newspapers: some of the troops stationed in Canada, displeased with the judgment of a civil court in sentencing one of their officers to prison, had entered the judge's house and cut off his ears and slit his nose.[47] Was money needed in the British exchequer, Dulany asked, so that troops could be "employed in the national Service of Cropping the Ears, and Slitting the Nostrils of the Civil Magistrates, as Marks of Distinction?" [48] Sometimes in these slashing attacks Dulany hit below the belt, as when he attributed to Thomas Pownall views which the latter had never held.[49] Nevertheless, fair or unfair, his blows struck home, and in spite of all digressions he hammered out his main point, that Parliament's authority in the colonies had limits this side of the right to tax.

It was only when he came to discuss the question of what steps the colonists ought to take if Parliament overstepped its bounds, that Dulany touched a note of moderation. Even here he spoke as though he meant to propose a vigorous resistance. "Instead of moping, and puling, and whining to excite Compassion; in such a Situation we ought with Spirit, and Vigour, and Alacrity, to bid Defiance to Tyranny, by exposing it's Impotence, by making it as contemptible, as it would be detestable." [50] How then were the colonies to make tyranny contemptible? "By a vigorous Application to Manufactures." [51] The colonists must go to their looms and spinning wheels and make Britain tremble for the loss of her colonial customers. Even this measure Dulany thought would be improper for the colonial assemblies to direct, but the assemblymen might at least set an example: "The Sight of our Representatives, all adorned in compleat Dresses of their own Leather, and Flax, and Wool . . . would excite, not the Gaze of Admiration, the Flutter of an agitated Imagination, or the momentary Amusement of a transient Scene, but a calm, solid, heart-felt Delight." [52]

This was something of a comedown from the warm words with which Dulany had blasted Grenville and his adherents. After arguing that virtual representation did not extend to America, Dulany seems

---

47. *Maryland Gazette,* July 18, 1765.
48. *Considerations,* 42.
49. *Ibid.,* 13.   50. *Ibid.,* 47.   51. *Ibid.,* 47.   52. *Ibid.,* 48.

to have found no inconsistency in recommending a course of action which assumed that it did. By reducing purchases of British manufactures, he thought, the Americans would be able to alarm the British merchants and enlist their support in Parliament. He apparently did not see that the success of such procedure might serve as a partial refutation of his argument that American interest could not be felt by a Parliament elected entirely in Great Britain. Actually economic pressure was already being applied before his recommendations appeared, and did help to bring about repeal; but by that time it was no longer necessary for him to explain his inconsistency, for Parliament had ceased to justify its authority over the colonies by the doctrine of virtual representation. Virtual representation had become a dead issue, and Dulany had helped to kill it.[53]

Meanwhile Dulany's pamphlet was bought by his countrymen as they had scarcely bought any pamphlet before. Its articulation and justification of their own instinctive view of colonial rights delighted them. Already before its publication they had begun in their assemblies to do what Dulany did, to draw a line between Parliamentary authority and American rights. When they had done with argument and debate, it appeared that the united determination of Americans from Georgia to New Hampshire agreed with the private opinion of Daniel Dulany.

53. See below, chs. 15, 16, and above, n. 25.

SEVEN

RESOLUTION

PARLIAMENT had not rejected the American petitions; Parliament had simply refused to consider them at all, and thereby made painfully clear how much its members cared for the rights of the colonies. The early news reports showed that the Ministry had not only swept aside the colonial petitions but had pushed through the Stamp Act with no opposition worthy of the name. Had the members been satisfied with Grenville's fatuous talk about virtual representation? Had they supposed that the colonists would submit tamely to an act which violated the very basis of constitutional government? Had they thought that by refusing to hear the petitions they could silence two and a half million voices? Evidently they had. It would be necessary, then, to show them that Americans would not be satisfied with virtual representation, would not submit tamely, would not be silent.

In Williamsburg, Virginia, the House of Burgesses was going through the routine business of the May session—bills for building roads, docking entails, selling surplus military supplies, offering bounties on wolves—when news arrived that the petitions over which the Assembly had labored the previous year had not received a hearing and that stamp duties would be collected in America.[1] The

1. According to Edmund Pendleton, writing in 1790, the news of the Stamp Act came in a letter from Edward Montague, the Virginia agent, toward the end of the session, after many members had already gone home. E. S. Morgan, "Edmund Pendleton on the Virginia Resolves," *Maryland Historical Magazine*, 46 (1951), 71-80. It may be that Montague's letter took from early February until late May to reach Virginia, but the news it contained was printed in the *Pennsylvania Gazette* on April 18, the *Maryland Gazette* on April 25, and the *Georgia Gazette* on May 2. Copies of the *Virginia Gazette* for these months are not extant, but it is inconceivable that the news did not reach Virginia before the end of May.

Burgesses left no record of what they thought about the treatment of their petitions, but one may guess that they felt the same indignation that other colonists expressed. For example, William Smith, Jr., one of the authors of the New York petitions, wrote to a friend in England:

When the Americans reflect upon the Parliament's refusal to hear their Representations—when they read abstracts of the speeches within doors [inside Parliament], and the ministerial pamphlets without, and find themselves tantalized and contemned, advantages taken of their silence heretofore, and Remonstrances forbidden in time to come; and above all, when they see the prospects of innumerable loads arising from this connection with an overburdened nation interested in shaking the weight off of their own shoulders, and commanding silence in the oppressed Beast on which it is cast; what can be expected but discontent for a while, and in the end open opposition. The boldness of the Minister amazes our people. This single stroke has lost Great Britain the affection of all her Colonies.[2]

But William Smith did not propose immediate opposition, and similarly the men who had drawn up Virginia's petitions do not appear to have felt the need for replying at once to the Ministry's challenge. Most of the Burgesses, when the calendar of routine business was nearing completion, packed their bags and left the heat of Williamsburg for the comfort of their plantations. It was not the authors of the petitions but a new member who insisted on translating them without delay into a declaration of rights. Most of the old members had already departed when Patrick Henry, who had been admitted to the House only nine days before, rose to introduce a series of resolutions against the Stamp Act.

What Henry said and what the Burgesses did are clear in legend but cloudy in history. Thirty-nine Burgesses were present in the Chamber, and several spectators were watching in the lobby, but so far as we know today only one, a visiting stranger, wrote down any part of what he heard and saw. The first newspaper to report what happened was some five hundred miles away. The first attempt to reconstruct the event was twenty-five years and a revolution later, and the second attempt was forty to fifty years later and only succeeded in giving form to a legend. James Madison made the first attempt in 1790, by writing to Edmund Pendleton, one of the authors of the petitions of 1764. Pendleton answered as best he could, but it turned out that he was one of those who had already left for home when it happened and could only reply with dimly remem-

2. Massachusetts Historical Society, *Collections*, 4th ser., 10 (1871), 570-571.

bered hearsay.[3] Madison did not pursue the inquiry further, and by the time that William Wirt took it up in 1805, there were only two or three old men who could remember. Of these Thomas Jefferson, who had watched from the lobby, had the most vivid recollection, but forty-year-old recollections, however vivid, are apt to be compounded of fact and fantasy; and when Wirt put together his findings in a life of Patrick Henry, he drew a picture which merely perpetuated the legend that had already developed.[4]

The legend was one of Patrick Henry pouring forth torrents of sublime eloquence and bidding defiance to the shouts of "treason!" which rang from all corners of the House. The legend in all its appealing and dramatic simplicity still lingers for the schoolboy, but is now denied to adults, for in 1921 a contemporary eye-witness account turned up in the journal of an unknown French traveller, who had stood with Jefferson in the lobby of the House of Burgesses on May 30 and 31, 1765. Of all the spectators and of all the thirty-nine Burgesses, this anonymous stranger was the only one who left a message for future historians, and though his account contains at least one recognizable error of fact, it is the only direct road that we can follow back to those critical days when Virginia pointed the way to freedom.

May the 30th. Set out Early from halfway house in the Chair and broke fast at York, arived at williamsburg at 12, where I saw three Negroes hanging at the galous for haveing robed Mr. Waltho of 300 ps. I went imediately to the assembly which was seting, where I was entertained with very strong Debates Concerning Dutys that the parlement wants to lay on the american Colonys, which they Call or Stile stamp Dutys. Shortly after I Came in one of the members stood up and said he had read that in former times tarquin and Julus had their Brutus, Charles had his Cromwell, and he Did not Doubt but some good american would stand up, in favour of his Country, but (says he) in a more moderate manner, and was going to Continue, when the speaker of the house rose and Said, he, the last that stood up had spoke traison, and was sorey to see that not one of the members of the house was loyal Enough to stop him, before he had gone so far, upon which the Same member stood up again (his name is henery) and said that if he had afronted the speaker, or the house, he was ready to ask pardon, and he would shew his loyalty to his majesty King G. the third, at the Expence of the last Drop of his blood, but what he had said must be atributed to the Interest of his Countrys Dying liberty which he had at heart,

3. *Maryland Historical Magazine*, 46 (1951), 74.
4. *Sketches of the Life and Character of Patrick Henry* (Philadelphia, 1817).

and the heat of passion might have lead him to have said something more than he intended, but, again, if he said any thing wrong, he beged the speaker and the houses pardon. some other Members stood up and backed him, on which that afaire was droped.[5]

This account gives us a ringside seat in the House of Burgesses for long enough to deflate the legend of Henry's daring. Unfortunately it fails to tell us exactly what he proposed that the Burgesses do about the Stamp Act. From the official records we can discover that they passed four resolutions on that afternoon, and if we are to believe Henry himself and the recollections of Pendleton and Jefferson, Henry was arguing for the passage of these resolutions in his famous speech. In the printed Journals of the House they stand as follows:

Resolved, That the first Adventurers and Settlers of this his Majesty's Colony and Dominion of *Virginia* brought with them, and transmitted to their Posterity, and all other his Majesty's Subjects since inhabiting in this his Majesty's said Colony, all the Liberties, Privileges, Franchises, and Immunities, that have at any Time been held, enjoyed, and possessed, by the people of *Great Britain.*

Resolved, That by two royal Charters, granted by King *James* the First, the Colonists aforesaid are declared entitled to all Liberties, Privileges, and Immunities of Denizens and natural Subjects, to all Intents and Purposes, as if they had been abiding and born within the Realm of *England.*

Resolved, That the Taxation of the People by themselves, or by Persons chosen by themselves to represent them, who can only know what Taxes the People are able to bear, or the easiest Method of raising them, and must themselves be affected by every Tax laid on the People, is the only Security against a burthensome Taxation, and the distinguishing Characteristick of *British* Freedom, without which the ancient Constitution cannot exist.

Resolved, That his Majesty's liege People of this his most ancient and loyal Colony have without Interruption enjoyed the inestimable Right of being governed by such Laws, respecting their internal Polity and Taxation, as are derived from their own Consent, with the Approbation of their Sovereign, or his Substitute; and that the same hath never been forfeited or yielded up, but hath been constantly recognized by the Kings and People of *Great Britain.*[6]

Was this, then, the action which Henry urged upon the Burgesses? Or was this a compromise representing something less than he asked

5. *American Historical Review,* 26 (1920-21), 745.
6. John Pendleton Kennedy, ed., *Journals of the House of Burgesses of Virginia, 1761-1765* (Richmond, 1907), 360.

for? Or was it perhaps more? The printed record is silent, and the manuscript record has disappeared, but a letter from Governor Fauquier to the Board of Trade, on June 5, indicates that the four resolutions in the Journals must originally have been followed by a fifth:

On Wednesday the 29th of May, just at the end of the Session when most of the members had left the town, there being but 39 present out of 116 of which the House of Burgesses now consists, a motion was made to take into consideration the Stamp Act, a copy of which had crept into the House, and in a Committee of the whole House five resolutions were proposed and agreed to, all by very small majorities. On Thursday the 30th they were reported and agreed to by the House, the numbers being as before in the Committee; the greatest majority being 22 to 17; for the 5th Resolution, 20 to 19 only.[7]

What was this fifth resolution which passed by so narrow a majority and which is missing from the records? When Patrick Henry died, he left behind a paper on which five resolutions were written, four of them (with slight verbal alterations) as they stood in the Journal, the fifth one reading:

Resolved Therefore that the General Assembly of this Colony have the only and sole exclusive Right and Power to lay Taxes and Impositions upon the Inhabitants of this Colony and that every Attempt to vest such Power in any other Person or Persons whatsoever other than the General Assembly aforesaid has a manifest Tendency to destroy British as well as American Freedom.[8]

This resolution, it may be, was the fifth one, which passed by so slender a margin. Though it does not differ much from the others, it is more specific in its assertions and may therefore have earned fewer votes. We have the Frenchman's word for it that the debates were "very strong," and Jefferson even forty years later recalled that the debate on the fifth one was "most bloody." [9] Jefferson also remembered how Peyton Randolph walked into the lobby afterward exclaiming, "by God, I would have given 500 guineas for a single vote." [10] A single vote would have divided the house evenly on the fifth resolution, and Randolph knew that John Robinson, the Speaker, would then have been called to cast the deciding vote and would have voted against it.

7. *Ibid.*, lxvii.
8. *Ibid.*, frontispiece.
9. *Pa. Mag. of Hist.*, 34 (1910), 389.
10. *Ibid.* Nine years later Jefferson recalled it as 100 guineas, *ibid.*, 399.

Why Randolph, Robinson, Robert Carter Nicholas, and even Richard Bland and George Wythe, all of whom are said to have opposed the resolutions, should have been so hostile to them is not apparent. Most of these men had been active in drawing up the petitions of the preceding year, and Henry's resolutions did little more than paraphrase the petitions. George Wythe, who had drawn the petition to the House of Commons, told Jefferson that his first draft had required toning down because the other members of the committee thought it treasonable.[11] And Richard Bland was soon to express in print a view of Parliament's authority which was at least as restricted as that taken in the resolutions.[12] The argument of the opposition, if correctly recalled by Jefferson and Edmund Pendleton, was that the petitions of the preceding year were a sufficient statement of the colonial position and that no further step should be taken until some answer was received to these. But this argument was specious, for the Burgesses knew that the petitions had not received a hearing. In all probability, the opposition is not to be explained so much by the measure itself as by the men who were backing it. Henry and his friends were upstarts in Virginia politics, and their introduction of the resolves constituted a challenge to the established leaders of the House of Burgesses.[13]

In any case Randolph and the others who opposed the resolutions were so much upset by their failure to defeat them that they determined, possibly with the advice and approval of the Governor, to get them reversed. On the morning of May 31 when Jefferson went to the House to see what was coming next he found Peter Randolph, a member of the Governor's Council (and a cousin of Peyton's) thumbing through the Journals in search of a precedent for expunging a vote of the House.[14] Though Jefferson stood with him at the clerk's desk for an hour or two till the House bell announced the opening of the meeting, he could not recall whether Randolph found the precedent or not, but when the Burgesses met they did carry a motion to erase the fifth resolution. The Burgesses' Journal is entirely void of any mention of the Stamp Act under May 31. The votes of that day were either not recorded or were erased along with the fifth resolution. But Jefferson's recollection of the expunging is confirmed by Governor Fauquier's letter, which states that on the thirty-first, "there having happened a small alteration in the House

11. *Ibid.*, 400.
12. *An Inquiry into the Rights of the British Colonies* (Williamsburg, 1766).
13. See Carl Bridenbaugh, *Seat of Empire* (Williamsburg, 1950).
14. *Pa. Mag. of Hist.*, 34 (1910), 399.

there was an attempt to strike all the Resolutions off the Journals. The 5th which was thought the most offensive was accordingly struck off, but it did not succeed as to the other four." [15]

Governor Fauquier does not say how the small alteration in the House occurred, but Jefferson remembered in 1805 that Patrick Henry himself left Williamsburg on the evening of the thirtieth.[16] If Jefferson was right, then Henry himself may be held partly responsible for the rescinding of the fifth resolution, for assuming that no one else changed sides, the loss of his vote would have split the house. Did Henry leave because he thought that the matter had been decided and would not be reconsidered? Did he pair his vote with some other departing legislator from the other side? Or did Peyton Randolph perhaps find a way of spending his five hundred guineas for a single vote?

We will probably never know the answer, but of one thing we can be certain, that though the conservatives were able to get the fifth resolution rescinded before the House dissolved on the first of June, they were not able to keep it out of the newspapers. Word spread to the other colonies, and copies of the resolves were being passed around in Philadelphia by the middle of June.[17] One Philadelphian sent a copy to a friend in Newport, and here on June 24 the *Newport Mercury* gained the distinction of being the first newspaper to print them. Most of the other papers picked up the story from the *Mercury,* but the *Maryland Gazette* ran its own version on July 4, from a source closer to the original.

The puzzling thing about the resolves as printed in the newspapers is that they were not four in number as in the Journals of the Burgesses, or five, as in Patrick Henry's copy, but six in the *Newport Mercury,* and seven in the *Maryland Gazette.* The complete text, as given by the *Gazette,* has a slightly different wording from the five resolves we have considered and includes two new ones.

RESOLVES of the House of Burgesses in VIRGINIA, *June* 1765.

That the first Adventurers & Settlers of this his Majesty's Colony and Dominion of *Virginia,* brought with them, and transmitted to their Posterity, and all other his Majesty's Subjects since inhabiting in this his Majesty's Colony, all the Liberties, Privileges, Franchises, and Immunities, that at any Time have been held, enjoyed, and possessed, by the People of *Great Britain.*

15. *Journals of the House of Burgesses,* lxvii.
16. *Pa. Mag. of Hist.,* 34 (1910), 389.
17. Thomas Wharton and Joseph Galloway sent copies to Benjamin Franklin on June 15 and June 18, respectively (Franklin Papers, American Philosophical Society, I, 152, 147).

That by Two Royal Charters, granted by King *James* the First, the Colonies aforesaid are Declared Entitled, to all Liberties, Privileges and Immunities, of Denizens and Natural Subjects (to all Intents and Purposes) as if they had been Abiding and Born within the Realm of *England*.

That the Taxation of the People by Themselves, or by Persons Chosen by Themselves to Represent them, who can only know what Taxes the People are able to bear, or the easiest Method of Raising them, and must themselves be affected by every Tax laid upon the People, is the only Security against a Burthensome Taxation; and the Distinguishing Characteristic of *British* FREEDOM; and, without which, the antient Constitution cannot exist.

That his Majesty's Liege People of this his most Ancient and Loyal Colony, have, without Interruption, the inestimable Right of being Governed by such Laws, respecting their internal Polity and Taxation, as are derived from their own Consent, with the Approbation of their Sovereign, or his Substitute; which Right hath never been Forfeited, or Yielded up; but hath been constantly recognized by the Kings and People of *Great Britain*.

Resolved therefore, That the General Assembly of this Colony, with the Consent of his Majesty, or his Substitute, HAVE the Sole Right and Authority to lay Taxes and Impositions upon It's Inhabitants: And, That every Attempt to vest such Authority in any other Person or Persons whatsoever, has a Manifest Tendency to Destroy AMERICAN FREEDOM.

That his Majesty's Liege People, Inhabitants of this Colony, are not bound to yield Obedience to any Law or Ordinance whatsoever, designed to impose any Taxation upon them, other than the Laws or Ordinances of the General Assembly as aforesaid.

That any Person who shall, by Speaking, or Writing, assert or maintain, That any Person or Persons, other than the General Assembly of this Colony, with such Consent as aforesaid, have any Right or Authority to lay or impose any Tax whatever on the Inhabitants thereof, shall be Deemed, AN ENEMY TO THIS HIS MAJESTY'S COLONY.

The *Mercury,* and the papers copying from it, printed six of these in approximately the same form as the *Maryland Gazette* [18] but omitted altogether the third resolve.

The question is where the two extra resolves came from. Possibly they were part of a set of original proposals prepared by Henry and whoever was working with him. The records of the Burgesses indicate that the resolves were amended before their passage, and the amendment may have consisted of striking out the last two as given

18. The most notable difference is in the fourth resolution where the phrase "internal polity and taxation" as given in the *Maryland Gazette* and in the *Journals of the House of Burgesses* is altered to "taxation and internal police."

in the newspaper version. Governor Fauquier, who was not himself present, reported that the initiators of the resolutions had two more "in their pocket, but finding the difficulty they had in carrying the 5th which was by a single voice, and knowing them to be more virulent and inflammatory; they did not produce them." [19] Fauquier was right in supposing that the extra resolutions were more violent than the others, but he was wrong in supposing that they were not introduced, for the Frenchman, who like Jefferson returned to the Burgesses on the thirty-first, reported:

May the 31th. I returned to the assembly today, and heard very hot Debates stil about the Stamp Dutys. the whole house was for Entering resolves on the records but they Differed much with regard the Contents or purport thereof. some were for shewing their resentment to the highest. one of the resolves that these proposed, was that any person that would offer to sustain that the parlement of Engl'd had a right to impose or lay any tax or Dutys whats'r on the american Colonys, without the Consent of the inhabitants thereof, Should be looked upon as a traitor, and Deemed an Enemy to his Country. there were some others to the same purpose, and the majority was for Entring these resolves, upon which the Governor Disolved the assembly, which hinderd their proceeding.[20]

Unquestionably this refers to the seventh resolution. It is possible that the Frenchman recorded this event under the wrong date. The latter part of the entry for May 31 refers to events of succeeding days, and he may have written the whole entry some days later. In so doing he could have ascribed to the thirty-first what he actually heard on the thirtieth. But there is no reason to doubt that the Burgesses did debate the seventh resolution. If the Frenchman was right in dating the debate on the thirty-first, and if Fauquier was right in asserting that only five resolutions were proposed, then the fact that the seventh resolution was discussed would indicate that it was the one passed on May 30 and rescinded on May 31.

In 1814 Jefferson offered Wirt another theory about the identity of the rescinded resolution: "the 5th has clearly nothing to justify the debate and proceedings which one of them produced. but the 6th is of that character, and perfectly tallies with the idea impressed on my mind of that which was expunged . . . my hypothesis then is this, that the two disagreed to were the 5th. & 7th. the 5th. because

19. *Journals of the House of Burgesses,* lxvii-lxviii.
20. *American Historical Review,* 26 (1920-21), 745-746.

merely tautologous of the 3d. & 4th. and 7th. because leading to individual persecution, for which no mind was then prepared." [21]

If either of the above hypotheses was the case, then the Burgesses were ready on May 30 to go much farther in asserting their rights than has generally been supposed, for both the sixth and the seventh were much more radical than the fifth. But neither of these theories can be considered conclusive: the first rests on slim, albeit entirely contemporary evidence; the second rests on recollection too distant to be trustworthy. On the other hand, the evidence that the fifth resolution was the one rescinded rests solely on the copy found among Henry's papers. The copy is not in Henry's hand and is undated, and Henry's endorsement on the back (which states that these were the resolutions passed) was made many years after the episode. It is certainly not free enough of suspicion to be conclusive evidence.

It would be useful to know which resolution the Burgesses were willing to pass but not to retain after second thought, for it would help us to assess their temper, but unless new evidence appears no positive answer can be given. Of one thing we can nevertheless be certain: they did debate the question of resistance, for the seventh resolution which the Frenchman heard them discuss, presupposed that the Stamp Act would be resisted.

What remains as the indubitable position of the Burgesses with regard to Parliament's authority is the first four resolutions. Fauquier expressed the hope that the House at its next session would reverse these four as it had the fifth.[22] But when the Burgesses met again, he was disappointed. They did not adopt or reaffirm any of the radical extra resolutions, but neither did they revoke the four.

Here then was Virginia's position, and in all essentials it was the same as that defined later in more detail by Daniel Dulany. In phrases borrowed largely from the petitions which had been so fruitlessly delivered to Parliament, the Virginians claimed the rights of Englishmen, and affirmed that one of these was the right to be taxed only by "persons chosen by themselves to represent them" (no room for virtual representation there). The resolutions did not attempt to state what powers Parliament did have in Virginia but only what powers it did not have. As for the action people might take when Parliament went beyond its powers, the resolves said nothing. The unapproved ones had called for resistance, a course which Virginians

---

21. *Pa. Mag. of Hist.*, 34 (1910), 398.
22. Fauquier to Henry Seymour Conway, November 24, 1765, House of Lords Manuscripts, February 6, 1766, Library of Congress transcripts.

as private citizens might still adopt, but without the official approval or disapproval of their government.

Although the Burgesses had stopped short of recommending resistance, the resolves were too much for Joseph Royle, the conservative editor of the *Virginia Gazette*. He failed to print them, and consequently the other colonies, instead of obtaining a relatively reliable text from a publication in the colony itself, got news of Virginia's action from the more ardent supporters of the resolutions. Henry and his friends, having failed to secure passage of their most radical items in the House of Burgesses, were able to get them passed unanimously in the newspapers: every newspaper which carried the resolutions printed the fifth, sixth, and seventh as though they had been adopted. When Royle complained that the other papers were stuffed with false news about Virginia, the radicals could reply that "If Mr. *Royle* had been pleased to publish those Resolves, the *Authenticity* of his *Intelligence,* would have been undisputed, and he would not have had any Reason of complaint on that Score." [23]

To the other colonists, then, the Virginia Burgesses appeared much bolder than they had actually been, and their supposed example stirred up other assemblies to a degree of emulation which sometimes surpassed the original. The first colony to imitate Virginia was Rhode Island, where the resolves had first been printed. The Rhode Island Assembly met in May and June, after passage of the Stamp Act had been reported but before news of Virginia's action, and took no notice of the Act. It was not until the September session that the members from Providence, by instruction from their town meeting, moved a series of resolutions copied after those attributed to Virginia.[24] As adopted, the Rhode Island resolutions included the first, second, fourth, fifth, and sixth, all of which had been printed in the *Newport Mercury;* but Rhode Island, not being a royal colony, saw no reason to include the phrase, "together with his Majesty or his Substitutes" contained in Virginia's fifth resolution, and in the sixth resolution, the one calling for resistance, Rhode Island inserted the word "internal" before the word taxation. In the preceding resolutions, which denied Parliament's authority to tax, no distinction was made between kinds of taxation, but the appeal for resistance was directed against "internal taxation." In order to implement the general purpose of this resolution the Rhode Islanders added another and final one, which read:

23. *Maryland Gazette,* October 3, 1765.
24. *Newport Mercury,* August 19, 1765.

That all the officers in this colony, appointed by the authority thereof, be, and they are hereby, directed to proceed in the execution of their respective offices in the same manner as usual; and that this Assembly will indemnify and save harmless all the said officers, on account of their conduct, agreeably to this resolution.[25]

Rhode Island alone, by endorsing resistance, dared to speak to Parliament as impudently as everyone supposed that Virginia had spoken, but even Rhode Island did not go so far as to declare that supporters of the Stamp Act were guilty of treason. The other colonies stopped short, as Virginia had in reality, of approving resistance, but every colony which later participated in the Revolution, with the exception of Georgia, North Carolina, Delaware, and New Hampshire, eventually passed declaratory resolutions defining their rights, and in all of these the limits set on Parliament's authority excluded the right to tax the colonies.[26] Those colonies which had made somewhat limited objections to Parliamentary taxation in 1764 now set the matter straight. Rhode Island had been one of these. Connecticut was another, and she clarified her position in a set of resolutions also copied in part from those of Virginia.[27] It was Massachusetts, however, that had been most equivocal the previous year, in omitting all mention of rights in their address to Parliament. And in Massachusetts the effect of the Virginia Resolves was electric.

The House of Representatives in the Bay had never been happy about the address which Lieutenant-Governor Hutchinson had persuaded them to adopt. When they saw the spirited assertion of rights that New York had sent to Parliament shortly after theirs, they were ashamed of their own moderation. Governor Bernard, however, had assured them that their message would be well received and have good effects.[28] When the Stamp Act was passed and the members refused to hear any petitions at all, many of the representatives in the Massachusetts Assembly must have felt that it would have been far better to assert their principles and to hang for a sheep instead of a lamb.[29] Oxenbridge Thacher, who had penned the original asser-

25. *Records of the Colony of Rhode Island*, VI, 451-452.
26. I have discussed these resolutions in "Colonial Ideas of Parliamentary Power," *William and Mary Quarterly*, 3d ser., 5 (1948), 311-341. See pp. 320-325. The governor prevented action in North Carolina by keeping the Assembly prorogued. Delaware participated in the Stamp Act Congress, and Georgia and New Hampshire officially approved the proceedings of the Congress.
27. *Public Records of the Colony of Connecticut*, XII, 421-425.
28. Alden Bradford, ed., *Speeches of the Governors of Massachusetts from 1765 to 1775* . . . (Boston, 1818), 28; Bernard to John Pownall, November 17, 1764, to Richard Jackson, November 17, 1764, Bernard Papers, III, 260-264, Harvard College Library.
29. Thomas Hutchinson to Thomas Pownall, March 8, 1766, Massachusetts Archives, XXVI, 200-206.

tion of colonial rights, for which Hutchinson's timid plea had been
substituted, lay on his deathbed when news of what the Virginians
had done reached Boston. "They are men!" he cried.[30] And he or
some other patriot quickly penned a column for the *Boston Gazette,*
repudiating the shameful work of the previous year, and decrying
the imputation of treason which Boston conservatives had pronounced on Virginia's action:

The People of Virginia have spoke very sensibly, and the frozen
Politicians of a more northern Government say they have spoke
Treason: Their spirited Resolves do indeed serve as a perfect Contrast for a certain tame, pusillanimous, daub'd insipid Thing, deli-
cately touch'd up and call'd an Address; which was lately sent from
this Side the Water, to please the Taste of the Tools of Corruption
on the other—Pray Gentlemen, is it Treason for the Deputies of
the People to assert their Liberties, or to give them away? . . . We
have been told with an Insolence the more intolerable, because dis-
guis'd with a Veil of public Care, that it is not prudence for us to
assert our Rights in plain and manly Terms: Nay, we have been told
that the word RIGHTS must not be once named among us! Curs'd
Prudence of interested designing Politicians! [31]

Although Governor Bernard was a believer in this cursed prudence,
he was no more pleased with the Stamp Act than the Americans. He
had assured the members from Boston the previous summer that
the Ministry would much prefer to let the colonies tax themselves.
He had even recommended as much himself, and he was convinced
that his reorganization of the colonies was necessary before such
a measure as this could be successful. He himself had no doubts
about Parliament's authority, but he knew that the colonists did.
Until that authority was firmly established along the lines he had laid
down in his ninety-seven propositions, it was folly to pass an act
like the Stamp Act.

These were Bernard's private sentiments, which he uttered in
bitterness to his friends in England.[32] But since the Ministry chose
to ignore his warnings and gave him the Stamp Act to enforce, he
felt obliged to do his best by it. In point of fact he had not received
a copy of the Act or official notification of it and never did; but he
did not doubt the authenticity of the newspaper reports and though
the temptation must have been great, he did not attempt to shirk

30. John Adams, *Works,* C. F. Adams, ed. (Boston, 1850-1856), X, 287.
31. *Boston Gazette,* July 8, 1765.
32. To John Pownall, August 18, 1765, to Richard Jackson, August 24, 1765, to the
Earl of Shelburne, January 4, 1764, Bernard Papers, IV, 11-15, 18-20, 293-296.

his duty by taking refuge in the technicality of the Ministry's neglect. Trying to put the Act in what he thought the best possible light, he even explained it to the General Assembly as a step in his cherished scheme for reorganizing the colonies. Though the Act was far from fitting into his plans, he told the Assembly: "The general settlement of the American Provinces, which has been long ago proposed, and now probably will be prosecuted to its utmost completion, must necessarily produce some regulations, which, from their novelty only, will appear disagreeable. But I am convinced, and doubt not but experience will confirm it, that they will operate, as they are designed, for the benefit and advantage of the colonies. In the mean time a respectful submission to the decrees of the Parliament, is their interest, as well as their duty." [33]

During the summer of 1765 it became apparent that peaceful submission to the Act, when it should go into effect on November first, was dubious. To assist him in enforcing it, Bernard called together the Assembly on September 25, 1765, and told them frankly that it was not his business to consider the desirability or undesirability of the Stamp Act. "I have only to say," he explained, "that it is an act of the Parliament of Great Britain, and as such ought to be obeyed by the subjects of Great Britain. And I trust that the supremacy of that Parliament over all the members of their wide and diffused empire, never was and never will be denied within these walls. The right of the Parliament of Great Britain to make laws for the American colonies, however it has been controverted in America, remains indisputable at Westminster." [34]

The House of Representatives, in answering this exposition of the constitution, showed that they had thrown off the conciliatory mood in which they had been persuaded to appeal for privileges instead of declaring their rights the year before. In a message of considerable dignity they replied:

You are pleased to say, that the stamp act is an act of Parliament, and as such ought to be observed. This House, sir, has too great a reverence for the supreme legislature of the nation, to question its just authority: It by no means appertains to us to presume to adjust the boundaries of the power of Parliament; but boundaries there undoubtedly are. . . .Furthermore, your Excellency tells us that the right of the Parliament to make laws for the American colonies remains indisputable in Westminster. Without contending this point, we beg leave just to observe that the charter of the province invests

33. Bradford, *Speeches of the Governors,* 34.
34. *Ibid.,* 40.

the General Assembly with the power of making laws for its internal government and taxation; and that this charter has never yet been forfeited. The Parliament has a right to make all laws within the limits of their own constitution; they claim no more. Your Excellency will acknowledge that there are certain original inherent rights belonging to the people, which the Parliament itself cannot divest them of, consistent with their own constitution: among these is the right of representation in the same body which exercises the power of taxation. There is a necessity that the subjects of America should exercise this power within themselves, otherwise they can have no share in that most essential right, for they are not represented in Parliament, and indeed we think it impracticable.[35]

The Assembly did not proceed to "adjust the boundaries of the power of Parliament" by putting these views into the form of resolutions until a month later. By that time three of their members had attended a meeting in New York. That meeting, known ever since as the Stamp Act Congress, was suggested by the Massachusetts Assembly, and it established a more definitive statement of colonial rights than the Virginians had furnished in May.

The leading politicians of Massachusetts had long been aware of the advantages which the colonies might gain by collective action. For a single colony to deny the power of Parliament would be futile; for all to deny it together might not be. As early as May 24, 1764, the town of Boston had called for united efforts against the Sugar Act; the town meeting instructed its representatives in the Assembly: "As his Majesty's other Northern American Colonys are embark'd with us in this most important Bottom, we further desire you to use your Endeavors, that their weight may be added to that of this Province; that by the united Applications of all who are Aggrieved, All may happily obtain Redress." [36] Probably as a result of these instructions the House of Representatives had sent a circular letter to the other colonies, urging them to ask their agents in England "to unite in the most serious Remonstrance" against the Sugar Act and the proposed Stamp Act.[37]

This would appear to have been a perfectly unexceptionable proposal, but Governor Bernard sensed that it might have dangerous consequences. He knew that the representatives from Boston were behind it, and he had already come to believe that anything the

35. *Ibid.*, 45.
36. *A Report of the Record Commissioners of the City of Boston containing the Boston Town Records, 1758 to 1769* (Boston, 1886), 122.
37. Connecticut Historical Society, *Collections*, 18 (1920), 284-285.

Boston politicians proposed would end in trouble. "Altho' This may seem at first sight only an Occasional measure for a particular purpose," he wrote to the Lords of Trade, "yet I have reason to believe that the purposes it is to serve are deeper than they now appear. I apprehend that it is intended to take this opportunity . . . to lay a foundation for connecting the demagogues of the several Governments in America to join together in opposition to all orders from Great Britain which don't square with their notions of the rights of the people. Perhaps I may be too suspicious; a little time will show whether I am or not." [38]

Within a year Bernard saw his suspicions borne out. The proposal had indeed produced no immediate effect: though some colonies had urged their agents to cooperate with each other, neither the agents nor the assemblies had formed a union. But on June 8, 1765, having received news of the Stamp Act, the Massachusetts House of Representatives sent another circular letter to the assemblies of North America inviting them to meet in a congress at New York the following October, "to consider of a general and united, dutiful, loyal and humble Representation of their Condition to His Majesty and the Parliament; and to implore Relief." [39]

Of the thirteen colonies which later took part in the Revolution, nine responded to the invitation. New Hampshire declined but formally approved the proceedings after the congress was over.[40] Virginia, North Carolina, and Georgia were prevented from participating, because their governors refused to convene the assemblies to elect delegates.[41] Delaware and New Jersey met the same obstruction but sent representatives anyhow, chosen when some of the assemblymen defiantly held an informal election of their own. In New York the Assembly's Committee of Correspondence nominated themselves to attend. Twenty-seven delegates in all took part in the congress, and according to one of them they were "an Assembly of the greatest Ability I ever Yet saw." [42]

38. June 29, 1764, Bernard Papers, III, 157.
39. *Pennsylvania Archives*, 8th ser., 7 (1935), 5765.
40. Nathaniel Bouton, ed., *Provincial Papers: Documents and Records Relating to the Province of New Hampshire* (Nashua, 1873), VII, 92.
41. The North Carolina Assembly later rebuked the governor for preventing their sitting during the crisis. *Colonial Records of North Carolina*, VII, 347. The Georgia Assembly approved the proceedings of the congress and sent copies of the petitions to their agent in London. Allen D. Candler, ed., *The Colonial Records of the State of Georgia* (Atlanta, 1904-1915), XIV, 315-318.
42. George H. Ryden, ed., *Letters to and from Caesar Rodney, 1756-1784* (Philadelphia, 1933), 26. The delegates were James Otis, Oliver Partridge, and Timothy Ruggles from Massachusetts; Metcalf Bowler and Henry Ward from Rhode Island; Eliphalet Dyer,

Governor Bernard had watched with misgivings while the Massachusetts Assembly proposed this congress but felt himself helpless to prevent it. He had accordingly made the best of a bad business by taking the lead in it, so as to control the choice of the Massachusetts delegates. He was able to report to the Board of Trade on July 8, 1765, that the Massachusetts delegation, owing to his efforts behind the scenes, contained two "prudent and discreet men such as I am assured will never consent to any undutiful or improper application to the Government of Great Britain." [43] The men were Timothy Ruggles and Oliver Partridge, whom Bernard had gauged correctly. The other member of the delegation—there were three altogether—was James Otis. Otis appears to have been the first to suggest the congress, and may have been sent to it for that reason. His presence might normally have been expected to offset that of the other two members, for he had a great reputation as a rabble-rouser. Fortunately for Bernard, however, Otis had recently changed his tune. In May, even before Otis had proposed the congress, Bernard had been able to report to his friend John Pownall that "the author of the Rights of the Colonies now repents in Sackcloth and ashes for the hand he had in that book. . . . In a pamphlett lately published he has [begged pardon] in humblest Manner of the Ministry and of the Parliament for the liberties he took with them." [44] Bernard's report was correct. When news of the Virginia Resolves reached Boston, Otis is said to have called them treasonable; and though he apparently continued to speak fire in anonymous contributions to the *Boston Gazette*, his public statements extolled the power of Parliament, and before he left for the congress, he was heard to say that "If the government at home don't very soon send forces to keep the peace of this province they will be cutting one anothers throats from one End, to the other of it." [45]

Otis was always unpredictable, and the insanity that clouded his later years may already have been affecting him, but it would seem that his role at the congress was as subdued as Bernard could have

David Rowland, and William Samuel Johnson from Connecticut; Robert R. Livingston, John Cruger, Philip Livingston, William Bayard, and Leonard Lispenard from New York; Robert Ogden, Hendrick Fisher, and Joseph Borden from New Jersey; John Dickinson, John Morton, and George Bryan from Pennsylvania; Thomas McKean and Caesar Rodney from Delaware; William Murdock, Edward Tilghman, and Thomas Ringgold from Maryland; Thomas Lynch, Christopher Gadsden, and John Rutledge from South Carolina.

43. Sparks mss., 43, British mss., IV, Harvard College Library.

44. Bernard Papers, III, 289.

45. Bernard to John Pownall, October 19, 1765, Sparks Mss., 10, Chalmers, I, Harvard College Library.

wished. According to John Watts, a New York merchant, he endeavored to get himself elected chairman of the meetings, but failed because the other members thought that "as he had figured much in the popular way, it might give their meeting an ill grace." Watts noted, however, that "it is observed Otis is now a quite different man, and so he seems to be to me, not riotous at all." [46]

The man whom the congress finally chose as chairman instead of Otis was Timothy Ruggles, whose election to the Massachusetts delegation had been engineered by Governor Bernard. As chairman of the meeting Ruggles was in a good position to carry out the instructions Bernard had given him: to get the congress to recommend submission to the Stamp Act until Parliament could be persuaded to repeal it.[47] Had he been successful in dominating the men who made him their chairman, probably the congress would have confined itself to arguing for repeal of the Stamp Act and Sugar Act on the grounds that they would hurt Anglo-colonial trade and bankrupt the colonies. As it turned out, the men who took the lead after the meetings were organized showed a different temper. General Gage exaggerated only a little when he wrote to Secretary of State Conway, "They are of various Characters and opinions, but it's to be feared in general, that the Spirit of Democracy, is strong amongst them." By "Democracy" Gage did not mean a belief in rule by the people so much as a belief that the colonists were beyond the control of Parliament, for he went on to inform Conway that the question which the congress was debating was not one "of the inexpediency of the Stamp Act, but that it is unconstitutional, and contrary to their Rights, Supporting the Independency of the Provinces, and not subject to the Legislative Power of Great Britain." [48]

After the members had elected Ruggles as chairman and seated all the delegates, they began drawing up a statement of the "rights and privileges of the British American Colonists." For the next twelve days, excluding Sunday, they argued and scribbled and crossed out and filled in and finally produced the following declarations:

The Members of this Congress, sincerely devoted, with the warmest Sentiments of Affection and Duty to his Majesty's Person and Government, inviolably attached to the present happy Establishment of the Protestant Succession, and with Minds deeply impressed by

46. John Watts to Governor Monckton, October 12, 1765, Massachusetts Historical Society, *Collections*, 4th ser., 10 (1871), 579-580.

47. Bernard to Ruggles, September 28, 1765, Bernard Papers, IV, 72.

48. October 12, 1765, Clarence E. Carter, ed., *The Correspondence of General Thomas Gage with the Secretaries of State, 1765-1775* (New Haven, 1931), I, 69-70.

a Sense of the present and impending Misfortunes of the *British* Colonies on this Continent; having considered as maturely as Time will permit, the Circumstances of the said Colonies, esteem it our indispensable Duty, to make the following Declarations of our humble Opinion, respecting the most Essential Rights and Liberties of the Colonists, and of the Grievances under which they labour, by Reason of several late Acts of Parliament.

I. That his Majesty's Subjects in these Colonies, owe the same Allegiance to the Crown of *Great-Britain,* that is owing from his Subjects born within the Realm, and all due Subordination to that August Body the Parliament of *Great-Britain.*

II. That his Majesty's Liege Subjects in these Colonies, are entitled to all the inherent Rights and Liberties of his Natural born Subjects, within the Kingdom of *Great-Britain.*

III. That it is inseparably essential to the Freedom of a People, and the undoubted Right of *Englishmen,* that no Taxes be imposed on them, but with their own Consent, given personally, or by their Representatives.

IV. That the People of these Colonies are not, and from their local Circumstances cannot be, Represented in the House of Commons in *Great-Britain.*

V. That the only Representatives of the People of these Colonies, are Persons chosen therein by themselves, and that no Taxes ever have been, or can be Constitutionally imposed on them, but by their respective Legislature.

VI. That all Supplies to the Crown, being free Gifts of the People, it is unreasonable and inconsistent with the Principles and Spirit of the *British* Constitution, for the People of *Great-Britain,* to grant to his Majesty the Property of the Colonists.

VII. That Trial by Jury, is the inherent and invaluable Right of every *British* Subject in these Colonies.

VIII. That the late Act of Parliament, entitled, *An Act for granting and applying certain Stamp Duties, and other Duties, in the British Colonies and Plantations in America, &c.* by imposing Taxes on the Inhabitants of these Colonies, and the said Act, and several other Acts, by extending the Jurisdiction of the Courts of Admiralty beyond its ancient Limits, have a manifest Tendency to subvert the Rights and Liberties of the Colonists.

IX. That the Duties imposed by several late Acts of Parliament, from the peculiar Circumstances of these Colonies, will be extremely Burthensome and Grievous; and from the scarcity of Specie, the Payment of them absolutely impracticable.

X. That as the Profits of the Trade of these Colonies ultimately center in *Great-Britain,* to pay for the Manufactures which they are obliged to take from thence, they eventually contribute very largely to all Supplies granted there to the Crown.

XI. That the Restrictions imposed by several late Acts of Parliament, on the Trade of these Colonies, will render them unable to purchase the Manufactures of *Great-Britain*.

XII. That the Increase, Prosperity, and Happiness of these Colonies, depend on the full and free Enjoyment of their Rights and Liberties, and an Intercourse with *Great-Britain* mutually Affectionate and Advantageous.

XIII. That it is the Right of the *British* Subjects in these Colonies, to Petition the King, or either House of Parliament.

Lastly, That it is the indispensable Duty of these Colonies, to the best of Sovereigns, to the Mother Country, and to themselves, to endeavour by a loyal and dutiful Address to his Majesty, and humble Applications to both Houses of Parliament, to procure the Repeal of the Act for granting and applying certain Stamp Duties, of all Clauses of any other Acts of Parliament, whereby the Jurisdiction of the Admiralty is extended as aforesaid, and of the other late Acts for the Restriction of *American* Commerce.[49]

To define these fundamentals was evidently no great problem for the twenty-seven delegates. For that matter it would have been difficult to find an American anywhere who did not believe in them—as far as they went. The principal disagreement which kept the congress arguing for nearly two weeks was whether to balance the denial of Parliament's authority to tax the colonies with an acknowledgment of what authority it did have. But to formulate an acknowledgment which could not be misconstrued to the prejudice of colonial rights proved impossible. According to Robert R. Livingston, one of the New York delegation,

What gave us most trouble was whether we should insist on a Repeal of all acts laying Duties on Trade as well as the Stamp Act all agreed that we ought to obey all acts of trade and that they should regulate our Trade but many were not for making an explicit declaration of and an acknowledgment of such a Power. I thought and many with me that if we did not do it there was not the least hopes of success, for except Britain could regulate our Trade her colonies would be of no more use to her than to France or any other power, and that it is impossible to suppose that she would ever give up the point of internal taxes except the other were fully secured and acknowledged. I find all sensible people in town to agree with me in this but we had some who were much too warm to do any good.[50]

49. *Proceedings of the Congress at New York* (Annapolis, 1766). This was the first printing of the Journals. They are reprinted in Hezekiah Niles, *Principles and Acts of the Revolution* (Baltimore, 1822), 451-461.

50. To ——, November 2, 1765, Bancroft Transcripts, New York Public Library.

From this statement one may gather that all members of the congress accepted the authority of Parliament to regulate the trade of the empire, but that the majority thought it unwise to make any express acknowledgment of such an authority. Undoubtedly what made them unwilling was the double purpose of the Sugar Act. Here was an act which served both to raise revenue and to regulate trade. An admission of Parliament's authority in the regulation of trade might be construed as an admission that the taxes levied under the Sugar Act were constitutional.

It is possible to follow the course of debate in two early drafts of the declarations. Both are in the hand of John Dickinson of Pennsylvania, and it may be that he was the first to formulate a statement for the other members to consider. The first draft is not radically different from the final version except in containing specific acknowledgment of Parliamentary authority in the words: "all Acts of Parliament not inconsistent with the Rights and Liberties of the Colonists are obligatory upon them." In the second draft this was changed to "all Acts of Parliament not inconsistent with the Principles of Freedom are obligatory upon the Colonists." Finally these statements were replaced by the acknowledgment in the first resolution that the colonists owed "all due Subordination to that August Body the Parliament of *Great-Britain*." [51]

The first change probably represents an unsuccessful attempt of the conservative members to satisfy the radicals by a more general statement: some colonies could count on "privileges" derived from their charters; others had no charters and wished to base the declaration on a broader principle. Christopher Gadsden of South Carolina seems to have been the leading opponent of any explicit statement. After the congress he wrote, "I have ever been of opinion, that we should all endeavor to stand upon the broad and common ground of those natural and inherent rights that we all feel and know, as men and as descendants of Englishmen, we have a right to, and have always thought this bottom amply sufficient for our future importance. . . . There ought to be no New England men, no New Yorker, &c., known on the Continent, but all of us Americans; a *confirmation* of our essential and common rights as Englishmen may be pleaded from the Charters safely enough, but any further dependence on them may be fatal." [52] Gadsden thought that the desire of the "eastern gentle-

51. Both drafts are in the Dickinson Papers, Free Library Company of Philadelphia. A third draft, printed in Historical Society of Pennsylvania, *Memoirs*, 14 (1895), 183-187, is in the Library of the Historical Society of Pennsylvania.

52. Gadsden to Charles Garth, December 2, 1765, R. W. Gibbes, *Documentary History of the American Revolution* (New York, 1855), I, 8.

men" for the explicit statement of subordination was the result of their placing too much dependence on their charters, and a letter from William Samuel Johnson confirmed this view.[53]

In all probability, then, the second of Dickinson's drafts, with the substitution of "Principles of Freedom" for "Rights and Liberties of the Colonists," was an attempt to meet demands by Gadsden and others that the rights of the colonies be rested on a broader footing than the "privileges" granted in colonial charters. The modification, however, was still unsatisfactory, for it committed the colonists to obedience so long as Parliamentary legislation did not violate the principles of freedom. Since these principles were not clearly defined and were in fact the subject of the dispute between England and America, it would be unwise to make so positive a commitment. The final solution, of course, was to make no mention of Acts of Parliament and to leave colonial subordination undefined except by the weasel-word, "due."

This solution was evidently resisted by Robert R. Livingston, as we can tell from his letter. It was also resisted by Timothy Ruggles and by Robert Ogden of New Jersey, for both Ruggles and Ogden refused to sign the proceedings of the congress because of the omission of any precise acknowledgment of Parliament's authority.[54] Ruggles and Ogden were probably the strongest supporters of Parliament present. The other members, even those who opposed Gadsden, were so anxious to see a unanimous assertion of colonial rights that they accepted the majority view. William Samuel Johnson, writing to Ogden ten days after the congress broke up, wished that they "had adopted the other Plan of admitting the general superintendance of Parliament and limiting their Power by the Principles and Spirit of the Constitution which sufficiently excludes all Constitutional Right to Tax us, and effectually secures the fundamental Priviledge of Trial by Jury as well as every other Right Essential to British Liberty." But in the interests of unity Johnson had acquiesced in the Declarations.[55]

53. Johnson to Gadsden, January 10, 1766, William Samuel Johnson Papers, Connecticut Historical Society.

54. Ruggles and Ogden were both rebuked for their stand by their respective assemblies. See Bernard to Board of Trade, March 10, 1766, Chalmers Papers, II, Harvard College Library; *Boston Gazette*, February 17, 1766; Governor Franklin to Board of Trade, December 18, 1765, *Archives of the State of New Jersey*, 1st ser., 9 (1885), 525; Donald L. Kemmerer, *Path to Freedom* (Princeton, 1940), 287-288. The delegates from New York, Connecticut, and South Carolina were not authorized by their assemblies to sign, so that their names also are missing from the documents.

55. Johnson to Robert Ogden, November 4, 1765, to Eliphalet Dyer, December 31, 1765, William Samuel Johnson Papers, Connecticut Historical Society.

After the congress had agreed on what their official position should be, they appointed three committees to draw up a petition to the King, a memorial to the House of Lords, and a petition to the House of Commons.[56] At this point Christopher Gadsden objected to the admission of Parliamentary authority that would be implied in petitioning that body. The rights of the colonies, he said, were not derived from Parliament; besides, the House of Commons had shown how little it cared about petitions from America when it refused even to consider the colonial petitions of the preceding year. The other members of the congress were not ready to join in such a wholesale snub to the supreme legislature of Great Britain. Gadsden could afford to be generous in this question, for he had already won the major battle of the congress in the debate over the Declarations. For the sake of unity he now gave way, and in the short space of four days the two petitions and the memorial were drafted and accepted.[57] The delegates from Connecticut, New York, and South Carolina were not authorized to sign the documents, and official approval by those colonies had to await action by their assemblies, but the other members, with the exception of Ruggles and Ogden, put their signatures to the proceedings, and returned home with copies for transmittal to England.

Although the congress had refused in their official statements to make any specific acknowledgment of Parliament's authority, they left behind, among the waste paper that such a conference begets, one document which suggests what some of them thought about the subject. William Samuel Johnson, having labored over the "Report of the Committee to whom was refer'd the Consideration of the Rights of the British Colonies," [58] carried it away with him and preserved it among his papers. Its eleven pages had evidently been too wordy to satisfy the congress, but they quarried it for phrases and sentences to incorporate in the Declarations and petitions, and one phrase they took was the crucial "due subordination." Seen in their original context these nebulous words take on greater precision.

Altho the due subordination of the Colonies to the Crown and Parliament and the dependancy of the Colonies on Great Britain are

56. Niles, *Principles and Acts*, 457-460.
57. Gibbes, *Documentary History*, I, 7-9.
58. There is no record of the appointment of this committee in the journals of the congress. After the adoption of the Declarations, Johnson was appointed to the committee to draw up the petition to the King, but the report referred to here is clearly not the report of that committee. It appears, rather, to be an attempt, probably earlier than any of those in Dickinson's hand, to formulate a declaration of rights. It is now in the William Samuel Johnson Papers, Library of Congress.

what every Intelligent American [wishes] . . . Yet it is most humbly
conceived that this subordination and dependency is sufficiently secured by the Common Law, by our Allegiance, by the Negative of
the Crown on the Laws of most of the Provinces, but above all by
the general superintending power and authority of the whole Empire indisputably lodged in that August Body the Parliament of
Great Britain which Authority is clearly admitted here so far as in
our Circumstances is Consistent with the Enjoyment of our Essential Rights as Freemen and British Subjects, and we farther humbly
Conceive that by the Constitution it is no further admissible in
Great Britain itself. It is also submitted whether there is not a vast
difference between the Exercise of Parliamentary Jurisdiction in general Acts for the Amendment of the Common Law, or even in general Regulations of Trade and Commerce for the Empire and the
Actual Exercise of that Jurisdiction in levying External and Internal
Duties and Taxes on the Colonists while they neither are nor can be
represented in Parliament. The former may very well consist with a
reasonable Measure of Civil Liberty in the Colonies but we must beg
leave to say that how the latter is consistent with any degree of Freedom we are wholly at a loss how to Comprehend.

Here the due subordination of the colonies is expressed in terms of
Parliament's superintending authority over the whole empire, and it
is specified that such authority includes the right to pass legislation
regulating trade but does not include the right to tax. This distinction between taxation and legislation was implicit in the abbreviated
assertions of the Declarations, particularly in the sixth resolution,
"that all Supplies to the Crown, being free Gifts of the People, it is
unreasonable and inconsistent with the Principles and Spirit of the
British Constitution, for the People of *Great-Britain* to grant to his
Majesty the Property of the Colonists." The delegates were saying
here that acts of taxation, unlike other acts of a legislature, are gifts
and that they can be granted only by the representatives of the people
who make the gift. The distinction was made explicit in the petition
to the House of Commons, where a more extensive borrowing from
the Report produced the query, "Whether there be not a material
Distinction in Reason and sound Policy, at least, between the necessary Exercise of Parliamentary Jurisdiction in general Acts, for the
Amendment of the Common Law, and the Regulation of Trade and
Commerce through the whole Empire, and the Exercise of that Jurisdiction by imposing Taxes on the Colonies." [59]
Due subordination, then, meant submission to Parliamentary leg-

59. *Proceedings of the Congress at New York*, 23. Niles, *Principles and Acts*, 460, has
garbled this passage.

islation but not to Parliamentary taxation. The line between the two might be difficult to perceive in Westminster, but it was plain in America. The congress could see it; Daniel Dulany could see it; and the several colonial assemblies could see it, as they showed by endorsing the proceedings of the congress or by resolutions and petitions of their own or by both.[60]

The Americans did not mean that any kind of legislation was allowable. Legislation, for example, which took away the right of trial by jury or any other acknowledged constitutional right went beyond the limits of Parliament's authority anywhere, whether in England or in the colonies. There was also the contention made in the Virginia Resolves, and copied from them into the resolves of several other colonies, that Parliament could not interfere with the "internal polity" of the colonies. The meaning of this phrase was not entirely clear in 1765, and because Parliament did not happen at the time to be interfering with whatever was meant by internal polity, it was not clarified. Apparently, however, none of the Parliamentary legislation which was on the books in 1765 came within the scope of this phrase, unless the Stamp Act itself was regarded as doing so, for the constitutional objections raised by the colonists both in the colonial assemblies and in the congress were aimed at the Stamp Act and the Sugar Act. The great distinction, then, which marked off the authority of Parliament in Great Britain from its authority in the colonies was the distinction between legislation and taxation: for Great Britain Parliament might levy taxes as well as make laws; for the colonies it could only make laws.

For the most part the colonial protests argued for the rights of Englishmen on a constitutional basis, but they did mention another kind of rights which Parliament was violating—the rights of man. Although the Americans were confident that the British constitution guaranteed the right to be taxed only by consent, they regarded this

60. The petition from New York to the House of Commons, adopted by the assembly on December 11, 1765, made the point most sharply by declaring "That all parliamentary Aids in Great-Britain, are the free Gifts of the People by their Representatives, consented to by the Lords and accepted by the Crown, and therefore every Act imposing them, essentially differs from every other Statute, having the Force of a Law in no other respect than the Manner thereby prescribed for levying the gift.

"That agreeable to this Distinction, the House of Commons has always contended for and enjoyed the constitutional Right of originating all Money Bills, as well in aid of the Crown, as for other Purposes.

"That all Supplies to the Crown, being in their Nature free Gifts, it would, as we humbly conceive, be unconstitutional for the People of *Great-Britain*, by their Representatives in Parliament, to dispose of the Property of Millions of his Majesty's Subjects, who are not, and cannot be there represented." *Journal of the Votes and Proceedings of the General Assembly* (New York, 1766), II, 800.

right as a product of natural as well as of British law. In the third resolution the congress stated that "it is inseparably essential to the Freedom of a People" as well as "the undoubted Right of *English-men*," that they should be taxed only by consent. This appeal to a wider basis for their rights is notably absent in the petitions to King and Parliament, where the congress, like Dulany, asked only for their rights as Englishmen. In two other sets of resolutions, however, those of Massachusetts and Pennsylvania, the colonists grounded their statements on the natural rights of man. Pennsylvania, on September 21, 1765, declared "That the Inhabitants of this Province are entitled to all the Liberties, Rights and Privileges of his Majesty's Subjects in *Great-Britain,* or elsewhere, and that the Constitution of Government in this Province is founded on the natural Rights of Mankind, and the noble Principles of *English* Liberty, and therefore is, or ought to be, perfectly free." [61]

Massachusetts likewise, on October 25, the day that the Stamp Act Congress adjourned, resolved, "That there are certain essential rights of the British constitution of government, which are founded in the law of God and nature, and are the common rights of mankind," and "That the inhabitants of this province are unalienably entitled to those essential rights, in common with all men; and that no law of society can, consistent with the law of God and nature, divest them of those rights." [62] Though their representatives at New York might side with the conservatives, the Massachusetts Assembly was siding with Gadsden.

Thus by the fall of 1765 the colonists had clearly laid down the line where they believed that Parliament should stop, and they had drawn that line not merely as Englishmen but as men. The line was far short of independence, and there was no suggestion in any of the resolutions of the congress or of the assemblies that the colonists wished to cease being Englishmen. Nevertheless, if England chose to force the issue, the colonists would have to decide—and in that winter many were trying to make up their minds—whether they would be men and not English or whether they would be English and not men.

61. *Pennsylvania Archives,* 8th ser., 7 (1935), 5779.
62. Bradford, *Speeches of the Governors,* 50.

A NOTE ON INTERNAL AND EXTERNAL TAXES

It has been argued by Carl Becker in *The Declaration of Independence* that the Stamp Act Congress confined its objections against Parliamentary taxation to internal taxes only. This argument presupposes that the first eight resolutions are based on constitutional principles and apply only to the Stamp Act and that resolutions 9-12 are based on economic considerations and apply only to the Sugar Act. By this reasoning there appears to be no constitutional objection in the resolutions to the "external" taxes levied by the Sugar Act. In all probability this interpretation was influenced by the supposition which was already current in England by 1766 and which was nurtured and perpetuated, that the colonists in 1765 differentiated between internal and external taxes and had no objections to the latter. I have examined this supposition elsewhere and shown it, I think, to be unfounded.[1] As far as the resolves of the Stamp Act Congress are concerned, it appears to me unlikely for several reasons that the first eight resolutions were intended to apply only to internal taxes and resolutions 9-12 to external. It seems more probable that in the first eight resolutions or at least in the first seven, the congress was stating unqualified constitutional objections to all taxes and that in resolutions 9-12 it merely added the economic objections. This contention is borne out by the petition to the House of Commons and the memorial to the House of Lords. In the petition to the Commons the congress begins by reciting constitutional objections and then proceeds to economic objections with this paragraph:

But were it ever so clear, that the colonies might in Law, be reasonably deem'd to be Represented in the Honourable House of Commons, yet we conceive, that very good Reasons, from Inconvenience, from the Principles of true Policy, and from the Spirit of the British Constitution, may be adduced to shew, that it would be for the real interest of *Great-Britain,* as well as her Colonies, that the late Regulations should be rescinded, and the several Acts of Parliament imposing Duties and Taxes on the Colonies, and extending the Jurisdiction of the Courts of Admiralty here, beyond their ancient Limits, should be Repeal'd.[2]

Similarly in the memorial to the Lords the economic objections are introduced in this way: "But your Memorialists (not waving their

---

1. "Colonial Ideas of Parliamentary Power 1764-1766," *William and Mary Quarterly,* 3d ser., 5 (1948), 311-341; "The Postponement of the Stamp Act," *ibid.,* 7 (1950), 353-392. See the letter by Curtis P. Nettels and my reply, *ibid.,* 6 (1949), 162-170.
2. *Proceedings of the Congress at New York,* 22.

Claim to these Rights, of which with the most becoming Veneration and Deference to the Wisdom and Justice of your Lordships, they apprehend they cannot Reasonably be deprived)." [3]

Another indication that the congress was not confining its constitutional objections to internal taxes lies in the fact that William Samuel Johnson's lengthy statement of principles repeatedly objects to "external and internal duties and taxes." The resolutions themselves make no use of the words "external" or "internal," but shorten Johnson's phrase to the one word "taxes." [4] If there had been an intention to distinguish between internal and external taxes, it is reasonable to suppose that these words would have been used. Since Johnson thought that the resolutions in their final form went too far,[5] it is unlikely that he construed their objections to Parliamentary taxation as more limited than those which he himself had penned. Certainly when the resolutions and petitions reached England, Parliament thought that they made no distinction and refused to consider them partly for that reason. It is perhaps worth noting also that John Dickinson, who drafted the resolutions, did not believe that the constitutional objections were confined to internal taxes. By 1767 the English were already condemning the colonies for inconsistency in abandoning this distinction which in reality they had never held. Dickinson replied in his Farmer's Letters by quoting the resolves of the Stamp Act Congress and then pointing out that there was "no distinction made between *internal* and *external* taxes" in them.[6]

It is difficult, in the face of this evidence, to believe that Carl Becker would have found a distinction between internal and external taxes in the resolves of the Stamp Act Congress if it had not been for the traditional belief that the colonists were making such a distinction at this time.[7]

3. *Ibid.*, 20.
4. William Samuel Johnson Papers, Library of Congress.
5. See letter to Robert Ogden, November 4, 1765, William Samuel Johnson Papers, Connecticut Historical Society.
6. Historical Society of Pennsylvania, *Memoirs*, 14 (1895), 331-332.
7. For Carl Becker's argument see *The Declaration of Independence* (New York, 1922), 90.

PART II

Road to Revolution

⇾ EIGHT ⇽

ACTION

Boston Sets the Pace

THE resolutions which the clerks of colonial and intercolonial
assemblies were recording in the summer and fall of 1765 were
outspoken denials of Parliament's right to tax the colonies. But
only in Rhode Island did the Assembly approve outright resistance.
It was one thing to define a right and another to fight for it, particularly if you must fight against a body which you had hitherto accepted as supreme and to which you still acknowledged "all due subordination." Nevertheless, while men like James Otis blew hot and
cold, now for colonial rights and now for Parliamentary supremacy,
and while others followed Daniel Dulany in affirming colonial rights
but wishing only passive resistance, a substantial number of men in
every colony recognized that the time had come when more than talk
was needed. They had been convinced by Dulany and Otis and by the
Virginia Resolves and the declarations of the Stamp Act Congress that
Parliament had no right to tax them. They also knew that there was
no branch of government higher than Parliament to prevent Parliament's doing what it had no right to do. The burden therefore was
left to those whose rights were endangered: they must resist Parliament to preserve their rights, and if that meant an end to Parliamentary supremacy, then that was what it meant.

It would be too much to say that these men wished to throw off
the authority of Parliament altogether. Perhaps some of them did,
but there is no reason to suppose that they were not content with the
constitutional position which their representatives had defined, denying Parliament's right to tax but allowing its right to regulate trade
and to pass other general legislation affecting the empire at large.
The only point at which they went a step further than the resolutions

was in their determination to prevent the supreme legislature from doing what it had no right to do. In this determination they ignored the distinction which Dulany had drawn between propriety and power. But if anyone had told them that in spite of the impropriety of its action, Parliament's power was supreme, they might have answered that supremacy in power cannot be determined by argumentation or declaration. If Parliament lacked the authority to tax America, then its power to do so would have to be tested in American fields and streets. And this was precisely where they proposed to test it.

Although the Virginians had been first to suggest resistance, it was not in Williamsburg but in Boston that argument first gave way to action. The Massachusetts radicals saw that if the colonists were to defeat Parliament's attempt to tax them, they could not rely on their representative assemblies to do the job. The assemblies might resolve, as that of Rhode Island did, that officers of government should carry on business as usual, as though the Act had never been passed. But what if the officers of government who had to use the stamps lay beyond the immediate control of the assemblies? Most of the documents which would require stamps after November first were papers used in legal proceedings. In some colonies the assemblies might withhold the salaries of the judges as a means of bringing them into line, but in others the judges of the superior courts were not appointed by the assemblies, and in all the colonies the independence of the judiciary was regarded as a principle of the British constitution which could be tampered with only at the peril of civil liberty. The assemblies were also powerless to control the royally appointed customs officers who must issue clearances for all ships leaving American harbors. According to the Stamp Act, clearance papers issued after November 1 would have to bear a stamp. If the customs officers chose to comply with the law, and as royal officials they doubtless would comply, what could the assemblies do about it? The duties of customs officers did not fall within their jurisdiction, and royal governors would certainly have vetoed any orders from the assemblies which attempted to regulate matters beyond their authority.

Clearly the radicals who had determined to turn from words to deeds could expect little more than words from their assemblies. For action they must look elsewhere, and where was not hard to guess. In Boston particularly the answer was clear, for in the past the good people of that city had frequently turned from the niceties of theological controversy to achieve some necessary social reform in their own way. Perhaps a few inhabitants could recollect with some amusement how they had laid out a street through Jonathan Loring's barn

near Love Street some thirty years before. The selectmen had surveyed the proposed street and found Loring's barn square in the way.
There was some doubt whether they had a right to seize the barn, but
a gathering of the townspeople resolved the question without argument. Under cover of night and with blackened faces, a technique
they had already learned and would employ again in 1773, they
levelled the building, and the road went through.[1] In 1747 Boston
had demonstrated that even the British Navy must watch its step in
Massachusetts. Commodore Knowles in that year anchored his fleet off
Nantasket and sent press gangs ashore to fill gaps in his crews. When
the Governor and Council would not, as they could not, prevent
him, a mob arose in Boston which ruled the city until Commodore
Knowles released the men he had seized.[2]

Bostonians sometimes seemed to love violence for its own sake.
Over the years there had developed a rivalry between the South End
and the North End of the city. On Pope's Day, November 5, when
parades were held to celebrate the defeat of Guy Fawkes' famous gun-
powder plot, the rivalry between the two sections generally broke
out into a free-for-all with stones and barrel staves the principal
weapons. The two sides even developed a semi-military organization
with recognized leaders, and of late the fighting had become increasingly bloody. In 1764 a child was run over and killed by a wagon
bearing an effigy of the pope, but even this had not stopped the
battle. Despite the efforts of the militia, the two sides had battered
and bruised each other until the South End finally carried the day.[3]

When Boston had to face the problem of nullifying the Stamp Act,
it was obvious that men who fought so energetically over the effigy
of a pope might be employed in a more worthy cause. The problem
was to make them see the threat to their liberties that the Stamp Act
presented and to direct their energies accordingly. Sometime in the
early summer of 1765 a group of men got together in Boston to prepare for the day when the Stamp Act was supposed to go into effect,
November 1. An organization was formed which first called itself
The Loyal Nine and later, when its ranks had expanded, the Sons of
Liberty. The Nine were John Avery, Jr., Thomas Crafts, John Smith,
Henry Welles, Thomas Chase, Stephen Cleverly, Henry Bass, Ben-

1. Petition of Jonathan Loring and Jonathan Jackson to Governor Belcher and Council, September, 1732, Curwin Papers, III, 97, American Antiquarian Society.
2. Thomas Hutchinson, *History of the Colony and Province of Massachusetts Bay*,
L. S. Mayo, ed. (Cambridge, 1936), II, 330-333.
3. *Massachusetts Gazette and Boston News-Letter*, November 8, 1764; Governor Bernard to John Pownall, November 26, 1765, Bernard Papers, V, 43-46, Harvard College
Library.

jamin Edes, and George Trott.[4] They were not the most prominent
citizens of Boston, nor were they the men who did most of the talking
against the Stamp Act. In general they were artisans and shopkeepers,
and they shunned publicity. The names of James Otis and Samuel
Adams were conspicuously missing from the list. So was that of John
Adams. Perhaps this division of labor was deliberate, in order to
keep the radical leaders of the Assembly, who were always conspicuously in the public eye, from bringing too much attention to the
group. Or perhaps the effectiveness of the radical leaders in the Assembly might have been impaired if they were openly associated with
an organization engaged in the treasonable activities which the Loyal
Nine envisaged. Whatever the reason, no conclusive alliance can be
proved between the leaders of the Assembly and the organizers of the
popular demonstrations, but it is probable that the Nine maintained
close communications with both Otis and Sam Adams, and on one
occasion at least, John Adams spent an evening with them at their
headquarters in Chase and Speakman's distillery on Hanover Square.

Only two members of the Loyal Nine enjoyed any local distinction: John Avery, Jr., was a Harvard graduate, class of 1759, and both
his father and grandfather were also Harvard men—a sufficient pedi-
gree in Boston; Benjamin Edes was the printer, along with John Gill,
of the *Gazette,* Boston's most enterprising newspaper. Avery's membership lent respectability to the group; Edes's gave it a mouthpiece.
Of the two, Edes's contribution was doubtless the more valuable, for
his paper published a continuous stream of articles to stir up feeling
against the Stamp Act.

By August 14 the Nine felt that Boston was ready for action. They
were confident that the well-to-do stood behind the moves which they
were contemplating, and that the propaganda published in the *Gazette* had aroused the mass of the people. More important, they had enlisted the services of the man who had led the South End mob to
victory over the North-Enders the preceding November. Ebenezer
McIntosh, a South-End shoemaker, was soon to become notorious as
a man who could control his two thousand followers with the precision of a general.[5] The Nine had persuaded him that he might do his

4. On the Loyal Nine see John Adams, *Works,* C. F. Adams, ed. (Boston, 1850-1856),
II, 178-179; William Gordon, *The History of the Rise, Progress, and Establishment of
the Independence of the United States of America* (London, 1788), I, 175; and George
P. Anderson, "A Note on Ebenezer Mackintosh," Colonial Society of Massachusetts,
Publications, 26 (1927), 348-361.

5. See George P. Anderson, "Ebenezer Mackintosh: Stamp Act Rioter and Patriot"
and "A Note on Ebenezer Mackintosh," Colonial Society of Massachusetts, *Publications,*
26 (1927), 15-64, 348-361.

country a real service by forgetting local quarrels and directing his strength against that hated Act which was designed to rob Americans of their constitutional rights.

On the morning of August 14 the signal for impending action was given by the hanging of an effigy on a tree near Deacon Elliot's house on Newbury Street. It represented Andrew Oliver, the man who, according to reports from England, had been appointed Distributor of Stamps for Massachusetts; alongside hung a piece of symbolism designed to connect Oliver and the Stamp Act with the most hated man in England. It was a large boot (a pun on the Earl of Bute), with the devil crawling out of it.[6] When Governor Bernard heard of the event he took it seriously. Some members of his council assured him that it was only a boyish prank, not worthy the notice of the government, but in view of the incendiary pieces appearing in the newspapers Bernard thought otherwise. So did Lieutenant-Governor Hutchinson. Hutchinson, as Chief Justice of the Colony, ordered the Sheriff to cut the image down; Bernard took an easier way out: he summoned the Council and turned the problem over to them. Before the Council could gather together in the afternoon, the Sheriff returned with the breathless news that his men could not take down the image without endangering their lives.[7]

Governor Bernard urged upon the Council the seriousness of the situation, but for various reasons they preferred to do nothing about it. Some thought it a trifling matter which would subside by itself if no notice were taken of it. Others admitted its seriousness, but felt that the government was not strong enough to force the issue and had better not risk the attempt. Unwilling, however, to have it go on record that they had done nothing, they passed the problem on to the Sheriff, advising that he be instructed to summon the peace officers. They could scarcely have expected the peace officers to have any effect on the crowd that was gathering about the tree where the

6. "Diary of John Rowe," August 14, 1765, Massachusetts Historical Society, *Proceedings*, 2d ser., 10 (1895), 61; Benjamin Hallowell to the Commissioners of the Customs, September 7, 1765, Treasury Papers, Class I, Bundle 442, Library of Congress transcripts.

7. Governor Bernard to Halifax, August 15, 16, 1765, Bernard Papers, IV, 137-144, and similar letters to the Lords of Trade, same dates, House of Lords Manuscripts, January 14, 1766, Library of Congress transcripts. For the events of August 14 and 15, described in the ensuing five paragraphs see these letters and also *Connecticut Courant*, August 26, 1765; *Boston Gazette*, August 19, 1765, supplement; Hutchinson to _____, August 16, 1765, Massachusetts Archives, XXVI, 145; Cyrus Baldwin to his brother, August 15, 1765, Miscellaneous Manuscripts, XIII, Massachusetts Historical Society. On the location of buildings and streets in Boston see Justin Winsor, ed., *The Memorial History of Boston* (Boston, 1881), II, i-lv.

image hung, but some gesture must be made in order to save face. Even as they sat in the Council Chamber the gentlemen could hear the rising voices outside, for the effigy had been cut down from the tree, and taking it with them the mob marched ominously to the Town House, gave three huzzas to let the Council know who was running the town of Boston, and then passed on.

Andrew Oliver had recently constructed a building at his dock on Kilby Street, intending to divide it into shops and rent them. Under the circumstances it was plausible enough to suggest that this was the office where he intended to distribute the stamps. From the Town House then, with McIntosh in the lead, the mob moved on to Kilby Street, and in five minutes Oliver's venture in real estate had gone the way of Jonathan Loring's barn. The next stop was Oliver's house, in the nearby street which bore the family name. Standing in the street the leaders presented those inside with a bit of pantomime, in which Oliver's effigy was beheaded, while the rest of the crowd showered stones through the windows. From here Fort Hill was only a step, and taking what was left of the effigy the mob moved on to the summit where they ceremoniously "stamped" on the figure and burned it in a bonfire, made appropriately of wood which they had carried from the building on Kilby Street.

For the more genteel members of the mob, disguised in the trousers and jackets which marked a working man, this seems to have been the last stop on the evening's excursion. But McIntosh had not yet completed his work. With his followers he now returned to Oliver's house. Both Oliver and his family had meanwhile retired to a friendly neighbor's, leaving the house in charge of a few trusted friends, who barricaded the doors. Finding the entrance blocked, the mob proceeded to demolish the garden fence and then systematically beat in the doors and windows and entered the house, swearing loudly that they would catch Oliver and kill him. The trusted friends quickly departed, and the mob were preparing to search the neighboring houses when a gentleman informed them that Oliver had gone to Castle William and thus saved his life.

It was possible to take revenge on his house, and this they did, destroying the furniture, including "a looking glass said to be the largest in North-America," and a large part of the wainscoting. Governor Bernard meanwhile had sent a message to the Colonel of the Militia ordering him to beat an alarm. The Colonel, a realistic man, replied that any drummer sent out would be knocked down and his drum broken before he could strike it—and besides the drummers were probably all up at Oliver's house engaged in what they would consider more worthwhile activities. With this, having made his gesture, Governor Bernard retired to Castle William, safely isolated from mobs by the waters of Boston harbor.

Lieutenant-Governor Hutchinson was more foolhardy. About eleven o'clock, when the tumult seemed to be subsiding, he took the Sheriff with him and went to Oliver's house to persuade the mob to disperse. He had no sooner opened his mouth than one of the ringleaders, perhaps McIntosh, recognized him. "The Governor and the Sheriff!" went the cry, "to your Arms my boys," and a rain of stones descended on the two men as they hurried off into the darkness. The mob was thus left to have its way and continued to make sport of the Stamp Distributor's house until about midnight, when McIntosh evidently decided to call it an evening.

Thus ended the opening move in the program to defeat the Stamp Act. Everyone agreed that it was the most violent riot the town had ever seen. The next day a number of gentlemen called on Andrew Oliver and persuaded him that what had occurred was only the beginning and suggested that he immediately resign his office. Oliver, like other stamp distributors who later followed his example, must have been somewhat confused by the fact that he had not received his commission and thus really had nothing to resign. He promised, however, to write home for leave to resign and in the meantime to do nothing toward executing the Act. This satisfied the Loyal Nine, but their followers could not understand this devious language. In the evening they built another fire on Fort Hill—Governor Bernard, watching from Castle William, knew that the mob was out again—but the leaders who had produced the previous evening's entertainment were able to dissuade their followers from turning the site of Oliver's house into a vacant lot. Instead the mob diverted themselves by surrounding the house of the Lieutenant-Governor. Hutchinson listened to them beating on the doors and shouting for him to come out, until finally a neighbor convinced them that he had fled, and they gradually drifted away.

During the next ten days McIntosh proved his worth by keeping his followers quiet, and the Loyal Nine could rejoice in a job well done. They had obtained the resignation of the Stamp Distributor a good two and a half months before the Act was scheduled to take effect. Moreover they had made plain what would happen to anyone who dared take Oliver's place. When one gentleman let it be known that he would not have been intimidated had he been the stamp master, they gave him a chance to see how Oliver had felt by fixing the date when his house should be pulled down. The gentleman

quickly recovered from his courage and retracted his statement.[8] Few
people could be found in Boston who would condemn the proceedings of the fourteenth. Even some of the ministers gave their bless-
ing,[9] and the Loyal Nine, feeling their oats, began to think of other
grievances that needed redressing. The officers of the customs and of
the admiralty court were obvious targets, and during these days there
was much talk of the malicious reports they had sent home about the
Boston merchants.[10] Then there was Thomas Hutchinson, a man to
reckon with.

The conduct of the Lieutenant-Governor, in ordering the images
cut down and in attempting to stop the pillage at Oliver's house,
marked him as a friend of the Stamp Act and an enemy of colonial
rights. It was insinuated that his letters home had encouraged passage
of the Act.[11] Still, the Loyal Nine may not have intended to give
Hutchinson the treatment they had handed Oliver. On the evening
of the twenty-sixth, Hutchinson himself heard the rumor that the
mob was to be out that night, and that the officers of the customs and
of the admiralty court were to suffer, but that nothing was contemplated against him.[12] On the other hand, Ebenezer Parkman, the minister of Westborough, thirty-five miles from Boston, heard on the
twenty-sixth that Governor Bernard, Lieutenant-Governor Hutchinson, and Mr. Story, the Deputy Register of the Admiralty Court
would be attacked. The information came in a letter from a friend
in Boston, dated the twenty-fourth.[13]

Neither Hutchinson's nor Parkman's information proved entirely
correct. On the evening of the twenty-sixth the mob rallied around a
bonfire on King Street and then proceeded in two separate bodies.[14]
One went to William Story's, and in spite of the fact that Story had
published an advertisement in that day's papers denying that he had

8. Bernard to Halifax, August 22, 1765, Bernard Papers, IV, 144-148.

9. Ibid.

10. Hutchinson, History, III, 89-90; Bernard to Halifax, August 31, 1765, Bernard
Papers, IV, 149-158.

11. Hutchinson, History, III, 88; Hutchinson to _____, August 16, 1765, Hutchinson
to Thomas Pownall, August 31, 1765, Massachusetts Archives, XXVI, 145, 149.

12. Hutchinson to Richard Jackson, August 30, 1765, Massachusetts Archives, XXVI,
146.

13. Diary of Ebenezer Parkman, August 26, 1765, photostat in Massachusetts Historical Society.

14. On the riot of August 26 see "Diary of Josiah Quincy, Jr.," August 27, 1765,
Massachusetts Historical Society, Proceedings, 4 (1860), 47-51; Benjamin Hallowell to
Commissioners of the Customs, September 7, 1765, Treasury Papers, Class I, Bundle
442; Thomas Hutchinson to Richard Jackson, August 30, 1765, and Thomas Hutchinson,
"A Summary of the Disorders in the Massachusetts Province," Massachusetts Archives,
XXVI, 146, 180-184; Bernard to Halifax, August 31, 1765, Bernard Papers, IV, 149-158.

written home ill reports of the Boston merchants, they destroyed a great part of his public and private papers and damaged his house, office, and furniture. The other group went after the Comptroller of Customs, Benjamin Hallowell. His house was acknowledged to be one of the finest in town—before they got there. Afterwards the windows, sashes, shutters, and doors were gone, the furniture broken, the wainscoting ripped off, the books and papers carried away, and the wine cellar all but empty.

It is possible that the men who originated the program for this evening had intended that it should go no further, but the letter which Parkman received shows that someone at least had planned what now occurred. McIntosh, who was still master of ceremonies, after the work at Story's and Hallowell's was completed, united his two companies and led them to the Lieutenant-Governor's. Whether he did this on his own initiative or at the request of the Loyal Nine or at the request of some other group will probably never be known. In later years William Gordon, who came to Boston in 1768 and knew most of the persons who were active in the revolutionary movement there, stated that ". . . the mob was led on to the house, by a secret influence, with a view to the destruction of certain papers, known to be there, and which, it is thought, would have proved, that the grant to the New Plymouth Company on Kennebec River, was different from what was contended for by some claimants." [15] The connection between the New Plymouth Company and the riot remains a secret. It may be that McIntosh saw no harm in killing two birds with one mob. He may have attacked the customs and admiralty officers for the Loyal Nine and Hutchinson for someone else.

Certainly in leading the attack on Hutchinson he had an enthusiastic following. Hutchinson was a cool and haughty man, about whom it was easy to believe any evil. McIntosh and company went about the work of wrecking his house with a zeal that far surpassed their previous height of August 14. They destroyed windows, doors, furniture, wainscoting, and paintings, and stole £900 in cash, as well as clothing and silverware. They cut down all the trees in the garden, beat down the partitions in the house and had even begun to remove the slate from the roof when daylight stopped them.

The fury of the attack on Hutchinson alarmed the best people in town. It looked as though the mob had got out of control and was bent upon transforming a commendable hostility to the Stamp Act into a levelling revolution. Rich men began to send their most valuable possessions to the homes of poorer neighbors where they might

15. William Gordon, *History*, I, 180.

be safer.[16] The town of Boston held a meeting and disavowed the attack on Hutchinson, though many of the participants in the pillaging must have been present at the meeting.[17] Hutchinson himself concluded that "The encouragers of the first mob never intended matters should go this length, and the people in general express the utmost detestation of this unparalleled outrage." [18] Three companies of militia and a company of cadets were called out to patrol the town and thereafter for many weeks the streets of Boston echoed with the steps of marching men. Even the children were caught up in the excitement. As one harassed parent complained, "the hussa's of the mobbs, the rattleing of drums, the clamour of the soldiers—who comes there—we are all well—and the continual hubub takes up all their attention. . . . As for James, wee cannot keep him from amongst the hurly burly without I would chain him. Thers no getting them kept to their sett times of schooling, eating, goeing to bed, riseing in morning in the midst of this disorder and confusion." [19]

Governor Bernard meanwhile met the crisis with his customary decisiveness by calling a meeting of the Council. Here it came out that McIntosh had led the assault on Hutchinson, and the Council ordered a warrant issued for his arrest. Sheriff Greenleaf found him on King Street and took him up without resistance. McIntosh was evidently so sure of himself that he felt no need to resist. It had already been rumored that the custom-house would be pulled down. Those who felt that the riots had gone far enough were ready to prevent this by use of the militia, but they were not ready to see McIntosh, who could name the instigators of both riots, tried in court. The word accordingly went around that unless McIntosh was released, not a man would appear to defend the custom-house. At this the officers of the customs went to the Sheriff and asked him to release his prisoner. Sheriff Greenleaf agreed and went to the Town House to tell the Governor and Council what he had done. "And did you discharge him?" asked Hutchinson.

"Yes," said Greenleaf.

"Then you have not done your duty."

16. James Gordon to William Martin, September 10, 1765, Massachusetts Historical Society, *Proceedings*, 2d ser., 13 (1900), 393; Hutchinson to Richard Jackson, September 1765, Massachusetts Archives, XXVI, 150.

17. *A Report of the Record Commissioners . . . Boston Town Records, 1758 to 1769*, 152; Hutchinson, *History*, III, 91.

18. Hutchinson to Richard Jackson, August 30, 1765, Massachusetts Archives, XXVI, 146.

19. James Gordon to William Martin, September 10, 1765, Massachusetts Historical Society, *Proceedings*, 2d ser., 13 (1900), 393.

"And this," Hutchinson wrote later, "was all the notice taken of the discharge." [20]

McIntosh thus went free, and no one was ever punished for the destruction of Hutchinson's property. But from this time forward the persons directing the mob were careful to keep matters more firmly under control, an accomplishment made possible by the willingness of the militia and of McIntosh to cooperate. Further demonstrations of violence were in fact unnecessary, for the Loyal Nine had made it plain that they were not afraid to bring out the mob against anyone who dared oppose them. Governor Bernard, retired in the safety of Castle William, was ready to admit that he did not have the command of ten men and was governor only in name. [21]

By the end of August, then, Boston was ready for the Stamp Act. With both the Stamp Distributor and the mob under control nothing remained to be done until the first of November, when it would be necessary to adopt a more vigilant watch to see that the Act should not be obeyed in any instance. A minor crisis occurred toward the end of September when the stamped papers arrived on a Boston merchantman. Governor Bernard was prepared for this and had announced earlier that he would lodge them in Castle William for safekeeping, since Oliver had disclaimed any responsibility. Fearing that Bernard would make an attempt to distribute them from the Castle, the Loyal Nine hinted that the people would storm the Castle the moment the papers were landed there and destroy them; but the Governor promptly stated in the newspapers that he was not authorized to distribute them and would make no attempt to do so. With this assurance the Loyal Nine were apparently satisfied, and when the papers arrived they were landed safely at the Castle under cover of two men-of-war in the harbor. [22]

In the ensuing weeks Boston waited uneasily for November first. Governor Bernard, brooding in Castle William over his grand scheme for reorganizing the empire, felt bitter about the mess which George Grenville had made of things. Although he had written to Richard Jackson on August 24, "to send hither Ordinances for Execution which the People have publicly protested against as illegal and not binding upon them, without first providing a power to enforce

20. Peter O. Hutchinson, ed., *The Diary and Letters of Thomas Hutchinson* (London, 1884-1886), I, 70-71.

21. Governor Bernard to Halifax, August 22, 1765, to Conway, November 25, 1765, Bernard Papers, IV, 144-148, 170-174.

22. Bernard to Lords of Trade, September 7, and September 28, 1765, House of Lords Manuscripts, January 14, 1766.

Obedience, is tempting them to revolt," [23] yet he could not quite believe that the people of Massachusetts would be so foolish as to prevent the execution of the Act. At first he told himself that the rest of the province would disavow the hot-headed proceedings of the Bostonians. There had always been a split between the coast and the country, and the country had always been more moderate. Bernard had hopes of getting some backing for law and order from the sober farmers of the interior when the General Assembly should meet. "I depend upon the Assembly to set these Matters to right," he wrote to his friend John Pownall after the first riot, "as I really believe that there is not one out of twenty throughout the Province but what will disapprove the Proceedings of Boston." [24]

When the Assembly came together on September 25, he pointed out to them that the doctrines of the *Boston Gazette,* however appealing they might be in Boston, would never find acceptance in Westminster. Though Parliament may have made a mistake in passing the Stamp Act, it was still an act of Parliament and the General Court of Massachusetts ought to see to its enforcement.[25] When his speech was over, it appeared that the radicals had won over a majority of the farmers in the Assembly, and so, as they prepared to draw up an answer to the speech, Bernard adjourned them.[26] Eventually he had to confess that the country people were even more violent in their opposition to the Stamp Act than the Bostonians: "They talk of revolting from Great Britain in the most familiar Manner, and declare that tho' the British Forces should possess themselves of the Coast and Maritime Towns, they never will subdue the inland." [27]

When he became disillusioned about the interior sometime in September, Bernard still clung to the idea that economic necessity would force the people of Massachusetts to accept the Act. He understood well the dependence of Massachusetts on trade. After November first, no ships would be cleared until the Stamp Act was accepted. Then Massachusetts would repent of her folly:

If the Ports and the Courts of Justice are shut up on the first of November, terrible will be the Anarchy and Confusion which will ensue; Necessity will soon oblige and justify an Insurrection of the Poor against the rich, those that want the necessaries of Life against

23. Bernard Papers, IV, 18-20; cf. Bernard to John Pownall, August 18, 1765, *ibid.,* 11-15.

24. Bernard to John Pownall, August 18, 1765, Bernard Papers, IV, 11-15.

25. Alden Bradford, ed., *Speeches of the Governors of Massachusetts . . .* (Boston, 1818), 39-43.

26. Bernard to Lords of Trade, September 28, 1765, Bernard Papers, IV, 162-165.

27. Bernard to Conway, January 25, 1766, Bernard Papers, IV, 201.

those that have them; But this is not all, it is possible that, when all the Provisions in the Province are divided amongst the People without regard to Property, they may be insufficient to carry them through the Winter, by cutting off the Resources from Pennsylvania and Maryland, upon which this Province has great dependance, a Famine may ensue. Less obvious causes, but very lately, were so near producing one, even with the help of the usual importations, that many perished for want: And who can say that the present internal stock of the Province, is sufficient, without importations to support the Inhabitants through the Winter only? [28]

Bernard was shrewd enough to see that the men directing the opposition to the Stamp Act wanted no insurrection of the poor against the rich. What he did not see was that these men would be able to turn the hatred of the poor against the British government instead of against the rich. It was true that if the ports were closed, famine would be the result in Boston, but before the poor should rise against the rich their fury would be aimed against the men who had closed the ports. In the face of that fury the ports would not stay closed, and neither would the clearances be on stamped paper. Bernard knew how to analyse the difficulties in the British imperial system, but when it came to analysing the immediate political situation he was helpless. His opponents had taken his measure correctly in the last weeks of August, and they knew that when the crisis came, his way of meeting it would be to pass the buck.

As the first of November approached, and word spread that there would be a grand parade and pageant that day, Governor Bernard performed his usual gesture. He called the Council and pointed out the danger that such a parade would end in more violence. To make matters worse, November 5 (Pope's Day) would follow hard after and give fresh occasion for riot. In order to forestall both these outbreaks, Bernard and the Council decided that several companies of militia should guard the town from October 31 to November 6.[29] On the thirty-first the officers of the militia came to the Council Chamber and, as might have been expected, announced that the militia could not be raised. The first drummer sent out had had his drum broken, and the others were bought off.[30] If Bernard had chosen, he could have had 100 regulars on hand. On September 10, General Gage had sent his aide-de-camp to offer that many troops for the maintenance of order. Bernard refused them, because, as he said, things had quieted down then, and because he was afraid that so small a number

28. Bernard to Lords of Trade, September 7, 1765, Bernard Papers, IV, 158-161.
29. Bernard to John Pownall, November 1, 1765, Bernard Papers, V, 16-21.
30. *Ibid.*

would only irritate the people without providing adequate protection to the government.[31] When November first came, then, Bernard was helpless. He was assured that his image would not be paraded, but nevertheless he retired to Castle William—not that he was afraid, he hastened to assure his correspondents, but he did not wish to be present when insults should be offered to His Majesty's government.[32]

As if to demonstrate how well they had the situation in hand, the Loyal Nine—or the Sons of Liberty, as they now began to call themselves—maintained perfect order in Boston on November first. The day was ushered in by the mournful tolling of church bells. The images of George Grenville and John Huske (whom the Bostonians took to be an instigator of the Stamp Act) were hung on the tree which had held those of Oliver and Bute on August 14. The tree had since been named the Liberty Tree, and a copper plaque commemorating August 14 (but not August 26) hung around the trunk. At two o'clock in the afternoon the images were cut down, and a procession of "innumerable people from the Country as well as the Town," marching in exact order, carried them through the streets to the gallows, hung them again, and then cut them to pieces. On November 5, there was a similar orderly demonstration, in which the union of the South End and the North End was celebrated with all the decorum of a church supper.[33]

No one in Boston supposed for a minute that these polite celebrations were the end of the Stamp Act troubles. The Sons of Liberty had begun to plan for the next step on their program as soon as they had forced Oliver to resign. On August 26, the day when Hutchinson's house was attacked, Benjamin Edes's paper had carried this item:

Since the Resignation of the Stamp Officer, a Question has been thrown out—How shall we carry on Trade without the Stamp'd Papers? — Carry on no Trade at all, say some, for who would desire to increase his Property, at the Expence of Liberty. — Others say, that in Case there shall be no Officer to distribute the Stampt Papers after the first of November, a regular Protest will justify any of his Majesty's Subjects, in any Court of Justice, who shall carry on Business *without* them? [34]

Governor Bernard naively supposed that the colonists would attempt to defeat the Stamp Act by ceasing all activities which required the use of stamps, but the Sons of Liberty had the second alternative

31. Bernard to Lords of Trade, September 28, 1765, Bernard Papers, IV, 162-165.
32. Bernard to Lord Colville, November 1, 1765, Bernard Papers, IV, 84.
33. Bernard to John Pownall, November 1, 26, 1765, Bernard Papers, V, 16-21, 43-46; *Boston Gazette*, November 11, 1765.
34. *Boston Gazette*, August 26, 1765.

in view—to proceed as though the Stamp Act had never been passed. Before attempting to achieve this by direct action, they tried to persuade the Assembly to effect it by law, as the Rhode Island Assembly had done by their promise to indemnify anyone who suffered by disregarding the Act. When the Massachusetts Assembly convened again on October 23, a committee of both houses was appointed to consider a resolution declaring that since the Stamp Distributor had resigned, whereby the people were prevented from obtaining stamps, it should be lawful to do business without stamps, the Act of Parliament to the contrary notwithstanding. Governor Bernard, still not recognizing the boldness of the people with whom he was dealing, supposed that this was simply another means of harassing him. "It is true," he wrote to John Pownall, "that they who bring in this Bill know that I cannot and shall not pass it: But what of that? it will answer their purpose; which is to bring upon me all the odium of the inconveniences, losses and miseries which will follow the non-usage of Stamps. The People will be told that all these are owing to me, who refused passing an Act which would have prevented them, and no notice will be taken of my incapacity to pass such an Act: so that I shall be made to appear to bring on these Evils, which I have taken so much pains to prevent." [35]

To Bernard's surprise the resolve did not pass the House, but the reasons for its failure were not calculated to reduce his uneasiness. The representatives rejected it, because they felt that it implied a right in Parliament to levy the tax. If the reason for ignoring the Act was simply that the stamp officer had resigned, the legality of the Act was admitted. If the resolution were adopted and a new Stamp Distributor should be appointed, it would be morally incumbent upon the Assembly to support him. These complex considerations could be avoided only by an open defiance of the Act, and this was more than the Assembly wished to put on its records. [36] The matter was left therefore, for the Sons of Liberty to resolve in their own way.

The most pressing problem would be the opening of the ports so that the trade which was Boston's lifeblood might go on. By putting every possible vessel to sea before November first the merchants gained a little time in which to consider the risks of ignoring an act of Parliament. The risks seemed to diminish in importance as ships returned from voyages to lie dismally idle, accumulating wharf-charges instead of profits; and the conviction that the Stamp Act must be ignored grew stronger.

35. Bernard to John Pownall, October 26, 1765, Bernard Papers, V, 13-14.
36. Bernard to John Pownall, November 1, 1765, Bernard Papers, V, 16-21.

While the Sons of Liberty waited for public pressure to rise, the customs officers, the Attorney General, and the Governor engaged in an elaborate rigmarole, in which the question of clearing vessels without stamps was tossed from one to the other and back again with graceful and disgraceful gestures, each person trying to shift the unpleasant decision from himself. The whole procedure is only to be understood in the light of the personal feud which had been going on for over a year between the Governor and John Temple, Surveyor General of the Customs.[37] Temple's headquarters were in Boston, but he supervised the collection of the customs in the entire Northern District from Nova Scotia to Connecticut. Bernard was jealous of Temple's power and did all he could to subordinate it to his own inside Massachusetts. Temple, on the other hand, regarded Bernard as a corrupt and grasping politician who had sabotaged the collection of the King's revenue (one example was the slowness with which he had moved to the support of John Robinson when Robinson had been put in the Taunton jail at the suit of Job Smith). Knowing that sooner or later either he or Bernard might have to take responsibility for clearing ships without stamps, Temple was anxious, if possible, to put the onus of the decision on Bernard.

The whole situation was further complicated by the fact that the only knowledge of the Stamp Act in Boston was hearsay. Two copies of the Act had come in private letters and from one of these the Act was printed in the newspapers, but Governor Bernard had received no official copy. From the newspapers he discovered that he was obliged by the terms of the Act to take an oath to support it, and accordingly he did so, but he naturally felt somewhat less responsible than he might have, had he known for certain what he was supposed to support. The same was true of Temple, and to a less degree of Oliver himself. Oliver received a notice of his appointment from the Secretary of the Stamp Office in England, but by November first he had not received his official commission as distributor. He surmised that this might be in the packet of stamped papers which was stored in Castle William, but neither he nor anyone else cared to break open the packet and find out.

Although everyone concerned with enforcing the Stamp Act could thus plead ignorance on November first, no one seriously doubted that the Act which had been printed in the newspapers was genuine, and it was plain that the customs officers whose duty it was to grant clearances would have to decide in the near future what course they

37. On this feud see Bernard Papers, III, *passim*, and Public Record Office, Treasury Papers, Class I, Bundles 441, 442.

should take. Accordingly on October 29 Benjamin Hallowell, Comptroller, who had already tasted the fury of the mob, and William Sheaffe, Collector, asked John Temple what they should do.[38] He replied that "as I have nothing in Charge from my Superiors concerning the Stamp Act, I can give you no other Advice or direction, for your Conduct than that of strictly observing all Acts of Parliament that have any Relation to the Duty of your Office, and wherein you may be at a loss for the true meaning of any Act of Parliament, I recommend you to the Advocate and Attorney General for their Advice." No help there.

The next day, October 31, Sheaffe and Hallowell went through the formality of asking Oliver for the stamped papers needed in their office. Oliver replied the same day that he had no commission as distributor and even if he did would not be able to handle the stamps. The next step was to ask Governor Bernard what should be done. He replied as quickly as Oliver that he had no authority to appoint a distributor or to distribute them himself. Sheaffe and Hallowell accordingly sent copies of their correspondence with Bernard and Oliver to the Attorney General, Edmund Trowbridge, and to the Advocate General of the Admiralty Court, Robert Auchmuty, and asked for their advice—all this by the evening of October 31.

On November 1, while Boston was diverting itself with the effigies of Grenville and Huske, Trowbridge sent his answer: ask Mr. Temple, the Surveyor General. As Auchmuty did not choose to make any reply at this point, the Collector and Comptroller were now back where they had started from, and here a disturbing thought occurred to them. Suppose they should refuse to grant clearances on the ground that they had no stamped paper. To grant clearances was their job, and no one else could do it. If they refused would they not be liable to suits for damages from every individual who applied for a clearance and was refused? On the other hand, suppose they granted a clearance on unstamped paper, and suppose further that the ship proceeding under this clearance were seized by the British Navy and condemned for proceeding under improper clearance papers. Would they not be liable in such a case to a suit for the value of the ship? Whatever they did were they not thus liable to innumerable suits? And were not the New England merchants notoriously quick to sue customs officers whenever they could?

Hastily they put their questions to the Surveyor General. Without hesitation he replied, "With regard to the Queries you have put to

38. The account of events in this paragraph and the ensuing eight paragraphs is based on the original letters in the House of Lords Manuscripts, March 13, 1766.

me, as they are mere points of Law, I must refer you to the Advocate and Attorney General." To the Advocate and the Attorney General they went, and this time obtained a reluctant opinion, that the Comptroller and Collector would not be liable to damages if they cleared ships on unstamped paper, provided they certified that no stamped paper was available. Having received this opinion, which of course was only an opinion and not a guarantee, Sheaffe and Hallowell still hesitated to proceed without some authorization from either the Surveyor General or the Governor. Accordingly they told Temple of the legal advice they had received, and he of course referred them again to the Governor. The Governor gave them the same answer that Temple had previously: "It is the Business of the Attorney General and the Advocate General to advise you in matters of Law and not mine."

It was now the nineteenth of November, and the merchants were becoming restless. Temple still refused to take responsibility. On his advice Sheaffe and Hallowell approached Bernard again on November 22, saying that they were afraid he might not have read Auchmuty's opinion at the time when he told them to go to the Attorney General and Advocate General for advice. Bernard was not to be caught in this trap: "I must again repeat to you that it is not my business to advise you in matter of Law. . . . I have perused the opinion of the Attorney General and Advocate General but desire to be excused giving my opinion upon the case myself."

Sheaffe and Hallowell next pressed the Attorney and Advocate for more explicit instructions, about how the clearances should be drawn up, and whether bonds as well as clearances might be unstamped. The only result was that Trowbridge got cold feet and withdrew his former advice. On November 30 he wrote, "I do not look upon myself as the Proper Person by whose advise You (in an affair of such importance, and which seems to be at present a matter rather of prudence than of Law) are to govern yourselves and therefore must be excused advising you either to grant Cockets or Clearances upon unstamped Papers or to refuse to do it."

On this same day, November 30, Andrew Oliver's commission finally arrived. Sheaffe and Hallowell again hopefully applied for stamps, but Oliver replied quickly enough that though he had received his commission it was still impossible for him to exercise it. Sheaffe and Hallowell therefore went back to plying Auchmuty and Trowbridge with questions. This time Trowbridge folded up completely. They received an answer written by a friend of Trowbridge's who was directed "to inform you that last Monday night he was seized with the Rheumatism in his right Arm and Shoulder to such a degree, as that he hath not ever since been able, either to write as much as his Name or attend to any business, wherefore he must be excused considering or answering those Questions."

By now the pressure was acute, and the Sons of Liberty were almost ready to take action. On December 11 Sheaffe informed the Surveyor General "that the Town was in an uproar and that there was a meeting of the Merchants and that the Mob intended at night to storm the Customhouse." Temple promptly sent the news to Bernard, with the additional intelligence that there was over six thousand pounds sterling of the King's money in the custom-house. As it grew dark, and the King's customs officers listened for the approaching rumble of the mob, Bernard penned his answer: "I will call a Council tomorrow."

But December 17, not December 11, was the day which the Sons of Liberty had scheduled for opening the custom-house, and the night of December 11 passed calmly. On December 13 Sheaffe and Hallowell made one more nervous attempt to get the stamps out of Oliver or to put the blame more squarely upon him. This time they got a categorical response: "In answer to your Letter of this date demanding my determinate and absolute answer to this question, whether I will or will not deliver you any stamp'd papers after having answered it twice already: I say No."

This was plain enough as far as Sheaffe and Hallowell were concerned, but the Sons of Liberty wanted a public statement. Before they put the final pressure on Sheaffe and Hallowell, they wanted to be certain that there would be no stamped papers available. On December 16, therefore, Benjamin Edes published an anonymous letter in the *Gazette,* asking whether Oliver intended to execute the commission he had lately received. Before publishing the letter Edes secured an answer from Oliver, which he also published, stating "that altho' he had now received a Deputation to act as Distributor of the Stamps for the Province of the *Massachusetts,* He had taken no Measures to qualify himself for the Office, nor had he any Thoughts of doing it."

To the Sons of Liberty this did not appear to be a satisfactory answer. They met in their headquarters at the distillery on Hanover Square and wrote another letter to Oliver:

Hanover Square Dec. 16, 1765

Sir,
The respectable Inhabitants of the Town of Boston, observe your Answer to an anonymous Letter published in Messi'rs Edes and Gill's

News-Paper of Today, which we don't think satisfactory; therefore desire that you would, To-morrow, appear under Liberty Tree, at 12 o'Clock, to make a public Resignation. Your Non compliance, Sir, will incur the Displeasure of *The True-born Sons of Liberty*. N.B. Provided you comply with the above, you shall be treated with the greatest Politeness and Humanity. If not . . . . .! [39]

When a messenger knocked at Oliver's door and handed his servant this letter, it was too late in the evening and the weather too dirty for Oliver to consult the Governor.[40] The next morning, the weather still stormy, notices were found posted up all over town, reading:

St-p! St-p! St-p! No.

Tuesday Morning, Dec. 17th, 1765

The true-born SONS of LIBERTY are desired to meet under Liberty Tree at XII o'Clock This Day, to hear the Public Resignation, under Oath, of Andrew Oliver, Esq; Distributor of Stamps for the Province of the *Massachusetts-Bay*. . .
A Resignation? Yes.[41]

Oliver realized that he had no way out. He sent for his friend John Avery, whose son was one of the Loyal Nine. The father, he surmised, would be able to act as an intermediary between himself and the Sons of Liberty. Avery came to him at nine o'clock and told him that effigies were already prepared as a signal for a riot in case he failed to appear at the Liberty Tree. In a last-minute attempt to save his dignity Oliver offered to make his resignation at the court house. This was not acceptable, and so at 12 o'clock noon, escorted by the redoubtable McIntosh himself, Oliver marched through the streets, the rain beating down tempestuously, and read his resignation from an upper window of the house which stood next to the Liberty Tree. In spite of the rain two thousand people had assembled, and when he was finished they gave three huzzas. Oliver replied with a polite, if somewhat bitter, statement that "I shall always think myself very happy when it shall be in my power to serve this people," upon which there were more cheers, and the crowd departed.[42]

39. *Boston Gazette*, December 23, 1765.
40. Andrew Oliver to Governor Bernard, December 17, 1765, House of Lords Manuscripts, February 10, 1766.
41. *Boston Gazette*, December 23, 1765.
42. Andrew Oliver to Bernard, December 17, 1765, and December 19, 1765, and to the Stamp Office, December 19, 1765, House of Lords Manuscripts, February 10, 1766 and February 14, 1766; *Boston Gazette*, December 23, 1765; Massachusetts Historical Society, *Proceedings*, 12 (1872), 246-247. The *Boston Gazette* gives Oliver's speech as follows: "I shall always think myself very happy to serve this People, when it shall lie in my Power."

Meanwhile messengers had been hurrying back and forth through the rain from Sheaffe and Hallowell to Temple, Trowbridge, Auchmuty, and Bernard. Auchmuty alone seems to have had the courage to advise flatly that the clearances be issued without stamps. Trowbridge still had the rheumatism, and Temple and Bernard refused to offer any advice. Sheaffe and Hallowell were still afraid to take the responsibility themselves. But when two thousand people could assemble on a rainy day to watch Oliver resign for a second time, present danger loomed larger than future damage suits. On the afternoon of the seventeenth the custom-house opened for business, and in the evening the Sons of Liberty sat down in their headquarters to a dinner of celebration, to which they invited their good friend Sam Adams and spent the evening drinking healths.[43]

With the ports open, the Sons of Liberty wasted no time in arranging for the opening of the courts. On the morning of the eighteenth the town of Boston, by petition of "a number of Inhabitants," held a special meeting in Faneuil Hall, at which a memorial to the Governor was drawn up. The memorial stated that "Law is the great rule of Right, the Security of our Lives and Propertys, and the best Birth right of Englishmen." By the closing of the courts the rule of law must cease; therefore the Governor was requested to order the opening of the courts.[44] Since the memorial was addressed to the Governor in Council, Bernard gratefully seized upon this opportunity to avoid a decision and appointed the next morning, December 19, for a Council meeting. When the Council met, Bernard informed them that he would leave the matter entirely to them. Since most of the members present were no more anxious to face the question than Bernard himself, and since many were absent, the meeting broke up with a decision to call in all the Councillors who lived within twenty miles of Boston for another meeting the following afternoon. As the gentlemen descended from their chamber in the upper story of the Town House, they could find a hint of what was expected of them in a paper hung up in the room below:

> Open your Courts and let Justice prevail
> Open your Offices and let not Trade fail
> For if these men in power will not act,
> We'll get some that will, is actual Fact.[45]

---

43. House of Lords Manuscripts, March 13, 1766; Henry Bass to Samuel P. Savage, December 19, 1765, Massachusetts Historical Society, *Proceedings*, 44 (1911), 688-689.
44. *Boston Town Records, 1758 to 1769*, p. 159.
45. Bernard to Conway, December 19, 1765, Bernard Papers, IV, 184.

When the Councillors assembled the next day, the lawyers of the town of Boston presented them with a long harangue on the necessity of opening the courts. The arguments were by now familiar. John Adams told them that the Stamp Act was "utterly void, and of no binding Force upon us; for it is against our Rights as Men, and our Priviledges as Englishmen." Parliament, he said, could err, and when it did, need not be obeyed. "A Parliament of Great Britain can have no more Right to tax the Colonies than a Parliament of Paris." James Otis, moved to tears by his own eloquence, argued that "The shutting up of the Courts is an Abdication, a total Dissolution of Government," and he too affirmed, as a principle well known to lawyers, "that there are Limits, beyond which if Parliaments go, their Acts bind not." [46]

Listening to these arguments, Governor Bernard perceived that the lawyers had given him another loophole. What they had said, he told them, "would be very pertinent to induce the Judges of the Superior Court to think the Act of no Validity, and that therefore they should pay no Regard to it; . . ." The question at issue was a matter of law, and it would not do for the executive branch of the government to determine a matter of law. In short the judges must decide the question.[47] The Council welcomed this solution, and adopted a resolution to the effect that the memorial presented to them was none of their business. In order to appease, as they hoped, the wrath of Boston, they added a recommendation that the judges of the several courts determine the question as soon as possible.[48] When the answer was delivered to the town meeting, on Saturday afternoon, December 21, the meeting considered the extraordinary question of whether the Council's reply was satisfactory, and came to the unanimous conclusion that it was not.[49]

The Superior Court of the province was not scheduled to meet until March, so that there was no immediate necessity for the justices of this court to make a decision, but the Inferior Court of Common Pleas for Suffolk County was to meet in Boston during the second week in January, and the session of the Probate Court of Suffolk

46. Josiah Quincy, Jr., *Reports of Cases Argued and Adjudged in the Superior Court of Judicature of the Province of Massachusetts Bay Between 1761 and 1772* (Boston, 1865), 200-209.

47. *Ibid.*, 206; Bernard to Conway, December 21, 1765, Bernard Papers, V, 66-68.

48. Bernard to Conway, December 21, 1765, Bernard Papers, V, 66-68; Thomas Cushing to John Cushing, January 28, 1766, Cushing Papers, Massachusetts Historical Society; *Boston Town Records, 1758 to 1769*, p. 160.

49. *Boston Town Records, 1758 to 1769*, p. 160.

County was already overdue.[50] In the Probate Court the obstinate figure of Thomas Hutchinson again appeared in the path of the Sons of Liberty. Hutchinson as Chief Justice of the Colony could postpone acting until March. Hutchinson as Judge of the Suffolk County Probate Court, would have to take his stand at once. His friends told him he must choose between four things: "to do business without stamps, to quit the country, to resign my office, or —" Here one may assume the friends supplied a significant gesture.[51]

Hutchinson was not an easy man to scare, but his friends assured him that he had no time to deliberate. His brother, Foster Hutchinson, did not share his unwillingness to do business without stamps. Governor Bernard suggested therefore that Hutchinson deputize his brother to act for him, but Hutchinson could find no precedent for such a proceeding. The Governor then offered to appoint Foster Hutchinson as Judge of the Probate Court for one year only. Such a limited appointment, Governor Bernard persuaded himself, could be made without stamped paper. Hutchinson complied with this arrangement, and so the Probate Court opened.[52]

Meanwhile the Boston town meeting had made inquiries—one suspects that the questions were heavily weighted—and discovered that the judges of the Inferior Court of Common Pleas in Suffolk County were ready to proceed without stamps.[53] When the next town meeting was held on January sixteenth, both the Probate and the Inferior Courts in Suffolk County were open for business as usual, but the courts in the other counties of the province were still closed. Since the only way in which the Bostonians could bring pressure upon these courts was through the General Assembly, the town meeting instructed their representatives in the Assembly to use their influence "that Measures may be taken that Justice be also duly Administred in all the County's throughout the Province and that enquiry may be made into the Reasons why the course of Justice in the Province has been in any Measure obstructed." [54]

50. The records of the Inferior Court of Common Pleas of Suffolk County for this period are not preserved, but the summonses are preserved, and they show that this court was scheduled to meet on the second week in January. On the probate court see Thomas E. Atkinson, "The Development of the Massachusetts Probate System," *Michigan Law Review*, 42 (1943), 425-452, and Quincy, *Reports*, 573-579.

51. Hutchinson to _____, January 15, 1766, Cushing Papers, Massachusetts Historical Society.

52. Excerpts from Council Records, and from Hutchinson's Correspondence (Massachusetts Archives, XXVI, 193), concerning this episode are in Massachusetts Historical Society, *Proceedings*, 2d ser., 16 (1902), 111 n.

53. *Boston Town Records, 1758 to 1769*, pp. 160-161.

54. *Ibid.*, 161.

The House of Representatives was by this time so thoroughly in accord with the town of Boston that on January 24, 1766, a resolution was passed by a vote of 81 to 5, stating that the courts of justice in the colony, and particularly the Superior Court, ought to be opened. When the resolution reached the Council, there again stood Thomas Hutchinson, prepared to block it. He wished the Council to reject it at once, but the other members postponed consideration until January 30.[55] The *Boston Gazette* immediately went to work on Hutchinson with a highly colored story to the effect that he had said that the resolution was "Impertinent and beneath the Notice of the honorable Board, or to that effect." [56] The *Gazette* had attained such a degree of power by this time that the Council thought it necessary to answer the charge. Governor Bernard, recognizing his old enemy Otis as the author, wanted the Council to have him arrested,[57] but the Council was no more ready than Bernard himself to assume responsibility for so dangerous a move, and contented themselves with passing resolutions in which they denied that Hutchinson had ever said anything derogatory to the House of Representatives.[58]

At the same time the Council thought proper to inquire of the judges of the Superior Court whether they would proceed with business when the next scheduled meeting should come up on March 11. The judges were as reluctant as everyone else to take a stand on the question but delivered their opinion that if the "Circumstances" of the colony remained in March what they were in January, and the lawyers should wish to proceed, they would be obliged to do so.[59]

This report from the judges was published without any mention of the provision that made opening contingent upon the wishes of the lawyers.[60] Actually the judges were shifting the responsibility back to the lawyers who had pleaded so eloquently before the Council for the opening of the courts. When March 11 rolled around, rumors of the repeal of the Stamp Act had already begun to arrive, and the revolutionary tension had relaxed to the point where the lawyers were dubious about risking their interests in an irregular procedure when a regular one might be obtained by waiting. Hutchinson, the Chief

55. *Boston Gazette*, January 27, 1766; *Journal of the Honourable House of Representatives* . . . (Boston, 1765 [*i.e.* 1766]), 214-215.

56. *Boston Gazette*, January 27, 1766.

57. Quincy, *Reports*, 213; Hutchinson to _____, February 27, 1766, Massachusetts Archives, XXVI, 199-200.

58. *Massachusetts Gazette*, January 30, 1766.

59. Quincy, *Reports*, 213.

60. *Massachusetts Gazette*, February 13, 1766. The whole incident is described by Hutchinson in a letter to Thomas Pownall, not sent, dated March 8, 1766, Massachusetts Archives, XXVI, 200-206.

Justice, manufactured an excuse to be absent from the March session —much to the annoyance of John Adams, who found himself as a lawyer in the dilemma which Hutchinson had escaped as a judge.[61] When the judges, perhaps perceiving the hesitation of the lawyers, declared themselves ready to proceed, even James Otis, who had led the movement to force the opening, was unwilling to plead. Finally a case was dug up which had been continued from the previous session, and after disposing of this, the Court postponed other civil business until April and from then successively until June.[62] The newspapers announced that "all the courts of Justice in this Province are now to all Intents and Purposes open." [63] With this token victory, which everyone could hope was the prelude to a real victory in Parliament, the agitation for opening the courts subsided, and Massachusetts waited for the news of repeal.

61. Quincy, *Reports,* 215; Adams, *Works,* II, 189.
62. Quincy, *Reports,* 216.
63. *Massachusetts Gazette,* March 20, 1766.

NINE

CONTAGION
Riots and Resignations

HEN the people of Boston began to pull down houses, they transformed the debate over Parliamentary authority into a test of Parliamentary power. What they challenged on Kilby Street, on August 14, was not simply the authority of Parliament—that was a matter for the colonial assemblies and the Stamp Act Congress—but the ability of Parliament to enforce the authority it claimed. For a few days after taking the step, they must have wondered whether they would stand alone. If so, if one colony alone rebelled, the power of Parliament would surely be too much for it. If all rebelled together, it might not be so easy for the English lawmakers to demonstrate their absolute authority.

Boston had to wonder for only a few days. Before two weeks were out, Rhode Island, the pariah of New England, which had helped save Massachusetts from the Pequots a hundred and thirty years before, again came to her rescue. As soon as news of the attack on Andrew Oliver reached Newport, the conservatives there began to hear rumors that their effigies would hang on August 27, as Oliver's had hung on August 14. What would follow the hanging they might guess for themselves. They knew the men who were planning the affair and expostulated with them. They even pleaded with the Governor to prevent it, but all in vain.[1] On August 26, the day before it was to take place, Martin Howard, Jr., appealed to the public, through an advertisement in the *Mercury*, defending his right to speak and publish his opinions and expressing his surprise "at the mistaken notions of those, who, under a Pretence of serving the Cause of Liberty, would take away the Right of private Judgment, and stop the Avenues to

1. Thomas Moffat, Manuscript account of the Newport riots, Chalmers Papers, Rhode Island, New York Public Library.

Truth, by instigating the Populace, and endeavouring to point their Fury against the Person and Interest of a Man, meerly because he happens to differ in Opinion from his Countrymen." The advertisement went on to say, "The Writer does not retract any Position contained in the *Halifax Letter;* and therefore does not meanly sollicit any Favour or Exemption from the Abuse intended him, because if his Person and Interest become the Objects of popular Revenge for these Sentiments, he thinks he shall never lament the Cause, whatever may be the Consequences." Howard was nothing if not proud, but his bold defence left his enemies unmoved, except by a desire to see whether he might not, under proper persuasion, lament those sentiments.

On the evening of the day Howard's advertisement appeared, the people of Boston put on their second riot, in which the house of Lieutenant-Governor Hutchinson was attacked. On the following morning, August 27, before news of the Hutchinson riot could have reached Newport, the inhabitants were treated to a parade in which three effigies were carried through the streets with halters about their necks and then suspended from a newly-erected gallows in front of the courthouse, while three leading merchants marched back and forth below the scaffold with clubs on their shoulders. The figures swinging above could be recognized by the labels conspicuously attached to them. One was Augustus Johnston, who had been appointed Distributor of Stamps for Rhode Island. The second was marked "That fawning, insidious, infamous Parricide, Martinus Scriblerus," meaning Martin Howard, Jr., and the third "that maw gazeen of Knowledge, Dr. Murphy," in other words, Dr. Thomas Moffat. The epithets had been drawn from James Otis's scurrilous pamphlet attacking the Newport group, but the artists who constructed the images added one original touch of their own. They connected Howard's neck with Moffat's by a rope bearing another label with their final verdict on the O.Z. letters. Howard and Moffat were supposed to be saying, "We have an hereditary, indefeasible right to an Haltar; besides we encouraged the growth of Hemp you know." [2]

The gentlemen who had been so suggestively portrayed feared the

2. For the events described in this and the ensuing six paragraphs, except as otherwise noted, see the following: *Newport Mercury,* September 2, September 9, 1765; *Boston Gazette,* September 2, 1765; *Connecticut Courant,* September 9, 1765; William Almy to Elisha Story, August 29, 1765, Massachusetts Historical Society, *Proceedings,* 55 (1923), 235-237; Chalmers Papers, Rhode Island, New York Public Library; Augustus Johnston to Commissioners of Stamps, August 31, 1765, Treasury Papers, Class I, Bundle 439, Public Record Office, Library of Congress transcripts; John Robinson to Commissioners of Customs, August 28, 1765, Treasury Papers, Class I, Bundle 442.

worst and retired to the safest places they could think of, Moffat to his farm across the Bay in Kingstown, the others to the man-of-war in the harbor. John Robinson went aboard the *Cygnet* too, "well knowing," as he said, "the Disposition of the People towards all Kings Officers, and the Danger to be apprehended from an inflamed Multitude." Evidently, however, the multitude was not as inflamed as the organizers of the show had expected. During the afternoon, therefore, they provided refreshments, with the hope of drawing a larger crowd. According to Doctor Moffat, they sent out runners to invite the people to this free picnic and served "strong drink in plenty with Cheshire cheese and other provocatives to intemperance and riot." When the party was well under way, the effigies were cut down and burned in a bonfire. After this, in spite of the strong drink and the cheshire cheese, the crowd dispersed, news having been spread that the principal characters required for any further activities had gone aboard the men-of-war. The next morning Moffat, Howard, Johnston, and Robinson returned home and found everything calm, but during this day, in all probability, news of the exciting riot at Boston reached Newport and further aroused the ambition of Newporters to take a more dramatic stand against the conservatives.[3] The events which began around dusk that evening occurred so rapidly that people later found it difficult to trace them in exact order.

As it was growing dark John Robinson and Martin Howard, Jr., in company with two other gentlemen who may or may not have been Moffat and Johnston, were walking down Queen Street. A man by the name of Samuel Crandall, who bore a private grudge against Robinson—for what reason is not apparent—stepped up at the head of a small party of men and collared the customs officer. Howard and Robinson's other companions succeeded in prying the man loose, and while Robinson hurriedly made his way home, Howard gave the bystanders a lecture on their unseemly behavior. He paid for his daring at once. A mob quickly collected, and with faces painted and broad axes in their hands, they poured down the street to Howard's house and gave it the same treatment that the Boston mob had given Hutchinson's, though Howard himself made his escape.

This was only a beginning. At Doctor Moffat's, where the mob made their next call, they found material worthy of their efforts. Moffat was something of a collector, and the hiss of ripping canvas

3. A letter in the Stiles Papers, Yale University Library (J. Avery to J. Collins, August 19, 1765), suggests that the instigators of the Newport riot may have been in correspondence with the Loyal Nine in Boston.

could be heard in the din as their axes tore through "Venus Sleeping," "Cleopatra," "Polly Peacham," "The Judgment of Hercules," and "The Countess of Coventry." There were also various intricate scientific gadgets of an appealing fragility (known to the times as "philosophical instruments"), such as telescopes, microscopes, barometers, thermometers, compasses, and hydrometers. These and the fine china from the Doctor's cabinet made a satisfying clatter, and there was also a library of valuable books, some of which splashed at the bottom of the well, while others enlarged the libraries of those who themselves had a taste for collecting.[4]

When there was no more fun to be had at the Doctor's, the mob surged on toward John Robinson's. His housemate, Lieutenant Wickham, warned him of their approach in time for him to make his way to safety aboard the *Cygnet,* where Wickham shortly joined him, for Wickham too, by virtue of his associations, was obnoxious. Deprived of the opportunity to manhandle the Collector, the mob spared the house, which did not belong to Robinson anyhow, and went on to the Comptroller, John Nicoll. But he too had fled.

Finally they got around to the Stamp Distributor. Augustus Johnston had already left, but his friends were there, frantically trying to hide his most valuable possessions in neighboring houses. The mob carted off much of what remained; but the house itself was spared, and when his friends promised that he would resign the next morning the crowd departed. By eleven o'clock, still going strong, they had made a full circle and found themselves back at Howard's ready to attend to any details that had been overlooked in the first visit. But the details had been well attended to so that they had to exert themselves on the more basic job of tearing up floors, hearths, and chimney pieces. Then on to Moffat's once more, to finish up there in the same way. They finally wound up about 2 A.M. at Howard's again, their broad axes still sharp enough to cut down the tough young locust trees that lined his yard. After triumphantly stuffing the ends of these into the cannons on the Parade, they marched home to the peaceful sleep of exhaustion and drink.

As the principal members of Newport's most exclusive club gathered together one by one aboard the *Cygnet,* they must have looked ruefully backward at the town where the mob was doing God only knew what with their possessions. None of their number had been killed or injured, but their worst forebodings about the mad "Herd" which ruled Rhode Island had been confirmed, and the town of Newport had lost its attraction for them. Moffat and Howard, thinking

4. Treasury Papers, Class I, Bundle 437.

doubtless of the hostile faces which they had encountered ever since their publication of the O.Z. letters and the Halifax Letter, decided that Newport was not worth saving. Without going ashore they left by the first ship for England. Augustus Johnston, who despite his office was less unpopular than his companions, went back to town and publicly resigned, though he, like Andrew Oliver in Boston, had not yet received his official appointment.

For Robinson the future was not so easy. The riot had begun with an attack on him by Samuel Crandall. And though Crandall was not himself a merchant, Robinson suspected that he had been egged on by the merchants in hope that the customs officers would be intimidated into overlooking smuggling activities. This suspicion was confirmed when, the morning after the riot, a message came to him from Crandall, saying "that if we would agree to receive our Fees agreeable to their Will and Pleasure,[5] and would also deliver up the Sloop Polly and her Cargo, now under Prosecution before Doctor Spry at Halifax, I might come on Shore in Safety, and rely on their Protection." [6] This was a truly outrageous proposal, to threaten the life of the Collector unless he would disobey an act of Parliament, and unless he would deliver the *Polly*, which had already caused him so much grief. Robinson sued out a warrant for the arrest of Crandall and issued a notice offering a hundred dollars reward for information leading to the conviction of other rioters, but the Sheriff returned the warrant as impossible to execute under peril of his life, and no one appeared to claim the hundred dollars.[7]

The behavior of Governor Ward was almost as disgraceful as that of the mob.[8] He had refused to take action to prevent the display of the effigies, even though he knew all about the plans days in advance. He had left town after the hanging and did not return until the rioting was over. When Robinson applied to him for protection against the men who were trying to intimidate him, he answered with empty

5. This may have meant a proposal that the customs officers should compound with the merchants for a certain annual sum in lieu of duties, or it may have meant that the customs officers should allow the merchants or the Rhode Island Assembly to set the fees which the customs officers collected for their services in clearing and entering vessels. In the preceding year acts had been passed regulating the fees which officers of government, including customs officers, could charge for performance of official duties. John R. Bartlett, ed., *Records of the Colony of Rhode Island and Providence Plantations in New England* (Providence, 1856-1865), VI, 413.

6. John Robinson to Commissioners of Customs, September 5, 1765, Treasury Papers, Class I, Bundle 442.

7. *Ibid., Newport Mercury*, September 9, 1765.

8. On Ward's behavior and his exchanges with Robinson and Leslie described below, see Moffat's account in Chalmers Papers, Rhode Island, and *Records of the Colony of Rhode Island*, VI, 453-457.

assurances, "that everything is perfectly tranquil, and that you may immediately return to town with all the safety imaginable." Robinson and the other customs officers replied that "while one Samuel Crandall, a principal fellow amongst the mob, dares, to this moment, to threaten the collector; and also on his and their behalf, prescribe the terms on which he may come on shore, we cannot consider the riot quelled, or that we may attend to the execution of our offices, either with safety to our persons and property, or to the King's revenue." To this communication, which should have resulted in an order for Crandall's arrest, the Governor answered that he had talked with Crandall, and "upon examining him, he assures me, that he has not the least intention of raising any disturbance or riot, or of doing any kind of injury. . . . He says Mr. Robinson has personally used him ill, and he shall insist upon proper satisfaction; but has not even a thought of taking any illegal or riotous method for obtaining it." The Governor again assured the Collector that there was no danger of another riot and that he might safely come ashore, and yet on the same day that he said this, September first, Captain Leslie of the *Cygnet* informed him of a plan in which Crandall was involved, to rescue the *Polly*. Though the case was being tried before Judge Spry at Halifax, the *Polly* was still in Newport harbor, lying under the guns of the *Cygnet*. According to the plan reported to Leslie, the mob was going "to man and arm a number of boats or vessels, and possess themselves of the fort; and in case they find a resistance on my part, when such boats or vessels are endeavoring to take away the said sloop (which will certainly be the case, when we discover any such attempt being made,) that then the guns at the fort are to be fired at His Majesty's ship under my command. This, I own, appears very surprising; but from the repetition of the report, and what happened last year to His Majesty's schooner *St. John*, I must own I think the madness of the mob may carry them to such lengths, without the interposition of the government's authority."

Governor Ward dismissed this communication as he had those from Robinson. But as long as Robinson stayed aboard the *Cygnet*, the customs office in Newport stayed closed, and the merchants were unable to clear any of their vessels for departure. Bold as the merchants might be, they did not at present dare send their ships to sea without clearance papers. The British Navy would seize ships without papers wherever they found them, and there was no mob available on the high seas to force the Navy to give them back. Consequently as long as Robinson kept the custom-house closed, foreign trade in Newport was at a standstill.

Robinson could afford to wait. He employed his time by writing an account of the riot and also of the *St. John* episode to the Lords of the Treasury in England. The occasion was an appropriate one for supporting his friends' petition for a royal government, and he assured the Lords that all the riots sprang "from the principles of the constitution of the government, which is the most popular that can be formed," and "that the same causes will be the sources of future riots and disturbances." [9] While Robinson was enjoying the hospitality of Captain Leslie and writing his letters, the merchants were clamoring for the custom-house to open. After four days the clamor reached the ears of the Governor, and since Robinson would not come ashore without a bodyguard, the Governor was obliged on September 2 to provide "5 Or 6 civil Officers," to protect him.[10]

With the custom-house open again, business proceeded, but everyone knew that a new crisis was not far away. The people were evidently determined to prevent the use of stamps after November first. The Stamp Distributor had resigned; the Governor had refused to take the oath required of him to assist in enforcing the Act;[11] and the Assembly had passed a resolution directing all officers to ignore the Act.[12] But John Robinson was not an officer of the Colony of Rhode Island; he was an officer of the King. If he refused to disregard the Stamp Act, all trade out of Newport would be at an end. In anticipation of the crisis merchants loaded as many of their ships as possible and hurried them out of port before the November first deadline.[13]

The tension increased when news leaked out that the stamped papers for Rhode Island had arrived in Boston and at the direction of Augustus Johnston had been brought to Newport and placed aboard the *Cygnet*—this in spite of his resignation. The stamped papers had of course been shipped before his resignation, and friends in England had given bond for their safety. When he received word of their arrival, he had to do something about them lest they be destroyed and his friends forfeit their bonds. The safest place for stamped papers as well as for stamp distributors, was aboard a man-of-war, and so he had

9. *Acts of the Privy Council of England, Colonial Series,* VI, 387.

10. John Robinson to Commissioners of Customs, September 5, 1765, Treasury Papers, Class I, Bundle 442.

11. According to Ezra Stiles, Governor Ward was upheld in his refusal to take the oath by the Assembly, which voted that he was included in the promise of indemnity in the resolution directing all officers of government to ignore the Act. See above, ch. 7, and Ezra Stiles's Stamp Act Notebook, Stiles Manuscripts, Yale University Library.

12. *Records of the Colony of Rhode Island,* VI, 452.

13. The listings of clearances in the *Newport Mercury* for the last weeks in October, 1765, are much larger than in previous weeks and much larger than in the corresponding weeks of previous years.

them delivered to the *Cygnet*. Although it is difficult to see how he could honorably have done less, the people of Newport feared that he intended to act in the office he had publicly resigned.[14] During the night of Saturday, October 19, someone posted a paper on the draw-bridge at Long Wharf, where Sunday-morning strollers could not fail to notice it. It warned Johnston that his life would not be worth much in Newport, should he attempt to distribute the stamps. It also communicated some resolutions adopted by the "respectable populace," with regard to the Collector of Customs. There was no indication as to who comprised this respectable populace or as to when and where they adopted their resolutions, but the resolutions themselves were not ambiguous:

That the C---r of N-- shall use none of them [stamps] in his office, upon pain of our highest displeasure.

That if he will clear no vessels upon paper without Stamps, that he shall be drove out of town with a high hand.

That any merchant clearing out his vessel upon St--p papers, shall meet with our highest displeasure.[15]

When the fatal day of November first arrived, the merchants had already cleared out all available vessels, so that there was no immediate necessity of facing the issue. However, as more vessels kept coming into port, Robinson realized that he would have to give unstamped clearances or else leave town. On November 21 he went through the formality of applying to Augustus Johnston for the proper stamped papers. Johnston could only answer that it would be dangerous to his life and property to supply them.[16] Faced with the same dilemma as Sheaffe and Hallowell in Boston, Robinson capitulated, and by November 25 was carrying on business as usual at the custom-house.[17]

14. Captain Charles Leslie of the *Cygnet* and Thomas Moffat, both stated that Ezra Stiles, the pastor of the Second Congregational Church at Newport, harangued the crowd after Johnston's original resignation and warned them that it was no resignation at all, that in spite of it Johnston would be able to resume the office whenever he pleased (*Calendar of Home Office Papers of the Reign of George III, 1760-1765*, London, 1878, pp. 610-611; Chalmers Papers, Rhode Island, New York Public Library). Stiles denied that he had anything to do with the violence against Johnston (letter to Benjamin Franklin, November 6, 1765, Stiles Manuscripts), but Johnston's letter to the Commissioners of Stamps, August 31, 1765, suggests that Johnston did intend to carry on the office if popular hostility subsided (Treasury Papers, Class I, Bundle 439; see also *Newport Mercury*, December 30, 1765).

15. *Newport Mercury*, October 21, 1765.

16. *Records of the Colony of Rhode Island*, VI, 476-477.

17. This fact has been ascertained from evidence in the Aaron Lopez Invoice Book, Newport Historical Society, and from letters of Ezra Stiles to different persons which indicate the sailing dates of ships from Newport, Stiles Manuscripts.

After Boston and Newport had shown the way, the mere threat of violence was sufficient in most other colonies. In New York James McEvers did not wait to be asked before resigning as Stamp Distributor. He knew that the invitation would probably be similar to that extended to Andrew Oliver. On August 26, while Boston prepared for its second riot and Newport for its first, McEvers publicly announced his resignation, and wrote to a friend in England asking him to secure the appointment of someone else. He recounted what had happened to Oliver and expressed his belief that other distributors would receive the same treatment by November first. The consequences for himself, he said, would be disastrous, "as I have a Large Store of Goods and Seldom Less than Twenty thousand Pounds Currency value in it with which the Populace would make sad Havock with Respect to my own Person I am not much Concern'd About it, but I must Confess I am Uneasy about my Store, as a Great Part of What I have Been Labouring hard for, is Center'd there, . . . if it is Practebil Should be Glad to have Some Other Person Appointed in my Place which I Immagen would be Attended with Little Difficulty as there are many who are not in so good a Way of Business and not so Large a Store at Risque that would gladly undertake it, (by the Present Disposition of People here it Appears that a Stranger would be more Agreable than a Native)." If transportation then had been what it is now McEvers might have closed his letter here, but it occurred to him that by the time his letter reached England he might already have suffered the loss of his property; in that event he would be glad to have the income which the office of stamp distributor would provide if the Act should be enforced. "If this Letter Should Come to your hands too Late," he wrote, "and I cannot *Probably* be Releav'd at or about the time the Act is to be in Force in Such Case I Beg you will not make Any Application for my Releasement, as the First month or Six Weeks Service in the Office will be the most Dangerous and Disagreeable Part of it." [18]

McEvers' letter must have made painfully clear in England the folly of a decision which George Grenville had made the preceding March. After he had driven the Stamp Act through Parliament against the objections of the colonial agents, he had determined to make another appeal for colonial good-will, this one more genuine than his suggestion that the colonies tax themselves. He had summoned the agents and announced that he would appoint native

18. James McEvers to Barlow Trecothick, August, 1765, Treasury Papers, Class I, Bundle 439.

Americans as stamp distributors.[19] The offices would not be sinecures, but they would be lucrative, and Grenville supposed that the appointment of Americans would be taken as a friendly gesture. Grenville was a politician, and in the world of politicians the distribution of offices is the principal cement of friendship. What he failed to realize was that by making his stamp masters native Americans he was giving the colonists a lever by which to pry them loose from their positions. If the stamp masters had been Englishmen, strangers to the country, with no property or interests invested in it, they could have withstood the pressure of the populace much longer. But the office was not sufficiently valuable in the eyes of most Americans to make it worthwhile sacrificing the property they had accumulated in a lifetime. John Robinson, an Englishman, could have held out indefinitely aboard the *Cygnet* against the Newport mob. Augustus Johnston, though he might come aboard to save his skin, could not bring his house and business with him. And while the mob made off with some of his property, they left enough to work on in case the first night's attack did not produce his resignation. After the Boston mob had shown the way to deal with an American stamp distributor by pulling down Andrew Oliver's new building, the distributors in other colonies, as McEvers' letter reveals, had to weigh the value of their property against the value of the fees they might or might not collect. There were other factors in the equation, a man's honor and dignity for example, and even his life, but no one could neglect to consider the loss in pounds and shillings which accepting the stamp office might entail.

McEvers, by resigning before a mob demanded it, was able to save something of his dignity, and all of his property. William Coxe, his neighbor in New Jersey, did the same. On August 24 he was writing to the Secretary of the Stamp Office in England that "no spirit of undutifulness or disrespect has yet appeared . . . from the People of New Jersey." [20] On September 2 he resigned, though Governor William Franklin maintained that he had received no threats or insults to cause him to do so.[21]

Other distributors, not so far-sighted or not so timid, stuck it out longer and consequently suffered losses or were obliged to eat humble pie. When Zachariah Hood of Maryland refused to resign after his

19. New Haven Colony Historical Society, *Papers*, 9 (1918), 323, 337.
20. Treasury Papers, Class I, Bundle 455.
21. William Franklin to Benjamin Franklin, September 7, 1765, Treasury Papers, Class I, Bundle 442.

house had been pulled down on September 2, the mob effectively prevented him from acting by forcing him to flee for his life with only the clothes on his back.[22] Lieutenant-Governor Colden of New York gave him refuge in that colony at Fort George, but this was not a very convenient place from which to distribute stamps for Maryland. At first Hood hoped that a man-of-war might be anchored off the Maryland coast from which he could officiate, but by November 10, he had given up this idea as impracticable, and on November 26 the New York mob sought him out and helped their neighbors to the south by forcing his resignation.[23]

George Meserve, Distributor for New Hampshire, owed his appointment to the fact that he was visiting England when the Act was passed. Even before he set foot again in America, he discovered that he had accepted a liability. The pilot who came aboard to guide his ship into Boston harbor on September 8 delivered a letter from the principal gentlemen of Portsmouth, saying that it would not be safe for him to come home until he had first relinquished his office. The rebellious temper of America became even more apparent when the Boston mob forced his ship to lie for two days in the harbor, under protection of the men-of-war there. Not until they were persuaded that the stamped paper for New England was not aboard would they permit her to dock. Awakened to his danger, Meserve announced his resignation before going ashore, whereupon the Bostonians received him with acclamations and conducted him to the Exchange Tavern for a celebration.[24] He found his fellow colonists in New Hampshire equally determined but less cordial. Although he agreed to all their demands, he nevertheless slept uneasily, always with arms by his side, and he dared not engage even in private business for fear of having his "Interests destroyed by a mob." [25]

Jared Ingersoll of Connecticut, in spite of being threatened and burned in effigy in various parts of the colony, held his ground for several weeks but was finally obliged to resign on September 15, when

22. *Maryland Gazette,* September 5, 1765; Zachary Hood, probably to Captain Kennedy, September 2, 1765, Sedgwick Papers, Massachusetts Historical Society.

23. *Ibid.,* and Zachariah Hood to Benjamin Franklin, September 23, 1765, to Commissioners of Stamps, November 10, 1765, Treasury Papers, Class I, Bundle 442; *Maryland Gazette,* January 30, 1766.

24. *Massachusetts Gazette and Boston News Letter,* September 12, 1765; George Meserve to Commissioners of Stamps, September 30, 1765, Treasury Papers, Class I, Bundle 442; James Gordon to William Martin, September 10, 1765, Massachusetts Historical Society, *Proceedings,* 2d ser., 13 (1900), 393.

25. George Meserve to Stamp Office, December 3, 16, 1765, House of Lords Manuscripts, February 14, 1766, Library of Congress transcripts.

a mob accosted him on his way to the meeting of the Assembly and prepared to lynch him.[26]

John Hughes, a proud man with a sharp tongue, was able to avoid bowing to the Philadelphia mobs until October 7, when they wrung from him a promise that he would not execute the Act unless the other colonies did. Since he was Distributor for Delaware as well as Pennsylvania, he was obliged to give an assurance to the people of that colony that his promise included them too.[27]

George Mercer of Virginia, like George Meserve of New Hampshire, had been in England when the Act was passed, and not anticipating opposition, he too had accepted an appointment as Distributor. Mercer did not arrive in Williamsburg until October 30, two days before the Act was to go into effect. Unfortunately for him, his arrival coincided with a meeting of the General Court which had filled the town with people from all over the colony. They met him in the street even before he had reached his lodgings and demanded his resignation at once. He asked time to consult his friends, and then, followed by the crowd, he walked to the Coffee House, where the Governor and most of the Council were sitting on the porch. These high officials received him warmly, to the chagrin of those below, and when the mob prepared to seize him, Governor Fauquier stepped forward and taking him by the arm, conducted him safely through the awed assembly, to the accompaniment of angry murmurs. The two men walked to the Governor's mansion and there talked the matter over. "He asked me what he should do," Fauquier reported to the Board of Trade. "In return I asked him whether he was afraid for his Life, if he was it was too tender a point for me to advise him; if not his Honor and interest both demanded he should hold the office; and if that should be his resolution he must not regard the reasonings of his Father and Brother two Lawyers attending the Court, who were both frighted out of their senses for him. He left me that night in a State of uncertainty what part he should act."

By the next morning the state of uncertainty was gone. Either from a different view of honor and interest or because his father and brother had communicated their fears on the point too tender for the Governor's advice, George Mercer resigned.[28]

The populace of Charleston, South Carolina, had two stamp men

26. *Connecticut Courant*, September 23, 1765. See below, ch. 14.
27. *Pennsylvania Gazette*, October 10, 1765. See below, ch. 13.
28. Fauquier to Lords of Trade, November 3, 1765, House of Lords Manuscripts, January 27, 1766; *Pennsylvania Journal*, November 14, 1765.

to take care of, for both Caleb Lloyd, Distributor for the colony, and George Saxby, Inspector of Stamps for North Carolina, South Carolina, and the Bermudas [29] resided in their town. Lloyd fled for his life on October 20 when the arrival of the stamps precipitated a mob bent on destroying both him and the paper. He dared not return to town, and George Saxby, arriving from London on October 27, joined him at Fort Johnson. There, after two days of willing imprisonment, both stamp men agreed to suspend their duties until the petitions of the Stamp Act Congress (which had just finished its meetings at New York) had been sent to England and Parliament's determination on them returned. Hoping to exonerate themselves in England, they wrote to the British Stamp Office that they had given in only "after two days being prisoners in the fort, to prevent Murther and the destruction of the town which we were well informed by our friends would certainly have happened the Inspectors house having been already rendered uninhabitable himself burnt in Effigie and the Mobs further resolution of pulling the same to the Ground and putting us to death unless we agreed to suspend. . . ." [30]

November first arrived before the people of North Carolina and Georgia knew who their distributors were to be. Henry McCulloh, the original appointee for North Carolina, had declined the office. Dr. William Houston, who had been fixed on in place of McCulloh, did not hear of his own appointment until summoned from his home in Duplin County to Wilmington, sixty miles distant, to claim a letter from the Stamp Office. The wary citizens of Wilmington, suspecting the contents of the letter, had intercepted it and turned it over to the Mayor for delivery. When Houston arrived on November 16 and opened it, their suspicions were confirmed, and they required him to resign forthwith. [31]

In Georgia, as November first approached and passed without news of stamps or stamp distributor for the colony, nervous radicals conducted their demonstrations with nameless effigies and sent threatening letters to a number of conservative citizens suspected of secretly holding the office or of harboring stamps. Finally, on November 7, the *Georgia Gazette* informed its readers that one George Angus was their man. Angus was not available for threatening, because he had not yet left England. Furthermore, he was not a native of the prov-

---

29. House of Lords Manuscripts, January 29, 1766.

30. George Saxby and Caleb Lloyd to Commissioners of Stamps, October 29, 1765, Treasury Papers, Class I, Bundle 455; William Bull to Lords of Trade, November 3, 1765, House of Lords Manuscripts, February 14, 1766.

31. *New Hampshire Gazette*, December 27, 1765; William Houston to Commissioner of Stamps, November 20, 1765, House of Lords Manuscripts, February 14, 1766.

ince, the lone exception to Grenville's ruling on this point, and hence he was not susceptible to property damage. But it was not property damage that Governor Wright feared for him. To secure him from violence the Governor made elaborate preparations, so that when his ship arrived at Tybee on January 4, he was whisked away to Wright's house before his presence became generally known. There he immediately took the required oaths of office and distributed stamp papers to the customs officers. In spite of this successful beginning George Angus quickly discovered that his new occupation was not a healthy one, and before two weeks were up he had left for parts unknown.[32]

The infection did not spread so alarmingly north of New England or south of Georgia, but in the colonies which later participated in the American Revolution there was no one able or willing on November first to put the Act into execution. And in most of these colonies, or so the royal governors claimed, it was the contagious example of Boston which had set off the troubles.

The royal governors, to be sure, were not the most disinterested observers. Each of them was anxious to exonerate himself and his administration from any blame, and Boston provided a convenient scapegoat; yet the charge probably was justified to a large degree. It may even be true, as Governor William Franklin suggested to his father, that "the Presbyterians of New England have wrote to all their Brethren throughout the Continent, to endeavour to stir up the Inhabitants of each Colony to act as they have done, in hopes of thereby making it appear to the Ministry too difficult a Matter to call them to account for their late outrageous Conduct." [33] Probably, however, it was not necessary to write private letters. The printers of colonial newspapers sent exchange copies to one another, and the news of what had happened in Boston, together with the inflammatory remarks of Boston's patriots, was sent from one end of the continent to the other in the *Boston Gazette*. The effect of the news in so distant a colony as South Carolina, was described by Governor Bull in a letter to the Lords of Trade on November 3, 1765:

Accounts had been received from Boston of the Outrages committed there on the 14th and 26th of August last, and also of those at Rhode Island to show their determined Resolutions to prevent or elude the Execution of the Stamp Act in those Provinces, and also of the Intentions, which other Provinces at the Northward had ex-

32. *Georgia Gazette*, October 31, November 7, 14, 1765; James Wright to Secretary of State Conway, January 31, 1766, in Charles C. Jones, Jr., *The History of Georgia* (Boston, 1883), II, 60-64.

33. William Franklin to Benjamin Franklin, September 7, 1765, Treasury Papers, Class I, Bundle 442.

pressed to the like purpose; tho not with so much violence; . . . New England vaunts its Numbers, and arrogates glory to itself in taking the lead of North America. For before those accounts came, the People of this Province, tho' they conceived it too great a burthen, seemed generally disposed to pay a due obedience to the Act, and at the same time in a Dutiful and respectful manner to represent to his Majesty the hardships, which it would lay them under, and to pray relief therein . . . But by the Artifices of some busy Spirits the minds of Men here were so universally poisoned with the principles, which were imbibed and propagated from Boston and Rhode Island, from which Towns, at this time of the year, Vessels very frequently arrive, that after their Example the People of this Town resolved to seize and destroy the Stamp Papers, and to take every means of deterring the Stamp Officers from executing their Duty.[34]

Boston and Rhode Island could take credit for the initial leadership, but people in South Carolina, and for that matter in the other colonies, would scarcely have been ready to follow such distant leaders if the direction of march had not been agreeable.

34. House of Lords Manuscripts, February 14, 1766. Cf. James Wright to Lords of Trade, November 9, 1765, *ibid.;* Fauquier to Secretary of State Conway, December 11, 1765, House of Lords Manuscripts, February 6, 1766.

≫ TEN ≪

NULLIFICATION
Ports and Courts

ALTHOUGH Massachusetts took the lead in violence, several other colonies were putting their ships to sea with clearance papers unstamped before Sheaffe and Hallowell finally opened the Boston custom-house. The speed with which merchants were able to resume business as usual after November first, was measured by their own determination, by the contrary determination of their customs officers and governor, and by the economic needs of their particular colony. In Georgia where, on November first, there were no stamps, no stamp distributor, and indeed no copy of the Stamp Act itself, Governor Wright and his Council felt justified in authorizing the clearance of ships without stamps. The customs officers simply continued to use old forms, with a note to the effect that no stamps were available.[1]

In Georgia this procedure was temporary, and the ports closed on November 30, after Governor Wright and the customs officers received definite notices of the Act;[2] but in Virginia the Act was consistently violated, so far as shipping was concerned, from November second onward. The way was smoothed here by the fact that George Mercer, who brought the stamps for Virginia with him, claimed to have none for the custom-house, so that the necessity of proceeding without them appeared to arise from neglect in England rather than from violence in America.[3] The procedure was facilitated too by the straightforwardness of the Governor and Surveyor General. The lat-

1. *Georgia Gazette,* November 7, 14, 1765; *Colonial Records of Georgia,* IX, 435.
2. *Colonial Records of Georgia,* IX, 439-440, 454-456.
3. Certificate by Fauquier, House of Lords Manuscripts, February 14, 1766, Library of Congress transcripts.

ter, Peter Randolph, when he could not at first persuade the Governor to share the responsibility, did not wait but on November 2 advised the collectors on his own initiative to clear vessels as usual, and to give a certificate that no stamped paper was available. At the same time, he told them, they should take from the master a waiver of damages in case the vessel should be seized at its destination for lack of a proper clearance. Randolph sensibly concluded that "impossibilities will not be expected of us, and that from the Nature of the Case our Conduct will stand justified." [4] Governor Fauquier quickly saw the reasonableness of Randolph's action, and on November 7 added his sanction to it. Thereafter the certificates testifying to the lack of stamps bore the Governor's signature under the province seal. [5]

Rhode Island followed Virginia by the last week in November, and in the first week of December Pennsylvania, New York, and New Jersey did likewise. [6] In Philadelphia, by an ingenious device not apparently thought of elsewhere, trade had been kept moving throughout November. In all colonial ports merchants had cleared out every ship they could load before November first, but in Philadelphia they cleared ships which were only partially loaded. Although clearances were not supposed to be granted until the entire cargo was declared, all the ships in Philadelphia which had any part of their cargoes aboard obtained clearance papers in the last days of October. When the cargoes had been completed, the owners went to the customhouse and had undated additions entered on their papers. The Collector, John Swift, at first refused to cooperate in this scheme unless the merchants would engage to pay whatever penalties he might undergo as a consequence, but when the Governor failed to back him up he gave in. [7] Since it normally took three to four weeks for a ship

4. Peter Randolph to Collector of Customs at Norfolk, November 2, 1765, *Pa. Mag. of Hist.*, 2 (1878), 298-299.

5. Fauquier to Lords of Trade, November 11, 1765, House of Lords Manuscripts, February 14, 1766; Andrew Eliot to Charles Stewart, December 6, 1765, Philadelphia Custom House Papers, Historical Society of Pennsylvania.

6. Abel James and Henry Drinker to John Clitherall, December 3, 1765, James and Drinker Letter Books, Historical Society of Pennsylvania; Collector and Comptroller of New York to Archibald Kennedy, December 10, 1765, and Collector of Perth Amboy to Commissioners of Customs, December 7, 1765, House of Lords Manuscripts, February 14, 1766.

7. Joseph Shippen to Edward Shippen, Jr., November 9, 1765, Shippen Papers, Historical Society of Pennsylvania; Thomas Clifford to Walter and Samuel Franklin, November 12, 1765, Pemberton Papers, Historical Society of Pennsylvania; Samuel and Jonathan Smith to Nathaniel Holmes, November 2, 1765, Samuel and Jonathan Smith Letter Book, Library of Congress; Abel James and Henry Drinker to Parvin and James, November 2, 1765, James and Drinker Letter Books.

to complete her cargo, there was relatively little pressure in Philadelphia until the end of November. On November 28 several vessels, with clearance papers dated before the first, were still waiting to finish loading.[8] By this time, however, the number of vessels which had reached port after the first was beginning to mount. On December first the Collector and Comptroller wrote to the Commissioners of Customs describing their troubles:

We have not yet done anything since the first of November, but people who have Vessels loaded begin to be very uneasy and Clamorous, The Winter is near at hand, and We may expect in a short time, that Our Navigation will be stopt by the Ice. The Harbour is full of Vessels, and if We don't begin soon to permit them to depart, they will probably be shut up all the Winter, which will occasion great distress and perhaps Ruin, to many of His Majesty's subjects, and at the same time be a means of lessening the Revenue of Customs.

What we have said above is on a supposition that it is in our power to detain them, but that is not the case, We dare not do it if we would; People will not sit quiet, and see their Interests suffer, and perhaps Ruin brought upon themselves and Famalies, when they have it in their power to redress themselves. . . . So that upon the whole We are of opinion that it will be best to let the business of the Custom house go on as usual, till We receive Instructions to the Contrary: The Surveyor General is of this opinion, but he does not chuse to give Us any Orders, as he cannot undertake to Indemnify Us against the Penalties of an Act of Parliament.[9]

By the next day the Collector and Comptroller accepted the necessities of the situation and began to issue clearances.[10] Before another week went by the Surveyor General, Charles Stewart, also screwed up his courage and sent out orders to all the officers of the Middle District (New Jersey, Delaware, Pennsylvania, New York) to clear vessels on unstamped paper if they thought it prudent.[11] Though he warned them that his order would not indemnify them in case of suits for damages, they all found it prudent to do as he suggested.

Stewart, in explaining his action to the Commissioners of Customs, pointed out the losses that would be entailed not only in the mainland colonies but in the West Indies, and in England, by keeping the ports closed, but he emphasized the fact that he had really no choice

8. Abel James and Henry Drinker to Neate, Pigou, and Booth, November 28, 1765, James and Drinker Letter Books.

9. Treasury Papers, Class I, Bundle 442, Library of Congress transcripts.

10. Abel James and Henry Drinker to John Clitherall, December 3, 1765, James and Drinker Letter Books; Philadelphia Custom House Papers, IV; *Pennsylvania Journal*, December 5, 1765.

11. House of Lords Manuscripts, February 19, 1766.

in the matter. One hundred and fifty sail of vessels were rotting in Philadelphia harbor, and if these should remain over the winter the consequences would be appalling: "Nothing is more certain than that so great a Number of Seamen, shut up for that Time in a Town destitute of all Protection to the Inhabitants . . . would commit some terrible Mischief, or rather that they would not suffer themselves to be shut up, but would compel the Officers to clear Vessels without Stamps—This would undoubtedly have been the Consequence of a few days longer Delay, . . ." [12] Idle sailors were a problem in every port, but the bigger the port the bigger the problem. Though the customs officers at New York began to receive threatening letters as soon as the Stamp Distributor resigned, some even demanding that they remit duties which had been collected under the Sugar Act, they were able to hold out until word came that the Philadelphia officers had begun to clear ships and that the Surveyor General approved. After they opened the port, on December 4, they wrote to the Commissioners of the Customs: "This step, we thought the more adviseable as we understood the Mob (which are daily increasing and gathering Strength, from the arrival of Seamen, and none going out, and who are the people that are most dangerous on these occasions, as their whole dependance for a subsistence is upon Trade) were soon to have a Meeting." [13] From such a meeting the officers knew what to expect.

Once the Collector and Comptroller began to issue clearances the pressure of the mob in New York slackened, but the situation was complicated by the action of Captain Archibald Kennedy of His Majesty's Ship *Coventry*. Captain Kennedy stopped all vessels he could catch leaving New York, and upon finding the clearance papers unstamped, refused to allow them to proceed. At the same time he allowed vessels to enter unmolested even when their papers, though dated after November first, were unstamped.[14] There continued therefore to be a large floating population of seamen in New York City, who kept the officers of government uneasy.

Duncan Stewart, the Collector of New London, held off the anxious merchants of that port for several weeks, awaiting instructions from John Temple, the Surveyor General in Boston. While Temple, Bernard, and the customs officers in Boston tossed the problem back and

12. Charles Stewart to Commissioners of Customs, December 8, 1765, House of Lords Manuscripts, February 19, 1766.

13. Collector and Comptroller of New York to Commissioners of Customs, November 6, 1765, Treasury Papers, Class I, Bundle 442; same to same, December 20, 1765, House of Lords Manuscripts, February 14, 1766.

14. *Ibid.*

forth, Stewart was forced to give way and opened the port on December 14, three days before Boston.[15] Within two weeks New Haven, the only other port of any consequence in Connecticut, had also resumed business.[16]

The custom-house at Portsmouth, New Hampshire, which was also under John Temple's jurisdiction, remained closed for a few days after the opening in Boston.[17] But New Hampshire ships had not all been gathering barnacles in port. Somewhere around December fourth Captain John Langdon had put his ship *Hector* out of Portsmouth Harbor for Montserrat, apparently without clearance papers of any kind, and was shortly sending back information about what ports in the West Indies could be safely entered without stamps, so that when officers at Portsmouth began issuing clearances, a fleet of New Hampshire vessels was ready to drive southward to resume the interrupted trade.[18]

Maryland and the Carolinas were last to issue unstamped clearances. On January 30, 1766, the *Maryland Gazette* announced that vessels had cleared last month from Oxford and Pocomoke without stamps and were now clearing from Annapolis in the same way, employing certificates that no stamps were to be had. The issue was not forced until February in the Carolinas. Peter Randolph, as Surveyor General for the whole Southern District from Florida to Maryland, could conceivably have speeded up the opening of these ports the way he did in Virginia. There is some evidence that he attempted to, but was foiled by zealous governors and customs officers. In January Randolph had made a trip to Charleston and dropped some strong hints to the effect that trade should proceed. These excited the people there, who thought as Henry Laurens acidly observed, that Randolph "had power to annihilate Acts of Parliament." There ensued a verbal battle between the Governor on one side and Randolph and the Assembly on the other, the latter buttressed by petitions from the merchants and the owners and masters of vessels and by the increas-

15. Duncan Stewart to John Temple, December 19, 1765, House of Lords Manuscripts, March 13, 1766.

16. *Connecticut Courant,* February 10, 1766.

17. Benning Wentworth in a letter to the Lords of Trade, December 16, 1765 (photostat in New Hampshire Historical Society) said that the port was still closed. *New Hampshire Gazette,* December 20, 1765, printed a notice of three ships entered at the Custom House during the preceding week, but none cleared out. Subsequent issues of the *Gazette* omitted the customary Custom House records. The port was probably opened as a result of a popular demonstration on December 26, 1765, described in a letter of that date from George Meserve to the Stamp Office, House of Lords Manuscripts, February 14, 1766.

18. See shipping agreements and correspondence of John Langdon in the Langdon Papers, New Hampshire Historical Society.

ing commotions of the populace. The Governor capitulated after Caleb Lloyd issued a public notice "that he adhered to his former resolution not to distribute Stamp'd Paper," and on February 4, began issuing certificates to be attached to clearance papers, testifying to the unavailability of stamps. One difficulty remained: the Collector still refused to budge until some superior should give him written orders. Randolph by this time was getting cold feet, and though he repeatedly advised the Collector to proceed, he would not order him to do so, and neither would the Governor. How this impasse was overcome is not apparent from the surviving records, but it was overcome, for by the last week in February vessels from South Carolina were arriving in other colonies.[19]

In North Carolina Governor Tryon at first attempted to secure submission to the Stamp Act by a shrewder strategy than any other governor devised. Sensing that the Assembly might imitate the Virginia Resolves or send delegates to the Congress at New York, he kept them prorogued. At the same time he summoned fifty leading gentlemen from Brunswick, New Hanover, and Bladen counties to meet with him on November 18. After wining and dining them, he explained his own disapproval of the Stamp Act and his particular concern for the people of North Carolina. He would write to England, he said, in terms that would bring a "favorable indulgence and exemption" for North Carolina, whether the Act were repealed or not, provided, of course, that the people did not frustrate his efforts by their own conduct. He recommended that they accept the stamps during the brief period before Parliament repealed the Act or exempted them from it. By so doing they would enjoy unusual opportunities for trade, while the merchants of other colonies twiddled their thumbs. As a further inducement he offered to pay from his own pocket the cost of the stamps on documents from which he derived a fee as governor, such as deeds, wills, and licenses.

The temptation to break ranks and use the stamps must have been great; yet the gentlemen who dined with Governor Tryon answered him the next day with a firm and dignified refusal. To submit to any part of the Act they said, "would put it out of our Power to refuse with any Propriety, a Submission to the Whole; and as we can never consent to be deprived of the invaluable Privilege of a Trial by Jury,

19. Henry Laurens to John Gervais, January 31, 1766, to Rosset and Gervais, February 4, 1766, Laurens Letter Book, Historical Society of Pennsylvania; extracts from the Journals of the Commons House of Assembly of South Carolina, and correspondence between Peter Randolph and Governor Bull, in Colonial Office Papers, Class 5, vol. 649, Library of Congress transcripts; *Virginia Gazette* (Purdie), March 14, 1766; *Maryland Gazette*, March 13, 1766.

which is one part of that Act, we think it more consistent as well as securer conduct to prevent to the utmost of our Power, the operation of it."

The North Carolinians refused to seek prosperity at the expense of the other colonies. In fact they were still twiddling their own thumbs with the custom-houses closed for several weeks after most other colonies had resumed trade. But by February 12 all ports except Cape Fear were open. The matter did not come to a head there until February 21. Early in January Captain Lobb of His Majesty's Sloop *Viper* had seized three ships entering the Cape Fear River, because their clearance papers, issued in other ports, were unstamped. On February 15 the King's Attorney, Robert Jones, gave his opinion that the seizures were legal and that William Dry, the Collector at Brunswick, should prosecute the vessels in the Admiralty Court at Halifax. As a result the men from Brunswick, New Hanover, and Bladen counties assembled on February 18 in Wilmington where they formed an association to prevent the operation of the Stamp Act. Their organization perfected, they marched on Brunswick a thousand strong and for the next three days were in complete control of the town and port. With the Collector in their power they ransacked his desk for the papers of the seized ships and, having found them, secured from Dry and Lobb not only the release of the vessels but a promise that the port would henceforth be stamp-free. Finally, on February 21, they rounded up all available customs and court officers and forced them to swear an oath not to execute the Stamp Act. Satisfied by this wholesale abjuration, they dispersed, many of them sailing triumphantly back to Wilmington on the liberated sloops.[20]

As previously noted, Georgia, without official notice of the Act, had carried on her shipping as usual until the end of November. When Governor Wright put an end to the unstamped clearances on November 30, neither stamps nor distributor had yet arrived; but Wright, once having learned what England expected of him, adhered strictly to his duty, and Georgia merchants, ship-owners, and captains petitioned in vain for business to proceed as it did in Virginia. When George Angus finally did arrive and under close guard distributed stamps for the customs officers, the latter were able to clear some sixty ships on stamped paper between January 17 and January 30. The Savannah merchants were willing to play the role which those of North Carolina had disdained, and they earned the hatred and contempt of the other colonists for this betrayal of American unity. The country people of Georgia, who were also outraged, gathered in all

20. *Colonial Records of North Carolina,* VII, 127-130, 168-183.

parts of the province for a march on Savannah. On January 27 Governor Wright heard that there were at least six hundred of them, all armed, and without waiting for them to arrive, he rushed the stamped papers to Fort George on Cockspur Island and from there to His Majesty's Sloop *Speedwell*. By this move he saved the papers from destruction but also saved them from use, for on the island and the warship they were as effectively removed from circulation as the mob could wish.[21] The *Pennsylvania Journal* of February 27, reporting this episode, stated that as a result of it the port was operating without stamps.[22]

The opening of the ports in defiance of the Stamp Act had been accomplished in most colonies within less than two months of the date when the Act was supposed to have gone into effect and in all the colonies before the Act was repealed. The interval from November first to the time when officers began to issue clearances, was not a comfortable time for anyone, except perhaps the wheat farmers of the middle colonies. Events which cause trouble for the rest of the population frequently blow their saving good in the direction of the farmers. In the summer of 1765, when it began to appear that New England's ports might be closed on November first, merchants there began to buy heavily in the Philadelphia and New York flour markets. The result was a scarcity of flour and booming prices even before the first of November. In Philadelphia the ships which had obtained their clearance papers with nearly empty holds continued the competition throughout November; and when clearances were issued again in December the prospect of the ice closing the port more effectively than the stamps had, caused the merchants to raise prices again in order to get the farmers to bring their crops to market before it was too late.[23]

This boomtime for farmers was accompanied by high prices and short rations for the rest of the population. In New York the export of flour before November 1 had been so large that there was a shortage of bread, and at the same time the accumulation of ships in the

21. *Pennsylvania Journal*, February 13, 1766; *Colonial Records of Georgia*, IX, 454-456; James Habersham to Daniel Roubadeau, December 17, 1765, to William Knox, January 29, 1766, Georgia Historical Society, *Collections*, 6 (1904), 56-58; Percy Scott Flippen, "Royal Government in Georgia, 1752-1776," *Georgia Historical Quarterly*, 13 (1929), 142-149; Jones, *History of Georgia*, II, 60-64.

22. Though newspaper accounts during these days were not wholly reliable, the report seems to be substantiated by records of shipping bonds posted during February, March, and April. See Georgia Historical Society, *Collections*, 8 (1913), 259 ff.

23. Thomas Clifford to Harper and Hartshorn, October 8, 1765, November 1, 1765, Pemberton Papers; Abel James and Henry Drinker to Lewis Teissier, December 18, 1765, James and Drinker Letter Books.

harbor under Captain Kennedy's ban increased the population and the demand for bread. The winter of 1765 was a lean one for New Yorkers and probably for the people of other colonial cities.[24]

The colonial merchants, in spite of their success in resuming trade, were by no means happy about the risks they were running. In most cases they had to waive all claims for damages in case their imperfect clearance papers should result in seizure of their vessels. At first they hardly knew where to send their ships. Rumor had it that vessels arriving in the West Indies without stamped papers were being seized, and to send ships to England would be asking for trouble. Many diverted their vessels to the Lisbon trade or the Irish; or to carrying provisions to the northern colonies. Some sent their captains to nose their vessels cautiously into West Indian ports; but all felt the danger of seizure hanging over them and had to choose between that and idle hulls.[25]

In the West Indies the repercussion of the continental opposition to the Stamp Act was felt not merely in similar outbreaks of violence but in a shortage of supplies. The temporary closing of North American continental ports and the reluctance of American merchants to risk their ships in West Indian waters with unstamped clearance papers cut sharply into the flow of provisions and lumber upon which the Islanders depended. A planter in Antigua wrote on December 22, 1765, "Our Crop promises well, but we are likely to be Miserably off for want of Lumber and Northward Provisions, as the North Americans are determined not to submit to the Stamp Act, and of course cannot clear out their Vessells, shou'd this be of any continuance, the Islands (nay the Merchants in England as our Remittances principally center there) will feel the Effects severely, for there is not One tenth part of the Lumber in the Islands that will be required for the next crop . . . when we're deprived of a Trade from the Northward, the Estates here can never be supported." [26]

Meanwhile trade returned to normal. Quebec, Nova Scotia, Florida, Barbados, Grenada, and Jamaica consistently made use of the stamps—to the great disgust of the other colonies—but even in these

24. William Bayard and Co. to John Henniker, December 21, 1765, House of Lords Manuscripts, February 14, 1766.

25. *Maryland Gazette*, January 30, 1766; Abel James and Henry Drinker, letters dated December 7, 27, 28, 1765, January 1, February 8, February 20, May 14, 1766, James and Drinker Letter Books; Thomas Clifford to Captain John Harper, December 16, 1765, Pemberton Papers.

26. Treasury Papers, Class I, Bundle 452. Part of the shortage in the West Indies was due to resentment by the continental colonies against those of the islands, especially Barbados, which had submitted to the Stamp Act. See *Maryland Gazette*, January 30, 1766; *Georgia Gazette*, June 11, 1766.

places ships arriving with unstamped papers from other American ports were unmolested.[27] Before the Act was repealed, American ship captains discovered that they could land in England itself without stamps,[28] and enterprising Philadelphia firms were issuing insurance against seizure at the rate of $2\frac{1}{2}\%$, sufficient evidence that the British Navy was not making much effort to enforce the Act.[29] The temporary closing of the ports, besides upsetting the course of trade and causing unexpected scarcities in various regions, had only one important effect, an effect which could scarcely have pleased the authors of the Stamp Act: it caused an increase in smuggling and a corresponding decline in respect for British authority. Though the customs officers finally gave way before the pressure, they waited long enough for the colonists to exhibit their contempt for an unconstitutional law. The officers at New York reported that "vessells were continually going and coming without any regard to the Customhouse or the Laws of trade, and we didn't dare neither would it have been prudent to take any Notice of them;"[30] and from Philadelphia the officers wrote plaintively that so long as the Americans were determined not to use stamps, "we must now submit to necessity, and do without them, or else in a little time, people will learn to do without either them or us."[31]

In the other colonies, as in Boston, the Sons of Liberty were less successful in opening the courts without stamps than they were in opening the ports. One reason for this defection may have been the occupational conservatism of lawyers and judges. This, however, was only one reason, and perhaps not the most important. When the Revolution did come ten years later, the people of Berkshire County, Massachusetts, kept the courts closed for five years, and not because

27. *Virginia Gazette* (Purdie), March 7, March 21, April 4, 1766; *Maryland Gazette*, March 13, 1766; *Pennsylvania Journal*, March 6, 1766; Lord Colville to Philip Stephens, February 10, 1766, Admiralty Secretary In Letters 482; Governor of Barbados to Charles Lowndes, February 24, 1766, Treasury Papers, Class I, Bundle 452; Colonial Office Papers, Class 5, LXVI, 273 (the last three are in the Public Record Office, Library of Congress transcripts); Massachusetts Historical Society, *Collections*, 69 (1914), 143; W. B. Kerr, "The Stamp Act in Quebec," *English Historical Review*, 47 (1932), 648-651; W. B. Kerr, "The Stamp Act in Nova Scotia," *New England Quarterly*, 6 (1933), 552-566.

28. *Pennsylvania Journal*, March 6, 1766; House of Lords Manuscripts, March 5, March 7, 1766.

29. *North Carolina Gazette*, February 26, 1766, quoted in *Colonial Records of North Carolina*, VII, 168 f.; *Pennsylvania Journal*, April 10, 1766.

30. Collector and Comptroller of New York to Commissioners of Customs, December 20, 1765, House of Lords Manuscripts, February 14, 1766.

31. Collector and Comptroller of Philadelphia to Commissioners of Customs, December 1, 1765, Treasury Papers, Class I, Bundle 442.

of any lingering loyalty to Great Britain. The temporary closing of the ports benefited only the farmers, and even this benefit would have turned to disaster if the closing had been more than temporary. The closing of the courts, on the other hand, was a decided advantage for a great many people. The proceedings in criminal courts did not require stamps so that the community suffered no interruption in the prosecution of criminals, but the admiralty courts, like the civil courts, could not properly function without stamped papers. The effect of closing the courts, therefore, was to render the opening of the ports less risky, for with the admiralty courts closed the means of enforcing both the Stamp Act and the Acts of Trade was removed. The Court at Halifax was still open, to be sure, for the stamps were in use there, but there was great inconvenience in carrying cases so far, and the impossibility of trying them in local courts left the naval and customs officers in a quandary. If they seized a vessel, whether for smuggling or for sailing without stamped papers, they could not tell how long it would be before they would be able to have her condemned in court, and they were uncertain how long they were entitled to hold her without trial. In these circumstances they were apt to overlook violations which they might otherwise have stopped.[32]

Besides facilitating the movement of trade in this way, the closing of the courts benefited everyone who was in debt. Henry Laurens even suspected that the champions of resistance to the Stamp Act intended to "obtain a Credit during their own pleasure by the distruction of the Stamp'd Papers," [33] for as long as the courts remained closed it was impossible for creditors to bring suit, and if the amount of litigation in colonial courts is any indication, colonial debtors seldom paid until a judge ordered them to.

In colonies where a large number of people were indebted to creditors outside the colony there was a decided advantage in keeping the courts closed. William Samuel Johnson in Fairfield, Connecticut, wrote to his friend Eliphalet Dyer (both were active opponents of the Stamp Act), "Our being so excessively in debt to the Neighbouring Governments seems to be a Reason peculiar to us why we sho'd be less hasty than others in opening the Courts of Law, but I am not fully determined what is best in this matter." [34] Even before the pas-

32. See letters from the Deputy Collector at New York to the Attorney General, no date, Philadelphia Custom House Papers, IV, and from Captain Sterling of the *Rainbow* to the Lords of the Admiralty, November 5, 1765, House of Lords Manuscripts, January 29, 1766.

33. Henry Laurens to Joseph Brown, October 22, 1765, Henry Laurens Letter Book.

34. December 31, 1765, William Samuel Johnson Papers, Connecticut Historical Society. Cf. Lawrence H. Gipson, *Jared Ingersoll* (New Haven, 1920), 214-216.

sage of the Stamp Act, the indebtedness of Connecticut had caused a shortage of currency and recourse to barter.[35] The closing of the courts gave a temporary respite from the drain of money out of the colony. Although the radicals felt obliged for the sake of political consistency to demand that the courts ignore an unconstitutional law,[36] it is not surprising that Connecticut courts remained closed. When they opened again, after repeal of the Stamp Act, Johnson reported that there were "Riots and Tumults among the People who having so long been loose from the curse of the Law unwillingly submit again to its necessary restraints." [37]

The same shortage of currency which Connecticut felt because of her outside indebtedness was created or aggravated in the colonies south of New England by the new Currency Act. Since this was not an act of taxation, the colonists made no attempt to nullify it as a measure beyond the authority of Parliament, but the closing of the courts in some measure helped to ease the problems which it presented. While the Currency Act tended to raise the value of money and thus make the payment of debts more difficult, the closing of the courts prevented the collection of debts and thus tended to reduce the demand for, and the value of, money.

The fact that the creditors of colonial debtors were in many cases English merchants was another reason for keeping the courts closed. If the Stamp Act prevented English merchants from collecting their debts in the colonies they would be all the more anxious to secure repeal of the Act. This line of reasoning operated strongly in Virginia where, as is well known, the tobacco planters were heavily indebted to English creditors. George Washington, anticipating as early as September 20, 1765, that the Stamp Act would close the courts, saw the consequences clearly: "if a stop be put to our judicial proceedings I fancy the Merchants of G. Britain trading to the Colonies will not be among the last to wish for a Repeal of it." [38]

Of course the English merchants were not the only ones to suffer by the suspension of judicial proceedings. No one engaged in commerce on a credit basis was apt to be entirely a creditor or entirely

35. Connecticut Courant, March 11, May 20, June 10, August 26, September 2, 1765; Oscar Zeichner, Connecticut's Years of Controversy, 1750-1776 (Chapel Hill, 1949), 46-48.

36. Sons of Liberty of Norwich, Connecticut, to Sons of Liberty of Portsmouth, New Hampshire, March 3, 1766, Belknap Papers, Massachusetts Historical Society; Resolves of the Meeting at Pomfret, Boston Gazette, January 13, 1766.

37. June 25, 1766, William Samuel Johnson Papers, Connecticut Historical Society.

38. John C. Fitzpatrick, ed., The Writings of George Washington (Washington, 1931-1944), II, 426. Cf. the extract of a letter from Philadelphia in London Chronicle, December 5-7, 1765.

a debtor. If the closing of the courts freed a man from paying one debt, it might also prevent him from collecting another, and, depending upon the exact condition of his current legal obligations, he might be either ahead of the game or far behind. If he had just lost a suit at law and was thereby obliged to pay, it would be impossible for him to collect from his own debtors; and it might be equally impossible for him to borrow money, because the bond which might be required as security also had to be stamped. Thus Abel James and Henry Drinker, Philadelphia business partners, wrote on October 14, 1765, of their melancholy thoughts "on the many Mischiefs that will attend us in that we shall not be able to commence Actions against Persons who are indebted to us nor proceed legally in many other Respects, until it is some Way Settled. In Short we know not whose Lot it may be to be ruin'd. . . ." [39] After the courts were closed, these lamentations were justified, for another Philadelphia business man reported on December 11, 1765, that "No writs are issued, No land can be Conveyed, No Bonds can be taken; Some take the Opportunity to walk off without paying their debts, others dont pay knowing they can't be sued, thus we are in the utmost confusion." [40]

A few creditors who were shrewd enough to perceive in advance the exact consequences of the suspension were able to make a good thing of it. The *Connecticut Courant* reported on February 17, 1766, from Amenia precinct, New York, that

Men of very considerable Interests (having become Surety for large Sums of Money, to be paid to Gentlemen in New York, barely to oblige a Friend in Connecticut) have unreasonably suffered, by those Gentlemen in New York, who were foresighted enough to procure Executions in Season; so that they might get their Money, notwithstanding the Stamp Act; and those men of Interest are not now in a capacity to recover their Dues in Connecticut, or elsewhere, on account of said Act. Four or Five Hundred Pounds worth of Estate, is bid off at Vendue, for just such or such a Sum of Money as the most monied Man there present seems to be possessed of—and that Sum seldom exceeds a Tenth of the real Worth, and the Buyer commonly appears to be the Officer, or Vendue-Master, frequently an Under-Sheriff, or Bum-Bailiff, and made up of the most Trickish of our Species.

39. To David Barclay and Sons, James and Drinker Letter Books.
40. Letter Book of John Reynell, Historical Society of Pennsylvania. For similar complaints, see Daniel Roberdeau to John Gill, November 27, 1765, Roberdeau Letter Book, Historical Society of Pennsylvania; Abel James and Henry Drinker to Stephen Skinner, March 10, 1766, James and Drinker Letter Books; William Samuel Johnson, letters to clients, dated November 21, 1765, January 10, February 10, 12, March 11, 1766, William Samuel Johnson Papers, Connecticut Historical Society.

It was not the speculators alone who profited from the suspension of justice in New York. According to a writer in the *New York Gazette* on February 20, 1766, "a large Majority of the Inhabitants of the Colony where I live, esteem the present Cessation of Business as a Kind of Jubilee." The farmers of the Hudson Valley, who enjoyed high prices for their produce because of the scarcity caused by closing the ports, seem to have obtained also a brief respite in the payment of their rents. Certainly landlords were unable to evict any who refused to pay, and when the reopening of the courts in the spring of 1766 brought evictions, riots broke out in the Hudson Valley which required troops to suppress.[41]

The economic confusion created by closing the courts echoed the confusion in the minds of lawyers and judges about the reasons for closing them and the extent to which they should be closed. No one suggested that the courts should make use of stamped papers even if they could be had, but opinions varied widely on the question of whether to shut down entirely or to proceed without stamps. Edmund Pendleton, writing to James Madison on December 11, 1765, thought it unwise to close completely, because "the appearance of courts may convince the people that there is not a total end of laws tho' they are disabled to act in some instances, I think they should be held for that purpose and as many things done as can be without stamps, particularly wills, which may be proved and ordered to be recorded, tho' they can't be recorded nor any order made for the appraisement. Administrations can't be granted because the Bond can't be taken. Grand jurys may be sworn and all proceedings had on their presentments and on all criminal matters or breaches of the peace. Justices may issue and trie any warrants or Attachments relative to themselves, but not attachments returnable to Court. . . ."[42]

By February 15, 1766, Pendleton wanted the courts to proceed in all business without stamps but admitted that this might lead the Governor to revoke the commissions of the judges, "and as none that are fit for it will and others dare not succeed them, a total privation of majestracy must follow, and [not] even the peace must be kept, . . ." Pendleton was also bothered by the problem which must arise by the inferior courts opening—as many of them did—without the superior court agreeing to do so: everyone who lost his suit in the inferior court would appeal, and the superior court would disallow the decision because of the lack of stamps on the proceedings. In spite of

41. William Samuel Johnson to Christopher Gadsden, June 25, 1766, William Samuel Johnson Papers, Connecticut Historical Society.

42. Massachusetts Historical Society, *Proceedings*, 2d ser., 19 (1905), 109.

these difficulties Pendleton thought that the courts should open. He had taken an oath to determine cases according to law, and since he believed that Parliament had had no authority to pass the Stamp Act, he could not regard that Act as a law and felt that it would be a violation of his oath if he refused to proceed because of it.[43] In his own county, as in most counties of Virginia, the other judges were more cautious and thought it best to wait a little longer; but in Accomac County the judges opened court and even warned the lawyers "that any attorney neglecting to carry on his business in court, under pretence of wanting stamps, should have his suits dismissed." [44]

In general it was the lawyers rather than the judges who gave the appearance of being most anxious to open the courts, though it was only an appearance. The lawyers in Boston had argued persuasively for opening on the same ground that Pendleton urged, that the Stamp Act was ipso facto null and void and that the judges should perform something like judicial review by ignoring it. Other lawyers wanted the courts to proceed without stamps on the ground that none were available, and that plaintiffs should not be denied justice simply because of the action of a mob. Still others pointed out, what in most cases was true on November 1, that the colonial governments had not been officially notified of the Stamp Act and that the distributors, even had they wished to execute their offices, had not received commissions, so that in terms of law the Act was only a rumor and not deserving of recognition. On one ground or another most colonial lawyers agreed that the courts should open without stamps, but when it came to action, their eloquence left them. As we have seen, when the Superior Court of Massachusetts gave way to popular pressure and agreed to do business without stamps, even those who had argued for the opening were unwilling to risk their own future or their clients' interests by trying a case.[45]

The lawyers in other colonies showed much the same vacillation. In Philadelphia they had a meeting on October 16 to decide what they should do after the first of November. According to Edward Shippen, Jr., who was present:

A Variety of sentiments at first appeared, but after some Debate it was carried by a Majority that tho we might perhaps be justified in America in practising in our usual way without stampt paper when none is to be had; Yet if the Parliament of England should determine

43. Pendleton to James Madison, Sr., February 15, 1766, *ibid.*, 109-111.
44. *Pennsylvania Journal*, March 20, 1766. Cf. *Connecticut Courant*, November 1, 1765; *Virginia Gazette* (Purdie), March 21, 1766.
45. See above, ch. 8.

to force the Act down our Throats, they would immediately set Pros-
ecutions on foot against the principal civil-officers who had ventured
to risque the Penalties, in order to strike a Terror into the other Inhabitants; and in that Case they would undoubtedly make Equity
and Law give way to Policy, in their Determinations—And what
American Fortune could withstand them—So that, upon the whole
we determined to do no Act whatsoever after the first of November
in our several Offices to hazard the penalties—However we are shortly
after that to have another Meeting. . . .[46]

The Philadelphia lawyers had several meetings after the first of
November, but in spite of a general agreement that they ought to act
without stamps could not quite bring themselves to do so. On November 25, at what was evidently a typical meeting, the only voices
against proceeding without stamps were those of John Ross and
Joseph Galloway. Ross was too drunk to argue effectively, so that the
entire burden fell upon Galloway. His arguments were demolished
by the rest of the company, but the meeting nevertheless agreed to
desist "till some other Government had sett us the Example." [47] The
neighboring governments of Delaware and Maryland did set the example,[48] but the Pennsylvania courts—with a few exceptions among
the inferior, county courts—stayed closed.

In New Jersey, as in Pennsylvania, the lawyers made a loud public
noise about their opposition to the Act, but they opposed it by ceasing to do business in court, even though the judges declared themselves ready to act. When a promise was finally extracted from the
lawyers to proceed after April first, the news of repeal extricated
them from their dilemma.[49] In New York the lawyers passed a resolution in December to do business without stamps, but according to
William Samuel Johnson, the purpose of this was simply to take the
embarrassing problem from their own hands and pass it on to the
judges.[50]

46. Edward Shippen, Jr., to Edward Shippen, October 17, 1765, Shippen Papers, XI,
Historical Society of Pennsylvania.
47. Richard Peters, Jr., to Jasper Yeates, November 26, 1765, Yeates Papers, Historical Society of Pennsylvania. Cf. Ernest H. Baldwin, "Joseph Galloway the Loyalist
Politician," Pa. Mag. of Hist., 26 (1902), 290-291.
48. Edward Shippen, Jr., to Edward Shippen, February 22, 1766, Shippen Papers, XI;
Pennsylvania Journal, February 27, March 20, 1766; Maryland Gazette, December 10,
1765, April 3, 1766; Charles A. Barker, The Background of the Revolution in Maryland
(New Haven, 1940), 308-311.
49. Richard Smith to the Sons of Liberty in New York, March 15, 1766, William
L. Clements Library; Archives of the State of New Jersey, 1st ser., 9 (1885), 531-533, 536-
548; 24 (1902), 639-640, 660-662; 25 (1903), 30-31, but cf. p. 36.
50. William Samuel Johnson to Eliphalet Dyer, December 31, 1765, William Samuel
Johnson Papers, Connecticut Historical Society.

In most cases the judges were no more eager than the lawyers to make the dangerous decision of proceeding without stamps or the increasingly dangerous one of not proceeding at all. Wherever the courts were bent on evading the problem, they did so by successive adjournments until news of repeal arrived. The first news of that event reached the colonies early in April, and the interval of five months was not much longer than the normal interval between sessions.

Where the courts did wish to disregard the Act, they were sometimes prevented by the tactics of the royal governors. In New York some of the judges of the Court of Common Pleas had prepared to take the lawyers at their word and to open in January. They drew up a memorial to justify the action, and since they happened to be members of the Governor's Council as well as judges, proposed to present the memorial to the Governor and have him enter it in the council minutes, "as if," stormed Governor Moore, "so wretched an expedient could be any justification for their disobedience to an Act of Parliament." Moore anticipated this stratagem by collaring the Chief Justice and warning him that any judge who sat upon a case in which the documents were not properly stamped, could expect to lose his seat in the Council as well as his seat on the bench. The threat apparently worked, for on February 20, Moore wrote to Secretary Conway, that "what I then said to the Cheif Justice had the proper effect on him as well as on his bretheren." [51]

In South Carolina the Governor joined with the Clerk of Court to prevent the opening, though not without causing a lively controversy. On November 13, the Court of Common Pleas had met at Charleston with Chief Justice Shinner alone on the bench. Shinner caused an order to be entered in the books stating that because of the lack of stamped papers, which the Distributor had refused to supply, it was necessary to adjourn the Court until December 3. Thereafter adjournment was successively continued until March 4, 1766. On that date three new Associate Justices appeared and after taking their seats prepared to hear cases without the use of stamps. The Attorney General objected to this procedure, and in view of the possibility of a repeal of the Stamp Act in the near future the Court once more adjourned, this time until April 1. On that date, having assembled once more the Associate Judges determined to proceed in spite of the dissent of the Chief Justice. They would doubtless have succeeded had it not been for the Clerk, Dougal Campbell, who refused to issue

51. E. B. O'Callaghan, ed., *Documents Relative to the Colonial History of the State of New York* (Albany, 1856-1887), VII, 806, 811.

a Writ of Venire for the jury. Without the Writ there could be no jury, and without a jury there could be no trial. The judges requested Lieutenant-Governor Bull to suspend Campbell, but Bull stood by the Clerk, and the Court put the matter before the General Assembly. The Assembly was already considering a memorial presented by the merchants and traders of Charleston, objecting to the closing of the courts. It was not, said the merchants, the business of litigants to provide stamps for the Court, and since the Court did not have the stamps itself, it must go on without them. The Assembly was sympathetic to the merchants, and they too appealed to Bull; but he remained firm, and they were obliged to content themselves with resolutions in favor of the Court's right to make all orders for the regulation of its own practice. The Court itself imposed a fine of £100 sterling on Campbell when they met in May after repeal of the Stamp Act, but Governor Bull had the last word by suspending the punishment.[52]

Rhode Island was the one colony which kept all its courts open without interruption. Fortified by the resolution of the General Assembly which promised indemnity to all officers who disregarded the Stamp Act, the judges both of the inferior courts and the superior court held their sessions according to the regular schedule. The only impediment to the sitting of the courts is recorded laconically in the journal of the Superior Court held at Providence on the third Monday in March: "The Kings Attorney being absent, at this Term the Court appointed Silas Downer to act as Attorney General in his Room." [53] The King's Attorney, as it happened, was Augustus Johnston. It would have been asking too much to expect that the Stamp Distributor should appear in court as attorney, to flout the very law under which he had been appointed. The appointment of Silas Downer in his place was an act of ironical boldness: Silas Downer was the Corresponding Secretary of the Providence Sons of Liberty.[54]

The only other colonies in which all courts were opened before news of repeal had arrived were New Hampshire, Maryland, and Delaware. The New Hampshire Superior Court was apparently

---

52. Governor Bull to Lords of Trade, May 20, 1766, and Minutes of Inferior Court of Common Pleas, Treasury Papers, Class I, Bundle 445; Henry Laurens to John Lewis Gervais, September 1, 1766, Laurens Letter Book; Edward McCrady, *The History of South Carolina under the Royal Government, 1719-1776* (New York, 1899), 572-575.

53. Records of the Superior Court, Office of the Clerk of the Supreme Court, Providence.

54. See documents in his hand in Rhode Island Historical Society Manuscripts, XII, and Peck Manuscripts, III, Rhode Island Historical Society.

closed until February, but on February 6, it met, with Chief Justice
Theodore Atkinson presiding. At this meeting the Clerk behaved
precisely as Dougal Campbell later behaved in South Carolina: he
refused to issue writs or summonses without stamped paper. But the
judges of the New Hampshire Court quickly put him in his place by
requiring him to enter the following order on the record in extra
large script:

The Justices considering the Necessity and Expediency for the
Preservation of the Peace and good Order of the Province of holding
this Court and the having Business done as usuall and No Stampt
Paper to be had, in this Province, do order and Command the Clerk
of this Court to issue all Writs, Processes and Copies as usual, without Stampt Paper.[55]

Two days later the Portsmouth Sons of Liberty reported that "Law
and Justice go on in their proper course without obstruction." [56]

The Delaware Courts, according to the newspapers at least, were
opened in February at the insistence of the Grand Jury. In most colonies there was no interruption in the trial of criminals, for the
Stamp Act imposed no tax on the documents used in criminal cases.
It was only the civil courts which were closed. The Grand Jury of
Delaware, charged with indicting criminals, refused to perform their
task until they were assured that the civil courts would be opened.[57]

In Maryland some of the inferior courts began to open as early as
November, but the Superior Court held out until the Sons of Liberty from all over the colony staged a meeting at Annapolis on April
1, and demanded its opening. Though the judges at first refused,
they changed their minds when the Sons of Liberty repeated the demand with "united Hearts and Voices." Four days later news of repeal arrived to ease the consciences of the judges.[58]

With the exception of scattered inferior courts in the other colonies,[59] these were the only courts which opened in defiance of the
Stamp Act. It is apparent, however, that if the Act had continued on

55. Superior Court Records of New Hampshire, New Hampshire Historical Society.
On New Hampshire inferior courts see *New Hampshire Gazette*, January 24, 1766; Otis
G. Hammond, ed., *Probate Records of the Province of New Hampshire*, VIII (Concord,
1940), shows several wills proved between November 1, 1765 and May, 1766.

56. To Sons of Liberty in Boston, Belknap Papers.

57. *Pennsylvania Journal*, February 27, 1766.

58. *Maryland Gazette*, December 10, 1765, April 3, 1766; Barker, *Background of the
Revolution in Maryland*, 308-311.

59. I have found evidence of inferior courts being open in North Carolina, Virginia,
Pennsylvania, and New Jersey.

the books for a month or two longer, the courts of every colony which later participated in the Revolution, might have been forced to ignore it. Popular demonstrations had already opened many courts, and it is probable that further demonstrations were forestalled by news of repeal.

It is doubtful that the closing of the courts in any colony worked excessive hardships, except perhaps those involved in the foreclosures in Amenia Precinct, New York. Their suspension may have thwarted the colonists' fondness for litigation, but the law's delay has always been one of the facts of life, as inescapable as death and taxes. An additional five months probably meant little to anyone except the radicals. They worried about the tacit admission of Parliamentary authority that was involved. Charles Carroll of Carrollton, for example, argued that "A suspense from business implies a tacit acquaintance of the law, or at least the right of the power of imposing such laws upon us." [60] And Richard Henry Lee wished that the Virginians could let the northern colonies know that the closing of Virginia's courts did not proceed from any regard to the Stamp Act but was simply the best way for Virginians to bring pressure on English merchants to demand repeal.[61] Even had the courts been opened, however, it would have been no great victory for the view which denied the authority of Parliament to tax the colonies, unless the judges had taken advantage of the occasion to declare the Stamp Act null and void. The judges who forced the opening in New Hampshire and those who tried to force it in South Carolina proceeded on the ground that justice should not be stopped simply because no stamps were available. William Samuel Johnson pointed out to his friend, Christopher Gadsden that the South Carolina justices would have played a more worthy part by "demonstrating the unconstitutional nature of the Stamp Act, and thence deducing the Legality of proceeding in Business without taking any Notice of it." But he admitted that "it would have been a very delicate point for a Judge to have Insisted upon in a Court of Law." [62] Marbury vs. Madison was still a long way off.

The closing of the courts and ports was the direct and foreseen result of forcing the stamp distributors to resign. The colonists pried open the ports before the closing had caused serious damage. It seems

60. Barker, *Background of the Revolution in Maryland*, 309.
61. R. H. Lee to Landon Carter, February 24, 1766, James C. Ballagh, ed., *The Letters of Richard Henry Lee* (New York, 1911), I, 15.
62. June 25, 1766, William Samuel Johnson Papers, Connecticut Historical Society.

apparent that they would have forced the opening of the courts also in time to prevent any very grave consequences. But by the time they had begun to be irritated by the lack of litigation, they were faced with a more serious problem, also proceeding from the resignation of the stamp distributors and also not wholly unforeseen. Parliament, it appeared, had recognized the challenge to its authority and might shortly call the unruly children to account.

ELEVEN

DIRECTION

Sons of Liberty

WHEN news of American resistance to the Stamp Act reached England, George Grenville and his friends had been replaced in the government by the men who had opposed the passage of the Stamp Act—though not because they had opposed it. To General Conway, who was now revered all over America, fell the embarrassing task of dealing with the rebellious colonists whose cause he had upheld. Conway, as Secretary of State for the Southern Department, wrote to the colonial governors, deploring the treatment of the stamp distributors. "It is hoped and expected," he said, "that this Want of confidence in the Justice and Tenderness of the Mother Country, and this open Resistance to its Authority, can only have found Place among the lower and more ignorant of the People; the better and wiser Part of the Colonies well know that Decency and Submission may prevail, not only to redress Grievances, but to obtain Grace and Favour; while the Outrage of a publick Violence can expect nothing but Severity and Chastisement." [1]

Conway probably believed that the riots in Boston and those that followed elsewhere were spontaneous outbursts of the rabble. If he read the dispatches which the colonial governors were soon sending to the Lords of Trade, he must have known better by the end of the year.[2] The episodes of violence which defeated the Stamp Act in America were planned and prepared by men who were recognized at

1. October 24, 1765, Connecticut Historical Society, *Collections*, 18 (1920), 362.
2. These may be found most conveniently in the House of Lords Manuscripts for the months of January and February, 1766, Library of Congress transcripts. For a somewhat different view of this subject, see Philip Davidson, *Propaganda and the American Revolution* (Chapel Hill, 1941), ch. 4, and "Sons of Liberty and Stamp Men," *North Carolina Historical Review*, 9 (1932), 37-55.

the time as belonging to the "better and wiser part." In every colony there appeared a group who designated themselves as the "Sons of Liberty," and in every colony, the Sons of Liberty, if they were not composed of prominent and well-to-do citizens, at least had their backing. Members of the assembly, who might scruple as assembly-men to call for open rebellion, had no hesitation in planning the nullification of the Stamp Act through mob violence. Merchants, law-yers, and plantation owners may have appeared seldom enough in the actual work of destruction, but that they directed the show from behind the scenes is suggested by every surviving piece of evidence.

Governor Bull of South Carolina, describing the treatment of the Stamp Distributor there, wrote, that "Altho these very numerous Assemblies of the People bore the appearance of common populace; Yet there is great reason to apprehend they were animated and en-couraged by some considerable Men, who stood behind the Cur-tain." [3] Crusty old Henry Laurens, who later became President of the Continental Congress but who disapproved of the violent resistance to the Stamp Act, knew by more than conjecture that the Sons of Liberty came from the higher ranks. At midnight on the twenty-third of October, 1765, he was awakened by a violent thumping and con-fused roar at his chamber window. Opening it, he heard the cries of "Liberty, Liberty, and Stamp'd Paper." He assured the crowd below that he had no stamps, and when they were not satisfied, "accused them with cruelty to a poor Sick Woman far gone with Child and produced Mrs. Laurens shrieking and wringing her hands." He offered to have it out with any one of them with a brace of pistols, and told them "it was base in such a multitude to attack a single Man." To this he received the answer that they loved and respected him and bore him no grudge, "but that they were sent even by some of my seemingly best friends to search for Stamped Paper which they were certain was in my custody." Perceiving that they were ready to force an entrance, Laurens let them in, and while two of them held a pair of cutlasses against his chest, he surprised the others by pene-trating the "Soot, Sailors habits, slouch hats &c." with which they had disguised themselves, calling nine of his acquaintances by name. [4]

In North Carolina, when the continued paralysis of the port at Cape Fear brought on the crisis already described, the lead was taken by fifty gentlemen of Wilmington, who made no attempt to conceal

3. To the Lords of Trade, November 3, 1765, House of Lords Manuscripts, February 14, 1766.
4. Henry Laurens to Joseph Brown, October 28, 1765, Laurens Letter Book, Historical Society of Pennsylvania.

their identity but signed an open letter to the Collector of Customs, demanding that ships be cleared. When this failed to bring action, they formed an association of "all the principal Gentlemen, Free-holders and other inhabitants of several counties," and forced the issue. Leading the crowd were several prominent citizens: John Ashe, Colonel James Moore, Colonel Hugh Waddell, Alexander Lilling-ton, Colonel Thomas Lloyd, Cornelius Harnett, Moses John De Ros-set and others. Most of these men were members of the Assembly, Ashe being the Speaker. De Rosset was Mayor of Wilmington. Two of the number averred that they had been compelled to assume the leadership of the movement, but others were obviously zealous in the cause. Maurice Moore, an Assemblyman and Judge in Salisbury Dis-trict, was so intemperate in supporting the opposition to the Stamp Act that the Governor suspended him from office. The Governor also found the merchants of the colony "as assiduous in obstructing the reception of the Stamps as any of the Inhabitants." [5]

In Virginia too the better and wiser sort did not bother to hide be-hind the curtain. Describing the men who forced Mercer to resign, Governor Fauquier said, "This Concourse of People, I should call a Mob, did I not know that it was chiefly if not altogether Composed of Gentlemen of Property in the Colony—some of them at the Head of their respective Counties, and the Merchants of the Country whether English, Scotch or Virginians, for few absented them-selves." [6] John Hughes of Pennsylvania carefully pointed out to his superiors in England the true character of the Philadelphia "mob," "as the Great Men here wou'd fain have it Term'd, and believ'd on Your side the Water, and I make no doubt, but it will be so repre-sented by the Proprietary Governor and his Friends." [7] Actually the directors of the Pennsylvania mob were men of standing in Phila-delphia: James Tilghman, attorney at law, Robert Morris, Charles Thomson, Archibald McCall, John Cox, and William Richards, all merchants, and William Bradford, the printer.[8] In New Hampshire the Reverend Samuel Langdon, minister of the Congregational Church and later President of Harvard College, was one of the lead-ers; and after one of the public demonstrations in Portsmouth when the Sons of Liberty had stepped from behind the scenes and shown themselves openly, the *New Hampshire Gazette* reported that they

5. *Colonial Records of North Carolina*, VII, *passim*, especially 143, 168-183, 199.

6. Fauquier to Lords of Trade, November 3, 1765, House of Lords Manuscripts, January 27, 1766.

7. To Commissioners of Stamps, November 2, 1765, Treasury Papers, Class I, Bundle 441, Public Record Office, Library of Congress transcripts.

8. Hughes to Commissioners of Stamps, October 12, 1765, House of Lords Manu-scripts, January 14, 1766.

were "no other than the principal Inhabitants of the Town and the Representatives of the Country." [9]

In Boston the Loyal Nine, who directed the activities of Ebenezer McIntosh, were probably themselves subordinate to the merchants and politicians. This at least was the opinion of Thomas Hutchinson, who had a somewhat more than academic interest in the matter. In a letter directed to ex-Governor Pownall on March 8, 1766 he wrote,

It will be some amusement to you to have a more circumstantial account of the present model of government among us. I will begin with the lowest branch partly legislative partly executive. This consists of the rabble of the town of Boston headed by one Mackintosh who I imagine you never heard of. He is a bold fellow and as likely for a Massianello as you can well conceive. When there is occasion to hang or burn effigies or pull down houses these are employed; but since government has been brought to a system they are somewhat controuled by a superior set consisting of the master-masons carpenters, &c. of the town. . . . When anything of more importance is to be determined as opening the custom house or any matters of trade these are under the direction of a committee of merchants Mr. Rowe at their head then Molyneux Solomon Davis, &c. but all affairs of a general nature opening all the courts of law &c. this is proper for a general meeting of the inhabitants of Boston where Otis with his mobbish eloquence prevails in every motion, and the town first determine what is necessary to be done and then apply either to the Governor and council or resolve that it is necessary the general court should meet and it must be a very extraordinary resolve indeed that is not carried into execution. [10]

There is abundant evidence that the merchants of Boston were at least partly responsible for the riots. Governor Bernard in describing the events of August 14 and 26 to the Secretary of State, told how an old quarrel between the merchants and the admiralty and customs officers had broken out anew just prior to the riots. [11] The attack on Story and Hallowell on August 26 was the payment of a score which the merchants had long held in account against the custom-house. Hallowell's friends, inquiring in town about the reasons for the attack, were told that it stemmed from his strictness in enforcing the Laws of Trade. [12] Hallowell himself wrote to the Lords of Trade on

9. *New Hampshire Gazette,* January 10, 1766. The letters written by the Sons of Liberty in New Hampshire to those in other colonies were written by Langdon, Belknap Papers, Massachusetts Historical Society.

10. Massachusetts Archives, XXVI, 207-214.

11. Bernard to Halifax, August 31, 1765, Bernard Papers, IV, 149-158, Harvard College Library. One of the merchants responsible for reviving the quarrel was Briggs Hallowell, Benjamin's brother.

12. Treasury Papers, Class I, Bundle 442.

September 7, 1765, that "the leaders or Conductors of the Mob offered to take any Kind of Goods liable to Seizure under their protection and bid defiance to the Officers of the Customs," [13] and Bernard reported on November 26, 1765, that people were saying, "let us see now who will seize Merchants Goods, what Judge will condemn them, what Court will dare grant Writs of Assistance now." [14]

In New York Robert Livingston professed to be unacquainted with the "secret party" that conducted the riots, but noted that one of their public posters had evidently been written by a person of education.[15] Actually his brother William and the two other political leaders of the Assembly, John Morin Scott and William Smith, both men of the first rank, must have known more than a little about the secret party and the men who composed it.[16] The documents do not reveal whether or not they had a directing influence in it, but popular opinion gave the Livingstons and their wealthy friends credit for forming it. One Dutch farmer who, like other farmers in the Hudson Valley, felt himself oppressed by the great landlords of the province, complained to the Attorney General that one of the Livingstons (it is not clear who) "has spoke treasonable words against king and parliament we must rase a Rebellion against the damned stamp act and I wil shed the blood against it and turn us sels tu a free republic as Holland this is the vue of Livingstons familie the robbers and murders of common poor people. . . ." [17]

Both Cadwallader Colden, the Lieutenant-Governor of the province, who had reason to hate the Livingstons, and General Gage, who was perhaps a more impartial observer, shared the view that the New York riots were directed by men of standing. Both diagnosed the trouble as coming from the lawyers, who at this time belonged to the wealthiest families in the province. Colden wrote to Conway on November 9, "I have the strongest presumption from numerous Circumstances to believe that the Lawyers of this Place are the Authors, Promoters, and Leaders of it. People in general believe it, and many must with certainty know it." [18] Gage went further than Colden and blamed the trouble in every colony on the lawyers. "The Lawyers,"

13. *Ibid.*

14. Bernard to John Pownall, November 26, 1765, Bernard Papers, V, 43-46.

15. To Governor Monckton, November 8, 1765, Massachusetts Historical Society, *Collections*, 4th ser., 10 (1871), 560.

16. See Dorothy R. Dillon, *The New York Triumvirate* (New York, 1949), 91-99; Davidson, *Propaganda and the American Revolution*, 70.

17. Howenburgh to J. T. Kemp, Sedgwick Papers, Massachusetts Historical Society.

18. To Secretary Conway, November 9, 1765, O'Callaghan, ed., *Documents Relative to the Colonial History of the State of New York*, VII, 773; New York Historical Society, *Collections for the year 1877* (1878), 61-62.

he said, "are the Source from whence the Clamors have flowed in every Province. In this Province Nothing Publick is transacted without them, and it is to be wished that even the Bench was free from Blame. The whole Body of Merchants in general, Assembly Men, Magistrates, &c. have been united in this Plan of Riots, and without the Influence and Instigation of these the inferior People would have been quiet. Very great Pains was taken to rouse them before they Stirred. The Sailors who are the only People who may be properly Stiled Mob, are entirely at the Command of the Merchants who employ them." [19]

Gage and Colden were talking about the mob in New York City, but up the river, Albany likewise had its Stamp Act riots, and here too the Sons of Liberty were drawn from the best families in town. They bore the names of the old Dutch mercantile families and many of them were officeholders or relatives of officeholders in the local government. [20]

The most complete information that has been preserved about the Sons of Liberty in any colony is that which Ezra Stiles set down about the group in Newport. Stiles, who had a fortunate penchant for collecting information that would be useful to later historians, not only set down the names of the Newport Sons of Liberty but contributed a biographical sketch of each. His account was written early in 1767 and included only those who were active in the "Committee" at that time, but the members were probably much the same as they had been the year before:

The Committee contained some Gentlemen of the first Figure in Town for opulence, Sense, and Politeness: and without Question was as respectable as could have been chosen in Newport, and the most respectable Committee of the Sons of Liberty on this Continent. Secretary Ward and Mr. Bowler were deputed by the General Assembly of Rhode Island, and attended the grand Congress of provincial Commissioners at New York in October 1765 which formed the Resolves of the Congress and the Addresses to the King Lords and Commons at that dangerous and memorable Crisis. Colonel Lyndon aetat 65, has been many years Clerk of the General Assembly of the Colony, and of the Inferior Court of common pleas of the County of Newport, a Gentleman of an amiable and respectable reputation, of Politeness and of a good Estate. — Mr. Crook is a Merchant of figure

19. To Secretary Conway, December 21, 1765, Clarence E. Carter, ed., *The Correspondence of General Thomas Gage with the Secretaries of State, 1763-1775* (New Haven, 1931), I, 79.

20. Beverly McAnear, "The Albany Stamp Act Riots," *William and Mary Quarterly*, 3d ser., 4 (1947), 486-498.

and of good Connexions. He and Mr. Bowler, with two or three more, were the only Sons of Liberty of Consequence among the Churchmen in Town. The Messrs Ellerys were Sons of the late Hon. Dep. Gov. Ellery who possessed an Estate of Twenty Thousand Pounds Sterling. William Ellery Esq. was educated at Harvard College, and for Literature and sound Judgement equal to any Man in Town, and really of the most weight and Firmness of any of the Committee: his Brother Captain Ellery was vigorous, intrepid and bold. Mr. Channing aetat 53 was a Gentleman of the greatest Politeness, a true Friend of Liberty, of free and genteel Elocution, and a Merchant of the largest Business, transacting a Commerce of Four Thousand Sterling a year. Mr. Collins a hearty and zealous and sensible Friend of Liberty—once in the Fall 1765 he had a little Fit of Timidity; but recovered himself intirely and become a glorious Champion in the Cause. Major Otis is a very sensible worthy Man, of a very personable Aspect, a Man of Religion, and an honor to his Country; stedily firmly and immutably attached to Liberty. — He is a Remote Relation to the honorable James Otis of Boston, who first proposed the Congress. Mr. Spooner was from among middling and lower Life, and united in himself the whole Confidence of the plebians—he was cautious and on his Guard, but his whole soul was in Liberty—he was vigorous and circumspect, safe but enterprizing. a man perhaps aetat 30. He was very necessary, and perhaps as important as any Man of the Committee, as they without him would not have had so intirely the Confidence of the Populace. Mr. Marchant aetat 26 was a judicious sensible and steady and bold Assertor of Liberty, his Intermarriage in a church Family secured him from that Torrent of Church Ribaldry Bellowing and Reproach which they poured forth like a Tempest on the Sons of Liberty, calling them Rebels, Traitors, Republicans, and worthy to be carried home in Chains and tried for their Lives. Of this last number was Maudsley, whom the Sons elected into the Committee for his own Mortification.[21]

Although gentlemen seem to have held the reins among the Sons of Liberty, they could not have succeeded in their ambitions without the support of their social inferiors. Their plans required the use of violence, and violence was not their forte. The wiser and better sort were not accustomed to throwing brickbats or smashing furniture, nor would they have wished to risk their reputations by openly indulging in such uncouth activities. As members of a legislative assembly they might be willing to proclaim the unconstitutionality of Parliamentary taxation, but resistance to Parliament was a larger order,

21. Ezra Stiles, Stamp Act Notebook, Stiles Papers, Yale University Library. Where Stiles uses the words "church" and "churchmen" he refers to the Anglican Church. One notable leader of the Sons of Liberty whom Stiles does not mention here was Samuel Vernon, another merchant. Moffat listed Vernon and William Ellery as "two of the Chief Ringleaders," Chalmers Papers, Rhode Island, New York Public Library.

in which the support of the "lower and more ignorant" might be needed.

General Gage testified that the lower and more ignorant had taken a good deal of prodding before they could be brought to act, and Ezra Stiles said that Major Spooner was indispensable to the Newport Sons of Liberty in order to gain the support of these lower ranks. Actually the lower classes probably had little to lose directly by the Stamp Act. They might feel some concern over the restriction of trial by jury, but they did not commonly engage in the legal business transactions which required a stamp. They would not have worried about the extra cost of matriculating at a university or entering a corporation or alienating a piece of land. They might have worried about the stamps on dice, playing cards, and newspapers, but they probably read newspapers supplied by the management in their local coffee house, and a pair of dice will last a long time. How then did the Sons of Liberty rouse these people to fury, and more important, how did they control that fury once they had aroused it?

In order to bring the people in general to a sense of the dangers which the Stamp Act held for the colonies, it was necessary to show them the consequences which must inevitably follow if Parliament's right to tax were acknowledged. The Sons of Liberty were far-sighted enough to see the issues involved in the Stamp Act, to see that in the long run it would be to Parliament's advantage to draw as large a proportion of revenue as possible from a people who were not close enough at hand to protect themselves through protest or pressure or the ballot box. The more money Parliament could draw from the Americans the less they would have to draw from their own constituents in England. The Americans could thus be bled dry for the benefit of their fellow subjects in England.

The only way to prevent such a calamity was to defeat the Parliamentary tax at its inception, and this is precisely what the Sons of Liberty urged so successfully upon the people of the colonies. Their method of ringing the alarm was that which their forebears in England had used in the 1630's, the press. But the colonists had a great advantage over the English revolutionists in that they could obtain nearly automatic circulation of their writings through the newspapers. In Boston one of the Sons of Liberty was Benjamin Edes, the printer, with John Gill, of the *Boston Gazette,* which Governor Bernard tagged as "the most factious paper in America." [22]

22. To John Pownall, July 20, 1765, Bernard Papers, IV, 7-9. On the activities of the press see A. M. Schlesinger, "The Colonial Newspapers and the Stamp Act," *New England Quarterly,* 8 (1935), 63-83.

In Providence William Goddard, printer of the *Providence Gazette,* was also a Son of Liberty,[23] and in Philadelphia, William Bradford, printer of the *Pennsylvania Journal,* belonged to the group.[24] Even where the printer of the local paper did not belong he generally cooperated. In Newport Samuel Hall, who had printed the propaganda of the Royalist group there, even including Martin Howard's *Letter from a Gentleman at Halifax,* was wholeheartedly supporting the opposition to the Stamp Act by the summer of 1765.

A printer who refused to cooperate was apt to regret it, for the Sons of Liberty might also be the leaders of the legislative assembly. Many printers relied upon the business of printing the legislative records of the provincial assemblies to keep them going, and those who opposed the Sons of Liberty might lose that source of income. Conversely those who cooperated could expect to be favored. James Parker, a friend of Franklin's, despaired of setting up a press in New York in 1766, because "the Sons of Liberty carry all before them, Mr. Holt [John Holt, printer of the *New York Gazette*] has gained very great Popularity, and being back'd by them, seems to have a Run of Business." [25]

A few newspapers suspended publication after November first, in order to avoid the use of stamps, but most printers ignored the requirement that news sheets be stamped and continued business as usual. Where the Sons of Liberty were well organized, the printers may have thought it safer to continue than to suspend. John Holt, though himself an ardent opponent of the Stamp Act, received a warning on October 31 saying, "should you at this critical time shut up the press, and basely desert us, depend upon it, your house, person, and effects, will be in imminent danger. We shall therefore expect your paper on Thursday as usual...." [26] Peter Timothy, printer of the *South Carolina Gazette,* who ceased publication during the operation of the Act, was still feeling the loss of business from the hostility of the Sons of Liberty three years later.[27] Andrew Steuart, printer of the *North Carolina Gazette,* had the most trying experience of all. He had suspended publication, allegedly because of illness, before November first. On November 16, the mob which forced the resignation of the Stamp Distributor on that day let him know that he must resume publication—or else. When he did

23. Rhode Island Historical Society Manuscripts, XII, 63.

24. See note 8.

25. Massachusetts Historical Society, *Proceedings,* 2d ser., 16 (1902), 210.

26. Isaac Q. Leake, *Memoir of the Life and Times of General John Lamb* (Albany, 1850), 13-14.

27. September 3, 1768, Franklin Papers, II, 139, American Philosophical Society.

so, and opened his pages to all who wished to contribute, one vigorous upholder of Parliamentary authority sent in a letter. Because he published it, he was threatened with a horse-whipping. He appealed to his readers in bewilderment: "What part is he now to act?— Continue to keep his Press open and free, and be in danger of corporal punishment, or bloque it up and run the risk of having his brains knocked out?" Two weeks later the Governor and Council answered his question by suspending him for printing a letter that was too radical! [28]

The printers who cooperated with the Sons of Liberty published many serious articles demonstrating the dangers of the Stamp Act to American rights, but like journalists of later ages they did not stop with appeals to reason. The *Boston Gazette* fed the people a steady diet of incendiary exhortation, directed not only against the local Stamp Distributor, but also against Governor Bernard, Lieutenant-Governor Hutchinson, and even against England itself. As one epigram on the Mother Country put it:

> Spurn the Relation—She's no more a Mother,
> Than Lewis to George a most Christian Brother,
> In French Ware and Scotch, grown generous and rich,
> She gives her dear Children Pox, Slavery, and Itch.[29]

And to George Grenville the *Gazette* offered this couplet:

> To make us all Slaves, now you've lost Sir! the Hope,
> You've but to go hang yourself.—We'll find the Rope.[30]

The papers appealed for action in a variety of ways. When the *Boston Gazette* printed a simple quotation labelled as a warning once made to Cardinal Wolsey, "Great Sir, Retreat or you are Ruined," the reader could readily take it as an invitation to help ruin Governor Bernard, in case that harassed official should attempt to prevent nullification of the Stamp Act.[31] When a stamp distributor was advised in the paper to appear before the Liberty Tree at twelve o'clock, every patriotic citizen would take pains to join him there. The *Providence Gazette* suggested the resignation of Augustus Johnston in the strongest possible terms simply by announcing that he had agreed not to execute the Act—five days later he fulfilled the prophecy.[32]

28. *Colonial Records of North Carolina*, VII, 123-124, 168a, 187.
29. *Boston Gazette*, December 2, 1765.
30. *Ibid.*
31. *Boston Gazette*, January 6, 1766.
32. *Providence Gazette Extraordinary*, August 24, 1765.

By printing highly colored news of the daring deeds of other colonists, the papers encouraged similar exploits by their own subscribers. The most conspicuously successful example of this type of propaganda was the printing of the Virginia Resolves in a version far different from that which had actually passed the House of Burgesses. By representing the Virginians as more radical than they had actually been, the newspapers succeeded in bringing about resolutions and riots in their own colonies that surpassed what had happened in Virginia. Some papers even extended their exhortations to neighboring colonies. The *Boston Gazette* offered Connecticut good advice about how to deal with Jared Ingersoll,[33] and Governor Franklin of New Jersey complained bitterly that his people had become nearly as much inflamed as those of the other colonies because of the way in which the papers in New York and Pennsylvania had ridiculed them for their moderation, insinuating that he had given them "a Dose of Poppies and Laudanum." [34]

While newspapers served as a constant stimulus to popular indignation, the Sons of Liberty knew that it was not enough simply to stir people up. It was necessary for someone to take the lead in whatever violence was necessary to intimidate the stamp masters and nullify the Act. The Sons of Liberty might in some cases be able to do this themselves, but the social gulf that stood between them and the masses could be a handicap. Ezra Stiles's comments about the importance of Major Spooner to the Newport Sons of Liberty suggests that birth and breeding were already political liabilities. The Boston gentlemen who disguised their rank with trousers when they marched in the mob on August 14, were probably seeking to conceal their part in a disreputable business, but they may also have been making a bid for popularity. It is, at any rate, a fact that in at least two colonies the Sons of Liberty made use of a genuine workingman to lead the mob.

In Boston Ebenezer McIntosh, the shoemaker, already had a reputation as the impresario of the South End mob, when the Stamp Act was passed. McIntosh was evidently willing to work for his betters, for throughout the crucial months from August, 1765, to April, 1766, he followed the orders of the Sons of Liberty, or, as they originally called themselves, the Loyal Nine. It is possible that on the night of August 26 he slipped the reins for a time; but it is evident that the Sons of Liberty, with the assistance of the militia, quickly regained control, and when it became necessary to force Oliver's resignation

33. *Boston Gazette*, August 26, September 9, 1765.
34. To Grey Cooper, January 15, 1766, Treasury Papers, Class I, Bundle 452.

for a second time on December 17, the affair was carried out under McIntosh's direction without a hitch. Two days later Henry Bass, one of the Sons of Liberty, confided to a friend that "the whole affair transacted by the Loyall Nine, in writing the Letter, getting the advertisements Printed, which were all done after 12 o'Clock Monday Night, the Advertisements Pasted up to the amount of a hundred was all done from 9 to 3 oClock." Bass urged his friend to "keep this a profound Secret." "We do every thing," he said, "in order to keep this and the first Affair Private: and are not a little pleas'd to hear that McIntosh has the Credit of the whole Affair." [35]

How the Sons of Liberty in Boston were able to keep McIntosh so well under control is not apparent. He must have known how powerful he really was when the Sheriff did not dare to hold him for more than a few hours on August 27. His submission to the Sons of Liberty, whether willing or unwilling, is rendered the more impressive by the failure of the Newport Sons of Liberty in their experiment with a demagogue. [36] Ezra Stiles mentions Major Spooner as the intermediary between the Newport Sons of Liberty and the lower classes, but he does not mention John Weber who enjoyed a brief but terrifying rule as leader of the Newport mob. Weber was a young Englishman who had been in Newport for only three or four days when the riot of August 29 occurred. He may well have been a sailor with some reputation as a leader among other sailors; and perhaps was employed on a vessel belonging to one of the Sons of Liberty. One account has it that he was a "deserted convict, aged about 20 Or 21 years." In any case, if we are to believe Augustus Johnston, Weber must have been hired by the Sons of Liberty to lead the mob in attacking Robinson, Johnston, Moffat, and Howard. Though his employment was probably supposed to terminate with this exploit, he evidently enjoyed his work too much to stop. As soon as Augustus Johnston had resigned his office on the morning of August 29, Weber began to grow insolent and insulted several persons, "some of whom," says Johnston, "were the very people concerned in beginning the Riot, by preparing the Effigies, &c. and now began to fear for themselves." These gentlemen, Johnston continues, "were weake enough to immagine, that if they should

35. Massachusetts Historical Society, *Proceedings*, 44 (1911), 688-689.

36. The account of events in Newport in this and the next three paragraphs is based on *Newport Mercury*, September 2, 1765; Augustus Johnston to Commissioners of Stamps, August 31, 1765, Treasury Papers, Class I, Bundle 439; Charles Leslie to Lord Colville, September 5, 1765, Admiralty Secretary In Letters 482, Public Record Office, Library of Congress transcripts; and *Calendar of Home Office Papers of the Reign of George III, 1760-1765* (London, 1878), 610-611.

secure this Fellow, who had exerted himself a good deal in the Disturbances—That it would in some measure attone for the part they had Acted; And accordingly they with the Assistance of the sheriff seized him and carried him on board the Cygnet Man-of-War, he exclaiming that he was betrayed by the very people who first set him to work."

The Sons of Liberty shortly discovered that their problem could not be solved so easily. Weber in his brief night of glory had gained a number of loyal followers. These now gathered together and announced that if Weber were not released forthwith they would give the gentlemen who planned the riot a taste of their own medicine by destroying *their* houses. The threat was effective. A few of the gentlemen went aboard the *Cygnet* and informed Captain Leslie that they had mistakenly apprehended the wrong man. The authorities in town, they said, were now in pursuit of the ringleaders and would bring them aboard as soon as they were taken up. Captain Leslie swallowed the story and released Weber, who was hailed with cheers as he came ashore.

The Sons of Liberty were now in a more desperate position than before. As soon as Weber landed he threatened to pull down their houses. Panic-stricken, the gentlemen offered this monster everything that he wished, gave him money, ordered him clothes, and begged and prayed him to be satisfied. But John Weber with the Newport mob at his back was not to be satisfied by cringing condescension, not even when Sheriff Wanton pleaded "What would you have of me? I will do everything to satisfy you; I will lay myself down, and let you tread on my neck, if that will satisfy you."

Perceiving that appeasement would get them nowhere the gentlemen took a firmer stand and prepared to defend themselves in case the mob should not disperse. The challenge was not accepted, and the crowd were finally persuaded to go quietly to their homes. Nothing happened that night, though the Sons of Liberty must have slept uneasily. The next day Augustus Johnston heaped coals of fire on the heads of his tormenters by rescuing them from the predicament in which their attack upon him had placed them. Johnston had formerly been a popular man in Newport—the town of Johnston, Rhode Island, was named after him—and he had probably regained some measure of his popularity by resigning the stamp office. Moreover he was still Attorney General of the colony. Meeting with Weber alone in the street, he seized him and carried him off to jail. Curiously enough, Weber's followers made no immediate attempt to rescue their hero, and the Sons of Liberty could breathe a sigh of relief. There was of course the danger that Weber, if brought to trial, would reveal the names of his employers, but evidently the Sons of Liberty were able to scare him out of this, for when he was asked for his story, he refused to give it, saying "I shall be tore to Pieces by those who set me on but if my Person can be secured I will say what I know." Charles Leslie, Captain of the *Cygnet,* told Augustus Johnston that he would give Weber protection on the *Cygnet,* if he could be got aboard. But Johnston intended to go on living in Newport and perhaps thought it best to let matters stand for the moment as they were.

The atmosphere remained highly charged. Weber lay in jail, while the Sons of Liberty endeavored to maintain popular feeling against the Stamp Act without touching off another riot. As November approached, everyone sensed the explosiveness of the situation. There must have been a tightening of jaws when the Sons of Liberty learned that Sheriff Wanton had received two letters threatening that unless he released John Weber, his house would be destroyed and the doors of the jail forced.[37] On November first, in order to forestall any possible riot, the Sons of Liberty attempted to divert popular feeling into an orderly demonstration, by staging "a grand funeral of Freedom." A procession of mourners marched through the streets to the burying ground following a coffin marked "Old Freedom." Upon arrival at the place of interment, according to the description in the *Mercury,*

A Son of LIBERTY emerging from the horrid Gloom of Despair, addressed himself thus: 'Oh LIBERTY! the Darling of my Soul!— GLORIOUS LIBERTY! admir'd, ador'd, by all true Britons!—LIBERTY dead! it cannot be!'—A groan was then heard, as if coming from the Coffin; and upon closer attention, it proved to be a Trance, for old FREEDOM was not dead—The Goddess Britannia had order'd a guarding Angel to snatch Old FREEDOM from the Jaws of frozen Death, to the Orb of the rising Sun, to remain invulnerable from the attacks of lawless Tyranny and Oppression.[38]

After this agreeable diversion the afternoon was spent in rejoicing, with bells ringing and the courthouse ornamented with flags. In the evening a number of persons patrolled the streets to prevent the gathering of a mob, and the night passed quietly. Weber after two months in jail was reaching the point of despair. When no

37. *Newport Mercury,* November 4, 1765.
38. *Ibid.*

rescue party attempted to release him on November first, he tried
to hang himself in his cell, but was prevented. On the following
evening his friends rallied for a last effort. A crowd of twenty or
thirty prepared to storm the jail, hoping no doubt to gather reinforcement as they went. But Weber's magnetic personality could
not exert its attraction from within the walls of the jail. An alarm
was given and the incipient mob dispersed, minus two of their
number, "who were seized; and instead of releasing their Associate
in Prison, were forced to take up their Residence in the same
Place." [39] This was the last to be heard of John Weber. Doubtless
he was released after the Stamp Act troubles were over, but until
then the Sons of Liberty in Newport were careful to direct all opposition to the Stamp Act in person. They celebrated Christmas day by
making Augustus Johnston resign his office again, though he had
still received no commission from the Treasury Department in
England.[40] In January they gave warning through the *Mercury*
"That no Son of Perdition among us, of what Character in Life
soever, shall ever mention that destestable Pamphlet, called a *Stamp
Act*, with Applause, nor in any Way, by Word or Writing, Sign or
Token, ever aid or assist in the Prosecution of the Contents thereof,
without our highest Indignation." [41] When a ship arrived from the
West Indies with stamped clearance and bond, the Sons obtained
the papers and ceremoniously burnt them, along with two copies
of Martin Howard's *Letter from a Gentleman at Halifax*.[42] Never
again, however, did the Sons of Liberty in Newport risk a riot. One
John Weber was enough.,

According to General Gage, the Lawyers and Merchants who
started the mobs in New York also became uneasy about the extraordinary power which they had called into being. Once the violence
had begun, a number of demagogues appeared, not distinguished
by birth or breeding and only too eager to call out the mob on
any pretext. The more conservative merchants and lawyers had to
exert themselves continually to prevent a complete breakdown of
civil order. At one point the seamen got so far out of hand that
it was necessary to enlist the influence of the ship captains in regaining control. Gage thought that the better sort would have preferred to end all riots, but that they would never call in troops to
suppress the mob, for fear of losing their main objective, the defeat

39. *Ibid.*
40. *Newport Mercury,* December 30, 1765.
41. *Newport Mercury,* January 6, 1765.
42. *Newport Mercury,* March 24, 1765.

of the Stamp Act.[43] Like the Newport Sons of Liberty the New Yorkers had to steer a middle course. They must use the power of the mob to defeat the power of Parliament, but they must not allow the mob to escape from their own direction and upset the delicate balance of social classes within the colony.

How nice a problem this became is well illustrated by the events which occurred when two New York merchants executed a customs bond on stamped paper. The Sons of Liberty could not afford to allow this breach in the opposition to pass unnoticed, and they ordered the two merchants to appear before them at a local coffee house. John Holt, printer of the *New York Gazette,* wrote the following account of what ensued in a private letter to Mrs. Benjamin Franklin:

The Matter was intended to be done privately, but it got wind, and by ten o Clock I suppose 2000 people attended at the Coffee House, among them most of the principal men in Town—The Culprits apologies did not satisfy the people, they were highly blamed and the Sons of Liberty found it necessary to use their Influence to moderate the Resentments of the People. Two Men were dispatch'd to the Collector for the Stamp'd Bonds of which he had 30 in all, he desired Liberty to confer with the Governor, which was granted. The Governor sent Word, if the Stamps were deliver'd to him, he would give his Word and Honour they should not be used; but that if the people were not satisfied with this, they might do as they pleased with them—The message being returnd to the gathering Multitude, they would not agree to the Governors Proposal, but insisted upon the Stamps being deliver'd and burnt, one or two men attended by about a thousand others were then sent for the Stamps, which were brought to the Coffee House, and the Merchant who had used them was order'd himself to kindle the Fire and consume them, those filled in and all, this was accordingly done amidst the Huzza's of the people who were by this Time swell'd to the Number I suppose of about 5000, and in another hour I suppose would have been 10,000—The people pretty quietly dispersed soon After, but their Resentment was not allay'd, Toward the Evening . . . tho' the Sons of Liberty exerted themselves to the utmost, they could not prevent the gathering of the Multitude, who went to Mr Williams's house, broke open the Door and destroyed some of the Furniture, but thro' the Influence of the Sons of Liberty and on his most earnest Entreaty and promise in the most publick manner to ask pardon next day, or do whatever they should require

43. To Conway, December 21, 1765, January 16, 1766, Carter, ed., *Correspondence of Gage,* I, 78-79, 80-83. Cf. New York Historical Society, *Collections for the year 1881* (1882), 339-371.

of him, they were prevail'd on to leave the House, and then went to the Merchants where after huzzaing for some time, they were prevail'd upon to forbear doing any mischief—on Consideration that both the men were well beloved in Town, and bore fair Characters, that the Merchants Wife was not in good Health, and very near her Time and that if the Sons of Liberty undertook under the penalty of £2 [the manuscript is clipped here; the sum was probably at least two figures] that they would both ask the pardon requir'd the next Day mounted on a Scaffold, and do whatever else the people could reasonably desire—Accordingly today about 11 OClock they appear'd in the Fields, and attended by three Clergymen got out of a Window upon a pint House, before many thousand people and declared their Sorrow for what they had done, promised to do so no more and humbly ask'd pardon of the People. It was fear'd they would have been ill used but there was not the least Insult or incivility offer'd them.

The people were generally satisfied and soon dispersed—but many of those of inferior Sort, who delight in mischief merely for its own sake, or for plunder, seem yet to be in such a turbulent Disposition that the two mortified Gentlemen are still in some Danger, but the Sons of Liberty intend to Exert themselves in their Defense.[44]

Even where no large and excitable crowds existed, the Sons of Liberty frequently had to deal with people who tried to turn the existing confusion to their own advantage. Though the term "Sons of Liberty" was claimed in every colony by an organized group seeking to prevent the execution of the Stamp Act, the phrase nevertheless came to have the more general meaning of anyone who opposed the Stamp Act, and some individuals who perceived that certain kinds of lawlessness had become popular made the mistake of supposing that they could do as they pleased simply by calling themselves Sons of Liberty. Thieves who broke into a house in Maine and stole £ 700 worth of goods, followed up their crime by sending threatening letters to the victim in the name of the Sons of Liberty; [45] and in South Carolina a group of sailors formed a mob to collect money from people in the streets.[46] The Sons of Liberty in every colony felt obliged to suppress disorders of this kind, especially when carried on in their name, and by the end of the year 1765 they were sometimes referring to themselves as the "true" or the "true-born" Sons of Liberty, to distinguish themselves from those

44. February 15, 1766, Franklin Papers, XLVIII, 92. According to the account in the newspapers the thirty blank forms for bonds and Mediterranean passes had been shipped to Charles Williams, the "naval officer" of New York "without any mention of their being stamped." *Pennsylvania Gazette*, February 27, 1766.

45. *Virginia Gazette* (Purdie), May 9, 1766.

46. *Pennsylvania Journal*, January 2, 1766.

who abused the name.[47] They had no intention of allowing the hatred of the Stamp Act to be diverted into a pretense for criminal or anti-social activities.

In order to keep popular sentiment flowing in the channels they had marked out for it, they took pains to keep themselves constantly in the public eye. In many colonies this purpose was achieved by the clamor for opening the ports and courts. The fact that the British government had been so slow about commissioning the stamp distributors also furnished a suitable occasion for public demonstrations. When the commission reached a distributor after he had resigned, there was a question of whether the first resignation was binding, and the Sons of Liberty usually found it necessary to have a second one, again conducted in public with great ceremony. Many of the activities in which they engaged were harmless enough in themselves. There was, for example, no injury done to anyone in the public burning of occasional stamped papers which arrived on ships from Nova Scotia or Jamaica, nor was anyone harmed by the meeting in Boston on February 20, 1766, when Grenville and Bute were hung in effigy and "Long Life, Health and Prosperity" was drunk to all the Sons of Liberty in America, while the friends of the Stamp Act were toasted with a wish that they might have "a perpetual Itching without the Benefit of Scratching." [48]

These mild diversions did not mask a fact that became increasingly evident to all officers of government during the winter of 1765-66. As the Sons of Liberty perfected their own organization, that of the regular governments was dissolving. Everywhere colonial governors sent home reports of their helplessness. Governor Bernard prepared to flee from his province.[49] Lieutenant-Governor Hutchinson wondered whether authority could be restored even if the Stamp Act were repealed.[50] And from other colonies came the same story. Governor Wright could not rely on the support of more than ten men in Savannah and dared not call the militia for fear of arming his enemies.[51] Governor Wentworth in New Hampshire averred that no governor on the continent could depend upon his

47. Cf. Davidson, *Propaganda and the American Revolution*, 69.

48. *Boston Gazette*, February 24, 1766.

49. Massachusetts Archives, XXVI, 183; Bernard to Lord Colville, November 1, 1765, to Conway, December 19, 1765, Bernard Papers, IV, 84, 184.

50. Hutchinson to ——, February 27, March 26, 1766, Massachusetts Archives, XXVI, 199, 216.

51. To Lords of Trade, February 7, 1766, *Georgia Historical Quarterly*, 13 (1929), 148; to Conway, February 7, 1766, Jones, *History of Georgia*, II, 60-64. Wright had seventy Rangers and was promised twenty men from the warship *Speedwell*, but could muster only ten supporters among the inhabitants of Savannah.

militia, "because the Militia are the very People on the other Side the question." [52] Even in Connecticut where all the officers of government were popularly elected, it was reported that "the principal Men are obliged to throw cold water, and to use the utmost Address to extinguish and prevent the Flames breaking out.... Men of Eighty are ready to gird the sword ... the very Boys as well as the hardy Rustic are full of fire and at half a Word ready to fight." [53] Governor Colden of New York admitted that he had no power outside the fort in which he guarded himself.[54] In Pennsylvania Governor Penn thought "we are not more than one degree from open Rebellion." [55]

In this situation wisdom dictated that the nominal authorities should avoid occasions for demonstrating their weakness. A few governors like Franklin of New Jersey and Tryon of North Carolina rode out the storm by openly expressing disapproval of the Stamp Act or at least keeping silent about it.[56] Others like Francis Bernard and Cadwallader Colden invited disaster not only by showing their fear of the mob, but by lecturing the people on the duty of obedience. Colden virtually challenged the New York mob to attack Fort George by ordering extensive preparations for defense, and it was only the coolness of the officers within that prevented the American Revolution from beginning on October 31, 1765, with an attack on it. A milling crowd of several thousand people stood outside and "knocked at the gate, placed their hands on the top of the Ramparts, called out to the guards to fire, threw bricks and stones against the Fort and notwithstanding the highest provocation was given, not a word was returned to the most opprobrious language." [57] Major James, in command at the time, testified before Parliament that if he had fired he could have killed 900 of the mob on that night, but he added that the opposition could thereupon have assembled 50,000 fighting men from New York and New Jersey alone, and that it would have been impossible to hold out against such

52. To Lords of Trade, October 5, 1765, House of Lords Manuscripts, January 14, 1766.

53. Ezra Stiles to Benjamin Ellery, October 23, 1765, Stiles Papers.

54. Collector and Comptroller of New York to Commissioners of Customs, November 4, 1765, Treasury Papers, Class I, Bundle 442.

55. Richard Penn, Jr., to [Thomas Penn], December 15, 1765, Penn Manuscripts, X, 19, Historical Society of Pennsylvania.

56. William Franklin to Benjamin Franklin, November 13, 1765, Franklin Papers, I, 168; Colonial Records of North Carolina, VII, 127-128. Cf. Fauquier to Conway, December 11, 1765, House of Lords Manuscripts, February 6, 1766.

57. Robert R. Livingston to Governor Monckton, November 8, 1765, Massachusetts Historical Society, Collections, 4th ser., 10 (1871), 559-567.

a force.[58] This opinion was supported by General Gage himself, who wrote to England that fire from the fort could have meant the beginning of Civil War.[59] Gage knew that in such a civil war the troops which he commanded would have been all but massacred. Twenty years later, when the fighting that began in 1775 had ended with the Americans victorious, Gage may have looked back and regretted that they had not got it over with in 1765; but at the time there was still hope that British authority might be preserved for the future by suspending it in the present. Men like Gage and Governor Franklin of New Jersey realized that "for any Man to set himself up as an advocate of the Stamp Act in the Colonies is a meer Piece of Quixotism" [60]—even if the man were a colonial governor, sworn to support the authority of Great Britain. Those who do not carry a big stick are well-advised to speak softly, and every colonial governor who understood the smallness of his power, spoke in a whisper or not at all.

With the regular government all but extinguished, the Sons of Liberty steadily tightened their own control. Within their respective colonies, though there may have been uncomfortable moments when a Weber or a McIntosh seemed to be getting out of line, they kept the upper hand. They acted, of course, more arbitrarily than the regular government would have dared to do: they seized private mail, restricted the freedom of the press, and terrorized their enemies without mercy. But this is only to say that they were beginning a revolution. They had seized the power which once belonged to the royal governments, and they were prepared to keep it by fair means or foul until their end, the defeat of the Stamp Act, was accomplished.

How far they were prepared to go became apparent when England responded to the news of American riots. The threats of violence by which the Sons of Liberty exercised authority in America were transformed by three thousand miles of ocean into an impertinence, and Parliament, which had dealt with mobs before, replied to the challenge with talk of cramming stamps down American throats. When the Sons of Liberty heard this, they knew that they might have to fight for their rights not against a few helpless stamp distributors, but against the British Army. To be sure they probably surmised

58. Additional Mss., 33030, British Museum.

59. Quoted in Colden to Conway, November 4, 1765, Treasury Papers, Class I, Bundle 447. Cf. Gage to Conway, November 4, 8, 1765, Carter, ed., *Correspondence of Gage*, I, 70-73.

60. William Franklin to Benjamin Franklin, Franklin Papers, I, 168.

that the Rockingham government might repeal the Stamp Act before any attempt was made to enforce it. Nevertheless there were already British regulars in America under General Gage, and if repeal should fail, action might come fast. Consequently it was important that they be prepared to fight or give up when the time came and not lose the decision by default. In the winter of 1765-66, therefore, the Sons of Liberty throughout the colonies sponsored meetings of townspeople in which the citizens put on record their determination to defend their rights.

The Sons of Liberty in Connecticut seem to have taken the lead in holding meetings of this kind. The resolutions adopted show that they appreciated what the defense of their rights might cost. The meeting at New London on December 10, 1765, asserted the natural right of a people to set bounds upon their government and their duty, if lawful methods failed, "to reassume their natural Rights, and the Authority the Laws of Nature and of God have vested them with." [61] The people of Pomfret, Connecticut, asserted on December 25, 1765, "That God and Nature brought us into the world Freemen," and the English constitution confirmed their rights, "nor shall it be in the Power of any to deprive us of them, but with our lives." [62] In Wallingford the Sons of Liberty resolved on January 13, 1766, "That we will oppose the same [Stamp Act] to the last extremity, even to take the field." [63] In the opening months of 1766 the Sons of Liberty in other colonies followed the example of Connecticut with similar resolutions. Meetings were reported at Providence, New York City, Oyster Bay, Huntington, New Brunswick (New Jersey), Cecil County (Maryland), Leedstown and Norfolk (Virginia), and Wilmington (North Carolina), enunciating the readiness of the people to resist the Stamp Act "to the last extremity," "at any Risk whatever," "to the utmost of our power," "with our lives and fortunes," "at every Hazard, paying no Regard to Danger, or to Death." [64]

Such sentiments could be made effective only by a union of the Sons of Liberty, not merely within each colony but among all the colonies. The Americans might cry "liberty or death," but if they preferred the former, they would be most apt to get it by uniting. How early the Sons of Liberty in any colony began to think of intercolonial union is hard to say. The Stamp Act Congress brought to-

61. *Boston Post Boy*, December 16, 1765.

62. *Boston Gazette*, January 13, 1766.

63. *Connecticut Courant*, February 3, 1766.

64. *Newport Mercury*, March 31, 1766; *Maryland Gazette*, January 30, March 20, March 27, April 10, 1766; *Pennsylvania Journal*, January 30, March 6, 13, April 17, 1766.

gether a number of radicals who may have discussed plans for armed resistance in the odd hours when they were not drawing up the declarations of right and the appeals to King and Parliament. The congress was preceded by the issue in New York of a news sheet called the *Constitutional Courant,* which repeated the famous Franklin cartoon of 1754, of the snake cut in pieces, with the motto "Join or die." And the paper itself was filled with articles of an inflammatory nature.[65] But the congress, at least formally, did not consider a union in arms, and even James Otis, in a letter written shortly after to William Samuel Johnson, deplored the violence at Charleston and New York, and expressed the fear that "Parliament will charge the Colonies with presenting petitions in one hand and a dagger in the other." [66] Nevertheless, even before the delegates could all have returned to their homes, demonstrations of a strikingly similar character were staged in several colonies. The congress broke up on October 24, 1765. On November first, the day when the Stamp Act was to take effect, the Sons of Liberty in Portsmouth, Newport, Baltimore, and Wilmington, North Carolina, all held mock funerals of Liberty, perhaps by coincidence, perhaps as the result of a circularized suggestion.[67]

The first definite move to organize colonial resistance to the Stamp Act on a continental basis took place in a tavern in New London on Christmas day of 1765. Two delegates from the New York Sons of Liberty met there with some of the Connecticut Sons of Liberty and subscribed an agreement of mutual aid. They promised each other "to march with the utmost dispatch, at their own proper costs and expence, on the first proper notice, (which must be signified to them by at least six of the sons of liberty) with their whole force if required, and it can be spared, to the relief of those that shall, are, or may be in danger from the *stamp-act,* or its promoters and abettors, or any thing relative to it, on account of any thing that may have been done in opposition to its obtaining." In addition they promised that they would "endeavour to bring about, accomplish, and perfect the like *association* with all the *colonies* on the continent for the like salutary purposes and no other." [68]

For the next three months the Sons of Liberty all over North

65. Albert Matthews, "The Snake Devices, 1754-1766, and the Constitutional Courant," Colonial Society of Massachusetts, *Publications,* 11 (1910), 409-453.

66. November 12, 1765, Bancroft Transcripts, New York Public Library.

67. Davidson, *Propaganda and the American Revolution,* 68.

68. William Gordon, *History of the Rise, Progress, and Establishment of the Independence of the United States of America* (London, 1788), I, 197-198. Connecticut Historical Society, *Collections,* 18 (1920), 384-386.

America were sending letters back and forth, perfecting their organization, offering assistance to one another, and proposing boycotts against any colony that submitted to the Act. The New Yorkers who had been at New London went on to Boston and secured the allegiance of the Boston Sons to the association. Boston in turn wrote to all the towns in Massachusetts and to Portsmouth, New Hampshire in order to bring them into the organization.[69] Connecticut likewise produced a colony-wide organization, with a convention at Hartford on March 25, which drew up resolutions supporting the intercolonial associations.[70] In March the Providence Sons of Liberty sent out circular letters to the Sons in other places, proposing correspondence and declaring that "We shall be ready at all Times not only to vindicate ourselves, and the People under our more immediate Inspection, from lawless Might, but as Occasion may require to give aid to the other Colonies, for the rescuing them from every Attempt against their Liberties." [71] There is evidence that the correspondence was carried as far south as South Carolina, and that the South Carolinians offered 500 men to assist the Georgians in getting rid of their stamps.[72] In Maryland a colony-wide organization was effected as a means of forcing open the courts and customs, and New Jersey worked out an organization almost identical with the one which she used for establishing an independent government ten years later.[73]

No central intercolonial organization was established in the three months before the first news of repeal, but plans for a "General

69. Belknap Papers.

70. *Connecticut Courant*, March 10, 1766. See below, ch. 13, note 42.

71. Rhode Island Historical Society Manuscripts, XII, 64.

72. Davidson, *Propaganda and the American Revolution*, 69-73; Leake, *John Lamb*, 19; Belknap Papers; Wright to Conway, January 31, 1766, Jones, *History of Georgia*, II, 60-64; Wright to Lords of Trade, February 7, 1766, *Georgia Historical Quarterly*, 13 (1929), 148. The Georgians outside Savannah did stage a march on the town, but found upon arrival that Governor Wright had already put the stamps aboard the sloop *Speedwell* where they could be neither destroyed nor distributed. Consequently there was no need of assistance from South Carolina. Nevertheless, because of Georgia's temporary compliance with the Act the South Carolinians voted to boycott the entire colony. Although there were local Sons of Liberty in Pennsylvania the intercolonial organization seems to have made little headway there. Governor Penn wrote to his uncle on March 21, 1766, "There is a very impudent set of people to the northward who call themselves sons of liberty, whose business seems to be, to stir up as much discontent and uneasiness as they possibly can. They are not satisfied with the mischief they do at home, but are travelling from one end of the Continent to the other sowing dissention wherever they go. Two of them were here some days ago, but were not received in the manner they expected as the people are determined to wait patiently the Issue of the Stamp Act. They correspond with most of the Colonies from New Hampshire to Georgia and their purpose is to form a general plan of Opposition if ever the stamp act should be attempted to be put in execution, and I am really afraid it would be the Case." Penn Manuscripts, X, 33.

73. Davidson, *Propaganda and the American Revolution*, 72.

Congress" were under discussion,[74] and there can be no doubt that the colonists were getting ready to fight the British Army. What they would be fighting for seemed clear to most of them. In their messages to one another expressions of loyalty to the House of Hanover and defiance of Parliament were judiciously mingled on every page. They were assuring themselves, and perhaps protesting a little too much, that they were not rebels, for the resistance they envisaged was resistance only to an unconstitutional enactment of Parliament. The Sons of Liberty in Portsmouth, New Hampshire, expressed the common attitude when they wrote to their companions in Boston, on February 8, that since the Stamp Act violated the fundamental privileges of British subjects, it was "Therefore void of all Lawfull Authority, so that depending upon Meer Force it may Lawfully be oppos'd by Force." [75] The Sons of Liberty, like other revolutionaries, claimed that law and tradition and constitutional precedents were on their side. Ostensibly at least, they had no wish for independence, and they rejected indignantly the accusation commonly made in England that the colonies were scheming for independence. But the wiser among them must have recognized that if it came to war, the House of Hanover would not back them against Parliament, and that independence might be the inescapable outcome.

Most Americans would have looked upon such an outcome as undesirable, but many could see that unless Parliament backed down the colonies would be driven to it. John Dickinson, who later withstood the movement for independence until the last moment, could see the direction of events as early as December, 1765. In an appeal to William Pitt, the man who was regarded as most likely to save the empire, Dickinson warned that although independence would be unfortunate for America as well as England, there could be no doubt of the Americans' ability to achieve it.[76] Inter-colonial rivalries and recriminations had hitherto kept them divided, but their quarrels were giving way before their common concern for Liberty. "No colony," he pointed out, "apprehends that any other has Designs upon its Liberty. Their Contests are of an inferior Nature, and will vanish when one more dreadful to them commences." Americans would not seek for independence "unless excited by the Treatment they receive from Great Britain," but if once they made the attempt, "The Strength of the Colonies, their Distance, the wealth

74. Leake, *John Lamb*, 19. New York Sons of Liberty to Boston Sons of Liberty, April 2, 1766, Lamb Papers, New York Historical Society.

75. Belknap Papers.

76. Dickinson to Pitt, December 21, 1765, Historical Society of Pennsylvania.

that would pour into them on opening their Ports to all Nations, the Jealousy entertained of Great Britain by some European Powers, and the peculiar Circumstances of that Kingdome, would insure success." [77] Dickinson anticipated with horror the results of such success: "A multitude of Commonwealths, Crimes & Calamities, Centuries of mutual Jealousies, Hatreds, Wars of Devastation; till at last the exhausted Provinces shall sink into Slavery under the yoke of some fortunate Conqueror."

The only way that such a future could be avoided, in Dickinson's opinion, was for Parliament to give way and repeal the Stamp Act. Dickinson was a lawyer and knew well enough the arguments for and against Parliament's authority to tax the colonies, but he was able to see by December of 1765, that the authority, whatever basis it might or might not have in law and political theory, could not be supported in fact. Rather than put it to the test which the Sons of Liberty were preparing, it would be better for Parliament to abandon it voluntarily. "It may be said," Dickinson wrote to Pitt, "that Great Britain by repealing that Act will tacitly acknowledge, that she has no Right to tax the Colonies. If the Repeal should be construed as such an Acknowledgment, it will only be renouncing a Right, the Exercise of which can never be repeated without throwing the Colonies into Desperation. This I hope Great Britain will never do; and therefore she cannot lose any thing by such a Renunciation. . . . If this shall be thought by the Parliament too light a Pretence for the repeal, and that their authority may be wounded by such a Condescension, I am afraid they cannot hereafter rely on the affection of the Colonies."

For three months after Dickinson wrote, the colonies hung in the balance, hoping for peace, preparing for war. By the time the news of repeal arrived a great many things had happened, things that might not be remembered in the moment of jubilation but that could not be easily forgotten in the months and years that followed. While affection for Great Britain was being proclaimed on all sides, the Sons of Liberty would remember with some pride their success in defying Parliament. The unfortunate individuals upon whom they had demonstrated their defiance would remember too, and perhaps with as much pride, their own behavior during those trying months.

77. For similar views of the likelihood of American success in the event of revolution, see John Penn to Thomas Penn, March 21, 1766, Dickinson Papers, Historical Society of Pennsylvania, and a letter from New York, November 8, 1765, Additional Mss., 35911, British Museum.

PART III

Patterns of Loyalty

» TWELVE «

THOMAS HUTCHINSON

IN the summer of 1765 there were two courses open to Americans who believed, as most Americans did, that Parliament had no authority to tax them. They could fight, or they could submit and accompany their submission by humble requests for repeal of the Stamp Act and the Sugar Act. The Sons of Liberty chose to fight, and they began to fight so early that their more peaceable countrymen were given no opportunity to try the alternative. Most of those who would have taken the course of submission sat back in silence and helplessly watched the approach of rebellion. A few, because of the offices they held, because of a greater sense of responsibility, or because they had more courage, tried to halt the approach of disaster. The results in every case were ruined lives.

The men who suffered for upholding the authority of Parliament in 1765 were not simply transplanted Englishmen, sighing for love of the mother country. They were Americans, many of them with deep roots in the American past and all of them bound by ties of blood and affection and business and honor to the American life of the day. They had both friends and enemies among their countrymen, for no man who has the character or the wealth or the prominence to influence his fellow men can be without enemies; but in each case their enemies were to be found among the Sons of Liberty and their friends among the peaceable but helpless. Perhaps one reason why they spoke up as they did was that they saw their enemies on the other side, the side of rebellion. And as they saw their enemies, their enemies saw them. When the Sons of Liberty attacked in the summer of 1765, they were attacking not merely the spokesmen of Parliamentary supremacy, but men who, in one way or another, had earned their hatred long before. How else can one account for what happened to men like Thomas Hutchinson, John Hughes, or Jared Ingersoll?

Thomas Hutchinson was not the kind of man who made friends easily. His thin, handsome face, handsome in spite of its long nose, and his tall spare frame held precisely erect, combined to give an impression of remote dignity—a cool man this, who could swallow half the offices in the province and look as though they belonged to him by divine right. And yet he was as free of malice as any man. After the dust had settled on the ruins of his house on the morning of August 27, he must have tried to recall the things he had done to make himself so hated that people wanted to tear his house to pieces. What had made them so angry with him? He had, of course, a few personal enemies. There was James Otis, currently the leader of the Massachusetts House of Representatives. Otis thought that Hutchinson had cheated his father, James Otis, Senior, out of a seat on the Superior Court. Governor Pownall had promised a seat to the elder Otis whenever one should become vacant, but Pownall was no longer in the governor's chair when a vacancy occurred in 1760, and Governor Bernard did not feel bound by his predecessor's commitments. When he offered the position to Hutchinson, the latter remembered the promise and spoke of it, but Bernard for some reason had determined against Otis. He told Hutchinson that whoever received the place it would not be Otis; if Hutchinson refused, it would go to someone else. Under these circumstances he had accepted, but Otis never forgave him. Since then the younger Otis had gone into politics, and as a member of the House of Representatives had taken every opportunity to attack the man who he thought had cheated his father.[1]

James Otis, Jr., was not a man to be nice about his methods, and he used every trick of innuendo and snide suggestion to communicate his own hatred to the people at large. Probably he was partly responsible for the outrage of August 26 simply by virtue of the feeling against Hutchinson which he had helped to create. Yet he was not solely responsible. Hutchinson could remember occasions, even before Otis turned against him, when he had made himself odious simply by adhering to his convictions in the face of popular opposition. In 1748 he had done Massachusetts a great service which nevertheless rendered him extremely unpopular in certain quarters. In

1. Hutchinson, *History of Massachusetts-Bay*, L. S. Mayo, ed., III, 63-64. The affair is dealt with most extensively in Malcolm Freiberg, Prelude to Purgatory: Thomas Hutchinson in Massachusetts Politics, 1760-1770, Ph.D. dissertation, 1950, Brown University Library.

that year Massachusetts received reimbursement from the British Treasury for her part in capturing the French fortress of Louisburg in 1745. The capture of Louisburg had been almost entirely the undertaking of Massachusetts. It was the only notable success of British arms in the War of the Austrian Succession, and enabled the British to secure by exchange the return of Madras in India from the French. A grateful Parliament therefore voted to reimburse Massachusetts for her pains, in the sum of £ 183,649, 25s. 7d. Heretofore, like other colonies, Massachusetts had had to rely on a wholly unstable paper currency which every year depreciated further, to the great grief of all creditors. When the British Treasury turned over the sum, all in silver, Hutchinson and other far-sighted individuals saw the opportunity to get rid of paper money in Massachusetts. Hutchinson pressed hard to persuade the Assembly to take this step, and succeeded, with two results: Massachusetts had the soundest currency in North America, and Massachusetts debtors, who lost heavily by the change, hated Hutchinson cordially as the author of their misfortunes.[2]

That had been seventeen years ago. The memory still rankled, but it was not enough to make people suddenly burst out in a wild rage. A more recent event which contributed to the people's dislike was Hutchinson's part in preventing the courts of Massachusetts from violating an act of Parliament. The customs officers in Boston had received strict orders in 1761 from William Pitt to prevent clandestine trade with the enemy. To assist them in discovering such trade they were instructed to apply for writs of assistance (general warrants) empowering them to break open any building they chose to search for contraband or smuggled goods. Such writs had been authorized by an act of Parliament in 1696 but had never been employed before, and it was doubtful whether the colonial courts had authority to issue them. Some of the other justices of the Superior Court favored a blank refusal, but Hutchinson persuaded the Court to postpone a decision until they obtained more information from England, with the ultimate result that the Court did issue the writs. James Otis, Jr., his new-found enemy, was advocate of the Boston merchants in the case, arguing against the writs of assistance as violations of the natural rights of man. Up to this time Otis had been advocate of the Admiralty Court, a position which would have obliged him to argue in favor of the writs, but he re-

2. Hutchinson to Conway, October 1, 1765, Massachusetts Archives, XXVI, 155; Andrew McF. Davis, *Currency and Banking in the Province of the Massachusetts Bay* (New York, 1901), chs. 10-12.

signed in order to argue against them. As a result Otis gained in popularity what Hutchinson lost.[3]

By his support of hard money in 1748 Hutchinson had earned the dislike of the debtors; by his stand on the writs of assistance he had earned that of the smugglers. According to some estimates, if these two groups were subtracted from the population of Massachusetts, there would be scarcely anyone left. And yet even the episode of the writs of assistance passed without any violent demonstration against him. He had been unpopular, but no one thought of pulling his house down. As a matter of fact, only a year and a half before the riot there had been proof that the people respected his integrity, even though they might not love him. In February, 1764, the House of Representatives with only eight members dissenting asked him to go to England to argue the colony's case against the molasses duty. He had been unable to leave at once, and before he was prepared to go news of the Sugar Act arrived.[4] Yet the vote demonstrated that the people knew him for an honest man. It was what happened in the following year that turned them so bitterly against him.

As Hutchinson considered what he had done during this year to win the reward of August 26 he must have felt some bitterness himself. He was no friend of the Sugar Act or the Stamp Act. When the Massachusetts Assembly voted to send him to London to oppose the Sugar Act, they had not picked the wrong man. Hutchinson was a merchant himself and knew what the Sugar Act would mean to New England commerce. He thought it was a piece of folly which Parliament would repent of. As for the Stamp Act he had been one of the first to see the dangers of that. He had never told the people of Massachusetts of his efforts to prevent it or of his efforts to secure repeal of the Sugar Act. It would not have been fitting for him, as a servant of the Crown, to encourage the people of the colonies in their resistance to acts of Parliament by letting them know he was on their side; yet he was just as convinced as his demagogical enemies that Parliament had had no constitutional right to pass either the Sugar Act or the Stamp Act.

During the spring of 1764, when Governor Bernard was setting down his 97 propositions and James Otis was writing his *Rights of*

3. Hutchinson to Conway, October 1, 1765, Massachusetts Archives, XXVI, 155; see Freiberg, Prelude to Purgatory, ch. 1, and O. M. Dickerson, "Writs of Assistance as a Cause of the Revolution," in R. B. Morris, ed., *The Era of the American Revolution* (New York, 1939), 40-75.

4. Hutchinson to ———, February 6, 7, 1764, Massachusetts Archives, XXVI, 76-78; Bernard to Jackson, February 2, 1764, Bernard Papers, III, 123-127, Harvard College Library.

the Colonies, Hutchinson too was writing about the rights of the colonies.[5] Perhaps he too did some of his writing in Concord, for like Bernard and Otis he was attending the meetings of the Assembly there. Bernard had sent his propositions to Richard Jackson on July 9, suggesting that he get them printed if they were approved in the proper quarters. Hutchinson sent his piece to Jackson too—Jackson knew everybody—on July 23, and enclosed a copy of Otis's pamphlet which had just been rushed into print. It was Hutchinson's intention that Jackson should get his paper printed, provided Jackson thought that it would be helpful in preventing taxation of the colonies, but Hutchinson wanted the authorship kept secret. He wrote the piece in a form common in political writing at the time, as a letter from a gentleman to his friend. At first he wished Jackson to make it appear as coming "from some other colony rather than the Massachusetts, which might prevent fixing upon the author," but upon second thought added that it might be safer if it were made to appear as a production of someone in England. This might be done if "some stroke or other could be inserted having reference to some very late transaction with you of which there could not be time for advice in the colonies." [6]

Hutchinson's uneasiness about having his name connected with the piece may well have arisen from the fact that it affirmed the rights—not the privileges—of the colonies in very explicit terms. In fact there was scarcely any argument used in the later colonial struggle against the Stamp Act that Hutchinson did not anticipate. The only thing that marked him off from the radicals was the calmness with which he stated the case. In the opening paragraph he even apologized for the warmth with which Otis had written: "Before I enter upon the Subject," he wrote, "give me leave to observe to you that the Colonists like all the rest of the human race are of different spirits and dispositions some more calm and moderate others more violent and extravagant. and if now and then some rude and indecent things are thrown out in print in one place and another I hope such things will not be considered as coming from the Colonists in general but from particular persons warmed by the intemperate zeal shall I say of Englishmen in support of what upon a sudden appears to them to be their rights."

Although he thus attempted to undo the damage which he felt

5. I have published the manuscript, along with some of the observations on Hutchinson made in this chapter, in *New England Quarterly*, 21 (1948), 459-492. All quotations from the manuscript will be found here.

6. Massachusetts Archives, XXVI, 99-100.

would result from Otis's heated phrases, Hutchinson's own position was in every important particular identical with Otis's. Both paid tribute to the standard Whig doctrine of the supremacy of the British Parliament. Hutchinson thought it reasonable that "British Colonies should ever remain subject to the controul of Britain and consequently must be bound by the determinations of the supreme authority there the British Parliament." Otis agreed that "The power of parliament is uncontroulable, but by themselves, and we must obey. They only can repeal their own Acts." [7] Otis, while acknowledging the supremacy of Parliament, argued in terms derived from Locke that Parliament ought not to violate the natural rights of the subject.[8] Hutchinson likewise affirmed that Parliament should have a tender regard for "all rights natural and acquired of every Subject." Hutchinson went on to state that the colonists "claim a power of making Law and a Privilege of exemption from taxes except by their own Representatives." This power, he said, was what they deserved as Englishmen and had been confirmed to them by the charters which stated that the colonists should have the same privileges as natural-born Englishmen. This did not mean that Parliament had resigned all authority over the colonists, but according to Hutchinson Parliament had suspended a part, at least, of the authority which it would have exercised had they remained in England. This authority had been transferred from the home government to the colonial governments, just as in the case of the Roman colonies. And Hutchinson went into the analogy of the Roman colonies in considerable detail, emerging with the conclusion "that it does not seem to be an unreasonable proposition, that the inhabitants of [a] Colony are intitled to all the privileges they enjoyed in their mother Country which will consist with their dependance upon it."

Hutchinson, again like Otis, dismissed the distinction between internal and external taxes favored by some English writers and notably by his friend Richard Jackson. According to this distinction Parliament might levy external taxes, that is, customs duties, on the colonists but not internal or direct taxes. Otis had said: "There is no foundation for the distinction some make in England, between an internal and an external tax on the colonies." [9] Hutchinson put the argument more directly in terms of popular rights. "Is it any difference to me," he asked, "whether I pay three pounds ten shillings duty for a Pipe of wine to an officer of Impost or whether I pay the same Sum by an

7. *The Rights of the British Colonies Asserted and Proved* (Boston, 1764), 39.
8. *Ibid., passim,* especially 25-31.
9. *Ibid.,* 42.

excise of ninepence per Gallon to an excise Officer or would an old Roman have thought his Privileges less affected by the Portorium than by the Stipendium or Decumae?" Hutchinson was more diplomatic than Otis in stating that if there appeared to Parliament to be an essential difference between internal and external taxes, he was willing to accept it; he was willing to take half a loaf as better than none, but, he queried, remembering no doubt that Parliament had already passed the resolution for a stamp tax, "are we sure of retaining even this?" Are we sure in other words, of retaining an exemption even from internal taxes?

Hutchinson next pointed out the weakness of the argument, which apparently had been advanced in England already, that the colonies were as much represented in Parliament as were the nine Englishmen out of ten who had no vote in Parliamentary elections. Hutchinson showed that every important interest in England was represented in Parliament, "but what Member," he asked, "can be said to be the representative of the Colonies more than all the rest?" This passage bears a striking resemblance to General Conway's speech against the Stamp Act on February 15, 1765, when Conway asked, "Will any man in this house get up and say, he is one of the representatives of the colonies; when so far from being an object of their choice, the most sensible man in the colonies scarce knows such a gentleman exists." [10]

In the first part of his manuscript Hutchinson had advanced constitutional arguments against Parliamentary taxation. In the remainder of the paper he dismissed the question of constitutional right and showed the inequity of levying taxes upon colonies which already contributed heavily, through the mercantilist regulations of trade, to the wealth and power of the mother country, and which had been planted, with the exception of Georgia and Halifax, entirely at the expense of the colonists themselves. In this part of the paper Hutchinson anticipated the arguments urged by Colonel Barré in his speech in Parliament on February 6.[11] Hutchinson understandably made no charge of corruption against colonial governors, as Barré did, but he did show that the colonies had been planted by the enterprise of the colonists, not by any care on the part of the mother country; and he also showed that for a hundred years the colonists had defended themselves against the Indians without assistance from England and that the late French and Indian War, in which the colonists contributed both men and money, had been fought as much for the benefit of the mother country as for that of the colonies.

10. *Georgia Gazette*, August 1, 1765.
11. See above, ch. 5.

The resemblance between Hutchinson's arguments and those used in the House of Commons by General Conway and Colonel Barré was perhaps more than a coincidence. Jackson evidently decided that no good purpose would be served in England by printing the manuscript, but apparently he passed it around discreetly among persons of influence. Arthur Savage of Boston, who arrived in London early in 1765, found that "People seem generally agreed that at the present Junto no Man is so sutable or so likely to Serve the Province as Mr. Hutchinson who is in high Repute here—which is greatly strengthned by a Letter of his to Mr. Jackson . . . which is highly spoken of." [12] The person to whom Jackson finally entrusted the manuscript was His Majesty's new Secretary of State for the Southern Department, General Conway. Exactly when he did so Jackson neglected to say, but he did tell Hutchinson that he had let Conway in on the secret of who the author was. "This was a Piece of Confidence in him," wrote Jackson, "that I thought proper, and have no reason to be sorry I reposed it." [13] Whether Isaac Barré saw the manuscript or not is uncertain but altogether likely, since he along with Conway was known as a friend of the colonies. In November, 1765, after hearing of the assault on Hutchinson's house, Jackson wrote to Governor Bernard: "Nothing can be more unjust than the Treatment of the worthy and unfortunate Lieutenant Governor, nothing can be a greater proof of the Blindness of the Rabble: I know that He has used the weightiest Arguments against the obnoxious Act, and that they have been used at Home from his Materials." [14] Jackson's testimony that Hutchinson's manuscript had assisted the opponents of the Stamp Act in England was later confirmed by General Conway himself. On May 24, 1776, while his countrymen were preparing to declare their independence, Hutchinson was in England, dining with Sir George Hay, who told him that Conway had observed in a speech in Parliament "that he had received from me in the time of the Stamp Act, such reasons against the passing of it as were irresistible." [15]

In 1765, as he passed the shell of his once handsome house or caught the hostile glances of people on the street, Hutchinson must have reflected with some bitterness on the irony of his situation. He stood in the eyes of his countrymen as a traitor, while Barré and Conway basked in a shower of fulsome tributes. Town-meetings all over

12. To S. P. Savage, January 12, 1765, S. P. Savage Papers, II, Massachusetts Historical Society.
13. Massachusetts Archives, XXV, 65.
14. Massachusetts Archives, XXII, 456.
15. Peter O. Hutchinson, ed., *The Diary and Letters of Thomas Hutchinson* (London, 1884-1886), II, 58.

America including that of Boston had passed votes of gratitude to these gentlemen.[16] And the only thing that Barré and Conway had done was to urge in Parliament the arguments which he had advanced long before. In fact it was not unlikely that they had derived their arguments from his manuscript.

Hutchinson would certainly have been justified in thinking that he deserved better at the hands of Massachusetts. And yet in a perverse way the mob had been right. Mobs never act reasonably, for they would not be mobs if they did. The mob which destroyed Hutchinson's house was right in attacking him, because he was a man of strength: the people of Massachusetts had sensed that a showdown was near and that when it came, the strength of Thomas Hutchinson would be against them. Whatever his feelings about the expediency or constitutionality of the Stamp Act, he would be found defending law and order. When the barricades were up, Thomas Hutchinson would be on the other side. And in the summer of 1765 it looked as though the barricades were going up. It was his prudence, his moderation, his fundamental conservatism that made Hutchinson an enemy of the people in 1765, because the time for prudence had suddenly passed. The face of revolution had appeared; he who was not a friend was an enemy; and Hutchinson was an enemy not to be dealt with lightly.

He had demonstrated his moderation in the most positive manner during the year preceding the assault on his house. In the summer of 1765 the people of Massachusetts were thinking of the numerous occasions when he had urged them to submit peacefully to the chains which Parliament was clearly forging for them. The instance in which he had exerted his influence most forcefully was in toning down the petition which Massachusetts sent to the King in November, 1764.[17]

It is interesting that Hutchinson insisted on leaving the word "rights" out of the petition and on confining the objections against taxation to internal taxes. In his own essay he used the word rights and ridiculed the distinction between internal and external taxes. Even more curious is the fact that only a little more than a week after he had finally persuaded the Massachusetts House of Representatives to drop their declaration against the external taxes of the Sugar Act, he wrote to his friend Ebenezer Silliman in Connecticut, chiding him for the fact that Connecticut confined its arguments to internal taxes. Silliman was a member of the committee which

16. *A Report of the Record Commissioners of the City of Boston, containing the Boston Town Records, 1758 to 1769*, p. 157.
17. See the discussion in ch. 3, above.

worked with Governor Fitch in writing *Reasons why the British Colonies, in America, should not be charged with Internal Taxes, by Authority of Parliament.*[18] "Your distinction between duties upon trade and internal taxes," Hutchinson wrote,

agrees with the opinion of People in England, particularly your Agent [Richard Jackson]. and with the opinion of most People here Mr. Bernard is full with you in it. I think it imprudent to oppose it and therefore am silent but it is for this reason only. I am for saving as much of our privileges as we can and if the people of England make the distinction I think it tends to strengthen us in our claim to exemption from internal taxes. Really there is no difference and the fallacy of the argument lies here it is your supposing duties upon trade to be imposed for the sake of regulating trade, whereas the Professed design of the duties by the late Act is to raise a revenue. Can I possibly cause any difference to the subject to impose a duty of £5 on a pipe of wine to be paid as an impost or to impose a duty of excise of 12d a gallon to be paid by the licensed inland vendor. The consumer pays just the same supposing the pipe to be 100 gallons in the one case as the other and the rights of the people are alike affected in both cases. If they will stop where they are I would not dispute their distinction with them, but if they intend to go on there will be a necessity of doing it for they may find duties on trade enough to drain us so thoroughly that it will not be possible to pay internal taxes as a revenue to them or even to support government within ourselves.[19]

In view of Hutchinson's performance in persuading the Massachusetts House of Representatives to adopt an address which objected only to internal taxes, his letter to Silliman is remarkable. He tells Silliman that "most people here" agree with the distinction between internal and external taxes, yet the House of Representatives had approved Otis's pamphlet in which the statement occurred that "there is no foundation for the distinction some make in England, between an internal and an external tax on the colonies," [20] and in the petition originally approved by the House it was stated with regard to the external duties levied under the Sugar Act, that "we look *upon those Duties as a Tax,* and which we humbly apprehend ought not to be laid without the Representatives of the People affected by them." [21]

18. (New Haven, 1764); *Public Records of the Colony of Connecticut,* XII, 256, 651-671.

19. November 9, 1764, Massachusetts Archives, XXVI, 117-118.

20. *Rights of the British Colonies,* 42; *Journal of the Honourable House of Representatives* (Boston, 1764), 53, 66.

21. Massachusetts Archives, XXII, 412-418.

In the address which Hutchinson had just persuaded the House to accept there was no suggestion that the duties of the Sugar Act were regarded as a tax. The address pleaded against the Sugar Act solely on economic grounds and confined its constitutional objections to internal taxes. Hutchinson had thus persuaded the Assembly to accept a statement which fell short of what he himself believed to be their due. In the paper he sent to Jackson he declared that all Parliamentary taxation of the colonies, internal or external, violated the rights of the people. In the letter to Silliman he said that the rights of the people were no less affected by external than by internal taxes, and yet he persuaded the House of Representatives not to use the word "rights" and to plead for exemption from internal taxes only. Since the people of Massachusetts knew nothing of Hutchinson's private views, it is no wonder that they thought he was ready to sacrifice their rights. Even if they had known of his efforts to prevent the Stamp Act, they might have continued to think so, though perhaps with less bitterness—and they would not have been wrong.

Until the Stamp Act had become a law Hutchinson had been on the side of the colonists. He had opposed the Act, because he believed that it would violate their rights, not merely their charter rights but their natural rights as men. But he also believed in the supremacy of Parliament, believed in it to the point where defiance of Parliamentary authority, however that authority was exercised, became synonymous with revolution. When Parliament did tax the colonies, Parliament was in the wrong, but that was no reason for the colonies to commit the further wrong of resisting. The only way out of the dilemma, as Hutchinson saw it, was to persuade the members to undo the injustice they had committed. And the most effective means of persuasion was not defiance but prudent submission and humble supplications.[22]

Prudence in the last analysis was Hutchinson's solution for the impasse between Parliamentary supremacy and colonial rights. He prevented the Massachusetts Assembly from asserting their rights, because he did not think it prudent to assert them. He went along with Governor Bernard and Richard Jackson in their distinction between internal and external taxes, though he believed it without foundation, because it was prudent to do so. He did not publish his paper on colonial rights, because he did not think it prudent. His was the attitude of honest friends of the colonies in England, who likewise had to reconcile Parliamentary supremacy with colonial rights. Richard Jackson did not think it advisable to publish Hutchinson's man-

22. Hutchinson to Champion and Hayley, April 9, 1765, *ibid.*, XXVI, 135.

uscript even with the authorship secret. Instead he gave it to Conway, from whom the sentiments expressed in it would come more graciously than from a colonist.

The friends of the colonies in England were distressed by the aggressive declarations of right pouring from America in the summer of 1765,[23] and Hutchinson was distressed by them in Massachusetts. He knew that they would make repeal of the Stamp Act more difficult, and he tried to persuade his countrymen to be more discreet. As he confided to his business correspondents in England, "It can be to no purpose to claim a right of exemption when the whole body of the people of England are against us." [24] It was this attitude which gave Hutchinson his reputation in Massachusetts as an enemy of the people's rights. He thought it foolhardy for people to seek a head-on collision with Parliament by abstract declarations of their rights or by exercising those rights in defiance of an act of Parliament. He even took advantage of his position as chief justice to lecture them on the consequences of such actions. In addresses to the grand juries of the several counties, he let them know, as he put it, "the nature of the offence of opposing by force and violence the execution of an Act of Parliament the supreme legislature of the British Dominions." [25]

Thus as his fellow-countrymen grew more outspoken, more determined to defend their rights, Hutchinson grew more and more prudent. There can be no doubt that his judgment was correct so far as concerned the immediate goal of repealing the Stamp Act. The colonial declarations of right and the violence against the stamp distributors only served to embarrass the men who were attempting to bring about repeal in England. What Hutchinson failed to understand was that in the year 1765 the American colonies had reached political maturity. Hitherto they had not been obliged to determine exactly what their rights were. But when Parliament taxed them, they found out where they stood; and having done so, they were unwilling to accept prudence as a solution to their troubles. They did not want privileges; they wanted rights. Hutchinson never understood this. In 1774 he was in England, still seeking to mitigate the harshness of British measures against the colonies, still urging the colonies to forget about their rights and seek accommodation through prudence. When he heard of the Continental Congress, he wrote to a friend in America warning of the ill effects to be expected from such an assembly. "I know it is expected," he wrote, "that the more de-

23. See below, ch. 15.
24. To Champion and Hayley, April 9, 1765, Massachusetts Archives, XXVI, 135.
25. Hutchinson to Conway, October 1, 1765, *ibid.,* 155.

termined the Colonies appear, the more likely it will be to bring the Government here to their terms. I do not believe it." [26]

Hutchinson of course was right in 1774 as he had been in 1765. The British Parliament would not give way in the face of colonial determination. If the colonists had followed Hutchinson's advice, perhaps they might have preserved their attachment to the mother country without necessarily suffering an unfair burden of taxation. Through humble petitions and silent economic pressure they might have been able to obtain the redress of their immediate grievances. But they would have obtained it as a favor, not as a right. Hutchinson's mistake was in supposing that the colonies were willing to accept favors in place of rights. Fifty years before, they might have been, but never after the passage of the Stamp Act. The colonies had come of age; and Thomas Hutchinson was still trying to play the role of guardian. The price of his mistake in 1765 was a house in ruins; the ultimate price was a life completed in exile.

26. *Diary and Letters*, I, 217 (August 8, 1774).

THIRTEEN

JARED INGERSOLL

WHEN William Samuel Johnson went to England in the fall of 1766, he was shocked at the gulf that separated rich from poor. He wrote about it to his old friend Benjamin Gale, of Killingly, Connecticut, and Gale wrote back like a trueborn Son of Liberty: "the Common people of England are a very different sett of Men from the people of America, otherwise they never would submitt to be taxed in the Manner they are, that a few may be loaded with places and Pensions and riot in Luxury and Excess, while they themselves cannot support themselves and their needy offspring with Bread, I thank God we are not such Jack Asses in America, and I hope in God we never shall be brought to submit to it, . . ." [1]

It is difficult to believe that a man who could denounce British taxation with such zest could curse the Sons of Liberty with equal vigor. Yet in this very letter Benjamin Gale bemoaned the fate of Connecticut under a government in which the Sons of Liberty had the leading hand. He found comfort only in the fact that the governor was very old, and "as age is Honorable," Gale concluded, "I wish he was as old again as he now is."

Benjamin Gale had been no advocate of a stamp tax. For that matter what American had? But for Gale as for many other Americans the Stamp Act had turned the world upside down. In a political and social situation which was precarious at best the Stamp Act had confounded wise and foolish, just and unjust. Connecticut plunged wildly through convulsions of hate, envy, and ambition; and suddenly, senselessly the men against whom Gale and his friends had been fighting for twenty-five years emerged victorious. These men,

1. Benjamin Gale to William Samuel Johnson, December 1, 1767, William Samuel Johnson Papers, Connecticut Historical Society.

he was sure, had no claim to be sole champions of liberty or justice or reason, and yet the appointment of Jared Ingersoll as Distributor of Stamps had enabled them to appear on the side of the angels while Gale and his friends were forced into the outer darkness. You really had to live in Connecticut to understand what had happened. In fact you had to be a Yale man to understand it properly, for it had all begun at Yale back in the winter of 1741-42, when Jared Ingersoll was a senior there. Thomas Clap was Rector of Yale in those days.[2] He had been installed in 1740, after serving for fifteen years as pastor of the church in Windham, where he had already outlived one wife and married a second. His first wife had been a niece of Colonel Joseph Whiting of New Haven, and as family relations figured largely in Connecticut, this connection with a prominent New Haven family was of some importance in the events that followed. Clap was a strong-minded man, apt to be pig-headed at times, but always a man to reckon with. He was orthodox in religion, abhorring equally the "Arminian" notions of free will which were beginning to appear in sophisticated quarters and the "enthusiastic" evangelism which was already stirring up thousands in England. The year he became rector enthusiasm crossed the ocean and broke like a tidal wave on his college and his country.

This was the year of the Great Awakening: George Whitefield who had excited so many souls in England, was now cutting a swath through the colonies, and New Haven lay in his path. The students responded as avidly as the rest of the population, and when Whitefield had departed, they sent an invitation to Gilbert Tennent, a native evangelist who was currently splitting the Presbyterian church in Pennsylvania with his denunciations of an unconverted ministry. Tennent came to New Haven and left the students, or some of them at least, in agonies of despair and delight. After him came the wildest enthusiast of them all, James Davenport, who embarrassingly enough was a Yale graduate. Davenport, whose manners did not comport with President Clap's idea of either a Christian or a Yale man, made himself particularly obnoxious by denouncing the minister of the New Haven church, the Reverend Joseph Noyes.[3]

2. On Clap see Clifford K. Shipton, *Biographical Sketches of those who attended Harvard College in the Classes 1722-1725*, (Boston, 1945), 27-50; Franklin B. Dexter, "Thomas Clap and his Writings," New Haven Colony Historical Society, *Papers*, 5 (1894), 247-274.

3. On the Great Awakening in Connecticut see Joseph Tracy, *The Great Awakening; a History of the Revival of Religion* (Boston, 1842); Ellen D. Larned, *History of Windham County, Connecticut* (Worcester, 1874), I, 393-485; Edwin S. Gaustad, The Great Awakening in New England, 1741-1742, Ph.D. dissertation, Brown University Library; Maria L. Greene, *The Development of Religious Liberty in Connecticut* (Boston, 1905), 220-272. The best original accounts of the Awakening at Yale are the following:

The effect of all this excitement on the students was what might have been expected. When they attended the New Haven Church, as they regularly did, they found Mr. Noyes's preaching as cold as Davenport had said it was. And from here it was only a step to making the same judgment about the prayers which the President and tutors conducted at college. There is no record that anyone had the audacity to consider Thomas Clap dull, but some of the students who had been most deeply moved by the revivalists could not forbear making invidious comparisons with regard to the tutors. David Brainerd, who later enjoyed a brief but distinguished career as missionary to the Indians, found Tutor Chauncy Whittelsey a man of little grace. When another student spoke warmly of Whittelsey's performance at prayers, Brainerd retorted that "He has no more Grace than this chair." The statement was overheard by a freshman, who told it to someone in the town, who told it to Rector Clap. Rector Clap had already clamped down on the students' attendance at revival meetings, and he now made an example of Brainerd by expelling him from the college.[4] Three years later, Clap exerted his authority in an even more dictatorial manner by expelling John and Ebenezer Cleaveland. Their only offense was that they had attended the meeting of a "New Light" revivalist church at Canterbury, Connecticut, during the spring vacation.[5]

Although Clap's action was characteristically high-handed, the General Assembly of the colony approved it. The Assembly in 1742, shortly after Brainerd's expulsion from Yale, had passed an act to outlaw itinerant preaching and preaching by any minister not properly ordained. The majority in the Assembly were "Old Lights," hostile to the Awakening, and the following year, in order to prevent the formation of New Light churches, they repealed an act of toleration passed thirty-five years earlier.[6]

With feelings running so high it was not possible for a man to be neutral. Young men in college are not apt to be cautious about forming or disclosing their opinions anyhow, and although Jared Ingersoll was circumspect by nature, that very trait doubtless inclined him

---

Samuel Hopkins, Works (Boston, 1852), I, 15-18, and Jared Ingersoll, An Historical Account of Some Affairs Relating to the Church, Especially in Connecticut, together with some other Things of a Different Nature, Ms, Library of Congress.

4. Jonathan Edwards, An Account of the Life of the Late Reverend Mr. David Brainerd (Boston, 1749), 20.

5. Larned, History of Windham County, I, 417-427.

6. Public Records of the Colony of Connecticut, VIII, 454-457, 521-522.

toward the Old Lights. During his junior year the students who had been most deeply stirred by the revival were meeting secretly and openly for religious discussions. Samuel Buell, in the class before him, and Brainerd, in the class below, went about visiting the rooms of all the students, inquiring after their spiritual condition, and urging them to repent. Most of the students seem to have borne these visitations patiently and humbly; Samuel Hopkins, who was to become the leading New Light theologian of his generation, was deeply affected by them.[7] But to a man of Ingersoll's temper they were probably distasteful. The kind of life which the New Lights would have had him lead was one in which the pleasures of polite social intercourse would have been all but eliminated. Whitefield on his first visit to New Haven had spoken expressly "against mixed dancing and frolicking of males and females together." [8] Ingersoll was no wanton, but he and his friends doubtless sided with Rector Clap in deploring the misguided zeal of the Revival movement.[9] The kind of men whom Ingersoll was friendly with were not the earnest young devotees who were to spread the New Light through America in the ensuing years. Ingersoll preferred the company of men like John Whiting (brother of Colonel Joseph Whiting), and of Nathan Whiting, John's cousin and a brother-in-law of Rector Clap. Later, while the Hopkinses and the Buells were making a name for themselves in the pulpit, Nathan Whiting would be winning fame on the field of battle in the French and Indian Wars. And at the end of the war Whiting would write to Ingersoll from South Carolina for news of Connecticut, "how is the State? do the Saints Govern, or do some of you Men of the World, take upon you Worldly matters? ... What for a Commencement had you? was it in the old Stile? were you allowed to dance, kiss the Girls, and drink Wine?" [10] One gathers that Ingersoll and the Whiting boys had had some opportunity to frolic with females during their years at college, and probably without incurring the frowns of Rector Clap. Nathan Whiting had been brought up mainly by his sister Mrs. Clap, and later became Clap's son-in-law as well as his brother-in-law, by marrying the daughter

7. Hopkins, *Works*, I, 16-18.

8. *Ibid.*, 15.

9. Ingersoll's "An historical Account of Some Affairs Relating to the Church, Especially in Connecticut" takes a characteristically objective attitude but is punctuated by parenthetical disclaimers ("as was supposed" or "as they thought it") in stating the position of the New Lights. Indispensable for the study of Ingersoll is Lawrence Gipson's *Jared Ingersoll: A Study of American Loyalism in Relation to British Colonial Government* (New Haven, 1920).

10. New Haven Colony Historical Society, *Papers*, 9 (1918), 303.

of the Rector's second wife.[11] Family relations were often complicated in New England.

Within a year after he graduated from college Ingersoll himself became a member of the Clap-Whiting clan by marrying Hannah, John Whiting's sister, and eight years later John confirmed the bond by marrying Ingersoll's sister. And to complete the entente which had begun in college, Tutor Whittelsey, the man whose piety Brainerd had dismissed so harshly, married Elizabeth Whiting, another sister of John.[12]

When Ingersoll settled in New Haven after graduation to study and practice law, it was a foregone conclusion that he would join the church of which Mr. Noyes was then pastor. His wife was already a member; her brother John was to be Deacon for thirty years; and Chauncy Whittelsey was ultimately to succeed Noyes as pastor. In 1742, while Ingersoll was still in college, a separate church had been set up in New Haven by those who agreed with James Davenport's judgment of Mr. Noyes. Similar secession movements had occurred all over the colony, and although the government with its majority of Old Lights had refused to recognize them or to give them official standing as churches, the separations proceeded in defiance of authority. Ingersoll, always on the side of law and order, stood by Mr. Noyes and became a tower of strength to the church in its long-drawn struggle with the New Light group.[13]

Ingersoll was a bright young man. Possessed of the right family connections he moved rapidly upward in his profession, and in 1751, probably through the influence of John Whiting (now clerk of the New Haven County Court), he became King's Attorney for New Haven County.[14] Thus at the age of twenty-nine Ingersoll had become a leading member of the community. He was definitely associated with one side of a continuing religious controversy, but this was nothing against him, for everyone in the colony was associated with one side or the other. The only inauspicious omen for his future lay in the fact that the side which he had chosen was dwindling. The New Lights with their vigorous preaching were steadily growing in numbers and securing more and more strength in the legislature. However, the trend was not so pronounced that

11. Franklin B. Dexter, *Biographical Sketches of the Graduates of Yale College with Annals of the College History* (New York, 1885), I, 750-751.

12. Gipson, *Ingersoll*, 36, 38; Dexter, *Biographical Sketches*, I, 615, 656.

13. Gipson, *Ingersoll*, 42; Leonard Bacon, *Thirteen Historical Discourses on the Completion of Two Hundred Years, from the Beginning of the First Church in New Haven* (New Haven, 1839), 198-242.

14. Gipson, *Ingersoll*, 42.

anyone would have dared to predict that the Old Lights were on the way out.

Then in 1753 an upset occurred which strengthened the New Lights immeasurably and embittered the Old Lights. Rector Clap, who had opposed the Awakening so effectively in the 1740's, swung his weight to the side of the New Lights. The shift must have been the more bitter to Ingersoll and to John and Nathan Whiting because they had been in college at the time when the Awakening began and had then formed their judgments and taken their stand under Clap's direction. Nathan had been brought up in Rector Clap's family. Since then he had married Mrs. Clap's daughter and had gone into business in New Haven with Mr. Noyes's son-in-law. To the religious issue was thus added the bitterness of a family quarrel. Clap's desertion may have been consistent with his religious principles, for the New Lights had by this time lost their excessive emotionalism and were probably closer to orthodoxy than the Old Lights; but to the men who had been supporting Mr. Noyes in New Haven, the religious issue was probably overshadowed by what appeared to be personal treachery.

Clap's about-face took the form of a move to establish Yale College as a church with a professor of divinity as pastor. Hitherto there had been no professors at Yale, the president and tutors carrying on all the duties of instruction, and no pastor, the students being required to attend Mr. Noyes's church. What Clap wanted was to establish Naphtali Daggett, a New Light of the class of 1748, as Professor of Divinity, and at the same time to cut off the students from Pastor Noyes's Old Light sermons. Raking up a number of old precedents of the kind that scholars can always find, he proclaimed that a college was an independent ecclesiastical corporation, in short a church, as well as an institution of learning. Jared Ingersoll joined with Benjamin Gale, an Old Light Yale man of the class of 1733, to combat this sophistry; but Clap was able to carry his point, and in 1756 Daggett settled down in New Haven as Professor of Divinity and pastor to the students. One may surmise that he brought with him no love for the New Haven lawyer who opposed his appointment.[15]

15. Clap's move was defended and attacked in a series of pamphlets: Thomas Clap, *The Religious Constitution of Colleges, Especially of Yale-College in New Haven in the Colony of Connecticut* (New London, 1754); Benjamin Gale, *The Present State of the Colony of Connecticut Considered. In a Letter from a Gentleman in the Eastern Part of said Colony, to his Friend in the Western Part of the same* ([New London], 1755); Clap, *The Answer of the Friend in the West . . .* (New Haven, 1755); Gale, *A Reply to a Pamphlet entitled the Answer of the Friend in the West . . .* ([New London], 1755); Noah Hobart, *A Congratulatory Letter from a Gentleman in the West to His Friend in the East* (New Haven, 1755).

The controversy did not cease with Daggett's arrival, but Ingersoll was suddenly removed from it in 1758 by appointment as the colony's London agent. The next three years in London were delightful ones. Though he was far from his family and missed them, he was also removed from the bitter political squabbles that were going on in the colony and was able to indulge in a social life with a glamour unknown to New Haven. The time not engaged by business was agreeably filled with attendance at the Court of St. James's, official balls, plays, operas, and country weekends. In spite of his provincial upbringing, Ingersoll fitted perfectly into the high life. He was a man of grace and dignity, amply built—both in face and figure, attentive to dress and fashion, a man who talked well, who made friends easily. Probably his moments of greatest pleasure came from his nightly "patrole of the Strand" and lingering hours at one of the coffeehouses, where he enjoyed the conversation of men like himself, who appreciated good wine and good company. Ingersoll made many friends in these years, friends who lay beyond the feuds and fights of provincial Connecticut. In fact he had some right to think that the company he kept was rather distinguished. There was Benjamin Franklin, serving as agent for Pennsylvania, with his son William, who would shortly be appointed governor of New Jersey. There was Richard Jackson, who knew everybody and everything, who had corresponded with Benjamin Gale's father-in-law Jared Eliot, and for whom Ingersoll secured appointment as his successor in the agency in 1760. John Temple, who became Surveyor General of the New England Customs, was another friend, and so was Thomas Whately, who was to be under-secretary of the Treasury when George Grenville took office. Ingersoll used to dine of an evening with Whately and his other friends at the Crown and Anchor Tavern, perhaps rubbing elbows with the famous Samuel Johnson and the men who hung about him.[16]

There were other visiting Americans too, with whom one could talk of home: Joseph Harrison of Newport, at present living with the Marquis of Rockingham but soon to return to America as Collector of Customs for the port of New Haven, and Godfrey Malbone, also of Newport and later the moving spirit in the founding of the Episcopal church in Pomfret, Connecticut. Ingersoll's tastes were catholic. He made friends both with Benjamin Franklin and with Franklin's political opponent, James Hamilton, who had already served in Pennsylvania for five years as the Proprietors' governor and would

16. See Ingersoll's correspondence in New Haven Colony Historical Society, *Papers*, 9 (1918), 234-304.

shortly serve for four years more. He also knew Alexander Wedder-
burn, who denounced Franklin before the House of Commons in
1774. Ingersoll even made friends with his landlady, Ann Davies,
and she later sent him stays of the latest London fashion for Mrs.
Ingersoll and wrote him a long description of the coronation of
George III, which occurred just after he had left for home. She told
him how his friend Harrison rode out in the procession to meet the
new Queen when she landed from Germany. Harrison "rode by the
side of Coach for half a mile and he says she is very agreable but
as not much buety." And Mrs. Davies added, with less restraint, that
"Thair was two Gentman of my acquatance as says they wold not
gave two pance for her, was she to be had." [17]

It was a pleasant life, but there were times when Ingersoll became
homesick, and felt that he would not give twopence for the whole
island, let alone its Queen; he used to argue with Mrs. Bridges,
Richard Jackson's sister, about the superiority of America to England,
and his preference for New Haven above all the rest of the world.
Even so he stayed in England for a year after he secured the transfer
of the agency to Richard Jackson, working at business negotiations
which later proved fruitless. It was not until the fall of 1761 that
he returned to New Haven to find the quarrels which he had left
proceeding with increased bitterness.

During his absence the New Lights had made a concerted effort
to gain control of the governor's chair and the upper house of the
Assembly. They had failed, no thanks to Rector Clap he felt sure,
but their strength was still growing, and the situation at Yale had
gone from bad to worse, with Clap becoming more dictatorial every
day. Ingersoll's friends were now preparing an appeal to the legislature, asking for the establishment of a committee of visitation to
inspect the college regularly and reform abuses there. Ingersoll
wrote to Benjamin Gale for ammunition in the battle and presented
a petition to the Assembly in May, 1763. It was no use. The New
Lights now had a majority in the lower house, and would never
consent to interfere with Yale while they regarded Clap as their
friend. It was remarkable how the New Lights had developed their
political organization. William Samuel Johnson, himself an Anglican,
observed at this time, that "The N. L. within my short memory were
a small Party merely a religious one, honored within and restrained
by Laws and Decrees of Assembly yet fresh in everybody's Memory,
then looked upon as far off from the Establishment as the Churchmen, and in this short period by their continual struggles they have

17. *Ibid.*, 244, and *passim.*

acquired such an Influence as to be nearly the ruling part of the Government owing to their superior Attention to Civil Affairs and close union among themselves in Politicks." [18] This party naturally regarded Ingersoll as their enemy.

At the same time Ingersoll had become obnoxious to another influential group in the colony. Back in 1754 when Clap was opening his campaign for a professor of divinity at the College, a group of Connecticut speculators had purchased land from the Indians in the Wyoming Valley of Pennsylvania. This group, incorporated as the Susquehannah Company, secured the endorsement of their claims to the region by a resolution of the Connecticut Assembly in 1755. The Assembly overlooked the fact that the land had been purchased from the Iroquois, though the Delawares were in possession of it; they also overlooked the fact that it was in Pennsylvania. According to the theory upon which the Susquehannah Company proceeded, the land was really in Connecticut, because the Connecticut charter of 1662 provided for the extension of the colony westward as far as the Pacific Ocean. Connecticut had not objected when Pennsylvania was chartered in 1685, but the Susquehannah Company thought that it was not too late to object now, and prepared to send settlers to the area.[19]

Jared Ingersoll and Benjamin Gale both owned stock in the company, and when Ingersoll went to England in 1758 he was instructed to promote the Company's interests. But it seems doubtful that either Gale or Ingersoll was a strong supporter of the Company at any time, and when he arrived in England, Ingersoll found that the authorities there thought even less of the project than he did. His friend Thomas Hamilton and the Penn brothers probably argued with him at some length about the unfortunate consequences that might proceed from a disregard of the Pennsylvania charter. Certainly no one thought very highly of a claim that had lain dormant for seventy-five years.

Consequently, when Ingersoll returned to Connecticut, he was not prepared to give the Susquehannah Company much encouragement. The Company had already determined to send a special agent to England to apply for a charter from the King, and Ingersoll, who

18. To J. Beach, January 4, 1763, William Samuel Johnson Papers, Connecticut Historical Society. On the Yale College controversy, see New Haven Colony Historical Society, *Papers*, 9 (1918), 276-277; Benjamin Gale, *A Calm and Full Vindication of a Letter* . . . (New Haven, 1759); John Graham, *An Answer to Mr. Gale's Pamphlet* (New Haven, 1759).

19. On the Susquehannah Company see Julian Boyd, ed., *The Susquehannah Company Papers* (Wilkes-Barre, 1930-33).

was now placed on a committee to prepare arguments for the company's rights to the land, evidently distinguished himself by pointing out the various reasons why the company had no rights. He wrote to his friend James Hamilton, who was back in Pennsylvania as Governor again, that he thought the Susquehannah project would blow over.[20] This conjecture was supported not only by the eloquence of his own arguments against the project but also by the fact that the Connecticut Assembly, at the insistence of General Amherst (Commander-in-Chief of British forces in America), had issued a proclamation warning the inhabitants of the colony against settling in Pennsylvania, though not actually forbidding them to do so.[21] The Earl of Egremont, then Secretary of State for the Southern Department, soon followed Amherst's demand with a letter to Governor Fitch, requiring him to exert every legal authority against the prosecution of settlements.[22] A delegation of Indians came to Hartford to protest the invasion of their lands, and though many settlers were already on the spot, it began to appear that the project really would fall through. But to the consternation of Ingersoll and other conservatives, opposition only made the speculators more eager to press their claims.[23] Ingersoll attended a meeting of the Company and delivered one final harangue against the project. When the members remained unmoved, he sold out his stock and departed.[24]

With this move Ingersoll became the open enemy of the Susquehannah Company, and by an unfortunate coincidence most of the members of the Company already had reason to dislike him. The Susquehannah Company drew the majority of its members from Windham County, the center of the New Light movement in Connecticut. The Company, of course, had no connection with any church and contained many Old Lights from all over Connecticut, but the bulk of the membership could be found on Sundays in the New Light churches of Windham County, where Ingersoll's name already called up unpleasant memories.

Ingersoll believed his dealings with the Company had been fair and above-board. He had not taken any active measures to injure it, apart from communicating on friendly terms with Governor Hamilton of Pennsylvania, the Company's arch-enemy. Nevertheless he was developing into an unpopular figure: New Lights and mem-

20. Thomas Penn to James Hamilton, September 9, 1762, to Richard Peters, September 10, 1762, Boyd, *Susquehannah Papers*, II, 161, 163.
21. *Ibid.*, xxvii, 135.
22. *Ibid.*, 194-196.
23. Ezra Stiles to Pelatiah Webster, May 21, 1763, *ibid.*, 229-230.
24. *Ibid.*

bers of the Susquehannah Company actively disliked him, and the rest of the population could hardly love a man who moved in spheres so far beyond their own experience. His years abroad, some people said, had given him airs; he was too much a man of the world, too much interested in English affairs above American. To be sure in a country which still called England "home," it was no great sin to have been in England, and yet there was a certain uneasy distrust of this man, who had fought against the Great Awakening, who dismissed the colony's claims to the West, and who hobnobbed with English politicians. None of these liabilities was enough to sink a man of Ingersoll's undoubted integrity, and had he been able to keep out of public affairs, he might have gone his way unmolested if unloved. But Ingersoll was too big a man and too closely associated with the Old Light party to withdraw entirely from public life, and his enemies had only to wait for the right opportunity to impart to the rest of the population their own violent hatred of the man.

When George Grenville took office in the summer of 1763, events began to occur which ultimately gave Ingersoll's enemies their chance. Grenville appointed Thomas Whately, his friend and Ingersoll's friend, as under-secretary in the Treasury Office. Then he turned over to Whately the task of drawing up the Stamp Act, and Whately wrote to Ingersoll for advice. From this innocent beginning Ingersoll was gradually drawn into the snare which time had set for him. Ingersoll liked Whately. Before he heard of Whately's appointment, he had written to him, recalling the many cheerful days they had passed together and assuring him that he would like to dine with him some night at the Crown and Anchor, provided that after dinner he could take a chair to New Haven. Whately answered him with news of their common friends, many of whom had since gone to America, Hamilton for example, who was also writing to Ingersoll, urging a visit to Philadelphia and regretting the want of good company and conversation in America. Whately proposed in jest a tour of the colonies, when he should spend many hours with Ingersoll, and assured him, "I would not disgrace mine Host by English Libertinism; I am a Chip you know of the old Block; my Great Grandfather at the farthest was an Oliverian: and his Posterity is not so degenerated but that I could look as demurely on Sundays, or bundle as merrily on the Week Days, as any the best of the Puritans." [25]

How was Ingersoll to know that this delightful correspondence

25. New Haven Colony Historical Society, *Papers*, 9 (1918), 292; Boyd, *Susquehannah Papers*, II, 142-145.

was paving the way for his disgrace? When Whately asked him about the Sugar Act and the proposed stamp tax, he answered in terms that should have satisfied any American, that the 3d. duty on molasses was more than the trade would bear and that Parliament would better have given a premium than imposed such a duty. As for the imposition of a stamp tax, he could only say that it had caused great alarm in the colonies, that people considered it beyond the authority of Parliament, and that it would be difficult to say how many ways could be invented to avoid the payment of it.[26] Perhaps one of the ways which Ingersoll did not think of was that of threatening to kill the tax collector.

In October of 1764 Ingersoll set sail for England in order to look after a private business venture. Even before he landed, the Connecticut Assembly learning of his trip instructed the Governor to write and ask him to assist Richard Jackson in opposing the Stamp Act. The previous May the Assembly had asked him to serve on the committee which drew up the colony's arguments against the Stamp Act, even though he was not a member of the Assembly. It would appear, then, that the majority of the Assembly still trusted his fidelity to the colony, in spite of the distrust which might be felt with regard to his religious views or his attitude toward the Susquehannah Company.[27]

Upon arrival in England and even before he heard of the Assembly's action Ingersoll cooperated with the other agents in agitating against the Stamp Act, and was one of the four agents who met with Grenville early in February in a last-minute attempt to stave off the blow. At the same time he resumed his acquaintance with Whately, and at Whately's request wrote a description of the methods of taxation currently in use in Connecticut and calculated the amount which the proposed stamp tax might be expected to produce. According to his figures, the British government might expect to draw £ 3439. 10s. annually from Connecticut by a stamp tax.[28] When it became apparent that George Grenville was determined to have such a tax, Ingersoll took advantage of his friendship with Whately to get the Act cast in as agreeable a form as possible. He was able to get the duty entirely removed from three items which were included in the original draught of the bill: marriage licenses, commissions of justices of the peace, and notes of hand. On other items he per-

26. New Haven Colony Historical Society, *Papers,* 9 (1918), 299.
27. Gipson, *Ingersoll,* 124.
28. Treasury Papers, Class I, Bundle 433, ff. 406, 410; Public Record Office, Library of Congress transcripts.

suaded the Ministry to set the duties at a lower rate than they had intended.[29]

Ingersoll believed with some reason that he had done his country good service. Though he had not succeeded in preventing the stamp tax, he had done more than any other man to reduce the size of it. It was perhaps with a feeling of righteousness produced by this reflection that he accepted from Grenville the office of Stamp Distributor for Connecticut.

The news of the appointment reached Connecticut shortly after news of the Act itself. The first reaction of a number of citizens, some of whom later distinguished themselves for their opposition to the Act, was not unfavorable to Ingersoll. William Samuel Johnson, who was to attend the Stamp Act Congress as one of Connecticut's delegates, wrote to Ingersoll offering to serve as his "subaltern" for the town of Stratford. "Since we are doomed to Stamps and Slavery," he wrote, "and must submit, we hear with pleasure that your gentle hand will fit on our Chains and Shackles, who I know will make them set easie as possible." [30] This was precisely the reaction Ingersoll must have expected from the people of Connecticut when he took the job. But when he returned to New Haven early in August, he found that this attitude of resignation had passed. The change was apparent in Boston, where his ship landed,[31] and his arrival in New Haven was signalized in the *Connecticut Gazette* by a letter which maliciously interpreted his acceptance of the stamp office as treason against his country. With maddening ingenuity the author of the letter discredited in advance whatever defense he could make: "Have three hundred Pounds a Year, or even a more trifling Consideration been found sufficient to debauch from their Interest those who have been entrusted with the most important concerns by the Colonies? . . . No you'll say, *I don't delight in the Ruin of my Country, but, since 'tis decreed she must fall, who can blame me for taking a Part in the Plunder?* Tenderly said! why did you not rather say— *If my Father must die, who can accuse me as defective in filial Duty, in becoming his Executioner, that so much of the Estate, at least, as goes to the Hangman, may be retained in the Family?*" [32] The letter was signed "Cato," but Ingersoll doubtless knew who wrote it. It

29. New Haven Colony Historical Society, *Papers*, 9 (1918), 314.

30. *Ibid.*, 324. Several other persons also applied to Ingersoll for subordinate positions (*ibid.*, 324-327).

31. *Boston Gazette*, August 12, 1765.

32. *Connecticut Gazette*, August 9, 1765, reprinted in *Connecticut Courant*, August 26, 1765.

was Naphtali Daggett, the Professor of Divinity at Yale, whose enmity Ingersoll had earned ten years before.[33]

The letter was a signal for Ingersoll's other enemies to close in. Though the newspapers printed his and his friends' letters of explanation and defense, though he announced that he would not execute the Act against the wishes of the people, the tide rose rapidly against him. His effigy—his "virtual representative" the newspapers called it—was hanged in Lebanon, Windham, New London, and Norwich; [34] and in Windham County and New London County, where the New Lights and the Susquehannah Company were strongest, a movement was set afoot to force his resignation. Ingersoll heard that companies from Windham, Norwich, and New London were planning a march on New Haven. His fellow-townsmen, he knew, whatever their sentiments about the Stamp Act, would resent this interference by the easterners. There would undoubtedly be a clash with a possible loss of life and property, including his own. In order to avert this, he sent messages to his advancing enemies, proposing to meet them at Hartford, where the Governor had called a special session of the Assembly for September 19. Here he hoped to turn over his problems to the legislators. If they wished to nullify the Stamp Act, he would not stand in their way. If they wished to support it, then they could deal with the mob themselves. In either case the responsibility would be off his shoulders. Unfortunately he was able to ride only as far as Weathersfield before meeting an advance contingent of the easterners, about five hundred in number, some in the uniform of militia officers and all armed with staves. Ingersoll was not a timid man, and he held out for some time, arguing, explaining, expostulating, asking "if they thought it was fair that the Counties of Windham and New-London should dictate to all the rest of the Colony?" The only answer he received was "It dont signify to parly—here is a great many People waiting and you must resign." Ingersoll replied with some warmth "that I could Die, and perhaps as well now as another Time; and that I should Die but once." But after all he held no brief for the Stamp Act and decided upon second thought that if he must be a martyr it should be in a better cause.[35] By resigning his office and giving three reluctant cheers Ingersoll was able to send the mob home, though not until he had been con-

---

33. Gipson, *Ingersoll*, 158.

34. *Newport Mercury*, August 26, September 2, 1765; *Connecticut Courant*, September 2, 1765.

35. New Haven Colony Historical Society, *Papers*, 9 (1918), 341-349.

ducted to Hartford and obliged to repeat the performance before the Assembly House for the benefit of a larger audience including the assemblymen within.

Jared Ingersoll's troubles were not yet over. The men who organized the march against him and who called themselves the Sons of Liberty had more in view than the defeat of the Stamp Act. They looked toward new lands in Pennsylvania and New Light in religion. With Ingersoll the most unpopular man in Connecticut, they saw the opportunity to unseat a substantial number of those persons in the government who shared his views both on religion and on the Susquehannah Company. For some time now the New Lights had been in control of the Lower House of the Assembly, but the Old Lights still controlled both the governor's council, and the governor's chair itself. Ingersoll's appointment as stamp agent was a disaster for the Old Light Party. Only by repudiating him completely and themselves leading the opposition to the Act could they possibly have maintained their position thereafter. Ebenezer Devotion, the Old Light minister in the New Light stronghold of Windham, showed the way by speaking so earnestly for colonial rights that the town sent him to the Assembly as its representative in 1765. But the Old Lights more commonly preferred passive resistance to the Stamp Act, fearing that open resistance would give England the excuse she was looking for to revoke Connecticut's precious charter.[36] Consequently the Sons of Liberty who organized resistance to the Act appear to have been mostly New Lights, and they took such pains to identify their party with the opposition to the Stamp Act, that by January of 1766, it was reported from New Haven that "a Man's religious Principles are made the Test or shall I rather say badge of his political Creed. An Arminian, and a Favourer of the Stamp Act signify the same Man." [37]

Governor Fitch gave the irreparable blow to his own career and to the Old Light party when he complied with the Act by swearing to enforce it. Such an oath was required of every governor by the terms of the Act, upon penalty of £1000 sterling. When Fitch called the Council together in order to be sworn in their presence, only four councillors would participate. These four and the Governor himself therefore became the political targets of the Sons of Liberty.[38]

36. Franklin B. Dexter, ed., *The Literary Diary of Ezra Stiles* (New York, 1901), I, 55; Zeichner, *Connecticut's Years of Controversy*, 54-59.

37. Franklin B. Dexter, ed., *Extracts from the Itineraries and Other Miscellanies of Ezra Stiles* (New Haven, 1916), 509-510.

38. Ingersoll to Jackson, November 3, 1765, New Haven Colony Historical Society, *Papers*, 9 (1918), 357-360; Zeichner, *Connecticut's Years of Controversy*, 56-59.

Ingersoll was not a member of the Assembly or the Council, but his association with the Old Lights was so well known that it was advantageous to keep popular feeling against him at a high pitch. His mail was watched and evidently opened, for a rumor spread that he had written to England suggesting that people might submit to the Stamp Act if some of the duties were reduced. Actually his suggestion had been that *if* Parliament did not repeal the Act, they should at least reduce the rates.[39] But it was no use telling this to the Sons of Liberty. A committee of these gentlemen, hailing from Windham County, called upon him and demanded copies of his recent letters. He gave them up when the committee assured him, after reading them, that the populace would be quieted by hearing the true contents. With impudent malice they then held public meetings to which they read excerpts of the correspondence lifted from context in such a way as to make them appear damaging to Ingersoll's character. In response to the reading of such passages the meeting at Litchfield resolved

That if any Person in this Colony has represented that the People in it, might, under any possible Circumstances, become willing to have the aforesaid Act executed upon them, or to have one Farthing of their Property taken from them, except by their own Consent, given as aforesaid; they are perswaded that such Representation must have been the Result of extreme stupid Ignorance, or dictated by a malignant apostate Spirit.[40]

The ostensible purpose of the meetings sponsored by the Sons of Liberty was to defeat the execution of the Stamp Act, but behind these engineered gatherings of righteously indignant citizens the guid-ing spirits were preparing for political revolution in the spring elec-tions of 1766. Evidently their plans leaked out a little prematurely, for early in the year it was reported that the New Lights, who con-trolled the Sons of Liberty, were preparing to take advantage of the excitement against the Stamp Act for their own purposes. A writer in the *Connecticut Courant* on January 13 suggested this and warned the people not to let "blind Enthusiasm, or a low, mean, party Spirit, like a Torrent, sweep all before it." The Old Lights naturally re-sented the attempt to play politics in the midst of the crisis, for they too abhorred the Stamp Act, and many had joined the Sons of Liberty as a movement which transcended party lines. They were able to get the same meeting at Litchfield which denounced Ingersoll

39. Ingersoll to Whately, November 2, 1765, to Jackson, November 3, 1765, New Haven Colony Historical Society, *Papers*, 9 (1918), 353, 357-360.
40. *Connecticut Courant*, February 24, 1766.

to dissociate itself from political maneuvers by adopting a resolution which expressly denied any intention "to bring about the least alteration in the Legislative Body of the Colony." [41] In spite of such protests, the political organization of the Sons of Liberty went forward, by means of conventions held on an ever-widening basis. Meetings of the people in a particular town or village were succeeded by meetings of a whole county with delegates from each town. Finally, in a convention of representatives from the whole colony at Hartford on March 25, the Sons of Liberty uncovered their plan for getting rid of Old Light control in the council and the governorship.

The meeting had already agreed upon a resolution in favor of corresponding with the Sons of Liberty in other colonies, when a vote was carried requiring all spectators to withdraw. After this order had been carried out, some of the delegates wanted to know why it had been done. The leaders of the meeting then stated that they "ment to collect the Minds of the People, for Unity, and by that Means be able to give the Freemen a Lead in the ensuing election, since, should they run upon different Men, the Persons desired might not be elected, by the Freemen." In other words the Sons of Liberty proposed to nominate a slate of candidates for the coming election. When some of the delegates objected strenuously to this plot for a government dominated by New Lights, the political architects of the meeting wisely adjourned it until the following day. They spent the ensuing evening profitably, for the following day without further discussion of the proposal the convention nominated candidates for governor and deputy governor. The delegates from Litchfield, remaining true to the resolves of their convention, four weeks before, voted nine to four against the measure, but a majority of the convention approved it, perhaps because more delegates attended from New London and Windham counties than from any others. Some members would have gone further and named a slate for the Council too, but the opposition was so great that it was finally decided not "to make too great an Alteration in the Body Politick at once." [42]

The scheme was of course successful in spite of everything that Ingersoll and the Old Lights could do. It was useless for Ingersoll to demonstrate his sincerity by publicly urging the courts to open in defiance of the Stamp Act,[43] useless for his friends to protest that

41. *Ibid.*

42. Gipson, *Ingersoll*, 218-221; Zeichner, *Connecticut's Years of Controversy*, 70-75.

43. Emmet Papers, 4897, New York Public Library; New Haven Colony Historical Society, *Papers*, 9 (1918), 376.

"there are a great many brave Hearts in this Colony that hate a stamp-man, but love Mr. Ingersoll." [44] In the eyes of many people Ingersoll's character was ruined and the men with whom he was associated were correspondingly tainted. Guilt by association, as more than one American has learned, cannot be washed away by a mere demonstration of innocence. There might still be many brave hearts that loved Mr. Ingersoll and that loved Governor Fitch, but not enough to win an election, in 1766 or ever after.

44. Gipson, *Ingersoll*, 189.

» FOURTEEN «

JOHN HUGHES

WHEN the news reached Philadelphia in the spring of 1763 that France and England had finally made peace, John Hughes, like other Americans, could rejoice. Not only had Great Britain become the greatest power in the western world, but in Pennsylvania the men of good will whom Hughes respected had been able to keep their grip on the reins of government. Politics in Pennsylvania, at all times a tricky business, had been especially difficult during the war, and the formal closing of hostilities brought a welcome lightening of the tension for John Hughes and his friends. Hughes was no longer a young man as he surveyed the prospects opened by the peace. Less than two years later he was to describe himself as "an old Fellow, born and Educated, in the Wilds of America, at a Time, when the Schools were but few." [1] He had watched Pennsylvania grow, watched the German settlers landing on the banks of the Delaware by the thousands, watched the turbulent Scotch-Irish pour into the interior. He had seen the city of Philadelphia mushroom around him, expanding in all directions, becoming the second city of the British Empire. Any place which grew as rapidly as Pennsylvania was bound to have growing pains, and if it had not been for the wise and steady leadership of his Quaker friends, Pennsylvania would have felt the pains sharply long before.

Hughes was no Quaker himself. He gave his faith to the Church of England, but he had lived with the Quakers in Pennsylvania long enough to respect them. These Pennsylvania Quakers were not the

1. Hughes to Commissioners of Stamps, January 13, 1766, Treasury Papers, Class I, Bundle 452, Public Record Office, Library of Congress transcripts.

wild fanatics who had marched naked through the streets of England in Cromwell's time. They were sober men, industrious, thrifty, wise in the ways of the world but still retaining the firmness of conviction that had led their grandfathers to cross the ocean. It was because of their fundamental decency that Pennsylvania had been able to grow up so rapidly and yet so comfortably. In particular their honesty in dealing with the Indians had prevented the bloody clashes which punctuated the advance of the frontier in other colonies. The Quakers, from the time of William Penn, had treated the Indians as human beings, and the Indians had responded in kind. It was only when the Scotch-Irish Presbyterians moved out to the frontier and began to throw their weight about that Indian warfare came to Pennsylvania.

These Presbyterians, Hughes felt, were the principal trouble-makers in Pennsylvania politics. Until 1758 the Presbyterians had been relatively easy to handle; until that year they had been split into two factions—the Old Lights and the New Lights—and the two had distrusted each other more than they did outsiders. The split began early in the forties when George Whitefield was storming through the colonies, leaving behind a trail of shrieks and groans and hallelujahs. After the hallelujahs had come dissension and schism to the Presbyterians of Pennsylvania, as to the Congregationalists of Connecticut, and the Presbyterians had consequently been immobilized as a political force. In 1758 when the two sides made peace, with the New Light group in the ascendancy, they became a major force in politics.[2]

Fortunately, as Hughes saw it, the Presbyterians' strength lay in the West; and since the western counties of Pennsylvania did not have as many representatives in the Assembly as the eastern counties, the Presbyterians by themselves, even after the reunion of 1758, did not command anything approaching a majority. Hughes feared, however, a possible coalition between the Presbyterians and some other faction. The largest such group in the colony, the one which might swing the legislature one way or the other, was the Germans. The Germans hitherto had found the rule of the Quakers congenial. Many of them belonged to the Mennonite sect, which had religious principles in common with the Quakers. They lived for the most part in the portion of the colony that lay between the Quakers of the East and the Scotch-Irish Presbyterians of the West. Politically, too, they were a middle group. Lacking aggressive leaders of their own,

2. G. S. Klett, *Presbyterians in Colonial Pennsylvania (Philadelphia,* 1937); L. J. Trinterud, *The Forming of an American Tradition* (Philadelphia, 1949).

they had hitherto looked to the East for leadership, but what if they should turn in the other direction and ally themselves with the Presbyterians, thereby giving the latter control of a popular, and perhaps a legislative, majority? [3]

Another place where the united Presbyterians could look for support—Hughes sadly faced the fact—was in his own church. Only a year or two after the Presbyterians healed their own division, the Church of England in Pennsylvania was split by precisely the same issue that had troubled the Presbyterians fifteen years earlier. The trouble, as a matter of fact, came from a renegade Presbyterian who had taken orders in the Church of England, a man by the name of MacClenaghan, who appeared in Philadelphia in 1760 and began to preach revival sermons. Though he was strenuously opposed at first, the Philadelphia Anglicans had gradually caught the fever, and by 1763, it had to be admitted, were strongly tainted with New Light ideas. It was characteristic of New Lights to dislike the prudent and rational members of their own denominations and to embrace the wildest fanatics of other denominations. Consequently, though the Anglicans outside Philadelphia did not become illumined by the New Lights and continued to look upon Quaker rule as better at least than Presbyterian, the Philadelphia Anglicans stood ready to join with the Presbyterians. [4]

The great danger to the Quaker regime lay in the combination of the Presbyterians with the Anglicans of Philadelphia and with the Germans of the middle region. The danger was rendered acute by the fact that the Presbyterians had obtained the support of the family which exercised the greatest political and economic power in all Pennsylvania. William Penn, who founded the colony, had been one of the leading Quakers of his time, but his grandchildren, remaining in England, had deserted the faith to become members of the Church of England. If they had adhered faithfully to the interests of that church, Hughes could have found it easier to excuse their other faults. Instead they carried on a flirtation with the Pennsylvania Presbyterians in order to defeat the measures of the Quakers who controlled the Assembly. The Penn family owned all the public land in Pennsylvania and theoretically were entitled to an annual quitrent on all private land. They also appointed the governor of

3. On Pennsylvania politics in this period see C. H. Lincoln, *The Revolutionary Movement in Pennsylvania* (Philadelphia, 1901); W. R. Shepherd, *History of Proprietary Government in Pennsylvania* (New York, 1896).

4. William S. Perry, ed., *Historical Collections Relating to the American Colonial Church*, Vol. II—*Pennsylvania* (Hartford, 1871), 305-311, 319-324, 341, 354-355, 364-365, 392-393, 413-414.

the colony, who had authority to veto any laws passed by the Assembly. This vast power they frequently abused. In particular they consistently refused to make any contribution to the expenses of government by allowing their lands to be taxed, as the lands of all other Pennsylvanians were. This attitude had led to continuous conflict between the Assembly and the governor. Since the Presbyterians were as much at odds with the Quaker-dominated Assembly as the Proprietors were, the two had sought each other as natural allies. As a result the most lucrative offices in the appointment of the proprietary family went to Presbyterians, and William Allen, the political leader of the Presbyterians and perhaps the wealthiest man in the province, was also the Chief Justice of Pennsylvania.[5]

The combination of Proprietors, Presbyterians, and Philadelphia Anglicans with the potential addition of the Germans provided a formidable opposition which had hitherto been unsuccessful. The most trying time had been during the late war. The Quakers, because of their pacifist principles, were not well constituted to run a government at war. They themselves recognized this fact and turned over the actual leadership of the Assembly to well-disposed allies, men like John Hughes and Joseph Galloway and Benjamin Franklin. By this means Pennsylvania had been able to make as great a contribution to the war effort as other colonies. If such a comparison was faint praise, at least the Quakers were not to blame for any deficiencies. The Proprietors and the Presbyterians might scream that the cowardly pacifism of the Quakers was responsible for military failures, but Hughes knew that the greed of the Proprietors in refusing to contribute their share of taxes was at the bottom of the troubles; and he could see that other Pennsylvanians shared his views when they continued to support the Quaker party. Nevertheless, pacifists do not generally win popularity contests in wartime, and all friends of the Quaker regime could breathe a sigh of relief when the war ended with the Quakers and their friends still in the saddle.

Unfortunately the year which opened so auspiciously was to see the most savage Indian attack in history carried out all along the western frontiers of the American colonies, with Pennsylvania hit especially hard. Pontiac's rebellion was a last desperate attempt by the Indians to hold the interior of the American continent against

5. See correspondence of William Allen with the proprietors in Penn Papers, Historical Society of Pennsylvania. The alliance between Allen and the Penns was so notorious that Thomas Penn, the Proprietor, advised his nephew, Governor Richard Penn, not to marry Allen's daughter, lest this further evidence of the connection cause criticism. On the other hand he urged his nephew to take Allen's advice in all matters. Penn Correspondence, V, 67, 69; VIII, 78-85.

the English. Striking in June, 1763, the Indians by the end of the month had compelled the Pennsylvanians to abandon some of the finest country in America. As always they hit without mercy, killing men, women, and children. No troops were immediately available to stop them, and the survivors pouring eastward brought with them an understandable bitterness against the people who thought that Indians should be treated fairly. With unreasoning rage a group of Presbyterians from Paxton and Donegal townships, unable or afraid to march against the Indians who were ravaging the Western frontier, fell upon a small and thoroughly tame village of twenty Indians near Lancaster, and murdered the six individuals they found at home. The remaining fourteen were rounded up by the Sheriff at Lancaster and placed in the workhouse for their own protection, but the Paxton boys broke into the house and murdered them too. This apparently proved to be so satisfactory a way of expressing their feelings, that the Paxton boys next set their sights on another body of 140 peaceful Indians. In order to protect these from the fate of the others the government moved them to Philadelphia and transferred three companies of Regular troops to Philadelphia to watch over them. In the face of what was going on to the westward, the frontiersmen could only regard this shift of troops as a painful demonstration that the government of Pennsylvania was more interested in protecting the Indians from the frontiersmen than it was in protecting the frontiersmen from the Indians. In wrath some seven hundred men collected and prepared to march on Philadelphia.[6]

This was in February of 1764, two months after the massacre at Lancaster. The governor of the colony, feeling his own inadequacy in the situation, called upon Benjamin Franklin to organize a popular force. Franklin had already published a bitter narrative of the Indian massacres, describing the Paxton boys as "Christian White Savages." [7] The pamphlet had helped to arouse popular feeling against the brutal conduct of the frontiersmen so that Franklin and Hughes found the Philadelphians ready to defend themselves and the Indians who had taken refuge with them.[8] However, Franklin had no desire for civil war; he met the Paxton boys at Germantown and persuaded them to return home. Having done so, he seized the opportunity to

6. Carl Van Doren, *Benjamin Franklin* (New York, 1941), 306-311.

7. *A Narrative of the Late Massacres in Lancaster County* (Philadelphia, 1764), reprinted in Albert H. Smyth, ed., *The Writings of Benjamin Franklin* (New York, 1905-1907), IV, 289-314. See p. 310.

8. Hugh Neill to the Secretary of the S.P.G., June 25, 1764, Perry, *Historical Collections*, II, 360-361; James Pemberton to Samuel Fothergill, March 7, 1764, Pemberton Papers, XXXIV, 128, Historical Society of Pennsylvania.

aim a blow which he hoped would give the *coup de grâce* to the Proprietary-Presbyterian combination. The Governor in the crisis had been unable to direct the defense of the province. At the same time he was refusing to sign a bill passed by the Assembly for raising troops, because the bill provided for taxation of proprietary estates in order to help defray the cost. Under Franklin's leadership the Assembly passed a series of resolves and drew up a petition to the King, asking for the establishment of royal government in Pennsylvania.[9]

Franklin had timed the move with a perfect sense of the situation. The Governor's weakness in the crisis and his obstruction to the raising of troops put people out of patience with the proprietary family. The decision to seek a royal government was so generally concurred in that the resolves passed the Assembly with only four dissenting votes. The move was likewise well timed with respect to the situation in England. Franklin, like other well-informed Americans, believed that the mother country was preparing to overhaul the whole imperial system. Rhode Island was petitioning for royal government, as Franklin's friend Martin Howard had informed him. Governor Bernard was advising a revision of all charter governments. Maryland was becoming dissatisfied with proprietary rule. A more auspicious time for getting rid of the baleful influence of the Penn family could scarcely have been chosen. And John Hughes was confident that if the Penns were deprived of their governmental privileges, the Presbyterians would be less formidable.

The Presbyterians were not slow to understand the significance of the move. They hurried to the defense of the proprietary charter with counter-petitions and with scurrilous broadsides and pamphlets attacking both Franklin and the Quakers.[10] From the frontier counties they sent in petitions complaining of the fact—and it was a fact —that the three eastern counties, with a minority of the population, elected a majority of the representatives in the legislature. Hitherto this disproportion had not excited jealousy. In fact the westerners frequently failed to send even their allotted number of representatives. But now a great furor was raised against the oligarchical rule

---

9. *Pennsylvania Archives*, 8th ser., 7 (1935), 5591-5607; Carl Van Doren, ed., *Letters and Papers of Benjamin Franklin and Richard Jackson, 1753-1785* (Philadelphia, 1947), 150-152, 211-212.

10. On the counter-petitions see Penn Correspondence, VIII, *passim,* and Hugh Neill to the Secretary of the S.P.G., October 18, 1764, Perry, *Historical Collections*, II, 364-365. For the voluminous pamphlet literature see Evans, *American Bibliography* (Chicago, 1903-1934), III and IV, items indexed under Pennsylvania, "Tracts in favor of proprietary government."

of the eastern counties, which, the Presbyterians claimed, were seeking to overthrow the foundations of the colony by their petition to the King.[11]

In the Assembly itself the debates were lively. William Allen assured the members that Pennsylvania would find the little finger of the King heavier than the loins of the Proprietor. Allen had no sooner finished than John Hughes was on his feet to cry treason. No one but a rebel, he said, would be guilty of such a statement.[12] But perhaps Hughes did not realize how many Pennsylvanians had misgivings about the petition which he and Franklin were pushing. There was not the same attachment to the charter in Pennsylvania that there was in Rhode Island, where all the charter privileges belonged to the people as a whole. In Pennsylvania the charter was a benefit principally to the proprietary family. Nevertheless the people had gained many rights in the government set up under it; in particular they had gained all the procedures established by William Penn in the famous Charter of Liberties of 1701. If the proprietary charter were revoked, it might be impossible to retain these procedures. No one could tell what form of government the King might provide, especially at a time when Parliament was showing intentions of extending its control over the colonies. In the eyes of many Pennsylvanians, including even some leading Quakers, the petition for royal government was a rash and dangerous move.[13]

During the summer of 1764 the words flew hot and heavy, and when the elections to the Assembly were held in the first week of October it became apparent that the Presbyterians had scored a minor victory: Franklin and Joseph Galloway, the two principal leaders of the Quaker party, had been defeated for re-election. The campaign against royal government had won enough votes for the Presbyterian-Anglican-Proprietary combination in Philadelphia to defeat the men who had proposed the change. But in the rest of the colony the party of Franklin and Galloway and Hughes held fast. The westerners were apparently not seriously displeased with their representatives who had favored the petition for royal government, nor were they aroused by the indictment of Pennsylvania's unequal

11. Theodore Thayer, "The Quaker Party of Pennsylvania," *Pa. Mag. of Hist.*, 71 (1947), 19-44.

12. Hughes to Commissioners of Stamps, October 12, 1765, House of Lords Manuscripts, January 14, 1766, Library of Congress transcripts. Cf. Allen to Thomas Penn, December 13, 1764, Penn Manuscripts, Official Correspondence, IX, 290.

13. John Reynell to Mildred and Roberts, November 23, 1764, Letter Book of John Reynell; James Pemberton to Samuel Fothergill, June 13, 1764, Pemberton Papers, XXXIV, 131; and letters of John Griffith and John Churchman, Pemberton Papers, XVII, 63, all in Historical Society of Pennsylvania.

system of representation. Except in Philadelphia the Quakers had been able to discredit the Presbyterian charges as a mere device to distract public attention from the shameful actions of the Paxton boys. Consequently when the Assembly convened, the Quaker party still commanded a large majority, and among that majority was Franklin's old friend John Hughes.[14]

Hughes did not propose to see the talents of the wisest man in Pennsylvania cut off from the services of the Assembly, and it was Hughes who now persuaded the Assembly to send Franklin to England to assist his friend Richard Jackson in prosecuting the appeal to the King for a royal government.[15] However, while the Pennsylvanians had been slaying one another in print, something had occurred in England which could not be overlooked. George Grenville had persuaded Parliament to pass the Sugar Act, and he had announced that a stamp tax might be necessary in the near future. Though the issue of proprietary vs. royal government in Pennsylvania seemed the more important issue to Hughes, the taxation of the colonies by Parliament was a move which must be resisted vigorously. When he arrived in London Franklin must not only push forward the business of royal government but must also do everything possible to get the Sugar Act repealed and to prevent the passage of the Stamp Act.

After Franklin left on his dual mission, in November, 1764, the factions continued their quarrel with the same virulence. William Allen persuaded one of the Presbyterian propagandists to publish a libellous piece calling Franklin an "inflammatory and virulent man, whose views are not those of peace and reconciliation" and accusing him of misusing public funds, of stirring up political controversies for his own gain, and of taking advantage of his position to win favors for himself and his family.[16] John Hughes came quickly to his friend's defense. On December 20 he published in the *Pennsylvania Gazette* an advertisement in which he offered to pay £ 10 to

14. Thayer, "Quaker Party of Pennsylvania"; Lewis B. Walker, ed., *The Burd Papers: Extracts from Chief Justice William Allen's Letter Book* (n.p., 1897), 62-65; Thomas Balch, ed., *Letters and Papers Relating Chiefly to the Provincial History of Pennsylvania* (Philadelphia, 1855), 204-206; Allen to Thomas Penn, September 25, 1764, Penn Manuscripts, Official Correspondence, IX; Benjamin Marshall to Joseph G. Wanton, October 5, 1764, *Pa. Mag. of Hist.*, 20 (1896), 207.

15. Hughes to Commissioners of Stamps, October 12, 1765, House of Lords Manuscripts, January 14, 1766; *Pennsylvania Archives*, 8th ser., 7 (1935), 5687-5690.

16. *An Answer to Mr. Franklin's Remarks on a Late Protest* (Philadelphia, 1764), probably by William Smith. The "late protest" was a protest by the minority in the Assembly against Franklin's appointment as agent, Historical Society of Pennsylvania, *Memoirs*, 14 (1895), 151-154. The *Remarks on a Late Protest* was published by Franklin before leaving for England, Smyth, ed., *Writings*, IV, 273-285.

the provincial hospital for every accusation against Franklin that could be proved correct, provided that Allen would come out from behind his anonymity and pay £5 for every charge that could be proved false. The challenge was accepted only by another anonymous letter to the newspaper, which Hughes promptly answered with a further attack on the cowardly anonymity of the author.[17]

As Hughes made his bold, defiant gestures the issue which had hitherto seemed a minor irritation beside the major struggle against Proprietor and Presbyterians was rising to overwhelm him. The same torrent that overturned the lives of Francis Bernard, John Robinson, Jared Ingersoll, and Thomas Hutchinson picked up John Hughes and swept him helpless before the fury of the Presbyterians. Franklin, in London, felt the groundswell of the movement before it reached America. He did everything in his power to prevent passage of the Stamp Act. He pleaded with Grenville and proposed alternatives, but the Minister was adamant.[18] Franklin, ever the realist, fought while the fighting was worth while. Even after the Act was passed he worked for its repeal, but meanwhile he made the best of a bad situation. When George Grenville asked him to name a man for stamp distributor in Pennsylvania, he must have seen an opportunity to gain a move in the contest he was simultaneously carrying on with the Proprietors of Pennsylvania. The Penn brothers had also taken an active part in the effort to prevent the stamp tax,[19] but when the campaign had been lost, Grenville did not give them an opportunity to name a candidate for any of the offices which the Act created. Franklin named John Hughes, and Grenville immediately made the appointment. When Thomas Penn later complained to Grenville that this must appear as a reward for Hughes's opposition to the Proprietor, he had to be content with Grenville's promise to write Hughes and warn him that the appointment was not made with any such view in mind.[20] Franklin to all appearances had gained a point in his duel with the Proprietors and the Presbyterians. It was some months before he realized how costly that victory would prove for his friend.

17. *Pennsylvania Gazette*, December 27, 1765, January 3, 10, 1766; *Pennsylvania Journal*, same dates.

18. Verner Crane, "Benjamin Franklin and the Stamp Act," Colonial Society of Massachusetts, *Publications*, 32 (1937), 56-77; Verner Crane, ed., *Benjamin Franklin's Letters to the Press* (Chapel Hill, 1950), xxxiii-xlvi, 25-30, 63-73; John Fothergill to James Pemberton, February 27, 1766, Penn Manuscripts, X, 35.

19. See letters of Thomas Penn, dated February 8, 15, March 9, 1764, Penn Correspondence, VIII, 33, 35, 205, 217.

20. Thomas Penn to John Penn, April 13, 1765, to Mr. Hockley, September 22, 1765, to William Young, September 28, 1765, Penn Correspondence, VIII, 244, 310, 315-316.

When Hughes received news in May, 1765, that he had been nominated Distributor of Stamps for Pennsylvania, he saw no better than Franklin that this was the end of his political career. He wrote with some satisfaction to his friend Anthony Wayne that his appointment had given the proprietary party "no small pain."[21] Though his own party had suffered a minor setback in the October election of 1764, they quickly reformed their ranks, and even their opponents admitted that Franklin and Galloway, though no longer members of the Assembly, still ran the show from behind the scenes. In the spring and summer of 1765 the Presbyterians worked furiously to naturalize friendly Germans who agreed to vote for them, but in spite of all their efforts the Quakers held the line and even succeeded in re-electing Galloway that October. Hughes's party was firmly entrenched, and was to remain so until the Revolution, but Hughes himself was already a liability. In his appointment as Distributor of Stamps the Presbyterians had seen an opportunity to attack the Quaker party, and had he not withdrawn his candidacy in this election the Presbyterians might have been successful in crucifying his party along with him.[22]

Early in September Hughes had begun to receive suggestions that he ought to resign. By this time he could perceive the danger in which his appointment had placed him. His position was all the more difficult because the stamps were reported on their way, and yet he had not up to this time received his commission as distributor. In fact he had had no official communication on the subject from the government. On the eighth of the month he wrote to Franklin:

You are now from Letter to Letter to suppose each may be the last you will receive from your old Friend, as the Spirit or Flame of Rebellion is got to a high Pitch amongst the North Americans; and it seems to me that a sort of Frenzy or Madness has got such hold of the People of all Ranks, that I fancy some Lives will be lost before this Fire is put out. I am at present much perplext what course to steer: For as I have given you Reason to expect I would endeavour to put the Act in Execution, and you no doubt have inform'd the Commissioners; I cannot in point of Honour go back, until something or other is done by the People to render it impossible for me to proceed.

21. June 1, 1765, Hughes Papers, Historical Society of Pennsylvania.
22. John Hughes to Lords of the Treasury, February 20, 1766, Treasury Papers, Class I, Bundle 452; William Young to Thomas Penn, December 14, 1765, Penn Manuscripts, Private Correspondence, V; Israel Pemberton to Joseph Pemberton, September 25, 1765, Pemberton Papers, XVIII, 53; Samuel Purviance, Jr., to Colonel Burd, September 20, 1765, Balch, *Letters and Papers*, 208; John Reynell to James Shirley, May 14, 1765, Letter Book of John Reynell.

But perhaps when a Mob is on foot, my Life and Interest may fall a Sacrifice to an infatuated Multitude. —and I know of no way to prevent it but absolutely declaring off as all the rest have done to the Eastward. But as yet I cannot prevail upon myself, notwithstanding the Threats of some, and the Persuasions of others, to do an Act that appears to me neither loyal nor reputable.

I have hitherto kept matters easy by saying I had nothing to resign, for I have neither received my Commission or any other kind of Writing from the Stamp office. But when it is known I have received my Commission, I fancy I shall not escape the Storm of Presbyterian Rage. And as Captain Friend [who was reported to be bringing the Stamp papers] is expected every day, my Doom will soon be known, but whether I may live to inform you, is yet in the Womb of Futurity.[23]

By the time the Assembly met on September 9, a majority of the members, though not Presbyterians, had caught the infection which was sweeping the other colonies. Though they still wanted a royal government, their irritation with the Proprietor was momentarily overshadowed by their resentment against the Stamp Act. On September 10, by a vote of 15 to 14, they resolved to send a delegation to the Stamp Act Congress at New York.[24] Hughes was foolish enough to oppose this move,[25] and the Assembly snubbed him by appointing John Dickinson, George Bryan, and John Morton as delegates. Dickinson was one of the four who had voted against the petition for royal government, and Bryan was an up-and-coming Presbyterian politician.

On the same day that the Assembly chose its delegates to the congress, Captain Friend arrived—without the stamp papers.[26] The crisis was thus postponed, but the tension continued. Hughes heard rumors that his house would be pulled down, upon which he announced without hesitation that he would defend it with his life. His friends the Quakers were taking no part in the commotions. As a matter of fact he had many friends in Philadelphia, and if the worst came to the worst, he would not fight alone. The same men who had gathered with him and Franklin to meet the Paxton Presbyterians were ready

23. Treasury Papers, Class I, Bundle 442.

24. *Ibid.; Pennsylvania Archives*, 8th ser., VII (1935), 5767.

25. Samuel Purviance, Jr., to Colonel Burd, September 20, 1765, Balch, *Letters and Papers*, 208.

26. Except where otherwise noted the events described in this and the ensuing paragraphs are based on letters to and from John Hughes in Treasury Papers, Class I, Bundles 441, 442, 452, and in House of Lords Manuscripts, January 14, 1766. Some of these letters were printed in a supplement to the *Pennsylvania Journal*, September 4, 1766.

to stand by him against the Philadelphia Presbyterians. On September 16 the test came. When it was spread about that Hughes's house would be destroyed that night, Joseph Galloway and his other friends, to the number of seven or eight hundred, organized to protect it. As might have been expected the governor, mayor, and other civil officers did nothing. But Hughes's friends posted themselves in different places, prepared to resist the gathering mob. Hughes himself stayed indoors, ready to fight as soon as the house should be entered. From time to time he wrote reports of what was occurring to his friend in London:

I for my Part am well arm'd with Fire-Arms, and am determin'd to stand a Siege. If I live till to-morrow morning I shall give you a further Account, but as it is now about 8 a Clock, I am on my Guard, and only write this between whiles, as every Noise or Bustle of the People calls me off.

9 0 Clock. — Severall Friends that patroll between my House and the Coffee House, come in just now, and say, the Collection of Rabble begins to decrease visibly in the Streets, and the Appearance of Danger seems a good deal less than it did.

12 a Clock. There are now several Hundreds of our Friends about street, ready to suppress any Mob, if it should attempt to rise, and the Rabble are dispersing.

Sept. 17. 5 in the morning — We are all yet in the Land of the Living, and our Property safe. Thank God. —

There was more trouble to come. Hughes now fell ill and for the next three weeks was confined to his bed. He wrote to the governor the day after his all-night vigil, saying that any reports to the contrary notwithstanding, he had not received a commission from the Stamp Office in England, and that if the stamps should arrive, it would not be his duty to care for them. In Hughes's absence the Assembly adopted their radical resolutions of September 21, against the constitutionality of the Stamp Act,[27] but no popular demonstrations occurred until it was reported that the vessel bearing the stamp papers was beating up the river. On October 5 the stamps arrived and, ominously enough, so did Hughes's commission. Even before he received the document its arrival was announced on the strength of the large packet of mail addressed to him. Accordingly, the gentlemen who had appointed themselves to prevent his execution of the Act, met at the coffee house run by William Bradford, the printer, and

27. *Pennsylvania Archives*, 8th ser., 7 (1935), 5779-5780.

sent out orders for muffled drums to be beaten through the streets and for the bells of the churches and state house to be tolled with muffled clappers. At this signal a mob collected, chiefly composed, according to Hughes, of "Presbyterians and proprietary Emissaries with the Chief Justices (Mr. William Allens) Son at their Head animating and encouraging the lower Class." The Governor and Mayor as usual made themselves scarce. The only attempt by any magistrate to interfere with the proceedings was that of Benjamin Shoemaker, an Alderman of the city and a Quaker. Shoemaker, according to Hughes's account, "met with the Drummers, as they were allarming the City and took them to task, requiring to know by what authority they were endeavouring to raise a Mob, they answered if He would go to the State House, He might know, He then asked who ordered them to beat about Streets, they said they had their orders from the Coffee House. . . Mr. Shoemaker then forbid them to proceed any farther, and said He would go immediately to the Mayor, and have them committed, they answered they could get the Mayor's orders when they pleased; But Mr. Shoemaker could not find the Mayor, nor any Officer to assist him, and therefore was obliged to desist, least He should draw the Mob upon Himself and Family and to have his house pulled down."

By three o'clock in the afternoon a sizeable mob had collected at the state house, and a deputation of seven prominent Philadelphians was sent to ask Hughes for his resignation as Distributor of Stamps. Since Hughes knew that the feeling against him was by no means universal, even though the feeling against the Stamp Act might be, he decided to see how long he could hold out. Lying in bed he told the gentlemen that he had indeed received his commission but that two friends in England had given bond to the sum of £500 for him to perform his duties. He would not resign unless the gentlemen would indemnify his friends. This they of course refused to do. After arguing unsuccessfully with him for an hour the delegation finally told him that he need not resign but only promise not to put the Act into execution until the King's further pleasure was known or until the Act should be executed in the neighboring colonies. Technically this would be only a temporary suspension of office. Hughes could look at it that way if he chose and feel that he had not been derelict in his duty. The delegation who had to deal with this peppery Tory were willing to settle for something less than an outright resignation, partly no doubt because they feared him a little, partly because they knew that popular indignation would prevent use of the stamps anyhow. Hughes agreed to their compromise, perhaps softened a little himself by word from his friends that the mob intended to proceed to the last extremity if he refused. The delegation then withdrew and shortly after sent him a written request for a promise, to be delivered the following Monday (it was then Saturday), that he would not execute the Act. Hughes did not fail to notice that this demand asked for more than he had agreed to. He had merely consented not to execute the Act until the King's further pleasure was known or until it should be executed in the neighboring colonies. Hughes saw Charles Thomson, one of the delegation, in private and called the change to his attention.

On Monday when the group called upon him again, Hughes was prepared with a statement. Fully aware of the rebellious nature of the proceedings against him, he had determined to make his opponents as uncomfortable as possible about what they were doing. He therefore opened his statement with a preamble which said that he was acting under the demand of James Tilghman, Esqr. attorney at law, Messrs. Robert Morris, Charles Thomson, Archibald McCall, John Cox, and William Richards, merchants, and Mr. William Bradford, printer. Moreover in making his promise not to execute the Act he included the conditions of the original agreement. When he presented this statement to the gentlemen, he had the pleasure of watching them squirm over the inclusion of their names: ". . . after some consultation amongst themselves they objected to their names being inserted, I said why come Gentlemen you have not done a thing you are ashamed to own, not in the least they said, but there was no necessity for their names to be inserted, nor would they receive that Resignation, whereupon I said to Mr. Tilghman come Sir take the Pen and please yourself for I see you are determined to be arbitrary."

While Tilghman was drafting a more satisfactory statement, Hughes continued to needle his opponents by asking them what they intended to do with the stamps, now that they had assumed supreme power in the province. "They then look'd at one another for a while, and seemed somewhat confounded." Tilghman at last said, "Let Mr. Hughes take care of them. I answered Gentlemen that cannot be, as you have now fixed matters. For were I to take the Stamps into my Care I should have your Party come about my House to pull it down and destroy both me and them, well says another let the Governor take care of them, another then said perhaps the Governor will call upon Mr. Hughes to put the Act into execution, and when he declines the Governor will perhaps appoint an Officer and the Act may take place, here a general pause ensued, but at last one and all cryed out, let us see who will dare put the Act in execution upon the Governor's Appointment, we will take care of that."

By this time Tilghman had written a statement, and Hughes signed it, promising simply that he would not execute the Act until it was executed in the other colonies. His tormentors were now satisfied, and Hughes himself had at least retained some degree of dignity. He only wished that he knew whether the British government itself would back down before the pressure of the American mobs. If Parliament was going to repeal the Act, it would be foolish for him to risk his life and career by defending it. For the present he still had friends in Pennsylvania who would stand by him, but already the riotous inhabitants of Virginia and Maryland had threatened "that if they ever catch me there, they will make a Sacrifice of me." As time went on he would lose his friends in Pennsylvania too. He was willing to stick by his guns if Britain was prepared to back him, but if Parliament repealed the Stamp Act, he would have suffered for nothing.

There was unfortunately no way of telling what Parliament would do. John Hughes stayed in Philadelphia maintaining his dignity as best he could, and missing no opportunity to let his enemies know the full implications of what they had done. He was a sociable man, quick-tempered but voluble, and he could sometimes be seen in the streets and coffee houses arguing with the men who opposed him. He occasionally confided the contents of his conversations to his superiors in England:

I sometimes tell some of our Warm Blades, that it is a piece of Inconsistency in them to call themselves Englishmen, Because Gentlemen say I, If you are Englishmen you must be bound by Acts of Parliament until that Parliament releases you, from that Obedience, which has not yet been done as I know of,

To this they reply, our Charters have done it,

absolutely no Gentlemen, Your Charters are but the Declaration of the Kings that Granted them, and they cannot be Tortured to mean no more then that the Kings of Great Britain, would not arbitrarily and without Law raise money on the Subject in America, And this is all our forefathers, seem to have asked, when they left Britain, and Indeed it is all the Kings of Great Britain can legally promise, for the King cannot Bar the Rights of the Lords and Commons, any more then they can his Prerogatives, the Answer then is you are an Enemy to America, and ought to have your brains beat out. . . .

One Reason assign'd for not paying Obedience to this Act of Parliament, is that we have no Representatives in Parliament, I then say let us Petition for Representatives O no we will not agree to that, because we have Representatives of our own, and have always given money when we have been cald upon by the King or his Ministers, and if that will not do let us have a House of Commons in America to settle what shall be the Quota of each Colony when Money is wanted &c.

No Gentlemen you have foreclosed yourselves of that, for you have demonstrated your Proprietary [propensity?] to Rebellion to that Degree that it is my opinion the Ministry never can advise his Majesty to Unite you more than you now are, But if they know'd our Circumstances Rightly they wou'd devide us yet more, by forming New Colinies out of Virginia, and Perhaps some others that are already but too large.

Hughes continued to see the proprietary government as the source of Pennsylvania's troubles, and he did his best to turn the whole episode into an argument for royal government. Knowing that the proprietary governor had been required by instructions from England to assist in the enforcement of the Stamp Act, and knowing also that the governor had failed to give him any protection against the mob, Hughes took pains to place the responsibility for nullification of the Act on the governor's shoulders. When the delegation of October 7 had extracted his promise not to enforce the Act, he wrote the governor a letter, stating what he had done and why he had done it.

Hughes now considered his own responsibility discharged until the government of Pennsylvania should make it possible for him to distribute stamps. When the customs officers on November 4 asked him in writing for the stamped papers on which they were supposed to issue clearances for ships leaving Philadelphia, he took delight in writing them an official account of why he could not deliver the papers. He described first the way in which the mob had assembled to demand his resignation and then went on:

Secondly altho it was currently reported, thro' the City on the 4th October last that Captain Holland with the stamp papers &c. would be up the next day and that a Mob would be raised to destroy them, Yet neither the Governor, the Supream Judges, the Mayor, Recorder, Aldermen, nor any other Justiciary Officers (Benjamin Shoemaker Esquire excepted) took the least notice therof, nor used any means to preserve the Peace of the City: . . . but as you may be unacquainted with the Situation of the Stamp Papers, I do myself the pleasure of informing you that his Honour the Governor, has committed them to the care of Capt. Hawker Commander of his Majesty's Ship Sardine and I would likewise Gentlemen, beg leave to acquaint you, That he has taken as I am informed, a Solemn Oath "to do his utmost that all and every of the Clauses contained in (the Stamp Act) shall be bona fide observed" — Wherefore I must refer you to him (as I am for the reasons already assigned at *present* incapacitated to supply you with stamp papers &c) for a more full answer if necessary to your letter.

Hughes doubtless wrote this letter with one eye on the officials in England to whom he surmised that it would be transmitted. From time to time he sent reports directly to the stamp commissioners in England, and here he took care to draw the conclusions which he merely implied in his letter to the local customs officers. Thus on November 2, 1765, he wrote, "It is my private Opinion, that if the province of Pennsylvania was changed from Proprietary to a Royal Government and some Person Appointed to Govern it, that had both Interest amongst the People, and a perfect knowledge of them, [Dr. Franklin, for example?] so as to be able to displace the Disloyal, and put into Power and Commission, such only as cou'd be depended on, and have Demonstrated their loyalty to their King, such a Person after the Changes Aforesaid might easily Govern this Province and preserve the Peace of it, and keep it in Subjection to his Majesty which I think we hardly are at this Time."

Besides pointing out the shabby behavior of the proprietary government Hughes kept up a running fire at the Presbyterians. The Proprietors were only interested in maintaining their own selfish interests, but the Presbyterians were downright rebels, if not Republicans. They had become "as averse to Kings, as they were in the Days of Cromwell, and some begin to cry out, *No King but King Jesus.*" The dangerous thing was the close alliance between these rebels and the proprietary government. The danger was demonstrated early in January when another consignment of stamped papers arrived in Philadelphia. Hughes reported the incident in a letter to the Stamp Office on January 13, 1766, in which he first told of the dangerous republicanism of the Presbyterians and then went on:

And as the Presbyterians, are united with the people in power, and are many of them, in power themselves, in this province, these and the others, countenance, and privately encourage, Riots, so that I really know not, what may be the Consequence, for a few Days ago, the London Ships came up, with some Stamps, and one of the Captains happening, to put a Box of Stamps on Shore, Instantly, the two printers, Messrs Bradford and Hall, got a Drum, and caused it to be beat, about the streets, and raised a Rabble of Boys, Sailors, and Negroes &c. to destroy the Stamps, but they were taken on board again, and the captains notwithstanding, were obliged to take an Oath, that they would not land them in the province, But not one single Magistrate, gave or shewed, the least Disapprobation of this Conduct, Nor is the Justice who swore them, Mr. George Bryan (who is a Red hot presbyterian by the by) any ways blamed by the Governor, for his proceedings on the Occasion, which I think may clearly shew, how far his Honour approves these Measures secretly.

By his waspish defenses of Parliamentary authority Hughes was steadily aggravating the feeling against himself, not only in Pennsylvania but in the neighbouring colonies as well. John Holt, an old friend of Franklin's and a leader of the Sons of Liberty in New York (where Hughes's brother was also one of the Sons of Liberty), begged Mrs. Franklin to use her influence on Hughes to make a complete renunciation of his office.[28] He had conceded on November 21 that he would not execute the Act even if the other colonies did, unless the people of Pennsylvania called upon him to do so;[29] but still, to the disgust of the Sons of Liberty in neighboring colonies, he had not made an outright resignation. Every day he received anonymous messages and letters threatening him with "a mob of several thousand people, from the Jerseys, New York, and New England." "I think," he wrote to the Stamp Commissioners, "my Friends, and Relations, and my Credit, and popularity, in this province, will prevent such a step from being taken, but if Presbyterians Schemes succeed, I shall in a little Time fall a Sacrifice, unless I can fly to Britain for Shelter."

Hughes, like Thomas Hutchinson and many others who suffered from the Stamp Act, was far from thinking that the colonies had been justly treated by Great Britain. In letters to his superiors in England he urged a number of reforms in the colonial system. Though he acknowledged the supremacy of the British Parliament, he asked that representation in Parliament be extended to the colonies. He also suggested ways in which England could raise money in America without causing the unnecessary discontent created by the Stamp Act. One method might be to establish an American port to which goods might be shipped, subject to import duty, directly from Europe. Another method was the one favored by his friend Franklin, the establishment of loan offices for the issuance of bills of credit, the interest on which should accrue to the British Treasury.[30] In either of these schemes the advantages received by the colonists would outweigh whatever grievances might be attached to them. In all seriousness he also suggested that the Prince of Wales be made Prince of North America as well. This he said, "would naturally attach the Minds of the People to the person of the King of Great Britain, and it would

28. February 16, 1766, Franklin Papers, XLVIII, 92, American Philosophical Society.
29. *Pennsylvania Journal*, November 21, 1765.
30. Verner Crane, "Benjamin Franklin and the Stamp Act," Colonial Society of Massachusetts, *Publications*, 32 (1937), 56-77.

be the Interest, of every King of Great Britain, to make the Tour of North America, whilst prince of Wales, whenever his Circumstances admitted his so doing."

Throughout the Stamp Act troubles Hughes continued to think in terms of local politics. Yet he perceived that the Presbyterians had created or at least caught hold of something bigger than themselves. Somehow or other their attack on the Quaker party and upon himself in particular had been transformed into a broader enveloping movement which threatened to destroy the whole foundation of British authority in America. From his vantage point in Pennsylvania, where everything evil seemed to spell Presbyterianism, Hughes looked at the other colonies and interpreted what he saw as the fruit of one great Presbyterian conspiracy.

By February 20, 1766, he was writing to the Stamp Commissioners that "these Sons of Liberty, who were chiefly composed of Presbyterians at first Onset, aim'd at Sovereignty, and they Dayly succeed in Drawing the weak and unwary amongst other Societies into League and Covenant with them, so that their Numbers begin now to be very formidable and will soon be more so, for they now, in some colonies, have stated Meetings and appoint Committees of Correspondence from one part of the Continent to the other, so that the. Spirit of Rebellion (as I call it) is propagated publicly with the Gratest Industry."

As this spirit of rebellion gathered momentum, Hughes saw that his own career had become inseparably attached to the fate of the British Empire. He was content to have it so. He wanted no part of a Presbyterian republic.

In one of his earliest reports to the Stamp Commissioners he had warned of what would happen if Great Britain allowed the Presbyterians to get their own way by mob violence. "If Great Britain can or will suffer such kind of Conduct in her Colonists to pass unpunished," he wrote, "a Man need not be a Prophet or the son of a Prophet to see clearly that her Empire in North America is at an End." When Parliament repealed the Stamp Act in March, 1766, Hughes must have felt that both the British Empire in North America and his own political career were at an end. His party might continue, but henceforth he would be a millstone about its neck, and it was best that he withdraw from the scene. He did not understand this new American world where resistance to Parliament was rewarded by leniency. For the next eight or nine years he wandered through it, wearing his proud red coat, his head high, and proclaiming his loyalty to George III. He died before the Republic he dreaded became an actuality. Had he lived to see it, he would doubtless have said that the Presbyterians had finally got their way.

Hutchinson, Ingersoll, and Hughes were not the only Americans who suffered in 1765 for supporting the supremacy of Parliament, nor were Massachusetts, Connecticut, and Pennsylvania the only colonies where a political faction was able to take advantage of the Stamp Act to belabor its opponents. In every colony the Stamp Act forced men to decide where their final allegiance would be given, to themselves or to Parliament. If the Act had been enforced, there would have been many more to suffer as these three did and as Cadwallader Colden and Zachariah Hood and Thomas Moffat and Martin Howard suffered. There would have been many more too, who would have joined with the Sons of Liberty to uphold their rights at the cost of their subordination to Parliament. Before the Stamp Act was repealed, the men who would have counted most in the struggle that seemed to be approaching must have made up their minds as to which side they would take. But because it was repealed many of them did not have to reveal their decisions and probably most of them thought that the choice they had made could now be forgotten and the whole episode pushed back into oblivion. Unfortunately the question of Parliament's power in the colonies, once raised, could not be dropped, and the way in which Parliament went about repealing the Stamp Act demonstrated clearly to anyone with the heart to look, that the difficult decisions of 1765 would continue to be relevant.

PART IV

Revolution Delayed

❯❯ FIFTEEN ❮❮

REPEAL

THE passage of the Stamp Act had little effect on the tortuous course of British politics in the summer of 1765. While the Americans were cursing George Grenville and planning rebellion, George III was becoming dissatisfied with his Prime Minister for altogether different reasons. The King had never liked Grenville, and shortly after the passage of the Stamp Act the Minister inflicted upon him an insult which was not easy to forgive. Grenville, at the King's request, drew up a bill giving the King the right to appoint a regent in case he should become incapacitated—George had already had the first of those fits of insanity which were to cloud his later life. Grenville insisted on qualifying the bill to exclude the possibility of the King's appointing his mother as regent. The King's mother was widely believed to be the mistress of the Earl of Bute, who was perhaps the most cordially hated man in British politics. Grenville's insistence on excluding her may have been aimed at excluding the influence of Bute, but it was a direct affront both to her and the King. George, who already controlled a large bloc of seats in Parliament, was able to secure the insertion of his mother's name in the bill, from the floor of the Commons, and thus to defeat his own Minister. The bill carried in that form with little opposition.[1]

The King was confident of his power. Although Grenville had

1. On British politics of the period 1765-66 see W. T. Laprade, "The Stamp Act in British Politics," *American Historical Review*, 35 (1930), 735-757; D. A. Winstanley, *Personal and Party Government* (Cambridge, 1910), 204-275; L. B. Namier, *England in the Age of the American Revolution* (London, 1930), and *The Structure of Politics at the Accession of George III* (London, 1929); L. S. Sutherland, "Edmund Burke and the First Rockingham Ministry," *English Historical Review*, 47 (1932), 46-72. I have relied extensively on these in this account of repeal.

hitherto encountered no opposition in Parliament worthy of the name, George knew that he could dismiss him any time he chose. When Grenville seemed to regard the influential Duke of Bedford as his master, rather than the King, George knew it was time to be rid of him. The problem was whom to put in his place.

The only man who could challenge the power of the King was William Pitt. Fortunately for George, Pitt was not an able politician. He was a colossus, a man to whom everyone had turned in time of crisis, but who could not hold a majority in time of peace. During the Seven-Years War he had ordered Parliament about like a drill-sergeant, knowing that the members had no choice but to obey him. As soon as victory was in sight he lost his grip; yet he still loomed in the House of Commons as the most formidable opponent that any ministry could face. If the King could tame this giant, make him a minister but dependent on the King's support for a majority in Parliament, then George's authority would be complete. He would be able through the regular channels of Parliamentary politics to accomplish what his seventeenth-century predecessors had tried, and failed, to do by disregarding Parliament.

Pitt, then, was the man whom George would have liked to see at the head of the new ministry, but Pitt's own following in Parliament, while great in talent, was so small in numbers that, even with the support of the King, Pitt would have had to work with others, in particular with the group headed by the Duke of Newcastle and the Marquis of Rockingham. Pitt was, as usual, unwilling to play unless he could make his own rules, and as a result the King had ultimately to devise a ministry headed by the Marquis of Rockingham and including, besides Newcastle, General Henry Seymour Conway and the Duke of Grafton, both of whom were ardent followers of Pitt. Conway indeed had only been induced to enter the ministry, as Secretary of State, on condition that Pitt should be allowed to join it the moment that he expressed a wish to do so.

When the Rockingham Ministry took office early in July, the members of Parliament had retired from the heat of a London summer and would not come together again until December. Until that time Rockingham and his followers would have no opportunity to test their strength, but no one who knew the workings of Parliament had very sanguine hopes for their success. The Duke of Newcastle admitted to a friend "that the administration may have a considerable majority in both houses: but that majority must be made up of their enemies, creatures of the two last administrations, and such as are influenced only by their employments and their interest. Such a majority will last no longer than they find the administration carries everything clearly and roundly. The moment there is the least check, they return to their vomit; . . ." [2] This being the opinion of one of the new ministers it is not surprising that politicians outside the administration, particularly the followers of George Grenville and the Duke of Bedford, should hold it in the utmost contempt. Even before it was formed the Earl of Sandwich had called it "the most rash attempt that ever was made," and by the end of August he was writing to Bedford that "the general language seems turned to ridicule the new ministry, and to pronounce their existence to be of a very short duration." [3] He might have added that his own chaplain, James Scott, under the name of Anti-Sejanus, was writing the most stinging ridicule of the new Ministry in the London newspapers. [4]

By the time Parliament came together in December, the strength of the Ministry had by no means improved, but the need for strength was desperate. The news of the riots in America had turned all talk in that direction, and the Rockingham government was faced with the problem of quieting a rebellion which their opponents had called into being. The absence of Pitt now became more conspicuous than ever. Lord Chesterfield had remarked in the preceding summer that the new Ministry was without a keystone. The keystone, he surmised, would have to be added in the course of the winter, and the keystone would have to be William Pitt. [5] In November the Ministry tried to persuade Pitt to come in. Newcastle even agreed to back out if he would accept a place, but Pitt preferred his solitary glory.

The Ministry, then, must meet the American problem by themselves, supported only by their small following of friends and the placeholders who would be obliging only as long as the King wished. If Rockingham displeased the King, he would fall. If he displeased Pitt, he might also fall, for Pitt's opposition would be a signal not merely for his own followers but for all half-hearted supporters to desert. Feeling himself on such shaky ground, Rockingham took a new step. Since he had no real power in Parliament, he looked for it outside Parliament.

2. Quoted from Additional Mss., 32969, f. 392, British Museum, in Winstanley, *Personal and Party Government,* 242n.

3. John Russell, ed., *Correspondence of John, Fourth Duke of Bedford* (London, 1846), III, 304, 316. Cf. Thomas Whately to John Temple, July 12, 1765, Stowe Collection, Huntington Library: "The Newcastle Party are now in Office, how long they will continue so is another question . . . ."

4. Fred J. Hinkhouse, *The Preliminaries of the American Revolution as Seen in the English Press* (New York, 1926), 70-71.

5. Bonamy Dobrée, ed., *The Letters of Philip Dormer Stanhope, 4th Earl of Chesterfield* ([London], 1932), VI, 2658.

The Old Whigs, as Rockingham's group were called, had some reputation among the people as defenders of freedom. They had supported John Wilkes, in spite of his somewhat shady character, in the
fight for freedom of the press. In that fight they had been allied with
the merchants of London, who were also generally to be found on
the side of freedom and against the government. They were a group
of men whom Parliament could neglect only at the expense of the
country's prosperity and of the revenues which derived from that
prosperity. As Canning later called in the New World to redress the
balance of the Old, Rockingham now called in the merchants who
traded with the new world to redress the balance of Parliament.[6]

The alliance of Rockingham and the merchants was grounded on
a common repugnance to the Stamp Act. Conway, the Secretary of
State, had of course been one of the principal speakers against passing it. George Grenville, the father of the measure, would undoubtedly be a leader of the opposition in Parliament, and the best way to
discredit him would be to discredit his Act. The merchants had even
stronger motives than the Ministry for disliking it. This was one
point upon which the merchants trading to North America and
those trading to the West Indies could heartily agree. They might be
at odds over the Sugar Act, which benefited the islands at the expense
of the mainland, but the Stamp Act was pinching them all alike.

The merchants trading to North America, already troubled by the
post-war depression, were further vexed by the non-importation
agreements which the Americans had adopted as a means of promoting repeal. The Americans had begun to cut down imports and
to advocate an increase in home manufactures as soon as the Sugar
Act was passed. With the coming of the Stamp Act, they had taken
more drastic action. The day before the Act was to go into effect, two
hundred New York merchants signed an agreement to import nothing
more from Great Britain until the Stamp Act should be repealed.
The Philadelphia merchants and retailers subscribed similar agreements the next week, and the Boston merchants in December, to be
followed by those of Salem, Marblehead, Plymouth, and Newbury.[7]

The English merchants held no hard feelings towards the Americans for their non-importation agreements but blamed everything on
George Grenville's ill-advised schemes. In order, therefore, to force
a repeal of the Stamp Act, the London merchants on December 4
organized a committee of twenty-eight to mobilize mercantile sentiment and deluge Parliament with petitions for repeal. Barlow Tre-

6. Sutherland, in *English Historical Review*, 47 (1932), 46-72.
7. Schlesinger, *Colonial Merchants and the American Revolution*, 76-80.

cothick, a leading merchant who had been born in Boston, was chairman. Meeting with the Marquis of Rockingham, Trecothick drew up a circular letter which he directed to thirty trading and manufacturing towns throughout the kingdom. As a result petitions came to Parliament not only from the merchants of London but also from the merchants and manufacturers of over twenty other British towns and cities. The petitions made no mention of the rights involved in the Stamp Act but stressed the fact that the North American trade, which suffered under the Grenville measures, was the source of England's prosperity, and that unless Parliament took action, the merchants and manufacturers and all dependent upon them faced ruin.[8]

This was a language which Parliament was willing to talk, but unfortunately the Ministry could not expect Parliament to judge the Stamp Act simply by its economic effects. Probably one of the principal reasons why George Grenville had pressed the Act was in order to settle once for all the question of right. Certainly that was a principal reason why Parliament passed it. The Americans themselves had raised the question in the summer of 1764 by objecting to Parliament's authority to tax them. Once raised, the question could not easily be ignored, and it had become for many members of Parliament the central issue. They might agree that the Act was ill-advised, they might accept every claim made by the merchants, but they could not afford to give the appearance of backing down before a colonial mob; and they would not abandon the authority which they had claimed in passing the Act.[9]

The dilemma of the Rockingham government, therefore, was to find a way to redress the grievances of the merchants, and at the same time assuage the injured honor of Parliament and maintain at least the semblance of authority. As soon as Parliament met on December 17, though the purpose of the meeting was to issue writs of election to fill vacant seats, George Grenville made it plain that he would not allow the members to forget the colonial affront. In opening the session the King referred to the "matters of importance" which had lately occurred in some of his colonies in America. Grenville imme-

8. *Journals of the House of Commons,* XXX, 462-503. Sutherland, in *English Historical Review,* 47 (1932), 62-65; Thomas Penn to William Allen, December 15, 1765, Penn Correspondence, VIII, 338-339, Historical Society of Pennsylvania; *Boston Gazette,* February 24-March 3, 1766 Supplement; Additional Mss., 33030, ff. 208-211, British Museum. Library of Congress transcripts.

9. This view is supported by a host of letters from the friends of the colonies in England. See those in G. H. Guttridge, ed., *The American Correspondence of a Bristol Merchant, 1766-1776* (Berkeley, California, 1934), 10, 14; *Boston Gazette,* February 24, 1766; Massachusetts Historical Society, *Proceedings,* 2d ser., 11 (1897), 446-448; Massachusetts Archives, XXII, 453-460; Penn Correspondence, VIII, 330.

diately wished to know why His Majesty had been advised to speak so leniently on this subject. And the Duke of Bedford called for all papers that had been sent to America since the passage of the Stamp Act to be laid before the House, the purpose being, obviously, to discover some means of embarrassing Conway, the Secretary of State.[10]

Fortunately the House adjourned to January 14, 1766, without agreeing to this motion. The Ministry was thereby given a few more weeks in which to arrive at a formula which would satisfy both merchants and Parliament. At first, apparently, they planned merely to modify the Stamp Act in order to render it less objectionable. As late as January 11, three days before Parliament met, Richard Jackson was writing to Governor Thomas Fitch of Connecticut.

I am informed by the best Intelligence I can procure that the Stamp Act will not be repealed, every other Relief may be, I think, expected, and even this Law will probably be reduced to nothing more, than a Proof of the Power of Parliament to impose Taxes as well as make other Laws for America. Something to Assert this Power is judged necessary by leading Men in both Houses, I wish that some other means of attaining the same End may be thought of rather than this, but I fear no other will.[11]

Rockingham and his followers were considerably handicapped in drawing up a program by the fact that they could not tell what position Pitt would take. They had repeatedly sought his advice and asked him to enter the Ministry, and he as often refused to communicate with them or imposed conditions tantamount to dissolving the Ministry. Consequently when Parliament opened on January 14, they still did not know what line he proposed to follow. The King opened the session with a speech which reflected the ministers' intention both of asserting Parliament's constitutional authority and at the same time of pursuing economic measures which would revive colonial trade. The Ministry followed by introducing the usual address of thanks in which they repeated their intention of combining a zeal for the authority of Parliament with "the utmost attention to the important objects of the trade and navigation of these kingdoms." The opposition opened debate on the address by insisting at once that the Stamp Act should be enforced unless repeal were sought

10. *The Parliamentary History of England* . . . (London, 1813), XVI, 83-90; *Maryland Gazette*, March 6, 1766.

11. Connecticut Historical Society, *Collections*, 18 (1920), 383; Cf. Thomas Penn to William Allen, December 15, 1765, Penn Correspondence, VIII, 338-339; Edmund Pendleton to James Madison, February 15, 1766, Massachusetts Historical Society, *Proceedings*, 2d ser., 19 (1905), 111; Richard and John Samuel to John Yeates, December 4, 1765, Yeates Papers, Historical Society of Pennsylvania.

simply as a favor. The tenor of the opposition was set by Mr. Robert Nugent's contention that though the Stamp Act might produce little in revenue, "a peppercorn, in acknowledgment of the right, was of more value, than millions without." [12]

Before the Ministry could come to their own defense, William Pitt took the floor for one of his most famous speeches. With relentless eloquence he succeeded in the triple task of supporting the address of thanks, flaying the Ministry, and commending the Americans for their rebellion. The address he said was good, but the Ministry should have called the House together earlier on so important a matter. The Ministry, he made it plain, did not have his confidence. "Pardon me, gentlemen," he said, bowing to them, "confidence is a plant of slow growth in an aged bosom: youth is the season of credulity; by comparing events with each other, reasoning from effects to causes, methinks, I plainly discover the traces of an over-ruling influence." (The last was presumably a reference to Lord Bute, or to the Duke of Newcastle.) On the other hand, his contempt for the preceding ministry was even deeper. Turning to George Grenville, who sat only one seat away from him, he thundered, "as to the late ministry every capital measure they have taken, has been entirely wrong!" With the government and the opposition thus disposed of, Pitt went on to extol the Americans, and before the day was over he had pronounced his famous dictum, "I rejoice that America has resisted." In conclusion the great commoner gave his recommendations. They were:

. . . that the Stamp Act be repealed absolutely, totally, and immediately. That the reason for the repeal be assigned, because it was founded on an erroneous principle. At the same time, let the sovereign authority of this country over the colonies, be asserted in as strong terms as can be devised, and be made to extend to every point of legislation whatsoever. That we may bind their trade, confine their manufactures, and exercise every power whatsoever, except that of taking their money out of their pockets without their consent.[13]

When Pitt had done, the Ministry knew at last where he stood, but the revelation merely added to their difficulties. While they had hoped to minimize the importance of the riots in America, Pitt had glorified them. If he had coupled his encomiums for the Americans with a word of praise for the Ministry, he might have contributed

12. *Parliamentary History*, XVI, 90-97; Winstanley, *Personal and Party Government*, 256-259; Laprade, in *American Historical Review*, 35 (1930), 749-750.
13. *Parliamentary History*, XVI, 97-108; W. S. Taylor and J. H. Pringle, eds., *Correspondence of William Pitt, Earl of Chatham* (London, 1838), II, 363-373.

toward effecting the relief of the colonies. As it was, Anti-Sejanus was able to pillory the Ministry in his newspaper columns with a deadly and embarrassing series of questions:

Have they proved that Mr. Pitt, upon whose shoulders they have endeavoured to exalt themselves, will support either them or their system? Has not he more than once hinted at some private influence which they are under, and ridiculed them in the most notorious and public manner? Have they been able by wheedling and fawning, by cringing and crouching, with supple and abject servility, to draw one single drop of comfort from that popular gentleman? Will he espouse their cause and support them in P—t, or leave them to shuffle and scramble for themselves? Dare they adopt his idea, or dare they confront it? Will they not rather, lest they should offend the Idol, find out a middle way, and retain the shadow of power over the colonists, while they give up the substance? [14]

In the face of such taunts, the Ministry once again besought the colossus to join them, but the colossus once again laid down impossible terms, demanding among other things that Newcastle should be dismissed and that Lord Temple, who was George Grenville's brother, should be admitted if he chose to come in. The last demand was the most ironical, for at the same time that Pitt in the Commons was rejoicing over the resistance of the Americans, Temple in the Lords had been speaking in favor of continuing the Stamp Act.[15]

Rockingham was thus obliged to carry on unassisted by the prestige which Pitt's support would have brought him, and hampered by the demands of the merchants and the irritation of Parliament. Since Pitt had always been the favorite of the merchants, his speech intensified their zeal against the Stamp Act, while in Parliament it merely shocked the members by its justification of rebellion. The solution Rockingham devised to bridge this gap, though it was perhaps the only one open to him, promised trouble for the future.

On January 17 the leading ministers met at Rockingham's house and came to an agreement. Rockingham described it in a letter to Charles Yorke, the Attorney General: "The ideas we join in are . . . a declaratory act in general terms,—afterwards to proceed to considerations of trade, etc., and finally determination on the stamp act, i.e. a repeal." [16] The formula Rockingham had fixed upon was, except for one particular, the one which Pitt had asked for in his speech

14. *London Chronicle*, January 28-30, 1766.
15. Winstanley, *Personal and Party Government*, 260-262.
16. Quoted from Additional Mss., 35430, f. 31, British Museum, in Winstanley, *Personal and Party Government*, 262n.

of January 14. Pitt had demanded a total repeal of the Stamp Act combined with an assertion of the legislative authority of Parliament. So far Rockingham was ready to oblige. Pitt had also asked "that the reason for the repeal be assigned, because it [the Stamp Act] was founded on an erroneous principle." To have stated the reason that Pitt assigned would have been asking the members of Parliament to display a humility they had never possessed. Rockingham was obliged, in fact, to emphasize the economic reasons for repeal and so far as possible to keep Parliament from considering the question of principle. It was this necessity which made the repeal of the Stamp Act almost as fruitful of evil consequences as the passage.

Rockingham did not introduce the resolution for the Declaratory Act until February 3 and that for repeal of the Stamp Act until February 21.[17] In the interval between the decision of January 17 and the resolution of February 21 the administration did its best to make Parliament feel the great public demand for repeal, while the opposition accused the Ministry of aiding and abetting the colonial rebellion. The Stamp Act had produced more discussion in the press than any other American measure heretofore. Much of the ablest discussion came from the friends of Grenville: the writings of Anti-Sejanus were undoubtedly the cleverest things appearing in the London papers during the winter of 1765-66. Anti-Sejanus aimed at Parliament more than at the public, and closely followed the proceedings in each House, pouncing upon any bit of testimony or argument that offered an opportunity for ridicule or rebuttal. The failure of the Stamp Act he blamed on the Ministry, alleging that they had not taken proper steps to enforce it. When it came out in Parliament that Governor Moore had been sent to New York without instructions and that Governor Bernard had never received a copy of the Act, he lashed the "inaction and somnolency" of a ministry that would "send off a Governor to one of the principal provinces in America, without any instructions; and let another remain without even a copy of the act, which it was his duty to enforce? A Lieutenant Governor could not act, because he had not proper instructions: and behold, when the Governor himself came—he had no instructions at all." [18] Anti-Sejanus repeatedly warned the members of Parliament of the consequences of appeasing the Americans. "Can it be supposed," he asked, "that the Colonists will ever submit to bear any share in those grievous burdens and taxes, with which we are loaded, when they find that

17. William J. Smith, ed., *The Grenville Papers* (London, 1853), III, 357, 373.
18. *London Chronicle*, February 22-25, 1766.

the G--nt will not, or dare not assert its own authority and power? Have we not reason to expect, that they will shake off all dependance and subjection, and neither suffer a limitation of their trade, nor any duty to be imposed upon their commodities? Is not this want of spirit and resolution, a direct encouragement of the mob, to redress every imaginary grievance, by force and violence?" [19] These telling arguments were bolstered by satirical ballads such as "America Triumphant; or Old England's Downfall, to the Tune of There was a jovial Beggar," which contained the verses

> Who'd stay in musty England,
> And work himself to death,
> Where, choaked with debts and taxes,
> No man can fetch his breath
> > *And to America we'll go* &c.

> Then to America we'll go,
> Where we will merry be;
> Since there no taxes need be paid,
> As wise men all agree.
> > *And to America we'll go* &c.

> Then fare thee well, Old England,
> Where honesty can't thrive;
> Farewell roast-beef, and bread, and beer,
> We'll go to yonder hive.
> > *And to America we'll go* &c.[20]

The Whigs countered with essays on the rights of Englishmen and with reprints of colonial pamphlets.[21] Throughout the heated debates, from the latter part of 1765 until the final victory of repeal, the *London Chronicle* carried in every issue a notice which read:

TO WHOM IT MAY CONCERN,

MEN OF ENGLAND, THE COLONIES, BRETHREN

Consider well the Reverse of a Dutch medal,
struck in their early troubles.
'Two earthen vases, floating on the waters.
Inscription. Frangimur si collidimur.'

19. *Ibid.,* January 11-14, 1766.
20. *Ibid.,* February 18-20, 1766. Cf. "The World Turned upside down, or the Old Woman taught Wisdom," *ibid.,* March 8-11, 1766.
21. Hinkhouse, *Preliminaries of the American Revolution as seen in the English Press,* 52-80. The most able newspaper spokesman for the colonists wrote under the name of "Aequus" in *London Chronicle,* November 28-30, December 10-12, 28-30, 1765, January 4-7, 9-11, 1766.

By and large the Whigs found their greatest strength not in the press but in the organized petitioning of the merchants and in the actual fact of economic depression. The opposition did their best to discredit the petitions by pointing out, with some reason, that these had been inspired by the government itself in order to bring pressure on Parliament.[22] But whatever the origin of the petitions, there was no denying their existence nor was there any denying the economic power of the merchants who presented them. No government can thrive on hard times, and the members of Parliament could not fail to be impressed by the evidence that times were getting harder. They listened to a series of manufacturers quoting discouraging statistics on unemployment. The Ministry expressed the belief that if the Act were enforced Parliament would have to face 20,000 starving Englishmen petitioning for its repeal. It was even hinted that 100,000 unemployed workmen would soon march on London.[23]

In addition to these depressing facts and predictions, Parliament had to consider the testimony of military experts that it would be impossible to enforce the Stamp Act unless more troops were sent to America to do the job.[24] With times so hard already, it was appalling to contemplate raising more troops to enforce an act which showed no signs of bringing in large revenue anyhow. Edward Shippen, off in the wilds of Pennsylvania, knew what he was talking about when he told his father that the British would think twice about enforcing the Act when they realized that it would have to be done "by a mighty army raised from among themselves, for the levying of which they must be *forced* to open their own purse-strings, and this, too, before they have recovered themselves, from the last expensive wars with France and Spain." [25] Nor could Parliament any longer dismiss the hostility of the colonies as mere impertinence. The rebellion there was assuming serious proportions, and while no one would wish to countenance rebellion, only a fool would provoke it unnecessarily. The colonies were admittedly an important source of Britain's strength, but colonies in rebellion could strengthen only Britain's enemies. For a variety of reasons, therefore, the Ministry found Parliament ready to give their proposals a careful hearing.

22. *The Annual Register . . . for the Year 1766* (London, 1772), 37; cf. *London Chronicle*, December 3-5, 14-17, 24-26, 1765, January 4-7, 1766.

23. *Georgia Gazette*, June 4, 1766; Henry Cruger, Jr., to Henry Cruger, February 14, 1766, Massachusetts Historical Society, *Collections*, 69 (1914), 139-142. Cf. Chesterfield to his son, February 11, 1766, *Letters*, Dobrée, ed., VI, 2711-2713.

24. Additional Mss., 33030, British Museum.

25. December 25, 1765, Balch, ed., *Letters and Papers Relating Chiefly to the Provincial History of Pennsylvania*, 212-215.

The members did not lack for information. In addition to the petitions from English merchants and manufacturers, they heard petitions from Edward Montague, agent for Virginia and William Knox, agent for Georgia, both carefully phrased so as to avoid any imputation of Parliament's authority and both asking for repeal of the Act. The Ministry paraded some forty merchants, colonial agents, and visiting Americans before the bar of the House of Commons. Even Thomas Moffat and Martin Howard, Jr., appeared to give their first-hand accounts of the American riots. So did George Mercer, who assured the Commons that the Act could not be enforced without troops. Barlow Trecothick and Nicholas Ray, both of whom had lived in America and had since become prominent London merchants testified to the need for repeal. The star performer, however, was Benjamin Franklin, whose carefully rehearsed performance, made a great impression and was quickly published.[26] The Board of Trade reported on the revenues which had been derived from the customs service in America in the preceding quarter century year by year, together with the costs of conducting civil government and military defense in America, and the amount of the public debt in each colony. In addition Conway laid before the House all the communications from royal governors and stamp officers describing the troubles in America.[27] A great deal of this information, and the testimony of some of the witnesses, Moffat and Howard for example, must have been far from soothing to the injured dignity of Parliament. The Ministry could not afford, however, to suppress any evidence, for their opponents would have been quick to bring it to light. The most that they could do was to maximize the disastrous economic consequences of the Stamp Act and minimize the colonists' denial of Parliament's authority to tax them.

The picture of colonial views about taxation which the ministers and other friends of the colonies endeavored to paint for Parliament was a good deal less clear and a good deal less radical than the views actually expressed by the colonists through their assemblies and through the Stamp Act Congress. The colonies had distinguished between the power to tax and the power to make laws. The latter, they said, belonged to Parliament for the whole empire, but the power to tax was the exclusive power of the local representative assembly in each part of the empire. The House of Commons might levy taxes on

26. *Journals of the House of Commons,* XXX, 455-602; Additional Mss., 33030, British Museum.

27. These papers, preserved in the House of Lords, constitute one of the principal sources for the study of the Stamp Act crisis.

the people of Great Britain, but only the Massachusetts Assembly could tax the people of Massachusetts. This was the argument not merely of the various colonial assemblies, but also of Daniel Dulany and other colonial pamphleteers. One of Dulany's readers had been William Pitt, and Pitt had argued for the colonial position in his speech of January 14. "It is my opinion," he said, "that this kingdom has no right to lay a tax upon the colonies. At the same time, I assert the authority of this kingdom over the colonies, to be sovereign and supreme, in every circumstance of government and legislation whatsoever. . . . Taxation is no part of the governing or legislative power." [28]

This was the view of Pitt, and this was the view of the Americans, but to most members of Parliament it was a novel idea and a dangerous idea to distinguish between the power to tax and the power to legislate. There was, however, another and slightly less dangerous distinction which had already been proposed, probably on the floor of Parliament, and which it was possible to confuse with the distinction between legislation and taxation: the distinction between internal and external taxes. When it was first suggested that Parliament might tax the colonies externally but not internally is uncertain. Richard Jackson, the agent for Connecticut, expressed his belief in this distinction in a letter to Franklin December 27, 1763, averring that "the Mother Country may prohibit foreign Trade, it may therefore tax it. And the Colonys have a Compensation, in Protection but I dread internal Taxes." [29] At the time when he wrote these words Jackson was a member of Parliament. Governor Bernard made use of the distinction in the plan for reorganizing the colonies which he sent to Halifax; and by the spring of 1764 when James Otis was writing his *Rights of the British Colonies Asserted and Proved* the distinction was sufficiently well known so that Otis could disavow it as a "distinction some make in England." [30]

Evidently some of the friends of America, perhaps Richard Jackson, had already rehearsed in Parliament the notion that external taxes on the colonies were constitutional but that internal taxes were not; for when Pitt made his speech in defense of the Americans, the other members of Parliament thought that he was adopting this distinction, or rather they confused this distinction with the one which he did expound, that between taxation and legislation. Pitt actually

28. *Parliamentary History*, XVI, 99; *Chatham Correspondence*, II, 366.
29. Van Doren, ed., *Letters and Papers of Benjamin Franklin and Richard Jackson, 1753-1785*, 123-124.
30. *Rights of the British Colonies Asserted and Proved*, 42.

made two speeches on January 14. In the first, according to the records of the debate, he did not even mention the words external and internal.[31] Yet Grenville, who of course was attacking the Ministry as well as Pitt, said in answer, "I cannot understand the difference between external and internal taxes. They are the same in effect, and only differ in name." Pitt, taking the floor again, clearly dismissed these remarks as not applicable to what he had said. "If the gentleman," cried Pitt, "does not understand the difference between internal and external taxes, I cannot help it; but there is a plain distinction between taxes levied for the purposes of raising revenue, and duties imposed for the regulation of trade, for the accommodation of the subject; although, in the consequences, some revenue might incidentally arise from the latter." Pitt, like the Americans, would admit duties on trade for the purpose of regulation, but not taxes on trade or anything else if for the purpose of revenue.[32]

According to the records, the passage in which he dismissed responsibility for Grenville's failure to understand the difference between internal and external taxes was the only place in his speech where Pitt referred to this distinction or mentioned the words external or internal. Yet some members of Parliament came away with the impression that he had differentiated internal and external taxes, Lord George Sackville wrote to his friend General Irwin, on January 17:

It seems we have all been in a mistake in regard to the Constitution, for Mr. Pitt asserts that the legislature of this country has no right whatever to lay internal taxes upon the colonys; that they are neither actually nor virtually represented, and therfore not subject to our jurisdiction in that particular; but still, as the Mother Country, we may tax and regulate their commerce, prohibit or restrain their manufactures, and do everything but what we have done by the Stamp Act; that in our representative capacity we raise taxes internally and in our legislative capacity we do all the other acts of power. If you understand the difference between representative and legislative capacity it is more than I do, but I assure you it was very fine when I heard it.[33]

Here Sackville has obviously confounded and combined the two distinctions. Perhaps other members of Parliament did the same. In

31. The account of this speech as given in *Chatham Correspondence*, II, 363-373, and *Parliamentary History*, XVI, 97-108, is said to have been "almost verbatim." See Basil Williams, *The Life of William Pitt* (London, 1913), II, 336, 346 n.

32. *Parliamentary History*, XVI, 101, 105; *Chatham Correspondence*, II, 370.

33. Historical Manuscripts Commission, *Report on the Manuscripts of Mrs. Stopford-Sackville* (London, 1904), I, 104.

any case it was to the interest of the Rockingham Ministry and of anyone seeking repeal of the Act to foster this confusion, for the distinction between internal and external taxes limited the power of Parliament much less than the wholesale distinction between taxation and legislation. The Ministry therefore made no effort to show what the true position of the Americans was but preferred to let Parliament suppose that the Americans were denying the power merely to levy internal taxes and had no objection to external taxes.

It was evidently for this reason that Rockingham did not make use of the petitions from the Stamp Act Congress. A technical reason was discovered for not hearing them in Parliament, namely, that they were not properly signed. But Charles Garth, one of the special agents appointed to present the one to the House of Commons, told his constituents that the reason the Ministry failed to support the petition was "that it tended to question not only the Right of Parliament to impose internal Taxes, but external Duties. . . ." [34] Pitt, quite consistently, demanded that the petitions be heard, for Pitt had taken precisely the position which the Stamp Act Congress took, but his defense of the Congress only served to embarrass the Ministry in their attempt to keep the radical constitutional theories of the Americans in the background. [35]

The members of the opposition showed some astuteness in pointing out that the Americans actually went farther than merely internal taxes in their denial of Parliament's authority. From Martin Howard they extracted the statement that the colonists "made no Objection while they only Taxed by Customs But now they . . . have in Virginia denied all Taxes." One of the members asked him if they did not also object to the Navigation Acts, but Howard answered fairly enough, "They do not Extend it so far." [36] Hans Stanley, a member of the opposition from Southampton pointed out bluntly that "The Americans have not made the futile Distinction between internal and external taxes." [37] And in the House of Lords, Lord Lyttelton, who had taken the trouble to read Otis's pamphlet, reported that "The Americans themselves make no distinction between external and internal taxes. Mr. Otis, their champion, scouts such a distinction, . . ." [38]

These more accurate delineations of the American position were,

34. *Maryland Historical Magazine*, 6 (1911), 285.

35. George Thomas, Earl of Albemarle, *Memoirs of the Marquis of Rockingham* (London, 1852), I, 289-290; Historical Manuscripts Commission, *Stopford-Sackville*, I, 105.

36. Additional Mss., 33030, ff. 133-135, British Museum.

37. *American Historical Review*, 17 (1912), 566.

38. *Parliamentary History*, XVI, 167.

fortunately for the proponents of repeal, overshadowed by the spectacular performance of Benjamin Franklin, who managed to convey very forcefully the idea that the Americans objected only to internal taxes. Though Franklin must have known that the American objections to taxation were more sweeping, he was anxious to assist in the repeal, and he knew that the American claims of exemption were a stumbling block. For that reason, probably, he followed the Rockingham party in minimizing their extent. Much of his testimony had been rehearsed with members friendly to the Ministry, but he gave some of his most effective answers in dealing with questions posed by the opposition. One member asked him if the reasoning by which the colonists objected to internal taxes might not justify them in objecting to external taxes as well. Franklin's answer was so neat that it must have made a lasting impression. "Many arguments have been lately used here to shew them [the colonists], that there is no difference, and that, if you have no right to tax them internally, you have none to tax them externally, or make any other law to bind them. At present they do not reason so; but in time they may possibly be convinced by these arguments." The laughter which must have followed this rather telling blow probably diminished the effect of the next question, asked by a member who had evidently taken the trouble to look at some of the documents which Conway had laid before Parliament: "Do not the resolutions of the Pennsylvania assembly say, all taxes?" To this Franklin could only say, that if the Pennsylvania resolutions said all taxes, they meant only internal taxes. But Franklin had made his point, and somehow the impression remained that the Americans objected only to internal taxes.[39]

How much this misunderstanding of the American position contributed to the repeal of the Stamp Act would be difficult to say. Perhaps very little, for the evidence suggests that pressure from the merchants, rather than consideration for colonial rights, was the force behind repeal. The misunderstanding may even have been a genuine confusion in which the Rockingham Ministry shared, though the Ministry's stand on the petitions of the Stamp Act Congress suggests strongly that they understood the colonial claims better than they were willing to admit. In any case Rockingham was clearly responsible for another misunderstanding, the converse of that about internal and external taxes. In drawing up the Declaratory Act, he deliberately phrased it in such a way as to leave the meaning uncertain to those whom it might offend. The result was that the colonists at

39. *Ibid.*, 137-160; see pp. 158-159; Benjamin Franklin, *Writings,* Smyth, ed., IV, 412-448, see pp. 445-446.

first misunderstood Parliament's declaration of right, just as Parliament had misunderstood the colonists' declarations.

The idea of a declaratory act, affirming Parliament's authority over the colonies, seems to have occurred to Rockingham fairly early. Such an affirmation of Parliament's authority over Ireland had been made in a Declaratory Act in 1719.[40] With this example before him the Minister had apparently decided as early as December 27 that whatever accommodation he extended to the colonies should be accompanied by a declaration of Parliament's authority.[41] It was not Rockingham, however, but William Pitt who provided the immediate impetus for the act which was finally passed. In asking for repeal of the Stamp Act on January 14 Pitt had said, "At the same time, let the sovereign authority of this country over the colonies, be asserted in as strong terms as can be devised, and be made to extend to every point of legislation whatsoever.[42] Obviously Pitt did not mean that this assertion of sovereign authority should extend to taxation, for his whole speech had been a denial that taxation was a part of the sovereign power, and he demanded at the same time an express recognition that the Stamp Act was unconstitutional. The declaration which he called for was a declaration of Parliament's legislative authority, and Rockingham took care to frame his declaration precisely as Pitt had demanded. The resolution which Rockingham presented to Parliament on February 3 read "That the King's Majesty, by and with the advice and consent of the Lords spiritual and temporal and Commons of Great Britain in parliament assembled, had, hath, and of right ought to have, full power and authority to make laws and statutes of sufficient force and validity to bind the colonies and people of America, subjects of the crown of Great Britain, in all cases whatsoever." [43]

This was the declaration "in general terms" upon which Rockingham and his colleagues had decided on January 17. The fact that the resolution and the act which was framed from it made no mention of taxation was no accident, for the act was designed to satisfy everyone. The members of Parliament, or by far the greater part of them, had derided Pitt's distinction between legislation and taxation. Grenville had expressed the sentiments of the house when he said, "That this kingdom has the sovereign, the supreme legislative power over America, is granted. It cannot be denied; and taxation is a part of that

40. 6 George I, c. 5.
41. Winstanley, *Personal and Party Government*, 256.
42. *Parliamentary History*, XVI, 108; *Chatham Correspondence*, II, 373.
43. *Parliamentary History*, XVI, 164.

sovereign power." [44] The House should therefore be satisfied by the declaration of Parliament's legislative power even though it did not mention taxation specifically. Pitt and his followers, on the other hand, both in and out of Parliament, in both England and America, could be expected to agree to the declaration, since it merely asserted legislative authority.

Rockingham had taken great pains to keep the act in such general terms. When he sent the resolutions agreed upon by the Ministry to Charles Yorke, his Attorney General, for comments, Yorke noted that the assertion of the right to make laws for the colonies made no specific mention of taxation. Although Yorke doubtless subscribed to the notion that the right to tax was a part of the right to legislate, nevertheless the whole necessity for a declaratory act had arisen from a denial of Parliament's right to tax. Yorke accordingly suggested that the last phrase of the resolution be amended to read "as well in cases of Taxation, as in all other cases whatsoever." [45] This emendation would have left no room for doubt, but it would have offended Pitt and his followers, and Rockingham shrank from another bout with the Great Commoner. He therefore informed Yorke, in a letter dated January 25, that the word taxation could not appear. "I think I may say," he politely wrote, for his relations with Yorke were not altogether friendly, "that it is our firm Resolution in the House of Lords—I mean among ourselves—that that word must be resisted." [46]

Yorke was not the only Whig dissatisfied with the ambiguous character of the resolution. The Archbishop of Canterbury wrote to the Duke of Newcastle urging that the resolution be "sufficiently vigorous," lest the opposition introduce "extravagant and hurtful" ones and gain "the sole Merit of whatever may be good in those resolutions." [47] Though Rockingham spoke of the firm resolution of his party in the House of Lords, the Earl of Hardwicke, Yorke's

44. *Ibid.*, 101.
45. Albemarle, *Memoirs of Rockingham*, I, 285-287. In the Stowe Collection, Huntington Library, there is another draft of the resolution which contains the words "as well in all Cases of Impositions and Taxes, as in all other matters, and for all purposes whatsoever." Additional Mss., 35912, ff. 45-51, British Museum, marked "The within propositions vary in some particulars from those given to Mr. Yorke some time ago," proposes a resolution affirming Parliament's power "to make Laws (whether of Taxation, or not) binding upon all the colonies." The origin of these two documents is not indicated.
46. Additional Mss., 35430, ff. 37-38, British Museum. Albemarle, *Memoirs of Rockingham*, I, 287-288, prints this letter in a slightly different form: the words "must not be inserted" are substituted for "must be resisted." This may be a misreading of the manuscript, or perhaps Albemarle used a different copy of the letter. In either case the meaning is the same.
47. Additional Mss., 32973, f. 332, British Museum.

brother, to whom Rockingham later offered a seat in the Cabinet, likewise thought that taxation should be specifically mentioned. Hardwicke was so concerned about the matter that when he saw the resolutions which were to be introduced in the House of Lords, he wrote to his brother, observing that "The question about *the right* is in general terms—all cases *whatsoever*. I presume it is the same in your House. Tell me *what you will do*, if taxation is proposed to be inserted. The Ministers desire to flatter North America, not to make it subordinate to this country." [48]

Evidently Hardwicke thought it likely that the opposition would introduce a specific assertion of Parliament's right to tax and felt tempted to break ranks and vote for such a measure. As the event turned out, it became unnecessary for the opposition to propose any mention of taxation in the Declaratory Act, because of an unexpected move by the man who had all but dictated the terms of the Act: William Pitt. Colonel Barré, an adherent of Pitt, moved as an amendment, that the words "in all cases whatsoever" should be struck out. Barré, in arguing for his amendment, and Pitt in supporting him, both contended simply that Parliament had no right to tax the colonies.[49] In the House of Lords Lord Camden argued the same point.[50] Since the arguments were directed against the phrase "in all cases whatsoever," it became clear to Parliament that the inclusion of this phrase must mean that the declaration extended to the right of taxation. Why Pitt and Barré and Camden should have insisted on drawing out this explicit meaning from the words is not apparent. Pitt himself had said that the declaration should "extend to every point of legislation whatsoever." It is difficult to see how the Act which was passed departed from this prescription. The debate over the inclusion of "all cases whatsoever" only served to accomplish, for the members of Parliament at least, what Charles Yorke would have accomplished by a specific mention of taxation. If the Act had passed without debate on this point, it would have been possible for Pitt and other friends of the colonies to argue later that it did not include the right to tax. As it was, the meaning was entirely clear to the men who passed the Act, and the meaning was that Parliament had full authority to tax the colonies.

After passing the Declaratory Act, Parliament reluctantly agreed to repeal the Stamp Act: the issue was in doubt until the end. As

48. January 28, 1766, Albemarle, *Memoirs of Rockingham*, I, 291.
49. *Maryland Historical Magazine*, 6 (1911), 287-305; *American Historical Review*, 17 (1912), 565-574.
50. *Archives of Maryland*, XIV, 267-268; *Parliamentary History*, XVI, 177-181.

one of the merchants put it, "today the Ministry wou'd have the best of it, and things would look well; tomorrow Grenville and his Party wou'd gain the Power, and then of course *no* Repeal." [51] On one evening Grenville kept the House of Commons debating until eleven o'clock on a motion he introduced for enforcement.[52] The motion was lost by 140 votes, but as late as February 8 the *London Chronicle* reported the opinion that the Act would be enforced. The King, after signifying to the Ministry his approval of repeal, let it be known privately that he favored enforcement.[53] The Ministry, for a desperate moment, even considered resigning. Feelings ran high within Parliament and without. The debates went on night after night till the early hours. After it was all over, one weary merchant wrote to his American friends, "I have been one of those that have attended the House of Commons early and late, or rather late and early, about the American affairs, . . . I am glad this ugly affair is over, for we are heartily tired, and have slaved like horses, sometimes not coming home till two or three o'clock in the morning, and then perhaps fasting." [54] When the crucial debate on the resolution for repeal was held in the committee of the whole on Friday, February 21, the members began arriving at eight o'clock in the morning to reserve their seats. Repeal did not finally carry until two o'clock Saturday morning, by a vote of 275 to 167, with fifty-two of the King's placeholders voting with the opposition by his permission.[55]

Though the bill had yet to undergo three readings and passage by the Lords, it had survived the critical test, and the people of England did not wait to rejoice. Saturday morning, as soon as the news was abroad, the bells of London's churches began to ring and continued to ring all day. The captains of the West India ships in the Thames broke out their colors, and as the news reached other towns the rejoicing spread all over England. For in spite of the powerful opposition in Parliament, popular opinion had been overwhelmingly for repeal. The economic depression in England was acute and in the minds of the people who suffered most seriously from it, the Stamp

51. Henry Cruger, Jr., to Henry Cruger, February 15, 1766, Massachusetts Historical Society, *Collections*, 69 (1914), 139-142.

52. The debate took place February 7 (Albemarle, *Memoirs of Rockingham*, I, 298). It is described in Henry Cruger, Jr.'s letter, Massachusetts Historical Society, *Collections*, 69 (1914), 139-143; and the substance of the motion may be found in the papers of the Stowe Collection, Huntington Library.

53. Massachusetts Historical Society, *Collections*, 69 (1914), 139-142; Albemarle, *Memoirs of Rockingham*, I, 302-303.

54. *Georgia Gazette*, June 4, 1766.

55. *Virginia Gazette* (Purdie), April 25, 1766. Winstanley, *Personal and Party Government*, 268, 305-306; Chesterfield, *Letters*, VI, 2716.

Act was to blame. Manufacturers now began rehiring their workers, and ships put out for America with cargoes of British textiles and messages which would spread the rejoicing to America too. "It is repealed, my friend," said one of the messages, "to the universal joy of Britain . . . Had it not been so, there is the strongest reason to think that by this time there would have been more formidable commotions here than any that have been on your side of the Atlantick." [56]

Both Englishmen and Americans had cause to rejoice, for rebellion and civil war had been avoided and the strength of the empire preserved. Unfortunately repeal did not put back into the limbo of ambiguity the words which had been spoken so often in the preceding two years, "the rights of Englishmen" and "the authority of Parliament." Grenville had given a meaning to one phrase, and the colonists to the other, which repeal of the Stamp Act could not erase.

56. *Virginia Gazette* (Purdie), April 25, June 13, 1766.

⤜ SIXTEEN ⤛

CONCLUSION

ONE of the principal arguments which the opposition had used against repeal of the Stamp Act was that the colonies would interpret it as a sign of weakness, that whatever reason Parliament assigned for repeal, the Americans would believe that their own resistance had been the real cause. The friends of the colonies took care to inform their correspondents in America that the violence against the stamp distributors had prolonged the struggle for repeal and had even threatened to prevent it entirely. Letters sent by the committee of merchants in London to the merchants of the principal towns and cities of North America urged the Americans not to exult in the victory as a point gained over Parliamentary authority. Any such attitude would surely strengthen the hand of Grenville and his followers, who might still return to power and undo the great work of reconciliation. The merchants had had a hard fight, in which they had "pawned their words" for the colonies, and "I hope," one of them wrote, "nothing will be done, that may make them ashamed of the assurances they have given, that all would return to quiet and good humour. A contrary behaviour will hurt the present ministry, who are your true friends; and if they fall, your enemies will succeed, from whom you have everything to fear." In order to prevent such a catastrophe, the committee urged the Americans to send over expressions of "filial duty and gratitude to your parent country." [1]

These words were made more pointed by two protests issuing from the minority in the House of Lords against repeal of the Stamp Act.

1. Massachusetts Historical Society, *Proceedings*, 55 (1923), 215-223; *ibid.*, 2d ser., 11 (1897), 446-448; *Newport Mercury*, May 12, 1766; *Georgia Gazette*, June 4, 1766.

Some thirty-three peers published to the country at large, with the sanction of their own illustrious names, the accusations which Anti-Sejanus had been making in the London press. Repeal of the Stamp Act, they said, was a surrender of Parliament's supreme jurisdiction. The reasons the Americans had assigned for disobedience to the Act would extend "to all other laws, of what nature soever, which that Parliament had enacted, or shall enact, to bind them in times to come, and must, if admitted, set them absolutely free from any obedience to the power of the British legislature." By the Declaratory Act, they said, Parliament only "more grievously injured its own dignity and authority by verbally asserting that right which it substantially yields up to its opposition." [2] The total effect would be to push the colonies in the direction toward which they were already verging—independence. In the protests of the Lords the Americans could read the narrowness of their escape as well as their future peril, and they hastened to comply with the advice of the merchants, which had been seconded by Secretary Conway in sending official notice of the repeal. The assemblies of the various colonies drew up addresses of thanks to King and Parliament for their parental solicitude and gave assurance of their loyalty to the King and their submission to the authority of Parliament—though none of them specifically acknowledged that this authority included the right to tax them. [3]

In spite of the loyal sentiments of their addresses, the colonists would have been a little more than human if they had not given themselves some of the credit for repeal. "Had we tamely submitted," they asked themselves, "would the Justice of our Cause have procured us Relief?" [4] Probably few could find it in their hearts to say yes. Thomas Moffat, returning to New England in the latter part of the year, wrote back to a friend in London, "The prevailing notions about the persons, measures, and principles upon which the Stamp Act was repealed would extremely divert you who might not expect so godly a people to be left under so many or so great delusions." [5] Thomas Hutchinson, looking back upon the period some years later thought that repeal was interpreted throughout the colonies, not as an act of favor, but as a concession to the colonial view that taxation

2. *Parliamentary History of England*, XVI, 181-193.
3. See note 20 and *Colonial Records of Georgia*, XIV, 380-381; *Colonial Records of North Carolina*, VII, 332-334; *Pennsylvania Archives*, 8th ser., 7 (1935), 5884-5885; J. Almon, ed., *A Collection of Interesting, Authentic Papers,...* (London, 1777), 109-110; Nathaniel Bouton, ed., *Provincial Papers: Documents and Records Relating to the Province of New Hampshire*, VII (Nashua, 1873), 106.
4. *Virginia Gazette* (Rind), May 30, 1766.
5. December 12, 1766, Bancroft Transcripts, New York Public Library.

was the power only of a representative body.[6] The celebrations with which repeal was greeted were decent and orderly, as the committee of merchants had urged. True, the Sheriff of Falmouth (Portland, Maine) was inspired by what he had drunk to ride his horse into the Townhouse and up the stairs, but the rest of the celebrators quietly placed him in the stocks.[7] In Philadelphia, the newspapers reported that "notwithstanding the GREAT and GLORIOUS cause of our present Rejoicings, not one single instance of that Kind of Triumph, so much dreaded by our Friends, and wished for by our Enemies in England, has escaped the warmest Sons of Liberty in this City." [8] Up and down the Atlantic coast, houses were illuminated; paintings and verses composed for the occasion were exhibited; and toasts were drunk publicly to William Pitt and the other men who had championed the cause of the colonies in Parliament; but the most significant thing about the celebrations was that they were directed by the Sons of Liberty, the men responsible for the violent proceedings which according to the Committee of Merchants had hindered repeal. The Sons of Liberty showed no contrition for their sins. Not only did they direct celebrations of repeal in 1766, but they also staged celebrations upon the anniversary of repeal every year thereafter, until the Revolution began. In Boston they even celebrated the anniversary of August 14, the night of the first riot.[9] Thus the Sons of Liberty kept alive the memory of the glorious days when Americans had risen up against the threat of tyranny and had successfully asserted their rights.

This misinterpretation of the repeal of the Stamp Act was rendered the more easy by the general terms in which Rockingham had couched the Declaratory Act. After the debate over Barré's motion to omit the words, "in all cases whatsoever," the meaning of the Act was plain to members of Parliament, so plain that one unofficial report of the resolves which formed the basis of the Act summarized it as saying "That the King, Lords, and Commons of this realm have always had, and ought to have the undoubted right to tax the colonies." [10] But the session of Parliament in which the debate took place was a secret one with no visitors allowed. Hugh Hamersley, the secretary to Lord Baltimore, wrote to Governor Sharpe of Maryland that he could give

6. Hutchinson, *History of Massachusetts-Bay*, L. S. Mayo, ed., III, 121.

7. Joseph Kent to Charles Miller, May 23, 1766, Sullivan Papers, I, Massachusetts Historical Society.

8. *Pennsylvania Gazette*, May 22, 1766.

9. Massachusetts Historical Society, *Proceedings*, 2d ser., 10 (1895), 63, 66; John Adams, *Works*, C. F. Adams, ed., II, 218; *Boston Gazette*, August 21, 1769.

10. *Newport Mercury*, April 28, 1766.

him no report of what had happened in the House of Commons, because "they have throughout the business shut their doors against all strangers." [11] Reports did reach the colonies from members of Parliament who happened to be colonial agents. Charles Garth sent a full report of the debate to the Maryland Assembly.[12] But many colonists, unaware of what had passed in Parliament, were puzzled by the Declaratory Act. Though the early reports had said that it asserted Parliament's right to tax, when the actual texts of the resolution and of the Act were reported, it was apparent that Parliament had made no mention of taxation. Ezra Stiles noted that the Act "declared the most absolute parliamentary Authority in Legislation yet with a seeming Ambiguity, as to power of Taxation." [13] John Adams, reading the resolve in the Boston newspapers, observed that it asserted Parliament's right "to make laws for the Colonies in all cases whatever," and wondered "whether they will lay a tax in consequence of that resolution, or what kind of a law they will make." [14] James Otis, on the other hand, assured the Boston town meeting that the Act "had no relation to Taxes," or so at least Governor Bernard was told.[15]

If Otis and others placed such an interpretation on the Act, it was not without reason. Rockingham had deliberately omitted any mention of taxation, and Conway in speaking to Dennys De Berdt, an agent of Massachusetts, told him that the Ministry had been opposed to any Declaratory Act but had been obliged to accept one in order to get a majority for repeal. Conway hoped that the Americans would understand the Act in that light.[16] Richard Jackson, the other agent of Massachusetts, dismissed the Act as a formality. He wrote on March 3, 1766, that repeal "could not have been obtained without another act for declaring the right of Parliament to bind the colonies by laws in all cases whatsoever; which will probably as little prejudice them, as the power we claim in Ireland, the manner of exercising which you are acquainted with." [17] The Massachusetts Assembly was well acquainted with the extent of Parliament's authority in Ireland. They knew, and had stated in an address designed to be sent to the King in 1764, that Parliament "have never laid any Duty or Tax on the Sub-

11. February 20, 1766, *Archives of Maryland,* XIV, 272.
12. *Maryland Historical Magazine,* 6 (1911), 287-305.
13. Stiles to Samuel Langdon, May 24, 1766, Stiles Papers, Yale University Library.
14. *Works,* II, 192.
15. Bernard to Shelburne, December 22, 1766, Bernard Papers, IV, 282, Harvard College Library.
16. De Berdt to Samuel White, February 15, 1766, Colonial Society of Massachusetts, *Publications,* 13 (1912), 312.
17. Alden Bradford, ed., *Speeches of the Governors of Massachusetts,* 72; Massachusetts Archives, XXII, 458.

jects of Ireland, though that hath ever been deemed, and acknowl-
edgeth it self to be a dependent Kingdom." [18] Daniel Dulany, even
though he must have had access to Garth's letter describing the debate over the Act, later argued that the Declaratory Act did not
affirm an authority to tax, because if such were the case the Declaratory Act of 6 George I would give a similar authority to Parliament
in Ireland. Since it was admitted, he said, that Parliament had no
right to tax Ireland, similarly, in spite of the Declaratory Act, Parliament had no right to tax the colonies.[19]

There is no evidence that the Americans, in rejoicing over repeal
of the Stamp Act, accepted the right of Parliament to tax them. Many
of their loyal addresses of thanks upon the repeal, were phrased so as
to reject any such admission. They rejoiced at repeal of the "late unconstitutional Stamp Act," which had "Endanger'd both their Liberty and Property"; they expressed submission to "the rightfull Authority of the British Parliament" or "constitutional subordination"
to Parliament, but they maintained that their struggles against the
Stamp Act were "not those of Rebellion or Disaffection, But those of
Freemen," and were "compatible with the English Constitution." [20]
The vague terms of the Declaratory Act enabled them to accept it as
a statement of their own position: that Parliament had supreme legislative authority, but that taxation was not a part of legislation.

William Pitt himself had spectacularly supported the American
position in Parliament, and the American press like the British press
gave to Pitt the credit for carrying the repeal. He had asserted plainly
the power of Parliament in all branches of legislation whatsoever, but
he had stoutly denied Parliament's right to tax. Upon reading his
speech of January 14, John Adams wrote in his diary: "What has
been said in America which Mr. Pitt has not confirmed? Otis,
Adams, Hopkins, &c. have said no more." [21] Since they believed that
repeal was the work of Pitt many Americans must have found it hard
to believe that the Declaratory Act should be interpreted as a denial
of everything he had said. George Mason of Virginia observed that
the Act asserted the "legislative authority" of Great Britain in all
cases whatsoever, but he remembered that "a just and necessary Distinction between Legislation and Taxation hath been made by the

18. Massachusetts Archives, XXII, 415.
19. Letter to Conway, undated, Sparks Manuscripts, 44, Bundle 7, Harvard College
Library.
20. *Journals of the House of Burgesses of Virginia 1766-1769*, 34; *Archives of the
State of New Jersey*, 1st ser., 9 (1885), 560-561; Massachusetts Historical Society, *Proceedings*, 57 (1924), 353-355; Bradford, *Speeches of the Governors of Massachusetts*, 91-92.
21. *Works*, II, 191.

greatest and wisest men in the Nation," for surely Pitt was one of the greatest and wisest. Mason noticed, however, that the Act did not specifically disavow the authority to tax, and just as Charles Yorke thought that the Act should have specifically claimed such an authority, Mason thought it should have specifically disclaimed it. Such a disclaimer, he said "wou'd not have impeached or weakened the Vote of Right; on the Contrary it wou'd have strengthened it." [22]

When the Americans did come to realize that the Declaratory Act was intended to affirm the right of taxation, they were by no means ready to accept it. To some this realization came much earlier than is generally supposed. One Virginian apparently saw the Act in this light as soon as he read it. In a letter signed "A British American," which appeared in the *Virginia Gazette* on May 2, 1766, he advised the assemblies of all the American colonies "to take no further notice of the declaration of the British Parliament should it be laid before them than to pay it the respect of ordering it to be laid upon the table for the perusal of the members and without mentioning any thing of the proceedings of parliament to enter upon their journals as strong declarations of their own rights as words can express." This letter was reprinted in the newspapers of other colonies during the summer of 1766, and must have started the inhabitants thinking about the meaning of the Act. The Providence Sons of Liberty evidently gave some attention to the matter, for by July 21 their secretary Silas Downer was writing to the Sons of Liberty in New York, urging the necessity of maintaining their organization and their intercolonial connections, because of Parliament's "passing a Law, wherein is affirmed in the strongest Terms a parliamentary Authority and Right to Tax us, to the great prejudice of the Crown, and of the Liberties of America, so that a Way might be ready paved for such Impositions in future, as might coincide with their Systems of Wealth, Power, and Dominion." [23]

In South Carolina Christopher Gadsden pointed out to the local Sons of Liberty that the Declaratory Act was not as harmless as it seemed. He called attention to its preamble, which denied the validity of the colonial resolutions. If Parliament thought these invalid, then Parliament was still claiming the right to tax, and such a claim the colonies must never admit.[24]

22. Kate M. Rowland, *The Life of George Mason, 1725-1792* (New York, 1892), I, 383, original in Library of Congress.
23. Peck Manuscripts, III, Rhode Island Historical Society.
24. Edward McCrady, *The History of South Carolina under the Royal Government, 1719-1776* (New York, 1899), 590.

Those who perceived the true meaning of the Declaratory Act also perceived that the Americans had small reason to display the gratitude which the merchants had insisted upon, for both Parliament and the merchants had been motivated by a concern for the welfare of England rather than America. A Virginian who signed himself "Algernon Sydney" pointed out that "The Relief they have given is professedly for their own Sakes, not ours." [25] Silas Downer likewise saw that "the Merchants trading to America, whose only Business is the Accumulation of Wealth, solicited the Repeal from Principles of Convenience to themselves; at the same Time holding fast the deleterious Doctrine of a certain Supremacy of the British People over the Americans, and never urging the least Argument in our Favor, founded on the Views whereon the American Opposition was built, but utterly discounting any such." [26] And George Mason ridiculed the merchants for speaking to the colonists like schoolboys, as if to say:

We have with infinite difficulty and fatigue got you excused this one time; pray be a good boy for the future, do what your papa and mama bid you, and hasten to return them your most grateful acknowledgments for condescending to let you keep what is your own; and then all your acquaintance will love you, and praise you, and give you pretty things; . . . Is not this a little ridiculous, when applied to three millions of as loyal and useful subjects as any in the British dominions, who have been only contending for their birth-right, and have now only gained, or rather kept, what could not, with common justice, or even policy, be denied them? [27]

Not all Americans were able to see as soon as Mason and Downer the implications of what Parliament had done, and even they missed the larger significance of the Declaratory Act. Perhaps even Rockingham failed to understand that his Act assigned a greater authority to Parliament than Grenville had originally claimed with his Stamp Act. Grenville had justified taxing the colonies on the ground that they were represented—virtually—in Parliament. Repeal of the Stamp Act, unaccompanied by the Declaratory Act, could have been utilized as a demonstration that virtual representation worked. Though the Americans did not elect a single member, Parliament had been sufficiently sensitive to their interests, as expressed through the British merchants, to repeal a measure they disliked. What better answer than this to the American claim that virtual representation could not

25. *Virginia Gazette* (Rind), May 30, 1766.
26. To the New York Sons of Liberty, July 21, 1766, Peck Manuscripts, III.
27. Rowland, *Life of Mason*, I, 382.

cross the ocean? But the Declaratory Act precluded such an interpretation of repeal, for it rendered unnecessary the pretence of linking taxation and representation, and rested the authority of Parliament on a simple declaration of that body's sovereignty. It was no sooner passed than the *London Gazetteer* announced, "As we are informed it is now decided that the legislature of this Kingdom hath a right to levy taxes on America, we beg leave to inform our correspondents that we can no longer admit any letters in which that right is in any wise controverted." [28] In spite of this announcement public discussion of course continued, but officially there was no longer any doubt that Parliament had authority to tax the colonies, and there was no longer any need to justify that authority by the doctrine of virtual representation. The British government had abandoned the constitutional position which linked them with the Americans and had retreated to the heights of arbitrary declaration.

It is possible, of course, that if Rockingham and his friends had stayed in power the Declaratory Act might have remained a harmless gesture. But the mere fact that the Act had been necessary in order to get repeal through Parliament was a sign that Rockingham's desire to avoid the issue which it presented was not generally shared. His control of Parliament had been tenuous at best, and in the summer of 1766 he gave way to a ministry headed at last by Pitt. It was one of the ironies in the career of that ailing and temperamental genius that the next measure for taxing the colonies was passed by an administration in which he was nominally the leader. As the years went by the government fell more and more into the grasp of men who believed with George Grenville that the Stamp Act should have been enforced instead of repealed. In their hands the Declaratory Act became an official permit (presented to them by their opponents), authorizing them to secure from the Americans that "pepper-corn in acknowledgement of the right," which they regarded as of more value than millions without. It is not impossible that a ministry disposed to moderation might have obtained money from America without reviving the conflict between colonies and Parliament: in return for the voluntary contributions which the Americans offered to make if called upon in a constitutional manner, Parliament might have been persuaded to leave its avowed authority unexercised. But the men in control after the fall of Rockingham were not interested in voluntary contributions and would not leave the question of right alone.

In the eyes of these men the Americans had been aiming at inde-

28. Quoted by W. T. Laprade, *American Historical Review*, 35 (1930), 752. Cf. *London Chronicle*, March 4-6, 1766.

pendence ever since the Peace of Paris. It was a common observation in the mid-eighteenth century that the colonies would not forever remain as dependencies of Great Britain. No one who considered the extent of the North American continent and the rate at which its population was increasing could doubt the truth of the observation, though the separation was scarcely expected to take place in the eighteenth century. Many Englishmen had warned before the Peace of Paris that if Canada were not returned to the French the Americans would no longer feel the need of the British army and navy to protect them and would turn their faces toward independence.[29] When these warnings were ignored and the French menace was ended by the Peace of Paris, the prophets of doom saw their fears justified in the ensuing American resistance to the Stamp Act. Anti-Sejanus told the people of England that "The Americans imbibe notions of independance and liberty with their very milk, and will some time or other shake off all subjection. If we yield to them in this particular, by repealing the Stamp-Act, it is all over; they will from that moment assert their freedom."[30] Rockingham and the merchants by arguing that the Americans objected only to internal taxation had been able to persuade a majority of Parliament that repeal of the Stamp Act would not encourage the movement of the colonies to independence. When the colonies next objected to the external taxes levied by the Townshend duties, many members of Parliament must have been convinced that Anti-Sejanus had been right. The Americans, it appeared, were working their way by gradual stages to the point where they would be completely independent, first freedom from internal taxes, then from external taxes. The Acts of Trade would be next. Little by little the supremacy of the mother country would be whittled away until the last bond was severed. The movement must be halted or at least retarded before it went any farther. Granted that America would one day become independent, there was no reason why that event should take place while the American population was little more than a quarter of Great Britain's.

As the English thought that they saw the Americans inching their way toward independence, the Americans thought that they saw a sinister party in England seeking by gradual degrees to enslave them. There had been rumors of a plan to reorganize the colonies ever since

29. See Alvord, *Mississippi Valley in British Politics*, ch. 2.

30. *London Chronicle*, February 11-13, 1766; cf. *ibid.*, March 22-25, 1766; *Parliamentary History*, XVI, 181-193; Thomas Penn to John Penn, January 11, 1766, Penn Correspondence, Historical Society of Pennsylvania; Thomas Martin to Daniel Rindge, December 24, 1765, Wentworth Papers, New Hampshire Historical Society.

the fall of Quebec, and Governor Bernard had intimated that the Stamp Act was a part of that plan. Even so reasonable a man as William Samuel Johnson thought that the ministry must have had a "formal design" constantly in view for several years. "Fortunately," he wrote in January, 1766, "they have of late precipitated their Measures and by that means opened our Eyes. Had they proceeded by slow and insensible degrees as they have been wont to do perhaps in a course of years they might have effected their baneful purpose. But by pressing it too much and making more haste than good speed they have defeated the whole design and given such an Alarm as will forever keep America upon her guard." [31]

With the repeal of the Stamp Act many Americans, misinterpreting the meaning of the Declaratory Act, believed that the plot had been foiled, and when Rockingham was replaced by Pitt, they rejoiced that their fastest friend was now in control. When the attempt to tax them was renewed under a ministry with Pitt at the head, they could see that the repeal was only a pause in the relentless advance of the plot to enslave them, and the vagueness of the Declaratory Act an effort to lull them into delusions of security, while stronger chains were fastened about them.

Thus while Rockingham had been able to hide from Parliament the full extent of the Americans' objection to its authority and from the Americans the full extent of Parliament's assertion of it, he had actually heightened the incompatibility of the two positions. When this incompatibility became evident, as it soon did, the happy misunderstanding he had fostered served only to exaggerate the difference. The English were encouraged to believe that the Americans were seeking independence in easy stages and the Americans to think that the English were trying to enslave them by slow and insensible degrees. The situation was not irretrievable, but to retrieve it would have required an understanding on each side of the exact limits of the other's claims. Such an understanding was rendered difficult at best by the illusions that now existed on both sides of the water as a result of the Stamp Act. But even if an understanding could have been achieved, reconciliation would have required also a willingness to compromise, for while neither side had such extravagant aims as the other supposed, there was nevertheless a genuine and irreconcilable conflict between Parliament's insistence on its authority to tax the colonies and the Americans' denial of that authority.

31. To Christopher Gadsden, January 10, 1766, William Samuel Johnson Papers, Connecticut Historical Society.

Unfortunately the Stamp Act period had not merely created illusions about the aims of both Englishmen and Americans but had also impaired the disposition to compromise in both countries and had in some cases discredited the men who would have been willing to do so. The circumstances that enabled Lord North to retain power from 1770 to 1782 were complex, but undoubtedly one reason was the conviction of most members of Parliament after 1768 that the repeal of the Stamp Act had been a mistake. Certainly this conviction was expressed again and again on the floor of the House of Commons, and the Whigs felt obliged to apologize for the measure which had staved off revolution in 1766.

In America too the Stamp Act had discredited moderates and enabled extremists to gain greater influence than they had ever enjoyed before. To be sure there must have been many Americans who would have taken the side of England if worst had come to worst in 1766, and some of these, not having been obliged to declare themselves, retained whatever influence in colonial politics they may have had before. In some cases a man's political career might even survive an open opposition to the riots of 1765. Joseph Galloway continued to sit in the Pennsylvania Assembly and to play an important part in public life in spite of the aid and comfort he had given to John Hughes. But there can be no doubt that the Stamp Act destroyed the popular prestige of many men who might have kept a restraining hand on their countrymen in the years that followed. In Rhode Island those who had sought a royal government were flushed into the open and disgraced. In Massachusetts Governor Bernard could no longer account himself a popular governor, and Thomas Hutchinson, though people might think that the resentment against him had gone too far, could never again claim the prestige which his long public career had formerly assured him. John Hughes was no longer a factor in Pennsylvania. Jared Ingersoll and Thomas Fitch were politically dead in Connecticut.

The withdrawal of these men from public life was accompanied by the rise of bolder and more aggressive politicians who had made their reputation in resistance to the Stamp Act. The part that a man had played in 1765 was not the criterion of his political success in every colony; and it would be wrong to suggest that the American Revolution was brought about entirely by the men who led the resistance to the Stamp Act. By 1776 some of the leaders of 1765 had died and some, William Samuel Johnson for example and Daniel Dulany, had gone over to the other side. Nevertheless, of the twenty-seven members of the Stamp Act Congress, only two, Johnson and

Ruggles, are known to have become loyalists in 1776,[32] and Ruggles had refused to approve the proceedings of the congress. On the other hand several of the members: Gadsden, Rutledge, Dickinson, Bryan, Rodney, R. R. Livingston, Eliphalet Dyer, and Otis took leading roles in the subsequent pre-revolutionary agitation. Others who took no part in the congress but led the resistance to the Stamp Act within their own colonies were likewise conspicuous in the revolutionary movement. It seems particularly significant that the parties which brought on the revolution in the two leading colonies, Massachusetts and Virginia, gained their ascendancy at the time of the Stamp Act.

In Virginia the Stamp Act provided the opportunity for Patrick Henry to break the monopoly which Speaker Robinson and his cronies had held in the House of Burgesses. Perhaps the most significant thing about the conflicting stories of Henry's speech for the Stamp Act Resolves is the fact that it was later remembered as more violent than it actually was. Henry had a long and fiery career in Virginia politics, and when men looked back upon it after it was over, they remembered the Stamp Act as the time when he had first assumed the leadership of the House of Burgesses. Speaker Robinson's death soon after and the revelations which it brought of embezzlement from the colony's treasury helped to prevent the elder statesmen of Virginia from regaining control, but it was the Stamp Act which first gave Henry the hold on the Burgesses by which he and his friends pushed Virginia along the path to revolution.

Richard Henry Lee, Henry's right-hand man in the revolutionary movement, likewise stepped into political prominence at the time of the Stamp Act. The Lees, though socially prominent, had previously been excluded from the coterie of Tidewater gentry who dominated Virginia politics, and the alliance between Lee and Henry was a natural one: the excluded aristocrat of the Tidewater and the rising would-be aristocrat from the Piedmont united against an aristocratic clique that was losing its grip. Lee, like Henry, saw the Stamp Act as a threat to the rights of Englishmen, and like Henry also, he saw it as an opportunity to break his way into a position of greater influence. When he first heard of it, he was so oblivious to the principle involved that he applied for the position of Stamp Distributor, but soon —within a few days, he claimed—recognized his mistake and withdrew the request. Instead he took upon himself the leadership of the Sons of Liberty in Virginia, and organized riots to force the resignation of Mercer and to punish a merchant who expressed a wish to clear ships

32. I am indebted to an unpublished study of the subsequent careers of the members by David S. Lovejoy, Marlboro College.

with stamped papers. In vain did the Mercers later reveal to the public that Lee had applied for the position of Distributor. In the course of the resistance he had demonstrated his opposition to the Act so consistently that he remained a popular hero and finally offered the resolution at Philadelphia with which American independence began.[33]

In Massachusetts the men who had followed Otis's fitful leadership in the Stamp Act crisis made unequivocal use of the episode to crush their opponents after repeal. On April 14 and May 5, 1766, they inserted in the *Boston Gazette* a warning to the freemen not to vote for anyone in the coming elections who was known to be a supporter of the Stamp Act, and lest there be any doubt as to whom they meant, they explained that a supporter of the Stamp Act was anyone who had opposed vigorous measures against it.

James Otis continued to be the leading spirit in the Massachusetts Assembly until he lost his sanity in 1769. Then his lieutenant, Sam Adams, took over. Otis's political career had begun before the Stamp Act, but it was the Stamp Act which had given him the greatest power and notoriety in spite of his occasional lapses into a legalistic and obscure sort of loyalism. Sam Adams, on the other hand, seems to have first come into view as a political leader at the time of the Stamp Act, with the drafting of the Massachusetts Resolves of October 25, 1765. Between them Otis and Adams called the tune for the Massachusetts Assembly from the time of the Stamp Act to the final dissolution of that body by General Gage. During this time they made life miserable for both Bernard and Hutchinson as well as for John Robinson, who came to Boston as Commissioner of the Customs in 1768. Probably no American did more than Sam Adams to bring on the revolutionary crisis.[34]

Besides disposing the colonies to accept radical leadership the Stamp Act period furnished those leaders with a method for bringing pressure to bear in England. Hitherto the colonies had never been able to unite for any purpose, not even for their own defense against the French and Indians. The Stamp Act, much to their own surprise, enabled them to act together. "The Ministry never Imagined we would or could so generally Unite in opposition to their measures," William Samuel Johnson wrote exultantly, "nor I confess till I saw the Experiment made did I. . . ."[35] The most spectacular achieve-

33. Ballagh, ed., *Letters of Richard Henry Lee*, I, 16; *Virginia Gazette* (Purdie and Dixon), October 3, 1766.

34. John C. Miller, *Sam Adams, Pioneer in Propaganda* (Boston, 1936), 48-81.

35. William Samuel Johnson to Christopher Gadsden, January 10, June 25, 1766, William Samuel Johnson Papers, Connecticut Historical Society.

ment in unity was of course the Stamp Act Congress, but the non-importation agreements adopted by the merchants of Boston, New York, and Philadelphia were equally surprising and more effective. If the merchants in any of these cities had chosen to continue importations, they would have profited heavily from the abstinence of the others. Their unanimity affected British exports sufficiently to give the British merchants an urgent reason to wish for repeal. Still further unity had been achieved among the Sons of Liberty in preventing the use of stamps in any colony from Maine to Georgia and in beginning the intercolonial union which was projected at New London on December 25 and which was making rapid progress when the Act was repealed. Observing all these signs of the united strength of the colonies, Joseph Warren in March of 1766 wrote to his friend Edmund Dana that Grenville's measures had brought about "what the most zealous Colonist never could have expected! The Colonies until now were ever at variance and foolishly jealous of each other, they are now . . . united . . . nor will they soon forget the weight which this close union gives them." [36]

The colonies remembered the strength of union well enough, as they demonstrated later in their non-importation agreements against the Townshend Duties, in their continental congresses, and finally in their formation of a continental army. Yet in the last analysis the significance of the Stamp Act crisis lies in the emergence, not of leaders and methods and organizations, but of well-defined constitutional principles. The resolutions of the colonial and intercolonial assemblies in 1765 laid down the line on which Americans stood until they cut their connections with England. Consistently from 1765 to 1776 they denied the authority of Parliament to tax them externally or internally; consistently they affirmed their willingness to submit to whatever legislation Parliament should enact for the supervision of the empire as a whole. To be sure, by the time when the First Continental Congress was called in 1774 they had become convinced that Parliament had no more authority to legislate for them than to tax them (this had been the position of the most radical Americans in 1765). But even while thus extending their objections to Parliamentary authority, they agreed to waive their rights in this respect and submit to Parliament's supervisory legislation as they had before.[37] In spite of the radical temper of the colonial leaders the position taken in 1765 would have served as a basis for reconciliation at

36. Miscellaneous Manuscripts, 1765-1767, Massachusetts Historical Society.
37. W. C. Ford and Gaillard Hunt, eds., *Journals of the Continental Congress* (Washington, 1904-1937), I, 68-69.

any time until the Declaration of Independence. There was, how-ever, no middle ground, no intermediate line to which the colonists were willing to retreat in the face of British efforts to tax them. They "stood bluff" in 1776 on the line they had drawn in 1765, and when the Ministry this time refused to recede from its demands, they fought.

» SEVENTEEN «

EPILOGUE

WHAT, then, of the men who had urged submission and faith in the ultimate justice and wisdom of the mother country? These were the loyalists of '65 and this study would not be complete without a final reckoning of the price of their loyalty. England did what she could for them as she later did for the loyalists of '76. Parliament first recommended that the various assemblies reimburse anyone who had lost property in the riots. When it became apparent that the colonial governments would not comply, George Grenville was able to shame his fellow members into a resolution that the King should "bestow some mark of his favor upon those Governors and Officers in America who had suffered by their Loyalty." [1]

In accordance with this resolution, England conferred honors and offices upon the men who had tried to uphold her authority during the time of the Stamp Act. What England could do for them was a poor enough compensation for what they had lost. For nearly a lifetime they had dreamt their different dreams of power, prestige, and success and had suddenly found not only their dreams but their whole world gone up in the smoke of their burning effigies. England could not restore their dreams nor, try as she might, their world. But England could at least enable them to stay alive and wherever feasible help them to a new start in a different place.

Of those who appear in this book old John Hughes probably fared the best. After the riots and the threats had ceased, he retired to his

1. William Samuel Johnson to Samuel Johnson, May 18, 1767, Bancroft transcripts, New York Public Library; to Jared Ingersoll, May 16, 1767, New Haven Colony Historical Society, *Papers*, 9 (1918), 405-408.

country home, Walnut Grove, where he could be seen playing the farmer, an old man with a hoe hacking away at the weeds in his fields. Bewildered but unbowed, he would occasionally visit his Quaker neighbors, who still knew him for a friend if not a Friend, and enjoy the kind of bantering conversation in which he excelled. His reward came in 1769 when he was made Collector of Customs at Portsmouth, New Hampshire. He sold his house (where later the British troops would enjoy their last entertainment from the local loyalists before evacuating Philadelphia), and rode by coach to Portsmouth, enjoying as he passed the salutations of the gentry. "In going this long Journey," he wrote back to one of his old neighbors, "I often thought of ovids Metamorphosese and could hardly forbear Laughing when I recollected the old Gray headed fellow that used to be troting up and Down a meadow at Walnut Grove with the Resemblance of a Grubing hoe on his shoulder and his feet wet and Dirty and often times his Legs also but now Riding in Great State in a Coach and four pinked off like a Beau—and treated as a person of Consequence—with your most Humble Servant Mr Collector—you are heartily wilcome to our Town &c &c—then comes a Card—with the Compliments to the Collector &c &c to Request the favour of his Dining or supping with him as the time admitted—and as to see the old fellow sent to his lodgings in a chariot with a postilion behind and sometimes a Servant into the bargain—I say, when I considered these things Seriously I could not help Reflecting upon the folly and vanity of those persons who upon such a change (which is but Temporary) forget not only their former Acquaintance but themselves also and thereby Render themselves Ridiculous and Contemptible." [2]

John Hughes was not the man to forget his friends, and he had been more than a little hurt by the way in which his political party in Pennsylvania dropped him after the Stamp Act troubles, when they discovered that he was a liability. However, his engaging personality made him new friends quickly. In Portsmouth he was soon on the best of terms with Governor Wentworth, and when he left early in 1771 to become Collector at Charleston, South Carolina, he carried Wentworth's introduction to the best families there. Though he wrote to his old neighbors in Pennsylvania that South Carolina in the winter was certainly the worst place in the world "for it Rains almost without Intermission, and there is a kind of raw Moist Cold in the air," he was nevertheless very happy there. So at least he persuaded himself. There was just a touch of homesickness in one of his

2. To Jonathan Roberts, September 7, 1769, Hughes Papers, Historical Society of Pennsylvania.

last letters to his son, saying "Whatever may be the Sentiments of Pensilvanians Relative to me, I have now the pleasure to say, that in the greatest of my popular Credit in that province, I was not by any Means as happy as I am now, it is true whilst I sacrificed my time and consequently my fortune to support a party I was a clever fellow, But when it became me to Discharge my Duty to my Sovereign, I was then with both parties a very bad man, here I have the pleasure to know, that from the Governor to the Meanest Merchant I am highly esteemed, nor is there a single man in the province but heartily wish me to Remain Amongst them." Hughes remained amongst them for more than a year, nursing his pride and indulging his love for conversation, but by the spring of 1772 he had died, hoping to gain "an acquaintance with, Innumerable other beings, of much superior knowledge, abilities and Sincerity," superior certainly to the men who had persecuted him for doing his duty to his sovereign.[3]

Jared Ingersoll received a commission in 1769 as Judge of the Vice Admiralty Court at Philadelphia, but did not go there till 1771. When he did, the newspapers in Connecticut accused him of giving assistance to the enemies of the Susquehannah Company. The Philadelphians in turn could develop no great love for the Judge of an Admiralty Court. When the fighting began he hardly knew which way to turn. "I am Conscious," he wrote to his nephew in New Haven, "of having done no wrong to my Country and so I am inclined to fear none from it, . . . at the same time I consider myself like a Saint of old, as a Pilgrim and Stranger in the Earth having no Abiding City." In the end he sent his family back to New Haven but remained in Philadelphia himself, until Pennsylvania decided that she did not want him and shipped him off to Connecticut. He died there in 1781, having preserved, as his epitaph said, "a graceful and majestic Dignity," but still a man without a country.[4]

Governor Bernard stayed on in Massachusetts until 1770 trying to recover his lost popularity and succeeding only in sinking it further. James Otis and his crowd seized every opportunity to magnify the hatred against him. When Richard Jackson wrote that Bernard had helped materially in securing the repeal of the Stamp Act, the *Boston Gazette* sneered its disbelief,[5] and Otis maintained in public that he could name the very room in Bernard's house where the Stamp Act

---

3. John Hughes to Jonathan Roberts, February 1, April 13, September 25, 1771; to Isaac Hughes, July 25, 1771, Hughes Papers. Cf. *Pa. Mag. of Hist.*, 61 (1937), 468.

4. Gipson, *Jared Ingersoll*, 294-295, 323-326. New Haven Colony Historical Society, *Papers*, 9 (1918), 418, 456, 472.

5. *Boston Gazette*, April 28, May 5, 19, 1766.

had been drafted.[6] The Assembly sent letters to England asking for his recall, and when he finally departed, the people of Boston demonstrated their joy by a celebration which he could watch from the harbor.[7] Bernard was rewarded for his pains by a knighthood, a satisfactory compensation perhaps for the chorus of hatred he had endured in Boston, but scarcely the fulfillment of his dream of serving as the architect for a new empire. The final blow to this vision came when Parliament adopted one of his recommendations as a means of punishing Massachusetts for the Boston Tea Party. The Massachusetts Government Act, by giving to the King the authority to appoint the Governor's Council, put the Council at last out of the power of the House of Representatives. It was a measure which Bernard had urged for years, but coming when it did, as a punishment instead of a reform, it helped to bring on the revolution it was designed to prevent.

When Bernard left Boston, Thomas Hutchinson stepped into his place, first as acting governor, finally as governor. He had coveted the place since 1766, when his son, seeking compensation for his losses in England, had first received hints that the governorship might be his reward.[8] Hutchinson felt that his own understanding of the people of Massachusetts and the accumulated prestige of his long career might enable him to succeed where Bernard had failed. But he was indulging in wishful thinking. Otis had not been satisfied with Hutchinson's losses in the riots and fought him as consistently as he fought Bernard, blocking him from a seat in the Council, and blaming him, along with Bernard, for everything unpleasant that happened in Massachusetts. Hutchinson's career as governor was as unhappy as Sam Adams, who took up where Otis left off, could make it. When he finally had to go to England to defend himself against the charges which his enemies kept bringing against him, he found himself trapped there by the Revolution, obliged to sit helplessly in London, as news poured in of the unhappy events in America. He might console himself with finishing the History of Massachusetts, writing a volume to cover the years which he could remember too well, but he had to do without the letterbooks which might have assisted him in setting details straight. These were back in Massachusetts in the hands of his enemies, and would be used by another historian, of inferior talent, to help in writing the first history of the

6. Bernard to Shelburne, December 22, 1766, Chalmers Papers, II, Harvard College Library.

7. *Boston Gazette*, August 7, 1769; Thomas Young to John Wilkes, August 3, 1769, Massachusetts Historical Society, *Proceedings*, 47 (1914), 207.

8. Thomas Hutchinson, Jr., to Thomas Hutchinson, July, 1766, Massachusetts Archives, XXV, 86.

Revolution. Hutchinson was at least fortunate enough to die before it appeared.[9]

The victims of the Newport mob all received appropriate rewards: Thomas Moffat returned from London in 1766 to become Collector of Customs at New London;[10] Martin Howard, Jr., became Chief Justice of North Carolina, where he later handed out severe sentences to the rebels who fought at Alamance in 1771;[11] Augustus Johnston received a commission as Judge of the Admiralty Court in 1767 at Charleston; [12] and John Robinson was named to the newly formed American Board of Commissioners of the Customs, which sat in Boston and supervised the collection of His Majesty's revenue in the whole of North America.[13] It was John Robinson who settled in blood a debt which was owed not merely to himself but to his friends in Rhode Island and to Bernard and Hutchinson as well. When Robinson came to Boston, James Otis added his name to his blacklist and filled the newspapers with insulting accusations against the customs commissioners in general and against Robinson in particular. Robinson bore the attacks for a time; he found a few congenial men of his own sentiments in Boston, men who knew what loyalty to Great Britain meant. He even found a wife in the daughter of one of them. But in the face of Otis's vile attacks, he scarcely lived a happy or peaceful life. He finally took to going about armed and made no secret of his intentions to give Otis what he deserved when the occasion offered.

On the night of September fifth in the year 1769, Robinson and a number of other gentlemen were sitting in the British Coffee House, enjoying the fare and the conversation, when in walked Otis. As he saw the man, Robinson must have thought not only of his own recent experiences, but also of what had happened to his old friends in Newport. It was Otis's epithets that the mob had attached to the effigies of Dr. Moffat and Martin Howard; it was Otis's pamphlets which had excited the rage against them. Robinson marched up to the man and seized him by the nose. In the scuffle that followed the lights went out, but it was not too dark for Robinson to give his enemy a crushing blow on the head. Though Otis later sued him, the damage which

9. William Gordon, a Boston clergyman sympathetic to the Revolution, had access to Hutchinson's seized letters in writing his *History of the Rise, Progress, and Establishment of the Independence of the United States of America* (London, 1788). See Vol. I.

10. Frances M. Caulkins, *History of New London, Connecticut* (New London, 1852), 478; *Gentleman's Magazine*, 57 (1787), 277; Diary of Thomas Moffat, Library of Congress.

11. *Colonial Records of North Carolina*, VII, 427-428; VIII, 642-643.

12. New Haven Colony Historical Society, *Papers*, 9·(1918), 423, 432.

13. William Tudor, *The Life of James Otis* (Boston, 1823), 362-366; John Robinson to Joseph Harrison, October 5, 1769, Chalmers Papers, III, 38, Harvard College Library.

Robinson had done could no more be compensated than the damage which his victim had done to Moffat, and Howard, and Hutchinson, and Bernard, and indirectly to every loyalist in America. Otis recovered physically, but Robinson's blow had destroyed his mind, and he would never again serve as the leader of Boston's violent men. It was a piece of poetic justice, a token revenge in behalf of those who had in their own way "stood bluff," though not on their constitutional rights. Having completed his part, John Robinson sailed for England with his bride and drifted out of the stream of history.

INDEX

DATE DUE

OCT 11 1967		
OCT 25 1967		
NOV 27 1967		
NOV - 9 1969		
DEC 2 1969		
NOV 19 1973		
NOV 20 1974		
FEB 20 1975		
NOV 20-1975		
OC 17 '86		
GAYLORD		PRINTED IN U.S.A.

THE POWER

OF

STRATEGY

INNOVATION

A New Way of Linking Creativity and
Strategic Planning to Discover Great
Business Opportunities

Robert E. Johnston, Jr.
J. Douglas Bate

AMACOM
American Management Association
New York • Atlanta • Brussels • Chicago • Mexico City • San Francisco
Shanghai • Tokyo • Toronto • Washington, D.C.

Special discounts on bulk quantities of AMACOM books are available to corporations, professional associations, and other organizations. For details, contact Special Sales Department, AMACOM, a division of American Management Association, 1601 Broadway, New York, NY 10019.
Tel.: 212-903-8316. Fax: 212-903-8083.
Web site: www.amacombooks.org

This publication is designed to provide accurate and authoritative information in regard to the subject matter covered. It is sold with the understanding that the publisher is not engaged in rendering legal, accounting, or other professional service. If legal advice or other expert assistance is required, the services of a competent professional person should be sought.

Library of Congress Cataloging-in-Publication Data

Johnston, Robert E.
The power of strategy innovation : a new way of linking creativity and strategic planning to discover great business opportunities/ Robert E. Johnston, Jr., J. Douglas Bate.
    p.   cm.
Includes bibliographical references and index.
ISBN 0-8144-0768-4
1. Strategic planning.   I. Bate, J. Douglas.   II. Title.

HD30.28.J657   2003
658.4'012—dc21

2003004618

Printing number

10   9   8   7   6   5   4   3   2   1

Dedicated to:

Danielle, Rob, and Em:

Your energy, humor, and love inspire me.
—Bob

Bradley and Jeffrey:

You can accomplish anything you commit to doing.
—Doug

CONTENTS

ACKNOWLEDGMENTS

This book is possible only because of the contribution of numerous participants in strategy innovation initiatives across many different industries and dozens of companies reaching back to 1983. However, we wish to acknowledge here the special contribution and support of a few individuals who have helped us bring it to fruition.

We decided early on that the story was best told by some of the many pioneers who have championed strategy innovation on behalf of their companies. Individuals who contributed generously in terms of personal time and support include Bob Galvin, Motorola; Bill Coyne and Ron Baukol, 3M; Dieter Kurz and Marc Vogel, Carl Zeiss; Craig Wynett, P&G; Bob LaPerle, Eastman Kodak; Bruce Carbonari, Fortune Brands Home and Hardware; Maureen Wenmouth and Tim O' Brien, Moen; Dan Buchner, Design Continuum; Ken Cox, NASA; Gary Kaiser, Eli Lilly; Ray Siuta, Hewlett-Packard; Terry Tallis, Essential Possibilities, and Dana Seccombe, both formerly with Hewlett-Packard; and Garrett Bouton, Barclays Global Investors.

Although this book will highlight the stories of dozens of companies, we would like to express a special thanks to two companies: Moen and McNeil Consumer and Specialty Pharmaceuticals. At Moen, CEO Dick Posey, the executive staff, and the Periscope II team have been extremely supportive of our efforts. At McNeil, we would like to express our appreciation to CEO Bill McComb; Bob Carpenter, vice president of marketing; Amy Weiseman, manager of innovation and new product processes; and the entire Edison team for their commitment to the exploration of a role for strategy innovation in their company.

We were warned that writing a book is one of life's challenges that will test our character, fortitude, and sense of humor. Thanks to the wisdom and disciplined freedom afforded us by AMACOM's editorial director, Adrienne Hickey, the orchestration of associate editor Mike Sivilli, and the experienced professionalism of Niels Buessem, we found the process to be both enjoyable and fulfilling.

Published authors who provided seasoned support and encouragement include Chris Zook, Bain & Company; Sidney Parnes, Creative Education Foundation; Teresa Amabile, Harvard Business School; Stan Gryskiewicz, Center for Creative Leadership; Jonathan Low, Cap Gemini Ernst & Young; T. George Harris, University of California, San Diego; Lynne Lesvesque, Harvard Business School; and Brian Mattimore, consultant.

While the coauthors have collaborated for over fifteen years, anyone who worked a day with IdeaScope Associates has made a contribution to this emerging field of strategy innovation. Former colleagues who have provided us with special support include Chris Von Pichl, Meg Dunn, Maxine Teller, Amy Weiseman, and Harvey Ehrlich. A special thanks to Stephen Cornell, who was an early conceptual catalyst in the mountains west of Banff and provided important polish later on.

Individuals not already mentioned who provided us with valuable feedback for ways to strengthen our strategy innovation story include Peter Carey, Worth and Louise Loomis, Dorie Shallcross, Ted Colson, Jeneanne Rae, K.T. Conner, Burt Woolf, Will Clarkson, David Arnold, Bella English, Maura Grogan-Cornell, and Melinda Merino. A special thanks also to Paul Wentzell and Terry Tallis, who provided us with timely graphics support.

Additionally, we would like to express our deep gratitude to Chris von Pichl, Peter Carey, Deborah Frieze, Bruce Landay, and Bruce Crocker for their helpful counsel in advancing the mission and impact of The Visterra Group.

Finally, our wives, Ty Johnston and Anne Bate, carried the special burden of living with first-time authors, and we are genuinely grateful for their perseverance and care.

INTRODUCTION

We want you to use this book. Nothing would please us more than knowing that leading-edge companies around the world are developing their own Discovery processes for the pursuit of strategy innovation.

Strategy innovation is not a fad. It is not the latest management-program-of-the-month. It is a process of exploring your emerging future, understanding the changing needs of your customers, and using the insights gained in those explorations to identify new business opportunities for your company. That's it. Whereas many management programs help you shrink your costs to grow your bottom line, strategy innovation is aimed at growing your top line. New business opportunities help drive new company strategies, which drive future growth.

So, why aren't more companies doing strategy innovation? Because they don't have an internal structure or process to do it. Who in your company is responsible for the future? Who is feeding your strategic planning process with ideas that stretch your current strategy and get you into new markets? How are you going about identifying your next new business platform, the basis of your future growth and success?

What we describe in this book is a phase-by-phase approach to the process of strategy innovation, not step-by-step. We provide the blueprint and encourage you to customize it for the specific needs of your company and your industry. This blueprint has been evolving for more than a decade, based on our experiences in a wide range of companies and industries. We will share with you some of the stories that helped to create this process of strategy innovation. It is a process that works.

Creating a cross-functional process for strategy innovation in a corporate setting is not as simple as it sounds. This is especially true when the process ventures outside the current corporate strategy or business model. Escaping your "corporate gravity" and then avoiding your "corporate immune system" are two threats to the establishment of this process. We will point them out and help you address them.

We will also share what we have learned about selecting and preparing a "reconnaissance" team for this process. The alignment with senior management on which strategic frontier to explore is a critical consideration that will be explained in detail. We will show you where value-based insights can be found on your strategic frontier—with customers, with the emerging future, and with new business models. Taking the insights and turning them into new business opportunities is a crucial step, as is the creation of a strategic road map for the future. All of these elements form the basis of the five phases of the Discovery Process.

Through this book and the work of our consulting firm, The Visterra Group, we hope to advance the awareness and use of strategy innovation in corporations around the world. Whether you are a multimega global corporation or a cheese shop in Zurich, you can use this strategy innovation process to chart a future path of growth for your business. The fact that you are reading this book says that this is of interest to you. We hope to hear from you at www.the visterragroup.com

The Organization of This Book

Section One (Chapters 1 through 4) of this book outlines what strategy innovation is, what it is not, and how we propose that you integrate it to your organization. This section will be particularly important reading for senior management of a company or division.

Section Two provides specific guidance for implementing a strategy innovation initiative, which we call the Discovery Process. We begin in Chapter 5 with a real example of how the Discovery Process worked in a real company. Chapters 6 through 10 then provide details for the implementation of the five phases of the Discovery Process—Staging, Aligning, Exploring, Creating, and Mapping. Stories and examples are woven throughout these chapters to add a practical touch to the frameworks presented. Understand, however, that these stories focus primarily on the *process* of previous initiatives, as we consider the content generated in them to be proprietary information.

Section Three offers more in-depth discussion of the Discovery Process and strategy innovation in a corporate setting. In Chapter 11, we answer questions and share some additional insights related to the Discovery Process. Chapter 12 outlines the key considerations in formalizing a strategy innovation process in a company, moving the Discovery Process from an ad hoc initiative to an ongoing strategy innovation system. Finally, in the Epilogue, we challenge senior management in corporations everywhere as we share some of our thoughts about the future of strategy innovation.

Scattered throughout this book are boxes titled "Process Tip." They represent what we consider to be critical elements in the implementation of the Discovery Process. They come from more than a decade of experiences in the trenches and are things we would emphasize if we were talking to you. We put them in boxes so you wouldn't miss them.

If you are curious about the history of strategy innovation in corporations and its roots in the early work done in creativity and brainstorming, we encourage you to read the remainder of this introduction. It will provide a good context for understanding the evolution of innovation as it makes its way to the corporate boardroom.

The Migration of Creativity to Strategy in Corporations: Evolution to Revolution and Beyond

Many writers, researchers, innovators and strategists have recognized the value of an organization reaching beyond predictable, incremental growth to achieve greater profit in innovative ways. Gary Hamel, C.K. Prahalad, Constantinos Markides, Jim Collins, and Clayton Christensen all champion strategy innovation as a vehicle for creating "new value" and spawning new wealth. And, while most cite or imply the importance of a creative process in breaking the bonds of incrementalism, none prescribe an explicit process to do the job. As Hamel succinctly states, "No one seems to know much about how to create strategy."[1] To date, serendipity appears to be the secret solution to strategy innovation. In this sense, the relationship between strategy and creativity in the business literature is still somewhat remote. Few strategists have yet discovered or shared the decades of research in creativity and innovation that can be harvested for the purposes of creating new value and new profitability in their businesses.

Applying Imagination as a Skill

An emphasis on creativity first entered the corporate world in the 1940s and 1950s. The groundbreaking work on the creative process by Alex Osborn, cofounder of the advertising agency BBD&O, led to his fathering the process known as "brainstorming." His work also led to one of the first creativity guidebooks, the classic *Applied Imagination*.[2] While achieving legendary success with his creativity techniques in the advertising world, Osborn and his colleague, Sidney Parnes, recognized that every human being has the potential to be creative, if given the opportunity and the right environment. Their work was supported by the research efforts of J.P. Guilford, Paul Torrance, Don MacKinnon, Calvin Taylor, and others, which clearly proved that creativity is a developable skill inherent in everyone, not just a genius elite.

Parnes's research demonstrated, among other things, that creativity is a skill that can be strengthened with coaching and practice. Routinely, students in his courses were able to increase their idea-generating capacities by 100 percent or more. Of particular importance, Osborn and Parnes proved the value of a mental model for creativity, where "divergent thinking" is used to expand one's options, and "convergent thinking" enables the focus on a preferred, innovative choice. One believer, Robert Galvin, retired CEO and chairman of Motorola, used his imagination and inspired others to grow Motorola one-thousand-fold during his three decades of leadership. Galvin sagely observed, "Some think of this work of engaging the imagination to be the work of genius. Osborn demonstrated how it could be developed as a vocational skill." If creativity is a skill that can be developed, it becomes a tool that corporations can use for purposes of innovation.

Applying Imagination to Inventing

In the late 1950s, George Prince and William Gordon had the task of delivering proprietary new inventions to the clients of Arthur D. Little, Inc., in Cambridge, Massachusetts. As part of the R&D–focused Invention Design Group, they had the task of focusing on solving client problems in innovative, often patentable, ways. During many years of successful new product innovation, Prince and Gordon analyzed their process to determine the most effective thinking strategies for invention.

This research led to their founding in the 1960s of a new company they called Synectics, Inc. Synectics used the power of metaphor and analogy to spark creative thinking, leading to the identification of new products. They gave creativity a process that could be applied in corporations for the purpose of innovative inventions. In a span of a few decades, creativity had gone from an esoteric skill in an ad agency to the basis of a corporate process for generating innovative product ideas. Creativity was making progress but was still under the radar for most corporate managers.

Applying Imagination to Management . . .

In the 1960s Edward DeBono, a British neurologist, introduced the world to the concept of "lateral thinking," a fresh way to think about creativity. DeBono observed that in attempting to solve problems, most people think "vertically," in a straight line, probing deeper and deeper until the solution eventually presents itself. In problems involving a creative response, however, he noted that the solution is typically *not* at the end of a linear thought process, digging the same hole deeper and deeper. Instead, it involves "lateral thinking," digging a new hole somewhere else. Shifting the framework of the process often results in new and creative solutions.[3]

In thinking about thinking, DeBono believes that, between vertical and lateral approaches to creative thinking, lateral thinking is the more difficult to master but the more rewarding for innovation. DeBono has spent decades teaching corporate executives around the world the importance of "serious creativity" for inspiring innovative opportunities. During that time, the creativity message gained credibility with corporate managers as a tool for innovation.

In 1970, the Center for Creative Leadership in Greensboro, North Carolina, was founded to teach courses for individuals and teams to hone their creative talents. Stan Gryskiewicz—founding member, senior fellow, and vice president—organized and still leads a group called the Association for Managers of Innovation, which provides a forum for showcasing and networking of innovation practices across corporations. Corporate managers were beginning to recognize the potential for creativity in their organizations.

Applying Imagination to Strategy

According to Henry Mintzberg, former president of the Strategic Management Society, strategic planning is an oxymoron.[4] In most organizations it tends to neither provide a sufficient range of strategic options to consider nor present an engaging road map of a compelling future. This is not surprising since most strategic planning processes are numbers-oriented, lacking a creativity component. As a result, strategic planning in most companies is a process that merely extends the previous strategy into the future. Even when senior executives invite "out of the box" thinking, most managers do not know how to go about exploring beyond the existing strategic framework.

We had the opportunity, as a founding principal and associate at

IdeaScope, Inc., to work with senior executives of companies to discover and develop many new strategic opportunities. Initially, much of our work was product-centric. After working with many Fortune 100 companies on the creation of new product concepts, we had the privilege of assisting Procter & Gamble in the late 1980s with the development of an internal process called Concept Lab, for new product development across their many divisions.

Since we were known as leaders of a proven creative process in our product concept work, soon executives with *strategic* challenges began enlisting our services to provide the missing creativity ingredient from their analysis-based strategic planning approaches. Applying creativity to corporate strategy is more challenging than the identification of new products, and yet some of the process is similar. Through dozens of strategy innovation initiatives, we experimented with a variety of different processes and carefully analyzed the results. Then, following our departures from IdeaScope, we spent nearly two years researching and developing a new framework for strategy innovation—which represents a significant advance in the process. What you will see in this book is the result of more than a decade of work—a proven method for creating strategy innovation in corporations.

Early Pioneers of Applying Imagination to Strategy

From the mid-1980s on, companies like Eli Lilly, Procter & Gamble, 3M, Moen, BMW, Eastman Kodak, Hewlett-Packard, Fidelity Investments, General Mills, Dow Chemical, Motorola, Carl Zeiss, and Schott Glas have recognized the importance of infusing creativity into their development of new strategic opportunities. In a few of these companies, the quest for new strategic growth was vision-driven. Others were motivated by ambitious goals that extended beyond the reach of current capabilities. Still others were motivated by a severe competitive threat, which created an appetite for strategy innovation where none had existed before.

In every case, the organization was challenged by its situation to stretch beyond its self-limiting boundaries of how it viewed itself and the world. A shift to a new organizational self-image, a new industry perspective, or a new worldview was needed. The organization would then have to align on that new perspective, so it had to be a result of a credible, quality process.

Eli Lilly: An Early Strategy Innovator

In the mid-1980s, Eli Lilly and Company, a large and respected pharmaceutical manufacturer, speculated there could be a dramatic shift in drug discovery and development within infectious disease, home of its largest revenue stream. Most of Lilly's product portfolio for infectious disease was targeted to bacterial disease. Senior management wanted to explore the emerging trends in infectious diseases to determine if more attractive opportunities might exist in developing new products targeting viral and/or fungal diseases.

We were retained to act as "process architects" and "discovery guides" for the Infectious Disease Task Force, a half-dozen cross-functional teams assembled to create and develop new strategic options for Lilly in infectious disease. After much research of the available literature and the hosting of several panels of industry experts (called thought leader panels) sharing their views of the emerging future, the Lilly teams gained a new understanding of the opportunities for the future of pharmaceuticals. From this foresight, these scientists used creative techniques to generate a list of hundreds of new strategic options for Lilly, which they then refined to a few for presentation to management.

The advisory groups and senior management, up to and including the chairman of the board, committed to the new strategic opportunities developed by the teams. The organization was restructured around these new strategic options in infectious diseases, helping Lilly to remain a prominent player in that marketplace, as well as to anticipate and participate in the newly emerging field of biotechnology.

Impressed with the process of applying creative tools to strategy development, Eli Lilly later replicated the same strategy innovation process for both their cardiovascular business and for Elanco, their agricultural products business. Creativity had successfully entered the corporate boardroom.

Applying Imagination to the Economy

In his recent book, *The Rise of the Creative Class*, Richard Florida takes the importance of creativity and imagination to a new level, beyond that of corporate strategies to entire industries and our world economy. He writes:

> Many say we now live in an "information" economy or a "knowledge" economy. But what's more fundamentally true is that we now have an economy powered by human creativity. Creativity—"the ability to create meaningful new forms," as Webster's dictionary puts it—is now the decisive source of competitive advantage. In virtually every industry, from automobiles to fashion, food products and information technology itself, the winners in the long run are those who can create and keep creating.[5]

Creativity from the Mailroom to the Boardroom

Through this book we hope to extend this fifty-year migration of creativity in corporations. What started as a recognized, teachable skill in an advertising agency grew to become a tool for invention, and then a process for innovation throughout the company. This book will open the door for creativity in the boardroom, successfully marrying the processes of innovation and corporate strategic planning.

Although strategy and creativity may be strange bedfellows, the time is right for bringing them together in the corporate boardroom. It is not a matter of replacing your analytical, numbers-based strategic planning process with a less predictable, sometimes-serendipitous creative approach to strategy. The strategy innovation process outlined in this book will show how the two disciplines can be merged, with strategy innovation feeding the strategic planning process. The corporate need for innovation will demand this marriage, from a courtship that began long ago.

Endnotes

1. Gary Hamel, "Strategy Innovation and the Quest for Value," *Sloan Management Review*, Winter 1998.
2. Alex F. Osborn, *Applied Imagination*, 3rd edition (New York: Scribners, 1963).
3. Edward DeBono, *Lateral Thinking for Management* (New York: AMACOM, 1972).
4. Henry Mintzberg, *The Rise and Fall of Strategic Planning* (New York: The Free Press, 1994).
5. Richard Florida, *The Rise of the Creative Class* (New York: Basic Books, 2002).

PART ONE

THE WHAT AND WHY OF STRATEGY INNOVATION

CHAPTER 1

STRATEGY MEETS INNOVATION

> If an organization is to meet the challenges of a changing world, it must be prepared to change everything about itself except its basic beliefs. The only sacred cow in an organization should be the basic philosophy of doing business.
>
> —*THOMAS J. WATSON*

No corporate strategy lasts forever. Companies that get all the components of their business models working together can often drive their success for many years. But at some point, they start to run out of gas. Many companies are shocked to hear the financial engine sputter, having never paid much attention to their fuel gauge. Others have an eye on the gauge but don't have a clue where the next service station is located, so they coast along, hoping to get lucky.

Then there are companies that have scouted out the road ahead and know their refueling options. With their eyes watching the road, the map, and the fuel gauge, they fill up the tank before it gets too low. Even older models, with the proper tune-up and constant refueling, can remain cruising at the speed limit for decades.

Your company needs strategy innovation initiatives to understand the road ahead and know your options for keeping the product tank full and the financial engine running smoothly.

What is strategy innovation?

Strategy innovation is shifting a corporation's business strategy in order to create new value for both the customer and the corporation.

In a dynamic marketplace, every business runs the risk that its current business model will become obsolete. As long as there is customer value to be delivered, there will be companies interested in delivering it. New companies will create innovative, more efficient business models in order to compete in profitable industries. Consider the case of Wal-Mart. Starting as a discount retailer to the underserved population of rural areas, it needed to develop a new, more efficient retailing business model in order to survive in that segment of the retailing market. Using sophisticated technology and a streamlined distribution system, Sam Walton created a new business strategy in the retail industry that created value for both his rural customers and for his company. The superiority of their innovative business model ultimately led to Wal-Mart's domination of that entire industry. The strongest survive.

In other dynamic industries of the twenty-first century, new technologies, new materials, and new distribution channels are continually changing the competitive landscape. Companies such as Nokia, Charles Schwab, and IBM recognized the potential of these changes, altered their business strategies, and have been able to take advantage of the emerging growth opportunities in wireless communications, financial services, and computer services. Companies such as K-Mart, USAirways, and Digital Equipment Corporation either did not see the trends in their industries or refused to alter their business strategies in times of change, and they have suffered the consequences. As Jack Welch, the highly successful former CEO of General Electric, once said about companies in dynamic markets, "When the rate of change outside exceeds the rate of change inside, the end is in sight."[1]

A Fight to the Photo-Finish

An example of the importance of strategy innovation in dynamic markets can be found in the photography industry. Back in the

1980s, Kodak and Polaroid were two prominent, global players in that industry. Kodak dominated the silver halide, 35-mm market while Polaroid, protected by its patents, owned the instant photography segment. At about that time, a new, disruptive technology was just beginning to emerge via the computer revolution, one that would threaten to make both conventional film processing technologies obsolete—digital imaging.

Kodak took the initiative in the late 1980s to understand the potential implications of this new technology. In two, large-scale strategy innovation initiatives, cross-functional teams of Kodak managers used panels of experts in this new technology to explore the emergence of digital photography and identify the potential new business opportunities of the future marketplace. From this work, Kodak understood the ramifications of digital photography on the industry and made important changes in their corporate strategy. R&D spending was immediately shifted from a focus on new silver halide projects to an interim, "hybrid" strategy, balancing the needs of the still-strong silver halide business with the growing potential of digital photography.

In the decade that followed, Kodak became a force in the world of digital photography, including the development of Picture CDs, Picture Maker kiosks, the purchase of their Japanese partner Chinon to manufacture digital cameras, the purchase of online photofinisher Ofoto, and a joint venture with America Online called You've Got Pictures. As this book is being written, Kodak is transitioning with the market to digital photography, rather than being left in its wake. It shifted its business strategy to create new value for both Kodak and its customers.

Polaroid, on the other hand, ignored the early signs of digital photography and decided to stick with and protect their existing corporate strategy in instant photography. They did not understand how to create value in this emerging marketplace, preferring to compete using their old strategy, crafted in a very different era. On October 12, 2001, Polaroid filed for bankruptcy protection.

Companies that are attuned to the changes taking place in the market and see them as potential business opportunities are practicing strategy innovation. Companies that are eager to create new value for customers are practicing strategy innovation. Companies that are willing to redefine themselves and how they operate in order to pursue new, more vibrant growth initiatives are practicing strategy innovation.

Strategy Innovation Goes Beyond Product Innovation

It is interesting to note how many companies in recent years have adopted "innovation" as a core value or as part of their mission statements. If we as a society have moved from the Information Age to the Knowledge Age, then this relatively new emphasis on innovation is quite logical. When information is ubiquitous and is no longer a source of competitive advantage, it is the innovative use of that information (via knowledge) that differentiates people, companies, and nations. Innovation may become the basis of all competition in the future. Innovation is the new competitive arena where present-day gladiators, equipped with similar information and access to similar resources, try to outsmart one another to victory.

As we work with and read about corporations today, we see the focus of innovation being placed primarily on the *products* that they are creating. Go to a company's Web site. If they talk about innovation or have an Office of Innovation, it is frequently related to the work done in their Research & Development labs. Innovation is usually thought of as invention. Innovation is usually new technology being turned into something unique and tangible that the company can sell. For those companies with strong R&D departments, this focus on the invention of innovative products is probably a key element of their corporate strategy.

There are, however, other elements of a corporate strategy beyond innovative products that can help companies compete in their markets. Besides having a product to sell, companies have to make that product and then get it into the hands of customers (and meet their customers' needs). To do this, companies create specific functions such as manufacturing, sales, distribution, and marketing. These functions and how they interrelate make up the company's business model. The effectiveness and efficiency of the business model is a critical element of a company's strategy. Michael Porter, the corporate strategy guru at Harvard Business School, highlighted the importance of "fit" of the functional activities that make up a company's strategy when he wrote, "Strategic fit among many activities is fundamental not only to competitive advantage but also to the sustainability of that advantage. . . . Positions built on systems of activities are far more sustainable than those built on individual activities."[2]

The implication here is that the most innovative *product* on the market may not be able to compete against a less advanced product that has a unique or superior *business model*. Dell Computer is a successful company because of its innovative business model (selling customized computers via the Internet and use of a very strong supply chain management), not because of its superior computers. Therefore, companies that do not have a world-class R&D capability may still be able to compete effectively in markets if they focus their efforts on building a superior business model.

Given the strategic importance of a company's business model in its ability to compete in the marketplace, it is logical that efforts put into improving the business model could provide real value to a company. If that is true, then companies should place at least as much "innovation" focus on the other elements of the business model (and how they interact) as they currently do on the product side.

Strategy innovation is a process of applying innovative thinking to the entire business model of a company, not just to its products or inventions.

Strategy Innovation as a Strategic Advantage

Although strategy innovation may be critical for success (or survival) in dynamic markets, it can also be a source of competitive advantage in more stable markets. The company that understands how to create value for both their customers and themselves can change the basis of competition in their industry. By creating efficient business systems aimed at delivering this new value in a market, companies not only redefine value but lock out competitors who are unable to replicate the efficient business model that delivers it. Like Wal-Mart, they play the same game with a different set of rules, rules that give them a decided advantage.

Strategy innovation has done for business what the forward pass did for the game of (American) football. Without a change in the rules, football would not have survived its early start-up years. Note in the following story the parallels between the early game of football and many businesses today:

The game of football first emerged on college campuses in the early 1800s. Styled after the game of rugby that was being played in England at that time, football consisted of a group of people moving a ball past another group of people, using whatever means they could. As the game evolved, teams adopted wild and dangerous tactics, such as the flying wedge, for moving the ball up the field. Defenses would respond to these new schemes with actions that bordered on assault. Games were won and lost in violent interchanges around the line of scrimmage, with both teams using brute force to maintain their positions. Plays were predictable, and the ball usually moved slowly, incrementally up the field. Some compared the game to warfare in the trenches of World War I. Injuries were common in those early days, and fatalities became a growing problem. When the number of deaths related to football rose to 33 in 1905, President Theodore Roosevelt stepped in with a mandate. He threatened to ban the sport unless changes were made to the style of play.

In 1906, the Rules Committee of the organization that would become the National Collegiate Athletic Association approved the use of the forward pass for football. This changed significantly the way the game was played. Soldiers in the trenches now had support from their airborne units. Teams now had more options for moving the ball. Rather than having to rely on the standard offense of running-the-ball-up-the-middle for a small gain in yardage, a team could throw a pass over the defense for a larger gain. The game became more complex. Predictability of offensive plays gave way to surprise attacks. Quarterbacks and coaches now had to make decisions on what play to use in any given situation, based on the strengths and weaknesses of the competition and the distance to the goal line. John Heisman and Knute Rockne were some of the first coaches who found effective ways to make the forward pass an integral part of the game. Football became a game of strategy.

The forward pass rule changed the basis of competition in collegiate football. Teams with big, tough players who could become human battering rams no longer had an advantage. Now teams with small, agile, quick pass receivers could compete with the big guys. More colleges fielded football teams, competition grew, and the game survived.

Strategy innovation is the process of finding a way to "change the rules of the game" so that your company's products, competencies, and assets provide you with a competitive advantage in the marketplace. If you are not the mammoth "battering ram" of a company that can compete in a market on the basis of size, strategy innovation allows you to define a new business where "small, agile, and quick" is the only way to provide customers with value. Starbucks could not have outmuscled and outspent Procter & Gamble and General Foods to gain advertising awareness for their new coffee and shelf space in supermarkets. So they set up small cafes where they not only sold their premium coffees but provided customers with the added value of a European café experience. Similarly, Minnetonka, Inc., was able to outmaneuver the giant soap companies in the early 1980s by introducing the first liquid soap product, later purchased by Colgate and renamed Softsoap.

In his book *The Innovator's Dilemma,* Clayton Christensen suggests that this small company advantage is an important force in the marketplace. He writes, "Large companies often surrender emerging growth markets because smaller, disruptive companies are actually more capable of pursuing them. Though start-ups lack resources, it doesn't matter. Their values can embrace small markets, and their cost structures can accommodate lower margins.

Their market research and resource allocation processes allow managers to proceed intuitively rather than having to be backed up by careful research and analysis, presented in PowerPoint. All of these advantages add up to enormous opportunity or looming disaster—depending on your perspective."[3]

This is the essence of strategy innovation: "changing the rules" of how customers receive value and having a business model that delivers that value better than anyone else. In that way, you make your weaknesses in an established market irrelevant, and your innovative business model becomes the new basis of competition in a market that you started.

Constantinos Markides, a professor at the London Business School and author of *All The Right Moves*, calls strategy innovation "a fundamental reconceptualization of what the business is about, which in turn leads to a dramatically different way of playing the game in the industry."[4]

In his book *Leading the Revolution*, Gary Hamel cites a number of companies that have dared to reinvent themselves by adopting innovative strategies and creative new business models. He believes that this capability will be required to compete in the markets of the future. "Unless you and your company become adept at business concept innovation, more imaginative minds will capture tomorrow's wealth."[5]

Strategy Innovation as a Source of Corporate Renewal

Strategy innovation is often considered the calling card of start-up companies looking to enter already-existing markets. However, established companies also use strategy innovation to their advantage, if they have the instinct for it. We recognize this instinct as a strong, internal emphasis on corporate "renewal." The instinct for renewal is something beyond a cultural norm; it seems to be embedded in the organization's DNA, what it sees when it looks in the mirror. These companies are never completely satisfied with who they are today, but are more interested in who they are becoming.

Companies such as Procter & Gamble, IBM, and Nokia have not experienced their sustained success by merely evolving. They have taken bold, strategically innovative steps at critical points in their histories to redefine who they were. How else does one explain the radical shift in the business of these companies from their origins? Procter & Gamble was once exclusively a soap manufacturer. At one point in their history, IBM made scales and cheese slicers. Before Nokia was in mobile phones, they were a paper products company. These companies are more concerned with their future than their past. They are proactive. They believe that corporate renewal is healthy, if not critical to their ongoing survival and success. All have confidence that they will still be in business in 2050 without believing it will be the same business they are in today.

Companies with an instinct for renewal as part of their corporate DNA are not on a treadmill. They are vigilant in the examination of their business peripheries, expecting the boundaries to change as the marketplace changes. And, when more radical opportunities present themselves, they are poised to respond. That is how a soap manufacturer becomes successful in the pet food business, how a producer of cheese slicers wins Nobel Prizes for physics, and how a paper products company becomes a world-beater in wireless communications. They expect to renew through strategy innovation and, in the process, be more vital tomorrow than they are today.

Summary

- Strategy innovation is shifting a corporation's business strategy in order to create new value for both the customer and the corporation.

- Strategy innovation is a process of applying innovative thinking to the entire business model of a company, not just to its products or inventions.

- Strategy innovation is the process of finding a way to "change the rules of the game" so that your company's products, competencies, and assets provide you with a competitive advantage in the marketplace.

- While strategy innovation may be critical for success (or survival) in dynamic markets, it can also be a source of competitive advantage in more stable markets.

- Established companies with an instinct for corporate renewal use strategy innovation to remain vital and relevant over time.

- Strategy innovation can provide new growth prospects for companies in any marketplace and should be a capability, if not a core competence, of every company hoping to survive in the dynamic business world of the twenty-first century.

Endnotes

1. Jack Welch, from GE's *2000 Annual Report*.
2. Michael Porter, "What Is Strategy?," *Harvard Business Review*, November/December 1996.
3. Clayton Christensen, *The Innovator's Dilemma* (Boston: Harvard Business School Press, 1997).
4. Constantinos Markides, *All the Right Moves* (Boston: Harvard Business School Press, 2000).
5. Gary Hamel, *Leading the Revolution* (Boston: Harvard Business School Press, 2000).

CHAPTER 2

STRATEGY INNOVATION IS
MANAGING THE FUTURE

> There are always two parties—the party of the Past
> and the party of the Future; the Establishment and the
> Movement.
>
> —*RALPH WALDO EMERSON*

When do you know that you need strategy innovation? In most cases, it is when the projection of revenues for future products and services does not add up to the company's growth targets. When this happens, business leaders scramble around to find ways to address this "delta," the difference between the revenues they expect to generate and the revenues they need to generate (see Figure 2-1).

The Dreaded Delta and the Spiral of Incrementalism

The knee-jerk reaction to this revenue-target dichotomy is to pull together a team of people to brainstorm some new product ideas or acquisition targets to fill the dreaded revenue delta. Over the years, creativity in the form of brainstorming events has earned its reputation as a viable method of creating incremental new product

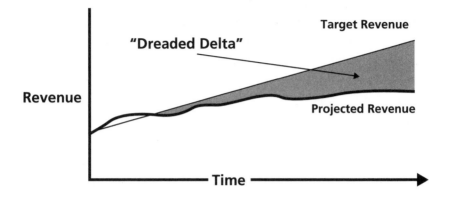

Figure 2-1. The dreaded delta.

and service ideas in corporations. However, the problem with many brainstorming efforts is that they are done within the context of the base brand or current business and tend to produce only line extension opportunities or incremental product improvements. They take current products and make them slightly more powerful, slightly more colorful, or slightly longer-lasting (at a slightly higher price). Often, these slightly better line-extension products can help fill the revenue delta, as long as the delta is not too big.

After years of creating line extensions to fill revenue gaps, corporations often evolve into "institutions of incrementalism." This is particularly true in companies that have had a successful product or brand on the market for many years. Whenever additional revenue is needed, a new line extension of the current product is introduced. With a strong brand, it is not too difficult to introduce a successful line-extension product. The line extension can usually use the same manufacturing facilities, the same distribution system, and the same sales force as the base brand, minimizing incremental costs. Because it leverages a known brand name, market acceptance is likely, and additional revenues (from the slightly higher price) are almost certain. Because it is similar to other products produced by this business system, the process for getting it to market is relatively easy, fast, and problem-free. A downside to leveraging the base brand through line extensions is the relatively low incremental revenue that results, as cannibalization of the base brand will account for some of the additional revenue.

Meanwhile, the business systems of the company adapt to this strategy of growth through incrementalism. We worked with a company once that had become a victim of its line-extension success. Its operations had become more efficient around dealing with line extensions, but less flexible in their abilities to accommodate new and unique products. Financial controls and hurdle rates for new products were set to the attractive level of line extensions, making it difficult for new products requiring additional costs or investment spending to be approved for development. The corporate culture, which rewarded people who quickly brought new line extensions to market, was less patient when nonincremental products had a longer time frame or required more attention or problem-solving to develop. When this happened, the company became caught in a spiral of incrementalism. It had become very efficient at developing low-volume, high-profit line extensions, and the internal systems prevented it from identifying, developing, or introducing significantly new products and services to the market. The company had lost its ability to significantly grow the business.

As long as the base brand remains vibrant with growth potential in the marketplace, the spiral of incrementalism can be an efficient and profitable way to run the business. If the brand saturates the market, the market undergoes some change, or the brand loses some of its previous vitality, growth slows, and the dreaded delta appears. Richard Foster and Sarah Kaplan, in their book *Creative Destruction*, write, "The reason IBM stumbled was that something was wrong with John Akers's view of the world—with his mental model. Akers believed in continuity in gradual, incremental change. But the world had become discontinuous."[1] When this happens, it is time to find a new growth platform for the company, a new "engine" to drive future revenues and profits. Akers's successor at IBM, Lou Gerstner, was successful in doing that and, as a result, was able to save the computing giant from break-up or collapse. By refocusing the company's expertise on computing services and its patents on technology licensing, Gerstner created significant new business platforms that will continue to drive growth in IBM's future.

The Corporate Dilemma of the Current Business vs. the Future Business

It is not easy for the senior management team of an existing company to navigate the whitewater conditions of a dynamic marketplace. Everything seems to be constantly changing—products, technologies, competitors, customer needs, distribution channels, and so on. How should the company respond? Is it better to take action or wait for the market to settle down? Should the company stick with their current strategy or move to a new one?

On the one hand, the company must manage its current business, which has been proven and time-tested in its ability to find a market and deliver a product or service to that market. This predictability represents a low-risk means for the company to meet its financial goals, ensuring its survival. It is the goose that laid the golden eggs. However, that current business is probably working off an older business model, created in the past when the market conditions were quite different. Being an older business model, it may have an infrastructure and overhead expenses that are inordinately high, keeping prices high and making the market an attractive target to new, leaner competitors. A start-up company with a Web site and access to cheap manufacturing capabilities overseas could replicate your products at lower prices and steal your market share. A global goliath could apply its considerable resources and technologies to offer your customers more than you can. All existing businesses are vulnerable, to some degree, to competitive pressures in a dynamic marketplace, making their futures uncertain.

On the other hand, there are countless ways for a company to create new business opportunities in a dynamic marketplace. Change in the status quo of any market component creates some degree of disequilibrium, which means that there are likely to be customers somewhere who are being underserved or business systems that are not working at full efficiency. This results in the potential to create value, which is the basis for new, future business opportunities. Revenue generated from these new ventures can help fuel the future growth necessary to keep the company financially vital and attractive to investors, suppliers, and employees. However, new business opportunities have a downside. They can introduce potential new risks to the company's financial equation, as the development and successful implementation of a new business opportunity is far from certain. Spending too much or taking too much time to pursue these new, untested opportunities may kill the goose, cutting off your golden egg supply.

This "tension" between focusing on the current, lower-risk (but vulnerable) businesses versus higher-risk new business opportunities is often a critical factor in the creation of a corporate strategy. It is the corporate strategy that identifies how the company will allocate and develop its resources to meet both current and future market needs, while keeping the company financially viable. Therefore, it is an important strategic imperative to consider how a company will balance the needs of today's business while pursuing the business needs of the future. Jim Collins and Jerry Porras, in their book *Built to Last: Successful Habits of Visionary Companies*, write, "Managers at visionary companies simply do not accept the proposition that they must choose between short-term performance *or* long-term performance. They build first and foremost for the long term while *simultaneously* holding themselves to highly demanding short-term standards."[2]

Although allocating time, attention, and resources to managing the future business will divert time, attention, and resources from managing the current business—and vice versa—this tension between the present and the future business is a healthy tension to foster in an organization. Linda S. Mayer, the senior vice president of marketing and product development at Moen, calls it the need for "bifocal vision." It requires everyone to always determine and strike a balance of the two, thus preventing the urgency of the present from overshadowing the importance of the future.

Business school professors Michael I. Tushman (Harvard) and Charles A. O'Reilly III (Stanford), in their book *Winning through*

Innovation: A Practical Guide to Leading Organizational Change and Renewal, address this difficult trade-off between the present and future businesses of corporations. "To succeed both today and tomorrow, managers must play two different games simultaneously." They go on to explain how the management of today's business requires a focus on efficiency and stability, aligning and improving the productivity of all facets of the business model. The business of the future, however, requires "streams of innovation," which can be a destabilizing force because they require corporate change. "Given these contrasting forces for change and stability, managers need to create ambidextrous organizations—organizations that celebrate stability and incremental change as well as experimentation and discontinuous change simultaneously."[3]

One way to foster this healthy tension is to create an internal corporate system focused on strategy innovation and the future. By formalizing such a system, senior management makes a corporate commitment to the importance of the company's future, while still running today's business. Chapter 12 outlines some important considerations in the formalization of a strategy innovation system.

Strategy Innovation Is Managing Your Business Toward the Future

Organizations that have found it difficult to focus on managing the future business provide a range of excuses, including:

- ◆ Corporate myopia
- ◆ Industry turbulence
- ◆ Future incompetence

Corporate Myopia

There are some companies that are so engrossed in managing today's business that they claim they cannot find the time or energy to think about tomorrow. We recently asked the senior management team of a billion-dollar corporation to speculate on the company's future, and on which direction it might take to identify new business opportunities. It was clear from our interviews that only two people on the team had spent any time thinking about the company's future beyond their current one-year planning period. This is probably not unusual. Especially in light of the downsizing and the relentless pressure to make the quarterly numbers in many organizations, the urgency of today's business supersedes the importance of tomorrow's business.

Industry Turbulence

Other companies, particularly those involved with fast-changing industries such as communications and technology, claim that attempts to understand the future are fruitless, given the chaos and unpredictability they see in their markets. With technologies, products, and pricing changing so rapidly, they maintain that it is impossible to speculate on where those markets might be in a three-to-five-year time frame. As a result, many of these companies take a reactive approach to the future, preferring to make decisions once market dynamics are clearer.

Future Incompetence

Finally, we have also run into companies that know it is important to understand the future and want to do it, but they do not know how to go about doing it. Their typical response is to try to find someone who "really understands the future," who can advise them on what to do about it. They want the answer delivered to them by an enlightened outsider. The search for this person is rarely "prophet-able." Futurists vary significantly in the assumptions they make and the factors they consider. None have the answer.

As a result of this lack of attention, the future is an unknown, mysterious place for many companies. The mystery even leads to some myths about the future, which can actually discourage its exploration. For example, many people see how sudden changes can have an impact on a market. Believing that these changes could not have been predicted, they assume that all "forecasts" of the future are too tenuous to be of value. Therefore, they do not bother to explore the possibilities of the future.

Assumptions About the Future

Strategy innovation can be a powerful means of managing your business toward the future. However, the effective pursuit of strategy innovation requires a few basic assumptions about the future.

1. *The future does not yet exist and can be created.*

   There are some people who feel that the future has already somehow been determined and will be revealed to us as it arrives. For them, the future is like an actor, with lines carefully rehearsed, waiting backstage for the right moment to enter the scene. Those who feel this way tend to be very *reactive* in their actions, for they fear that they cannot control the future. They will take no action until the future arrives. Then, they will "see what the future holds" and respond to it. Perhaps they feel the future is so powerful that it will nullify their actions, so why waste energy and resources now?

   By definition, the future does not exist and never will (once you experience tomorrow, it is no longer tomorrow, but today). Therefore, because the future is not a fait accompli, it can be influenced. Although maybe not a totally blank canvas, the future has considerable latitude for the artist to make an impact. Actions taken today by a company will result in some future effects in the marketplace. Therefore, *proactive* companies that take those actions today will have the greatest influence on the future. Reactive companies may survive into the future, but it is the proactive companies that will create that future. The proactive companies can, through their actions, "change the rules" in the marketplace, requiring the reactive companies to play the game a different way or perish.

2. *The future cannot be precisely predicted, but its forces can be identified.*

   If all trends were linear, constant, and noninteractive, it might be possible to predict the future. However, trends change, and so much of the future is shaped by events that cannot be predicted. We call these events discontinuities, things that shift the trend lines. They are inflection points that cause the future to be diverted from its previous path. The invention of the transistor, the evolution of the Vietnam War, and the development of the Internet were all discontinuities that had a significant impact on the future that we are now experiencing. The human genome project, the 9/11 terrorist attacks, and nanotechnology may have a similar impact on our children's future.

Although these elements cannot be predicted with any degree of certainty, the forces that led to them would have been quite easy to spot—by those who were searching for them. As we will discuss later in this book, we were involved in a strategy innovation initiative in the mid-1990s where an industry expert shared a concern that terrorist attacks could render city water supplies vulnerable. Back then, that seemed a very unrealistic possibility. But those who were in positions of responsibility recognized the potential because they were dealing with such issues every day. It is a valuable exercise to identify existing forces that could have an impact on the future. It is not the same as *predicting* the future, but it is gaining market foresight that can help understand and shape the future.

3. *The future is not one-size-fits-all, it is proprietary.*

When you see a cow standing in a field, what do you see? A farmer may see his chores. A toddler may see something scary. Ben & Jerry see a potential supplier. The point is that we all see things differently, based on our experiences and what is important to us (our values). The future is the same way. Companies perceive the future according to their past experiences, their core competencies, and their values and aspirations. Therefore, two companies from the same industry may see the same forces in the marketplace, but paint two totally different pictures of the future. The future you see is proprietary to you, based on your values. It cannot be delivered by a consultant, it must be discovered by you.

With these basic assumptions about the future, you are now in a position to explore the future for strategic opportunities that exist there.

Future Business Opportunities Will Drive a New Corporate Strategy

What does your company currently understand about its future? How might your markets change? What business opportunities will exist in these future markets? How will your company participate in these markets? Who in the company is focused on that question? These are important questions for all companies in all markets to consider as they create their business strategies.

In thinking about what your future business strategy might look like, there is often the question of which comes first—the new business opportunity or the new corporate strategy? Although not quite as perplexing as its chicken-egg cousin, this question might make for an interesting research project for an aspiring professor. Do corporations establish their strategies and then look for business opportunities to support those strategies or is it the other way around—first finding a business opportunity and then creating a new corporate strategy around it?

A case could be made for the strategy coming first. A quantitative analysis of markets done in the context of a strategic model (such as Michael Porter's Five Forces Model, or Bain & Company's Profit Pools Analysis) can identify "gaps" in the market, areas of profitability, or market segments where the company could have a sustained competitive advantage. In this case, a preferred company positioning in the marketplace can be identified first, leading to a search for new business opportunities to support that strategy.

However, we believe that new corporate strategies more often come from first identifying a new business opportunities. Many of the examples in this book reflect a new corporate strategy being created based on the identification of exciting new business opportunities. Having a portfolio of new business opportunities to choose from will provide senior management even greater flexibility in crafting a competitive strategy. Henry Mintzberg, a professor at McGill University and author of *The Rise and Fall of Strategic Planning*, observes that opportunities beget strategies. He wrote in the *Academy of Management Executives*, "Good strategies grow out of ideas that have been kicking around the company, and initiatives that have been taken by all sorts of people in the company. . . . That means that a lot of very effective, so-called strategists or chief executives don't come up with the brilliant new strategy."[4]

Robert Galvin, former CEO of electronics giant Motorola, claims that in his more than forty years at the helm, it was the new business options available to him that often drove his corporate strategies. He explained, "Strategy is determining the most worthy place to apply your resources. You allocate the resources to the ideas that have the most promising potential. Before allocating those resources, you should have surveyed all of your options and selected the best one."

Portfolio of New Business Opportunities: A Valuable, Intangible Strategic Asset

It stands to reason that if new business opportunities help drive the creation of new corporate strategies, then having a portfolio of many new business opportunities provides senior management with more options and more flexibility in their strategy-making. A portfolio of new business opportunities can provide the company with choices on how to grow the business. A diverse portfolio, consisting of shorter-term and longer-term opportunities as well as lower-volume and higher-volume options, can provide senior management with choices on how to meet the changing needs of the business.

The portfolio of business opportunities becomes, then, a strategic asset for the company. As an asset, it is worthy of investment by the company to develop, update, and maintain this portfolio. We believe that all companies should consider investing in a process of strategy innovation, either on an ad hoc basis or as an ongoing, core capability. Strategy innovation and the portfolio of new business opportunities created by a strategy innovation process is a valuable asset for competing in the future.

Much has been written recently about the growing importance of intangible assets on the ability of corporations to compete in today's economy. Tom Stewart, editor of *Fortune* magazine, wrote, "Intellectual capital—not natural resources, machinery, or even financial capital—has become the one indispensable asset of corporations."[5]

In their book *Invisible Advantage: How Intangibles Are Driving Business Performance*, Jonathan Low and coauthor Pam Cohen Kalafut write, "Threats and opportunities arise because intangibles have value. Value lies in the skill and knowledge of the people who manage a business and those who work for it. . . . It's built into how a company operates: the ideas that it pursues, the innovations it can bring to market, the information systems that tell managers what is going on in the world and in the organization."[6]

Low and Kalafut go on to say that intangible assets, including such things as products in the R&D pipeline, can have a significant effect on the company's valuation. In research they did for the Cap Gemini Ernst & Young Center for Business Innovation, Low and Kalafut found that "on average, 35 percent of professional investors' allocation decisions are driven by consideration of nonfinancial data or information about intangibles. In other words, more than one-third of the information used to justify these large-scale investment decisions is nonfinancial."[7]

We witnessed, in anecdotal form, the increase in corporate value that is possible based on the existence of intangible, strategic assets. Clinical Diagnostics was a division of Eastman Kodak when we first worked with them in the early 1990s to develop a ten-year strategic map for their business. Shortly after our initiative, Johnson & Johnson acquired Clinical Diagnostics to supplement their line of medical diagnostic equipment. According to José Coronas, the president of Clinical Diagnostics, Kodak received a premium price for their division because of the quality of their strategic map for the future.

Who Is Minding the Future?

Very few companies have a formalized process or infrastructure for creating new business opportunities for the future. Most are capable of generating new product ideas, which can often turn into new business opportunities. But few take the time to research the emerging marketplace and try to understand how it could differ from the markets of today and what opportunities might be available. Few take the time to understand customers and their unarticulated needs, which can lead to significant market opportunities of the future. Few examine the many ways that companies are rethinking and streamlining their business models in order to deliver customer value more efficiently and effectively.

Why is this the case? We believe it is because most companies do not have someone responsible for the future. In companies that phased out their corporate strategic planning departments in the mid-1980s (as Jack Welch did at GE), there is frequently nobody who is focused on the role that strategy can play in growing a business for the future. As a result, strategies are merely carried over from previous years and eventually become fixed as a way the company does business, something that is a "given" from year to year.

It does not have to be this way. Strategy innovation and its focus on the future can (and should) be senior management's responsibility and a core capability for any company. Finding innovative ways to deliver higher value to customers will create new markets and growth opportunities, giving the company first-mover advantage. It can also provide differentiation from competition, which keeps margins and profits strong. Companies with portfolios of new business opportunities will be more strategically agile in the nearer-term and better poised for corporate renewal in the longer-term.

Many companies invest heavily in R&D to identify innovative new *products* that can fuel future company growth. It only makes sense that companies should also invest resources to explore ways of creating innovative *strategies* for the future. Both are strategic assets that can be effective individually in a market but can be even more effective when they work together—an innovative product with an innovative business model.

To compete in tomorrow's markets, senior management needs a "road map" of the emerging future and a portfolio of new business opportunities aimed at creating value in that future. Being proactive and discovering new opportunities that fit the changing needs of a dynamic marketplace is the process of strategy innovation.

Summary

- At the point when companies experience the "dreaded delta," the gap between their projected revenue and the revenue required to maintain their businesses, they will need a capability for strategy innovation.

- If your business operates to annually introduce incremental product improvements (line extension products) to the marketplace, you may not have the business systems necessary to identify significant new business opportunities for strategy innovation.

- All companies must balance the needs of today's business with the needs of tomorrow's business. Strategy innovation can be a powerful means of managing your business toward the future.

- The effective pursuit of strategy innovation requires a few basic assumptions about the future:

  1. The future does not yet exist and can be created.
  2. The future cannot be precisely predicted, but its forces can be identified.
  3. The future is not one-size-fits-all, it is proprietary.

- The identification of new business opportunities in the future can drive new corporate strategies.

- Having a portfolio of future new business opportunities is an important corporate asset.

- To compete in tomorrow's markets, senior management needs a "road map" of the emerging future and a portfolio of new business opportunities aimed at creating value in that future.

Endnotes

1. Richard Foster and Sarah Kaplan, *Creative Destruction* (New York: Currency/Doubleday, 2001).
2. James Collins and Jerry Porras, *Built to Last: Successful Habits of Visionary Companies* (New York: HarperCollins, 1994).
3. Michael L. Tushman and Charles A. O'Reilly, *Winning Through Innovation: A Practical Guide to Leading Organizational Change and Renewal* (Boston: Harvard Business School Press, 2002).
4. Daniel J. McCarthy, "View from the Top: Henry Mintzberg on Strategy and Management," *Academy of Management Executives,* August 2000.
5. Tom Stewart (quote), www.vernaallee.com, January 2003.
6. Jonathan Low and Pam Cohen Kalafut, *Invisible Advantage: How Intangibles Are Driving Business Performance* (Cambridge: Perseus Publishing, 2002).
7. Ibid.

CHAPTER 3

STRATEGY INNOVATION IS NOT STRATEGIC PLANNING

> Strategic positionings are often not obvious, and finding them requires creativity and insight.
>
> —*MICHAEL PORTER*

Although the concept of strategy innovation as a corporate capability is intriguing, it is an elusive goal for most organizations. The reason for this is that most corporations have in place processes for doing strategic "planning," but not strategic "innovation."

The Strategic Planning Process Will Not Produce Strategy Innovation

In 1993, Bain & Company began a multiyear research project to measure the management tools being used by senior executives to improve the performance of their companies. In the results of the 2001 survey of 451 senior executives in companies around the world, "strategic planning" was the most frequently mentioned tool being used in corporations today, by 76 percent of executives.[1]

The Bain survey, however, does not specify what constitutes strategic planning in an organization. Our experience suggests that it encompasses a wide range of different activities across companies and even across different business units within the same corporation. On the one hand, some companies pull together their yearly budgets for the upcoming fiscal year and call that a strategic planning process. At the other end of the spectrum, there are companies that hire large consulting companies, such as Bain & Company, Boston Consulting Group, or McKinsey, and spend a significant amount of money analyzing the marketplace and competitors, and identifying any "gaps" in the marketplace that might suggest a new strategic opportunity. That is the deluxe version of strategic planning, done by larger corporations.

At the risk of overgeneralizing, we suspect that much of the strategic planning done in most business units of corporations is somewhere between these two extremes. It is likely that most strategic planning includes some review of the market and competition, such as updating market shares, revenue, and growth projections each year. It might also include a SWOT analysis (strengths, weaknesses, opportunities, and threats), reminding management where the company is strong relative to competition and where it is vulnerable.

However, the strategic planning in most companies is rarely an exercise in creating new and effective strategies for the future of the company. Instead, the strategic planning process is more often one that perpetuates, and at best revises, the current strategy every year. Richard Foster and Sarah Kaplan, in their book *Creative Destruction*, write, "Often today's strategic planning does not attempt to collect information that could challenge existing mental models. It focuses on reanalysis of the existing businesses and the analysis of similarly sized competitors, rather than attempting to understand what is happening at the periphery of the business and how it might change."[2]

Does your company have a standard "format" for the strategic planning presentation? Do you start this year's strategic planning process by referring back to tables and projections from last year's strategic plan? Are many of the tables already on spreadsheets that just need updating? If so, your strategic planning process is built around revising the strategy that is already in place. For a lot of companies, this is quite logical. If there are no dramatic changes in the market and the company is not hemorrhaging red ink, then continuing with last year's strategy is more efficient than starting from scratch. "If it ain't broke, don't fix it." Perpetuating the current strategy in your strategic planning process may be quite adequate for your market and your company's needs—but it won't lead to strategy innovation.

What financial targets are usually set for your business unit in the strategic plan? Do the targets encourage or require any risk-taking with the elements of the strategic plan? Is there any strategic "stretch" required? In many companies, there is an emphasis on steady, predictable financial growth from year to year. There are no surprises in the targets, which encourage no surprises in the strategic plan. Bets are placed on the tortoise, not the hare. These expectations send the business unit managers looking for incremental, predictable revenue growth each year. Introducing a lemon-flavored line extension of the current product does not raise corporate eyebrows the way an innovative, new-to-the-world product would. As a result of incremental financial targets, the strategic planning process in many companies encourages incremental growth within the existing strategy and business model.

Is number crunching an integral part of your strategic planning process? Do you spend a lot of time making all of the numbers in the plan "fit"? Numbers are frequently used in strategic planning to track sales, shares, and trends in a market. Those numbers are then used to make projections for the future of that market. When that is the case, the projections for the future are typically extrapolations of historical data. This process reinforces the notion that the future is expected to be an extension of the past. If it is believed that the future will look just like the past, then perpetuation of the current strategy is logical. However, strategic planning filled with statistics rarely leads to strategy innovation. Henry Mintzberg, in his book *The Rise and Fall of Strategic Planning*, wrote, ". . . nobody in the history of the world has ever created a strategy through an analytical process."[3] The analytical discipline of the strategic planning process with its year-to-year comparisons and extrapolations is one more reason why the strategic planning process is more of a perpetuation of the historical strategy and business model than the creation of the company's optimal strategy for the future.

Strategy Innovation vs. Strategic Planning

If you are intrigued by the potential of strategy innovation for your company, be aware that you will not get it from your current strategic planning process. You will have to create a separate process for strategy innovation, one that is:

- Creative
- Market-centric
- Heuristic (discovery-driven)

Creative

Strategy innovation requires a creative process, not an analytical one. It requires people to listen to customers in new ways, design new types of products, and envision strategies for markets that do not currently exist. It is a process that is as disciplined and structured as strategic planning but uses creativity, rather than analysis, as the primary tool. The raw materials for strategy innovation are insights, which are new perceptions and new understandings of value. Insights can come from listening to or observing customers—their words, actions, emotions, and wishes. Insights can come from listening to industry experts or thought leaders as they explain their understanding of the present and future dynamics of a marketplace. Insights can also come from listening to people who are not entrenched in your industry, company, or culture, as they are in the best position of offering a fresh perspective.

The quality of the insights necessary for strategy innovation cannot come from statistics. People with a strong analytical orientation can participate in the strategy innovation process (everyone has the potential for creativity), but they must check their quantitative tools and mind-sets at the door. They can have them back when it comes time to evaluate and quantify the business opportunities developed by the strategy innovation process. However, the process for strategy innovation is a creative one, not an analytical one.

Market-Centric

Strategy innovation requires a market-centric process, not one that is company-centric. For many, this shift is as significant as the Copernican revolution. You will recall from high school science class that Copernicus identified the sun as the center of the universe (heliocentric model). Just like people used to believe that the sun and stars revolved around the earth, many of today's corporate executives believe that their companies are the center of their business universe, and that all other stakeholders (shareholders, suppliers, customers, and employees) revolve around them. Customers must shop at hours most efficient for the company. Suppliers must change their delivery schedules to meet the company's needs. Employees must move to a new location if the company wants them to. Strategy innovation proposes, instead, that customers and the dynamics of the marketplace are the center of the business universe (market-centric), and that wise companies will consider setting their orbits around them. If customers need call centers to receive the service they need, companies should consider changing their business models to create them. If Third World markets need household products at lower prices, companies should explore innovative ways of providing them.

To be clear on this point, we are not suggesting that companies meet all customer needs or sacrifice sound financial management to fulfill those needs. Successful strategy innovation requires that a new business opportunity add significant value for *both the customer and the company* to be worthwhile. However, the *starting point* for that consideration should be the needs of the customer/market, not the company's needs.

Heuristic

The strategy innovation process is not as predictable and linear as the strategic planning process in most companies. Revising plans and updating numbers have a predictability that allows you to schedule strategic planning sessions months in advance. Strategy innovation is a grassroots, discovery ("heuristic") process that is dependent on the quality of the insights gained along the way. Sometimes it happens quickly, sometimes it takes many iterations before a breakthrough is achieved. Customer interviews might not reveal new expressions of value in the first month of trying. An examination of future market dynamics may suggest several very different future scenarios that will take a while to sort out and evaluate. There will be starts and stops, dead ends, and a need to revisit previous work done. The iterative nature of the process means that the imposition of deadlines may affect the quality of the output. That is, a team may be forced to stop exploring because of a deadline, rather than because they have already discovered all the great insights they need. Flexible timing is more accommodating to the heuristic nature of the strategy innovation process.

Another difference between traditional strategic planning process and a strategy innovation process is the orientation toward time. There is a natural tendency in the strategic planning process to start the planning with "today" and then make projections, based on historical trends and today's statistics, out to "tomorrow." It is starting with the known and working toward the unknown. This near-term to long-term work flow reinforces the evolutionary nature of the strategic planning process.

The strategy innovation process, on the other hand, works best in the other direction: It starts with "tomorrow" and then plans backwards to "today." To be successful, the search for new business opportunities cannot be constrained by today's corporate conditions or today's market conditions. The search for opportunities cannot get bogged down in arguments over resource allocation. Strategy innovation is decidedly future-oriented. It must be able to transcend today's conditions and imagine what is possible in the future. After identifying potential new business opportunities in the future, the planning works *backwards* to identify the key strategic milestones to get there. In this way, the more tangible appeal of new growth opportunities acts as a "future-pull," which will help the company in its decisions on resource allocation (see Figure 3-1).

Strategic Planning Process	Strategy Innovation Process
Analytical	*Creative*
Numbers-driven	*Insights-driven*
Company-centric	*Market-centric*
Logical/linear	*Heuristic/iterative*
Today to tomorrow	*Tomorrow to today*
Extend current value	*Create new value*
Fit the business model	*Create a new business model*

Figure 3-1. The strategic planning process vs. the strategy innovation process.

Where traditional strategic planning focuses on building value in current markets, strategy innovation focuses on creating new value in new markets. In the 1960s, Xerox had a near monopoly on the sales and servicing of large copy machines to large businesses. Their business model consisted of a direct sales force that sold leased, high-end equipment, and an extensive service network (profit center) to keep the equipment operating. In their strategic planning processes at the time, much of Xerox's focus was no doubt on determining how to extend or improve the current value delivered to current customers, e.g., faster machines, new sorting methods, faster service response, or better leas-

Process Tip:

Strategy innovation is best achieved by leaping ahead and working backward.

You cannot discover distant lands if you remain tethered to your current one. Often we believe that some invisible constraints prevent us from seeking new and unique solutions to our problems. Make a conscious effort to break the bonds that hold you to your current operating system or business model and explore far-reaching possibilities. Dare to dream. When you find a dream out there that fits or helps solve your problem, figure out a way to take it back to your world. Leap ahead, work backwards.

ing plans. These means of value-enhancement can help grow revenues while leveraging the company's current strategy and business model.

However, there are also other ways of delivering value to customers. Canon discovered a different way to deliver value in the copier market. Using their skills in microelectronics and optics, they developed a copier with a replaceable cartridge, which they sold as the first personal copier. Aimed at small businesses and individuals, these copiers were inexpensive, required little or no maintenance, and could be purchased through existing retail channels. Canon used strategy innovation to redefine value in the marketplace for copying machines. As with Canon, the opportunity to create new value has tremendous revenue potential. At the same time, it will likely require a company to consider the development of a new business model in order to implement the new strategy. Xerox stayed with their old business model for a long time and suffered for it.

Strategy Innovation and THEN Strategic Planning

Developing an internal strategy innovation process to identify new ways of competing in the dynamic markets of the future does not mean that strategic planning is obsolete. In fact, we believe the strategic planning process and the strategy innovation process both need to exist and to work together. The way we propose that they work is for a strategy innovation process to be established that will "plug into" the strategic planning process. In other words, do strategy innovation and THEN do traditional strategic planning (see Figure 3-2).

In this case, strategy innovation becomes the "fuzzy front end" of the strategy creation process within a company. Its creative, market-centric view of the future will provide a portfolio of new business opportunities that exist, which the company can consider. These new opportunities can then feed into the company's current strategic planning process. There, the focus on numbers and fit with current corporate capabilities can help refine, evaluate, and ultimately integrate the opportunities identified. The creative process leads to the evaluative process. The ideas meet the implementation details. The strategy innovation process finds new ways to provide

Corporate Strategy Creation

Figure 3-2. Integration of strategy innovation and strategic planning.

new value in the marketplace, and strategic planning determines if those opportunities provide new value for the company.

Corporations that choose to conduct strategy innovation on an ad hoc, initiative basis will want to consider planning a new initiative every few years to feed into the strategic planning process. They will find that the portfolio of new business opportunities they identify can remain robust for two to five years, depending on how quickly their markets are changing. At the end of that time, the market dynamics will have shifted, new technologies will be available, the strategic road map will have been played out, and it will be time to reexamine what the future might hold.

This was confirmed by Bob LaPerle, currently a corporate vice president at Eastman Kodak, who led two corporate-wide strategy innovation initiatives at Kodak in the 1990s. At that time, LaPerle noted, "I think it is valuable to do a study like this every two to three years, to look out five years. We need to challenge our paradigms every few years, especially if our business case is built on them or is sensitive to them. We should find out what the frontier looks like, challenge our thinking with outside experts, and see if our business case holds up."

For those companies that choose to conduct strategy innovation on an ongoing, formalized basis, they will want to find a way to integrate the strategy innovation process with their internal strategic planning process. It can be a formal "hand-off" of results from one group to the other, although that runs the risk of a not-invented-here reaction on the part of the receiving group. Preferably, there will be some inter-mingling of the strategy innovation and strategic planning groups, so that continuity is established and the opportunities flow seamlessly from their development stage to their evaluation stage. Since the 1990s, Eastman Kodak has moved from conducting strategy innova-tion initiatives to the development of a formalized strategy innovation process, which they call their Systems Concept Center. In it, they have created a separate venture board structure to help move new ideas from creation through to commercialization, providing the crucial link between strategy innovation and strategic planning. This center is beginning to play an important role in the identification and integra-tion of significant new business opportunities to Kodak.

Chapter Summary

- ◆ Strategic planning in most companies is rarely an exercise in cre-ating new and effective strategies for the future of the company, making it ineffective for strategy innovation.

- ◆ Strategic planning is typically a highly analytical, quantitative process that focuses on corporate issues of today and today's business model, extending out into the short-term future.

- ◆ For effective strategy innovation, companies must create a new process, one that is creative, market-centric, heuristic (discovery-driven), and focused on the future.

- ◆ A process of strategy innovation should be the "fuzzy front end" of an overall strategy creation process, leading seamlessly from opportunity identification and creation (strategy innovation) to opportunity evaluation and integration (strategic planning). Do strategy innovation and THEN do strategic planning.

Endnotes

1. Darrell K. Rigby, "Bain & Company Management Tools 2001 Global Results," Annual Survey of Senior Executives.
2. Richard Foster and Sarah Kaplan, *Creative Destruction* (New York: Cur-rency/Doubleday, 2001).
3. Henry Mintzberg, *The Rise and Fall of Strategic Planning* (New York: The Free Press, 1994).

Chapter 4

The Discovery Process

> Our quest for discovery fuels our creativity in all fields,
> not just science. If we reached the end of the line, the
> human spirit would shrivel and die. But I don't think
> we will ever stand still: we shall increase in complexity,
> if not in depth, and shall always be the center of an
> expanding horizon of possibilities.
>
> —*Stephen Hawking*

Do not outsource the strategy innovation process for your company! Regardless of how downsized, bogged-down, or downright busy your people are, they can find the time and energy to participate in a strategy innovation initiative. These initiatives are a welcome relief from employees' day-to-day responsibilities because they are opportunities to view the business from a much different perspective. Your people get to see the big picture, they get to see longer-term, and they get to embrace a companywide, cross-functional perspective that is often lacking in their functional silo-based daily activities. It is also a chance to explore, speculate, and imagine new possibilities for the future. A strategy innovation initiative is frequently the type of activity that pulls together organizations by aligning people and departments to a common goal, a shared purpose.

Try a strategy innovation initiative with an internal, ad hoc group before thinking about building a more formalized system for strategy innovation. Experiment with it. Try different approaches, with different teams of people—either sequentially or simultaneously. Every initiative will provide valuable insights and ideas to your company, which will turn into economic benefits. Some initiatives will yield short-term, business-building innovations, and some initiatives will produce the breakthrough, market-creating innovations of the future. After getting an idea of how strategy innovation can work in your company, then you can think about building a more permanent, in-house capability for it.

To launch a strategy innovation initiative in your company, you will need some resources (people and funding) and a process. If you supply the resources, this book will supply the process.

What Is the Discovery Process?

The strategy innovation process, which we have named the Discovery Process, is a method for creating a portfolio of innovative, new business opportunities that could become the basis for a new strategic direction for your corporation. Corporate teams that have taken these journeys liken themselves to reconnaissance teams, sent by their companies to explore the strategic frontiers of their industries. This imagery reminds us of Lewis and Clark, those brave explorers sent by U.S. President Thomas Jefferson in 1804 to learn what lay to the west of the Mississippi River, America's first frontier. The team gathered for that expedition was called the *Corps of Discovery*. Fast-forward several centuries to another frontier, outer space. Following the highly successful Apollo space program that placed Americans on the moon, NASA's space shuttle program launched the Hubble Space Telescope in 1990 to do reconnaissance work into inter-galactic space. The name of the space shuttle that delivered the Hubbell telescope was *Discovery*. It seemed appropriate to us that corporate reconnaissance teams would use the "Discovery" Process to explore and discover new business opportunities on their strategic frontiers, leading to innovative and competitive corporate strategies.

The Five Phases of the Discovery Process

The Discovery Process is a series of phases, not a linear series of steps (see Figure 4-1). By carrying out the phases, your company will avoid some of the process pitfalls that arise when doing cross-functional work at the strategic level. The specific steps to be taken within each phase must be determined by each company individually, as will be explained later in this chapter.

A summary of the five phases is as follows:

1. *Staging Phase.* In this phase, the Discovery team is selected, key roles are identified, the objectives of the initiative are established, and the team is prepared for the process.

2. *Aligning Phase.* The Discovery team and senior management align themselves on the focus and scope of the initiative, agreeing on the "strategic frontier(s)" to be explored.

3. *Exploring Phase.* The goal of this phase is the collection of new insights on the strategic frontier that can form the basis of new, value-producing business opportunities in the future. Depending on the strategic frontier and the scope of the initiative, teams will explore insights related to different exploration "vectors," including customer value, market dynamics, and/or business model innovation.

4. *Creating Phase.* Using the new insights gained, the Discovery team will create and refine a portfolio of new business opportunities for the future.

| Staging | Aligning | Exploring | Creating | Mapping |
| Phase | Phase | Phase | Phase | Phase |

Figure 4-1. The five phases of the Discovery Process.

5. *Mapping Phase.* In this final phase, the team will create a strategic road map outlining key events, trends, market discontinuities, and milestones to move the company into its new strategic future.

Flexibility of the Discovery Process

All phases of the Discovery Process must be implemented for a successful strategy innovation initiative. However, just like fingerprints, no two Discovery Processes are alike. The activities that take place within each phase will vary significantly, based on the individual circumstances of the company and the goals for the initiative. Accordingly, the costs and timing of the process will vary also, depending on the activities undertaken. The scope of a strategy innovation initiative that is right for your company will typically depend on the following factors:

- ◆ Size of company
- ◆ Size of industry
- ◆ Type of industry
- ◆ Strategic frontier
- ◆ Degree of innovation desired

Size of Company

In general, larger companies have more resources available for strategy innovation than smaller companies. Yet the process of identifying new business opportunities is equally important, if not more important, for smaller companies to consider. The five-phase Discovery Process presented here is not dependent on a certain level of resources being available. We recommend that all companies carry out all five phases, regardless of how much time and money is spent on each phase. However, larger companies with their greater resources can afford to do more, on a larger scale, than the smaller companies can.

Larger companies, for example, can usually identify up to a

dozen people across all their functional areas that can be assigned to participate on the Discovery team. It is not unusual for each team member to be able to dedicate up to 20 to 25 percent of their time over a six-to-eight-months period for this initiative. In the Exploring Phase, larger-company budgets will allow for team travel across the country or across the world to participate in professionally organized meetings and customer visits. Depending on the scope, these global initiatives can last a year or more.

Smaller companies would experience this process very differently. With fewer people available, they might select three company executives and a college-age intern to participate in their Discovery Process. To take advantage of the availability of the intern, they may want to complete the entire initiative over the course of a summer, which is quite possible on a focused initiative. Instead of elaborate meetings at customer sites around the country or abroad, teams from smaller companies might concentrate their exploration efforts more on local visits with some customers, telephone interviews with others, and literature searches on marketplace trends via the Internet.

The implementation of the Discovery Process for strategy innovation is extremely flexible and can accommodate the different resources available in different size companies.

Size of Industry

Similar to company size, the size of the industry will also play a role in the scope of the Discovery Process. By size, we mean both the revenues generated and the number of industry "participants."

As you might imagine, being a strategic innovator in the multi-billion-dollar automobile industry will require a more significant Discovery Process than being an innovator in the unicycle market. The automobile industry is very complex, with many stakeholders (customers, suppliers, dealers, manufacturers, after-market suppliers, etc.) and market segments to explore. The Exploring Phase in the automobile industry would likely be quite extensive and take a great deal of time to implement. The unicycle market, on the other hand, probably consists of only a handful of manufacturers, a relatively limited number of distributors, and a small core of user/enthusiasts. Insight gathering in the Exploring Phase would be much simpler for the smaller, simpler unicycle market, requiring a Discovery Process that is much more limited in its scope and scale.

At the same time, making a significant impact on the automobile market through strategy innovation could result in significantly more revenue growth than making a significant impact on the unicycle market. The potentially higher return in automobiles would justify a greater investment in the Discovery Process in that industry than might be justified in unicycles.

Type of Industry

In addition to size of industry, the type of industry will also help dictate the scope of the Discovery Process. Industries undergoing a greater degree of change or transformation will usually require a more extensive Discovery Process than more stable markets. The reason is that it is more difficult to gain an understanding of a market's future if changes are taking place more rapidly. Very dynamic markets such as the telecommunications industry will have very complex forces at work—new products, new companies, new regulations, new technologies, and what some believe is an inevitable merging with the computer industry. Each market expert in the telecommunications industry may well describe a different emerging market scenario, making it difficult for your Discovery team to agree on what the future holds for the company. In these more dynamic markets, it may take multiple exploration efforts and a longer period of time before the future becomes visible and new business opportunities can be identified.

More stable markets are much simpler to explore because there are fewer future-changing forces to consider. A Discovery Process in the insurance industry, for example, would be a smaller scale effort than one in the telecommunications world.

Strategic Frontier

The selection of one or more strategic frontiers to be explored in the Discovery Process will have a critical impact on the size, scope, and timing of the initiative. A strategic frontier is a market, product, technology, or business process that lies beyond a company's current corporate strategy and business model. The identification of a single frontier allows the Discovery team to focus their efforts and activities in the Exploring Phase, interacting with one set of customers, projecting the future of one market, and seeking insights on a minimum number of business models. The selection of multiple frontiers will result in multiple explorations in these areas in order to best understand the opportunities available.

Besides the number of strategic frontiers being explored, the type of frontier will often dictate the activities necessary. As will be described in more detail in Chapter 8, insights on value in the frontier can be found along three different exploration vectors: customer value, market dynamics, and business model innovation. Some frontiers, such as repositioning the brand name or product to a different target audience, might require exploration in only one vector: the customer value vector. The insights from the new target audience would be most critical for the creation of a new business opportunity. On the other hand, leveraging an emerging technology may require exploration in all three vectors. Getting customer insights on the technology (customer value vector), a picture of how the future market might emerge (market dynamics vector), and an understanding of how to best organize for the new venture (business model innovation vector) will make that Discovery Process more complex.

Degree of Innovation Required

We saved the most important consideration for last. The scope and complexity of the Discovery Process is directly related to the degree of strategy innovation desired. Companies looking to identify new business opportunities that will create new-to-the-world markets and provide them with a unique, sustainable advantage over competition will need to plan on a robust, larger-scale Discovery Process commitment. These more visionary market opportunities will not emerge from merely holding a brainstorming session or two. It may require a longer-term effort for a team, or the company may decide to form two or three Discovery teams to pursue this level of strategy innovation simultaneously.

On the other hand, companies that have a new business opportunity already in mind and are searching only for a unique, strategic twist that will give it a proprietary advantage in the market will often find it after a brief, more concise Discovery Process.

The degree of innovation being sought is usually one of the first questions to be considered because it has a direct bearing on not only the scope of the Discovery Process, but the selection of the activities in that process.

Strategy Innovation by Degrees: Strategic Opportunity Spectrum

While Wal-Mart, Charles Schwab, and Dell are often among the poster-children of strategy innovation in business, they are not necessarily the norm. Strategy innovation does not have to be high-risk, market-creating new ventures that land their CEOs on the cover of *Fortune*. Strategy innovation just has to be something beyond today's strategy that provides new growth opportunities and/ or a competitive advantage in the marketplace. When a company opens its first sales office outside its home country, it is strategy innovation. When Time Inc. introduced *People* magazine, it was strategy innovation. When Nike used its brand name to enter the new markets of clothing and equipment, they were practicing strategy innovation.

There is a wide range of the degree of innovation that companies can target. We define this range of strategy innovation as a Strategic Opportunity Spectrum, or SOS (see Figure 4-2). On one end of the spectrum are strategy innovations such as expanding sales offices, product offerings, and brand names into other markets. These are "visible" opportunities. They are not necessarily new-to-the-world markets or breakthrough products, but they do represent new value provided to customers and to your company, which makes them strategy innovations for you. Visible opportunities are likely to be

Figure 4-2. Strategic Opportunity Spectrum.

strategic options that management has been aware of for some time but which just need to be studied and defined before they can be introduced.

Parked at the other end of the Strategic Opportunity Spectrum are the classics of strategy innovation, such as Federal Express, amazon.com, and Starbucks, among many others. These are "visionary" opportunities because they required visionary thinking to create them. The markets that these companies dominate did not exist before they created them. They were created to provide value where customers did not realize they had needs. The moves were bold, considered risky by some, but resulted in the establishment of new-to-the-world products, services, and markets.

As with all spectra, the middle represents strategy innovations that fall somewhere between the visible and visionary ends. There are no hard-and-fast rules of how to categorize the level of innovation and where new innovative products or services belong on the spectrum. Think of this middle ground as consisting of products and services in already-existing markets, but ones that redefine those markets or represent a dramatic change over how that market has traditionally operated. Southwest Airlines is an example of a company that created an innovative strategy between the visible and visionary ends—a unique business model introduced to an existing marketplace. Digital cameras, wireless telephones, and electrostatic cloth sweepers might also be innovations that fall in the middle of the SOS.

Key Elements for Strategy Innovation

Strategy innovation can be done in a company on a one-time, ad hoc basis. Most of the examples contained in this book come from initiatives carried out by ad hoc teams. However, there is growing interest in the development of an internal capability for strategy innovation. Some of the elements necessary for developing a formalized, ongoing capability for strategy innovation can be found in Chapter 12.

Whether it is done on an ad hoc or ongoing basis, strategy innovation in any corporation must consist of the following four elements:

1. Management mandate
2. Corporate infrastructure
3. Innovation process
4. Corporate culture

Management Mandate

It is not until senior management in a company commits to strategy innovation that the company will respond. Employees will generally set their time commitments to be consistent with the perceived commitment of their management team. Therefore, the stronger the management mandate for strategy innovation, the sooner a higher-quality initiative will be accomplished. For a company looking to build strategy innovation as a core capability, this mandate must be built into its business systems.

Corporate infrastructure.

The infrastructure requirements for strategy innovation can be fairly simple, consisting of a team of people and some funding. Suggestions on finding the "right" people for the team will be examined in detail in Chapter 6, Staging Phase. For larger companies, the team should be a diverse, cross-functional team of eight to twelve people in upper-middle management who will have some responsibility for implementing new strategic initiatives in the company. Smaller companies will target teams of four to six people and include people who are directly involved with strategic decisions within the company. The team must have a captain to guide the process and a senior-level executive sponsor to fund it.

Funding requirements for a strategy innovation initiative will range significantly, depending on the size of the company, its industry, and how aggressive the team wants to be in exploring their strategic frontiers. Some companies have undertaken strategy innovation initiatives that cost in the $50,000 range, while others (usually large, global businesses) have had budgets well into the seven digits. It is the team that estimates the budget, based on the activities they identify as important to pursue.

Innovation Process

A good team needs a good process for how to go about creating new business opportunities that lead to strategy innovation. The Discovery Process is designated to meet that need. The five phases, described in detail in the next section, are designed to provide needed structure but allow for flexibility of activities within the phases to accommodate a wide range of industries and corporations.

Corporate Culture

If a strategy innovation initiative is being done on an ad hoc basis, the team can create for itself the type of creative, collaborative, and entrepreneurial environment or culture necessary for its success. However, if a company wants to develop a formalized strategy innovation capability, then there may need to be adjustments to the corporate culture to allow it to flourish. More cultural implications can be found in Chapter 12, Formalizing a Strategy Innovation System.

Output of the Discovery Process

The Discovery Process will yield a portfolio of new business opportunities that leverage the emerging trends in the marketplace and the needs of potential customers. In the Discovery Process, your team will seek out new insights on customer needs and their perception of value after talking to and observing potential customers in new ways. They will also learn of trends, market dynamics, and potential discontinuities in your industry as they work with experts to understand the emerging markets of the future. New business models being used successfully by companies in other industries will also offer insights on new ways of doing business.

Overall, there are three tangible outputs from this process:

1. The *insights* gained from the customer, market dynamics, and new business models are an important output of this process. Creating a database of these insights and sharing them with everyone in the organization will help stimulate new thinking and new ideas internally.

2. The insights will be used as the basis for the creation of a *portfolio of innovative new business concepts.* These concepts will range from short-term business opportunities to longer-term opportunities, providing your company with a valuable portfolio of strategic options for your future.

3. A third output of the Discovery Process is a *strategic road map* assembled by the team. On the basis of the new business opportunities that have strongest potential for the company, the team will create a strategic road map outlining a future plan based on implementation strategies and key marketplace factors.

The output from the Discovery Process will then advance to your in-house evaluation process for new business opportunities. There, the leading opportunities will undergo the quantitative scrutiny that is critical for determining market viability and financial attractiveness to your company. Business opportunities that receive the green light will then be ready for consideration in the company's strategic planning process (see Figure 4-3).

Although not every company is a Procter & Gamble, any company can be inspired by the success of their Corporate and Sector

Figure 4-3. The Discovery Process integrated to strategic planning.

New Venture groups. These groups have infused new thinking, new growth, and new profits into this global consumer products giant. They have achieved this by identifying new insights to support the development of a portfolio of strategically innovative new business concepts, including the Swiffer mop, Crest White Strips, and ThermaCare self-heating pads. Over a four-year stretch, these groups conceived, developed, and helped launch "a third of all new U.S. packaged products with yearly sales above $100 million." While, by almost any measure, this level of success would be labeled a string of "home runs," each innovation was inspired by a new insight of a basic human need.

Risks Involved in the Discovery Process

There is very little at risk with a strategy innovation initiative, other than the time and money invested by the team. The internal team sets the overall budget so that costs (primarily in the Exploring Phase) can be controlled to whatever level represents a reasonable investment in the company's future.

We have never encountered an initiative where discussions with customers and industry experts did not lead to valuable insights for the company. The only question is whether the impact of those insights represents a significant business opportunity for the company (or only a minor business opportunity) and whether the company will choose to follow up with them.

Other things to watch for as critical success factors that can affect overall results include:

- The selection of the Discovery team, where lack of diversity in functions and skills can limit the quality of the output.

- The breadth and commitment of the management mandate to the team, as small mandates tend to produce small results.

- Alignment with senior management perspectives on the business, which greatly enhances the usefulness of the resulting portfolio of new business opportunities.

- The pursuit of *new* insights on customers and the marketplace, using techniques that are new to the company.

- The creativity of the team's working environment, where the identification of new business opportunities is not constrained by the company's current business model.

- The collaborative nature of the team's working environment, so that opportunities have cross-functional internal support.

Type of Company to Benefit from Strategy Innovation

A strategy innovation process may not be right for every company. However, it is difficult to cite what type of company would not benefit from understanding their customers better, gaining valuable foresight about their emerging marketplace, and considering how changes in their business model could provide a competitive advantage. If your company fulfills these requirements, you can benefit from a strategy innovation initiative or an ongoing strategy innovation process.

Listed below are those types of companies where strategy innovation would be most valuable:

- Companies that no longer want to compete on the basis of a similar, "commodity" product in the market
- Companies that seek a sustainable competitive advantage
- Companies looking to change their strategic direction
- Companies searching for the next growth platform for their business
- Companies that need new growth opportunities to meet long-term revenue goals
- Companies that are in declining markets
- Companies that have streamlined and downsized their businesses to improve the bottom line and now need to find profit improvements in growing the top line
- Companies facing a competitive threat and that need to respond with new ways to deliver customer value
- Companies looking to aggressively increase market share
- Companies that need to define a corporate mission or vision
- Companies that value management collaboration in the development of strategy

The following corporate environments are impractical for, or resistant to, a strategy innovation process and the new thinking it provides:

- Companies with a command-and-control management style
- Companies that have chosen to be a "fast-follower" or "low-cost provider" in their markets
- Companies where the collaborative culture is overshadowed by corporate politics

So, while it may not be right for every company, a strategy innovation process can be applied to many different types of companies and address many different corporate situations where new growth in new ways is the goal. What type of company is your company?

How might strategy innovation be incorporated to your strategic planning process?

In the next chapter, we provide an actual case study that will provide you with an understanding of how the strategy innovation process can work in a company. Following the case, we outline how to carry out the process through a detailed explanation of the five phases of the process.

Summary

- The Discovery Process is a market-tested approach for creating a portfolio of innovative new business opportunities for your corporation, leading to strategy innovation.

- The Discovery Process is a series of phases to guide a corporate team in doing cross-functional work at the strategic level. It is extremely flexible and can accommodate the different resources available in different size companies.

- The Discovery Process consists of the following phases:

  1. *Staging Phase.* In this phase, the Discovery team is selected, key roles are identified, the objectives of the initiative are established, and the team is prepared for the process.

  2. *Aligning Phase.* The Discovery team and senior management align themselves on the focus and scope of the initiative, agreeing on the "strategic frontier(s)" to be explored.

  3. *Exploring Phase.* The goal of this phase is the collection of new insights on the strategic frontier that can form the basis of new, value-producing business opportunities in the future. Depending on the strategic frontier and the scope of the initiative, teams will explore insights related to different exploration "vectors," including customer value, market dynamics, and/or business model innovation.

  4. *Creating Phase.* Using the new insights gained, the Discovery team will create and refine a portfolio of new business opportunities for the future.

5. *Mapping Phase.* In this final phase, the team will create a strategic road map outlining key events, trends, market discontinuities, and milestones to move the company into its new strategic future.

- The scope, timing, and costs for each Discovery Process will differ, based on size of company, size of industry, type of industry, the strategic frontier identified, and the degree of innovation desired.

- There is a wide range of the degree of innovation that companies can target, defined here as a Strategic Opportunity Spectrum. On one end of the spectrum are "visible" opportunities, representing nearer-term, lower-risk businesses that often extend the current business into new but established markets. On the other end of the spectrum are "visionary" opportunities, those longer-term, higher-risk businesses that introduce breakthrough products or establish new markets or industries.

- Companies can implement the Discovery Process on an ad hoc, initiative basis to meet a product line need or formalize it as an ongoing strategy innovation system. In either case, strategy innovation requires attention to four key elements—process, infrastructure (resources), mandate from management, and culture.

- Three tangible outputs from the Discovery Process include the insights gained from the Exploring Phase (into customers, market dynamics, and business model innovations), a portfolio of innovative new business opportunities based on those insights, and a strategic road map outlining a future plan based on implementation strategies and marketplace factors.

- There is very little at risk and much to be gained with a strategy innovation initiative, and nearly any company can benefit from one—learning more about their customers, the emerging marketplace, and new business model options.

PART TWO

A GUIDE FOR IMPLEMENTATION

CHAPTER 5

THE DISCOVERY PROCESS

The Moen Story

> Transformation takes place when a new worldview re-
> places an old one.
>
> —*WILLIAM MILLER*

While Southwest Airlines, IKEA, Charles Schwab, and other high-profile entrepreneurial companies tend to be associated with the concept of strategy innovation, they are not the only examples that exist. Strategy innovation does not always begin with a visionary founder in a start-up mode—it can happen in fifty-plus-year-old companies. It does not always germinate in technology-oriented companies—it can happen in companies that bend metal for their main business. It does not have to create a whole new industry—it can happen in companies that just want to grow their businesses.

To illustrate how strategy innovation (specifically the Discovery Process) can be implemented within a corporation, we selected an example from a quality, existing company in a very common industry, plumbing products. The company is Moen, located in a suburb of Cleveland, Ohio. Here is their story.

The internationally known Moen corporation has a long history of "firsts" in the plumbing products industry. It created the first single-handle faucet, the first washerless cartridge system, and a "swing 'n spray" aerator, which can change a faucet's water flow from a stream to a forceful spray. It was the first company to develop a family of versatile faucets that could be lifted up to ten inches above a sink, and among the first to introduce pressure-balanced shower valves, as well as customer-friendly lifetime warranties and a toll-free help line.

Challenge for Growth

Yet in the early 1990s, this North Olmsted, Ohio–based company found itself in a challenging situation. Moen had just been purchased by American Brands (now Fortune Brands), and Bruce Carbonari had been installed as its new CEO. In assessing the company and its growth prospects, Carbonari quickly determined that he must transform the company in order for it to grow. The company was losing market share—it had become a distant number two brand in the market. It was also not positioned well for the changes that were beginning to take place in the market.

Moen's prior success had been achieved by focusing on faucet engineering and manufacturing. This was the approach to business that founder Al Moen established when he created that first single-handle faucet more than six decades earlier. The company's success as the number two brand in the plumbing products market was to make quality products and distribute them through plumbing wholesalers. Product styling, company marketing, and retail distribution were minor considerations in their business model.

But these old ways of competing would not sustain the new growth goals in the dynamic plumbing products market of the early 1990s. Female consumers were making more and more design decisions for kitchens and bathrooms, and they were looking for products that were as fashionable as they were practical. The number of shelter magazines and home shows was increasing to further fuel this interest in home renovation and design. At the same time, big-box retailers were changing how plumbing products were being merchandised and purchased, making them more accessible to the average homeowner. In a short time, Moen's strategic landscape had become dramatically more complex than simply selling a technically superior faucet to a plumbing wholesaler.

So CEO Bruce Carbonari started thinking about how to reposition the company for the future:

> These realities going on around us made it easier for us to start looking at change, because we knew we had no choice. We were the number two player, and dramatically smaller than the number one player. Roughly 90 percent of our sales were from products designed in the 1960s—and obviously not selling as well as we wanted. We needed to change, to evolve, and to get to a new and more sophisticated business model.
>
> But before we could change our product or how we do business, we had to change the way we viewed the business and, really, the entire culture of the company. Moen was a metal-bending company, not a consumer-driven one. We were a company with great faucet technology. But our faucets were of such great quality that most people only bought a new one every nine years. Our products were practical, but not designed with consumer input, and certainly not exciting. And exciting is what we needed.

The infrequent purchase rate of a Moen faucet, once every nine years on average, became a focus of Carbonari's new internal strategy for corporate transformation. Calling his new strategy *9-to-5*, he challenged his employees to create a company that produced such stylish and innovative products that consumers would be interested in purchasing new ones every five years, instead of nine years.

The company responded. New people and business processes were put in place to increase the flow of new, consumer-focused product lines. As new products were introduced to the market, sales increased, and Moen was back on a growth track. By 1994, however, Carbonari recognized that Moen needed even greater growth to achieve their corporate goals in the increasingly competitive marketplace.

Although Moen was doing a good job in developing new products, they did not have a reliable process for the identification of new products. Many different people within the company had many different ideas of what should be produced. They needed a way to determine a corporate strategy and accompanying product plan that would help them to meet the higher growth rate they desired.

Identifying Champions for Growth

The first thing he had to do was to get the organization aligned on the goal and get a group to lead the journey required to achieve it. To do this, Carbonari charged three members of his management team—Dan Buchner, director of new product concepts; Maureen Wenmoth, director of marketing services; and Tim O'Brien, director of technology innovation—to put together a diverse, cross-functional team from within Moen. Their challenge would be to lead the team in the creation of a "future product road map," outlining how Moen would achieve its growth goals over the next five-year period.

Carbonari and the Moen senior management team agreed that for the company to succeed, it needed the following from this internal team:

- ♦ A five-year strategic product road map
- ♦ A proactive competitive strategy
- ♦ Organization-wide commitment on the goal of being No. 1 in the industry
- ♦ Foresight on significant trends and events for the future
- ♦ An exploration of new technologies
- ♦ A shift from being "engineering driven" to being "consumer driven"

This last point—being consumer-driven—was very important to Carbonari. He believed that "you can be visionary, but if consumers aren't with you, and don't want your product, who cares?"

So with these considerations in mind, plus Carbonari's promise to provide the necessary support, Buchner, Wenmoth and O'Brien began wrestling with the identification of ingredients for success—engaging the right people, scheduling sufficient time, and allocating appropriate dollars. In other words, they had to figure out how to harness and organize Moen's talent and assets to move a plumbing fixtures company to a new level of excitement and innovation in the industry.

Organizing for Success

The tri-captains focused their initial efforts on forming the team that could meet this challenge. Buchner, Wenmoth, and O'Brien did not want employees who were comfortable with the status quo at Moen. They also did not want team members representing only senior management (senior vice presidents and above). Nor, for that matter, did they want team members whose contributions might be constrained by personal or political agendas for this project. They wanted to enlist individuals who were known to have "open minds," a track record for innovation, a collaborative style, and a passion about the future of Moen.

With these criteria and after a lot of back-and-forth, Buchner, Wenmoth, and O'Brien handpicked a team that represented a horizontal slice of directors, managers, and vice presidents from the marketing, research, product development, engineering, sales, operations, IT, finance, and advertising departments—a total of eleven team members. The group named itself the "Project Periscope Team," and appropriately so. Like a periscope, its mission was to examine Moen's future landscape from a position out of the direct line of sight. And like a submarine captain, Periscope team captain Buchner was at first unsure what the Moen Periscope team would see. According to Buchner:

> With a project this big, it's not initially possible to think too far ahead, or get a detailed implementation plan from the start. So the most important thing we needed to focus

on here was the people. We needed people who were flexible and available and committed. People who cared about the company, but weren't overly concerned about the impact change would have on their functional area. Several times, I had to go back to managers and say, "No, I want someone else from your department" because the person they recommended was not bringing the right level of talent to the team or was not passionate enough.

The group committed to meeting weekly, or more often as the process and activities demanded. Buchner, Wenmoth, and O'Brien, as tri-captains, would invest more time, typically by arriving to work before others did or working later. In addition to this critical Periscope role and responsibility, the tri-captains also kept their "day jobs."

Additionally, an Extended Periscope team was formed, consisting of the key "doers" and "decision makers" from within Moen. Their involvement was designed to deepen the alignment among the decision makers and accelerate the implementation of the strategy once the process was complete. Involving CEO Carbonari, the senior vice presidents, and a carefully selected cadre of proven Moen innovators, this extended team would be engaged primarily for those events designed to yield customer insights or to identify and examine future marketplace trends. They would then have the opportunity to provide assistance to the Periscope team in its task of conceiving and developing new business concepts based on this new knowledge.

How often does the level of talent and experience represented on Moen's Periscope team and Extended Periscope team come together in any organization to focus on the future? In Moen's history, this was a first.

With the teams identified, Buchner, Wenmoth, and O'Brien worked to develop a common foundation of Moen knowledge so that everyone involved in the process would have a baseline of information on which to build throughout the process. This briefing document covered topics that would make up the Periscope "lens" through which each participant might more accurately view Moen's preferred future. The composition of this lens included current company competencies, resources, talents, and strengths. It also outlined areas for possible strategic growth and, perhaps most importantly, acknowledged the company's weaknesses. One weakness brought to light by the process was Moen's practice of using the "gaps" or "holes" in a competitor's line of products to dictate the type of new products Moen would develop. According to Tim O'Brien:

> In essence, we were letting the competition create our business strategies, and that, obviously, is not how things should be done. The central lesson from the brief was that to do things differently, we needed to see things differently.

Gaining a New Perspective

To see things differently, Moen enlisted the assistance of someone whose profession was seeing human behavior in a deeper, more insightful way—a cultural anthropologist. This anthropologist visited more than twenty homes and businesses across the country to observe how people use water and what role it played in their lives. He watched and photographed people doing the dinner dishes, washing their pet lizards, filling their pools, running through the sprinkler, hosing down the driveway, washing their cars, and bathing their children, among other things. He tracked people's moods, happiness levels, and feelings of satisfaction while carrying out each of these activities, plus how they felt when they were done. He wrote down how long each action took, and documented how people moved and adjusted their water faucet for the needs of that activity. He rated the importance people placed on water safety, flow, and efficiency, as well as the effectiveness and aesthetics of each fixture. The fun factor of each activity was rated too. He observed and noted the differences between the habits of men and women in their handling of fixtures. The final report from the cultural anthropologist did an excellent job of cataloging water use

among consumers, providing the Periscope team with a much
broader understanding of the uses and implications of their product line. As Maureen Wenmoth noted:

> The results of this insight safari was that people wanted
> more than just functioning faucets. We thought we knew
> all about water and faucet needs, and why not? Moen had
> been in the water business for many decades. But, by never
> before conducting observational research, we really were
> missing out on a lot. We were also limiting ourselves by
> working in self-created boundaries. We were working
> under the pretense that water is a commodity element—
> something people want and need. But the reality is that
> it's not so cut-and-dried. Water is many different things to
> different people. Yes, it's something people need. But it's
> also something they want to enjoy using and receiving. The
> information confirmed that we needed to be consumer-
> driven and think not just about faucets, but how they re-
> late to a room, use, or surrounding space. Our future de-
> manded it.

Enlightened by a new perspective on consumer behavior in and
around water, the Periscope team wanted additional opinions or
information on how this behavior might evolve or be influenced to
change in the future. If this is our consumer today, who will be our
consumer tomorrow? What will the world look like five years from
now? What will be the key forces that could drive change in the
marketplace? To create a "future view" to add to their newly found
consumer worldview, the Periscope team decided to enlist the help
and stimulation of a dozen globally recognized "thought leaders"
from different areas of targeted expertise.

Bringing the Outside World Inside

Although the Periscope team was confident that an infusion of outside-the-company perspectives would be a positive stimulus, there

was still some anxiety around picking the right topics and the right people to represent those topics. Observed Buchner, "The selection of the thought leaders and anticipating their interaction with our internal staff was an anxious time. Could we create a good outcome? We had lots of strong-willed people who had ideas that vertical integration was the way for us to go. What happens when you throw someone like a futurist into that discussion?"

The team decided that twelve thought leaders would be invited to two separate events. The first event, designed to provide Moen with a comprehensive "macro" view ten years out, would cover a series of broad topics. To identify these topics, Moen employees were asked if they could somehow, magically, achieve perfect knowledge, what would be the most urgent questions, the hottest issues, and the most enlightening topics to be addressed by a team of outside-the-company experts? The result of this exercise was a series of topics for the first thought leader panel, which included water quality, cost and availability, environmental regulation, trends in residential construction and building techniques, the relationship between people and water, the evolution and emergence of distribution channels, functionality and design in the homes of the future, trends in consumer purchasing options, and technologies and materials development of the future.

The First Panel

At this point, the recruiting of six thought leaders for this first panel began. Hundreds of people were contacted in order to identify the six that could best cover the topic areas. Thought leaders were selected based on both their knowledge of the topics and their style in communicating it. Thought leaders, to be effective in this role, needed to be confident of their expertise, open to being influenced by other thought leaders and the Moen team, and able to communicate their knowledge in an easy-to-comprehend way. These desired attributes in a thought leader made the search more daunting, but in the end successful. The selected thought leaders were then coached very carefully on how to play the role of "provocateur" in this panel, instead of an "expert with the answer." The goal was to stir up the thinking of the Periscope team and the Extended Periscope team, not to tell them what to do.

The first thought leader event was very successful. The thought leaders shared their perspectives, covered the topics well, and, most importantly, caused the Moen teams to think more broadly about their business. They learned that people outside the company had important perceptions and experiences that could help drive the move to a new growth strategy for Moen. "Short of clairvoyance, this was the best process for determining future wants and needs," says O'Brien. "It enabled us to look at, and be guided by, the present and the future, rather than the past."

The Second Panel

The second thought leader event was designed to deepen and advance the learnings of the first event. While the first panel had been intended to provide a wide-angle perspective on the industry's future landscape, this second gathering of thought leaders was focused on what it would take to have Moen's new business concepts and models successfully developed and launched into the marketplace. The thought leaders for this event were recruited for their expertise in kitchen and bath design, changing consumer values and lifestyles, water regulation and conservation, and trends in construction and building design.

The Probability of Terrorism

During the second event, a trend surfaced that had the potential to become an industry-wide discontinuity in the future—"environmental terrorism." In 1995—almost seven years before 9/11—multiple thought leaders had forecast the probability of terrorists purposely polluting or poisoning a public water supply with the intent to harm or kill many people. Following such a catastrophic event, it would be hard to imagine a parent drawing tap water from a faucet and then handing it to a child. The Periscope team heard from multiple experts that, regarding environmental terrorism, it

was not a question of whether it would happen, but when. Consequently, it was not difficult for the team to see the need at some
point in the future for a product that would filter pollutants and
poisons from a home faucet and signal when it was safe to drink.
Maureen Wenmoth observed:

> These were people who saw, and knew firsthand, how peo-
> ple want to use water, from many different perspectives
> and areas of expertise. They gave us a deeper understand-
> ing of the topic. How people want water faucets that are as
> safe as they are attractive. How they want fixtures that
> don't actually look like fixtures. And so on. Water safety,
> in fact, was a recurring theme that really got us thinking
> and focusing on the potential importance of water filtra-
> tion.

With new perspectives and knowledge from the cultural anthropologist and the thought leader events, the Periscope team was
ready to start creating a robust portfolio of new business opportunities. In a series of sessions, they created a wide range of opportunities, spanning the short-, middle-, and longer-term time horizon
for their five-year plan. To combat the probable trend of environmental terrorism and assure water safety, the Periscope team conceived a new product/business concept they called "PureTouch." It
would be the world's first faucet with a built-in filter and electronic
signal to indicate when the water is safe to drink. Moen partnered
with Culligan, a leading water filtration company, to provide the
replaceable filter in PureTouch. The innovative business design for
PureTouch provided new growth potential for Moen via follow-up
filter purchases by those who bought the product.

Since Carbonari, his executive staff, and American Brands management had all been members of the Extended Team and involved
throughout the process, there was no need for the Periscope team
to do the traditional "selling" of their new business concepts up the
corporate ladder. Instead, the time and energy typically invested in
selling senior management at the back end of a process was freed

up to do more and better future planning. So the Periscope team, using tailored market research, did additional fine-tuning of their new business concepts and the five-year road map. The Moen Future Road Map described a preferred future for Moen as it looked to compete in the plumbing products market for the next five years. It outlined the major events, milestones, and potential conditions of the world and marketplace over that time, including such things as:

- Target launch dates for new products, with key milestones
- Anticipated trends and significant events at retail, with consumers, and in government regulations
- Probable competitive tactics and responses

As Dan Buchner explained:

> We took the output from the thought leader panels and built a detailed Future Map that captured our new learnings regarding the industry, the economy, and our competition, anticipating what might happen over the next five years. We updated the Future Map as part of our annual planning. It helped us focus and showed us the difficult decisions that we would have to make. Before, we had been trying to do everything in the marketplace, so the map helped us focus our attention and our efforts. The events on our Future Map played out faster than we expected. Three-quarters of the things happened, but in half the time that we expected.

It took several years of intense development and problem-solving for Moen to actually produce PureTouch. In the process, the company brought in new people with new skill sets to broaden its ability to create innovative products. They also set up systems to efficiently develop new products and take them to market. The Moen tradition of engineering excellence would remain essential to product development. But also added to their development strategies was a closer examination of water containment, water forming, the water-user interface, valving, product intelligence, installation/retrofit, treatment, temperature, and style.

It was the development and launch of PureTouch, along with other similarly innovative products, that significantly changed Moen. No longer did Moen view itself as merely a faucet company. With their new internal slogan H2O-4-U ("water for you"), team members were set to position Moen as a full-service water supply company, offering "Water the way you want it." In the market-place, this new product line and new company attitude signaled to consumers and the plumbing products trade that Moen was serious about their new, long-term strategy of "leadership through innova-tion."

Award-Winning Innovation Spurs Growth

The PureTouch Filtering Faucet System won *Popular Science's* pres-tigious "Product of the Year" award for 1999 (along with the new Volkswagen Beetle and Viagra!). Awards are nice, but for some on the team, it was almost as satisfying when the CEO of a leading competitor was discovered, by an after-hours security camera at a major trade show, fondling an early PureTouch model. And, within six months of PureTouch hitting the shelves, Moen became the number one brand in North American residential faucets.

Fast forward to the end of 2002. Moen has tripled in size and is pushing $1 billion in sales. Its market share is up 72 percent since the early 1990s, and the brand is now number one in consumer awareness in all of Moen's product categories. Bruce Carbonari is now the CEO of Fortune Brands Home and Hardware. Maureen Wenmoth and Tim O'Brien have been promoted to vice presidents at Moen, and Dan Buchner has taken a position leading the Indus-trial Design group for Design Continuum, an international design firm.

In assessing the success of the Periscope project, many believe that this strategy innovation initiative was the catalyst for creating

organizational alignment around a number of new growth platforms for the company. The resulting development of internal systems and capabilities for those platforms allowed the company to
launch a series of new products that fueled company growth for the
next five years, keeping Moen the industry leader and allowing
them to meet their financial targets.

As this book is being written, Moen has recommitted to its strategy of "leadership through innovation" by launching a new five-
year strategy innovation initiative, called Periscope II.

Strategy innovation can have a dramatic impact on a company's
growth and its future. Identifying the business opportunities for
strategy innovation is a process that can be carried out in any company willing to make the commitment to it. In the next five chapters, we describe the process used by Moen in their successful
transformation. Use it in your company to eliminate the dreaded
delta, navigate the whitewater of your changing marketplace, or re-
vitalize your business. You too can do it.

CHAPTER 6

THE DISCOVERY PROCESS

Staging Phase

> Producing major change in an organization is not just
> about signing up one charismatic leader. You need a
> group—a team—to be able to drive the change. One
> person, even a terrific charismatic leader, is never
> strong enough to make all this happen.
>
> —*JOHN KOTTER*

| Staging Phase | Aligning Phase | Exploring Phase | Creating Phase | Mapping Phase |

The Staging Phase is the creation and preparation of an internal team for a strategy innovation initiative. The Staging Phase consists of three important activities:

1. Creating the right team and support structure

2. Creating the right working environment

3. Implementing the staging meeting

These three activities are driven by the internal sponsor of the Discovery Process and coordinated by the Discovery team captain. Their efforts culminate in the launching of the strategy innovation initiative.

Initiating the Discovery Process: The Importance of a Management Mandate

It is senior management that is responsible for the creation of the corporate strategy. They have the corporate perspective necessary to understand the strengths and weaknesses of the current business model and its implications for the future. They can foresee when the current business model may be incapable of meeting the needs of all of its stakeholders. They know when the current corporate strategy may not be sufficient to remain viable in a dynamic marketplace. Therefore, it is essential that senior management initiate the call for new strategic options and commit to the pursuit of a stronger, more innovative corporate strategy.

Regardless of who first identifies the need for strategy innovation, it is critical that the senior management level makes a commitment to the effort. A successful initiative requires this commitment because it signals to the Discovery team and the rest of the organization that their efforts are important and are making a meaningful contribution to the long-term success of the organization. When the team sees that commitment, they, too, will be committed to the effort.

This mandate from senior management for strategy innovation may be the single most critical element in the ultimate success of the initiative. Teams that believe that their work will likely result in a positive impact on the organization will be much more engaged and productive than those who believe that their work is just another corporate program. At the very least, we encourage corporate CEOs to communicate the importance of this effort directly to the team. To the extent that this mandate for strategy innovation can be expressed even more forcefully—such as the commitment to enter one new market every two years or to have a certain percentage of revenue from products less than five years old—it will significantly boost the team's commitment and energy level.

A number of companies have benefited significantly from a senior management commitment to strategy innovation. At 3M, the most recent CEOs, Desi DeSimone and now James McNerney, carry the banner for breakthrough strategy innovation by inspiring the business units and labs to innovate beyond, for example, the next Post-it Note line extension. During his tenure as CEO of IBM, it was Lou Gerstner who, to drive innovation, would routinely visit IBM Research to communicate customer "needs" he had observed during his travels. At Procter & Gamble, it was CEO John Pepper and COO Durk Jager who sponsored and maintained a direct link with Corporate New Ventures, helping steer and support the discovery of "white space" opportunities for that consumer packaged-goods giant. At Moen, the CEO Bruce Carbonari championed the importance of strategy innovation to both dramatically grow his business and, importantly, remold his organization's culture from a commodity producer of faucets to a leading edge innovator of new kitchen and bath products. At Barclays Global Investors, it was the CEO for Global Individual Investor Business, Garrett Bouton, who sponsored and shepherded the creation of iShares, a breakthrough in publicly traded index funds. Indeed, the larger surprise for us would be the identification of a company with the capacity for strategy innovation where senior management is *not* directly engaged as champion and primary supporter of those efforts.

When senior management commits to a strategy innovation initiative, they are agreeing that there is value in each of the following:

+ Involving an internal team of managers in the development and implementation of corporate strategy

+ Using the emerging marketplace and the needs of customers in the formulation of a corporate strategy

+ Considering new business opportunities that may require some change to the current business model (infrastructure, processes, or resource allocation)

Of these three, it is senior management's unwillingness to consider changes in the current business model that most often derails successful strategy innovation initiatives. Discovery teams *will* identify exciting new business opportunities for the future. However, the pursuit of those opportunities often requires, for example, the creation of a new distribution channel, the licensing of a new technology, the outsourcing of a critical skill, or the establishment of a new partnership in order to meet these new customer needs. When management will not consider any changes to its current business model as part of the future strategy, they are wasting the potential of strategy innovation. It is better to observe and follow the lead of companies like 3M, IBM, P&G, Moen, and Barclays, among many others that we will present in these chapters, to consider new corporate structures when necessary to harness the full potential of strategy innovation.

Creating the Right Team and Support Structure

Why an internal team for strategy innovation? The history of strategy innovation in the corporate world is filled with examples of brilliant strategies identified by insightful and talented individuals. Sam Walton of Wal-Mart, Steve Jobs of Apple, Fred Smith of Federal Express, and Howard Shultz of Starbucks are frequently cited for their abilities to perceive a need in the marketplace and conceive of a unique business model to meet that need. Because of their success as individuals, wouldn't it seem better to assign one or two of your best people to do strategy innovation rather than create an internal team to do it?

A Corporate Team, Not a Lone Pioneer

We believe that a corporate team is the most successful approach for identifying and developing innovative business opportunities. A team of dedicated people can outperform an individual in identifying new business opportunities because of the following factors:

1. New ideas require different perspectives
2. Complexity requires support
3. Successful implementation requires alignment

Different Perspectives

Identifying innovative business opportunities requires a new way of looking at customers and the marketplace. Taking on a new perspective can be difficult for people who have developed or supported the current view of customers and the marketplace. A team of people with diverse perspectives is more likely than a lone pioneer to be able to see the world differently. In addition, the process of discovering new business opportunities requires both right-brain creative skills to identify a new customer need and left-brain rational skills to create the appropriate business model to meet that need. Unless the designated strategist is mentally gifted, a team of people with a mix of different perspectives and thinking skills is much more effective in this process of strategy innovation.

Complexity

The process of creating an innovative strategy for a corporation is not a simple one. There are many issues and questions to address, many options to consider, and much uncertainty in the decision-making process due to an inability to accurately quantify the future. In this complex and often ambiguous journey, a team of people can offer support and problem-solving ideas to each other where an individual would have to shoulder the entire burden alone.

Alignment

The most important reason for using a team is the need for gaining internal agreement or "alignment" with the strategy being developed. Many of the famous strategy innovators of the past started their own companies and did not have to deal with the often shark-infested waters of a complex bureaucratic organization. If you ever had an idea where you needed support from a variety of other functional areas in your company in order to implement it, you know that "convincing" others of a need to change is a daunting task. Aligning others, who often have a different set of needs and priorities, can take a long time. It often requires persistence, diplomacy, good luck, and maybe some political horse-trading to align all parties to bring a new idea to fruition. How many market-changing innovations have not seen the light of day because their inventors could not get the necessary cooperation or could not convince other functional groups of their viability?

Internal, cross-functional teams greatly enhance the internal alignment process. When the team members from different functional areas together hear customers complain about the call center or the redesigned packaging, they do not need to spend time understanding, questioning, or verifying the problem. Rather than trying to decide who is to blame and who must solve the problem, they brainstorm potential solutions together. When faced with reporting their findings back to management, they unite around their preferred solution together. The process of internal alignment for strategic action is made significantly easier when a cross-functional team is involved rather than a lone strategy creator.

Bob LaPerle was a director of business planning in the photographic products group at Kodak in the early 1990s when he helped organize a critical strategy innovation initiative for that photographic giant. He recalls:

> **Process Tip:**
>
> *People support what they help create.*
>
> If you have played a role in the creation or development of something, you are much more likely to be committed to it than if you were not involved. You know the thinking that went into it, the trade-offs that were made, the problems and issues that were addressed, the time invested. Your fingerprints are on it. You are proud of your group's output and want to see it implemented. You will help defend it, if necessary. People support what they help create.

> I had no staff and no budget, so how was I going to make a difference? Pulling together the folks from the business units and R&D in a cross-functional team was key. It made a huge difference when we went to the first thought leader panel. There we found out together what industries were likely to interface with photography in the future. As a result, we gained agreement on a dramatic change in the R&D spending. It was a significant shift in spending away from silver halide projects towards projects aimed at digital photography and hybrid approaches.

Think about the impact on your company if there were a team of people across all functional areas that was aligned around the company strategy and committed to its implementation. The strategy would have momentum from its wide-ranging support and would probably help speed the time to market. What if that small team were supplemented by a much larger group of managers that had also been involved in the process at critical points and felt a similar sense of "ownership" and commitment to it? The impact on the efficient and coordinated implementation of your corporate strategy would be significant. That is the power of a team approach to strategy innovation.

Key Roles in the Discovery Process

Participation in the Discovery Process will vary for each corporation based primarily on its size and reporting structure. For a small company with fewer layers of management, members of the senior management team would be directly involved in the process. Because these team members are also the strategy decision makers in the company, the Discovery team would, by definition, always be aligned with the interests and perspectives of senior management. In the case of smaller companies, the Discovery team needs only to select a cross-functional team and appoint a team captain.

In larger corporations with much more complex organization charts, the selection of the team and identification of roles requires more careful consideration. The primary reason for this is that Discovery team members who search for and create the new business opportunities will be different from the company's strategy decision makers. This requires the identification of a role (such as sponsor) that will act as a liaison between these two groups to help keep them aligned. Secondly, a larger corporation usually has a greater breadth and depth of functional areas that play important roles in the implementation of any corporate strategy. With more people who can have an important influence on the strategy, there needs to be a way to involve a larger group without making the team unwieldy (Extended Discovery team).

When planning a strategy innovation initiative, there are some roles that are crucial for success and others that are valuable but should be considered optional (see Figure 6-1).

Key Roles

- *Sponsor*
- *Team Captain*
- *Discovery Team*
- *Extended Discovery Team*

Optional Roles

- *Facilitator*
- *Advisory Team*
- *Support Team*

Figure 6-1. Staffing the Discovery Process.

Sponsor

Working closely with 3M CEO Desi DeSimone on bringing strategy innovation to the top of the innovation agenda was William Coyne, senior vice president for research. It was Coyne's active sponsorship of strategy innovation, with vocal and visible support from DeSimone, that led to the formalization of 3M's highly successful strategy innovation capability called Pacing Plus. As in this example with 3M, the sponsor is typically a higher-level management executive who has responsibility for the strategic growth of the corporation or of a division. Good sponsors understand that their personal futures, as well as the futures of their organizations, are at stake, and they are committed to the challenge. It is important that they have a vested interest in the outcome of the work.

In addition, the sponsor of the Discovery Process must believe that corporate growth should be achieved through strategy innovation, not just incremental improvements to the current corporate strategy. There will be pressures throughout the organization to look for short-term, incremental growth opportunities because they are the lowest-risk programs and easiest for the company to implement. The Discovery team will turn to their sponsor to defend their pursuit of innovative growth opportunities that meet the needs of customers and the emerging marketplace, not primarily the short-term, risk-reduction needs of the corporation. For Bruce Carbonari, CEO at Moen, there were numerous hurdles in the development of PureTouch, their innovative, prize-winning filtration faucet. Still, for him, as sponsor, it was never a question of whether this breakthrough opportunity would be launched as a new business, it was only a question of, "How breakthrough could it be?" It was his insistence on innovation and persistence through the hurdles that ultimately led to its introduction.

There are three primary roles of the sponsor in this Discovery Process:

1. Liaison
2. Mentor
3. Spokesperson

Liaison

As liaison, the sponsor is the primary point of contact between the Discovery team and both senior management and the Extended Discovery team.

Mentor

As mentor, the sponsor provides the guidance the Discovery team needs in the design of the initiative, the securing of resources, and their presentations to management. Additionally, in this mentoring role, if the organization or senior management has a vision for the company, the sponsor is the primary cheerleader of that vision to the Discovery team on behalf of the rest of senior management. If the organization lacks a vision, then it is incumbent on the sponsor to personally be visionary enough to not constrain the Discovery team. Typically, this means being open-minded and willing to be stretched by the team in the way he or she views the future of the enterprise.

At the Hewlett-Packard Inkjet Business Unit (HPIJBU), it was Dana Seccombe, as general manager and sponsor of a strategy innovation initiative, who provided the compelling future vision for computer printing—that some day printers will be given away for free, and, therefore, future revenue and profit must be generated by ink and paper. Understanding this fundamental trend before anyone else put HPIJBU in a strong position to strategically out-innovate the competition. Seccombe's vision, combined with his foresight to sponsor key strategy innovation initiatives, is part of the reason HP's Inkjet Business Unit was able to average 45 percent growth over ten years through 2000.

Spokesperson

As a spokesperson for the Discovery team, the sponsor plays a key role in the communication of the purpose, impact, and results of the Discovery Process to the rest of the organization, as appropriate.

However, sponsors are not considered members of the Discovery team and generally do not attend its regular meetings, unless invited for advisory purposes. The team must feel that they are driving the process and are not just there to carry out the directions and wishes of the sponsor. Sponsors stay in touch with the efforts of the team through the team captains.

As sponsors become engaged in the Discovery Process, it is critical that they adopt the innovative work style that the team has adopted. Be they CEOs, EVPs, or general managers, it is important when participating in Discovery Process activities that they not require the decorum that typically accompanies their title and office. Although this hierarchical demeanor might have value in the day-to-day running of the business, it has a countereffect on individuals and teams who are conceiving and developing new business concepts.

Consider the example of the CEO of a consumer products company that had assembled and charged a strategy innovation team with identifying new business opportunities. The CEO had requested to "observe" the team's meetings without any direct involvement. Think for a moment about how this type of participation would affect you, as a Discovery team member. Your sponsoring CEO walks into your meeting and sits at the back of the room without saying a word. Would that change the dynamics of the meeting? Would you feel more relaxed about offering the next speculative new business possibility on which the future of the organization will be based?

In this case, the CEO was advised to go ahead and attend the meeting *and* participate in the same manner as other participants at the meeting. In that particular meeting where the purpose was to generate a wide range of new business possibilities, this would specifically mean:

- Listening to others with an open mind for new learnings, surprises, and insights
- Offering ideas with the same frequency as other members of the team
- Being a model for risk-taking by offering speculative ideas along with others

The CEO took the advice and made valuable contributions to a highly productive session. The dynamics of the meeting greatly improved with his involvement. The team was even more fluent and targeted than it had been in prior sessions. The experience of their CEO listening, learning, offering ideas, and speculating on new, out-of-the-box possibilities seemed to energize and encourage the team. They were seeing the management mandate in action.

To optimize the contributions of a sponsor, sometimes even subtle changes in attitudes or behavior can have a positive impact on the output of the Discovery Process. There is a German manufacturing company that had, over its hundred-plus-year history, refined bureaucratic hierarchy to a new level. Higher ranks within the organization brought with them a deference bordering on reverence. However, the current CEO/chairman was determined that the future would be different in both strategic substance and style. He chartered a Discovery team and challenged them to create a process that would result in a new strategic portfolio for the company. One of the first signals to this team that the CEO was serious about creating a new future was a simple one: He agreed that in all the meetings where he and other sponsors (other executive officers and a general manager) were involved, titles would be dropped, and everyone would be on a first-name basis. This was a dramatic departure from traditional meetings in this company and indicated to the team that this was, indeed, a bold new initiative. The CEO reasoned that they were all in this project together and shared a common goal—the creation of an innovative portfolio of proprietary business opportunities that would fuel the growth of the enterprise for the next decade.

Team Captain

A crucial role in the success of a Discovery Process initiative is that of team captain. Dan Buchner, one of the team captains on the Moen Periscope project, had this to say about the role of team captain:

> The role of team captain was pretty exciting. We were at a point where we had to do something different, think in a different way, and we had a lot of support to do that. I was curious on how it would play out, in both the process and the results. I had organized and directed efforts like this before, so I was not scared or concerned. I value naiveté.

> If you take on big challenges, it is better to not know ex-
> actly what you are taking on.

Typically, the team captain is personally recruited by the sponsor, as the two of them will work closely in the coordination of the
initiative. Team captains need to be leaders who can command respect from team members and are enthusiastic about the initiative.
They need to be able to think strategically while simultaneously
managing the details of an organization-wide strategic effort. Because of the cross-functional and highly collaborative nature of the
team and its work, the team captain must be more of a "first among
equals" leader than a "command-and-control" leader.

Good team captains can come from any department or function
in the company, although in many companies it is the R&D section
leader or the senior marketing manager who fulfills this role. Even
though most of the team members continue to hold their "day
jobs" while participating in the Discovery Process, team captains
who are relieved of most of their other responsibilities during the
initiative are much more effective.

The team captain needs to be an enthusiastic supporter of the
initiative, a good communicator and listener, and someone able to
deal with both the "big picture" (corporate strategic options) as
well as the "little picture" (reserving conference rooms). Personal
characteristics of good team leaders include knowing how to get
things accomplished in the organization, being flexible in planning,
being willing to experiment and take risks, and being respectful of
the needs and different perspectives of others.

The sponsor should clarify to a prospective team captain what
the value of the initiative is to the organization and what the "risks
and rewards" are for him/her personally. This will begin to lay the
foundation for the trust and openness in their relationship, which
may be the most important one in the initiative. When this is done,
it greatly increases the probability of success for both the relationship and the initiative. We have seen team captains, after showcasing their talent in leading successful strategy innovation initiatives,

propelled to greater responsibility and positions at some of the largest and most respected global companies.

The Discovery Team

Recruiting the right mix of people to form the Discovery team is a critical element of the success of the initiative. On the topic of his Periscope team, Dan Buchner of Moen said, "I was quite concerned about who would be on the team. I was concerned about the right balance of perspectives in both functional areas represented as well as individual perspectives. It was also very important to me that team members be open-minded and have the ability to change. But there weren't a lot of people like that in our organization at the time. We had lots of debates internally on who should be on the team."

As for how he went about recruiting the team, Buchner explained:

> I would go to the head of a functional area and ask for their best person but often they would offer the person most loyal to the thinking and direction of that area. Sometimes I had to go back and say, "No, I want someone else." Another approach I took was to get the people I wanted on the team excited about the program, and then they would request to be on it. It's more about the people you put on the team than having a detailed implementation plan before you start the process—it's not possible to think that far ahead. If I were to form a team again, I wouldn't do anything differently. A key issue was the availability of people. We got the right group of people at the right levels in the organization. It would not have worked with the VPs. The manager and director levels are much better because there are no politics there and no one is overly concerned about the output of the program having an impact on their particular functional area. In addition, these are people who can get stuff done in the organization.

> At the higher levels in an organization, people have less
> time to be involved—plus people sometimes start ques-
> tioning their motives.

Think of the Discovery team as a reconnaissance group that is charged with exploring the future and reporting back the business opportunities they find there. Who from your company would you send on a reconnaissance mission? Because reconnaissance work is done in unknown, uncharted territories, you would probably want people who are comfortable with, and capable of, making observations and decisions in new environments and contexts. You would also probably want to include people who are excited about the opportunity to be involved in this type of work and would be committed to the responsibilities that it entails. Beyond that, team members should be selected based on both internal corporate considerations and the attributes the team needs to work effectively.

The following are key considerations when recruiting a highly effective Discovery team:

1. Cross-functional implementers
2. Diversity of its members
3. Team players

Cross-Functional Implementers

Cross-functional teams used in the Discovery Process will help facilitate the process of corporate alignment and implementation of a new strategy. When the Discovery team is made up of individuals from all major functional areas of the company, it will create business opportunities and a strategic future that reflects the interests, needs, and capabilities of the entire company, not just those of R&D or marketing. This pays significant dividends when it comes time to aligning the organization around a strategy for the purposes of implementing it. People support what they help create. When all functions have helped create the new strategy, they will be more easily convinced to support it in its implementation phase.

A key implementer for Discovery teams that is often overlooked is the public relations or corporate communications function. Having been part of the initiative and the creation of the new strategic direction, a team member from this function will speak with even greater knowledge and conviction when communicating the new strategy to both internal employees and external stakeholders.

Diversity of Its Members

The single most important attribute of the Discovery team is its diversity. This diversity, however, has nothing to do with being "politically correct" or sensitive to a broad representation of employees. Do not create team diversity in order to avoid age or gender discrimination lawsuits.

Diversity has a very tangible benefit for a Discovery team. Strategy innovation is a creative process, with a goal to identify markets, products, and business models that may not yet exist. Success will depend on the team's ability to ask new questions, perceive new insights, and imagine new solutions. It is very difficult for a group of individuals who all share the same backgrounds, thinking styles, and experiences to think new thoughts when they are together. They share the same assumptions and mental models of how things work. On the other hand, an "outsider" added to this group will likely introduce a new way of looking at something, which will help the group break out of their old patterns and consider new ideas. When the entire group is made up of "outsiders," the possibilities for new thinking increase exponentially. Having diverse perspectives, thinking skills, and expertise on the team will significantly enhance the group's creative potential.

An example of the importance of diverse thinking and new perspectives comes from Wilson Greatbach, the inventor of the cardiac pacemaker. He was an engineering student at Cornell when he would, on occasion, lunch with the students from the Cornell Medical School. Listening to the medical students discuss the dissection of cadavers where death was caused by cardiac arrest, Wilson heard the discussion, of course, not in medical terms but in his terms—engineering principles. His insight of an engineering solution to this medical problem led to the development of the first cardiac pacemaker. This invention became the core of a billion-dollar business and was the first of 240 patents granted Wilson Greatbach, an individual with a different perspective who was able to listen and make new connections between seemingly unrelated disciplines.

Having cross-functional representation on the team will automatically add an important element of diversity. However, also consider including people for reasons other than functional diversity. For example, perhaps the team could benefit from some company veterans and some newcomers, some big-picture people and some detail people, some older people and some younger ones, some from different cultures or backgrounds, some extroverted people and some more reflective ones, some conservatives and some liberals, or some right-brain thinkers and some left-brain thinkers. Often teams will use standardized aptitude tests or personality tests, such as Myers-Briggs, to help them define these dimensions. The more variety on the team, the greater your chance of finding innovative opportunities that can become practical new businesses.

Also consider going outside the company for recruiting Discovery team members. People from your advertising agency, design firm, or other suppliers can bring a valuable "outside" perspective to this effort. A Kodak team included a science fiction writer on the team to help them in imagining future marketplace scenarios. A P&G team included a major foods wholesaler who had been developing a "grocery store of the future." Blue Cross and Blue Shield of Virginia involved a maverick hotel entrepreneur to help them stretch their concept of "service."

Team Players

The third important consideration for a Discovery team is recruiting people who are team players. Effective teams interact well, respect each other, listen to each other, and create new things together. People who feel they have "the answer" or in some way try to control the output of the group will end up destroying the creative dynamic of the team. Focus on finding team members who look forward to discovering and creating the future together with others.

It is important to point out that Discovery team members do not have to have experience in, or even an understanding of, corporate strategy. The team will focus on identifying business opportunities that are stimulated by hearing about customer needs and emerging marketplace dynamics. Those opportunities will eventually be handed over to individuals or organizations with strategy experience for further refinement and evaluation for the company.

Size matters somewhat when it comes to a Discovery team. We have found that the ideal team for larger corporations or business units usually consists of eight to twelve members. Larger companies with many different departments find it difficult to provide good cross-functional representation with fewer than eight members. With more than twelve members, meetings can become unwieldy and team decisions more difficult.

In smaller companies, it may not be possible to identify eight available people to make up a Discovery team. It is difficult to say what the "minimum" number of members should be for a team, as it will depend on the people who participate. With fewer than five or six members, the team will not benefit

Process Tip:

Ask for a small portion of each team member's "mindshare" to be dedicated to this initiative on a 24/7 basis.

It is better to have 20 percent of someone's mind thinking about this initiative *all* the time than it is to have 100 percent of someone's mind for a meeting once every few weeks. Between meetings, team members should be scanning their world for new data, trends, insights, and connections that could affect the company's future. This turns initiative "downtime" into fruitful "incubation" time, when the brain subconsciously works on a problem and often finds solutions while we are doing something else.

from the diversity of perspectives and thinking styles that will foster innovative thinking. However, we can imagine that even four committed, curious, and open-minded individuals could be a dynamic and effective team. An alternative approach for a smaller company is to add outside expertise to the internal team, perhaps tapping talented people from advertising agencies, vendors/suppliers, or other affiliated companies.

Because most companies do not have the luxury of a dedicated staff to do this discovery work, they must find people who already have "day jobs," who can dedicate part of their calendar, energy, and passion to this effort. The part-time nature of the team working over an extended period of months can introduce issues of continuity and momentum. If the team only meets once every week or two, the pressures of the day jobs can steal valuable attention from the Discovery Process. To address this, we recommend asking team members to always keep the initiative on their mental radar screens.

The Extended Discovery Team

In most companies, there are people in management who will play a role in helping to decide on or implement the corporate strategy, but who cannot be included as a member of the Discovery team. Those people can still play an important role in the Discovery Process by being part of the Extended Discovery team. Typically a group of ten to fifty people from middle management up to senior management ranks, they participate in the process at the key review or alignment meetings, as well as in any high-profile exploration activities that might involve industry experts.

The Extended Discovery team consists of individuals who assist the Discovery Process in one of three ways:

- ◆ Their deep, sometimes specialized, experience enriches the quality of the Discovery team's work for generating insights and developing opportunities.

- ◆ They increase the Discovery team's sensitivity to implementation considerations.

◆   As stakeholders in the organization's strategic decision-mak-
    ing process, they will play a vital role in the future alignment
    of the organization on the preferred opportunities.

The Extended Discovery team provides a vehicle to involve a
greater breadth of expertise from the organization in the strategy
innovation initiative. Regardless of the size of the Discovery team,
there will always be a need for a valuable perspective outside the
team at various points along the way. The Extended Discovery team
is the way to efficiently enlist broader organizational expertise at the
appropriate time. Some strategy innovation initiatives are highly
technical in nature and might require a greater involvement of the
R&D community in the exploration phase. In others, a greater skew
toward the marketing side could be most appropriate when it
comes time to creating the business opportunities. Establishing an
Extended Discovery team will allow you to involve the types and
depth of organizational expertise that is necessary in the Discovery
Process.

In any successful Discovery Process, there is always "one eye" on
the implementation of new business opportunities throughout the
process. The Extended Discovery team is the way to involve individuals, sometimes deep in the organization, who are known to
play pivotal roles in the successful implementation of a strategy
innovation by the organization. Because members of the Extended
Discovery team will be involved in the implementation of the new
strategy, they should be part of its evolution. Their insights and
advice typically prove to be valuable to the Discovery team as it
helps them understand possible implications of the new business
model they are creating. Get them involved early.

Since the sponsor is often a single member of a much larger
senior executive staff, forming an Extended Discovery team will add
other key decision makers to the Discovery Process. This will enable
these decision makers to better understand the future forces that
will influence the new opportunities that they help create. In his
Kodak initiative, Bob LaPerle felt that having some involvement of
senior executives on the Extended Discovery team was particularly

valuable. "It was good to have senior managers at the thought leader panel, as it opened their eyes significantly that imaging as an industry was going to transform. It aligned them around that idea. Forcing them to participate in the process was a big step forward."

Optional Roles in the Discovery Process

Because every company is different, every strategy innovation initiative will be configured differently. Team members bring a mix of skills and talents that might or might not be sufficient for the needs of the Discovery Process. For that reason, other skills and talents must be recruited to provide the necessary help. The optional roles of facilitator, advisory team, and support team can play valuable roles.

Facilitator

The team captain is often the logical choice to facilitate the meetings of the Discovery team. In some companies, however, the team captain is not one who has the necessary experience to facilitate meetings with a team of managers through a lengthy process. If that is the case, then consider identifying a skilled facilitator to lead the team meetings.

The Discovery Process requires someone who can focus a team's energy, encourage unconventional thinking, and help a team reach consensus. Larger companies often have in-house meeting facilitators who can play that role. If you use an in-house facilitator, make sure the facilitator is experienced in leading dynamic processes and has a good sense of the overall business of the company.

If your company does not have anyone in-house who is "process-savvy," consider finding an independent facilitator who has these skills. That will free up the team captain to focus on the "content" of the meeting and be able to provide direction to the team without jeopardizing the preferred "neutrality" of the facilitator role. According to Dan Buchner of Moen, "We could not have carried out our project without an independent group leading the process."

Advisory Team

Some strategy initiatives are so crucial to the viability of the organization that senior-level management prefers to play a more hands-on role during the Discovery Process. In those cases, consider the creation of an advisory team. The advisory team could consist of the team sponsor plus a couple of senior managers who provide guidance, advice, and counsel to the Discovery team on an on-going basis, perhaps through update meetings with the team or the team captain.

For the German manufacturer mentioned earlier, an advisory team consisted of the CEO/chairman, the COO, a third board member, and the general manager of a highly entrepreneurial and successful business unit in the United States. They would meet periodically with the Discovery team to hear progress reports and provide seasoned advice. Additionally, this advisory team participated in key Discovery events and provided valuable insights and feedback to the Discovery team in the debriefing sessions at the close of each event. The CEO/chairman served as the leader of the advisory team and made himself available for frequent meetings with the team captain.

Although these meetings greatly facilitate the alignment of the Discovery team with management, it is important that the advisory team does not dictate all of the team's activities. The Discovery team must feel some autonomy in their work and be allowed to explore and discover new opportunities on the strategic frontier. If they are only carrying out the wishes of the advisory team, they will feel less ownership of the output, which will negate the alignment advantage of using a team approach.

Support Team

Some initiatives require frequent meetings, travel, and arrangements with external individuals or organizations. The administrative details involved may require the identification of a person or team to help coordinate these efforts. The support team can relieve the team captain of these administrative responsibilities and provide the Discovery team with a central point of control over production of meeting notes, communications, coordination, and budget tracking.

Figure 6-2 shows the various roles and how they interact in the Discovery Process.

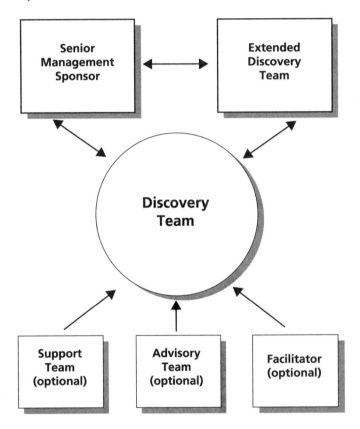

Figure 6-2. The Discovery team and support structure.

Funding the Initiative

The team's sponsor typically arranges for funding for the Discovery Process. Sometimes the funding is built into the annual budget, but other times the sponsor needs to go door-to-door seeking small change from management colleagues.

The "positioning" of the strategy innovation initiative will usually have an impact on its ability to be funded. Strategy innovation initiatives that are considered an investment in the future of the company tend to be funded more quickly than initiatives perceived merely as an expense item in this year's budget. Initiatives that fit the strategic agenda of senior management will be more compelling and of higher visibility than initiatives positioned as an experimental pursuit of a new internal process. When all functional groups in a company are committed to involvement in the process, it will attract funds faster than if it is primarily a project in one functional area, such as a marketing or product development activity. Perhaps because of the exploratory nature of strategy innovation initiatives, some corporations consider them to be similar to an R&D effort, and often look to the R&D budget for funding.

There is no "standard" cost for a Discovery Process. Focused initiatives at smaller companies or business units may generate exciting new business opportunities for less than $100,000, while large, global companies may spend over $1 million on exploration activities all around the world. It is the number and scope of the exploration activities undertaken by the team that will determine the overall cost of the initiative.

Creating the Right Work Environment

When Discovery team members are first asked to be part of a strategy initiative, it probably conjures up images of enough computer printouts to deforest Montana, spreadsheets endlessly calculating the impact of different sales estimates, and notebooks filled with presentation charts and tables. After all, strategic planning in the minds of most people is all about gathering and projecting numbers. Those numbers are related to today's corporate strategy and help identify how today's strategy must be adjusted to meet the projected needs of tomorrow.

However, as we emphasized previously, strategy innovation is not about incremental adjustment to today's strategy, and it is not about numbers. It comes about as a result of a process of exploring the future, discovering new business opportunities on your strategic frontier, and creating a strategic road map to move the company toward its preferred future. Therefore, the strategy innovation process (the Discovery Process) will differ significantly from a traditional strategic planning process, as outlined in Figure 6-3.

	Strategic Planning	Strategy Innovation
Process:	*Analytic/quantitative*	*Creative*
Based on:	*Current business model*	*New business model*
Goal:	*Extend current value*	*Create new value*
Focus:	*Company-centric*	*Customer-centric*
Assumes:	*Future similar to the present*	*Dynamic future*
Principles:	*Abide by rules/traditions*	*Break the rules*

Figure 6-3. Strategic planning vs. strategy innovation.

As a result, the Discovery team's working environment will be much different from a traditional strategic planning process. It will be:

1. Creative
2. Opportunistic
3. Dynamic
4. Collaborative

Creative

Because the team will be imagining new products, markets, and business models that do not currently exist, they will need to be creative together. All people are born with the potential to be creative, and it is the environment that will determine whether their creative abilities are realized. Environments that are highly judgmental or critical, risk-averse, or dominated by one set of beliefs will suppress creative potential. Therefore, it is important that the Discovery team create a working environment that welcomes all new thoughts and ideas, that is willing to experiment, and that is egalitarian in its operations.

There is one other aspect of a creative working environment that reflects the creative heritage of this Discovery Process. As with early "brainstorming" work done in corporations, a two-step, creative process consists of a "divergent phase" followed by a "convergent phase" (see Figure 6-4).

Divergent Phase

In the divergent phase, a team gathers together ALL ideas they can think of that will help solve the issue or problem they were dealing with.

> **"Rule of 100"**
>
> When Bob Galvin was CEO of Motorola, he once requested that his managers enter a meeting with at least a hundred ideas on how to solve a particular problem they would be addressing. This exercise forced people to "stretch" their thinking and be willing to entertain a wide range of options before committing to a decision. Said Galvin, "On that one, I tested things to the extreme, and it worked." This is the essence of divergent thinking, the critical first phase of the creative process.

Without regard to feasibility, practicality, efficiency, or effectiveness, the team creates a great quantity of new ideas, ranging from the ridiculous to the sublime. By ignoring the evaluation of each

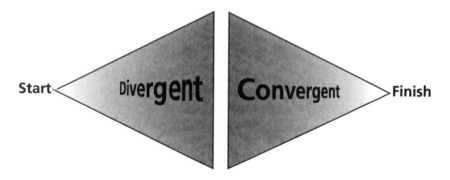

Figure 6-4. The creative process.

idea as it is presented, the divergent phase allows for a much greater quantity of ideas to be considered. Perhaps more importantly, however, deferring judgment on each idea allows the team to explore together and mentally wander into new and innovative ways of solving the problem. It is often the more absurd ideas offered in the divergent phase that will cause people to look at the problem differently, resulting in creative solutions. The divergent phase has a daydreaming quality to it that some people find exhilarating but more practical or action-oriented people find more frivolous. However, it is the crucial step that any group must take when they are interested in identifying innovative ways of solving problems.

Convergent Phase

As all business creativity must ultimately be feasible, practical, efficient, and/or effective to have value, the creative process must then move to a second phase—the "convergent phase." In the convergent phase, team members review the hundreds or more ideas generated in the divergent phase and apply some evaluation criteria to the list. It is the *quantity* of options created in the divergent phase that increases significantly the odds of finding an appropriate solution. This convergent phase is the work that most managers do well because their jobs typically require them to evaluate new options for appropriateness to the current business.

Divergent-convergent thinking should permeate all activities of the Discovery team. It is built into all the activities in the five phases of the Discovery Process outlined in this book. Try using it on your own activities. For example, if your team is considering where to go out for dinner some evening, first make a list of all possible restaurants that you could consider (even those that you normally would not consider) and then apply your team's decision criteria to that list. Innovation is a two-step process: Create, then evaluate.

Opportunistic

The Discovery team, acting in an entrepreneurial fashion, will be freed from any corporate constraints when exploring for new business opportunities. Without the pressure of having to find market-place needs that fit nicely into today's corporate business model, the team will be able to pursue any customer need, emerging mar-ketplace opportunity, or business model innovation that would cre-ate value at some point in the future.

Once team members can successfully disengage from corporate constraints, they are then able to disengage from marketplace or business model constraints also. After identifying a customer need, they look for the best way to meet that need, regardless of whether it uses traditional business practices or not. At this point, they are no longer "following the rules" or traditions in an industry but daring to "change the rules" in a way that creates customer and corporate value. This freedom from constraints creates a working environment that is highly opportunistic and filled with an any-thing-is-possible attitude among the team members. It is this atti-tude that is most conducive to the identification of innovative strategies.

Dynamic

Throughout the Discovery Process, new insights and information gathered will create an extremely dynamic working environment. The customer need that the team identified in Week One of the exploring process may appear worthless compared to what you found in Week Ten. Perhaps the new business opportunity you cre-ated with great enthusiasm fell apart when an industry expert said that the technology necessary would not be ready for ten years. In such a dynamic environment, Discovery team members must consider all ideas to be emerging and evolving, not fixed and un-changeable. We use the terminology of "building" ideas and oppor-tunities to reflect the fact that each new insight and fact can help improve an already-existing idea or start a new one. Thus, the working environment for the Discovery team is one of constant change and improvement rather than "we created it already, it's done."

Collaborative

The results of the Discovery Process are created by the entire Discovery team, not any individual. The collaborative working environment encourages everyone to "build on" or help improve any idea or concept that has been created. By the time the concepts are fully developed, many of the Discovery Process participants have their fingerprints on them and feel part of their development. This is not an environment where anyone tries to push a personal agenda or pet project. It is not one of internal coalitions or behind-the-scenes maneuvering for support for different positions. Ideas are created from new information and insights that the team discovers together. At the inception of the initiative, the canvas is blank. Through collaboration, the Discovery team creates the mosaic of the future together.

Collaboration is a critical element of the Discovery Process. It is offered here in contrast to more common corporate behavior of one group identifying or developing an idea or proposal and then "selling" or "handing off" that idea to another group. The process of having to sell ideas to other people or departments is frequently a challenging, politically charged, time-intensive process. Handing off ideas to a different department invites not-invented-here passivity and significant time delays until all of the development issues and questions are discussed and agreed upon. We have found that having all relevant parties present at key information-sharing and idea-creating events results in significantly greater alignment of those parties for decision making and enhanced implementation.

Implementing the Staging Meeting

At this point, the Discovery team has been recruited and understands the working environment for the Discovery Process. The final preparation step is the staging meeting, where team members:

1. Understand the scope of the initiative
2. Share the Discovery brief
3. Create the team

Understand the Scope of the Initiative

Senior management and the sponsor will "launch" the Discovery team at the staging meeting by outlining the reason for the initiative and the impact that it will have on the company. They will also share their expectations for the results of the Discovery Process. These expectations should be significant enough to challenge the team but not so significant that they feel overwhelmed by the task before them.

It is reasonable to expect that the Discovery team can identify three to five short to mid-term new business opportunities that would have an important impact on a company's revenues plus one to three longer-term opportunities that could have a dramatic impact on future business.

Share the Discovery Brief

The Discovery brief is a document containing information that would be helpful to the Discovery team as it begins the initiative. The document is prepared by the team members prior to the staging meeting and then presented at that meeting. Because the team is cross-functional, each function prepares information from their field or expertise that will educate their teammates on that area. The presentation of this information will provide a "working knowledge" of each area and give the Discovery team a common vocabulary for their discussions.

The Discovery brief has two distinct sections:

- The field of today
- The seeds of tomorrow

The Field of Today

In this first section of the Discovery brief, each department or functional area will prepare a short overview of the current conditions in that field. Marketing might share current market data, a short competitive review, and customer usage information. The R&D section of the Discovery brief might review how current products work, the materials/ingredients used, and consumer benefits. The sales department might outline how the various distribution channels have evolved over time.

The important focus of all areas should be to remove any "mystery" about how things work in that area and to introduce a working vocabulary for the Discovery team to use throughout the initiative. It is our experience that about one-third of the focus of the Discovery brief should be on the field of today.

The Seeds of Tomorrow

The remaining two-thirds of the Discovery brief should be future-oriented. Each functional area should share with the rest of their Discovery teammates what they see as possible influences on the business of tomorrow. Perhaps the operations group is aware of a new automated manufacturing process overseas that will allow for customized production. Product development may be working on a new product design that could provide customers with added benefits. Or finance has discovered a leasing company that is willing to finance some new equipment purchases.

The seeds of tomorrow are everywhere, once you start looking for them.

◆ What intangible assets do you have that could be leveraged in the marketplace?

◆ What trends are you seeing that could affect the future of the business (either positively or negatively)?

◆ What is taking place at the periphery of the market or within a small market niche that, if it were to grow, might have an impact on the future?

◆ What group of customers is changing their behavior for some reason?

◆ What are your suppliers or vendors doing that might affect you in the future?

◆ What new technologies or materials did you recently read about in a periodical?

◆   What is missing that your company could provide to the
    world?

The purpose of this part of the Discovery brief is to inventory
what the team already knows or has contemplated about the future.
It is not important at this point that these future seeds be certain
to or likely to affect the future—only that it is "possible." Waiting
for trends to become probable influences on the future is waiting
too long, putting your company in a reactive mode to the market
and competitors. It is the collection of these seeds before they have
germinated that gives a company a strong, proactive future-orienta-
tion.

When Eastman Kodak launched a strategy innovation initiative
in the early 1990s, called the Future Imaging Strategies Team
(FIST), it was the first broad-scale effort by management to assess
and develop a strategy for the impact of digital imaging technology
on their chemically based silver halide business. For over a century
Kodak had been expanding and protecting primarily a single technology in silver halide that had historically delivered over a 70 percent global imaging market share. The emerging Pacific Rim
technology for producing electronic images was soon to provide a
textbook technological disruption, which the FIST effort was
formed to address. The team captain, Robert LaPerle, noted that
the development of a briefing document had special value to the
team, given the scale of the threat to Kodak's traditional business.
"The planning brief got our mind-sets around 'digital' and the role
that it would have. We started to see it more as a long-term opportunity than a threat. It helped us to get senior managers exposed to
it and thinking about it. The brief took on a life of its own and was
distributed to individuals at the company who otherwise were not
involved in the FIST project."

By providing an inventory of the present and future elements
they have to work with, the Discovery team will begin to look at
their business differently. Dan Buchner of Moen claimed that the
writing of the Discovery brief for the Periscope project was one of
the "ah-ha" moments for the team. "We divided up the areas and

started digging in and came to realize how complex the issues were. We spent a huge amount of time pulling the planning brief together, and that helped a lot. We identified a lot of myths, things that were no longer true. We were running a company based on some ideas that were not true anymore."

In our experience of working with Kodak and Moen, as well as many other companies, in the development of a successful planning brief we have observed the following common threads:

- The quality of the Discovery brief is often "predictive" of the Discovery team's final output. A high-quality, thoughtful brief presented in the staging meeting dramatically increases the ultimate value of the initiative to the organization.

- The more candid the Discovery brief, the better. With the identification of corporate strengths, capabilities, competitive threats, knowledge gaps, and assumptions regarding the future, the brief becomes a metaphorical "mirror" that the Discovery team reflects on during the course of the process. Accuracy and honesty in this exercise sets the stage for greater strategic insights later on.

- The Discovery brief should not be a lengthy document. Attempts to fully educate teammates in the workings of a functional area can lead to confusion. Hit the highlights, keep it simple, and provide some sense of priority of information presented.

Create the Team

With the staging meeting being the first time the entire Discovery team has met as a group, time should be spent on issues related to the team and its working relationship. Team members need to establish how they will communicate with each other, the logistics of subsequent meetings, any ground rules for working together, and a first attempt at a time line and key milestones for the initiative.

Because the smooth interactions of the team members are so crucial for the success of the Discovery team, the staging meeting is a good time to begin to define the team. Just as Moen named their team "the Periscope team," your team might want to give itself a unique identity that bonds the members in its quest and captures the spirit of the initiative. We have been involved in some initiatives where the Discovery team, in an attempt to create more entrepreneurial thinking and be less tied to the constraints of their company, adopted a new company name for their team.

A final word regarding Discovery team chemistry. It is not uncommon for Discovery teams to experience a "bump" or two in their formation. Often, a functional area needs to be added, a team member needs to be replaced early in the process, or there are mild disagreements on the team's charter. These things generally work themselves out when team members become committed to the process and begin to work as members of a team. Occasionally, however, there are situations where it is obvious to the team captain and to the team that an individual is working contrary to the goals of the team or, put another way, not able to carry his or her weight in fulfilling the strategy innovation mission of the team. The sooner these individuals are replaced on the team, the better. One individual, consciously or unconsciously working to sabotage the Discovery Process, can derail the entire initiative. The team captain must act swiftly to either coach the individual toward being a contributing member of the team or replace that person.

Summary

- ◆ A mandate for strategy innovation from senior management is a critical first step to any strategy innovation initiative.

- ◆ A corporate team is the most successful approach for identifying and developing innovative business opportunities that lead to strategy innovation.

- ◆ The key roles in the Discovery Process consist of a sponsor, a team captain, the Discovery team, and the Extended Discovery team. Optional roles include a facilitator, an advisory team, and a support team.

- ◆ Key considerations in the creation of a Discovery team include the identification of cross-functional implementers, the diversity of the team, and the willingness of the members to be team players.

◆ Although there is no "average" cost for conducting a strategy innovation initiative, it is important that the team determines its needs and that management fund it adequately.

◆ Because the Discovery Process is a creative process, the team must establish a working environment that is conducive to teamwork and creativity. Specifically, the working environment needs to be creative, opportunistic, dynamic, and collaborative.

◆ The preparation of the team for the Discovery Process culminates in a staging meeting, where team members gain an understanding of the scope of the initiative, share the findings of a Discovery brief, and begin the formation of the team.

CHAPTER 7

THE DISCOVERY PROCESS

Aligning Phase

> The principal mark of genius is not perfection but
> originality, the opening of new frontiers.
>
> —*ARTHUR KOESTLER*

| Staging Phase | **Aligning Phase** | Exploring Phase | Creating Phase | Mapping Phase |

While the staging phase involved team preparation and primarily
process-related issues, the aligning phase focuses the Discovery
team on the *content* of the initiative. Where should the team begin
to explore for the best new business opportunities? What new areas
are most consistent with the mission, strategy, or capabilities of the
organization? What are the company's "strategic frontiers"?

The Aligning Phase consists of two important activities:

1. Identifying the company's strategic frontiers.

2. Aligning with senior management on the proposed strategic
   frontiers to be explored.

Current Corporate Strategy vs. New Corporate Strategy

One of the primary benefits of having a clearly defined corporate strategy is its ability to provide focus for the organization. It is the corporate strategy that aligns the behavior of all functional groups in the organization, coordinating how they spend their time and budgets. This focused and coordinated use of corporate resources will increase the likelihood of reaching corporate goals and help maximize the overall efficiency of the organization. A corporate strategy is a valuable tool for senior management to help control the activities and direction of the company.

Strategy innovation initiatives similar to the process presented in this book are intended to explore business opportunities that are *beyond* the current corporate strategy. They are initiated when the incremental execution of the current strategy will not provide the growth necessary for the company's future. Therefore, strategy innovation processes will venture outside the current corporate strategy, outside of the current purview of senior management, and sometimes outside the comfort zone of the organization.

This exploration beyond the current corporate strategy, beyond the current business model, beyond management control is an important consideration for the Discovery Process. Some companies encourage their people and teams to explore into new areas and welcome the discovery of new opportunities wherever they can be found. Other companies prefer to keep their exploring teams on a shorter tether, believing that exploring into areas that the company cannot (because of current resources) enter would be a waste of corporate resources. If your senior management team wants to maintain tight control over the strategic options it considers, then this is an important issue that needs to be discussed in the launching of a strategy innovation initiative.

This potential conflict between the exploratory work of a Discovery team and the narrow boundaries of acceptable results by senior management is a critical issue in strategy innovation initiatives. By its very nature and definition, strategy innovation involves searching for ways to "change the rules" of a current marketplace, in an attempt to increase value or market share for a company. Although strategy innovation can have a substantial positive impact on a company's growth, it may also require changes to the company's infrastructure or business processes to achieve that growth. While senior management desires the growth, they are also responsible for the current business model and are often wary of changes to it. This trade-off provides a "creative tension" that is present in all strategy innovation initiatives. The Discovery team needs the freedom to explore new business opportunities wherever they exist, *and* senior management needs to maintain some control over the process to protect against changes too risky to the business model.

Rather than try to resolve this "creative tension," we would argue that it is a necessary component for the success of the initiative. The Discovery team should know that senior management will not embrace every new business opportunity they identify, especially if the opportunities represent too radical a departure from today's core business. At the same time, senior management must understand that the Discovery team will need to recommend some changes in the current business model in order to create new value in the marketplace. These two forces should be held in a dynamic tension that keeps both groups from wandering too far away from their mutual goal, which is the identification of business opportunities that the company can implement to provide significant new value.

"Discovery Drift" and the Importance of Alignment

In some instances senior management has granted the Discovery team carte blanche at the beginning of the process to explore business opportunities wherever they can be found. This results in a very empowering and productive process for the team. Each new insight gained in the process uncovers value potential for customers, perhaps with only a slight change required to the current business strategy. After many months of exploring, all those *slight* strategic changes begin to add up so that by the end of the initiative, the Discovery team has identified some very exciting and significant business opportunities, but they are *very* different from today's corporate strategy and the company's current business model.

When the team presents its findings, senior management, not having been as involved in the process, notices the big shift in business strategy suggested by these opportunities and fears that the corporation cannot afford such dramatic changes. As a result, they may hesitate to endorse these new business opportunities, in spite of their significant revenue potential. Because senior management did not experience the gradual drifting from the current business strategy as the team did, they are not ready to make the big strategic leap to a whole new way of doing business. We call this movement away from the current business strategy "discovery drift," and we see it as one of the primary reasons why the output of such initiatives may not always be embraced by the company (see Figure 7-1).

To prevent this "discovery drift" and increase the possibility that the outputs of the Discovery Process will be embraced by senior management, phase two of the process establishes "alignment" between the Discovery team and senior management. By understanding the expectations of senior management for this initiative and the degree of stretch, change, and risk they are willing to consider,

Figure 7-1. Discovery drift and the need for alignment in the Discovery Process.

the team can appropriately focus their exploration and creation outside the current business strategy.

Senior management doesn't always play the role of curmudgeon in this process. We have seen cases where they had higher expectations for the team than what was delivered. We once worked with a team from a major consumer package goods company that had recently received FDA approval for a proprietary food technology. This technology, if leveraged properly into new products and businesses, promised to have a powerful impact on the company's profitability and shareholder value. However, senior management's charge and objectives to the team stopped short of suggesting, or even influencing, the new business areas that could be explored by the team. Without the encouragement to explore beyond the current business model, the team limited their explorations and their speculations to opportunities that fit the current business model. The result was that senior management was underwhelmed and unaligned with the new business opportunities developed by the team, feeling they were too close to existing businesses. The lesson from this experience is to engage and align senior management early on in determining the territory to be explored in the discovery work.

Alignment on the Flexibility of the Business Model

One way for the Discovery team to align with senior management around this question of how much change can be tolerated is to clarify what elements of the current business model they perceive as fixed and which they consider flexible. Either through a discussion with the Discovery team sponsor or a meeting with senior management, go through the elements of the current business model and ask how much change they would tolerate in that area. Will they consider serving a different customer base? Does a new business opportunity have to use current technology? Is senior management flexible in considering new business arrangements, such as joint ventures? Are they fixed in their insistence on using the company's current sales force or distribution channels for any new venture? Do the new products have to be manufactured in current facilities?

In this discussion, senior management will likely prefer to leverage all of the current elements of the business model because that represents the least change and will likely provide the greatest efficiency. However, if all of the elements of the current business model are to remain more fixed than flexible, the Discovery team has very little room to identify growth opportunities. The most important output of such a discussion is the sensitization by both senior management and the Discovery team that some changes will likely be necessary for the identification of new business opportunities. A second output is a prioritized list of business model elements that should remain fixed (or flexible). While the Discovery team will not necessarily use this list to limit their exploration of new business opportunities, they will use it as evaluation criteria to help screen and prioritize the opportunities they create in the Creating Phase.

Alignment on Business Assumptions

Another way for the Discovery team to align with senior management is to examine business assumptions together. Since no one can know the future, as previously noted, we all make assumptions about it. If not based on new knowledge, our assumptions about the future are typically based on our past experience. We assume that the competitive landscape of tomorrow will be similar to today's landscape. We assume that the channels of distribution today will be the ones we use to grow the business. We assume we will adapt our current manufacturing capabilities to meet the needs of future markets.

However, all markets are dynamic. Sometimes the changes will obsolete a business assumption that is crucial to the company's strategy. Moen ran into this situation in the plumbing fixtures market. Their previous strategy was based on the assumption that plumbers would continue to be a primary means of selling/influencing the purchase of plumbing fixtures to consumers. By offering the highest-quality faucet to the plumbers who appreciated this quality, the company believed that their business would continue to grow. Then along came Home Depot, offering consumers the opportunity to select the fixtures they wanted. Seeing products side-by-side on the shelf, consumers made decisions based more on style (what they could see) than on quality (what they could not see). What helped Moen turn around their business was their willingness to surface key business assumptions, question the viability of those assumptions for the future, and then make a strategic shift based on marketplace changes. As a result, their faucets became more stylish.

How many companies based their futures on the business as-sumption that the dot-com revolution would continue at its torrid pace?

Following some thought leader panels in the mid-1990s, 3M rec-ognized that they had many processes in place to identify customer insights but nothing in place to collect market foresight. As a result, the business assumptions for the future were inconsistent and sometimes contradictory across their many different divisions. In response, 3M formalized a corporate capability for generating pro-prietary foresight. A group was established to identify and track emerging trends and possible discontinuities, providing a clearer and more consistent basis for the establishment of future business assumptions across divisions.

The Discovery team should spend time with senior management discussing the assumptions on which the current and near-term business strategy is based. Then ask how confident they are that the assumptions will remain valid in the future. Gaining alignment with senior management on which business assumptions will likely remain valid, which will probably change, and which are question-able is a potent alignment exercise.

Strategic Frontiers

"What's next for your company?" Can you answer that question? Is your answer, "More of the same"? If so, you are stuck in an *incremental* way of doing business, trying to eke out a little more revenue from the same marketplace using your same business model. Roll out the next line extension, charge a little more for it, and hope that competition is asleep at the wheel. Incrementalism is a safe strategy designed for modest growth. In some markets (those that are more static than dynamic), this can still be a viable strategy. If it still works for your company, you are probably not getting much from this book. When your company's financials or growth prospects need a boost that your incremental strategy cannot provide, it is time to rethink your strategy and consider "what's next."

Beyond Incrementalism

Process Tip:

A strategic frontier is that unexplored area of potential growth that lies between today's business and tomorrow's opportunities.

We call this area a frontier because it is considered to have potential for growth but has not yet been fully explored. When we talk to people in companies, many have opinions on what are (or should be) their strategic frontiers. However, because there is no process in place to do it, they rarely discuss these frontier options with others. A discussion of the future should begin with a discussion of a company's strategic frontiers.

We have run into a few companies, such as 3M, that usually know "what's next." In their yearly planning process, the 3M business units are required to account for their progress in developing their *next* strategic business platform for growth. That platform is identified and developed so it is ready to be introduced when revenue from the current platform begins to wane. The next platform becomes the basis of their corporate growth in subsequent years. If you are in a company like that, you already know "what's next for your company." If not, the first step in understanding the next growth platform for your business is to identify your "strategic frontier."

Think of a strategic frontier as market, product, technology, or business process that lies just *beyond* your current corporate strategy and business model (see Figure 7-2). You probably have some reason to believe that moving to this strategic frontier could result in growth for your company, either because it works in other companies, because it addresses a problem you have, or because it addresses a need in the marketplace. However, you have never pursued this strategic frontier because it was always considered just outside your company's strategy. This was the case with the Pure-Touch product at Moen. While the company had preliminary designs in-house for a water filtration faucet, its development did not fit with the fast-follower strategy Moen was pursuing in the conventional faucet market at that time. When their exploration of the future marketplace identified a growing need for water filtration, that became the strategic frontier for Moen. As part of their new

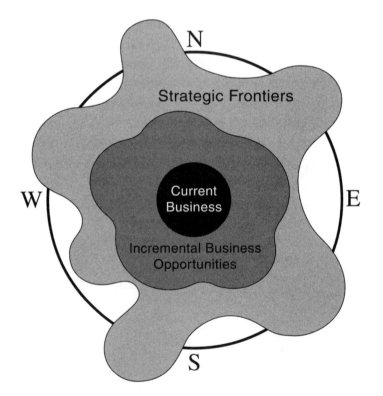

Figure 7-2. Strategic frontiers.

corporate strategy, the PureTouch concept was pulled out of moth-balls, developed, and introduced to the market.

A History of Frontiers: Terra Incognita

In the fifteenth century, mapmaking, or cartography, was anything but a science. Cartographers would gather the latest information from explorers returning from their journeys and update earlier maps by incorporating the new knowledge. Still, if you look at old European maps, you will see large sections to the west, north, and south labeled "terra incognita," or "unknown territories." These vast, empty expanses represented what the cartographers did not know. They were boundaries yet to be crossed or areas to be mapped by future explorers and cartographers.

Terra incognita or frontiers have played an important role in the development and growth of the United States. It was in 1803 that President Thomas Jefferson received congressional funding for the exploration of America's frontier at that time—the land west of the Mississippi River. Jefferson saw potential in that new frontier. In addition to any resources it may have contained, he had hoped that the frontier included a trade route to the Pacific Ocean. A "north-west passage" of inland waterways could eventually open up commerce to Asia. So he appointed his personal secretary, Meriwether Lewis, to lead a reconnaissance group to explore and chart the U.S. frontier. Lewis teamed with William Clark, a captain in the U.S. Army, and the two of them assembled a team of thirty-one people and a dog for the trip. This group, referred to as the Corps of Discovery, spent almost two-and-a-half years exploring this frontier. Although this discovery team did not find a "northwest passage," their maps of the frontier and knowledge of the native people and plants proved invaluable to the explorers, traders, and settlers who followed them to open up the American West.

As long as we can perceive "places" we have not been, we will always have frontiers to explore.

Imagine that your corporate cartographer has been assigned the task of drawing and illustrating a map of your organization's future.

Where are the frontiers? Does the resulting map cause you to feel more or less secure regarding the future of your organization beyond today's business? How much of your corporate future map is labeled "terra incognita"?

Today's Frontiers

Whereas frontiers of the past often referred to land or geography, many of today's frontiers in the world of business are invisible to the human eye. As this book is being written, wireless communications, genomics, and nanotechnology are three of the most significant frontiers that are likely to dramatically change the world in the decades to come. However, a strategic frontier does not have to change the world to be of value to your company; it just has to advance or grow your business. A new product category, a new target audience, a new distribution channel, or a new manufacturing process can be viable strategic frontiers for your business. Anything that could add value to your customers and would also add value to your company is a strategic frontier you should be considering for the future.

When Craig Wynett, general manager of new growth opportunities for Procter & Gamble, thinks of strategic frontiers, he considers them at three different levels: new products, new projects, and new platforms. Each of these levels requires a different corporate response and level of commitment. Creating new products is the easiest level because much of it can take place within the company's current business infrastructure and current business model. New projects become more challenging for a company as they often involve new organizational forms or processes, such as different business units working together or new distribution channels being created. The most challenging strategic frontier for a company is in new business platforms, where new organizational forms and new metrics for success must be considered. Determining how to enter a new industry, leverage a new technology, or create a new market takes more time and requires more corporate flexibility and commitment.

Strategic frontiers span a wide spectrum of business opportunities (see Figure 7-3). They can be near-term, low-risk business opportunities that the company has been considering for a while but for which it never created an effective strategy for implementation. At the other end of the spectrum, strategic frontiers can be breakthrough, industry-changing business opportunities requiring substantial investments in time and resources. What a company selects as a strategic frontier will reflect their business philosophy, industry, and available resources. The important point is that each company know its strategic frontiers and commit to an exploration of those frontiers.

It is important to note that the "company-specific" frontiers noted in Figure 7-3 are aimed at elements of the company's business model. Those elements become frontiers only when the company considers major changes in those areas that will result in significant new value-creation and growth for the company. Mere *improvements* of those elements fall into a category of operational efficiency, not strategic frontiers. For example, identifying a new, lower-cost manufacturing source to boost operating margins would be operational efficiency, improving what already exists. On the other hand, considering the outsourcing of manufacturing so the company can focus its resources on sales and marketing only would be a strategic frontier, a major innovation in the business model that provides growth opportunities.

Company-Specific	Company-Generic	Marketplace
New product	*Franchising*	*Artificial intelligence*
New product category	*Globalization*	*Biotechnology*
New distribution channel	*JIT manufacturing*	*Genomics*
	Mass customization	*Internet*
New manufacturing process	*Outsourcing*	*Nanotechnology*
	Partnerships	*Smart materials*
New positioning	*Patent exploration*	*Wireless communications*
New sourcing strategy	*Services*	
New technology		*Automation*

Figure 7-3. Examples of strategic frontiers.

Managing the Core Business AND the Strategic Frontiers

There are times when senior management, because of market or corporate financial conditions, must be conservative in running the business. Investing in today's "core" business with incremental product improvements or lower-risk new business opportunities can be the most prudent financial strategy, reinforcing and building the company's profitable core. However, there will likely come a time when company growth beyond what is achievable in the core business is deemed necessary. What will that business be? It is the management of "today's core business" with the active pursuit of "tomorrow's core business" that may be the single most important relationship for senior management to monitor and shape. When these two priorities are constantly balanced in the management of a company, they create a strategic tension in the organization that results in a focused, dynamic path to future growth.

In the mid-1990s, Rubbermaid was selected as *Fortune* magazine's "Most Admired Company." This was due, in part, to the fact that Rubbermaid had developed a well-deserved reputation for balancing the growth of its core businesses with growth into new categories and industries, including playground toys, sidewalk refuse containers, platforms for changing a baby's diaper in airports, and numerous other products. The senior management of Rubbermaid had developed a process that assisted them in fostering this strategic tension between managing the core business and creating tomorrow's new growth.

Senior managers who place all of a company's resources on today's core business and ignore the future run the risk that changes in the marketplace will leave them unprepared to enter the markets of the future. On the other hand, a company that starves today's core business because its resources are placed as bets on "the next big thing" may find the cash cow running dry before the bets are ready to pay off. It is the balance of these two factors that is so critical to corporate success—advancing today's core while strategically exploring and capturing new markets on the strategic frontier.

Identifying Strategic Frontiers

The specific activities pursued in the next phase of the Discovery Process, the Exploring Phase, will be dependent on the strategic frontiers that are selected as the highest priority for this strategy innovation initiative. This is the primary objective of this Aligning Phase—the identification and alignment with senior management on strategic frontiers to explore.

Companies that have spent time considering markets of the future will likely have some sense of what represents a promising strategic frontier for them to consider. For those that have not yet done so, the Discovery Process offers a great opportunity to speculate on what those frontiers might be.

Focused Exploration vs. Open Exploration

Senior management may already know the strategic frontiers they would like the team to explore. Because of their knowledge of the business, strategic insights, or some evolution in the marketplace, they will be clear about where the next, new marketplace opportunities are likely to be found. When senior management communicates the frontiers to the Discovery team, the process becomes a "focused exploration." The team will be able to focus their planning and energies on this predetermined strategic frontier.

For companies that have not explored beyond their current markets and current business models, this idea of a strategic frontier will be a new concept. Senior management could randomly select a strategic frontier for the Discovery team to explore, but then the team would be constrained in their exploration to an area that might not hold the greatest potential for the company. Instead, we recommend that the Discovery team first be charged with identifying possible strategic frontiers for the company to consider. In this case, the process becomes an "open exploration" for the Discovery team, and the Aligning Phase of this process takes on a much more important role. It is the identification and alignment with senior management on the most appropriate strategic frontier(s) to explore that will be critical for the ultimate success of this strategic innovation initiative.

Focused Exploration

In a focused exploration, a Discovery team is assigned a strategic frontier selected by senior management. The purpose of the Aligning Phase then is for the Discovery team to be as clear as possible on the reasons why this frontier represents growth opportunities for the company and to understand management's perception of the frontier boundaries. When senior management is able to provide a thorough background and rationale for the attractiveness of the strategic frontier, then this communication may be all that is needed for the team to proceed to the Exploring Phase.

Occasionally, senior management will have a strategic frontier in mind as the focus of the Discovery Process but will still request that the Discovery team move through the steps of an open exploration. This enables management to test the rationale for its proposed frontier and to see whether it will "stand up" to the growth opportunities in other strategic frontiers that the team identifies. This is an approach we recommend for a number of reasons. First of all, it is valuable for senior management to understand how the Discovery team (who may be the next generation of senior management) views future growth opportunities for the company. Their different perspectives on the business could add significant insights and suggest new strategic possibilities. Secondly, when the Discovery team feels that they have contributed to the identification of the strategic frontier they will be exploring, they will feel a greater sense of "ownership" of the process. Rather than carrying out someone else's mission, they will be carrying out their mission in the Discovery Process. This shift in perceived ownership of the process will lead to greater involvement and commitment by the Discovery team.

Open Exploration

In an open exploration, the Discovery team is charged by senior management to survey the world of possible strategic frontiers and recommend those they would like to explore through the Discovery Process.

The Discovery team should begin their process by identifying a long list of possible strategic frontiers for their company. How long should the list be? Use the "Rule of 100," introduced in Chapter 6, as a minimum. Each frontier should represent some degree of future growth potential for the company. Remember, these are areas that deserve further study or exploration because they are likely to yield new business opportunities for your corporation. You begin by building a list of possible frontiers. As you build this frontier list, keep in mind the following:

Process Tip:

Resist the urge to prejudge the potential of strategic frontiers.

When hearing about a new frontier, people have a tendency to make a split-second decision on its attractiveness. What happens in that split second is that the form of a product or service on that frontier is assumed, a market potential is estimated, and a comparison to the company's hurdle rate for new businesses is made. Break that chain of thought! The idea at this stage is to identify the frontier and, on the basis of a thorough exploration of it later, identify a way to "change the rules of the game" on that frontier. That rule-changing innovation is impossible to determine prior to the frontier exploration.

- Do not overanalyze the frontier options you add to the list.

- Do not consider *how* that frontier would be implemented by your company, but assume that you could acquire whatever skills or resources you would need.

- Do not judge the growth potential for each frontier as you build the list, as most would be too difficult to determine at this point.

Both of these latter two issues—implementation and growth potential—will be important topics of the Exploring Phase. Rather than be concerned with them now, stretch your thinking and list any area that could possibly provide you with new business opportunities in the future.

How do you go about building a list of strategic frontiers? It starts with the Discovery team sharing their points of view. Grab an empty conference room and a flipchart and spend the morning speculating. See how long you can make the list. Following that exercise, use both internal and external sources to help expand the list.

Sources of Strategic Frontiers

After the Discovery team does an internal listing of potential strategic frontiers, they should then seek out other sources of frontier options, both internal and external to the company (see Figure 7-4).

Internal Sources for Strategic Frontiers

There are a variety of internal sources that the Discovery team can tap in search of potential strategic frontiers to explore.

Management Interviews

Senior managers, with their experience, systemic perception of the company, and responsibility for its strategy, often have ideas on how to grow the business. Discovery team members should con-

Internal Sources	External Sources
Management Interviews	*Trends Search*
Company Vision	*Technology Search*
Corporate Drawing Boards	*Business Model Search*
Redefine the Business	*Outside Experts*
Core Competence	
Intranet Survey	

Figure 7-4. Sources of strategic frontier ideas.

duct personal (one-on-one) interviews with all of the senior managers to identify their suggestions for viable strategic frontiers. The Discovery team sponsor can help set up these interviews. Listen to the responses of these senior managers but also listen for the assumptions and perceptions that are behind those responses, as they will help you understand the company's current view of the future.

In one Fortune 50 company where we were asked to conduct these interviews with the top fifteen executives, there was some concern that the appointments would be difficult to arrange and that, due to near-term pressures on the business, our reception might be a chilly one. We were pleased to discover that every executive willingly created the time; in most cases, the one-hour meeting extended to ninety minutes or more so that all their input could be captured. These executives were eager for the opportunity to influence the company's future focus by suggesting possible new frontiers to be explored.

Company Vision

Another critical input for the identification of strategic frontiers is the company's vision or mission statement. If it is a good one, the vision will be a proactive one that contains a focus for the company's efforts and some indication of what success looks like when the vision is fulfilled. What path to the future is suggested by the vision/mission? Is it a relatively broad path that encourages the pursuit of a goal in a variety of different ways? Or is it a relatively narrow path that minimizes the company's flexibility and possible strategic options?

Corporate Drawing Boards

Talk to the people in R&D, new product development, and marketing. Ask them if they have any new product ideas that were developed or submitted but not considered to be a good fit with the company's current product line. Are there elements of those products that would suggest a strategic frontier for further exploration? Do any of these new ideas contain materials, technologies, or functions that would broaden today's business or open up new market niches? If so, it could be a strategic frontier.

Redefine the Business

Chris Zook, in his book *Profit from the Core*, describes the importance of knowing the definition of your core business. "Defining the business accurately is a way of creating a logical hierarchy of territories in and around your core business that help you target wise investments . . ." As an example, Zook asks the question, "Is Coca-Cola in the cola business, the soft drink business, the beverage business, or some other business?"[1]

This is a good exercise for the Discovery team to help explore possible strategic frontiers. The team should first narrowly define the business they feel their company is in right now. As an example, if your company is currently in the business of manufacturing coffee cups, the Discovery team should then define a larger business of which the coffee cups business is some minor portion or share. Perhaps it is the "beverage container" market, which would also contain glassware, paper cups, etc. Keep going and define the next higher-level business of which "beverage containers" is a relatively small share. That might be the market for "liquid conveyance devices," which would include milk bottles, picnic jugs, and even tank trucks. Following these expanded definitions of a company's market could suggest a strategic frontier to consider.

Terry Tallis, one of the leaders of a successful strategy innovation initiative at Hewlett-Packard's Inkjet Supplies Business Unit, notes about that project, "We were creatures of our past. This experience raised us up so that we could see what had been invisible to us. We had thought we were in the 'printer' business. We discovered we were in the 'printing occasion' business. We had 50 percent of the printer business but less than 1 percent of the printing occasion business. That was key to the whole growth initiative."

Core Competence

A core competence of a company can, with some effort, be turned into a *core excellence*, creating new value for customers and growth for the company. Take a look at what your company does well and determine if significant advances in that area might represent a significant growth opportunity. Rather than just have your Industrial Design group designing great products for you to sell, can they provide design services directly for your clients (as BMW does)? Can your internal inventory tracking system be offered as a service to customers on an out-sourcing basis (as Mrs. Fields does)? If so, these are potential strategic frontiers for your company to consider.

Intranet Survey

Ask your employees if they have any ideas on how the company might grow. A quick question placed on the corporate intranet is an easy, efficient way to gather new ideas for strategic frontiers and provides a way for the employees to feel involved in the process. In 1999, P&G launched an intranet site called myidea.com, which attracted over 9,000 possible ways to grow the business. It followed that by fostering new connections among 18,000 engineers by linking them via its Innovation Net.

External Sources for Strategic Frontiers

Using internal sources for the identification of strategic frontiers will frequently reflect a corporate myopia about the business. If you

---

Process Tip:

Core competencies and successful brands can be barriers to strategy innovation.

Often a logical starting point for the creation of new business opportunities is to leverage your current strengths, which frequently reside in core competencies and successful brands. However, core competencies and successful brands carry with them constraints or limits on how they can be used, so as to protect their "value" to the company. Be aware that these constraints may favor the incremental extensions of the current business over the pursuit of innovative new business opportunities.

have been with the company for more than a few years, you tend to believe that the way the company does business and the way the marketplace operates are "givens." If you were part of the company when many of the processes and infrastructure were established, you tend to believe that the company is already the best it can be. This makes it difficult to consider changes that could yield growth opportunities. It is important for the Discovery team to also explore external sources and perspectives in their search for potential strategic frontiers.

Many companies that have been in a business for a while, especially if they have been successful, consider themselves "experts" in the business. As experts, they believe that their opinions and perceptions of the market are superior to those of "outsiders," so that seeking outside perspectives is a waste of time. That may be true for managing today's business but it can be lethal in the pursuit of strategy innovation. The organizations that seek out new, outside perspectives as a stimulus to their strategic thinking tend to be the ones most prepared for dynamic shifts in their marketplace and the emergence of new frontiers. In the search for the next opportunity area, search outside the company.

Process Tip:

Visionary companies are seldom those that only talk to themselves.

Visionary companies tend to be proactive companies. They are often driven by internal goals but guided by the marketplace. It is their constant measurement and connection with customers and experts outside their company that helps guide their strategy development. Get outside of your four walls and talk to those who envision, create, and measure the future.

Trends Search

Trends reflect changes that are taking place in the marketplace or in the world. Changes within any type of system disrupt its stability and create some imbalance, which is the source of potential opportunities. Organize a subgroup of the Discovery team to scour publications and the Internet for trends in various cultures or societies, lifestyles, or demographics. Do any of the trends, if they were to continue or increase in intensity, suggest new customer needs or some difficulty by current companies in meeting their needs? Think through the implications of the trends and all their potential outcomes.

We know of a London-based communications company that dedicated a portion of its quarterly executive meetings to a presentation of key industry trends to stimulate a future focus. Once the presentation was completed, the group invested time in assessing the possible importance of those trends and their implications for the organization. This type of input into a Discovery initiative is ideal.

Technology Search

Set up a "scout team" to search for technologies or new materials that your company might use to greatly increase customer value and satisfaction. Look for technologies that could be used in a product or in the making and selling of a product. Talk with suppliers, vendors, other companies, and scientists in laboratories. Technologies that offer any potential for stimulating growth in your company should be captured as a possible strategic frontier.

One European company used a "scout team" approach as a way of seeking out both promising technologies and promising alliances, partners, or acquisitions. They identified candidate companies where a visit might be mutually beneficial and set up site visits by the Discovery team. Even where a longer-term relationship did not play out, the Discovery team benefited from the new knowledge and insights gained in the exchange.

At the same time, assign this scout team the task of identifying any possible or probable technological "dislocations" in your industry. New frontiers can often be found on the other side of these technological disruptions in the marketplace.

Business Model Search

In addition to investigating trends and technologies, set up a third search team to explore the business literature for new ways of running a business. Business periodicals routinely profile companies that defy conventional business wisdom and meet with success. Is there something they do that, if applied to your business, could result in significant growth? Seeing what companies in other industries are doing to increase the value of their business model can provide important insights about strategy innovation possibilities.

Following this type of research, one media company assigned a team to identify all the possible component parts to a business model in their industry. Then, from all the parts, they built up a model for each market competitor and, from role-playing the competitor's position, evolved the model out five years. Now, with a possible (maybe probable) competitive business landscape looking out five years, they conceived from scratch the optimal business model for their company in that industry. This business model perspective assisted the team in identifying the areas to explore in order to migrate from today's business to the more-competitive-in-the-future business.

Outside Experts

Consider engaging the services of an outside expert for gathering strategic frontier options. Strategy consultants, venture capitalists, financial analysts, technology experts, and magazine editors are just some of the people who can add a valuable outside perspective to supplement the internal search for strategic frontiers.

One major German automobile manufacturer enlisted the help of three expert resources to develop a probable scenario for the global automobile industry in 2010. Each had a different focus for surfacing emerging trends: manufacturing processes, the Asian market, or the U.S. market. The strongest and best-supported trends of each study were combined into a single presentation and used to "provoke" new thinking on future frontiers among a gathering of global executives. The executive conference proved to be a powerful combination of the newest innovations in the production pipeline married to an introduction of future forces to stimulate new thinking for future innovations.

Thought leader panels can also be very effective in identifying appropriate strategic frontiers. For example, the first Moen thought leader panel, referred to as the "macro" panel, was intended to bring outside, expert opinions to the company to help define areas of future growth opportunities. Recruiting experts from a mix of disciplines for a two-day exploration of the future will provide your company with a proprietary view of the future and clarity around possible strategic frontiers. Details on the thought-leader-panel methodology can be found in Chapter 8.

Prioritize the Strategic Frontiers

The list of potential strategic frontiers should be long, inspiring, yet somewhat daunting to the Discovery team. How can the team explore the range of opportunities available in the depth that would be necessary to understand the frontier? The answer is, they cannot. A Discovery team can explore only one or two, possibly three (depending on the scale of the project) strategic frontiers at a time. Pursuing more than three frontiers will typically stretch the team's resources so thin that the resulting exploration is too cursory to identify specific business opportunities. Therefore, the next step is to prioritize the list of strategic frontiers to narrow the focus for the initiative (see Figure 7-5).

The Discovery team can use any process they are comfortable with to help narrow the list. Be sure to clarify the criteria you will use to prioritize the frontiers: size of opportunity, degree of innovation, fit with current strategy, consistency with today's core business, etc. One option is to understand how senior management might assess the potential of a strategic frontier. However, do not be afraid to use the team's energy or passion with a frontier as a basis for prioritizing, as an energized Discovery team will generally excel in this process.

The next step is to involve senior management in the prioritization process. Set up a meeting with senior management to review

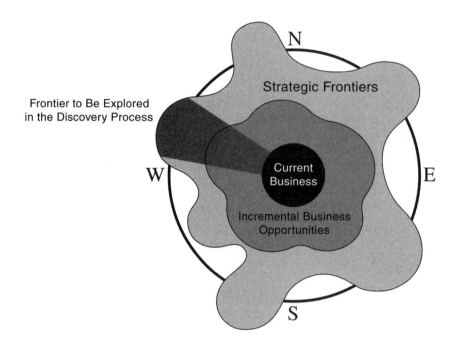

Figure 7-5. Strategic frontiers to be explored.

the strategic frontiers and share the Discovery team's prioritization efforts. Engage them in a dialogue about their views and priorities for these frontiers. Remind them that the exploration of this frontier will seek to understand how to create new value there. It will likely yield a range of short- to long-term opportunities, a range of low-risk to higher-risk businesses, and a range of conventional to innovative ideas. The objective of the meeting is to emerge with agreement on what strategic frontier(s) this Discovery team should explore in this Discovery Process. Keep in mind that this is not a commitment at this point to enter this area. It is only a commitment to explore its potential because of a belief that it may contain new growth opportunities.

This meeting with senior management is the first step in the all-important "alignment" that the team needs in order to keep the initiative relevant and to maximize the potential that their work can be implemented. Do not be surprised if the frontier decision takes more than one meeting. For many companies, this will be the first time that a proactive decision on the future has been made. It is an important strategic choice, so take whatever time is necessary to gain this early alignment.

Critical Role of Strategic Frontiers

The importance of this alignment of senior management and the Discovery team on the appropriate strategic frontiers for the company cannot be overstated. By authorizing this strategic initiative and focusing on strategic frontiers, senior management makes a commitment to the company's future. They agree to the challenge of managing today's core business while preparing for tomorrow's core business. It is much easier to focus on running today's business to satisfy short-term goals and let the future take care of itself. Being reactive about the future and what it will bring can be devastating to a company in a dynamic marketplace. Unexpected changes and shifts make a company vulnerable to new competitors, new technologies, and changes in customer behavior in a market. Being proactive about the future and creating the company's next growth platform will increase its chances of survival in a time of change.

Strategic Frontiers as a Corporate Vision

Much has been written about the positive role that a corporate vision can play in guiding the activities and development of a company. That compelling vision of an ideal future can motivate and influence employees as they make day-to-day decisions on behalf of the company. When we think of powerful visions, we think of how both Apple and Microsoft were purported to have been driven by the image of ubiquitous computers in the future. Corporate visions are particularly powerful for start-up ventures, but what about established companies? It is not easy to instill a new vision in an established company. Established companies cannot focus all their energies on creating a new company—they need to protect the ongoing business also.

Strategic frontiers are to established companies what corporate visions are to start-ups. A CEO of an established company can point to a previously unexplored strategic frontier and declare it to be the next growth area for the business. Distinct resources can be targeted to exploring and understanding that frontier while still maintaining the current business. Those resources can be guided in their search for business opportunities by the definition of that frontier.

When a company has both a current business *and* a strategic frontier, it is better able to balance the "current versus future" dilemma described in Chapter 2. Unless the future frontier is clearly identified, there is no reason for a company to dedicate attention and resources to the future. In fact, to allocate funding to a "fuzzy future" does not appear to be responsible spending. But allocating funds to a clearly delineated future frontier can make it a wise investment in the future. Senior management will be perceived by both employees and the investment community as leading the company, as taking a proactive stance.

> **Process Tip:**
>
> *Established companies should use strategic frontiers the same way that start-ups use corporate visions.*
>
> The identification of a company's strategic frontiers will turn a "fuzzy future" into a more "focused future." By naming the next growth area, senior management makes a bold, proactive statement to both employees and the investment community that they are leading the company to an attractive future, while still maintaining the current business.

The identification of a company's strategic frontiers will have other benefits also. It will provide a focus for the creative energies of the entire company by occupying some of the "mindshare" of the employees. If I am an employee and learn that wireless communication is our strategic frontier, everything that crosses my desk about wireless communication will now catch my attention, where it did not previously. If I am attending an electronics convention, I will wander by the wireless exhibits and booths. If I find a good article on wireless communication in a publication, I will share it with my colleagues. Identification of strategic frontiers can encourage employees to be more proactive and committed to the company's future. This results in a strong, intangible benefit to the company.

There is one more role that strategic frontiers can play in a company—the stimulus for change. Corporations are often quite resistant to the idea of change. It frequently requires a negative event, perhaps a major crisis or flirtation with bankruptcy, before change initiatives gain momentum. Strategic frontiers represent a positive stimulus for change in a corporation. Positioned by the senior managers as a challenge for the company that could have a very positive impact on its future, the successful penetration of a strategic frontier could provide a positive catalyst for corporate change.

Imagine, for a moment, the contrast between working for a company that is aligned on its future frontiers versus one that is clueless. Figure 7-6 illustrates some points of difference.

There is a choice. An organization can choose to wander into the future, letting today's events be the guide for their decision making.

Aligned on Near-Term Goals and Strategic Frontiers	Aligned on Near-Term Goals Only
Managing today's business with an eye on tomorrow	*Managing today's business only*
Sensitive to all changes in the business environment	*Optimizing today's competitive position*
Open to future perspectives	*Open to tactical perspectives*
Aware of evolving competitive landscapes	*Fixed on current competition*
Marketshare boundaries: dynamic	*Marketshare battle: Fractions of a percent*
Leadership: future focused	*Leadership: Wall Street–focused*
Innovation time horizon: long	*Innovation time horizon: short*
Future viewed as opportunity	*Future viewed as threat*
Organization's posture: proactive	*Organization's posture: reactive*

Figure 7-6. Impact of being aligned on strategic frontiers.

Or, an organization can choose to seize the future (carpe futurum!) by defining, exploring, and capturing the business growth opportunities on their strategic frontiers. It might take a few tries to identify the "right" strategic frontier for your company. Lewis and Clark did not discover the "northwest passage" they were hoping to find. But the mistake is in not starting this process, preferring to stay in your corporate comfort zone. If you are not searching your strategic frontiers, you will lose out to those who are.

Summary

+ The importance of alignment in the Discovery Process comes from an inherent tension in any strategy innovation process, where creating something new can have value to a company but can also represent potential risks.

+ In this process, the Discovery team will experience "discovery drift," where they embrace a series of small changes to the company's business model that lead to a major leap over the course of the initiative. In the meantime, senior management has not made that same mental shift, resulting in different expectations of the output of the initiative.

+ Agreeing on the elements of the business model that will remain fixed, on the business assumptions to be tested, and on the strategic frontier for the Discovery team to explore will help align the goals and expectations with senior management.

+ A strategic frontier is that unexplored area of potential growth that lies between today's business and tomorrow's opportunities. It is believed to have growth potential for a company but requires exploration by a reconnaissance group to determine if it is true.

+ Strategic frontiers span a wide spectrum of business opportunities from near-term, low-risk business ventures to breakthrough, industry-changing new businesses.

+ The identification of, and agreement on, the strategic frontiers to explore is the primary goal of this Aligning Phase. If senior management has not already identified that frontier, it is the role of the Discovery team to recommend options for them to consider.

- To identify potential strategic frontiers, the Discovery team should utilize a variety of internal and external resources for options.

- In addition to creating alignment between the Discovery team and senior management for the Discovery Process, the identification of a strategic frontier can play a significant role in the company by:

  - Signifying a commitment to managing the business of the future

  - Playing the role of a corporate vision within established companies

  - Focusing the activities and "mindshare" of employees

  - Providing a stimulus for corporate change, where necessary

- Established companies should use the identification and exploration of new business opportunities on a strategic frontier the same way that start-up companies use a vision statement: to focus the company's energy and efforts on the pursuit of a compelling future.

Endnote

1. Chris Zook, *Profit from the Core* (Boston: Harvard Business School Press, 2001).

CHAPTER 8

THE DISCOVERY PROCESS

Exploring Phase

> Many companies take their industry's conditions as given and set strategy accordingly. Value innovators don't. No matter how the rest of the industry is faring, value innovators look for blockbuster ideas and quantum leaps in value.[1]
>
> —*W. CHAN KIM AND RENEE MAUBORGNE*

| Staging Phase | Aligning Phase | **Exploring Phase** | Creating Phase | Mapping Phase |

With strategic frontiers that align with the aspirations of senior management for this initiative, the Discovery team is ready to begin exploring those frontiers. Where do they start? Who do they talk to? What do they look for?

While the Exploring Phase is often the most intellectually stimulating, it is also the most time and energy-consuming phase of the Discovery Process. It consists of the following steps:

◆   Preparing to be an explorer

  ◆ Adopting an exploratory mind-set

  ◆ Aiming for visionary opportunities

◆   Planning the exploration route

  ◆ Exploratory vectors

  ◆ Immersions and interactions

◆   Selecting exploration activities

  ◆ Customer value activities

  ◆ Market dynamics activities

  ◆ Business model innovation activities

◆   Discovering value on the frontier

  ◆ New insights

Preparing to Be an Explorer

Former astronaut and United States senator John Glenn would qualify as a modern-day explorer and space pioneer. The first American to orbit the earth in 1962 aboard the Friendship 7 Mercury capsule, Glenn returned to space thirty-six years later, at seventy-seven years of age, to explore research on aging on a Space Shuttle Discovery mission. He told PBS, "The urge to explore the unknown is part of human nature and has led us to many of the most profound changes in our standard of living."[2] What does it take to be a good explorer in unknown areas? Glenn believes curiosity plays a key role. "This has been the real hallmark of what's made this country really good—the curiosity of how we can do things better, whether it's a door knob or a TV camera or better chairs. I hope we don't lose that curiosity."[3]

Ken Cox, a technologist and futurist at NASA's Johnson Space Center, agrees that curiosity is an important component of the exploratory mind-set of pioneers. But Cox would add a number of other requirements for those who venture into the unknown. He believes that good explorers need to be open-minded, fearless, and comfortable with ambiguity. He points out that new information discovered in the unexplored frontier does not always fit into our old ways of thinking. As a result, an important skill for the explorer is to be able to discern new patterns in the new information being collected on the frontier. It is the identification of new patterns that often leads to the thrilling "eureka" response made famous by Archimedes.

Discovery team explorers will benefit greatly in this Exploring Phase by adopting these same attributes. As you look to learn more about customers, the emerging market, and new business models, be curious, open-minded, and fearless in your pursuit. Then, recognize that it might take some time to discern the new patterns in the new information, but keep at it because the discovery can be quite thrilling.

Adopting an Exploratory Mind-Set

Just as NASA rockets need to escape the earth's gravitational field to reach new planets, the Discovery team must escape the force of "corporate gravity" in order to discover new business opportunities. Corporate gravity is an invisible force that prevents employees from venturing too far from the current business model. As managers in charge of maintaining the integrity of the company's current operations, you spend most of your working days protecting the business model from anything that would have a negative impact on those operations. As a result of many years of doing this, you develop a knee-jerk reaction to anything that does not fit the current business model. The process is quite quick—you see something new, assess its fit with the current business model, and accept or reject it based on your expectations of its fit. If it would affect your efficiency or lower your ROI, you reject it. If it requires an infrastructure change, you reject it. If you can't quantify it, you reject it. This is corporate gravity. It acts as a filter for your perspective so that only corporate-friendly observations get through.

The Discovery team must first recognize this phenomenon of corporate gravity and then take steps to escape beyond it. One way

Process Tip:

In order to see more opportunities in the Exploring Phase, adopt the role of an independent, venture-backed entrepreneur.

Corporate managers often assimilate a shared view of the marketplace that helps streamline and coordinate their efforts. For example, most agree on what comprises a good (or bad) business opportunity, how customers behave, and what it takes to get a product to market. These shared assumptions, while promoting efficiency, can prevent the discovery of innovative (break the rules) new business opportunities. In order to minimize the impact of these corporate filters, team members should look at the market through the eyes of an entrepreneur. What would an entrepreneur trying to break into this market see in this Exploring Phase?

to do this is to adopt the perspective of a start-up entrepreneur, as outlined in the Staging Phase discussion in Chapter 6. By ignoring the constraints and restrictions imposed by your current corporate business model, you are free to perceive and consider new things in this Exploring Phase. Anything can inspire a potential business opportunity to a start-up entrepreneur. That is the mindset necessary for the Discovery team in this Exploring Phase.

Another way to escape the force of corporate gravity is to ignore any information you receive that is too "comfortable" for you. When you hear someone say that they are happy with the product that your company makes, politely ignore them. Instead, focus your energies on those who find it ineffective, too expensive, or too fragile—that is where the new business opportunities are located. If people tell you that the industry is healthy and stable, challenge them. Look for surprises, exceptions to the rule, possible market dislocations, and growing markets on the very fringes of the industry. If the corporate side of you would find it irrelevant or uncomfortable, the entrepreneur side of you would embrace it as the link to a potential opportunity. Practice being a contrarian with a mission.

Being a contrarian was a favorite ploy of Bob Galvin when he was running Motorola. He admired counterintuitive thinkers, claiming that "common wisdom holds back uncommon wisdom." When Motorola had big decisions to be made, Galvin would often look for the opposite approach.

> Frequently I would listen to my very intelligent associates to see how they were thinking out an idea. If they did a good job, we would go with it. If it were a very significant decision, the opposite thinking would often be the right approach. One of the consequences is that ultimately, the position that is right is a minority position—it is new and different. Most of us are not comfortable with the new and different. It takes courage to be a minority thinker to push it through. Every major Motorola decision when I was there were initially minority positions.

Aiming for Visionary Opportunities on the Strategic Opportunity Spectrum

The strategic frontier you identify will turn out to be an area containing a wide range of new business opportunities. Some opportunities will be short-term, some longer-term. Some will have large growth potential, others will be more modest. The way the Discovery team decides to explore the strategic frontier and the amount of time and effort put into the exploration will determine the number and variety of opportunities and variations they will discover. Achieving both a breadth and a quantity of options prior to making strategic decisions is a cornerstone of this Discovery Process. To ensure that the Discovery team aims for breadth and quantity, we suggest that they target their search to cover the entire Strategic Opportunity Spectrum (SOS) within each strategic frontier.

The Strategic Opportunity Spectrum is a method of categorizing the business opportunities you discover on your strategic frontiers (see Figure 8-1). On the left end of the spectrum are those business opportunities that are closest to today's core business. We call them "visible" opportunities because you probably know about them already and may have even considered them at some point. With a few minor changes in the current business model you can achieve a new growth opportunity on this frontier.

Visible opportunities, successfully brought to market, are all around us. John Deere's extension from professional-grade agricultural tractors to riding lawnmowers for the weekend farmer wannabe was a visible opportunity for them. Reese's Peanut Butter Cups have mined their "visible" boundaries from ice cream to breakfast cereal (after the Pieces and the Sticks). Zip-Loc used to mean airtight "bags" but now, with the introduction of reusable, hard plastic containers, it means airtight "containment."

Because the changes required to the corporate business model are relatively minor, the pursuit of visible opportunities is usually shorter-term and usually lower-risk. Markets for these products or services often exist already, customers are known, and the manufacturing and distribution infrastructure may have been established. These opportunities are the low-hanging fruit, easiest to harvest for your business. However, the existence of the market and the relatively low barriers to entry in that market often make visible opportunities lower-volume opportunities also. If someone else got to that market first, they probably captured the significant share of the revenue and profit potential.

"Visible" or not, we understand that senior management of some companies will quiver at the prospect of strategically extending beyond the most incremental of business innovations. What

"Visible"   **"Visionary"**

Low-Hanging Fruit   High Rewards

Figure 8-1. Strategic Opportunity Spectrum.

might be the impact on the base business? Diet colas were a visible opportunity for many years in the beverage category before a company made the leap to bring them into the fold. Remember Tab, the first commercially marketed diet cola? Coca Cola was so concerned that it might cannibalize Coke's market share that Tab's "flavor notes" were designed to not taste very good. You had to really, really want the diet benefit to tolerate the strange taste created for Tab. Of course, history has shown that the "diet innovation" of Diet Coke actually did not significantly cannibalize Coke's market share. It caused the category to greatly expand by attracting new weight-conscious consumers to the soft drink category.

On the other end of the spectrum lie the visionary opportunities. Visionary opportunities are typically based on the inspired imagination of the Discovery team. Markets, customers, and infrastructure for visionary opportunities do not currently exist, they must be imagined. We often see visionary opportunities arise in companies that are looking to fulfill a mission or cause in the marketplace. A visionary opportunity is often an "idealized" scenario of how a customer's needs can be fulfilled, based on a strongly held conviction that drives the company. Fred Smith of Federal Express dared to imagine a visionary opportunity of delivering mail overnight, and Apple's Steve Jobs imagined a computer in every home, based on his conviction of the value it would ultimately deliver. Both of these visionary company founders dared to dream of meeting customer needs in a new and unique way, even though the markets did not yet exist.

Visionary opportunities are not, however, exclusive to start-up companies. Motorola, originally a manufacturer of automobile radios, attained leadership in multiple "visionary" frontiers over the years, from televisions to wireless communications to microchips. And even though their early inventions were test-and-measurement devices, William Hewlett and David Packard committed their company to a vision of excellence in engineering that is both leading-edge and socially responsible. Because of this broad vision, Hewlett-Packard is now playing a leadership role in the once-visionary opportunities in computing, printing, and imaging industries, among others. 3M had humble beginnings as a mining venture that did not "pan out." It has been more successful replicating its innovation formula thousands of times into both "visible" and "visionary" frontiers, in industries ranging from sandpaper to pharmaceuticals.

Visionary opportunities are longer-term opportunities because they usually require the development of technologies, infrastructure, and customers that do not yet exist. From this standpoint, they also carry a higher risk compared to visible opportunities. However, visionary opportunities typically contain the possibility of *very* high rewards, both financially and psychologically, to those willing to take the risk.

The majority of new business opportunities identified in the Discovery Process lie somewhere between the two ends of the Strategic Opportunity Spectrum. They are opportunities that add value to customers in some way and require varying degrees of change and market development by the company in order to meet those needs. Opportunities in this middle range vary in the size of the market and revenue potential.

The Strategic Opportunity Spectrum is introduced here because the way the Discovery team thinks about the opportunities they will develop has a significant impact on the ultimate success of this process. Setting a goal of identifying a number of visible opportunities for your company will result in finding a few visible opportunities, but probably not much more. However, setting a goal

> **Process Tip:**
>
> *If you stretch your thinking to identify visionary opportunities, you will also identify opportunities all along the Strategic Opportunity Spectrum.*
>
> **Incremental thinking will produce, at best, incremental ideas. Stretch thinking that pursues the "big idea" in any marketplace will produce a large quantity of ideas, ranging from world-changing new industries down to incremental product improvements.**

of identifying a number of visionary opportunities will provide not only the visionary opportunities the team is looking for but also a large quantity of opportunities that fall all along the spectrum, including visible opportunities. It is the "stretch" in the thinking required by visionary opportunities that reveals the greatest quantity of new opportunities of all types (see Figure 8-2).

The *pursuit* of opportunities at the visionary end of the spectrum will establish the open-minded, anything-is-possible attitudes necessary for the team to "see" new opportunities everywhere. Often the visionary ideas they find will contain within them some element that the company can use today to improve their business. The process does not, however, work in reverse. Teams that are interested only in identifying short-term, visible opportunities close to their current core business are not likely to identify bigger, longer-term opportunities. Their desire to focus short-term prevents them from entertaining ideas that might fall to the right side of the spectrum, and they end up with a much smaller quantity of opportunities.

It does not matter whether senior management is seeking a visionary opportunity as part of their strategic portfolio or not. Even when the company will only consider developing the shorter-term, lower-risk, visible opportunities, it is important that the Discovery team aims to stretch their thinking and exploration to identify opportunities that lie on the visionary end of this spectrum.

Figure 8-2. Strategic Opportunity Spectrum: Setting stretch goals.

Some visionary opportunities are slow to be recognized or are missed entirely. All the major television networks missed the dedicated news network opportunity that Ted Turner developed in CNN. IBM missed the importance of software. Microsoft was slow to recognize the Internet. Motorola possessed the capability, but failed to see the market opportunity in inkjet printing.

Planning the Exploration Route

Like most explorations, the Exploring Phase of the Discovery Process is done "away from home." To gain new perspectives and discover new ways to think about your future business, the Exploring Phase must begin with an "external" exploration. It does not begin with an understanding of what a company does well (core competencies) or what it is currently able to do—that would be a capability in search of a market. The Discovery Process is a market-centric process that *begins* with an understanding of the emerging market and its needs, and then proceeds to a search for how the company might go about meeting those needs. This is an "outside-in" process for the Discovery team.

This is not an exercise to be conducted from your cubicle with a Web browser. The Exploring Phase will require the Discovery team to travel, meet with people, see what they see, and walk in their shoes. If yours is a regional business with local clients, the travel will be less. If yours is a global company, pack your bags and grab your passport.

There is no one formula or linear sequence of steps for the Discovery team to take in this Exploring Phase. Every industry is different, and every Discovery team will differ on how and where it finally chooses to explore. But where should they start?

Mapping the Route Along Exploration Vectors

To think about a starting point for the exploration process, take a step back and think for a moment about what business is all about. Business is about creating value for someone (a customer) and, in delivering that value, creating value for yourself. So identifying new business opportunities should focus on value—what it is and how it can be delivered or enhanced.

Where do you look for that value? Consider that a business transaction takes place between a customer and a company, in a marketplace. Therefore, the search for value should include explorations of the customer (customer value), the company (business model innovation), and the marketplace (market dynamics). We describe these three areas as exploration vectors, the pathways that a Discovery team should take to understand and identify value-creating opportunities on the company's strategic frontier (see Figure 8-3).

Customer Value Vector

Businesses do not exist without customers. Customers do not purchase goods and services unless those goods and services deliver value. Therefore, a logical starting point for exploring new business opportunities is to meet with potential customers and understand their perception of value. It is the new insights gained around emerging customer needs and their perception of value that can be the basis of exciting new business opportunities. Companies that are very customer-centric, and those that aspire to be, often begin the Exploring Phase with work in the customer value area.

Market Dynamics Vector

If strategy innovation is about creating the company's future, it should not be based on today's markets, today's products, or to-

**Exploring
Phase**

Figure 8-3. Exploration vectors.

day's customers. You need to understand the world of tomorrow and use those insights to drive the strategy innovation process.

In a stable world, the markets of tomorrow look a lot like the markets of today, minimizing the value to be gained by studying the future. In a dynamic world, changes in any aspect of the marketplace can have a ripple effect through not only that market, but all other markets that touch it. When world oil prices rise, sales at the local drive-thru restaurant can fall. Studying the future and the forces that affect markets will reveal the possibilities of change. Change is a two-sided coin (pun intended). On one side, it will have a negative effect on those who are vested in the old way of doing business. On the other side, it will cause market disruption and imbalances, opening up new business opportunities for those who are prepared to participate. Therefore, we strongly recommend that the Discovery team include market foresight in their exploration plan. Companies that feel they have a core competence to leverage and are very marketplace-centric often begin with the vector of market dynamics.

Business Model Innovation Vector

Many recent examples of strategy innovation have involved changes in the traditional business model used in those markets. Furniture was expensive and sold in showrooms until IKEA designed a line of inexpensive, Scandinavian-style, assemble-it-yourself home furnishings to be sold in large retail outlets to young buyers. Southwest Airlines rejected the standard hub-and-spoke system of air travel and concentrated on low-cost, local, point-to-point travel. A Belgian movie theater owner defied the industry logic of multiple-screen econo-boxes and built a hugely successful megaplex consisting of twenty-five screens and over 7,000 luxury seats. New business opportunities can come from old businesses, where changes in the traditional ways of doing business results in greater customer value and growth for the company.

This was the case with Cemex, an international cement company located in Mexico. They developed a sophisticated communications network and a strategically placed distribution system to be able to offer their customers on-demand cement delivery, within twenty minutes of the contractor's call. In his book *Value Migration: How to Think Several Moves Ahead of the Competition*, Adrian Slywotzky writes, "Value migrates from outmoded business designs to ones that are better able to satisfy customers' most important priorities."[4]

We recommend that you spend some exploration time examining the potential for new growth that comes from changing elements of your current business model. Companies that recognize their need to change or feel that the creation of new businesses is one of their core competences are often those who first explore business model innovation.

Setting Up New Activities

It is likely that your company has spent some time exploring customers, markets, and business models in the past, such as interviews or focus groups with your customers. In the Staging Phase, we mentioned that it is valuable to review old research to provide everyone on the team with an understanding of today's core business. However, *do not* use any previous work for the Exploring Phase. The reason is that the previous work was probably done to provide information for a specific reason, usually to support some aspect of the current business. For example, you may have used previous focus groups with current customers to test their reaction to a new line extension or new promotional materials. Chances are good that you talked to the types of customers you usually talk to and asked them some standard questions in order to get that information. This process was helpful for the core business at that time but it won't help you identify new business opportunities. The goal of strategy innovation on the frontier is to discover *new ways* of doing business. You cannot ask the same people the same questions and expect to learn something new. Instead, the Discovery team should concentrate their efforts on setting up new activities designed specifically for this initiative. Create new and unique events where you ask different questions of the same people, the

Process Tip:

To see things differently, you need to do things differently.

There are probably very good reasons why you take the same route to commute to work every day. However, if you ever get tired of the same old scenery, you won't be satisfied until you change your route. Looking for new business opportunities in the same places you have always found them will produce the same types of opportunities you have always found. To innovate, look elsewhere. Try different approaches.

same questions of different people, or different questions of different people.

The Discovery team should consider less conventional ways of doing their explorations in the Discovery Process. If the normal process for interacting with your customers is to watch a discussion from the other side of a one-way mirror in a focus group facility, consider meeting with customers on their turf—in their homes or in their offices. Or "immerse" yourself in their lives—follow them around for a day or night, to learn about their lifestyle, their needs, and the factors that influence them. By approaching them in different ways and/or asking them different questions, you'll gain new insights that could lead to exciting new business opportunities.

There are many marketing research and consulting companies that offer unique ways of exploring customers and the marketplace in search of insights for new business opportunities. The appropriateness of a technique will depend on the industry in which you work as well as the quality and experience of the company offering the technique. Searching books, journals, and Internet sites, as well as networking with colleagues, are the best ways to identify these exploratory techniques.

As an additional corporate benefit, this "fresh" look at customers, markets, and business models causes organizations to have new perspectives on their existing customers, markets, and business models. As a consequence of the Discovery Process, there is an infusion of "fresh thinking" into an enterprise for current, as well as future, growth. This is often a catalyst to an increased vitality felt throughout the organization and confidence about its prospects for the future. We have observed this even in organizations that specialize in visionary or innovation services. Become too static, and your products and your organization become "stale." Instead, challenge yourself to see new things in new ways, and the whole organization benefits from an infusion of fresh perspective.

The Goal: Identify Insights to the Creation of Value

Regardless of which activities the Discovery team uses in the Exploring Phase, the goal for all activities is to identify anything that could *create or enhance value*. In the customer value vector, it is learning what customers value, what is important to them and could cause them to take action. In the market dynamics vector, it is learning how the market will likely evolve and what technologies, market shifts, or emerging environments will create needs that will have value to those who are prepared for it. In the business model innovations vector, it is learning how new ways of configuring your business model can create greater value for both you and your customers (see Figure 8-4).

The identification of current, underlying, or emerging value is a good way to state the goal of the Exploring Phase. However, people do not usually talk directly about what has value to them or what would create value in the marketplace. When people behave or act

Vector	Focus
1. Customer Value	*Customer Needs*
2. Market Dynamics	*Emerging Marketplace (foresight)*
3. Business Model Innovation	*Company Structure/Processes*

Figure 8-4. Discovery Process exploration vectors.

in a certain way, they are often not aware of the values that cause them to act—they just act. And when you ask them why, sometimes they cannot articulate why. Therefore, it is often the goal of the Discovery team in these explorations to identify "hidden value." The Discovery team must become "detectives" to find evidence or clues in what they hear and see that could point to a cache of hidden value.

The Discovery team must focus on generating a large quantity of "insights" during the Exploring Phase. Insights are any new understandings about customers, market dynamics, or business models that could reflect some hidden value. When team members learn something new that *could* have some value potential, they should write it down as a new insight gained. It is *not* important that team members clearly know what that value potential is, how it could be delivered, or whether it would be worth pursuing. At the time they hear it, they should capture it as something that is new and different and has the *potential* for some value.

Team members should fight the urge to derive implications and conclusions from the insights gained. In their book *Radical Innovation*, authors Richard Leifer and colleagues speak to this issue:

> Ideas evolve, and they don't always evolve in predictable ways. Psychologists call the activities associated with idea development "loose associative thinking" processes. Associative logic is not sequential. It's jumpy. For a time, the maintenance of uncertainty is important. Closure is a killer, it strangles associative thinking in favor of arriving at "an answer." Early in the process, leveraging uncertainty, riding it, and valuing it are critical to developing robust ideas.[5]

The goal of the Exploring Phase is to generate a very long list of insights. Generating a large *quantity* of insights will result in more high *quality* insights, which are more likely to inspire innovative ideas.

Selecting the Exploration Activities

For each frontier being explored, your Discovery team will want to consider creating one or more activities in each of the three exploration vectors as a way to gain new insights. Setting up a worksheet, such as the one depicted in Figure 8-5, will help start the planning of the exploration activities.

This section is designed to share some of the techniques we have used with teams in previous initiatives. See Figure 8-6 for an overview of those techniques. It is by no means a complete listing of what is possible to do in the search for new insights! However, it may suggest ways in which your team can create its own exploration activities that fit your industry.

Process Tip:

Savor the insights you find and fight the urge to jump to product conclusions.

On hearing a customer express a need, just note the need they have. That is the insight. We all have a mental tendency to jump immediately to what product might fulfill that need, how large the market might be for that product, and whether our company would be interested in that market. All of that thinking happens within milliseconds, resulting in an unjustified judgment concerning the value of that insight. Fight the urge to assume, assess, and conclude—just focus on the insight. A month from now you might find a unique way to address that need.

Exploration Vectors

	Customer Value	Market Dynamics	Business Model Innovation
Strategic Frontier A			
Strategic Frontier B			

Figure 8-5. Exploration activities worksheet.

Exploratory Vectors

	Customer Value	Market Dynamics	Business Model Innovation
Interactions	ValueProbes Specialists	Thought leader panels	Benchmark calls Thought leader panels
Immersions	Safaris Lifestyle experiences Stake-outs	Experiments Conferences Guided journeys	Benchmark visits

Figure 8-6. Examples of Exploring Phase activities.

Interactions and Immersions

For each of the exploratory vectors, divide the exploratory activities into interactions and immersions. Think of interactions as "events" that are set up for the exchange of information. Any type of interview or meeting would be an interaction. If the Discovery team sets up group discussions with customers, interviews with marketplace experts, or telephone discussions with people in other companies to discuss their business model, think of them as *interacting* with others. Interactions are fairly standard means of gathering information and are very appropriate for this Exploring Phase. Interactions can be creatively tailored to produce either routine, baseline information in an unfamiliar area or advanced knowledge in a familiar one, determined by the Discovery team's needs in the Exploring Phase.

Another method of gathering insights to the exploratory vectors is for team members to "immerse" themselves in an environment of interest. Immersions allow the Discovery team to make *observations* in the various challenge areas, which can reveal insights or information that customers would not mention in a typical interaction. Instead of setting up a meeting with customers, an immersion might consist of spending a day with a customer, observing the customer in his/her own environment. In such a customer immersion, for example, team members might notice that the customer is working in a crowded office situation. Your company's product is seen buried under stacks of paper and is not easily accessible to the customer. This observation could lead to a redesign of your product line to minimize the product's "footprint," or perhaps introduce wireless remote access so that the product can be used more easily even when hidden behind stacks of paper. These are things that customers might not think to mention in a typical customer inter-action (such as interviews or focus groups) but that can be identi-fied in a customer immersion.

Customer Value Vector Activities

There will be a tendency on the part of the Discovery team to con-sider the current customers to be the customers of the future. This is one of the underlying assumptions of businesses that have been following a strategy of incremental improvements every year. It makes up part of the "corporate gravity" described earlier in this chapter.

Who Is the Customer of the Future?

Strategy innovation invites teams to question who the customer of the future is. Current customers remain an option but so are others. Perhaps there is an opportunity to sell your product to an under-served population, such as college students or customers in other countries. Perhaps there is an opportunity to turn nonusers of a product into users. Perhaps there is an opportunity to grow a small, niche market at the periphery of the business into a larger, more mainstream market. Spend time thinking about who on your stra-tegic frontier represents a potential customer and be sure to include them in this Exploring Phase.

Unarticulated Needs: The Holy Grail of Consumer Value

It seems as if it should be an easy process to identify new business opportunities. Just go to customers, ask them what they want, and give them what they ask for. There are some industries where this approach can still be effective. Talking to customers will almost always yield important information that can be used to help enhance a company's business in some way.

However, customer interactions frequently lead to changes that are more incremental in nature, not innovative. The reason for this is that customers have a relatively narrow frame of reference, based primarily on what they have experienced in the past. They can usually tell you what they like and do not like about your current product and how that compares to other products they have experienced. They will tell you they want the buttons on your product to be a little larger and easier to push. This will lead to some incremental product improvements for your next "new and improved model" but will usually not lead you to the new business platform that will drive company growth in the future. Terry Tallis, a former business manager with H-P, makes a similar point using the example of a Siberian ditch digger. If you talk to the ditch digger and ask him what products can improve his work, he will not likely mention a heavy-duty, diesel-powered, hydraulic-lift backhoe—because all he has ever known is a shovel.

Most customers are also more reactive than proactive. Show them a new product you have designed and they will react to it, giving you helpful feedback. However, they are unable to *speculate* on what innovative new products or services will better suit their needs than today's products. There is a tendency for people to want to ask customers to describe their "ideal" product. Again, that is a speculative exercise that might provide some incremental product improvements but seldom innovations. They will not be able to tell you, for example, that they want artificial intelligence built into your product so that it will adjust its performance as it is taken into different usage environments. You will have to figure that out for yourself. They will also not be able to tell you what products or services are *missing* from their lives, waiting for a company to invent them and make them wildly happy. In short, you cannot rely on customers to tell you what innovative products or services they would like to see created that will meet their needs. They will not design innovative new products for you.

Because most customers cannot describe the next-generation products you are looking to develop, the holy grail of the customer value vector is understanding their "unarticulated needs." What product or service would customers find valuable but, because they are not able to proactively describe it, remains unarticulated in most customer interviews? It is clear from sales figures over the past decades that customers have a need for a Sony Walkman, a Dodge Caravan, or a Starbucks grande latte. However, it is highly unlikely that, prior to their introductions, customers would have said they needed a portable stereo, minivan, or espresso with steamed milk. If companies are able to discern these unarticulated needs of customers, they can create significant new business opportunities.

Because of the importance of unarticulated needs to the creation of innovative products and services, it is worthwhile considering what they are and how they might be discerned. An unarticulated need can be considered something that has *value* to a customer. The early purchasers of a Sony Walkman were probably people who valued listening to good music. Prior to the Walkman, they accepted the fact that good, stereophonic music had to come from large components that took up a considerable amount of shelf space in the den. As a result, they planned their quality music experiences around being stationary in the den, where the stereo was located. That is the way things were in those days, and music lovers were satisfied with that arrangement because alternatives did not exist. They did not know any better; they did not have any idea of what was becoming possible with electronics. However, there was also something else that these customers valued—being mobile. If you had a traditional focus group on stereo music back in those days, chances are that customers would not have thought to mention their interest in going places and being mobile in their lives. After all, this was a focus group on stereo music, which had nothing to do with mobility in their lives. Therefore, the need for mobility would have remained unarticulated in that research venue. Had it been revealed in a discussion session, observers would have noted that the value of good music was in conflict with another value of customers, that of being mobile. This insight would have identified a conflict, which, if addressed, would have created greater value for the customer. Addressing this unarticulated need for mobility while listening to quality music created a new industry of the portable stereo (see Figure 8-7).

Value of   Value of   Unarticulated need
good music   mobility   for portable stereo

Figure 8-7. Unarticulated needs.

To identify unarticulated needs of customers, it is important to pursue an understanding of what they value. This pursuit of value must not be limited to current products or markets, as people tend to accept products and markets as they are, not speculate on how they can be. Finding new ways to explore customer values should be the focus of your exploratory efforts with customers.

Large-scale quantitative surveys of customers will *not* produce valuable insights into unarticulated customer needs. A survey is designed to get everyone to answer the same questions into precategorized answers, with little or no flexibility of responses allowed. It is often the exceptions to the questions or the subtle nuances of responses that can contain new insights that are so valuable for new business development. Quantitative surveys will not provide these new insights, but they do play an important role in the Creating and Mapping Phases, when metrics are required to evaluate the market opportunities and plan their implementation. The search for customer insights in the Exploring Phase should be personal, face-to-face encounters with customers.

Customer Value Vector: Interactions

The Discovery team should consider staging interactions with customers. The forms the interactions take can be traditional forms, perhaps one-on-one interviews, or group interviews, such as found in a focus group format. However, if you want to find new insights into customer needs and values, make sure that the line of questioning in those interactions is very nontraditional. Rather than just asking customers to react to current products and services in a market, extend the scope of the discussion to include an exploration of *what they value*. For example, if your business consists of selling widgets to small companies, don't spend time discussing only the widget market, the widget pricing, and widget delivery times. Also explore that customer's current business environment, how it is changing over time, and what they hope to do about it. Learning about the customer's customers, recent horror stories they have experienced, company priorities, and aspirations for the future all provide a valuable understanding of the context in which widget decisions are made. This broader line of questioning provides insights into what that customer values, helping you to see how you might redefine your widget business to provide greater value to your customers than it does now. That is the ultimate goal of the Discovery team—to redefine your business to provide the customer with greater value than you are now.

ValueProbes

One type of customer interaction we call ValueProbes (see Figure 8-8). They are discussion sessions aimed at exploring customer perception of what is valuable to them, to help them to articulate some of their unarticulated needs. By using a less traditional line of questioning or special, creative techniques, customers will articulate some of their previously unarticulated needs or opinions they might be reticent to express in a traditional interview setting. The key is to ask a different set of questions or use different techniques—not straight Q&A. There are many different techniques that can be used to foster these discussions, such as projective techniques, storytelling, role-playing, and photo-taking. When asked to express themselves in different ways from what they are used to doing, customers will sometimes reveal information that would

Exploratory Vectors

	Customer Value	Market Dynamics	Business Model Innovation
Interactions	ValueProbes Specialists		
Immersions			

Figure 8-8. Exploring Phase activities: Customer value interactions.

otherwise remain unconsidered and unspoken in the standard interview format.

In our work in the customer value vector, we have successfully used a technique of drawing combined with metaphors. For example, we have asked business customers to draw their company as a vehicle of some type, noting its important features that cause it to be better or worse than the "vehicles" of its competitors. We have seen organizations identify significant competitive weaknesses or threats, new target markets, the importance of new technologies, or ways to take advantage of a discontinuity using this indirect, creative technique. In any situation it can be helpful to know what, metaphorically, is an organization's steering wheel, its accelerator, its brakes, its power source, or its hood ornament. What is the road ahead like—a washboard surface of a dirt road or the smooth-banked turns of an autobahn? Are there any obstacles in the road? What is the weather like and what might it be like in the future? We have seen organizations, using this technique, depict themselves as Ferraris and, in one instance, a "parked Model T." How do you think today's customers would describe your organization using this vehicle metaphor? How would you like them to describe your company in the future? These nontraditional questioning techniques cause participants to think in new ways, often revealing new insights and values/needs that had previously been unarticulated.

Another tip for the identification of "hidden value" with customers is to zero in on the *emotions* that accompany their words. If you think about it, our emotions often reflect some underlying value that we have. If I am angry or frustrated when I describe using your product, it is probably because I value something different from what you are providing. If I am effusive in my praise of your product, it is because you have exceeded my expectations and delivered more value to me than others have ever done. If my emotions result from the difference between what I have and what I want, then they reflect what I value. Therefore, if you want to learn what is important to me, follow the trail of my emotions. Listen for my expressions of joy, anger, surprise, fear, excitement, and disappointment. Underneath may be a value that I have not articulated before.

One example of an exercise we have successfully used to identify emotions is to have customers draw their "emotional EKG" during a certain activity. For example, if your business is a restaurant, ask customers to reflect on a recent experience in your restaurant on a moment-by-moment basis. Have customers start from the moment they decided to go to the restaurant and continue to the moment they arrived back home again. Thinking about the emotional highs and lows of that experience, ask customers to represent those feelings as if they were generating a readout of their EKG. Then ask them to describe the output. What was your feeling when you decided to go to the restaurant? What caused the blip up when you first entered the front door? Why did your emotions dive when you were seated? The re-creation of this experience, using the emotional EKG metaphor, is a good way for customers to express their opinions and underlying values (see Figure 8-9).

Traditional focus groups spend a significant amount of time discussing *products* with customers, probing how they are used, likes and dislikes, and possible improvements. In a ValueProbe discussion, consider exploring the *environment* in which a product is used rather than the product itself. For example, let's say you sold sewing machines. Instead of asking customers about their sewing ma-

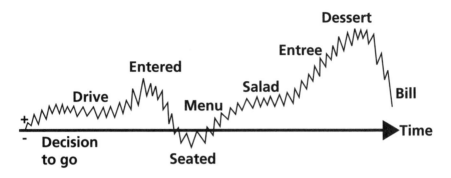

Figure 8-9. Emotional EKG: Restaurant visit.

chines, ask them about the act of sewing and the environment in which they do their sewing. Why do they sew? What role does sewing play in their lives? What are the "rewards" they get for sewing? When they think about sewing, what comes to mind? Where and when do they do most of their sewing? Where and when would they prefer to do their sewing? What do they aspire to sew some day? What is frustrating about the sewing process? What do they currently have to give up or sacrifice in order to sew? What are the most thrilling or magical moments in sewing? What would they put into their Sewing Hall of Fame? Questions like these help reveal the emotions and underlying values that surround the use of a product. That is the value to be gained by talking to customers, because they are the only ones who can talk about those values. Don't ask them to design a new sewing machine for you. But find out what problems, frustrations, or unfulfilled wishes they have, and then design the product or service that meets those needs and delivers them value. It is up to the Discovery team to connect the insights gained from customers to product or service features that will provide a new benefit or value.

Specialists

A second interactive approach in the customer value vector is the use of specialists. Instead of conducting these discussions yourself or with a trained facilitator, hire a specialist trained in a particular discipline to run them. A good psychologist or behaviorist leading these discussions, for example, can provide interesting new insights into how customers perceive a situation, why they act, or where and how they find value. In some work we did for a suitcase manufacturer, a psychologist revealed a series of customer needs around anxieties that customers encountered while traveling. With innovative products designed to allay these anxieties, customers perceived greater value in them.

The Periscope team from Moen successfully used a specialist interaction in their Exploring Phase. As described in Chapter 5, they had an anthropologist visit a number of people in their homes and observe the ways in which water was used and how it was valued by people. The anthropologist explored various uses of water in the home and some of the underlying symbolism and meaning of these acts. According to Dan Buchner, "What came out was fascinating. It opened people's minds and helped spotlight some myths we believed in terms of water use. We found that people really didn't care about things we thought they cared about."

Customer interactions can provide new insights to the perception of value if the questioning process employs new approaches or techniques. The techniques should be aimed at exploring customer value in new ways, attempting to get them to articulate what otherwise, using more conventional techniques, would probably remain unarticulated.

Customer Value Vector: Immersions

Whereas customer interactions typically rely on *discussions with* customers, immersions rely more on *observations of* customers. Immersions become a critically important component of the Discovery Process when the Discovery team agrees that innovative new business opportunities will likely be based on customers' unarticulated needs. Observations do not attempt to get customers to articulate their unarticulated needs. By entering the environment of your customers, you will *see* the context in which customers make their decisions and exercise their values. You walk in their shoes, see with their eyes. With these observations, you can better understand their needs and what could comprise value to them in new products and services (see Figure 8-10).

Maureen Wenmoth, director of marketing services at Moen, described how the Periscope project helped them focus more on observational research. "Now, when people come to me saying they want to do focus groups, we tell them we don't do that anymore." Instead, Moen sets up "real life laboratories where we can understand how people live and what they do." Video cameras set up in the homes of customers provide digital observations of people using Moen products in real-life, at-home situations. These tapes are then coded for the activities portrayed on the tape, such as hand-washing, use of the sink sprayer, or double-showering. When a team at Moen begins the development of a new product, they have instant access to videos of in-home use situations, which provides actual customer usage information that can help drive the creation of new and innovative product designs.

Safaris

The growing field of observational research is sometimes referred to as "ethnography," a term first used to describe a research method in the field of cultural anthropology. It refers to observing subjects in their own environments and attempting to understand

Exploratory Vectors

	Customer Value	Market Dynamics	Business Model Innovation
Interactions			
Immersions	Safaris Lifestyle experiences Stake-outs		

Figure 8-10. Exploring Phase activities: Customer value immersions.

their perceptual frameworks in order to understand their behavior. In its most basic form, the Discovery team could arrange to do ethnographic research via customer visits. Customer visits, which we often call "safaris," provide a more intimate understanding of customers than focus groups or interviews because they reveal insights of both the customers and their environments. Safaris also eliminate other problems typically encountered in traditional focus group discussions, such as customers forgetting (or overlooking) things or being embarrassed to mention something with other customers in the room.

When you sell to consumer households, it means setting up safaris to the homes of your customers. There are many market research companies that can set those visits up for you. Plan ahead what you hope to observe in these visits. Watch carefully how customers use (or misuse) your product. Note where it is stored. See what other products they are using in conjunction with yours. What can you learn about your customers from observing where and how they live? Can you get an idea of what is important to them? Can you determine what they value? As Yogi Berra is purported to have said, "You can observe a lot just by watching."

If your product is sold to other businesses, the Discovery team should arrange to visit customers in those business locations. Ask for a tour to see how your products are being used. Similar to home visits, note where the products in a business setting are being used, how they are stored, how they are tracked, when and how they are reordered. Also note the operating environment, the context in which the product is used. What is the space like? How many people are sharing the product? Have they made any adjustments to the product to make it work or fit better? Are your competitors' products there also? Are other products combined with yours to enhance performance?

When doing customer safaris, be sure to ask about things you find unusual or intriguing. It is like the story of the woman who cut the end off a pot roast before cooking it. When asked why she did it, she said that was the way her mother and grandmother before her had always cooked pot roast. A check with her grandmother revealed that she cut the end off because the cooking pan she had when she first got married was too small to hold an entire pot roast. In spite of changing conditions, some behaviors stay the same. Therefore, it is important to find out what drives behavior—a need, a perception, or a merely a habit carried over from the past.

Lifestyle Experiences

A second type of customer immersion is a lifestyle experience. Rather than visit the customer in one specific environment, observers "live" with their customers over the course of a day (or more). Go where they go, do what they do. Understand their world, what drives them, how they make decisions, what they value, how they are influenced. Ford Motor Company executives and designers visited malls, nightclubs, and other hangouts of young adults to understand their lifestyles and their needs in the design of their Focus model. Harley Davidson executives take to the road each summer to attend motorcycle rallies and spend time listening to their customers in their world.

Stake-Outs

A third type of immersion experience that the Discovery team should consider is what we refer to as "stake-outs." According to the strategic frontier you are exploring, identify where you can observe people using, considering, or buying products of interest to you. If your product is sold at retail, consider a stake-out in the store. Hang out in the store aisle and watch as people make their purchase decisions. Or, there are companies that will set up cameras in cooperating stores so that you can videotape this purchase-decision activity over a longer period of time. Better yet, see if you can work in a store for a week to gain a greater understanding of your customers and their shopping experiences.

Another stake-out option is to spend time observing your product being used in a public setting. For example, executives from a Honda U.S. design team spent time in the parking lot of Disneyland watching families there unload and load their vehicles. After watching people lift heavy cargo into the trunks of their cars, Honda redesigned their trunk so that it was lower and easier to load.[6]

A relatively new way to "observe" customer behavior is a stake-out via the Internet. People interact on the Internet, share opinions, and express their values there. You can have each member of the Discovery team log on to bulletin boards or take part in online chats. What is the focus of the discussions that you hear? Do people online have different perspectives about your product category? What can you learn from their complaints? We recently ran across a company that has developed software to monitor discussions about various product categories in chatrooms and bulletin boards on the Internet. The software will categorize the nature of those discussions and provide insights to trends, questions, and problems that are being discussed.

Customer immersion experiences will provide more of a "real-life" understanding of customers than interactive experiences will typically provide. However, the immersions tend to be more complex and time-consuming to implement than more standard interactions. The Discovery team must decide what mix of interactions and immersions with customers are likely to reveal the types of insights that will drive the creation of new business opportunities on your strategic frontiers.

Market Dynamics Vector Activities

The future cannot be predicted with a high degree of accuracy. There are always unforeseen forces that create "discontinuities" in the marketplace, causing current trends to accelerate or decelerate from expectations. However, there is tremendous value to be gained by understanding the forces that exist and that are likely to have an impact on the market.

In Search of Foresight

Bob Galvin, former CEO of Motorola, tells of learning the importance of anticipating the market from his father, the company's founder. "In the late 1930s, my father went to Germany and could tell that at some point we would be going to war. You didn't have to be a genius to see that something was going to happen. We knew something was going to happen, and we did something about it." What they did was develop some wireless technologies for the Army's Signal Corps. Even though the Army did not purchase their product initially, it gave Motorola a technology they would apply in World War II and quite profitably in future years. Galvin added, "A lot of the future is observable or guessable, but will anybody do anything about it? It takes the application of resources to make it happen—that is strategy."

Moen was also interested in market foresight. Tim O'Brien, vice president of technical innovation at Moen, explained that the Periscope team in their Exploring Phase was interested in determining which forces were likely to have the greatest impact on their market as it evolved to the future. Also of interest were the possible discontinuities, as being aware of them would help them in their planning process. O'Brien noted, "We need to make our boat watertight in case of future storms or hurricanes, even though we can't predict when they will actually happen." Recall that one of the potential dislocations identified by Moen in their Exploring Phase work (back in 1995) was the possibility of terrorists poisoning municipal water supplies. That predicted possibility has taken on new importance in the past few years.

Another company that has embraced the power of foresight in the creation of strategy is 3M. In the mid-1990s, they created the company's first corporate foresight division. In a recent interview with William Coyne, former senior vice president of R&D at 3M, he said, "We now have three people to do corporate foresight—not looking at today but just focused on the future and trends in technology, consumers, and geography. They then look at the business plans and find the disconnects with the future."

By market foresight, we mean gaining a better understanding of the emerging marketplace, your market of the future. What factors will likely drive its growth? How could technology change the dynamics of the market? How might globalization represent both an opportunity and a threat to your company's future? What impact will demographics have on usage and purchasing patterns? What new scientific discoveries are on the horizon? To make future plans without understanding the potential context of the emerging market is a risk to a company's financial health, and perhaps its survival.

Market Dynamics Vector: Interactions

Of all the market foresight work we have done for clients over the years, none has been more effective than a market interaction process we call thought leader panels (TLP).

Thought Leader Panels

These two-to-three-day meetings provide a very rich understanding of the evolving marketplace from a panel of "experts" recruited from a variety of different disciplines. The variety of their future views and the reconciling of their differences create among observers a shared understanding and appreciation of future forces and possible discontinuities. What emerges from this exercise is a proprietary view of the future that is shared by all in attendance, typically the Discovery team, the Extended Discovery team, and other senior management executives (see Figure 8-11).

In the case of Moen as outlined in Chapter 5, the Periscope team

Exploratory Vectors

	Customer Value	Market Dynamics	Business Model Innovation
Interactions		Thought leader panels	
Immersions			

Figure 8-11. Exploring Phase activities: Market dynamics interactions.

conducted two thought leader panels as part of their Exploring Phase. As Dan Buchner recalled:

> The thought leader panels worked well. We did two of them—one a high-level group and one more focused on implementation issues. We really needed the high-level view, the context in which we existed. We were a very tactically oriented company, and some people thought they would "put up with" the first (higher-level) panel in order to get to the more tactical one. However, we learned a lot from the first panel that caused us to change some of our thinking.

One of the important discoveries in this first panel was an understanding that the faucet business was undergoing a fundamental change in the 1990s, requiring Moen to reconsider its overall strategy. Buchner explained, "The thought leader panel allowed an open dialogue to take place around this issue. We explored the changes going on and discussed the myths that existed in our company with people who were outside our company. We agreed that these thought leaders were experts in the field so we had to listen to them. It allowed people to ask the hard questions and then believe what they heard. It wasn't about politics anymore, it was about a group making decisions together."

To conduct a thought leader panel, it is important that the Discovery team first identify the topics from the strategic frontier they feel are important to explore and understand in more detail. Topics usually consist of those areas that might have an impact on the development of future markets on the strategic frontier. Although every panel will differ, based on the issues within each industry, some common industry-wide topics frequently emerge, including technology, demographics, environmentalism, globalization, government regulation, retailing trends, and materials science. Panel topics can also focus on company issues related to the future, including marketing strategies, infrastructure expansion, technology development, retail channels, and human resource development. An ideal number of topics for a TLP would be five or six.

Once those topics have been identified, the next step is to recruit "experts" to represent each topic. Often, members of the Discovery team have some idea of who might be a good candidate to speak to the future of that topic. If not, searching books, periodicals, the Internet, and networking are the best ways to identify candidates. Telephone discussions with the candidates will reveal their qualifications and interest in participating. Other thought leaders could include demographers, magazine writers/editors, newsletter publishers, general futurists, representatives from similar companies in different industries, people who formerly held key positions, academics, authors, corporate leaders, psychologists, cultural anthropologists, Wall Street analysts, and government officials.

Don't be afraid to invite a "wild card" expert to your panel. A wild card expert is someone who has a perspective or skill set that is only indirectly related to your business but could help stimulate ideas. We have used a science fiction writer to help think about future scenarios, a database developer to help conceive of new market segmentation approaches, and an artist to help make intangible ideas visible. Another approach to consider is to invite someone who has "learned from experience." In one thought leader panel, a representative from a major company that had recently gone bankrupt provided very valuable insights into what a company should not do.

Experts from within your own industry should be used with extreme caution. They frequently work under the same assumptions and business model constraints as you do, restricting their abilities to conceive of new and innovative ways to create value in that industry. If you must include an industry expert, invite one who is focused on the future, has a good "big picture" perspective, or understands a part of the business that you do not.

Thought leaders should be asked to play the role of "provocateur" in the TLPs, not a consultant role. A consultant will sift through the possibilities of the future and, based on an understanding of the company's needs, offer the most appropriate "answer"

Process Tip:

No expert can adequately define a proprietary future for your company.

Your company is a unique blend of people, processes, culture, and spirit. No matter how knowledgeable they are, thought leaders or anyone else outside your company should not determine the future of your organization. Gather all the best insights you can from others but be sure that your future has been created by people inside your company. This makes it a proprietary future, one owned by your company because it reflects your interests, skills, values, and vision.

for a client. Thought leader panels are different. They focus more on creating the long list of possibilities for the future, not just a few answers that someone else feels is most appropriate for your company. In the language of the creative process, it is a "divergent" exercise aimed at exploring lots of options and possibilities. Toward the end of the panel, the Discovery team and Extended Discovery team will work to synthesize the list and identify the proprietary future that is most attractive to the company.

The thought leaders are asked to share their views of the evolving future in their areas of expertise, highlighting important trends and discontinuities that are possible. Subsequent interactions between the thought leaders usually reveal a deeper level of understanding about the future and the interaction of forces that could create it. Then sharing specific company issues with the thought leaders provides an opportunity for both thought leaders and company participants to imagine a future customized to the interests of the company. It is then up to the members of the Discovery team and the Extended Discovery team to craft a proprietary company future from the combined input and interactions of all of the thought leaders in the panel.

The proprietary future that emerges from a market interaction such as a thought leader panel is a powerful means to gain management alignment around the future. The outside expertise of the thought leaders provides a credible, objective, external view of the topics of interest on the strategic frontier. Attendees learn and react together to future possibilities, creating a common framework for internal strategic discussions. Bob LaPerle, a former director of business planning in the photographic products group at Kodak, observed, "The team members sitting with the experts and writing scenarios was very interesting and helpful to us. We had never done detailed scenarios before. They were plausible and had enough substance for new product generation. It was definitely a landmark event for the company."

At Moen, management decisions on the development of new products in the early 1990s were frequently based on personal opinions and available resources in the necessary departments. The thought leader panel's work with the Periscope project revealed a future where "water filtration" would be an important strategic frontier for Moen to consider. After that TLP, management decisions on new products shifted to this common framework. Said Tim O'Brien, "After Periscope, there was agreement on the trends so we needed to make decisions on products that were consistent with the trends. No longer could you put projects on the back burner for no good reason. If you wanted to cancel a product, you had to argue why that view of the future was no longer something worth believing in. The future became an arbiter and guide for our decisions."

Market Dynamics Vector: Immersions

Understanding the marketplace and its possible evolution can also be done with an immersion exercise. These immersions can take the form of "experiments" in the market, which are then monitored for their impact (see Figure 8-12).

Experiments

Immersion into a marketplace to understand its dynamics is more complex than many of the other processes outlined in this section.

Exploratory Vectors

	Customer Value	Market Dynamics	Business Model Innovation
Interactions			
Immersions		Experiments Conferences Guided journeys	

Figure 8-12. Exploring Phase activities: Market dynamics immersions.

The Discovery team needs to spend time at those places where the market is in action. For companies whose products are sold at retail, it may mean setting up your own retail experiment. If you are in the apparel industry, purchase or set up your own clothing store. Then experiment with leading-edge programs: new products, new methods of merchandising, new technology, new store layouts, and new marketing programs. Staff the store with people who are very customer-friendly and learn as much as you can about customers and their needs (customer immersion also). What you can learn from this experiment are valuable insights as to what the future may hold for that industry.

There are prototype stores in Japan called antenna shops that serve a similar experimental immersion function. Companies that manufacture products will open antenna shops to show prototypes of new, innovative products currently in development. Product design and marketing personnel interact with customers and learn their reactions to the prototypes before they go into production. Antenna shops provide customer insights on product innovations in the marketplace.

Conferences

Another immersion method to generate market foresight would be for the Discovery team to attend a variety of conferences on the topics of interest. If the conference has a future orientation to it, attendees can learn how that topic might evolve over time, key factors in that evolution, and the organizations that will play critical roles in that future.

Conferences require less of a cost and time commitment for the Discovery team than other methods of market foresight. However, the insights gained from conference attendance are generally fewer and less customized than the other methods mentioned here.

Guided Journeys

Guided journeys are useful when a Discovery team desires fast learning in a focused area of potential opportunity. The technique requires defining the area of opportunity as tightly as possible. Then a "guide," from inside or outside the company, is recruited to design and lead an immersion experience whereby the Discovery team experiences the key current problems, challenges, and forces that are likely to influence how the future of that area might unfold. On the basis of this experience, the team then speculates on what the emerging opportunities might be in that area. The experience can then be debriefed in the presence of "experts" who can affirm or challenge the learnings and insights.

One European company was interested in exploring the U.S. market for home security. Their team decided on a guided journey to gather market insights and spent a day touring residences in New York City. In the morning the team was led by a "beat cop" from Times Square, who directed them through the different boroughs of the city. From the Upper East Side to Harlem, the Discovery team saw examples of how New York City homeowners were at risk and, from a policeman's perspective, the simple steps that might be taken to reduce that risk. The afternoon was spent at New York City Police Headquarters, hearing firsthand from some of the department leaders what they considered to be the current and emerging threats to residents of the "Big Apple."

The Discovery team spent the next half-day debriefing its new learnings, surprises, and insights from their Guided Journey. They then used these insights as catalysts to generate innovative new opportunities for the home security market. The Discovery team then went on to explore several other frontiers in a similar fashion.

Business Model Innovation Vector Activities

The third exploratory vector for the Discovery team to consider including in the Exploring Phase is business model innovations. As mentioned previously, there are many examples in the business press about companies that have identified innovative new ways to conduct business in an established market. For example, Dell Computer pioneered a new business model in the established category of personal computers, serving as an example of the power of strategy innovation at the business model level. Instead of producing a line of computers for sale in a retail store, Michael Dell chose to offer custom-designed computers via the Internet. He then configured the rest of his business model to minimize the supply of parts on hand, the turnaround time for delivery, and the need for customer service. The result was an extremely efficient business model that produced handsome profits for many years.

Thinking About Remodeling

If you were an entrepreneur just entering your marketplace now, how would you structure your business to create greater value for customers and for your company? Which functions or business structures have you carried over from doing business in the past that are now draining cash from your bottom line and could be eliminated? Would customers respond to a new product configuration or sales process if it meant greater value for them?

Strategy innovation at the business model level can be scary for organizations because it implies changes to the organization, where change implies risk. As a result, it is usually only considered as a strategy of last resort. However, if there is *value to be gained* by an organization through the creation of a new business model, market dynamics suggest that it will eventually happen. Our capitalist system and the efficiency of financial markets dictate that unrealized value will eventually be realized. Therefore, it is important for companies to understand what is possible in this area and at least have a strategy ready for when that entrepreneur finally enters your market with a new way of doing business.

It should be noted here that many of the business opportunities identified in the other vectors (customer value and market dynamics) will also require some change in the company's business model. For example, learning that there is a market for your products in China will force you to consider the creation of a new element of your business model—a distribution network in China. It is a rare situation when a Discovery team identifies a great new business opportunity that requires no adjustment or change to the current business model.

The types of business model innovations we are talking about here are ways to reconfigure the system of functions and processes that make up your current means of doing business, rather than ways to increase the efficiency of your current processes. As pointed out by Harvard strategy professor Michael Porter, operational effectiveness is different from strategy. Operational effectiveness in the manufacturing area, for example, might mean finding ways to cut production time or costs. Business model innovation in the manufacturing area might mean asking the question of whether manufacturing should be outsourced completely or determining if there is some component of the manufacturing process that could be delegated to customers, such as having them assemble the parts at home. These innovations might help open up new markets or new distribution opportunities that would not be feasible under the current business model. Again, strategy innovation is about doing different things to create new value, not doing the same things a little better than before.

Houses built in previous centuries contained parlors, sitting rooms, and formal living rooms because those living spaces reflected how people relaxed and entertained in those eras. Does that floor plan fit the way families of today live? It can be difficult putting the large-screen television with surround sound in a parlor. Today's families need larger common rooms, kitchens for entertaining, outdoor living space—a different house design that fits the changing needs of today's lifestyles.

Is your current business model a relic from a previous business era? Are your current systems and departmental structures based on "the way we have always done things here"? Did they evolve over time based on corporate personalities or is it the best way to deliver value to your customers? Dare to look at your current business model and ask, "What if . . ."

Business Model Innovations Vector: Interactions

For most employees, the company's business model is invisible. They accept the processes, structures, and norms that shape their daily behavior and do not stop to think about whether it is the best way to achieve the company's objectives. The first step in considering strategy innovation at the business model level is to make it visible to the Discovery team. A good way to do that is to understand how other companies do business. Read business publications on how companies accomplished turnarounds, reengineered their processes, or cut costs dramatically compared to competition. Find out who those companies are and learn from them (see Figure 8-13).

Exploratory Vectors

	Customer Value	Market Dynamics	Business Model Innovation
Interactions			Benchmark calls Thought leader panels
Immersions			

Figure 8-13. Exploring Phase activities: Business model innovation interactions.

Benchmark Calls

The best way for the Discovery team to start exploring the possibilities of business model innovation is to contact companies that have done it before. Searching the business press for articles and stories of business model successes and failures will highlight companies that have attempted to do something that your team finds intriguing or a possible strategic frontier for your company. Call representatives of those companies and ask to learn more about the process. What worked and what did not? If they were to do it again, how would they do it differently? How did they handle the creation of the new business model so that it did not destroy the value still being created by the old one? Benchmarking calls like this will provide valuable insights into the attractiveness of business model innovation for your company.

Thought Leader Panels

Another, more powerful process for exploring business model innovation is to convene a thought leader panel (TLP). As discussed in more detail earlier in this chapter, TLPs consist of "experts" in a topic of interest attending a two-to-three-day meeting with the Discovery team and the Extended Discovery team plus senior management. Thought leaders in the business model innovation area would be representatives of companies that underwent a business model innovation. They would be asked to share their stories and what they learned from the creation of a new way of doing business.

The H-P Inkject Business Unit (IJBU) conducted two thought leader panels in their Exploring Phase that were aimed at building their business model. In their case, they were not interested in understanding how the *market* for inkjet printers would evolve, as they knew it would become a huge business, very quickly. Their challenge was to determine how to create the right business model and infrastructure to prepare for that growth and manage it for long-term success. Their first thought leader panel focused on the topic of "high market share." They recruited experts from major corporations, such as Coca-Cola, Intel, DuPont, and others, to share their stories of developing and maintaining a high share in the marketplace. From this panel, their team created a business vision and strategic plan for managing high market share in the inkjet printer market.

Shortly after that first thought leader panel, the team arranged for a second panel. Whereas the first one was aimed at marketplace activities that the company should undertake, the second had more of an internal focus. Called the "hypergrowth" panel, it also consisted of experts from major corporations (Cisco Systems, Microsoft, and Conner Peripherals, among others) that had to deal with the internal management of rapid corporate growth. From this panel, the team learned how to create systems and process strategies, as well as culture and infrastructure strategies, for handling rapid growth.

Terry Tallis, business planning manager for H-P, said, "We were intrigued with the idea of thought leader panels because they were so different from how we worked with other experts in the past." He said that the benefit of the thought leaders enabled IJBU to gain new perspectives, which in turn created a shared view of these new perspectives that ultimately altered their strategy. It was this new, shared view that ultimately led to the creation of a consensus strategy. According to Tallis:

> For the first time, the core team all had a common base of understanding. In our staff meetings, we would get information from different groups but it would all be filtered information. That did not happen with the thought leader panels, where we all heard everything at once. Thought leaders would ask insightful, naïve questions that were not politically motivated, such as, "Have you thought about it this way?" This was particularly helpful in the breakout sessions, as it really opened our eyes to new options. Later, people who attended the panels would recall quotes and advice from the thought leaders, instead of focusing on internal battles of who ought to be doing what.

Attendees at a business model thought leader panel will be able to make an assessment of the opportunities and risks involved with business model innovations. As with the market dynamics thought leader panels, the output of this work is an awareness of the variety of different ways that business model innovation can be done and an alignment by the senior management team on how it could work best within your company.

Business Model Innovation Vector: Immersions

Benchmarking Visits

Understanding business model innovations at a deeper level might consist of benchmarking innovative companies by visiting their operations (see Figure 8-14). Many companies will agree to provide tours or visits to other companies interested in benchmarking their operations. The advantage of an immersion (visit) over an interaction (telephone call) would be the opportunity to observe the operations, rather than just hear about them. As with the immersion visits with customers described earlier, Discovery team members should discuss ahead of time what information would be most valuable to obtain in a benchmarking visit. Note anything in the visit that could help your company understand the implications and implementation issues that might be associated with innovations in your current business model.

Exploratory Vectors

	Customer Value	Market Dynamics	Business Model Innovation
Interactions			
Immersions			Benchmark visits

Figure 8-14. Exploring Phase activities: Business model innovation immersions.

Discovering Value on the Frontier

The experiences you create in the Exploring Phase will expose your Discovery team to new ideas, new perspectives, new assumptions, and new mind-sets. Every one of these new understandings is potentially useful as the basis for the development of a new business opportunity. The key determination of its usefulness is its ability to create value for the customer and, as a result, value for your company.

The Discovery team should gather and record these new understandings during its exploration of the strategic frontier. After each interaction or immersion, conduct a debriefing session where team members share what they heard, what was new, what impressed them, and what surprised them (see Figure 8-15). We refer to all of these as insights gained from the exploration. There are no rules about what is, and what is not, an insight, so don't spend time debating what qualifies

Process Tip:

Insights are perishable, so share them in a debriefing session while they are fresh.

Immediately following any Exploring Phase activity, team members involved in that activity should plan a formal debriefing process. Create a list of what you learned, what has value, and what you consider at that point to be possible implications of what you learned. Writing down memorable quotes from the activity tends to extend their shelf life.

Insight		Implication
Convenience drives the purchase process.	→	*Make our product more accessible.*
The reward is a child's smile.	→	*Test it with children first.*
"I often spill it while opening."	→	*Consider a chewable version.*
All products are alike.	→	*Look into co-branding.*

Figure 8-15. Debriefing exercise.

as an insight. If it is new and thought to potentially have value in the marketplace, record it on a flip chart. Try to identify a long list of insights from each interaction or immersion—at least twenty from an individual customer interview, at least fifty from a Value-Probe session, and at least one hundred from a thought leader panel. These quantities of insights will force the team to listen and think carefully about all of what they heard and experienced.

As the team will eventually narrow this list of insights at a later time, it is a good idea to note during the debriefing session any possible *implications* for each insight generated. In that way, the implications will serve as a reminder of the potential value of that insight when used in the Creating Phase.

Summary

♦ To be able to perceive new opportunities on the strategic frontier, the Discovery team must escape "corporate gravity" through entrepreneurial and contrarian thinking.

♦ The Strategic Opportunity Spectrum (SOS) is a method of categorizing the business opportunities you discover on your strategic frontiers from "visible" opportunities to "visionary" opportunities.

♦ Stretch your thinking to identify visionary opportunities, and you will identify opportunities all along the Strategic Opportunity Spectrum.

♦ Business is about creating value for someone (a customer) and, in delivering that value, creating value for yourself. So identifying new business opportunities should focus on value—what it is and how it can be delivered or enhanced.

♦ Pathways for exploring for value on the strategic frontier can be found along three "vectors"—the customer value vector, the market dynamics vector, and the business model innovation vector.

♦ To gain a fresh perspective and unique insights, the Discovery team should consider less conventional ways of doing their exploration activities in this Exploring Phase. To see things differently, you need to do things differently.

◆ Exploration activities can be categorized as interactions or immersions. Interactions are events set up for the exchange of information while immersions are entering an environment in order to make observations.

◆ In the customer value vector, the goal is to identify unarticulated customer needs. To do that, consider interactions such as Value-Probes and specialists, and immersions such as safaris, lifestyle experiences, and stake-outs.

◆ In the market dynamics vector, there is tremendous value to be gained by understanding the forces that exist that may have an impact on future markets. To gain that understanding, consider interactions such as thought leader panels, and immersions such as experiments, conferences, and guided journeys.

◆ In the business model innovation vector, there is much to be learned about how other companies created a unique business model to capture greater value in the marketplace. To learn how to do that, consider interactions such as benchmark calls and thought leader panels, and immersions such as benchmark visits.

◆ Conduct a debriefing session immediately following every exploration activity so that team members can identify and share the insights gained from that effort.

Endnotes

1. W. Chan Kim and Renee Mauborgne, "Value Innovation: The Strategic Logic of High Growth," *Harvard Business Review*, January/February 1997.

2. John Glenn, www.pbs.org/kcet/johnglenn/rightstuff/faq/exploration .htm, January 2003.

3. John Glenn, www.floridatoday.com/space/explore/stories/1998b/102998k .htm, January 2003.

4. Adrian Slywotzky, *Value Migration: How to Think Several Moves Ahead of the Competition* (Boston: Harvard Business School Press, 1997).

5. Richard Leifer, et al., *Radical Innovation* (Boston: Harvard Business School Press, 2000).

6. Robert L. Shook, *Honda: An American Success Story* (New York: Prentice-Hall, 1988).

CHAPTER 9

THE DISCOVERY PROCESS

Creating Phase

> The purpose of divergent thinking is to define the possibilities and propose a promising solution that can be validated to the point of creating a business plan that will attract external investors.[1]
>
> —*RICHARD FOSTER AND SARAH KAPLAN*

| Staging Phase | Aligning Phase | Exploring Phase | **Creating Phase** | Mapping Phase |

Your explorations have ended. No more arranging of appointments and schedules. No more eating M&Ms in the viewing room of a marketing research facility. No more long lines at airport security. Your Discovery team may be weary, but their interactions and immersions over the past several months have provided them with a deep understanding of customers and what they value, the emerging marketplace of the future, and the potential for business model innovations. They have collected experiences and valuable insights

185

that now can be used to create the business opportunities of the future.

The Creating Phase is, as you might guess, a creative activity where imagination is used to envision and define businesses of the future. It consists of the following:

- Establishing the right environment
  - Creative
  - Collaborative
  - Entrepreneurial
- Collecting the necessary tools
  - Insights
  - Opportunity format
  - "Rough" evaluation criteria
- The creative process
  - Divergent phase: Identification of beginning ideas
  - Convergent phase: Concept development and evaluation

Establishing the Right Environment

Discovery team members will enter the Creating Phase as artists enter their studios. Their rich experiences in the Exploring Phase have helped them conceive of new opportunities that exist on the strategic frontier. Sometimes it is a specific, vivid image that only needs a medium and the time to recreate the image in their heads. In other cases, team members envision certain elements of the opportunities but cannot yet envision it in its entirety. In the Creating Phase, the artists of the Discovery team will give expression to these ideas.

Artists are usually very particular about the environments in which they work. Some prefer a rather plain, quiet studio so as not to be distracted by outside influences. Others prefer more stimulating, vibrant surroundings to feed and reinforce their creative impulses. The environment for the Creating Phase is a very important consideration. In order to facilitate the right interaction of team members and maximize the output of quality business opportunities, the working environment for the Creating Phase must be:

◆ Creative

◆ Collaborative

◆ Entrepreneurial

Creative

As described in Chapter 6, the Discovery Process is based on the principles of creativity applied in a business environment. Perhaps the creative element that is most useful to business is the two-step approach to identifying new ideas (see Figure 9-1). The first step, the "divergent phase," is the unbridled, unencumbered identification of a wide range of options to consider. Most people recognize it as a "brainstorming" type of activity. Without regard to practicality, feasibility, efficiency, or effectiveness, team members first identify a large quantity of ideas and options that could be used to run a business. It is through this divergent activity that participants "wander" beyond current constraints, ignore previous assumptions

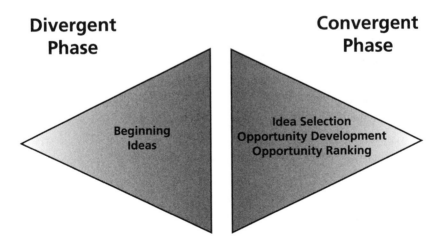

Figure 9-1. The Creating Phase.

about the business and discover new ways of doing business. When they do that, innovative ideas emerge. Without this permission to wander, speculate, and dream, options are few and tend to reflect old thinking patterns.

A senior manager of a large chemical company wondered why the room went suddenly quiet when, after challenging his team with an important problem, he exclaimed, "Now, everyone give me all your GOOD ideas!" He was oblivious to the importance of inviting all ideas without prematurely assessing whether they were good or not. As a result, each person in the room hesitated to offer any ideas, not knowing for sure how the manager would be distinguishing a "good" idea from a "bad" idea. The premature insistence on practical ideas led to a stifling of all ideas.

Because all business decisions must ultimately be practical, feasible, efficient, and effective, there is a second step to the creative process for business called the "convergent phase." This phase can be viewed as a "filtering" phase, as the great quantity of options identified in the divergent phase are filtered by the important business criteria. The team's options then converge on those ideas that make the most sense for the business.

Discovery team members are either extremely comfortable in the Creating Phase or they are somewhat uncomfortable. Inspired by the thrill of discovery they experienced in the Exploring Phase, some team members are easily convinced to continue this open-ended, anything-is-possible way of working. They will be eager to speculate and dream in the divergent phase about new business opportunities that could possibly exist. Other team members are anxious to take what they have discovered and identify the specific, practical, short-term implications for the current business. They do not want to think about new ways of doing business. They are ready to take action, to make specific recommendations to senior management. This latter group could be uncomfortable in the beginning of the Creating Phase. They must be patient, as their interests and skills will be used later in the Creating Phase and into the Mapping Phase, after a large quantity of new business opportunities have been created.

Collaborative

The new business opportunities that emerge from this Discovery Process must be viewed as being created by the entire Discovery team, not by particular members of the team. This is an important distinction to take into the Creating Phase because it establishes the most effective working environment for the team. The Discovery team will be "building" the opportunities together. It is a highly collaborative effort where all team member interactions are aimed at the same objective, creating the best future business opportunities possible from the insights gathered.

Think of the process of the Creating Phase as similar to the Discovery team creating clay sculptures together. While everyone will be asked to do the initial design and formation of their own sculpture, each will then spend time enhancing in some way the sculptures of all of the other team members. The sculptures are continuously evolving during the Creating Phase, with team members offering their insights that could lead to valuable refinements and revisions. Because the clay remains malleable until it is fired in the kiln, the team can decide when it is good enough, when it needs more work, or when it needs to be destroyed and the process started all over again. What emerges is a large quantity of works-of-art that everyone on the team supports, because everyone on the team has played some role in developing them. This is collaboration at its best.

To keep this spirit of collaboration alive in meetings, the Discovery team needs to adopt a new vocabulary. When someone on the team offers an idea and you see a way to enhance it, say, "I would like to build on that idea" and offer your addition. This acknowledges that what you heard was valuable and that you would like to contribute to its development—rather than your statement being perceived as a criticism or evaluation of what you heard. While it sounds subtle, we have found that using this "building" language enhances the team collaboration and incentive to maximize the business opportunities.

The synergy produced through collaboration is the most powerful approach for achieving high levels of team creativity. Of all the ideation tools and techniques we have used or heard about, none match the effectiveness of an inspired team collaborating toward a common challenge. From the many different perspectives represented on the team, they are able to identify ways to "build" and strengthen an idea by addressing collaboratively its gaps and points of weakness. You will recognize when your team achieves this level of teamwork by how the credit for an idea is given to the team, rather than to the individual. The individual egos become fused into one "team" ego. It is not dissimilar from the level of teamwork observed in many championship teams. In the 2001 NFL Super Bowl, the New England Patriots, heavy underdogs but the eventual winner, refused the traditional individual player introductions at the beginning of the game. Instead, they entered the field as one motivated mass of bobbing unity, recognizing that their strength was in the collaborative effort and not in superior individual performances.

Entrepreneurial

Using the insights gained about customers, the marketplace, and business models, the Discovery team will be identifying *business opportunities that will exist in the future.* The Discovery team is *not identifying business opportunities that your company should consider.* When you think only about opportunities for your company, you are unconsciously trying to "fit" a new insight into an old way of doing business. In doing so, you may be compromising the value inherent in the opportunity because of your company's current constraints or shortcomings. It is not difficult to imagine that in the years before Federal Express, the U.S. Postal Service could have identified the need for overnight mail service but expressed it as a one-day service because they were not set up for or capable of delivering overnight service. The need (and value) of the opportunity was for overnight service, not one-day service.

In assuming that someone else will be responsible for implementing the plan, adopt the mind-set of an entrepreneur. Assume

Process Tip:

You only dream to the level of your perceived implementation capabilities.

Try as hard as you want, it is very difficult to "think big" if you perceive that you will be the one responsible for implementing that big plan. Your subconscious concern of your ability to execute the plan will prevent you from ever articulating it in the first place. To create truly great and innovative business opportunities that will effectively deliver the value you envision, you have to assume for this Creating Phase that "someone else" will be responsible for implementing the plan.

that the capital, the skills, the partners, and the knowledge needed to fulfill that marketplace need will immediately become available as soon as you are able to "dream" it. Express the business opportunity in that way so that everyone is made aware of the opportunities that exist now or will exist in the future. It is then a separate strategic question to be addressed later of whether your company is willing to pursue that opportunity (and the resources required) or whether it is an opportunity that you will cede to another company.

One of our favorite ways to assist teams in adopting this entrepreneurial approach is to challenge them to become entrepreneurs for a fictitious company called Hurricane, Inc. Hurricane, Inc., is in the imagined business of providing emergency support to communities immediately following a storm of hurricane force. The company can assist a community in recovering from the aftermath of a storm's damage by supplying energy, food, water, and temporary housing. The team's challenge, as the Discovery team for Hurricane, Inc., is to identify new opportunities for new growth for the company.

Among a number of things, this imaginary challenge to the team helps determine whether the team is more comfortable "creating" at safe, near-term levels or at big-idea, breakthrough levels. Not surprisingly, all teams begin generating opportunities for Hurricane, Inc., that might be classified as visible opportunities on the Strategic Opportunity Spectrum—disaster insurance, home construction or reconstruction, and home meal delivery. Some teams are more aggressive in their strategy innovation, with ideas that extend disaster relief beyond just hurricanes, to include tornadoes and typhoons, or, a little further out, earthquakes, volcanic events, and avalanches. Teams that achieve a visionary level might identify opportunities such as a GPS–driven natural disaster forecasting, a warning and tracking service, or a systemic disaster-relief holding company that includes an integrated, cost-effective package of prevention planning, broad insurance coverage, and guaranteed property restoration.

When offering this type of creative challenge to a team, it is one thing to work with adults, it is quite something else to work with children. When the Hurricane, Inc., challenge was given to a class of fourth- fifth- and sixth-graders at Thacher Montessori School in Milton, Massachusetts, they generated a representative number of the above-mentioned ideas from visible to visionary. However, these children, unconstrained by the realities of business and eager to find "value" in a new situation, then stepped beyond to create two new spin-off opportunities for Hurricane, Inc.:

1. Hurricane Energy, Inc., is in the business of capturing and storing a portion of the megawatts produced as a hurricane moves through an area. This energy is then provided back to the community for emergency power or is sold to other parts of the country to help fund the recovery.

2. Hurricane Entertainment, Inc., is in the business of setting up "amusement parks" that harness a hurricane's force for purposes of recreational fun. Imagine a theme park with an area the size of a basketball court enclosed by netting rising thirty feet in height. Inside are rubber "bubbles," large enough for a large child or adult to get into. The stronger the hurricane winds, the wilder the experience for this "bumper cars in the air" amusement ride.

When you think you have reached visionary levels with your innovative, entrepreneurial thinking, remember how these children responded and push yourself to find what ideas are beyond those you have already.

Fresh Perspectives

As mentioned previously, consider inviting new team members to help identify new business opportunities in the Creating Phase. Someone from outside the company could provide a fresh perspective for the team. In addition, an outsider will not be affected by your "corporate gravity" and will be more likely to create business opportunities that fit the customer need, not the company's current business model. One company invited a science fiction writer to the Creating Phase for this purpose. Another enlisted a retired venture capitalist, who provided a breadth of business-model experience that was quite helpful.

When considering new team members, also consider internal employees, even senior management. Using our adage of "people support what they help create," you will want someone on the senior management team of your company to support the new business opportunities you create, so why not include him or her in their creation. One caveat to the involvement of senior executives, however, is that they must adopt the role of an "equal" to the other team members and abide by the rules of creativity and collaboration. If they prefer to play an advisory or evaluative role as "higher ranking" officials, the dynamics of the team and the process would be too compromised, and productivity would plummet.

Another outside perspective that can contribute significantly in this phase is that of a "visual illuminator." A visual illuminator is an artist who can bring to life the ideas being shared by the team. At this point in the process, ideas are intangible, incomplete, and fragile, as they have not yet been subjected to the critical scrutiny that further shapes and improves them. When a visual illuminator portrays that idea on paper, it takes on reality and becomes a tangible expression of what team members have created. They are now better able to understand it and to communicate it to others. We asked Harvey Ehrlich, a veteran visual illuminator, to describe the role that he plays in the Creating Phase for teams. He told us:

> In business, new ideas, whether they are tactile in nature or only philosophical, become easier to grasp and understand when, in addition to a carefully crafted verbal construct, a visual image is used. Visual illumination can cut through verbal camouflage and present an idea by means of a visual metaphor that can elegantly communicate. I have also found that humor, attached to both the visual and verbal images, embeds these ideas in the minds of the team much better than a verbal presentation can. The brain relishes what makes it laugh. To say more about visual illumination would require an image.

Collecting the Necessary Tools

With the appropriate working environment established, the Discovery team must then gather their tools for the Creating Phase. Unlike the myriad tools that artists have to provide expression to their ideas, there are only three "tools" necessary for this exercise: the lists of insights gathered from the Exploring Phase, an opportunity format, and some "rough" evaluation criteria.

Lists of Insights

As noted in the Exploring Phase, insights are new understandings of customers, markets, or business models that have the potential to create value for both the customer and the company. Insights from the Exploring Phase are the building blocks of the new business opportunities developed in the Creating Phase.

The Discovery team will have identified and recorded the new insights they gained in the various interactions and immersions of the Exploring Phase. A debriefing session immediately following each activity will have highlighted the insights gained and potential implications (way to create value) for each insight. With many hun-

Process Tip:

Add a visual dimension to your Creating Phase.

Invite an artist, cartoonist, or visual illuminator to join you in the creating process. It is not a frivolous expenditure. A talented (fast-working) artist can add a visual, tangible dimension to the creation of ideas and concepts that often has a dramatic effect on the team. Ideas come to life, color stimulates the environment, and humor can help the team think in new directions. The artist's output can also help dramatically in the communication of the new opportunities to the rest of the organization.

dreds of new insights identified by the team, the first step is to review them and identify which ones appear to have the most potential for further development into a new business opportunity.

Any process can be used to filter or converge around the most promising insights for your team to consider in the Creating Phase. We have successfully used a two-step sorting process based on the 3 Cs (clarity, confidence, and conviction) and an insight's value potential.

3 Cs

Using notes from all of the debriefing sessions, ask team members to first identify those insights on which, after all of the interactions and immersions, they have the most "clarity, confidence, and conviction." Either because of the frequency with which they were heard, the passion by which they were expressed, or the credibility of the source, some insights will emerge as creating a higher level of clarity, confidence, and conviction than others. The first step is to review the hundreds of the gathered insights and note which are selected by team members on this dimension and the frequency with which those insights appear within the team. The result will be a range of insights on the team's 3-C dimension.

Value Potential

A second filter is based on the team's perception of the potential value of a particular insight. Some insights may be able to generate only a slight, incremental value in the market, such as a new color option for a product. Other insights may indicate the potential for an entirely new product category or distribution system, creating significant value by reaching underserved customers. Sorting the insights that emerged from the 3-C filter into those with higher value potential and those with lower value potential will provide a matrix of insights for the team to consider (see Figure 9-2).

The insights that fall into the team's upper-right quadrant are those that, according to the team, have the most clarity, confidence, and conviction, as well as the greatest value potential in the market. This is one way for the team to narrow the number of insights so they can focus their energies on the Creating Phase.

Wild Cards

We believe that everyone on the team should have a wild card option in all sorting and voting activities in the Creating Phase. The purpose of the wild card is to allow everyone to pursue something that intrigues them or about which they have considerable passion,

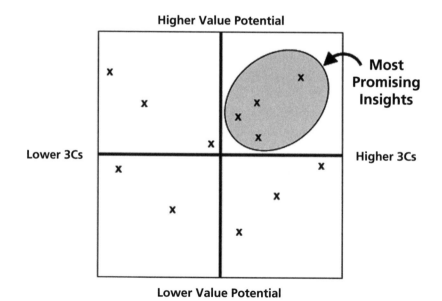

Figure 9-2. Value graph for insights.

even if it does not satisfy the sorting requirements or criteria the team establishes. For example, you may recall an isolated comment from a customer interview that you found particularly intriguing. Because you only heard it once, you don't yet have clarity, confidence, and conviction about this insight. So it technically would not pass your first sorting of the insights. However, you believe that this idea may have tremendous value potential if you could figure out a way to do it. In this case, you could use your wild card option to keep the insight under consideration by the team until you can further develop its possibilities later.

Opportunity Format

The second tool necessary for the Creating Phase is a format for the development of the new business opportunities. The purpose of the format is twofold. First, it helps guide Discovery team members in the creation of a new business concept. Because the team comes from a cross-section of the organization, there will be a number of members who have never had to describe a new business before. The format will take them step-by-step through the thinking process necessary to define the business opportunity. By filling out the format, they will have covered the important considerations of the business.

The second purpose of the opportunity format is to add a degree of standardization to what is created. This will be very important later in this phase when the team is asked to evaluate the opportunities. Having a common format makes cross-opportunity comparisons considerably easier. Standardization will also enhance the presentation of the new business opportunities to senior management at the end of the Discovery Process.

Every opportunity format is different. The nature of the industry will have the largest impact on what is important in the description of a business. The description of a new business opportunity in the restaurant business will include elements that are vastly different from the description of a new business opportunity in the biotech industry. The goal of the opportunity format is to consider the primary elements of the business model in that industry and the process requirements for its development. In restaurants, the focus could be on the theme, customers, ambiance, food, and service. In biotech, it could be the targeted disease and population, underlying science, clinical trials, regulatory issues, and partnerships.

Figure 9-3 illustrates a "generic" format that could be used as a starting point for the creation of a more customized format for your Discovery team.

Other elements that could be included in the opportunity format are unique point of differentiation, proprietary elements, current assets leveraged, reinforcing trends, conflicting forces, major internal constraints, major external constraints, and resources available. In addition, some industries may have critical success factors that should be included in the opportunity format. Keep the number of items included on the opportunity format to eight or ten so that the task does not appear too ominous to team members.

There are a variety of ways to create these business opportunities. Team members can develop them individually, in pair teams, or in small groups (of three or four people). When teams create the opportunities individually, they generate more opportunities overall and allow team

Process Tip:

Think BIG—but in phases and segments.

Team members often have difficulty describing the bold, ideal future they are asked to depict in these business opportunities. Because their day jobs consist of managing systems and assets of the company, they innately want to create realistic and feasible ideas that the company can implement. Tell team members not to think of big ideas as having to be implemented all at once, to all markets immediately. Instead, encourage them to describe that big, bold, ideal future but to break up its implementation into manageable phases and/or segments.

Your Name:
New Business Opportunity Format

1. **Code Name:**
   Strategic Frontier:
   Key Insight:

2. **Description of Opportunity:**
   (In 25 words or fewer, what is it and how does it create value?)

3. **Target Audience:**
   (Who is the primary target audience? Secondary audience?)

4. **Key Benefit(s) to Customers:**
   (What are the key benefits to customers in the opportunity? How will it help improve their lives?)

5. **Important Elements of the Opportunity:**
   (What are the products and/or services involved? Describe the elements that make it unique, useful to customers.)

6. **Competitive Advantage:**
   (How will your opportunity provide a competitive advantage over what competitors could offer?)

7. **Resources Required:**
   (What resources would be necessary to develop this opportunity—technology, budgets, parnerships, skill sets, etc?)

8. **Additional Information Required:**
   (What additional information will be necessary before the opportunity can be further developed?)

Figure 9-3. Opportunity format.

members to express their own points of view. In pair teams, everybody gets a teammate to help craft and refine the opportunity, each acting as a sounding board for the partner. Small group development of the opportunities is appropriate when the opportunities are quite complex, but it will cut down the total output because of the added time for groupthink and consensus-making. We recommend using opportunity development by individuals and pair teams wherever possible.

As team members craft these new business opportunities, remind them to develop them not to fit the capabilities of your company, but to fit the needs of the customer. Attempts to make them feasible for your company may compromise the business opportunity that exists. Instead, encourage team members to be bold and to envision how the opportunity could look at that point in the future when all the elements are in place and customers are being served. Using the Strategic Opportunity Spectrum concept presented in Chapter 7, the Discovery team should aim for creating visionary ideas, which will result in opportunities ranging from visible to visionary.

"Rough" Evaluation Criteria

Prior to the start of the Creating Phase, the Discovery team should know how they will go about screening or filtering the quantity of new business opportunities they create in this phase. The criteria they use will be based on the overall objectives of the strategy innovation initiative. They are just "rough" screening criteria at this point—used mostly for rank-ordering the ideas created and not for purposes of making market go/no go decisions. For example, if senior management and the Discovery team sponsor determine that the company needs a series of mid-term (over the next two to four years) opportunities that leverage a certain core competence and have the potential to eventually be a $30 million business, then those are the "rough" evaluation criteria that will be used to rank the opportunities created.

As with the opportunity format mentioned earlier, the rough evaluation criteria will be different for every company. Typically we would use three to five criteria for this initial screening. Some of the criteria to be used are:

- Time to market (specifying short-term, mid-term, long-term)
- Revenue potential
- Leverages a particular core competence, in-house technology, or brand profile
- Is unique in the market
- Will provide a proprietary advantage
- Leverages a customer or market trend

The identification of rough evaluation criteria just prior to the Creating Phase is a double-edged sword for the Discovery team. On the positive side, the criteria provide a focus for the development of new business opportunities and, when they are part of the team's objectives, increase the likelihood that the opportunities developed will be strategically valuable to the company. On the negative side, the evaluation criteria can diminish the latitude that the team feels in developing the best opportunities possible and could result in ideas that are less innovative.

As an example of the potentially constraining role that the criteria play, let's say that the Discovery team identifies an insight in the Exploring Phase that suggests a strong market opportunity for customized music CDs. Without any evaluation criteria to guide them, the team may develop the business opportunity to include an automated digital recording system connected to a Web site, where customers order their new CDs from their homes, and download the finished CD. However, if the evaluation criteria say that the new business should leverage the company's current retail distribution system, the customized music business opportunity that is created by the team will end up looking very different. It would likely involve a much more complex ordering process (at the store), less convenient for customers, and potentially a more expensive product. The point here is that evaluation criteria that are too stringent will prevent the team from identifying business opportunities that provide the greatest value for customers.

How do you deal with the *need* for evaluation criteria but the potentially constraining impact that the criteria could have on the process? Make the Discovery team *aware* of the evaluation criteria that will be used but at the same time make sure that they don't feel constrained by them in the creation of the new business opportunities. If a business opportunity, such as the Web-based CD system, is ultimately filtered by the evaluation criteria, the Discovery team can also use its wild card option to keep the idea alive for further consideration.

Innovation vs. Feasibility

The goal of a strategy innovation initiative is to identify innovative new business opportunities for a company to consider. However, highly innovative ideas, conceived as they are here outside the constraints of practical business considerations, could end up being impossible to implement or not financially viable. Thus, the need for innovation in these opportunities can be at odds with the company's need for feasibility. So how do you manage to keep ideas both innovative and feasible at the same time?

When faced with this innovation/feasibility trade-off, always go for the innovative. This was a principle of innovation used in early work at Synectics. Ideas will never be more innovative than they are during this Creating Phase. Free from the practical considerations of business and being encouraged to dream and think big, team members will be more likely now than at any other time to dream up innovative ideas.

At the same time, there is a natural, unconscious tendency for people in business to want to take new and innovative ideas and find ways to make them more "practical" or more feasible, quickly. They will say in response to an innovative idea, "Great idea—how can we implement it today rather than waiting for two years." These invisible *feasibility forces* will look for ways to refine the innovative ideas by substituting shorter-term, more feasible options.

> **Process Tip:**
>
> *It is easier to build feasibility into an innovative idea than to build innovation into a feasible idea.*
>
> In the Discovery Process, "feasibility happens." Faced with a highly innovative idea, people in business naturally try to find a way to make it more feasible so as to be able to use that idea. However, it is very difficult to take an idea that is already feasible and give it a booster shot of innovation. Therefore, the team should focus on creating the most innovative ideas possible instead of the most feasible, knowing that the feasibility forces will work their invisible magic.

The result is that longer-term, highly innovative ideas are usually refined and revised to become shorter-term and more feasible as they are further considered.

On the other hand, it is very difficult to build innovation into a feasible idea. If someone on the team suggests a feasible idea for a new business, chances are that it is more of an incremental product improvement than an innovation capable of changing the basis of competition in the marketplace. People are comfortable with its feasibility already and are reluctant to add innovative elements to it that will make the idea a less feasible, longer-term idea. In other words, there are usually no invisible *innovation forces* that will go to work and make a feasible idea more innovative.

Understanding this important mix between innovation and feasibility is important to keep in mind in the Creating Phase.

The Creative Process

Unlike the Exploring Phase, which can last from weeks to months, the Creating Phase is typically a two-day offsite meeting of the Discovery team (plus any other invitees). Another option for the team to consider is to start the Creating Phase during the Exploring Phase. For example, if your team is traveling to ValueProbe sessions in another city, you can debrief the insights gained from the sessions immediately after the sessions. Then, the next day, the team could meet again to begin to turn the insights into new business opportunities—while the insights and their implications are fresh in their minds. Whether you do it that way (create opportunities following each exploring event) or set aside a two-day session following all of the Exploring Phase work is up to the team. The process for the creating session is the same.

The Creative Process: Divergent Phase

The best way to describe the two-phased creative process used by the team to develop the new business opportunities is to think of it metaphorically as a funnel. The first phase, called the "divergent" phase, consists of filling up the funnel with a large quantity of "beginning ideas." A beginning idea is a small piece or portion of a business opportunity. It is not a finished description of the business opportunity. Do not attempt to move from an insight gained in the Exploring Phase directly to a completed new business description! For example, perhaps an insight gained in the Exploring Phase was "customers want their customer service problems resolved quickly." Rather than moving directly to the redesign of your customer call center or installing a new CRM system, create some *beginning ideas* based on that insight. One beginning idea from that insight might be, "Create an Internet-based customer service capability." Another might be, "Create the customer service equivalent of an emergency room triage system." Still another beginning idea off this same insight might be, "Assign an ombudsman to each customer when they call."

Don't spend time thinking through the implications, cost factors, or feasibility of a beginning idea. Just note the idea as a beginning idea, "throw it into the top of the funnel," and move on quickly to the next beginning idea. Go for quantity. Remember the Rule of 100, because eventually you will want several hundred beginning ideas in your funnel. Use a rapid-fire, brainstorming-like process for collecting these beginning ideas. Some will be very good ideas, some will be terrible ideas, and a lot will be in-between. Do not stop to judge any of the ideas. Judgment in this divergent phase will not only slow the process, it will dampen enthusiasm and drain creative energy from the team. Encourage dreaming, wishing, and rampant speculation. Ideas offered by one member of the team will usually inspire someone else to think of an opportunity. Allow this free-flowing interaction to take place. What are the many ways to create value in the marketplace?

The divergent phase should last into the afternoon of the first day. When the tsunami of beginning ideas becomes a ripple on the shore at low-tide, it is time to move to the second phase of this creative process, the convergent phase.

The Creative Process: Convergent Phase

Bob Galvin, former CEO of Motorola and great advocate of using creativity in business, described the creative process as, "Most ideas are grunt work, first getting a quantity of ideas and then looking for the quality ideas in there." The convergent phase is all about sorting through the quantity of the ideas you inserted into the funnel and finding the highest-quality ones.

At this point in the Creating Phase, you should have hundreds of beginning ideas written on flip chart paper and hung on the walls around the room. In the convergent part of this process, the team will go through the following steps to turn hundreds of beginning ideas into five to ten potentially viable business opportunities:

1. Select the most promising beginning ideas
2. Develop those ideas into concepts or opportunities
3. Rank-order the opportunities

Select the Most Promising Beginning Ideas

Any process can be used to narrow the list of beginning ideas to a more manageable number. One idea is to give out a quantity of colored adhesive circles—what we call "energy dots"—that team members can stick next to the beginning ideas they find "most intriguing." Don't use more stringent criteria at this point because beginning ideas are not yet ready to be evaluated by the evaluation criteria. They are not yet developed as business opportunities and thus cannot be expected to live up to the criteria for those opportunities. So for this first converging step, you could use the criteria of what the Discovery team finds interesting or intriguing. They have been close to consumers and market experts in the Exploring Phase and have developed a good idea of what would create value in the marketplace. It is also important for the team to feel some level of interest (or potentially, passion) about the beginning ideas. They will be the ones presenting their business opportunities to senior management and may have to defend them at some point.

Use this first convergent exercise to identify as many as thirty to fifty beginning ideas (if using the energy dots, list those that get at least one "dot" from the long list) that the team believes deserve more consideration and further development.

Develop Those Ideas into Concepts or Opportunities

The second convergent step is developing the most "intriguing" beginning ideas into business concepts. We call these concepts "business opportunities" and use the opportunity format presented earlier in this chapter as the basis of the exercise. Have Discovery team members select which of the beginning ideas they want to advance or more fully develop into business opportunities that can be evaluated. These opportunities can be new products or services, new target audiences, or new elements of a company's business model. Using the format and some quiet time, have team members think through what it might take for a company (not just *their* company but any company) to create value in the marketplace with the beginning idea they selected. What would it look like? How would it work? Who are the customers and why would customers like it?

A Discovery team will typically create between twenty and forty new business opportunities in a two-day Creating Phase session. Each idea is developed by either an individual or, at most, a pair team. It is much more efficient to develop the opportunities by individual or pair teams than in a large group. Managing who develops which beginning ideas will avoid duplication of effort and maximize the number of different opportunities created.

After the opportunity formats are completed, team members are asked to present their opportunities to the rest of the team. Following each presentation, team members can offer "builds" or suggestions on how to refine the opportunity to make it even stronger. It is a good idea to collect the builds and suggestions for improvement from the team and ask the authors of the business opportunities to then refine them as they see fit. It is the prerogative of the author to determine which builds are incorporated to create the refined business opportunity.

Rank-Order the Opportunities

The twenty to forty refined, new business opportunities are then ready for a screening process, the final convergent step in this process. Using the rough evaluation criteria identified earlier, the Discovery team will rate or rank all of the business opportunities they developed to provide a prioritization of those opportunities.

It is important to note here that this prioritization is not a go/no go decision for that idea. Many team members are disappointed when their concepts do not make the cut and mistakenly believe that they have failed because their opportunities have been rejected. This is not the case. That opportunity has been developed and should become part of a database or archive for this initiative. At any time, anyone can continue to work on that idea, refining it in ways that will better align with the evaluation criteria established or with the needs of a business. The creative process is an iterative process, where you can create, learn, and refine ad nauseam. Therefore, the screening out of an opportunity at this phase is not a "no go" decision, but merely a "not yet" decision on the part of the team.

Any process can be used for screening the business opportunities using the rough evaluation criteria. Some teams will very carefully evaluate every opportunity for every individual evaluation criterion, using complex, weighted, quantitative techniques and rating scales.

Other teams will just keep the criteria in mind as they select the three to five opportunities from the list that they like best. Whatever technique you use, the intent for this evaluation is to determine which of the twenty to forty opportunities are most aligned with the evaluation criteria that were established. Typically following this evaluation step, five to ten opportunities will emerge at the top of the ranking list as having the most potential for further consideration and development.

Don't forget the wild card option. Discovery team members, after evaluating the developed opportunities, may find that their favorite opportunities were far down the rankings. Perhaps an opportunity is very strong on most of the criteria but fell short in one area. The team needs a way to keep one or more ideas alive, if they have the passion for them. Let team members vote for one wild card opportunity they would like to keep in the running, based more on their passion for it than the evaluation criteria. Passion is a powerful, contagious force in innovation. A champion (or, better yet, a team of champions) with passion for an idea can build consensus and create momentum that will cause the organization to change.

At the conclusion of the Creating Phase, the Discovery team should have five to ten business opportunities that show some promise for the company. These opportunities are:

◆ Grounded in insights discovered in the Exploring Phase

◆ Part of a long list of beginning ideas

◆ Selected as "intriguing" or promising by one or more team members

◆ Developed by an individual (or pair team)

◆ Refined by suggestions from the entire Discovery team

◆ Screened by the rough evaluation criteria established earlier in the process

At this point, the team decides how many of the five to ten opportunities they want to move to the Mapping Phase, where they are placed on a time line and given a strategic context that will be important for their final evaluation stages.

Tim O'Brien from Moen noted the importance of this entire convergence process (which he referred to as synthesis) in the Periscope project. As he observed, "Synthesis must be a group activity, where the more people involved with it, the better, because you have that many more people making that many more connections. This synthesis resulted in management alignment on what we needed to move ahead."

Summary

◆ The Creating Phase is a time for Discovery team members to turn the insights gained in the Exploring Phase into new business opportunities.

◆ Establish the right working environment, one that is creative, collaborative, and entrepreneurial.

◆ Identify the business opportunities that will exist in the future, based on the insights gained in the Exploring Phase. Do not identify only those opportunities that fit your company's current capabilities. If the opportunity is attractive enough, you will find a way for your company to implement it.

◆ The only tools necessary for this creating process are the lists of insights gathered from the Exploring Phase, an opportunity format, and some "rough" evaluation criteria.

◆ Think of this process as moving through a metaphorical funnel. Begin by offering a large quantity of "beginning ideas," based on the insights gained, into the top of the funnel. This is the divergent phase of the creative process where the quantity of ideas is more important than the quality of each one. Innovation takes precedence over feasibility.

◆ Move the most promising of the beginning ideas "down the funnel" by selecting them and further developing them into concepts, using the opportunity format.

◆ The final step is to rank-order the opportunities using the rough evaluation criteria, allowing the strongest to emerge from the funnel for further consideration in the Mapping Phase.

Endnote

1. Richard Foster and Sarah Kaplan, *Creative Destruction* (New York: Currency/Doubleday, 2001).

CHAPTER 10

THE DISCOVERY PROCESS

Mapping Phase

> Make no little plans; they have no magic to stir men's
> blood and probably themselves will not be realized.
> Make big plans; aim high in hope and work, remem-
> bering that a noble, logical diagram, once recorded,
> will not die.
>
> —*DANIEL BURNHAM*

| Staging Phase | Aligning Phase | Exploring Phase | Creating Phase | **Mapping Phase** |

Your team has created a series of new business opportunities based on new insights about customers, foresight about the emerging marketplace of the future, and/or ways of reconfiguring existing business models in the market to increase value to customers and companies. These opportunities have been through a "rough" evaluation process that suggests that they may fulfill the needs outlined by senior management.

The Mapping Phase is the final step in the Discovery Process. It is a planning process for the implementation of the new business opportunity and consists of the following steps:

- ◆ Identify the critical strategic sectors
- ◆ Create road maps for each sector
  - ◆ Action items
  - ◆ Trends
  - ◆ Discontinuities
  - ◆ Milestones
- ◆ Develop measurement tools
- ◆ Present to senior management

A Strategic Road Map

Following the completion of this five-phased Discovery Process, senior management will have a portfolio of new business opportunities that can be found or created on their strategic frontiers. They must then consider how the company should respond to those opportunities. To do this, senior management will need information that will help them make those decisions.

Frequently the first piece of information that management will want is the market viability and potential revenue impact of these opportunities. Nearly every company has a means in place of estimating the potential size and profitability of new business opportunities. To be considered, a new business must pass certain hurdle rates, usually related to sales potential, margin requirements, or financial return requirements. We consider this fine-tuned, sharpen-the-pencil evaluation phase to be the next step that companies take *following* the Discovery Process. Because each industry and company differs in how they assess the viability of a new business opportunity, we do not believe that a "universal" evaluation process is possible within this process.

Beyond the internal financial implications, senior management will need to understand the marketplace in which these decisions will be made. What changes are on the horizon that could affect if, when, and why a business opportunity should be pursued? In a dynamic marketplace, this information is crucial to all strategic decisions that are made. To help management make these strategic decisions, the Discovery team should prepare a strategic road map for the frontier(s) they explored, as the final phase of the Discovery Process.

The Mapping Phase is so named as it engages in the preparation of a strategic road map for the company. This road map is a time line into the future that contains critical activities, milestones, and marketplace events that must take place for the new business opportunities to succeed. With a new business opportunity that appears viable and attractive to the company, the "big picture" view of the implementation plan provided by the strategic road map will uncover key issues that must be addressed. For example, a Discovery team might have been given a charge to identify a new business opportunity for introduction by the company in the next two to four years. In the Exploring Phase, they discovered a consumer need for a new medical device. It is in the mapping process that they learn that a clinical trial with patients must be conducted before the device will obtain government approval. That clinical trial may need to last for three years to prove efficacy and safety issues. Placing the three-year clinical trial on a two-to-four-year time line will very clearly indicate the timing necessary for the company to develop and implement this business opportunity. It uncovers potential conflicts, barriers, and constraints that the Discovery team will need to address, even by refining the business opportunity concept itself.

Dan Buchner, one of the team captains for the Moen Periscope project, describes the role of the strategic road map for Moen. "We took the output from the thought leader panels and built future maps, which we made part of our planning. They were quite detailed, helped us focus, and made it much more apparent what the difficult decisions were that had to be made. We had been trying to do everything in the marketplace, but the maps helped us focus our attention and our efforts." His boss, Bruce Carbonari, former CEO of Moen, added, "The nice thing about the maps is that everyone learned that the world is bigger than just Moen, and there are lots of things that cause other things to happen."

One of the important benefits of a strategic road map is that it makes tangible the company's proprietary future. No company can possibly monitor or manage all of the trends that will create the future. Instead, companies should focus on those areas and trends that are most relevant to *their* futures, the ones to be found on their strategic frontiers. The creation of a strategic road map captures the most relevant areas of their emerging futures and makes them available for the entire company to understand and track.

Another value of the strategic road map created by the Discovery team is that it provides a consensus "plan" from which all departments and functions in the company can operate. Recall that this was one of the primary reasons for creating a cross-functional Discovery team with people who will help implement the opportunity. The Discovery team is the ideal group to create this strategic road map for the organization because they understand the business opportunity (they created), and they understand what it would take for the organization to implement it. When this road map is created collaboratively by all members of the team, it provides the alignment necessary across all functional areas to quickly and effectively begin implementation.

If your company has a process for strategic mapping, we encourage integrating the findings from the Discovery Process to date in that process. For those companies that do not regularly map their future, we offer our model for the development of a strategic road map here.

Identify the Critical Strategic Sectors

The strategic road map offered here is a time line that consists of many bands or strata that represent important "sectors" that must be considered in the development of the business opportunity. As with most of the "tools" introduced in this Discovery Process, it must be customized to fit the specific industry and opportunity identified.

The first area of customization is the time line itself. It should be segmented by the relevant planning periods for operating in that industry. For highly dynamic industries such as electronics, the relevant time segments are probably in quarter years, if not months. In biotechnology, it will be years or perhaps decades. For many businesses, six-month intervals that stretch out over three to five years will often be an appropriate time line for the strategic roadmap.

In a mapping meeting, you can create time lines by taping together a number of flip chart pages and drawing the time line across the bottom (see Figure 10-1).

Identifying the critical strategic sectors is next. The team, using what they learned in the Exploring Phase, will determine the various areas that must be considered when developing, introducing, and competing in the marketplace of the future. Thought leader panels, described in the Exploring Phase, are extremely valuable in understanding the forces that will have an impact on the emerging marketplace. Some of the more common sectors that apply across many different industries include the following:

- Opportunity development (internal)
- Consumer/society
- Customer/marketplace
- Competition
- Technology
- Government/regulatory

Each industry may also have unique and important sectors to include on the strategic road map.

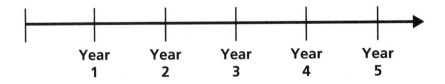

Figure 10-1. Time line.

The Discovery team should select those sectors that will likely play a role in developing the new business opportunity. If a sector can have an impact, either positively or negatively, it should be included in the strategic road map. In a mapping meeting, you can draw a series of "bands" on the flip chart paper just above the time line, labeling them with the sector names. An example can be seen in Figure 10-2.

Opportunity Development Sector

The opportunity development sector is the internal time line showing how your organization will develop the products, services, or new business processes that will take advantage of the new business opportunity identified. Included in this sector are the critical steps to be taken in the key functional areas of the company. Product development and R&D will show developmental milestones, testing processes, and intellectual property considerations. Marketing and sales will outline the key steps for advertising, packaging, promotions, sales, and merchandising strategies. Operations will identify a plan for manufacturing the product. Human resources, legal, and finance departments will indicate where and when they will play a

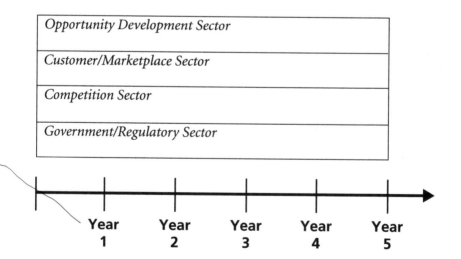

Figure 10-2. Strategic road map sectors.

role. Figure 10-3 shows the opportunity development sector broken out into these key areas that should contribute to this sector.

The Discovery team should include only the *critical* elements on the opportunity development sector, as too much detail makes the maps confusing and difficult to use. Each functional area should later develop a separate, more detailed time line for their internal planning purposes.

Consumer/Society Sector

The consumer/society sector of the strategy road map will consist of a variety of trends that are taking place in demographics, society, or lifestyles. If your customers are consumers, include those consumer trends that will have the greatest impact on the need, awareness, or acceptance of your business opportunity.

Customer/Marketplace Sector

Technology, globalization, and economic conditions are just some of the many factors that could have a dramatic impact on the marketplace in which you compete. It is important to try to predict

Opportunity Development Sector

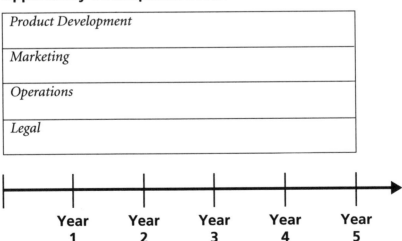

Figure 10-3. Strategic road map opportunity development sector.

how these forces might affect your market and customer base over the time frame of your strategic roadmap. Anticipating changes in distribution channels, sourcing options, supplier networks, and economic conditions could be critical for the success of your new business opportunity.

Competition Sector

In the dynamic marketplaces of the twenty-first century, it is unlikely that strategic actions by one company would not cause some reactions by its competitors. Faced with the possibility of losing business and/or customers, competitors will typically look to respond to new business introductions. Anticipating their responses and estimating their response times provides valuable information for the strategic road map. It establishes a "window" of time where competitive pressures are minimized and your company can maximize its market penetration. Think about which company will introduce a competing product and when. Which company will lower their prices? Which competitors will go out of business? Also think about what competitor (or new entrant to the market) might leapfrog your new product with a next-generation offering. All of these competitor reactions should be included, along with appropriate statistics, on the strategic road map.

Technology Sector

Because of the importance of technology for many new business opportunities, this sector is often one of the more critical ones on the strategic road map. It should highlight key trends in technology, availability dates of new technologies and capabilities, and dates of anticipated price drops in established technologies. Where one technology has not yet emerged as a standard, multiple technologies should be identified and tracked. Note which companies or organizations are developing and/or supporting these technological developments and anticipate any strategic moves they could make.

Government/Regulatory Sector

In many industries, there are government or regulatory issues that must be included on the strategic road map. It may be the testing process to satisfy the FDA, a wavelength licensing issue with the FCC, or a special ruling required from the EPA. In some cases, the process necessary is understood, and time frames are predictable. In others, decisions are heavily influenced by leaders and political considerations, which are less predictable. In either case, it is important to record on the strategic road map the factors and activities in this regulatory area that could have an influence on the development and introduction of your new business opportunity.

Create Road Maps for Each Sector

Following the identification of key sectors for the strategic road map, the Discovery team will focus on developing a road map within each sector. These sector road maps should include the following:

- Action items
- Trends
- Discontinuities
- Milestones

Action Items

Put the most critical action items in each of the sectors on the road map. Indicate items such as when the R&D group needs to apply for a patent, when the market research test begins and ends, and when manufacturing turns out the first production units. Also include on the strategic road map whatever actions trigger the commitment of resources or represent critical decision points in the development of the opportunity.

Action items can also be action taken by others. The anticipated response of competitors to your new business will take the form of action items to be included on the map.

Trends

It is also valuable to identify key trends on the road maps. If a trend is expected to have either a positive or negative impact on the development of the opportunity, it should remain visible to the team by being placed on the map. It is a good idea to quantify the trends by estimating their progress over time. For example, if a key trend for your business opportunity involves the use of DVDs in the home, estimate the household penetration level for DVD players at several different points on your time line.

Discontinuities

In addition to trends, the sectors of the strategy road map should also include any discontinuities that are possible. Discontinuities are those events that radically change the "normal" progression to the future because they quickly change perceptions and/or behaviors in society or the marketplace. The terrorist attacks of September 11, 2001, were the most significant, recent discontinuity that altered the emerging future of many, if not most, businesses. However, the introduction of the transistor, the home computer, and the growth of the Internet could also be considered discontinuities because they all caused shifts in how people lived or worked. Some discontinuities, such as new technologies, can often be anticipated, while others, such as major natural disasters or changes in governments, are much less predictable. If you know of the possibility of discontinuities, build them into the sector road maps.

Milestones

The strategic road map should also include milestones that mark progress. The timing of the identification of a strategic partner, for example, would be a milestone to include on the road map. You may also want to include go/no go decision points along the way or the points at which key financial decisions must be made (see Figure 10-4).

The best way we have found to build the sector road maps is to write the action items, trends, discontinuities, and milestones on Post-it Notes and apply them in the sector bands in the appropriate place over the time line. In this way, the elements can be shifted when the team discovers that their original timing estimates need to be adjusted. There will be a fair amount of adjusting and refining of the road maps as conflicts and sequence issues are discovered.

Work Backward

When creating the sector road maps and considering timing for various activities, we recommend working backward. Start with the launch date for the business, when you would like to be in the market. Then take the final steps and plot them on the road map, followed by the steps that precede them (in the development process). This will help the team create a more aggressive schedule and one more likely to hit the hoped-for market introduction. Otherwise, there is a tendency for team members to be conservative in

Opportunity Development   Select Manufacturing
                                   Partner

Finalize   Prototype Available   National Sales   PRODUCT
Product   In-Home Testing   Convention   LAUNCH
Specifications   Patent Filing   Assign Ad Agency

Customer/Marketplace
        Target Market   Excess Production Capacity   Industry Consolidation
        Reaches 3 million   Pricing War

Competition   GHInc. Introduces
      ABCorp.   New Product Line   JKLtd. Enters
      Introduces   US Markets
      New Website

Government/Regulatory
                    New EPA   Advertising
       Legal   Regulation Due   Federal   Claims Review
       Review   Elections

| Year 1 | Year 2 | Year 3 | Year 4 | Year 5 |

Figure 10-4. Strategic road map.

their estimates or even "pad" them for unexpected problems, which can extend significantly the timing of the development.

Develop Measurement Tools

What are the elements of this new business opportunity that are most crucial for its success? Perhaps it is a target audience of a certain size. Perhaps it is product cost under a certain target. Perhaps it is a global distribution network. Whatever the elements are that make the financial projections a viable business opportunity, those elements should be closely monitored during the development stages.

Along with identifying these key elements, we recommend creating a measurement tool to track those elements. A regularly scheduled market research survey can track key customer trends, behaviors, or attitudes. A phone call to the engineering department can update the latest product cost estimates. A new line item added to an existing monthly sales report can be used to track distribution progress. Put these measures in place so that results can be compared to the estimates placed on the strategic road map. It will highlight progress made and, more importantly, provide an ongoing assessment of the market potential for the business.

Strategic Road Maps as a Planning Tool

The process of creating a strategic road map will identify implementation issues that will need to be addressed for the development of a new business opportunity. Any issues that present significant hurdles to the process should be included on this road map for senior management, as they will need that information in their work of defining the corporate strategy.

In many cases, this strategic road map represents the "launching" of the first phase of development for the new business opportunity. With key action items and milestones available, people can be assigned to this new project, and work can begin.

It is important to consider the strategic road map to be a "living" document that changes and evolves along with the business development process. According to Moen's Maureen Wenmoth, "We used the future map for years, worked it as a tool. We updated it frequently as we found that some things happened faster than we predicted."

Presentation to Senior Management

With a portfolio of new business opportunities and a strategic road map, the Discovery team is ready for a presentation of their output to senior management. The Discovery team's sponsor can play an important role in this presentation by helping to guide its development. The sponsor can provide insights to the Discovery team on the following topics:

- How do the new business opportunities "fit" into the current thinking of management?
- What is the best way of explaining the insights that drove the development of these opportunities?
- How developed should the opportunities appear?
- Will senior management want to play a role in helping to refine the opportunities?
- Are there certain strategic options being considered that would make some of the opportunities more attractive to management than others?
- How aggressive is management feeling about new ventures?
- What level of risk is currently considered tolerable?
- What is the best way to introduce the visionary opportunities?

This presentation needs to be factual and accurate in the information shared, but special attention does need to be paid to making it engaging for senior management. The Discovery team has been through an intense and transformative process. They have learned a lot about customers, the future, and innovative ideas. They have points of view and, perhaps, even passion about these ideas. It is important to portray these elements in the presentation. Don't reduce your ideas to a few PowerPoint slides. Think of innovative and novel ways to communicate these opportunities. Identify a theme that runs through the presentation. Use video clips, bring in thought leaders or market experts (or get them on a conference call). Make sure that senior management feels the energy that was produced by the Discovery Process and the opportunities that exist for the future.

We recommend that the presentation to senior management include all members of the Discovery team and all members of the senior management team. The environment created for this meeting should be similar to that of the Discovery team in the creation process: creative, collaborative, and entrepreneurial. The business opportunities are not yet fully developed, as they have not been through the important financial evaluation process and refinements that may accompany their development. Therefore, the opportunities are not ready for senior management to provide a go/no go decision. The purpose of this meeting is to present to senior management the findings of the Discovery Process and begin to create some alignment around interesting new business opportunities that could lead to possible new corporate strategies.

Senior management should understand that they are being presented with business opportunities discovered on the company's strategic frontier, which the team believes will create value in the marketplace and value for the company (should they decide to pursue them). The business opportunities will not yet contain a detailed plan for how the company would implement them or the impact of the opportunity on the company's infrastructure or systems. We believe it is the role of senior management to identify how the company's business systems could be employed to implement a new business opportunity and to remove any internal barriers for its development. Decisions regarding the allocation of resources and redeployment of corporate assets to take advantage of market opportunities—the essence of corporate strategy—should be the primary role of the senior management team.

We favor a fairly structured process for the meeting with senior management but some teams prefer a more relaxed and informal interaction. In a more structured process, members of the Discovery team present the business opportunities, one at a time. Following each presentation, the senior management team is asked to first identify things they like about the opportunity, creating a list that is recorded on a flip chart. They are then asked to note issues and concerns they see with that business opportunity (or their perceived ability to implement the opportunity). Finally, senior managers are asked to identify "builds" or enhancements that might help address some of the issues and concerns they identified. This three-part process flow is used for each of the business opportunities presented.

At the end of the meeting, the senior management team provides direction for the next steps for the Discovery team. One possibility is that the team will be asked to further refine the opportunities, based on the feedback provided by the senior management team. Another is that the opportunities are sufficiently attractive to move to the next step, the evaluation stage.

Beyond the Discovery Process: The Evaluation Stage

The output from the Discovery Process is a portfolio of new business opportunities and the strategic road map based on the exploration of the strategic frontier. The strategy innovation process ends at this point, and the strategic planning process begins. Senior management will typically determine which of the business opportunities warrant moving to the evaluation phase. In the evaluation phase, market forecasts are made, revenue flows are determined, costs are estimated, and a quantitative business plan is crafted. The resulting key measures are compared to company hurdle rates for new businesses, and the attractiveness of the opportunities are determined.

Because every industry is dependent on different variables for success, and every business has a different evaluation system, it is impossible to suggest a best approach in this area. Some companies do this analysis internally, while others turn their new portfolio over to external consulting companies for help in evaluating and crafting strategic options.

Summary

- The Mapping Phase gets its name from the creation of a strategic road map for the company, making the proprietary view of the company's future tangible for all to see.

- A strategic road map is a time line into the future that contains critical activities and milestones that must take place for the business opportunity to succeed. The "big picture" view of the implementation plan provided by the strategic road map will uncover key issues that must be addressed.

- Begin the mapping by laying out the relevant time frame (often five years) and identifying the important sectors, such as the opportunity development, consumer/society, customer/marketplace, competition, technology, and government/regulatory sectors.

- For each sector, identify and place on the time line the action items, trends, discontinuities, and milestones that will play a role in the development of that business opportunity (or a portfolio of opportunities).

- Develop measurement tools to track the key elements placed on the strategic road map so that progress can be noted and actions taken.

- As the final step in the Discovery Process, present the portfolio of business opportunities and a strategic road map to senior management for their consideration. Frequently, these business opportunities will then undergo a quantitative assessment of their potential for the corporation, using in-house standards and evaluation criteria.

PART THREE

ADVANCED
STRATEGY
INNOVATION

CHAPTER 11

MAXIMIZING THE DISCOVERY PROCESS

Whenever you are asked if you can do a job, tell 'em, "Certainly I can!" Then get busy and find out how to do it.

—*THEODORE ROOSEVELT*

The preceding chapters described the basics of the Discovery Process—with sufficient detail to get you started. This chapter contains the answers to some additional questions we have been asked concerning the process.

Discovery Process and the Corporate Vision

Q. *What role does a corporate vision play in the Discovery Process?*

A. Vision statements in many corporations are ineffective because they are created to describe the current way of doing business rather than being an aspirational view of a desired future. Think about many of the vision statements you have seen. Nearly all of them talk about the same things:

We will strive to:

- Produce the highest-quality, most dependable products in the markets in which we compete

- Provide the highest level of service to satisfy the needs of our customers

- Be dedicated to the belief that our people are our most important asset

- Conduct our affairs in a manner consistent with the highest ethical standards

- Provide a fair, consistent rate of return to our shareholders.

What do these statements say? They say that the company is dedicated to doing the things that will help them stay in business. It is the equivalent of a person saying that their goal in life is to keep breathing. Too often vision statements are descriptions of how the company will be run, not a vision of where it is heading.

To be effective, a vision should describe some "future state" that is so appealing that the company stakeholders will be motivated and dedicated to the journey. And it needs to be more than "be number one in our industry" or "double our return on investment." Measures of this type are *by-products* of doing something else well, not a statement of what you want to do well. Investors may like financial measures as visions but most employees are not motivated by the prospect of making someone else wealthy.

The goal of a vision should be to identify what the company would like to achieve that will somehow have an important impact. Think of the purported early vision of Apple Computer, with a computer in every home (at a time when no one knew what a personal computer could do). Merck wants to eliminate diseases. Marriott wants every guest to leave satisfied. These are aspirational future states that have value. Moving toward these worthy goals can be very motivating. It stimulates our behavior by first engaging our emotions, our passions. Perhaps the real goal should be to have every corporation produce a passion statement, so that it is more likely to motivate.

So the question about a vision and the Discovery Process hinges on whether the company has a vision of a compelling future state or if it has a description of how it runs its business. If it is a vision of a compelling future state, it dovetails nicely into the Discovery Process. The future state will clearly identify the end goal for the company, making it much easier to define its next strategic frontier. If Merck wants to eliminate diseases, then assessing where diseases are right now versus the goal of "no diseases" will clearly outline what needs to be addressed in the near future. If Marriott has any unsatisfied customers, they can find out where their next strategic frontier needs to be on the way to their vision. When you know that the top of the mountain is your goal, you can usually tell where you need to go next as long as the peak is in sight.

If the corporate vision statement is not an ideal future state but merely a statement of how the company will operate, then it will not provide effective guidance to the selection of a strategic frontier. In fact, in these types of companies, it is the exercise of identifying the strategic frontier that helps the company gain a vision of where they are heading. Often it is the first time that management has looked up from their quarterly reports and balance sheets to think about where the company is headed next. The teams we have worked with are usually energized by thinking about and exploring the company's future, its next strategic frontier. It stimulates their thinking and engages their passions, just as a vision should. So, use the identification of your corporate strategic frontier as a worthy substitute for an ineffective vision statement.

Case in Point: Carl Zeiss

A different way to answer this question is to say that the Discovery Process can be used by a corporation to help identify its corporate vision. Carl Zeiss, a 150-year-old company headquartered in Oberkochen, Germany, is known as a pioneer in the field of precision optics. Their expertise in this area spawned a variety of new businesses over the years, including ophthalmic products, microscopes, photographic lenses, laser optics, and many more. Toward the end of the twentieth century, Zeiss was a global, 13,000-employee company consisting of six business units, all of which were the number one or two brand in their different industries. The business was quite strong in 2000, when a new board chair and CEO, Dieter Kurz, was appointed.

It was Kurz's assessment that the thriving business units were all pursuing different strategic paths in their respective industries and that there was decreasing value in being part of the Zeiss family of businesses, except for the brand name. As a result, he committed to the alignment of these distinct businesses on a single corporate vision and to create an opportunity road map to help guide corporate growth through the year 2010.

Outside the company's board of management, there was some skepticism of this initiative. The business units were thriving, the future looked positive, and managers were not convinced that dedicating resources to an effort that did not have a direct, bottom-line impact was a worthwhile expenditure.

Consistent with the Discovery Process, teams were formed for this initiative. They included the top three corporate officers, who committed a significant amount of their time as active steering committee members. Because of their involvement, there was no need for further management alignment, and the team moved quickly to the Exploring Phase.

The core team determined that the insights necessary to drive the creation of a corporate vision were not business-based, but value-based. Corporate values are taken very seriously at Carl Zeiss. This initiative first sought to understand the company values across all of the business units. Many employees were engaged in this assessment, which represented something of a turning point for the initiative. These interactions drew the company together as they discussed common values, obsolete values, and aspirational values as they looked to their futures.

With an understanding of key corporate values for the future, the core team sought to better understand the emerging global marketplace for their businesses. A thought leader panel was conducted to explore cutting-edge trends in demographics, technologies, lifestyles, globalization, and brands. Insights were generated, organized, and used to develop a series of scenarios out over the next decade. Managers from across the Zeiss business units were becoming clearer, both individually and collectively, on the forces most likely to influence their businesses. This consensus was an important foundation for the development of the corporate vision.

The vision team then gathered all of the values and marketplace insights and drafted a vision statement for Carl Zeiss. They worked through the benefits and impact of the vision on a wide range of stakeholders. They fine-tuned the statement through discussions with employees around the world, as well as with the help of experts in vision creation and communication. They also developed a future map, illustrating the key milestones on the way to an envisioned Carl Zeiss of 2010. The vision statement and the map were then presented at the first annual executive vision forum for the top 300 company executives. There, the board of management played the role of the primary presenters and proceeded to enlist everyone in the communication and implementation of the vision throughout the organization. Their new unifying vision is led by the charge, "We make it visible."

Staging Phase

Q. *While I agree that "people support what they help create," how can we possibly get enough people involved so that support is widespread? Our company has offices all over the world.*

A. Global companies can present something of a logistical challenge to the Discovery Process. The secret to creating broad involvement is in creating an infrastructure of teams, all with different responsibilities in the process. That was the case with Schott Glas, a one-hundred-plus-year-old manufacturer of high-quality specialty glass products, and a sister company of Carl Zeiss. Headquartered in Germany, the company's 18,000 employees are distributed over forty countries worldwide.

The objective of the initiative was to create a corporate vision for the company that would guide their strategy out through the year 2010. The sponsors of the initiative insisted that the new corporate vision be embraced by all of the company's offices, as the basis for new growth initiatives in the future.

The first step was to form a core team of four senior Schott executives, who would provide overall guidance for the initiative. Next, ten additional teams were formed, representing geographical, functional, and/or special interests within the organization. Each team participated in a two-and-a-half-day team workshop, held at six different locations around the world. In all, about 150 Schott employees from a wide range of levels within the company directly participated in the initiative, including representatives from all of the major offices.

Following the workshops, the captains of each team joined the Schott core team to form a new group called the visioning team. This visioning team met for three days to consolidate and integrate the work of the ten teams into a vision document. The document was then shared with an operating group within Schott's headquarters plus a thought leader panel of experts from other large corporations, providing valuable insights for clarification and refinement.

The unveiling of the new corporate vision, called Vision 2010, was made at a two-day worldwide annual conference of 200 of Schott's most senior managers. Conference attendees were also given a chance to provide feedback and refinements, extending the involvement of this key group in the creation of the vision. Because people support what they help create, take the time to involve as many people as makes sense in a strategy innovation initiative. Build in a variety of teams and a variety of events for providing input and feedback, but keep the "creation" element to a smaller core group.

Aligning Phase

Q. *We are having trouble focusing on one strategic frontier that we want to explore for the future. Any suggestions?*

A. Like many processes, the Discovery Process needs to find the right trade-off between breadth and depth of exploration. If you decide that you do not need a breadth of information (for example, one frontier), you can afford to explore it in more depth and detail. If you decide that you need more breadth in your search (more frontiers), then you may not be able to explore those multiple frontiers to the same depth and detail as you could with one frontier.

Although we have suggested that teams focus on one frontier, the process will also be successful with several (up to three) frontiers. The Discovery Process is a creative process, and creativity thrives on the ambiguity that results when focus cannot be attained. In fact, there can be value in pursuing multiple frontiers simultaneously and letting the explorations interact with each other. Often it is the intermingling of unlike things that causes people to make new connections among those things, resulting in innovative new concepts.

A popular exercise in creativity sessions is to ask people to intermingle unlike things. One way to get people to create innovative products is to tell them to combine their product (let's say, a flashlight) with another, random product (such as dental floss). What new product is suggested by the hybrid of these very different categories? Is it a flashlight on a rope, dental floss that glows in the dark, or perhaps a narrow flashlight that can be used and stored in tight places? New ways of thinking are sparked when unlike ideas are intermingled and forced to coexist. It is almost as if the human mind tries to give meaning to this unusual combination and finds a way for the items to make sense together. So take advantage of the variety of your strategic frontiers and explore several or all of them at the same time. As a result, you may identify a new hybrid product category that could make an interesting new business opportunity.

We experienced something similar in a strategy innovation session with a division of 3M in the mid-1990s. At that time, 3M was requiring all business units to identify new business platforms for their future.

This task of identifying large, new business platforms was particularly challenging to one of 3M's divisions, Electrical Specialties. Located in Austin, Texas, the Electrical Specialties Division (ESD) had a rather eclectic mix of products in its line. It sold electrical and thermal insulating tape, electrical connectors, cable ties, and electrical diagnostic and detection equipment for the electrical trade. It also sold static protection, and heat and conduction devices for use in integrated circuit manufacturing. Finally, its method of treating steel reinforcing bars (rebar) to resist corrosion made it a supplier to large construction companies involved in concrete building projects.

With such a diverse mix of products and technologies, how could it focus its exploration efforts for a large, new business opportunity platform? Which of the customer segments should it address? Which of the technologies should it leverage? Which market should it explore?

A cross-functional team was formed to help address these questions in the pursuit of new business platforms. The team decided to pursue a two-pronged attack. The first was to meet with customers in all three of their strategic business areas— electrical supply companies, circuit board manufacturers, and large construction companies. The team identified key customers in each group, split into teams of two to four people each, and made personal visits to each of these companies. While these meetings were helpful and identified a number of customer insights that helped ESD improve their customer relations and product lines, they did not identify any breakthrough insights that could lead to a robust new business platform.

The second part of the initiative was to gain market foresight. Where would these markets be going in the future? What market forces were in place that would affect product sales, distribution channels, competition, and technologies? How could ESD get "in front of the curve" and create the products their customers would need before competition?

To gain market foresight, ESD decided to conduct a thought leader panel. The panel would consist of six "experts" who could provide an understanding of market dynamics and potential future scenarios. But how do you conduct the thought leader panel with three diverse strategic business areas—one panel for each area? That would be a time-consuming and expensive effort, as each panel can take four to six weeks to plan and recruit. Selecting only one of the strategic business areas, however, would be the equivalent to making the decision on the future of the company. How should the thought leader panel be set up to provide the market foresight that ESD needed?

The team made the decision to include a thought leader from each of the three strategic business areas on the same panel: electrical, corrosion protection, and electronics. They also added thought leaders from three *other* areas they felt might have an impact on their future business: wireless transmission, power supply management, and environmental issues. Would this eclectic mix of thought leaders provide anything valuable to the ESD team? Would their selection of "breadth" of topics over "depth" of topics give them enough understanding of their future? How would the panel ever be able to focus its conversations?

As you might guess, the panel was a big success (otherwise we would not have included it here). The thought leaders presented their areas of expertise and then began to interact with each other. In these interactions, they discovered how their fields might intersect and affect each other. Many started looking, almost unconsciously, for synergies across the areas. The result was the identification of "smart materials" as a wave of the future. One of the thought leaders offered the idea that in the not-too-distant future, when a concrete-reinforcing steel bar in a bridge cracked, it would break a low-grade electrical current running through it, which would trigger the automatic notification of authorities by a wireless telephone call.

Innovations often result from combining things that have never been combined before. In the Exploring Phase, be sure to include variety in your explorations. Go for breadth over depth. Spice things up by intentionally introducing some ambiguity.

Always add a wild card thinker to every panel, someone who can act as a catalyst for fresh perspectives, new approaches, different ways of looking at the world. Experts in an area tend to gravitate toward "groupthink" unless there is someone to help them broaden their thinking.

Q. *Why can't you just do a traditional market analysis to determine whether a strategic frontier is attractive to your company?*

A. If the strategic frontier you selected is an established market with established products and an established way of doing business, doing a traditional market analysis may be helpful background information for the team to have. However, if that analysis goes from being background information for the team to the "rules" by which the team will identify new business opportunities, you will be abandoning the goal of identifying "innovative" business opportunities. By adopting the "established" nature of the market and its current rules, you are more likely to identify business opportunities in that market that use traditional products sold to traditional customers in a traditional manner. The ultimate potential for strategy innovation is finding a *new* way to enter that market, delivering new or greater value to customers than current competitors. Strategy innovation needs to break the current rules, not follow them.

Looking at the size of an established market may not be a good indication of its potential as a strategic frontier. A market analysis for transistor radios in the early 1960s, for example, would not have been a good measure of the market potential for a Walkman—because the Walkman broke the rules for the transistor radio market and greatly expanded it. If you assume that you will find a way to add new value to customers or bring more customers to the market, then a current market analysis may not accurately reflect the potential.

We suggest you be very careful with traditional market analyses in this Discovery Process. You run the risk that your team will begin to think conventionally about the market, rather than look for innovative breakthroughs and ways to change the rules. If successful in that, the size of the current market may not be indicative of the size of the potential market. With better products, different customers, different distribution channels, or lower costs, you can impact the market in a way that a traditional market analysis cannot anticipate.

Exploring Phase

Q. *It seems like there are so many activities to consider for the Exploring Phase, how should we decide which ones to use?*

A. Start with the strategic frontier selected for the initiative and the three exploratory vectors: customer value, market dynamics, and business model innovation. First decide which of the vectors would be appropriate for the strategic frontier. Would customer insights be critical to a business opportunity that your company might consider on that strategic frontier? If so, plan to do some activity on the customer value vector. Customer insight would be critical on the frontier of online shopping, for example, but not as critical on the frontier of biotechnology.

Do the same thing for the other vectors also. Will changes in the marketplace have an impact on your frontier? If so, plan a market dynamics activity. Is there a likelihood that making changes to your company's business model would allow you to experience an increase in value? If so, look into business model innovation activities.

Once you have determined which exploration vectors apply to your strategic frontier, then decide what type of activity in those vectors would likely yield you *new* insights. Try several different activities. For example, in customer value, do some ValueProbes to listen to people talk about their interests and values concerning a product category, but also set up some in-home visits to observe how they actually use those products. Also try to do something very different from what you normally do, such as interviewing people on the street or visiting online chatrooms.

On an ongoing basis, the Discovery Team should be identifying what it is that they don't know about the frontier—and wish they did. By debriefing after every exploration activity, the team can assess what they learned, what additional questions were raised, and what other information might be valuable to know. Let this information drive the decision on what other activities to do. If you have the luxury of time, you can make some of these decisions sequentially. This is the true spirit of exploration.

Keep adding activities until you are overwhelmed with fresh insights or have run out of time or money.

Q. *What are some of the things you do in a thought leader panel?*

A. We usually start out with individual presentations by each of the thought leaders, to allow them to share their perspectives and views of the future. Following that, we often engage the thought leaders in a panel discussion, asking them to respond to specific questions and issues from the members of the audience.

One of our favorite exercises is the business assumption test. Give each of the thought leaders an 8½-by-11 inch drawing of a fist with a thumb protruding from it. Then read to them a business assumption currently held by the company with regards to the future. For example, you might say, "The trend among adults for healthier eating will accelerate in the next five years." The thought leaders would then hold up their drawing in a thumbs-up "I agree" mode or a thumbs-down "I disagree" mode. No sideways thumb is allowed. Each thought leader would then be invited to share the thinking that contributed to his or her response.

As cited in Chapter 7, the identification of business assumptions for the future is a powerful way for the Discovery Team to align with senior management and to focus their exploration efforts. With the right thought leaders on the panel, this exercise can be one of the most powerful means of influencing Discovery Teams and their management as to the issues that lie between their current business and future opportunities. The key is being clear on the expertise best suited to play the role of sounding board.

The team must believe the thought leaders to be credible with regard to their future business assumptions. What is the right expertise for the panel? Can you benefit most from senior officers or board members from a parallel but noncompetitive industry? What if you could attract thought leaders who had successfully traveled a strategic path similar to the one you are on now? Or, what if you could find thought leaders who were unsuccessful in one of their ventures so that you could learn their hard-earned lessons before going down that path? We have been impressed with the value of this exercise and the willingness of world-class experts to play the role of sounding board for the future of other companies.

The results of this business assumption test are surprisingly predictable. Some of the assumptions are affirmed, often in new ways that gives management an even deeper conviction about staying the course. Some assumptions are challenged, often causing management to revise their assumptions to account for the new insights shared. And finally, some assumptions are outright rejected by the thought leaders as obsolete in a dynamic world.

Creating Phase

Q. *How can we identify more visionary opportunities?*

A. It sometimes takes a while (or a push) to get team members to think big and identify visionary new business opportunities. The strength of corporate gravity and the belief that ideas offered should be practical will keep team members from offering any "wild" ideas. Therefore, you need a way to force wild thinking.

A common approach is to ask people to define business opportunities that would appear far in the future. The nice thing about thinking in the future is that it contains none of the constraints that are felt so strongly today. With the idea that future technology will allow many things to happen that cannot happen today, people are usually more willing to offer more speculative and more visionary ideas.

Another way to get people to stretch their thinking is to go the opposite direction and actually *increase* the pressure of constraints. Tell your team you want ideas for a new widget that costs half of what today's widgets cost. This will require team members to abandon the current method of making widgets and rethink the entire process. In other words, unrealistic constraints will often force blank-page, innovative thinking to occur.

Finally, the work done by Clayton Christensen and colleagues on "disruptive" innovations can be a very effective stimulus for getting team members to identify more visionary opportunities for their companies. Christensen posits that most innovations are sustaining innovations, which are improvements to current products or services aimed at current customers in that market.[1] His work shows that disruptive technologies can have an even greater impact because they create new markets. The way that many disruptive technologies work is to provide a somewhat inferior but cost-effective product to people who are not currently customers in that market. By creating a business model that can sustain this new, lower-cost product, the disrupter will gain an important foothold in the market, dominate its segment, and be protected from its larger, cost-bloated rivals. Expose team members to some of Christensen's work, and they will be stretched in their thinking.

Q. *Do you have any examples of creating a new business model innovation?*

A. We were privileged to be part of a very important strategy innovation initiative with IBM Research in the 1990s. From its inception, IBM Research had been and nurtured for the purpose of pure research. For decades, their corporate parent was an arm's-length sponsor, proud of the Nobel Prize–winning efforts of its scientists. This relationship between IBM and IBM Research resulted in breakthrough discoveries in science, but was never expected to show a direct linkage with the corporation's bottom line.

That relationship was tested in the early 1990s when IBM fell on hard times. In 1992 and 1993, IBM lost over $13 billion, and in the prior three years, it had lost close to 50 percent of its mainframe market share. These losses led to layoffs of 45,000 IBM employees while red ink flowed and its market value sank. Seeking help, IBM brought in a new CEO, Louis V. Gerstner, Jr.

His first day on the job, Gerstner boarded a helicopter and flew to Yorktown, New York, to meet with Jim McGroddy, vice president of IBM Research at the T.J. Watson Research Center. "If there was a soul of IBM, this lab was it,"[2] noted Gerstner, who was uncertain at the time whether IBM Research should continue as part of the corporation.

The visit proved to Gerstner that there was marketable "value" to be mined from the intellectual property at IBM Research, and later he convinced McGroddy that Research was in need of a new "value model" in its relationship with the corporation. Research could no longer produce only science for the sake of science. The corporate parent wanted a return on its investment.

So, McGroddy challenged his organization to identify strategies that would enable IBM Research to double its value to IBM within one year. To address this challenge, McGroddy chartered a global team of ten fast-track researchers to create a blueprint for "Doubling the Value" of IBM Research. This cross-functional team, representing each major lab from around the world, gathered insights and data from its current and potential corporate customers. The team adopted a "guerilla" approach to the initiative—doing whatever it would take to create value-generating new concepts in a very limited amount of time. They planned to present their findings to McGroddy at a meeting of the global research council, less than a week away. Hours were long and meals, if any, were taken during working sessions. This working style galvanized the passion and commitment of the team to their goal.

The final phase of the process involved a multiday team immersion behind locked doors in San Jose, California, where the team focused on a continuous iteration of the proposed strategies. A pair team of scientists would advance a concept as far as possible and then, in round-robin fashion, pass it on to the next pair team. Each "Doubling Value" concept was iterated a half dozen times or more. All team members were able to add their fingerprints to every concept, multiple times. An artist was enlisted to bring visual life to each concept. The presentation was rehearsed and rerehearsed.

The output consisted of a series of novel and unique solutions in areas such as metrics for new patents and technology licensing, to be implemented by McGroddy and his executive staff. This new strategic direction also dovetailed nicely with Gerstner's view that "the IBM Research Division was far more fertile and creative than our ability to commercialize all of its discoveries. We were underutilizing a tremendous asset."[3]

Today, with Paul Horn having taken the leadership baton from Jim McGroddy in 1996, IBM Research has dramatically increased its tangible value to IBM. In 1999, IBM was able to generate $1.7 billion in patent licensing fees alone, and this vital revenue stream has continued to grow.[4] IBM Research created a radically different "business model" than the one originally envisioned by Thomas Watson, one that links leading-edge science to the corporation's financial vitality and new shareholder wealth.

Mapping Phase

Q. *Coming up with new business opportunities is not the problem in our company—implementing them effectively is our problem. Why doesn't the Discovery Process include an implementing phase?*

A. For many companies, the challenge of effective implementation of an innovation is more difficult than the identification of the innovation. We did not include an implementing phase in this process because we have found that it varies significantly by industry and by company within industries. Any implementing phase that we could develop would need to be generic enough to apply across industries and would probably not be specific enough to meet the needs of individual companies.

However, we have had experience successfully using elements of this process on implementation issues. One example is with the Hewlett-Packard Inkjet Business Unit (IJBU). This HP business unit designs, manufactures, and markets inkjet print cartridges for the HP family of printers, faxes, and large format plotters. In the early 1990s, the significant growth of HP printers for personal computers resulted in a 63 percent compound annual growth rate over five years. However, the next five years promised even greater growth, with revenues projected to increase from $1 billion to $6 billion by the year 2000. In the meantime, competitive companies were overcoming technological barriers and threatening to step into this market and benefit from this surge in demand.

In 1994, the IJBU was faced with a positive, but daunting, challenge—to keep up with the tremendous growth prospects in the market and maintain their dominant market position in a competitively charged environment. Dana Seccomb, general manager of IJBU at that time, recalled the challenge of moving a 10,000-employee company in one focused, strategic direction amidst the chaos of phenomenal growth. At one point, his management team had received fifty-six different proposals from the various functional groups on what needed to be done to grow the business.

Seccomb formed a team of ten of his direct reports to identify an implementation plan for the next five years. The team identified two key areas that would be critical to their success. The first was the development of their relatively weak marketing function so that they could remain competitive and hold on to their share as new companies entered the ink cartridge market. The second area was to create a plan for expanding the company's infrastructure and assimilating the new employees that would be required.

With the key areas identified, the IJBU team sought outside expertise in the form of two different thought leader panels. The first was a panel of experts in marketing at companies such as Coca-Cola, Kraft, Intel, and DuPont. A month later, the team held the second thought leader panel, addressing the issue of "hypergrowth," with experts from companies such as Cisco Systems, Microsoft, Atari, and Conner Peripherals. Each thought leader panel consisted of presentations by the experts and interactions between the experts and the IJBU team. These sessions were followed by debriefing sessions with the team to distill key learnings and insights and to align around next steps.

Using the insights from the experts who had lived through similar marketing and hypergrowth conditions, the IJBU management team established four strategic opportunity areas that they would develop to drive the business planning. Subteams were created for these four areas, and a total of eight "bridge strategies" were developed to move the company from a $1 billion business to a $6 billion business over the next five years. They included such things as the communication of the business vision, the expansion plans of each of the company's key business processes, and the communication and training vehicles to assimilate new hires into the distinctive HP culture.

These bridge strategies, the implementation plan, became the strategic road map for the IJBU. They were tracked quarterly by the management team and were reviewed and revised at each yearly strategic planning session.

Endnotes

1. Clayton M Christensen, Mark W. Johnson, and Darrell K. Rigby, "Foundations for Growth," *Sloan Management Review*, Spring 2002.
2. Louis V. Gerstner, Jr., *Who Says Elephants Can't Dance? Inside IBM's Historic Turnaround* (New York: HarperCollins, 2002).
3. Ibid.
4. "Eureka! Laboratories that Produce Profits: IBM Masters the Way to Make Research Pay Off Now," *The New York Times*, September 9, 2001, Section 3, p. 1.

CHAPTER 12

FORMALIZING A STRATEGY INNOVATION SYSTEM

Your system is perfectly designed to give you the results that you get.

—*W. EDWARDS DEMING*

For some companies, the pursuit of strategy innovation can be done on an as-needed, ad hoc basis. Pulling a Discovery team together periodically to explore the future of the market and customer needs will yield a portfolio of new business opportunities that could keep internal development teams busy for a couple of years.

However, there are many other companies where the intermittent pursuit of new opportunities is not enough. Industries that feature a new product line every year rely heavily on understanding their evolving market and customers. Companies that pursue a corporate strategy of market leadership and the commitment to innovation in their markets will need a more regular infusion of customer insights and market foresight to fulfill their goals. Companies in a turn-around situation will need to be constantly identifying and exploring their strategic frontiers for new business opportunities that will lead to their survival.

We believe that every company in the future will have strategy innovation as one of their core capabilities. Because most companies in the future will have access to information, technology, capital, manufacturing capabilities, and markets, it is the capability of a corporation to construct an innovative value proposition and a profitable business model that will determine success. And success will be fleeting, as competitors will attempt to replicate that success.

If your company could benefit from having innovation as a core competence, you should consider the *formalization of a strategy innovation system*. When strategy innovation is formalized, it has a home. Someone is accountable for it. People know where to go with questions, suggestions, or information needs. They also know where to go for results.

Hewlett-Packard's Inkjet Supplies Business Unit perceived the need to formalize strategy innovation after their initiative. Terry Tallis, business planning manager, said, "We tried to make it a process internally because the euphoria of the project can wear off rapidly. How do you get it ingrained in your day-to-day activity? Who do you go to for a new road map, a new strategy? What happens if the financial environment changes? Who owns responsibility for tracking these changes?"

The formalization of strategy innovation in an organization also contributes significantly to the culture of that organization. The number of companies that list "innovation" as one of their core values is mind-boggling. Everybody says they value innovation, and everybody wants their companies to pursue innovative ideas. However, very few companies to date have made a commitment to innovation by formalizing it, building it into the structure and the day-to-day operation of the business. Employees "hear" a lot from their senior management on how the company should behave. It is what they "see" from senior management that lets them know when they are serious and committed to what they say. A company with an ongoing, formalized practice for strategy innovation will provide a stimulus for fresh thinking in the organization and, thereby, invigorate its culture.

From the very beginning of the company, the culture at Motorola reflected the commitment that the Galvin family had to innovation. It has been a result of their constant pursuit of new technologies and new markets that the company has survived nearly three-quarters of a century in the volatile electronics industry. According to Bob Galvin, "You need to have a culture of renewal. My father, Paul, knew that he would be out of business in a year, so he had to find something else to do when that happened. He would always be in motion for motion's sake. He had to renew the day he opened up. Our driving thrust has always been renewal. How can we renew what we are doing?"

Penetrating the Corporate Immune System

Formalizing strategy innovation in a corporation appears, on the surface, to be a relatively easy process. Just hire a creative person, give him or her an office and a budget, and prepare for the breakthrough that will fund all the retirement accounts. Nothing could be further from the truth. Integrating any new function to an organization is a complex process of addressing reporting relationships, accountabilities, turf battles, salary disputes, and office locations. Integrating innovation is even more complex than most functions.

Innovation, by its very nature, "breaks the rules." Pablo Picasso has been quoted as saying, "The act of creation is first an act of destruction." What he meant was that creativity seeks to look at things a different way. By doing that, the creator is willing to "destroy" the old perceptions or assumptions about something in order to give it new and different meaning.

Think about this dichotomy for a moment. Corporations are created to standardize and control. In order to survive, the company must create consistent, reliable product to customers in a way that maintains the financial integrity of the organization. Internal systems are created to control internal processes—systems that are rule-driven with reporting processes that alert management to any deviation from the norm so that corrective action can be taken. "No surprises" is the operative mantra. Nearly everyone in the management of a company is responsible for preventing actions that might affect the company's standard operating procedures.

The result of these internal processes and controls is a corporate "immune system" that develops, protecting the company from surprises and deviations.

Clayton Christensen, in his book *The Innovator's Dilemma*, observed, "One of the dilemmas of management is that, by their very nature, processes are established so that employees perform recurrent tasks in a consistent way, time after time. To ensure consistency, they are meant *not* to change—or if they must change, to change through tightly controlled procedures. *This means that the very mechanisms through which organizations create value are intrinsically inimical to change.*"[1]

Innovation, however, is all about change and surprises. It is finding new ways of doing things, new ways to create value. It leverages surprises in the marketplace, and can create very positive surprises in the corporate boardroom—"what a great idea!"

But what happens when innovation tries to navigate the corporate hallways on its way to the corporate boardroom? To meet the changing needs of customers, someone in the company creates a new product design, signaling a change to your current product line. The innovation "champion" in the company then takes this new design concept to the R&D department, where she is told that the project will have to wait due to higher priority projects. She then shares it with the people in operations, where she is told that it will require new equipment that is not covered in this year's budget. The champion then goes to the finance group, which runs some numbers that show the projected ROI for the new design is not as good in the first year as the planned line extension

Strategic Point of Tension

Successful innovation can be very beneficial to a corporation but, in the process, will require it to change. Most corporate systems are established to *prevent* corporate change in order to maintain predictability. The challenge for management is to foster innovation and change without putting the organization at risk for its predictability.

that is coming up. Three strikes, and the champion is out. The immune system wins. Innovation cannot penetrate the corporate defense system, the controls designed to maintain the status quo and eliminate surprises.

This tale has played out thousands of times within companies across all industries. While well-intentioned senior managers desire the benefits that innovation can provide, they do not realize the systemic roadblocks that internal innovation champions encounter.

The Blueprint for Formalizing Innovation

It is possible to integrate innovation into any corporation. It must, however, represent a commitment on the part of senior management to provide the support and resources necessary to overcome the corporate immune system.

The following four elements must all be addressed for an innovation system to become *integrated* into the operating systems of a corporation:

1. Management mandate
2. Corporate infrastructure
3. Innovation process
4. Corporate culture

Management mandates for innovation will never get off the ground unless resources are provided via the corporate infrastructure. Information generated in an innovation process will dissipate without a receptive infrastructure. Even when the right infrastructure and processes are in place, the wrong corporate culture will ignore the new knowledge and kill the new ideas created by them. Innovation processes that begin at the company's grassroots with the support of the culture will wither without a management mandate. All four of these elements must work together for the integration of innovation to a corporation.

In the early 1990s, Eastman Kodak had an Office of Innovation, which was located outside the main headquarters building in Rochester. Although the staff there offered valuable advice and support to Kodak employees who had come up with new ideas, its ultimate demise was most likely due to its not being integrated into the mainstream corporate business systems. Recognizing their need for innovation and the shortcomings of the previous office, Kodak redesigned this group, integrating it more fully to the ongoing organization and its systems. Today, Kodak has a very impressive organization, called Systems Concept Center (SCC), aimed at identifying

> **Process Tip:**
>
> *Innovation needs to be integrated into your company, not merely added on.*
>
> Trying to add innovation to a company by setting up an innovation department would be like transplanting a human heart in a recipient but not attaching the important arteries and veins. Without somehow being integrally connected to the rest of the body on a constant, ongoing basis, the transplant will lose its nourishment and vitality and will ultimately fail.

and integrating innovative business opportunities. Funded by a portion of the R&D budget, the SCC identifies, develops, and screens innovative business opportunities and coordinates their smooth transition to the commercialization group. Unlike the original Office of Innovation, which was "added on" to the Kodak organization, the SCC is "built into" it and appears significantly more productive.

Management Mandate

The integration of strategy innovation into a corporation must begin with a management mandate. Because senior management is responsible for the corporate strategy, anything that helps feed the process of strategy creation must be initiated by them. In addition, senior management has the ultimate responsibility for the corporate infrastructure. Changes in the infrastructure that will be required for strategy innovation must have the proactive support of the senior management group.

What form should this "management mandate" take? We believe that management should *not mandate a process* for strategy innovation, but should *mandate the desired output*.

Employees in many corporations have been inundated with processes over the last several decades. In an effort to streamline operations and increase the bottom line, management has mandated quality control, reengineering, Six Sigma, and many other internal processes. The goal for strategy innovation is not to have employees implementing a new process. The goal should be focusing on an output—a portfolio of viable new business opportunities for the company.

Therefore, we recommend that the management mandate be for a specified *outcome* of a strategy innovation process. We most admire how the management mandate was carried out at 3M under the leadership of Bill Coyne. When Coyne became senior vice president of R&D for 3M in the early 1990s, he began looking for ways to improve the level of innovation in the company. As he talked with people across the business units and laboratories of 3M, he discovered that there were many exciting new technologies that were languishing in the labs because higher priorities were being placed on a large number of lower-risk line extension products. Although 3M had successfully evolved an innovation culture that was aggressively proactive and not constrained by a corporate "immune system," still it required fine-tuning to increase the emphasis on the nonincremental to breakthrough opportunities. Coyne explained, "We knew that we had to produce fewer, but better, products. Their time lines were longer, and they represented greater risk to the company, so the business units were not supporting these opportunities on their own." Knowing that the depreciation rate of technologies was increasing, Coyne searched for a way to stimulate the development and introduction of these technologies to the marketplace.

Building off a previous program already in place, Coyne created

what he called Pacing Plus programs throughout 3M. Pacing Plus
was an attempt to find one or two products or new business platforms in each business unit that were strong enough to make a
significant impact on the market. Specifically, Pacing Plus programs
were defined by the following characteristics:

- Capable of "changing the basis of competition" in a market
- Projected to generate $100+ million in revenues
- Global in scope
- Able to leverage a proprietary 3M technology

Proposals for Pacing Plus programs poured in and were given a
strict review to determine if they were of Pacing Plus caliber. Not
all the business units were able to identify one or two programs to
meet the corporate goal and were instructed by management to go
back and "try harder." Those that qualified were then provided
with corporate resources to support them. Coyne designated nearly
20 percent of the total corporate R&D budget to helping business
units develop and get these Pacing Plus programs to market. In
addition, they would get priority allocation of resources from the
corporation for engineering tech center support. With this assist,
business units were able to develop their higher-volume, higher-
risk programs to help break the cycle of reliance on incremental
line extensions to meet yearly growth targets. Without this support,
the business units were reluctant to support these programs because
of the longer time lines and greater risk to the company.

One of the first Pacing Plus programs to reach the market in
1996 was Dual Brightness Enhancement film, which increases the
brightness of LCD screens in laptops and other electronic displays.
A year later, the 3M Pharmaceuticals Division introduced Aldara,
an immune response modifier in cream form for the treatment of
genital warts. In 1998, CEO and board chair L.D. DeSimone announced that "Pacing Plus programs have the potential to reach
over $6 billion of annual sales at maturity."[2] Although current 3M
CEO Jim McNerney is using a different approach to innovation, his

corporate R&D commitment to the development of innovative new technologies at the business unit level has increased from 20 percent to 30 percent. While the form of strategy innovation initiatives will change as the market needs change, 3M's management mandate for innovation will continue.

In addition to stating the desired output of strategy innovation, the management mandate should include a tangible infrastructure change, clear accountability for results, an impassioned appeal, and the identification of a strategic frontier.

Tangible Infrastructure Changes

The management mandate for strategy innovation must include tangible infrastructure changes. Employees do not "hear" mandates; they recognize them when they "see" them. Tangible changes of some type from senior management represent a commitment to what they are proposing. The greater the tangible change that is made, the greater the perceived commitment. Examples of tangible changes to consider might include reallocation of budgets, the creation of a new group or department, or new guidelines for bonuses or yearly reviews.

When Procter & Gamble launched its Corporate New Ventures organization, a net was cast wide across the organization to identify the most capable P&Gers to staff the effort. While identification of the right individuals was easy enough, recruitment was a challenge. There was no precedent of successful career paths that went outside of a corporate sector and through an organization like Corporate New Ventures. The solution to this dilemma demonstrated a clear management mandate. Senior officers met with individual candidates and informed them that their promotion paths would likely accelerate due to this innovation assignment.

At Eastman Kodak in the early 1990s, R&D budget changes were implemented that helped stimulate the change in strategic direction of that imaging giant. Bob LaPerle explains, "There is no question that it takes a while to change the strategy and culture of a large organization. We were able to first make a dramatic change in the

R&D spending. By 1992, there was a significant shift in spending away from silver halide projects toward projects aimed at digital and hybrid approaches. QuickTake, the world's first digital camera, was an early success."

The Carl Zeiss company pioneered the science and business of optics in 1852. In 2001, the Zeiss board and management team, led by chairman and CEO Dieter Kurz, conducted a worldwide strategy innovation initiative that created a future road map and vision for the future of the company. The tangible infrastructure change that signaled this commitment to strategy innovation was the creation of a vision office, led by Vice President Marc Vogel. This office coordinates a series of global strategy initiatives, acts as a communications hub, and keeps the organization's scorecard on its metrics for success.

Clear Accountability

A successful management mandate must be clear about who is responsible for the results. Because new business opportunities involve most functional areas in the organization, it may not be clear to the functional groups that will be held accountable for the results.

At the same time, we recommend that the person or group responsible for the new business opportunities be involved in the establishment of the mandated results. Holding people accountable for unrealistic goals or providing them with inadequate resources to achieve those goals is counterproductive to the mandate and will jeopardize the formalization effort. Because people support what they help create, allow the responsible group to be part of the creation of the goals and identification of the required resources.

Impassioned Appeal

A mandate for innovation is different from a mandate for operational efficiency. Senior management can convince the company, through a myriad of charts and financial analyses, that they need to cut costs to remain competitive in their market. A rational, quantitative appeal will appeal to the rational, quantitative need for greater efficiency.

Strategy innovation is not a typical, quantitative goal, so it should not be communicated to employees in a rational, quantitative way. Strategy innovation is a bold leap into a new future. It is a rallying cry for growth, a clarion call to lead others into the future, to achieve new levels of performance and success. It is often vision- or mission-based. It speaks to what is possible to achieve. It taps into the wishes and aspirations of everyone—customers, employees, shareholders, and other stakeholders. For these reasons, we suggest that the management mandate for strategy innovation in a company include an impassioned appeal. Tap into people's aspirations, cite their need for challenge, or highlight the opportunity for everyone to make a difference (and grow in the process). Appeal to their hearts through emotions, not to their heads with numbers.

Strategic Frontier

The management mandate for strategy innovation should include reference to the company's strategic frontier. In 1961, U.S. President John F. Kennedy delivered his famous mandate for stimulating the growth of the U.S. space program by specifying a new strategic frontier, an American on the moon by the end of the decade. Highlighting the focus of strategy innovation will help people see that this is just not a random process being introduced to the organization, just in case it might help the company. Instead, identifying the strategic frontier as the goal to be achieved through strategy innovation will help employees see it as a tool to help the corporation get where it wants or needs to be in the future.

Corporate Infrastructure

There is no one-size-fits-all recommendation for corporate infrastructure to implement strategy innovation. Every corporation is different, sometimes radically different. For example, a small, highly entrepreneurial company may require only minor fine-tuning to integrate a system of innovation. On the other hand, a large, hierarchical corporation that has been successfully managing and line-extending one product over the last five decades will require dramatic changes to become an organization with the capability of strategy innovation.

The integration of strategy innovation to a company must include changes to the corporate infrastructure. Strategy innovation needs:

- A home
- Resources to operate
- Metrics to assess its performance

Home

Where should the responsibility of strategy innovation report within a corporate infrastructure? We believe it should report directly to the division or corporate president. Strategy innovation is a cross-functional effort, requiring the involvement of all major departments—R&D, product development, marketing, operations, sales, and finance. To have strategy innovation report to any of the functional silos would place more emphasis on that function, which may not be warranted.

Reporting to the division president will maintain the visibility of strategy innovation and perhaps also shield it from inappropriate budget squeezes. Whenever budget concerns force a company to make trade-offs in their spending, the budget for today's programs will always win out over the budget for future programs. The urgency of today triumphs over the importance of tomorrow. By reporting to the president, strategy innovation will be more shielded from this inclination, assuming that the president is being held primarily responsible for the future.

The location of the strategy innovation function is an issue that is handled differently by the companies we have worked with. Procter & Gamble set up their Corporate New Ventures (CNV) group on their main campus in Cincinnati, maintaining proximity to key people in the organization and reporting to the company's COO.

The story is told that Craig Wynett's CNV group originally shared office space with several corporate vice presidents, until they were asked to find a different office because of the enthusiastic noise they created.

In a different approach to location, Barclays Global Investors (BGI) sent the developers of iShares to a location down the street, away from the daily activities of BGI. The idea, according to Garrett Bouton, CEO of the Global Individual Investor Business of BGI, was a deliberate attempt to create a different, more entrepreneurial culture from the rest of the organization.

> We incubated iShares as a separate business outside the company and allowed it to grow independently. We put people in a different building and gave them a separate identity. They cooperated with BGI when necessary, acting more like a BGI client. It gained a lot of momentum, almost eclipsing the BGI in importance. After eighteen months, we brought them back to this building, where they were challenged to maintain that entrepreneurial spirit.

Regardless of where a company's permanent strategy innovation group is physically located, it is very important that they have their own space. Let the group design the space to fit their working style, which will likely include flexible, comfortable, stimulating common space in lieu of typical corporate-gray cubicles.

Resources

We include both people and funding as part of the resources for formalizing strategy innovation.

People

Because strategy innovation is a cross-functional effort, it should include representatives from the major functional groups. We have seen it work as either a matrix reporting relationship or a separate cross-functional group. If the strategy innovation group is not a full-time responsibility, it is critical to have a commitment from the people involved that it will nevertheless be a high priority in the allocation of their time and attention. If it is a full-time responsibility, you will want to carefully consider both career path and compensation issues involved, to be sure you are getting the strongest people possible in this group.

As for the type of people who should be involved in strategy innovation, it is not necessary to staff it with only "creative" people. Creativity plays an important role in the strategy innovation process but other skills are useful also. For example, you need to have people who are good at gathering insights, from customers and other information sources. You will also need employees skilled in evaluating or assessing market viability for new products and people who can help plan implementation strategies.

The people who are most effective in working in strategy innovation are those who are open-minded and comfortable dealing in ambiguity. Open-minded people are more likely to see the potential for opportunities in a situation than those who are more closed-minded and judgmental. Because the strategy innovation process is heuristic and iterative, there is no one pathway or progression of steps that will guarantee success. There will be dead ends and times of uncertainty, particularly when dealing with the future. People who appreciate structure in their work and need to follow a delineated plan will find the "fuzzy front end" of strategy innovation to be frustrating.

Funding

The other major resource component to formalized strategy innovation is funding. How much should you invest in strategy innovation? Obviously that will differ significantly by industry and by company within an industry. We have seen a spectrum ranging from tens of thousands of dollars to hundreds of millions of dollars. One way to approach this question would be to ask how much you would be willing to spend in order to identify a new business that would be capable of generating $XX million per year. What is that worth to you? Think of it in investment terms, perhaps looking at the net present value after calculating the discounted future cash flows.

Another approach to the funding dilemma is to consider how money is currently allocated to new products throughout the company. Some companies have five or six groups all pursuing, in an uncoordinated way, new products. By pooling funds and providing a focus for the work (the strategic frontier), you may find strategy innovation to be no more costly and much more efficient and prolific than the programs that are currently in place. Also consider carving out some portion of your R&D budget for this effort.

To find the right level of funding, think about experimenting with strategy innovation using a "beta" approach. Start small. Identify a few good people, give them some money to spend, and see what they come up with in terms of new opportunities for the company to consider. Then, debrief their process after a period of time and see what could have been done had additional funds been available. Decide if it would be worth the additional investment. If so, let them run a little longer and check their results again. Experiment, learn, adjust, experiment again. How ironic to think you might be able to create quantum leaps in your business through incremental steps in this beta process.

Metrics

Some people consider the "fuzzy front end" of new product development to be like a black hole in a black box. It draws vast quantities of people and resources into it but nobody is really sure what happens inside or when results can be expected. When asked, the people in charge of the process claim that it is a creative process and creativity cannot be rushed or scheduled. This only adds to the mystery.

We see it a little differently. It is true that because creative processes are heuristic and iterative, it is difficult to schedule exactly when "success" will be achieved. However, that should not imply that anything short of the final "success" does not have value. New business opportunities do not just emerge from nothingness. They evolve from earlier forms, which can be tracked and measured.

This book has outlined the strategy innovation process as a progression of outputs leading ultimately to new business opportunities (see Figure 12-1). For example, the first output is a prioritized listing of strategic frontiers. If you are in a company that knows its strategic frontiers, you have something valuable that remains a mystery to the vast majority of companies we talk to. Strategic frontiers are a goal; they are defined, and they can be tracked.

After strategic frontiers come insights. Each insight gained in the Exploring Phase has value to the company, because it represents value in the marketplace. Once identified, insights can be put in a database, where they will continue to have value until the marketplace changes significantly. Set a goal for the number of insights you want to generate per year and then track that number.

The next step in the evolution of new business opportunities is "beginning ideas." A beginning idea is an insight translated into an initial description of a business opportunity. However, because this initial description serves only as a stepping-stone to the creation of a finished business concept, we do not believe that there is value in archiving and tracking beginning ideas.

Finally, the output of the Discovery Process is finished business

Figure 12-1. Strategy innovation metrics.

concepts. These are the beginning ideas that have been further developed and refined, perhaps several times. Concepts are what you evaluate in your new product evaluation process. They represent new business opportunities and, as part of a portfolio of options, are significant assets to your company. Concepts should also be included in the metrics of the strategy innovation process.

At some point, the Discovery Process outlined in this book becomes a quantitative game. If you want to come up with one viable new business opportunity, that means you may have to generate at least twenty to thirty new business concepts. For each business concept, you may have to create more than twenty to thirty beginning ideas. Each beginning idea may require ten to twenty new insights. Of course, these numbers will vary by the size of business desired by the company.

According to Bob LaPerle, Kodak assumes that it will take 3,000 "beginning ideas" to create one significant new successful business opportunity. The numbers will vary by team but the point here is that the process is not an unpredictable black box. The components can be identified and appropriate metrics established. This aspect of the Discovery Process is quite similar to the approach of most successful venture capital companies that monitor their prospective investments.

Innovation Process

As mentioned earlier in the chapter, the management mandate should not specify that the company will take part in a strategy innovation process. It should specify the outcome that management desires and let the organization decide the appropriate process to achieve those results.

We highly recommend that you use the five-phased process outlined in this book for your strategy innovation process. That's why we wrote the book. It is a proven, hands-on technique that works. Whether you are using an ad hoc team or a dedicated team, have them go through the Staging, Aligning, Exploring, Creating, and Mapping phases.

Keep your focus aimed externally, on customers and markets. Don't try to force their needs into your system of doing things or your areas of competence. This is a very common way that teams want to start the search for new businesses—identifying their core competencies so they can understand what they have to leverage. This approach will significantly narrow your range of vision on the frontier, allowing you to see only those opportunities that fit your abilities. Besides, the way you operate (and your competencies) may no longer be valuable in a dynamic market. Ask travel agents, or companies that make typewriters or carbon paper.

Start the process with insights about customer and market needs, not with product ideas. Procter & Gamble's Craig Wynett shared with us his story of an "electronic suggestion box" created by his Corporate New Ventures group, called myidea.com. When it first started, they asked employees to contribute suggestions for new product ideas, such as ways to improve Tide or many of P&G's other products. The number of suggestions they received for product improvements was quite limited. So they changed the suggestion criteria and asked people to answer the question, "What do you see that is interesting and provocative?" The number of suggestions increased dramatically. People are more comfortable identifying insights than translating insights into implications for new products.

And don't start the process with one or two insights, start with more than you think you can ever use. The creative process described here is one of divergence (generate a great quantity) followed by convergence (selection of the best ones to meet your criteria).

Corporate Culture

Strategy innovation will thrive in an innovative culture. When people in a company celebrate newness and uniqueness, value nonconformity, practice tolerance and flexibility, and tolerate mistakes, innovation will flourish.

Stan Gryskiewicz describes the basis of a creative corporate culture in his book *Positive Turbulence: Developing Climates for Creativity, Innovation, and Renewal.* He suggests that corporate attempts to institute a sense of order, control, and focus on their current business will unwittingly eliminate the sources for innovation and renewal. Organizations need to introduce sources of turbulence, diversity, and dissenting opinions so that employees will constantly question how the company should change to address business opportunities of the future. He writes, "Every big trend starts as a small, one-of-a-kind blip on the screen, easy to overlook and easy to dismiss. Only those paying close attention to the turbulent periphery will see it, and only those predisposed to thinking that turbulence can be positive will see its strategic potential. The task for visionary leaders is to create an environment where new information is embraced, not feared."[3]

But strategy innovation can survive in a noninnovative culture too. The key to survival in a more rigid culture is to isolate and protect the corporate pioneers. Barclays Global Investors did this by sending its iShare development team to a separate location outside company headquarters. If off-site locations are not an option, consider creating a separate space in your building for this group. They need a place to call home that is not subject to constant comparisons with the rest of the organization.

While we do not pretend to be experts on corporate culture, we believe that corporate cultures are a by-product of how a company runs its business. If rules, strict controls, and punishment for mistakes are the primary tools used by senior management in running the business, the resulting culture will probably be risk-averse, fearful, and unwilling to experiment. If people are empowered to act, encouraged to take chances, and celebrated for both successes and failures, the culture will be much more innovative.

If it is true that corporate culture is a by-product of management activities, then it does no good to try to "change the culture" if you do not also change the management activities that drive it. We have heard of many attempts to make a corporate culture more innovative, through innovative awareness campaigns in the lunchroom or "innovation fairs" highlighting new ideas throughout the company.

Without a management mandate, infrastructure changes, or process changes, these efforts, while noble, will fail in their attempts to change the corporate culture.

BGI's Garrett Bouton says about corporate culture. "An innovative culture has to start at the top. The CEO has to want it and to celebrate new ideas that result. It could take years to establish but it's a valuable thing to have in an organization."

This positive reinforcement of innovations and special recognition of those who contribute (at any level) to innovation are valuable tools in establishing the right culture for strategy innovation. Senior management must be vigilant in communicating the company's goals and future vision, highlighting the need for constant innovation and change to reach them.

Beware of other cultural norms that might run counter to the goals of strategy innovation. For example, some corporations celebrate "heroes," those people who single-handedly champion a project and, against all odds, succeed. In an environment where people are looking for opportunities to be a hero, they will be less interested in joining a Discovery "team." Or worse, they will join a team and attempt to be its hero, destroying the collaborative dynamics that are critical to its success.

Teresa Amabile, Harvard Business School professor and author of *Creativity and Context*, says this about an innovation culture:

> Dynamics within a team can determine the creativity of both the individual members and the team as a whole. Our research in organizations suggests that the most effective creative teams are those that are composed of individuals who have diverse skills and perspectives and who are open to each other's ideas, able to constructively criticize those ideas, and eager to help each other. All of this is more likely to happen when the team members communicate freely, trust and respect each other, and feel that their teammates are committed to their project's success.

We have worked with a valuable tool for assessing the corporate culture as it relates to innovation. It is called KEYS to Creativity, is authored by Amabile and Gryskiewicz, and is available from the Center for Creative Leadership (CCL). This assessment tool measures six aspects of corporate culture that support the work environment:

- Organizational encouragement
- Supervisory encouragement
- Work group supports
- Sufficient resources
- Challenging work
- Freedom

It also measures two aspects of corporate culture that can undermine it: organizational impediments and workload pressure. The survey, taken by all members of a work environment, can be compared to other corporate environments in the KEYS database as well as serve as a "pre" level for any change management initiatives in innovation.

Summary

- For many companies, the intermittent use of ad hoc strategy innovation initiatives is not enough. If your company could benefit from having strategy innovation as a core competence, consider the formalization of a strategy innovation system.
- To be successful, a formalized strategy innovation system must penetrate and co-exist with the corporate "immune system," which protects it from undesirable change.
- The four elements that must all be addressed for an innovation system to become *integrated* into the operating systems of a corporation include:
  - *Management mandate*: The senior management commitment to strategy innovation, which could include tangible infra-

structure changes, clear accountability for those involved, an impassioned appeal, and the focus on a strategic frontier.

◆ *Corporate infrastructure*: The establishment of an infrastructure for strategy innovation so that it has a home, resources with which to operate, and metrics to assess its performance.

◆ *Innovation process*: The development of a specific process for identifying and evaluating new business opportunities, such as the Discovery Process.

◆ *Corporate culture*: The establishment of rules, norms, and recognitions in support of strategy innovation will ultimately create a culture that is supportive of strategy innovation.

Endnotes

1. Clayton Christensen, *The Innovator's Dilemma* (Boston: Harvard Business School Press, 1997).
2. L.D. DeSimone, 3M News, www.3m.com, May 12, 1998.
3. Stan Gryskiewicz, *Positive Turbulence: Developing Climates for Creativity, Innovation, and Renewal* (San Francisco: Jossey-Bass, 1999).

THE FUTURE OF STRATEGY INNOVATION

> I cannot manage the past. There are other people in my government who manage the present. It is my unique responsibility as the leader to shine a spotlight on the future, and marshall the support of my countrymen to create that future.
>
> —*MARGARET THATCHER*

We began this book in the Introduction by defining a migration over the last half-century for "imagination" in corporations—from a personal skill to the creation of strategy in the boardroom. What will happen in the next half century? We see a trend for which we have a high level of clarity, confidence, and conviction. A capability for strategy innovation will be a base requirement for those companies who are, or aspire to be, market leaders. What are some of the early indicators of this trend? We see strategy innovation being taught to the future leaders of corporations around the world.

In May 1999, INSEAD, a respected European business school, hosted a gathering of elite business leaders, academicians, and proven innovators to ask the "big" questions surrounding strategy innovation. Having observed the innovative strategic approaches of companies like IKEA, Swatch, and Southwest Airlines, INSEAD now wanted to intellectually examine, at a deeper level, the "how" behind strategy innovation. This conference examined such issues as:

+ What can the independent entrepreneur or the CEO of an established firm do to increase the odds of strategic innovation?

+ How should internal processes be reshaped, so that they generate and support the more radical and ambitious strategic innovations that lead to a sustained competitive advantage?[1]

The gathering at that conference included board members from Johnson & Johnson, Bayer, and Dentronic; executive officers from Glaxo Wellcome, Monsanto International, and BASF; and academicians from Oxford, the Wharton School, and the London Business School. What was the primary message that INSEAD received from this elite group? Strategy innovation is not only being encouraged in organizations, but it will be demanded in the corporate boardrooms of the future.

In addition to the INSEAD conference attendees, MBA students from Harvard, Duke, and Stanford business schools, to name a few, are being exposed to the concept of strategy innovation. As global businesses in technology-driven markets become more competitive, they will need more than management control systems and cost-cutting skills to deliver a consistent bottom line. These future business leaders will need to have strategy innovation as a corporate competence to expand and create markets, driving revenue growth.

The need for strategy innovation will not be limited to those companies that are very large and global in scope. The software firm in Ireland, the health food store in Singapore, and the fitness center in Rio de Janeiro can all benefit from strategy innovation. Strategy innovation will be driven by the company's desire to offer their customers greater value, keeping them one step ahead of current and future competition, or on a different playing field entirely.

These leading companies of the future will focus on, and be influenced by, their customer's current and emerging needs. They will be the ones with a capability to discern and assess the future forces in their dynamic markets. They will be the ones most agile in adapting their business models to these new customer and market insights. These companies will be diligent, proactive custodians of their future frontiers, constantly exploring for their proprietary and profitable futures.

By 2050, we believe that many of the companies whose stories we have shared in this book—3M, IBM, P&G, Carl Zeiss, Moen, Kodak, and others—will have maintained their leadership and vitality, but in different businesses with different business models from what are in place today. They will have strategically innovated to more profitable positions in current and future markets.

Finding those new positions and new markets must become a priority for corporations everywhere. Larger, global enterprises looking to be leaders in the marketplace will need to formalize or systematize a process for strategy innovation, making it a core competence. It can be done. P&G existed for 150 years before exploring any of the "frontiers" between their business sectors. Now, strategy innovation and creativity are embedded in the corporate vocabulary and associated with new markets, new growth, new shareholder wealth. As Craig B. Wynett, founding director for Corporate New Ventures at P&G, recently wrote, ". . . when a fast-track woman passed up the prestigious job of Tide brand manager to join CNV, we knew we were onto something."[2] When corporate language and preferred career paths change to provide an orientation toward strategy innovation, the organizational shift, we suspect, is profound and enduring.

Some of these larger companies will embrace a commitment to a system of strategy innovation faster than others. When senior management mandates this change, supports it with resources and infrastructure changes, and keeps the management of the future in balance with the management of today, it will happen. Other companies will struggle in their efforts to integrate strategy innovation, finding it difficult to effectively address and counter the effects of "corporate gravity" and the "corporate immune" system. Don't give up when you encounter these obstacles. Strategy innovation is not a quick fix. You are not putting a patch on a tire that is losing air; you are building a new tire—while the car keeps moving! Use your creativity to find ways to address these obstacles and keep moving toward your goal.

For a majority of companies, however, strategy innovation will not be integrated as a formalized system, an ongoing core competence with an infrastructure and a corporate career path. For these companies, strategy innovation will be used as a tool to greatly improve the strategic planning process. These smaller companies will form an ad hoc, internal team and charge them with identifying and aligning on the exploration of one or more strategic frontiers. The insights gained on the frontiers will be translated into a portfolio of new business opportunities and strategic road maps for the future that will add significantly to the strategic planning process. Having options of new growth platforms will help senior management craft leadership strategies, rather than relying on the default strategy of incrementalism.

Successful strategy innovation begins with a commitment to make your company more vital, more proactive, and more prosperous in the future than it is today. That's step number one. Step number two: Use this book!

Step number three would be to share the results of your strategy innovation journey with us. Let us know what worked, what did not work, and how you will do it differently next time. We have shared stories with you and would love to hear your stories of life on the strategic frontier. Contact us at www.thevisterragroup.com.

Endnotes

1. INSEAD conference brochure.
2. Craig B. Wynett, T. George Harris, "Yes, You Are a Creative Genius," *Spirituality & Health*, Winter 2003.

GLOSSARY

Aligning Phase—The second phase of the Discovery Process, where the Discovery team and senior management align themselves on the focus and scope of the strategy innovation initiative, agreeing on the strategic frontier(s) to be explored.

Bifocal vision—The ability of senior management to balance the realization of both near-term and long-term opportunities.

Business model innovation vector—One of three areas to be explored by the Discovery team for the identification of insights on how innovations in business models could add value to the company.

Business opportunity—Any new product, service, or significant change in a company's current business model that results in a new or improved revenue stream for the company.

Collaboration—A style of group interaction where all team members enter the process with an open mind and a willingness to explore together, define together, and select together the opportunities that will meet the shared objectives.

Convergent phase—The second step of any creative process, when the ideas and options generated in the first (divergent) step are prioritized, according to some evaluation criteria.

Corporate gravity—An invisible force that prevents employees from venturing too far from the current business model.

Corporate immune system—The role played by current corporate systems and processes to "repel" anything that threatens the current stability of the overall business system. While it repels things that threaten the system, it also acts to repel things that could improve the system.

Corporate myopia—A condition where the urgency of today's business supersedes the importance of the future business, resulting in a nearsighted perspective.

Creating Phase—The fourth phase of the Discovery Process, where the Discovery team uses its new insights from the strategic frontier(s) to create, refine, and develop a portfolio of new business opportunities for the future.

Creativity—The innate developable skill for generating novel ideas.

Customer value vector—One of three areas to be explored by the Discovery team for the identification of insights on what has value to customers.

Discontinuities—Events, products, or technologies that dramatically alter some aspect of the future because they cause large-scale changes in behavior.

Discovery brief—A document prepared by the members of the Discovery team that contains information that would be helpful to begin the Discovery Process initiative.

Discovery drift—The perceived gap between new strategies being considered by the Discovery team and the company's current strategy. If this gap becomes too large, senior management often rejects the new strategy as too much of a change for the company to handle.

Discovery Process—A five-phase process for the identification and mapping of new business opportunities that leads to strategy innovation. It is also referred to as a strategy innovation initiative.

Discovery team—The core group of people responsible for the implementation and results of the Discovery Process.

Divergent phase—The first step of any creative process, when new ideas or options are generated in great quantity, without regard for feasibility, practicality, efficiency, or effectiveness.

Dreaded delta—The gap between projected future revenues and the company's growth targets, which often triggers the need for strategy innovation.

Ethnography—The growing field of observational research, a term first used to describe a research method in the field of cultural anthropology.

Evaluation criteria—The screening criteria used by the Discovery team to prioritize the new business opportunities they develop in the Creating Phase.

Exploration vectors—The areas to be explored by the Discovery team for the identification of insights with value-adding potential. The three vectors recommended are: customer value, market dynamics, and business model innovation.

Exploring Phase—The third phase of the Discovery Process, where new insights are identified on the company's strategic frontier(s), providing the raw material necessary for the development of new business opportunities.

Extended Discovery team—A group of managers who participate in the Discovery Process on a part-time basis, typically attending high-profile exploration activities and review or alignment meetings. They are normally asked to be involved in the process because of their experience, expertise, or implementation responsibilities.

Focused exploration—A streamlined alignment process between the Discovery team and senior management based on the identification by senior management of the specific strategic frontier(s) to be explored by the Discovery team.

Foresight—An understanding of what is possible in the emerging future.

Formalizing—The process of creating a permanent, internal corporate system for strategy innovation.

Future-pull—The aspirational attraction that one feels towards the identification or creation of some compelling future state.

Fuzzy front-end—As part of the new product development process, often the name given to the early part of the process where new product ideas are first identified.

Immersions—In the Exploring Phase, the involvement of the Discovery team in a new environment (of customers' lives, in the marketplace, etc.) for observing new insights.

Incrementalism—The strategy of meeting revenue growth targets through the introduction of products that are only marginally different from (better than) existing products. Frequently the products are "new, improved" versions of current products, or line extensions.

Innovation—The process for implementing creative ideas.

Insight—Any new understanding or perception about customers, market dynamics, or business models that could reflect added value in the marketplace. Insights form the basis of new, value-creating business opportunities that, in turn, form the basis of strategy innovation.

Interactions—In the Exploring Phase, events set up by the Discovery team for the exchange of information (with customers, market experts, etc.) that could lead to insight identification.

Mapping Phase—The fifth phase of the Discovery Process, where the Discovery team creates a strategic road map, outlining key events, trends, market discontinuities, and milestones to move the company into its new strategic future.

Market dynamics vector—One of three areas to be explored by the Discovery team for the identification of insights on what could represent value in the marketplace of the future.

Open exploration—The alignment process between the Discovery team and senior management, where the Discovery team explores and recommends to senior management the specific strategic frontier(s) to be explored.

Opportunity format—A tool (form) used by the Discovery team in the Creating Phase for the development of new business opportunities.

Provocateur—The role played by outside experts (or thought leaders) in a thought leader panel, where the goal is to stimulate the Discovery team with provocative thoughts and insights rather than give coaching or advice.

Safaris—An immersion technique for the Exploring Phase, often consisting of customer visits for observing their environments.

Sponsor—The senior management individual who serves as liaison, mentor, and spokesperson for the Discovery team throughout the Discovery Process.

Staging meeting—The time when the Discovery team gathers to understand the scope of the initiative, to share the Discovery Brief, and to create the team.

Staging Phase—The first phase of the Discovery Process, where the Discovery team is selected, key roles are identified, the objectives of the initiative are established, and the team is prepared for the process.

Stake-outs—An immersion technique for the Exploring Phase, consisting of observing customers outside their living environments, such as retail stores or public places.

Strategic frontier—The unexplored area of potential growth that lies between today's business and tomorrow's opportunities. It is usually a market, product, technology, or business process that represents potential new growth for your company.

Strategic Opportunity Spectrum (SOS)—The wide range of new business opportunities that can result from the Discovery Process. The spectrum runs from shorter-term, lower-risk, market-entering opportunities that are on the "visible" part of the strategic frontier to the longer-term, higher-risk, market-creation opportunities on the "visionary" part of the strategic frontier.

Strategic planning—The process of deciding on the company's tactics for competing in the marketplace.

Strategic road map—A corporate time line into the future that identifies the crucial activities, milestones, and marketplace events that must take place for the new business opportunity to succeed.

Strategy innovation—Shifting a corporation's business strategy in order to create new value for both the customer and the corporation.

Team captain—The Discovery team member who is the leader of the team and primary contact for the Sponsor.

Thought leader panel (TLP)—An insight-gathering technique for the Exploring Phase, consisting of the interaction of five to six "experts" in a variety of areas relevant to the future of a strategic frontier.

Unarticulated needs—The opportunity areas for products and services that could add value to the lives of customers but that, because of their limited experiences and perceptions, customers are not able to describe or define.

ValueProbe—A customer interaction technique for the Exploring Phase, consisting of a group discussion with customers around what has value in their lives.

Visible opportunities—New business opportunities that are currently "visible" on the strategic frontier. They tend to be shorter-term, lower-risk opportunities, where markets are established but new value can be created.

Visionary opportunities—New business opportunities in a strategic frontier that are not currently visible. Visionary opportunities tend to be longer-term, higher-risk opportunities, where markets would need to be created.

Visual illumination—The process of graphically portraying an idea or opportunity to bring it to life and aid in its communication to others.

Recommended Readings

"Inspiring Innovation," *Harvard Business Review*, August 2002.

Amabile, Teresa, Constance N. Hadley, and Stephen J. Kramer, "Creativity Under the Gun," *Harvard Business Review*, August 2002.

Christensen, Clayton M., *The Innovator's Dilemma: When New Technologies Cause Great Firms to Fail*. Boston: Harvard Business School Press, 1997.

Christensen, Clayton M., Michael Raynor, and Matt Verlinden, "Skate to Where the Money Will Be," *Harvard Business Review*, November 2001.

Collins, James C., and Jerry I. Porras, *Built to Last: Successful Habits of Visionary Companies*. New York: HarperBusiness, 1997.

Collins, James C., *Good to Great: Why Some Companies Make the Leap . . . and Others Don't*. New York: HarperCollins, 2001.

DeBono, Edward, *Lateral Thinking for Management*. New York: AMACOM, 1972.

Dell, Michael, *Direct from Dell: Strategies that Revolutionized and Industry*. New York: HarperCollins, 1999.

Drucker, Peter F., "The Discipline of Innovation," *Harvard Business Review*, August 2002.

Florida, Richard, *The Rise of the Creative Class*. New York: Basic Books, 2002.

Foster, Richard and Sarah Kaplan, *Creative Destruction*. New York: Currency/Doubleday, 2001.

Gardner, Howard, *Creating Minds*. New York: Basic Books, 1993.

Gerstner, Louis V., Jr., *Who Says Elephants Can't Dance: Inside IBM's Historic Turnaround*. New York: HarperCollins, 2002.

Gordon, W. J. J., *Synectics*. New York: Harper, 1961.

Govindarajan, Vijay and Anil K. Gupta, "Strategic Innovation: A Conceptual Road Map," *Business Horizons*, July/August 2001.

Gryskiewicz, Stan, *Positive Turbulence: Developing Climates for Creativity, Innovation, and Renewal*. San Francisco: Jossey-Bass, 1999.

Guilford, J. P., *The Nature of Human Intelligence*. New York: Mc-Graw-Hill, 1967.

Hamel, Gary and C. K. Prahalad, *Competing for the Future*. Boston: Harvard Business School Press, 1994.

Hamel, Gary, *Leading the Revolution*. Boston: Harvard Business School Press, 2000.

——— "Strategy Innovation and the Quest for Value," *Sloan Management Review*, Winter 1998.

Johnston, Robert E., Jr., and Soren M. Kaplan, "Harnessing the Power of Strategic Innovation," *Creativity and Innovation Management*, June 1996.

Kaplan, Soren M. and Robert E. Johnston, Jr., "Dislocations—Drivers of Industry Evolution, Innovation, and Corporate Growth," *Strategic Change*, February 1998.

Kim, W. Chan and Renee Mauborgne, "Value Innovation: The Strategic Logic of High Growth," *Harvard Business Review*, January/February 1997.

Kotter, John P., "Leading Change: Why Transformational Efforts Fail," *Harvard Business Review*, March/April 1995.

Krinsky, Robert and Anthony C. Jenkins, "When Worlds Collide: The Uneasy Fusion of Strategy and Innovation," *Strategy & Leadership*, July/August 1997.

Leifer, Richard, et al., *Radical Innovation*. Boston: Harvard Business School Press, 2000.

MacKinnon, Don W., *In Search of Human Effectiveness*. Buffalo: Creative Education Foundation, 1978.

Markides, Constantinos, *All the Right Moves*. Boston: Harvard Business School Press, 2000.

———— "Strategic Innovation," *Sloan Management Review*, Spring 1997.

———— "Strategic Innovation in Established Companies," *Sloan Management Review*, Spring 1998.

———— "To Diversify or Not to Diversify," *Harvard Business Review*, November/December 1997.

McGrath, Rita Gunther and Ian MacMillan, *The Entrepreneurial Mindset: Strategies for Continuously Creating Opportunity in an Age of Uncertainty*. Boston: Harvard Business School Press, 2000.

Mintzberg, Henry, *The Rise and Fall of Strategic Planning*. New York: Prentice-Hall, 1994.

Osborn, Alex F., *Applied Imagination*, 3rd edition. New York: Scribners, 1963.

Parnes, Sidney J., *Source Book for Creative Problem Solving*. Buffalo: The Creative Education Foundation Press, 1992.

Peters, Tom, *The Circle of Innovation*. New York: Vintage Books, 1999.

Porter, Michael E., *Competitive Advantage*. New York: Free Press, 1985.

———— "What is Strategy?," *Harvard Business Review*, November/December 1996.

Prince, George, *The Practice of Creativity*. New York: Scribners, 1970.

Schwartz, Peter, *The Art of the Long View: Planning for the Future in an Uncertain World*. New York: Doubleday, 1996.

Slywotzky, Adrian J., *Value Migration: How to Think Several Moves Ahead of the Competition*. Boston: Harvard Business School Press, 1995.

Slywotzky, Adrian J. and Richard Wise, "The Growth Crisis—and How to Escape It," *Harvard Business Review*, July 2002.

Tucker, Robert B., "Strategy Innovation Takes Imagination," *Journal of Business Strategy*, May 2001.

Tushman, Michael L. and Charles A. O'Reilly, *Winning Through Innovation: A Practical Guide to Leading Organizational Change and Renewal*. Boston: Harvard Business School Press, 2002.

Utterbach, James M., *Mastering the Dynamics of Innovation.* Boston: Harvard Business School Press, 1994.

Wynett, Craig B. and T George Harris, "Yes, You Are A Creative Genius," *Spirituality & Health*, Winter 2003.

Zook, Chris, *Profit from the Core.* Boston: Harvard Business School Press, 2001.

INDEX